ERRONEOUS AND SCHISMATICAL OPINIONS

STUDIES IN THE HISTORY
OF
CHRISTIAN THOUGHT

FOUNDED BY HEIKO A. OBERMAN †

EDITED BY

ROBERT J. BAST, Knoxville, Tennessee

IN COOPERATION WITH

HENRY CHADWICK, Cambridge
JOHN VAN ENGEN, Notre Dame, Indiana
SCOTT H. HENDRIX, Princeton, New Jersey
BRIAN TIERNEY, Ithaca, New York
ARJO VANDERJAGT, Groningen

VOLUME XCIX

BARRY H. HOWSON

ERRONEOUS AND SCHISMATICAL OPINIONS

ERRONEOUS AND SCHISMATICAL OPINIONS

THE QUESTION OF ORTHODOXY REGARDING THE THEOLOGY OF HANSERD KNOLLYS
(C.1599 -1691)

BY

BARRY H. HOWSON

BRILL
LEIDEN · BOSTON · KÖLN
2001

This book is printed on acid-free paper.

Library of Congress Cataloging-in-Publication Data

Howson, Barry H.
  Erroneous and schismatical opinions : the questions of orthodoxy regarding
the theology of Hanserd Knollys (c. 1599-1691) / by Barry H. Howson.
    p.   cm. — (Studies in the history of Christian thought, ISSN
0081-8607 ; v. 99)
  Includes bibliographical references and index.
  ISBN 9004119973 (alk. paper)
    1. Knollys, Hanserd, 1599?-1691. 2. Dissenters, Religious—England–
–History—17th century. 3. Baptists—Doctrines—History—17th century.
4. Theology, Doctrinal—England—History—17th century. I. Title.
II. Series.

BX6495.K63 H69   2001
286'.1'092—dc21   2001035625
                                                                CIP

Die Deutsche Bibliothek - CIP-Einheitsaufnahme

Howson, Barry H. :
Erroneous and schismatical opinions : the question of orthodoxy
regarding the theology of Hanserd Knollys (c. 1599 - 1691) / by Barry
H. Howson. – Leiden ; Boston ; Köln : Brill, 2001
    (Studies in the history of Christian thought ; Vol. 99)
    ISBN 90–04–11997–3

ISSN   0081-8607
ISBN   90 04 11997 3

PRINTED IN THE NETHERLANDS

TABLE OF CONTENTS

Acknowledgements   ix

Introduction   1

Chapter One   Seventeenth-Century Background   17
   The Political and Religious Context   17
   The Theological Context   24
   The Historical Roots of Calvinistic Baptist Churches . .   28
   The Historical Beginnings of Calvinistic Baptists in
      England   32
   History of the Calvinistic Baptists from 1640 – 1689 . .   37

Chapter Two   Life and Writings of Hanserd Knollys   54

Chapter Three   Antinomianism   79
   The New England Antinomian Controversy:
      Its History   85
   The New England Antinomian Controversy:
      Its Theology   89
   Antinomianism in England: Its History   96
   Antinomianism in England: Its Theology 103
   Summary of Antinomian Tenets 114
   Hanserd Knollys and Antinomianism 115
   Conclusion 131

Chapter Four   Hyper-Calvinism 133
   High Calvinism: Its History 138
   The Theology of High Calvinism and Hanserd Knollys 139
   Hyper-Calvinism: Its History 158
   The Theology of Hyper-Calvinism and Hanserd
      Knollys 171
   Conclusion 192

Chapter Five   Anabaptism 194
   The Alleged Anabaptist Teachings of Knollys and the
      Calvinistic Baptists 203
   Knollys' Teachings Relevant to the Charges of
      Anabaptism 216
         Knollys' Doctrine of Baptism 217
         Knollys' Ecclesiology 221
         Knollys' Doctrine of the Ministry 229
         Knollys' Doctrine of the Trinity and of the Deity
            of Christ 235
         Knollys' Teachings On Church and State Issues .. 236
   Knollys and Anabaptism: Conclusion 241

Chapter Six   Fifth Monarchism 243
   General Survey of Knollys' Eschatology 248
   Knollys and Seventeenth-Century Eschatology
      Compared 252
         Nearness of Christ's Return 252
         Nature of Christ's Return 254
         Book of Revelation Comparison 255
         Signs of the End 263
         Date Setting 265
         Papacy 268
         Turkey 272
         Jews 274
         The Millennium 276
         Practical Piety 279
   History of Fifth Monarchism 284
   The Doctrine of the Fifth Monarchists and Hanserd
      Knollys 291
   Conclusion 303

Conclusion 307

Appendices
   Appendix A: Authors Cited or Quoted in
      Knollys' Works 315

Appendix B: The Question of Derivation of
   Anabaptist Teachings: Did Knollys and the
   Calvinistic Baptists derive their teachings from
   the Continental Anabaptists? 317
Appendix C: Survey of Knollys' Commentary on
   Revelation 335

Select Bibliography 345

Indices
   Index of Persons 365
   Index of Places 372
   Index of Subjects 375

ACKNOWLEDGEMENTS

This book is a reworking of my Ph.D. thesis completed at McGill University, Montréal, Canada. There are many people who have contributed to this work that I would like to thank. First, I am grateful for the support and encouragement that Breadalbane and Vankleek Hill Baptist Churches have been over the past five years to me and my family. Also I want to thank McGill's interlibrary loan staff, Maria De Souza, Janice Simpkins and Elizabeth Dunkley for their friendly and diligent work in providing me with materials outside of our library. In addition, I am grateful to Michael Novak, Stephen Brachlow, Murray Tolmie, Richard Land, and Baird Tipson for permission to copy their theses. I must also acknowledge the support of our parents, Richard and Alma Howson, and Roy and Marion Vanderlip who have stood by us, helping us in many ways during these years of study. I am very grateful for the encouragement and help of Dr. Michael Haykin, professor of Church History at Heritage Theological Seminary, Cambridge, Ontario, who has kindly read over this work. He has been a good friend, brother in Christ, and mentor to me. To Noreen Bider who has encouraged me in graduate studies from the beginning, and who so willingly read over this thesis looking for technical errors, I am very grateful. To Tim Dyck, who has become a very dear friend and brother in Christ, and always an encouragement to me while we have studied together at McGill for the past seven years, I cannot say enough.

I also wish to acknowledge the help of Dr. Edward Furcha who led me through the first two years of my Ph.D. studies before he unexpectedly passed away in the summer of 1997. And I want to give special thanks to Dr. William Klempa who willingly took over as my supervisor after leaving his position of Principal of the Presbyterian College and during his moderatorship of the Presbyterian Church of Canada. For his kind and helpful criticisms I am very grateful. With much appreciation I also want to thank

Dr. Torrance Kirby, the Church History professor of McGill's Religious Studies department, who above the call of duty helped me with the revision of this dissertation. Moreover, I would like to express deep gratitude to Professor Heiko A. Oberman for accepting this work into his series Studies in the History of Christian Thought. I am honoured by his acceptance. And my appreciation also to the people at Brill for their work on this project. For permission to reproduce material that has appeared already in article form, I would like to thank *The Evangelical Quarterly* and Particular Baptist Press (*The British Particular Baptists 1638-1910*, Vol 1).

Finally, I am so thankful to God for my family. My children, Natalie and Shawna, continue to be an encouragement to me. And my wife, Sharon, has been a true companion and support through these years of study. I am so thankful to God for providing me with such a helpmate. And most importantly, my hope is that this work will honour the Saviour that Hanserd Knollys loved and served (Revelation 5:6-14).

SOLI DEO GLORIA

B.H.H.
April, 2001
Vankleek Hill, Ontario, Canada

INTRODUCTION

> Would to God our religious Patriots assembled in Parliament would at
> length take care (as they have done of the Romish Emissaries) to suppresse
> [Anabaptists], that the name of God be not blasphemed: that they may not
> infect the simple people with their abhominable Errours.... The plague of
> Heresie is among us, and wee have no power to keep the sick from the
> whole.[1]

So writes the London Puritan Ephraim Pagitt in the mid-1640s of
English Anabaptists. One of those putative English Anabaptists and
harbinger of "errours" and heresies was Hanserd Knollys. Knollys,
a former Church of England clergyman, joined the Calvinistic Baptists sometime in 1644 and became one of their London pastors. In
his polemical treatise of 1645/46 against heresy entitled, *Gangraena*,
the Presbyterian Thomas Edwards accuses Knollys of Anabaptist
heresy:

> Whereas they [Anabaptists in England] plead a peaceable and quiet car-
> riage, I can prove a tumultuous disorderly managing their opinions, as in
> Mr. *Knols* [Knollys], and *Paul Hobson*, besides of many other Anabaptists in
> the Kingdom, which particulars I thought briefly to hint, as an Antidote
> against that Book for the present, intending suddenly a more full discovery
> of the fraud and fallaciousnesse of this *Confession of Faith of seven Churches*.[2]

Edwards charges Knollys with "fraud and fallaciousnesse" as a
leader of the confessional Anabaptist churches in England. This was
a serious accusation. The Anabaptists of Europe were considered
anarchists against the state, and heretics in their doctrine of God,

---

[1]   Ephraim Pagitt, *Heresiography: or, A description of the Heretickes and Sectaries of these latter
times* (1647), p. 37.
[2]   Thomas Edwards, *The First and Second Part of Gangraena or a Catalogue or Discovery of
many of the Errors, Heresies, Blasphemies and pernicious Practices of the Sectaries of this time, vented
and acted in* England *in these four last yeers*, 3rd ed. (1646), I, pt. 2, p. 109.

Christology and soteriology. Was this charge true? Was Knollys an Anabaptist?

Knollys was not only charged with Anabaptism but also with various other heterodox teachings which, for many English people, went hand in hand with Anabaptism. The 1645 *Minutes* of the Westminster Assembly refer to "Information against Mr. Knowles, his preaching in private, and venting his Antinomian opinions."[3] An Antinomian was a person who denied the practical use of the law of God given in the Scriptures. Consequently, an Antinomian was not only free to a live a scandalous life but also to reject both church and state authority. Again this was a serious charge made against Knollys. Was Knollys an Antinomian? In addition, a notation in the *Calendar of State Papers* of 1661 ascribes Fifth Monarchism to Knollys: "[The Fifth Monarchists] have bought a small ship to convey each other abroad. Mr. Knowles and others, who were in Newgate, are sent into Holland, where they are in good condition, but act their business more secretly than here; they only wait an opportunity."[4] Fifth Monarchism was an eschatological movement of the 1650s which espoused the bringing in of the millennium by physical force. Many English people, who were concerned for order in state and church, feared this type of millennialist enthusiasm as tantamount to sedition. Knollys and other Fifth Monarchists were "only wait[ing] an opportunity" to bring in the millennium by force. Again this was a serious charge levelled against Knollys, particularly after the Restoration of Charles II to the throne in 1660. Was Knollys a Fifth Monarchist?

Knollys has also been suspected of hyper-Calvinism. This teaching, an extension of the teachings of John Calvin, became popular in Calvinistic Baptist circles in the eighteenth century. Hyper-Calvinism taught that it was wrong for the preacher of the gospel to "offer" Christ or salvation to all people indiscriminately. Hyper-Calvinists believed that only the elect could respond to this offer, therefore this ministry was the Spirit's work, not the preacher's. The father of Baptist hyper-Calvinism was John Skepp, a successor to Knollys, who, in his book entitled *Divine Energy*, cites Knollys as the

---

[3]   Alex F. Mitchell & John Struthers, eds., *Minutes of the Sessions of the Westminster Assembly of Divines* (Edinburgh and London, 1874), p. 96.

[4]   Mary Anne Everett Green, ed., *Calendar of State Papers, Domestic Series, of the Reign of Charles II, 1661-1662* (London, 1860-1939), Vol. 41, No. 39, p. 87, Sept. 11, 1661.

one who previously laid the theological foundation upon which Skepp in the 1710s was building. This implicated Knollys as the grandfather of eighteenth-century hyper-Calvinism. The nineteenth-century Baptist historian Joseph Ivimey, and Knollys' biographer James Culross deemed it necessary to defend Knollys against this implication. And the twentieth-century Baptist historian Michael Haykin writes in an article on Knollys that his "high Calvinist soteriology [was] developed by many of his eighteenth century heirs into a hyper-Calvinism that all but paralyzed evangelism."[5] Was Knollys a proto-hyper-Calvinist? This is an important question, particularly for those confessional Baptist historians like Ivimey, Culross and Haykin who see evangelism as an important part of Baptist life.

The charges of Anabaptism, Antinomianism, and Fifth Monarchism were very serious ones. They would have caused much anguish and consternation for those who considered themselves orthodox Calvinists, as they did for Knollys who signed the 1644/46 *Confession*. This *Confession* declares in its title that the signatories are "commonly (but unjustly) called Anabaptists." This anguish is evident in the preface of the *Confession* where they take great pains to defend themselves from the charge of heresy:

> *Wee question not but that it will seeme strange to many men, that such as wee are frequently termed to be, lying under that calumny and black brand of Heretickes, and sowers of division as wee doo, should presume to appear so publickly as wee have done: But yet not withstanding wee may well say, to give answer to such, what* David *said to his brother, when the Lords battell was a fighting,* I Sam. 29.30. *Is there not a cause? Surely, if ever people had cause to speake for the vindication of the truth of* Christ *in their hands, wee have, that being indeed the maine wheele at this time that sets us aworke; for had any thing by men been transacted against our persons onely, wee could quietly have sitten still, and committed our Cause to him who is a righteous Judge, who will in the great day judge the secrets of all mens hearts by Jesus Christ: But being it is not only us, but the truth professed by us, wee cannot, wee dare not but speake; it is no strange thing to any observing man, what sad charges are laid, not onely by the world, that know not God, but also by those that thinke themselves much wronged, if they be not looked upon as the chiefe Worthies of the Church of God, and Watchmen of the Citie: But it hath fared with us from them, as from the poor Spouse seeking her Beloved,* Cant. 5. 6, 7. *They finding us out of that common road-way themselves walke, have smote us and taken away our vaile, that so wee may by them be recommended odious in the eyes of all that*

---

[5] Michael Haykin, "Hanserd Knollys (ca. 1599-1691) on the Gifts of the Spirit," *Westminster Theological Journal*, 54 (1992), p. 100.

behold us, and in the hearts of all that thinke upon us, which they have done both in Pulpit and Print, charging us with holding Free-will, Falling away from grace, denying Originall sinne, disclaiming of Magistracy, denying to assist them either in persons or purse in any of their lawfull Commands, doing acts unseemly in the dispensing the Ordinance of Baptism, not to be named amongst Christians: All which Charges wee disclaime as notoriously untrue, though by reason of these calumnies cast upon us, many that feare God are discouraged and forestalled in harbouring a good thought, either of us or what wee professe; and many that know not God incouraged, if they can finde the place of our meeting, to get together in Clusters to stone us, as looking upon us as people holding such things, as that wee are not worthy to live: Wee have therefore for the cleering of the truth we professe, that it may be at libertie, though wee be in bonds, briefly published a Confession of our Faith, as desiring all that feare God, seriously to consider whether ... men have not with their tongues in Pulpit, and pens in Print, both spoken and written things that are contrary to truth.[6]

In his 1672 autobiography Knollys, reflecting on his 1645 sufferings for Christ, wrote, "I was stoned out of the pulpit, and prosecuted at a privy session, and fetched out of the country sixty miles to London, and was constrained to bring up four or five witnesses of good report and credit, to prove and vindicate myself from false accusations [Anabaptism and Antinomianism]."[7] For Knollys and his Baptist brethren the charge of heresy was not taken lightly.

This question of Knollys' orthodoxy or heterodoxy has vexed historians from the eighteenth century to the present. The first historian who addressed this question was the Puritan biographer Daniel Neal who, reporting on Knollys' preaching in Suffolk in the 1640s, mentions that Knollys was "accounted an Antinomian and Anabaptist, his supposed errors were deemed as criminal as sedition and faction."[8] Shortly after Neal's work was published, the Baptist historian Thomas Crosby published his *History of English Baptists* in response to Neal's treatment of Baptists "in odious colours, ... writ[ing] many bitter things, even notorious falshoods concerning them, nay to fasten doctrines upon them, which they never ap-

---

[6] *The Confession of Faith* (1644) in W.L. Lumpkin, *Baptist Confessions of Faith* (Philadelphia, 1959), pp. 154-155.

[7] Hanserd Knollys, *The Life and Death of that Old Disciple of Jesus Christ, and Eminent Minister of the Gospel, Mr. Hanserd Knollys, who died in the Ninety-third Year of His Age written with his own hand to the year 1672, and continued in general, in an epistle by Mr William Kiffin* (1692), p. 33.

[8] Daniel Neal, *The History of the Puritans*, Revised, Corrected, and Enlarged (London, 1822), V, 136.

proved.''[9] Crosby gave an account of Knollys' ministry identifying him as "among the sufferers of *Antipaedobaptism*" and a "pious and learned" man, maintaining that as "a zealous opposer both of episcopacy and common prayer, ... all this could not exempt him from the rage of the *Presbyters*; [nor will Mr. *Neal*'s invidious representation do any harm to his character] because he was a Sectary and an Anabaptist." In further defence of Knollys, Crosby gives an example of his being arrested for preaching against Infant Baptism at Bow church in Cheapside. Crosby records that when brought before the Assembly of Westminster divines concerning questions of his authority to preach, the occasion of his preaching, and the doctrine he delivered in it, Knollys "gave such full answers, that they seemed *ashamed* of what they had done; and ordering him to withdraw, called in the goaler, reproved him sharply for refusing bail, and threatened to turn him out of his place." Crosby gives another occasion while in Suffolk in the 1640s of his being accounted "an Antinomian, and an Anabaptist" which "was looked upon to be *sedition* and *faction*, and the rabble being encouraged by the high-constable, set themselves zealously to oppose him." After his arrest "he made it appear by witnesses of good reputation, that he had neither sowed *sedition*, nor raised *tumults*, and that all the disorders which had happen'd, were owing to the rage and malignity of his opposers, who had acted contrary both to law and common civility."[10] Throughout Crosby's account of Knollys his purpose was to vindicate him from the charge of sedition that was attached to Anabaptism and Antinomianism; and in doing so he portrayed him as orthodox and pious.

The nineteenth-century Baptist confessional historians follow the same tack as Crosby, recording the charges against Knollys and vindicating him of heterodoxy. Early in the century Joseph Ivimey wrote his monumental work on English Baptists in order to correct some of the problems associated with Crosby's work, and in particular, to show that the Baptists were the first Christians to establish the principle of religious liberty. In *A History of the English Baptists* Ivimey uses more primary documents than Crosby in his study of Knollys, and brings together more material on him. In his first volume dealing with the history of adult baptism Ivimey records that

---

[9] Thomas Crosby, *History of the English Baptists* (London, 1738), I, A2, A3.
[10] Crosby, *English Baptists*, I, 226-232.

Knollys was "amoung the suffers of Antipaedobaptism," giving
Knollys' own account of his suffering for preaching against
paedobaptism in Suffolk. He vindicates Knollys with a record of
the House of Commons of 1648 that stated, "Ordered that Mr.
Kiffin and Mr. Knollys be permitted to preach in any part of
Suffolk, at the petition of the Ipswich men." He concludes by calling Knollys an "excellent man", and, quoting Knollys' own words,
maintained that he had "to prove and vindicate [himself] from false
accusations."[11] In volume two on the ministers and churches of the
English Baptists, Ivimey promotes Knollys' character calling him
the "pious and venerable Hanserd Knollys", an "eminent servant
of the Lord Jesus Christ", and a "good man." In this volume he
gives a sympathetic biographical account of Knollys, defending him
against the charges of Antinomianism and extreme Fifth Monarchism where they are mentioned or implied. For example, when
Ivimey touches on Knollys' time in New England where he was
considered to be an Antinomian, he quotes Cotton Mather approvingly concerning Knollys' "piety" and "respectful character." And
in accordance with his purpose for writing, Ivimey promotes
Knollys as one who was "zealous to defend civil and religious liberty" and who "survived all these political persecutions."[12]

In Ivimey's third volume which comprises the history of English
Baptists from 1688 to 1760, he gives a history of the pastors of
Knollys' church. In a footnote he mentions that Knollys "has been
stigmatized as of fifth-monarchy principles, and as the sentiments
of many godly ministers upon that subject are but little known, the
following extract from one of his works will explain them." Ivimey
then quotes from Knollys' *The Parable of the Kingdom of Heaven Explained* which delineates the three comings of Christ: his first coming in the flesh; his virtual and spiritual coming as the Bridegroom
to reign over the nations at the beginning of the millennium; and
his coming as Judge at the last day called His appearance the second time.[13] Ivimey believed Knollys held these principles. Further
along in the history of this church Ivimey looks at Knollys' third
successor, John Skepp. In his brief vignette of Skepp, Ivimey mentions the book he published, namely, *Divine Energy* and quotes from

---

11   Joseph Ivimey, *History of the English Baptists* (London, 1823), I, 172-174.
12   Ivimey, *English Baptists*, II, 261, 347-359
13   Ivimey, *English Baptists*, III, 360-361.

its preface where Skepp tells his readers that he is building on the foundation which Knollys had laid, thereby identifying Knollys' theology with his own. In a footnote Ivimey seeks to distance Knollys from Skepp's hyper-Calvinism. He writes,

> If Mr. Skepp meant to intimate that Mr. Knollys was of the sentiments propagated in the work on "Divine Energy," respecting the non-invitations of the gospel to the unconverted, nothing could have been more erroneous. Mr. Knollys was one of those ministers who, as Mr. Skepp expresses it, used an Arminian dialect in addressing the unconverted.

He then quotes a passage from Knollys' treatise *The World that now is, and the World that is to come*, where Knollys calls the unconverted to receive Christ, and tells lost sinners to consider that God offers Christ to them.[14] Ivimey wanted to show that Knollys did not hold Skepp's "no offer" theology.

James Culross, another nineteenth-century Baptist historian, wrote a sympathetic biography of Knollys as part of a series for the Assembly of the Baptist Union of Wales with the purpose of "illustrating the principles of Baptists." His goal was to cover the life of Knollys in its seventeenth-century context in order to instruct his readers to this purpose. He writes, "[The] tracing of his career shews us that truth and patient, suffering meekness are mightier unspeakably than the world's force."[15] Culross addresses all four of the charges levelled against Knollys in one way or another. He acknowledges that Knollys became an "Anabaptist" sometime in the late 1630s or early 1640s, and that it was "of all names the most hated, dreaded, and maligned."[16] His biography seeks to distance the Calvinistic Baptists and Knollys from the Continental Anabaptists, and in particular, the "excesses and enormities of the Munster men."[17] On the charge of Antinomianism Culross writes that Knollys' "Antinomianism was not more than that of Paul: 'Ye are not under the law, but under grace,'" and later quotes a passage from a sermon Knollys published under the title, *Christ Exalted*, (which at the time of delivery was supposed to contain antinomian teachings) concluding that "no one who understands the doctrines

---

[14] *Ibid.*, III, 364-365.
[15] James Culross, *Hanserd Knollys* (London, 1895), p. x.
[16] *Ibid.*, p. 30.
[17] *Ibid.*, p. 55.

of grace will set these views [that Christ abolished the ceremonies, penalties, curse, covenant and schoolmastership of the Law — our new schoolmaster, to whom we yield obedience of faith to His Father's will, is Christ] down as Antinomian."[18] Concerning hyper-Calvinism Culross again quotes a passage from Knollys' works to show that "though a decided Calvinist ... Knollys had no doubt or hesitation" about urging the unconverted to repent and believe in Christ.[19] Differing from Ivimey's representation of Knollys as a Fifth Monarchy man Culross more precisely defines what this teaching meant. Then he writes, "Some men dreamed of setting it up by force, and would have called 'the saints' to seize it. Knollys, too, believed in this kingdom, but *not* in setting it up by the sword." Culross then cites parts of Knollys' *Parable of the Kingdom of Heaven Expounded*, concluding, "This kingdom is not to be set up and sustained by the sword — as Venner and others dreamed of doing."[20] Unfortunately, the passage he quotes does not absolve Knollys of Fifth Monarchism.

The twentieth-century-historiographical approach to Knollys is more critical than that of its nineteenth-century counterpart. Pope Duncan published a sixty-page pamphlet entitled, *Hanserd Knollys: Seventeenth-Century Baptist.* Duncan believes that "to understand correctly the genius of Baptists, [one] must examine the lives, struggles, and thoughts of the people — even of individual persons." Hence, "This thin volume is designed as a simple illustration of the importance and relevance of such an individual as Knollys to the Baptist story."[21] Duncan states that his book does not pretend to be a full account of Knollys' life and work. He begins by briefly running through Knollys' life, setting it in its seventeenth-century context. In this section he notes that while in New England Knollys' "extreme religious views resulted in his being accused of being an antinomian."[22] In relation to his antinomianism Duncan acknowledges in a footnote the New England governor John Winthrop's claim regarding Knollys' "filthy dalliance" with two maids. Duncan gives several reasons why this might not have been true, not the

---

18 *Ibid.*, pp. 29, 47.
19 *Ibid.*, pp. 36-37.
20 *Ibid.*, pp. 96-98.
21 Pope Duncan, *Hanserd Knollys: Seventeenth-Century Baptist* (Nashville, 1965), p. 7.
22 *Ibid.*, p. 10.

least of which is that "Winthrop regarded Knollys as an antinomian and could hardly be a candid judge of him."[23] The next section of Duncan's little book examines three areas of Knollys'
thought: redemption, the church, and religious liberty. In this section he takes note of Knollys' "strong Calvinism", his belief in the
universal church, the gathered-visible-congregational-independent
church, his rejection of a presbyterial form of church government,
and the affirmation of the authority of the church over itself. Moreover, he mentions Knollys' rationale for believer's baptism by immersion, and Knollys' debate with John Saltmarsh over the difference between water baptism and Spirit baptism. When discussing
the subject of infant baptism Duncan writes, "The denial of infant
baptism was especially obnoxious to most of [the disputants of the
seventeenth century]. Knollys and other Baptists were, consequently, often treated with utter contempt and bitter invective."[24]
In addition, Duncan touches on Knollys' high view of the Baptist
ministry, the topic of discipline in the church, and inter-church relationships. He also notes the Baptist position on liberty of conscience, and Knollys' suffering for and encouragement of toleration. In Duncan's last section he looks at the relationship of Baptists
to more radical movements like the Seekers, Ranters, Familists,
Diggers, Levellers, Quakers, and the Fifth Monarchists. He addresses Knollys' involvement with this latter group by looking at
some of Knollys' eschatological writings, and noting some of his
activities in the 1650s. He queries, "The question of the exact relationship of the Baptists, and particularly of Hanserd Knollys, to
this movement is a complex one." After perusing some of Knollys'
writings, he writes, "It is clear that Knollys shared millennial views
which were in essential accord with those of the party of Fifth
Monarchy Men." However, he thought it was more difficult to ascertain "what specific relationship he had to the movement." After
giving some evidence for and against Knollys' participation with
the group, he concludes that whether "a party member or not, he
was so closely associated with the movement by thought and action
that he had to pay the penalty of being one both then and since."[25]

---

[23] *Ibid.*
[24] *Ibid.*, pp. 27-28.
[25] *Ibid.*, pp. 10, 46, 49-50, 50. Duncan also makes reference to Knollys and
Anabaptism but without defence or accusation (*Ibid.*, pp. 28).

Another critical Baptist historian of this century, who examined
Knollys in his Dr. Williams's Library Lecture of 1977 *Hanserd
Knollys and Radical Dissent in the Seventeenth Century*, is B.R. White, the
former principal of the Oxford Baptist college, Regent's Park.
White's approach is different from Duncan's in that he writes a
critical historical account of Knollys' life interspersed here and
there with quotations from his writings. The significance of this
study lies in White's critical knowledge and retrieval of primary
sources of the seventeenth-century context with respect to both the
Calvinistic Baptists and Knollys. On the question of Knollys' heterodoxy White addresses the subject of Fifth Monarchism. Like
Culross he defends Knollys against this charge. White writes:
"While there is no evidence that during the 1650s Knollys was any-
where near the heart of the Fifth Monarchy movement there is
some indication that his sympathies were with a number of those
who were themselves involved with it." White goes on to give evidence of these "sympathies" from Knollys' actions in those years.
He then challenges any notion of Knollys' commitment to the chief
doctrine of the movement (bringing in the millennium by force) by
quoting several passages from Knollys' work, *An Exposition of the First
Chapter of the Song of Solomon*, concluding, "Once more a Calvinistic
Baptist drew back from urging the use of physical force to inaugu-
rate Christ's millennial Reign."[26]

Having surveyed the historical landscape of important studies on
Hanserd Knollys, it is clear that all of the historians who have examined Knollys' life have sought on some level to address the question of Knollys' orthodoxy. The eighteenth- and nineteenth-century
historians have sought to vindicate him of these charges. The twentieth-century scholars have been on the whole more critical of
Knollys.

My approach to the question of Knollys' orthodoxy will necessarily be a synthesis of the historical and the theological. My aim is
to examine these charges regarding Knollys' orthodoxy in the light
of their historical and theological context. This means we will *sys-*

---

[26]   B.R. White, *Hanserd Knollys and Radical Dissent in the 17th Century* (London, 1977),
pp. 17-18. White also notes the charge of antinomianism levelled at Knollys in both the
1630s and 1690s but does not defend or accuse him of it (*Ibid.*, pp. 6-7). Muriel James
has written a recent account of Knollys' life as a defender of religious liberty (*Religious
Liberty on Trial: Hanserd Knollys — Early Baptist Hero* [Franklin, TN, 1997]). See chapter
two for an assessment of this work.

tematically and *comprehensively* weigh, in turn, each one of these charges of Antinomianism, hyper-Calvinism, Anabaptism, and Fifth Monarchism against Knollys' extant writings. Such a systematic approach has hitherto not been undertaken in relation to these charges made against him. The full historical and theological context of this catalogue of charges has yet to be studied. Former studies have only examined the question of Knollys' orthodoxy in a piecemeal fashion, frequently without due consideration to their theological context, or without due consideration given to all of his extant writings. Consequently, this present study undertakes the first consciously systematic and comprehensive approach to these various charges. In the end, it will enable us to assess the question of Knollys' orthodoxy with improved clarity.

Besides the need for a thoroughly comprehensive study of Knollys' thought in order to ascertain his orthodoxy, there is another important reason for such a study. Until recently most of the attention given to seventeenth-century English Baptists has been to the older General Baptists. As Leon McBeth writes, "Historians have tended to give more space to John Smyth and the General Baptists than to Richard Blunt or William Kiffin and the origin of the Particular Baptists."[27] However, in this century such scholars as B.R. White, Murray Tolmie, and W.T. Whitley have given more attention to the origins and history of the English Calvinistic Baptists.[28] Moreover, numerous dissertations have been forthcoming in the past thirty years by Michael Novak, Richard Land, Barry Vaughn and Paul Gritz. These studies have explored the thought of Calvinistic Baptists collectively and individually. We are grateful

---

[27] H. Leon McBeth, *The Baptist Heritage: Four Centuries of Baptist Witness* (Nashville, 1987), p. 39. In the twentieth-century such important Baptist historians as Robert Torbet, *A History of the Baptists* (Philadelphia, 1950); A.C. Underwood, *A History of the English Baptists* (London, 1947); Henry Vedder, *A Short History of the Baptists* (Philadelphia, 1907); and W.T. Whitley, *A History of the British Baptists* (London, 1923) give more attention to the General Baptists than they do to the Particular Baptists.

[28] For example, B.R. White, "The Origins and Convictions of the First Calvinistic Baptists," *Baptist History and Heritage*, 25, No. 4 (1990) pp. 39-47; "Organization of the Particular Baptists, 1644-1660." *Journal of Ecclesiastical History*, 17 (1966) pp. 209-226; *The English Baptists of the Seventeenth Century.* (London, 1983); "The London Calvinistic Baptist Leadership 1644-1660." *The Baptist Quarterly*, 32 (1987,88) pp. 34-45; W.T. Whitley, *Calvinism and Evangelism in England: Especially Amoung Baptists* (London, 1933); *A History of British Baptists.* (London, 1923); Murray Tolmie, *The Triumph of the Saints, The Separate Churches of London 1616-1649*; (Cambridge, 1977); "General and Particular Baptists in the Puritan Revolution" (unpublished Ph.D. dissertation, Harvard University, 1960).

for these works but more study needs to be done on this group in order to better understand seventeenth-century Calvinistic Baptist thought. Consequently, one way we can further our understanding of these Baptists is to examine the thought of one of their most re-spected leaders Hanserd Knollys. In this regard it is important to note that none of those dissertations examined a Calvinistic Baptist who signed both their *Confession*s and remained a leader for the first fifty years of their existence. For example, Richard Land has looked at Thomas Collier's thought. Collier joined the Calvinistic Baptists in the mid-1640s and became an important figure in the Western Association of Calvinistic Baptists during the Interregnum, but by the latter 1670s had become estranged from the group for his so-teriology and Christology.[29] Paul Gritz examined the thought of Samuel Richardson, an important figure during the Revolutionary years, signing the 1644 *Confession*, writing apologies on behalf of the Calvinistic Baptists, e.g., *An Apology for the Present Government* and *Brief Considerations.* However, Richardson died circa 1658, only approxi-mately fifteen years into the life of the Calvinistic Baptist group.[30] Barry Vaughn has written a dissertation on the thought of Benja-min Keach. He is an important figure in early Calvinistic Baptist history, but he did not join the group until about 1670, and conse-quently was not a part of the formative twenty years of the group's history.[31] Michael Novak has studied the writings of nineteen Cal-vinistic Baptists in order to understand the assumptions and theo-logical backdrop by which they came to their convictions on the church, baptism, and the relation of church and state. But he focussed his attention only on their first twenty years.[32] All of these studies elucidate the thought of seventeenth-century Calvinistic Baptists but none of them examines a Calvinistic Baptist leader who spanned their first fifty years.[33] For this reason alone Hanserd

---

[29]   Richard D. Land, "Doctrinal Controversies of English Particular Baptists (1644-1691) as Illustrated by the career and Writings of Thomas Collier" (unpublished D.Phil. dissertation, Oxford University, 1979).

[30]   Paul Linton Gritz, "Samuel Richardson and the Religious and Political Contro-versies Confronting the London Particular Baptists, 1643 to 1658" (unpublished Ph.D. dissertation, Southwestern Baptist Theological Seminary, 1987).

[31]   J. Barry Vaughn, "Public Worship and Practical Theology in the Work of Benja-min Keach (1640-1704)" (unpublished Ph.D. thesis, University of St. Andrews, 1989).

[32]   Michael J Novak, "'Thy Will Be Done' The Theology of the English Particular Baptists, 1638-1660" (unpublished Ph.D. dissertation, Harvard University, 1979).

[33]   Only one other person of historical significance in the denomination lived over

Knollys' thought ought to be explored more comprehensively.

In order to accomplish our primary task of ascertaining Knollys' orthodoxy the first two chapters will set Knollys in his historical context. The first chapter will briefly note the religious and political history of the seventeenth century, and then outline in some detail the history of the Particular (Calvinistic) Baptist denomination. An important part of this chapter will be to define the term "orthodoxy" in its seventeenth-century theological context against which Knollys' orthodoxy was measured by his contemporaries. The contemporary context is important because it provides the reader with an understanding of the theological standards according to which Knollys' orthodoxy was initially questioned. The second chapter will sketch Knollys' life and writings in the seventeenth-century context, using the presently available scholarship. Subsequent chapters will explore the specific context of the charges directed against Knollys' orthodoxy, with each chapter being devoted to one of the principal charges. Knollys' writings will be examined with each charge to see if it is valid. Chapters three through six will follow the Reformed Confessional order of soteriology, ecclesiology and eschatology. The reason for this order is twofold: Knollys' heterodoxy in the seventeenth century was being measured against this Reformed confessional orthodoxy; and the first charge historically made against Knollys was that of his Antinomianism while in New England.

The third chapter will address the charge of Antinomianism made against Knollys by his contemporaries in the 1630s, 1640s and the 1690s. First, we will explore the meaning of Antinomianism in the seventeenth-century context of both England and New England where Knollys was accused of this heresy. Then Knollys' writings will be compared with the antinomian tenets of his contemporaries to test whether their charges were in fact valid. We will also see something of Knollys' teaching on such subjects as justification, sanctification, and the relation of the law and sin to the believer.

Since the charge of hyper-Calvinism is closely related theologically to Antinomianism, we will examine it in the fourth chapter. Rooted in the teaching of Joseph Hussey in the early 1700s, hyper-

---

a comparable time period: William Kiffin (1616-1701). Kiffin's thought has not been explored, and as an important Baptist leader, needs to be.

Calvinism became an influential teaching in Particular Baptist churches in the eighteenth century. Was Knollys a High Calvinist like John Owen or did he go beyond High Calvinism and espouse a proto-hyper-Calvinism? This chapter will set out both High Calvinism in its seventeenth-century context, and hyper-Calvinism in the context of the late seventeenth and eighteenth centuries. In this latter context the works of John Gill and John Brine, the premier Baptist hyper-Calvinists of the eighteenth century, will be examined.[34] Seventeenth-century English High Calvinism and eighteenth-century Baptist hyper-Calvinism will be measured against the writings of John Calvin since his theology is the standard of orthodoxy on this particular charge. Knollys' writings will be compared in turn with the tenets of High Calvinism and hyper-Calvinism in order to examine whether he was a High Calvinist and/or a hyper-Calvinist. In this fashion we will be able to judge whether the charge of hyper-Calvinism is valid, as well as discern something of Knollys' thought on such doctrinal themes as evangelism, the work of the Holy Spirit in salvation, and election.

The fifth chapter will address the charge of Anabaptism made against Knollys. First, we will examine the specific Anabaptist teachings with which Knollys was accused as a subscriber to the 1644/46 *Confession* and a member of the Calvinistic Baptists. Then the writings of such protagonists of anti-Anabaptism as Robert Baillie, Thomas Edwards, Ephraim Pagitt and Daniel Featley will be examined in order to ascertain what this charge meant in the 1640s context. Finally, Knollys' writings will be examined in the relevant areas that address Anabaptism to see whether in fact this charge is valid. This chapter will also reveal Knollys' thought on various ecclesiological issues.

The sixth chapter will examine the eschatological issue of Fifth Monarchism, hence it's treatment last. Knollys was considered a Fifth Monarchist by his contemporaries and by several twentieth-century historians including A.C. Underwood and W.T. Whitley.[35] There is much circumstantial evidence to support this claim includ-

---

[34]   Gill's hyper-Calvinism has been questioned by some historians; but we will show from his writings that he espouses a Calvinism that certainly goes beyond High Calvinism, holding several tenets that were absent from it.

[35]   W.T. Whitley, *A History of British Baptists* (London, 1923), pp. 85-86, and A.C. Underwood, *A History of the English Baptists* (London, 1947), pp. 61, 109-110.

ing Knollys' eschatological terminology in some of his writings. In this chapter we will examine seventeenth-century English eschatology in general, and the teachings of the Fifth Monarchists of the 1650s in particular, comparing them with Knollys' eschatology in order to determine whether the remaining charge of Fifth Monarchism is valid.

The concluding chapter will summarize our findings, and seek to formulate an answer to the question of Knollys' orthodoxy. In addition, we will summarize what we have learned of his theology in order to further our understanding of seventeenth-century Calvinistic Baptist thought.

CHAPTER ONE

SEVENTEENTH-CENTURY BACKGROUND

The Political and Religious Context

The seventeenth century was a time of great change for the whole of British society. Christopher Hill considers the time between 1603 and 1714 "perhaps the most decisive in English history."[1] Politics changed from rule by King to rule by Parliament with the latter holding the purse strings; economics went from being highly regulated to *laissez-faire*; Britain grew from a second-class power to a world-class power by 1714 with colonies in Asia, America and Africa; uniformity of religion by the Church of England was replaced with toleration for Dissenters; central control by King became control by local officials; rule by divine right became rule by rational inquiry, utility, experience and common sense; worldviews changed from belief in the supernatural to belief in modern science, from a medieval cosmology to a Newtonian one; society changed from being predominately hierarchical to a more democratic and opportune one; writing went from the scholarly style of Hooker to the plain style of Bunyan and Defoe; and music changed from household chamber music to public performances of opera.[2] Of these changes the most important for this study involve religious and political developments. We will give a brief survey of the religious and political events of the seventeenth century in which Hanserd Knollys lived. It will be divided into three distinct time periods: 1603-1640, the early Stuart period; 1640-1660, the Puritan Revolution; 1660-1689, the later Stuart Restoration.

When Queen Elizabeth died in 1603, James VI of Scotland be-

---

[1] Christopher Hill, *Century of Revolution 1603-1714* (London, 1974), p. 13. For more on the history of this time see Godfrey Davies, *The Early Stuarts 1603-1660*, 2nd ed. (Oxford, 1959); S.R. Gardiner, *History of England 1603-1642*, 10 Vols. (London, 1883-4). For a social history see Christopher Hill, *Society and Puritanism in Pre-Revolutionary England* (London, 1969); and Keith Wrightson, *English Society 1580-1680* (London, 1982).

[2] Hill, *Century*, pp. 13-16.

came King of both countries. James, though raised under Presbyterianism, quickly embraced the Church of England hierarchical
church government because he believed that it accorded best with
monarchy ("No Bishop, no King"). At the Hampton Court Conference (1604), he sided with his Bishops refusing many of the Puritan
demands.

In these early years the Commons and the King clashed over
various issues primarily because of James' high view of the royal
prerogative. James sought to control both church and state. During
the reigns of both James and his son Charles Parliament sat for
only three and a half years in total.[3] James, though something of a
theological thinker, was primarily concerned with his political
power. Consequently, throughout his reign he was not particularly
rigid in his theological views but relatively tolerant of both Puritans
and Catholics as long as their actions or views did not impinge
upon his power. In addition, he believed he rightly owned the ad-
ministrative power of the Church. After the Hampton Court Conference the Puritans became an opposition party. At Hampton
Court James demanded that the clergy "acknowledge his temporal
and spiritual supremacy as well as the scriptural warrant for the
Prayer Book, the degrees of bishop, priest and deacon, and the Articles of Religion." Over the next few years, however, James did
implement some of the reforms for which the Puritans asked: for
example, he agreed to a new translation of the Bible (1611); some
textual variants to the Prayer book were amended; Bancroft attempted to remove pluralism and non-residence; James encouraged
a better preaching ministry; and Puritans were promoted to key
positions, e.g., John Preston (chaplain to Charles), John Abbot
(Archbishop of Canterbury), and Toby Matthew (Archbishop of
York). As a result opposition from Puritans was negligible until
about 1621.[4]

Throughout his reign, James was sympathetic towards Catholics.
For example, he was close to Catholics like the privy councillor
Henry Howard, the Earl of Northhampton or the Secretary of
State Sir George Calvert. James was not anti-Catholic because he

---

[3]   D.H. Pennington, *Seventeenth Century Europe* (Singapore, 1970), p. 392.
[4]   Kenneth Fincham and Peter Lake, "The Reigns of James I and Charles I," in *The
Early Stuart Church*, ed. Kenneth Fincham (Stanford, 1993), pp. 26-28.

believed that Catholics belonged to the true Church, professing the key doctrines of the Trinity and the Incarnation.

After the outbreak of the Thirty Years War on the Continent, James' hope for religious unity among Protestants and Catholics was shattered. However, he did seek to mediate between the two sides by pursuing a marriage between his son Charles and the Spanish Infanta. This policy, however, was criticised from both pulpit and press; it was another of his policies that seemed to "presage the triumph of Catholicism."[5] This was an important turning point in the Puritan/Parliament relationship with the crown and Court. In 1622 James sought to suppress Puritan dissent by giving the church a set of *Directions to Preachers* which told them to avoid discussing matters of state. In addition, he placed anti-Calvinists in key church positions. Moreover, James appreciated the two anti-Calvinist treatises by Richard Montagu, entitled, *A New Gagg for an Old Goose* (1624) and *Appello Cæsarem* (1625). These works identified Calvinism with subversive Puritanism. Consequently, when James died and Charles, his son, became King in 1625 the Puritans were quite alienated from the Crown. They were not hopeful that ecclesiastical policies would change, even though Parliament was dominated by Calvinists. With the attack on Calvinism, the teaching of Arminianism in the church became a major issue for Parliament up to 1629. Sir Robert Harley stated that Arminianism was a threat to the unity of the Church and the security of the nation. His concerns were echoed by other parliamentarians like Francis Rous, and clerics like Henry Burton and Jeremiah Dyke.[6]

When Charles dissolved Parliament in 1629 his eleven-year "personal rule" began. During these years he and William Laud, who became the Archbishop of Canterbury in 1633, sought to conform the Church to Arminian doctrine and sacramental worship. Their policies increasingly alienated the Calvinists in the country. One of the most offensive policies was the changing of the communion table into an altar permanently railed in at the east end of chancels. For Laud, the altar was the place where grace was dispensed and all could come and receive salvation. Other offensive issues included: baptism as a necessity for salvation; the denial of predesti-

---

⁵   Fincham and Lake, "The Reigns of James I and Charles I," pp. 28-34.
⁶   Nicholas Tyacke. *Anti-Calvinists: The Rise of English Arminianism, c. 1590-1640* (Oxford, 1987), pp. 157-158.

nation and perseverance; and the encouragement of private confession to a priest.[7]

Laud's policies were imposed not only on the English church but on Ireland and Scotland as well. This was the beginning of the end for Laud and Charles. In 1637 Laud imposed a liturgy on the Scottish church based on the English Prayer Book, and later he sought to place English bishops over the Scottish church. Scotland rebelled and invaded the North of England in 1639 thereby initiating the "Bishops Wars." By 1640 both England and Scotland were fed up with Charles' and Laud's ecclesiatical policies which, to many Protestants, appeared to be leading Britain back to Rome.

Charles called the Short Parliament in 1640 in order to fund his war with Scotland. Unfortunately for him Parliament wanted only to debate the history of his "Personal Rule."[8] Consequently, Charles dissolved Parliament after three weeks. About six months later in November, he called the Long Parliament which, over the next year, demolished the institutions of "prerogative rule." The High Commission, Star Chamber, other prerogative courts, unparliamentary taxation, and the political power of the bishops were abolished. In addition, Parliament voted and Charles accepted that the former could not be dissolved without its own permission. Moreover, Parliament drew up and passed the Grand Remonstrance which demanded a truly Parliamentary Monarchy. When, in the summer of 1642, no resolution could be made between the King and those on the side of the Grand Remonstrance the first Civil War broke out. By 1646 Parliament could claim victory due to the efforts of the newly formed New Model Army. Defeated Charles sought refuge in Scotland but by 1647 the Scots handed him over to the English Parliament. The army leaders and the active Independents in the Commons encouraged the country to bring Charles to trial for treason. Fearing the policies of the Independents and Army, some Presbyterians and Scots, in agreement

---

[7] See *Ibid.*, pp. 206-221.
[8] For a more detailed history of 1640-1660 see S. R. Gardiner, *History of the Great Civil War*, 4 vols., 2nd ed. (London, 1893) and *History of the Commonwealth and Protectorate*, 4 vols., 2nd ed. (London, 1903); Godfrey Davies, *The Early Stuarts 1603-1660*, 2nd ed. (Oxford, 1959); and Austin Woolrych, *England Without a King 1649-1660* (London, 1983). For a "worm's eye view" of the Revolutionary years see Christopher Hill, *The World Turned Upside Down: Radical Ideas During the English Revolution* (Harmondsworth, 1991). For a "view from the top" see David Underdown, *Pride's Purge* (Oxford, 1971).

with Charles, entered into a war with Parliament known as the Second Civil War (1648). This demonstrated to many Englishmen that Charles could not be trusted. In December the Army removed those members of Parliament (Pride's Purge) who refused to renounce further negotiation with the King. On January 30, 1649 Charles was executed by order of the Rump Parliament.

In 1649 a ten-year experiment with republicanism began in England and ended in failure. The Rump Parliament with its executive council primarily made up of army officers led by Oliver Cromwell sat until 1653. Cromwell dismissed the Rump and in its place a "Parliament of Saints" was nominated by the Puritan congregations which lasted only six months. In December of the same year, under a constitution called the *Instrument of Government*, Cromwell was declared Lord Protector. After two Protectorate Parliaments no agreement for a lasting government was accomplished among the members and Council of State. Cromwell died in 1658 and his son Richard made a feeble attempt to rule as the next Protector. By 1659 he resigned and the government fell into chaos. General Monck sought to resolve the problem by marching into England from his post in Scotland and restoring the Long Parliament and the King. Throughout the Protectorate years there was a large and increasing desire for Charles II's restoration. The government of the city of London which by now was Royalist played an important role in bringing about this Restoration. In March 1660 a new "Convention Parliament" was elected and it invited Charles to the throne.

During the Revolutionary years radical ideas in religion and politics flourished. For example, in politics a democratic movement known as the Levellers sought to bring about an English democracy. That is, they desired that sovereignty be given to the House of Commons which would be elected by universal suffrage. Prior to the 1640s such democracy was unheard of in Western Society. In religion, various sects emerged including Quakers, Fifth Monarchists, Ranters, Diggers, and Seekers.[9] In addition, groups like the General and Calvinistic Baptists were free to meet and worship. The Presbyterians, however, were not enthusiastic about this religious chaos and sought through Parliament and the Westminster

---

[9] For essays on these groups see J.F. McGregor & B. Reay, eds., *Radical Religion in the English Revolution* (Oxford, 1984), and Hill, *The World Turned Upside Down*, especially chapters 7, 9 and 10.

Assembly to bring about a Presbyterian uniformity of religion in the mid 1640s.[10] One of the key issues for which the Baptists and Independents fought in these years was religious toleration. Consequently, they resisted the Presbyterians in the 1640s and supported Cromwell throughout the Interregnum.[11]

Before coming to the throne, Charles II promised toleration to all Christians in his *Declaration of Breda*.[12] This, however, was not the will of the Cavalier Parliament, and consequently, no concessions were made to the Presbyterian leaders at the Savoy Conference of 1661. Many Presbyterians, Independents and Baptists were ejected from their livings; and the Church of England was once again established as a consequence of the Restoration. It was reinforced by the Clarendon Code which sought through various Acts to establish uniformity and quash dissent. However, the royal prerogative was not what it was prior to 1640. For instance, there were no prerogative courts or feudal exactions, and trafficking in offices no longer dominated the working of government.[13] This did not mean that there was no persecution for political or religious dissent. On the contrary, there were periods of time between 1660 and 1689 when persecution of dissenters was quite strong.[14]

During the seventies and eighties, a return to Roman Catholicism increasingly became a concern for English people.[15] Both Charles and his brother, James, had ties to the old religion which caused suspicion. For example, in the secret clauses of the *Treaty of Dover* (1670) with France, Charles promised in due course to declare

---

[10]   See C. Gordon Bolam, Jeremy Goring, H.L. Short & Roger Thomas. *The English Presbyterians from Elizabethan Puritanism to Modern Unitarianism* (London, 1968).

[11]   W. K. Jordon, *The Development of Religious Toleration in England*, 4 vols. (London, 1932-1940).

[12]   For the history of the Restoration period see George Clark, *The Later Stuarts 1660-1714*, 2nd ed. (Oxford, 1955); and Douglas Lacey, *Dissent and Parliamentary Politics in England, 1661-1689: A Study in the Perpetuation and Tempering of Parliamentarianism* (New Brunswick, 1969); David Ogg, *England in the Reign of Charles II* (Oxford, 1955). See also for church history C. E. Whiting, *Studies in English Puritanism from the Restoration to the Revolution, 1660-1688* (Cambridge, 1931); Peter Ole Grell, Jonathan I. Israel and Nicholas Tyacke, *From Persecution to Toleration: the Glorious Revolution in England* (Oxford, 1991); and Gerald Cragg, *From Puritanism to the Age of Reason: A Study of Change in Religious Thought within the Church of England* (Cambridge, 1950).

[13]   Pennington, *Seventeenth Century*, p. 409.

[14]   For example, in 1661-1667, 1670-1672, and 1682-1686. For more on persecution of Dissenters see Gerald Cragg, *Puritanism in the Period of the Great Persecution* (Cambridge, 1957), and Michael R. Watts, *The Dissenters*, vol. 1 (Oxford, 1978).

[15]   In particular, for James II reign see Hill, *Century of Revolution*, pp. 205-209.

himself a Catholic; and in 1672 Charles enacted a *Declaration of Indulgence* for Catholic and Protestant Dissenters. Moreover, Charles believed Catholicism was the best form of religion for defending the Restoration monarchy.[16] In addition, in 1678 Titus Oates' alleged Popish Plot, which falsely proclaimed that Catholics were planning to murder the King, was believed by many. In the eighties, when it appeared certain that James would take the crown upon Charles' death, there was even greater concern about Catholicism amongst not only Dissenters but also conformists. In 1673 James had married a Catholic and it was believed that James and a male heir from this union would lead England back into the Roman Catholic fold.

In 1685 Charles died and James ascended the throne. At first, things looked very promising for James. Parliament was generous to him, and the attempted rebellion by the Duke of Monmouth, Charles' Protestant bastard son, failed miserably. James, however, misread his subjects, and sought to promote his Catholic cause underestimating the loyalty of the Tories to the Protestant Church. His actions "did everything to unite the propertied class against him and to heal the split between Whigs and Tories."[17] For instance, he introduced Roman Catholic officers into his army, and he attacked the "privileges of the Anglican universities and the freehold tenure of fellows of colleges."[18] And to add more fuel to the Tory fire he tried to win support from Catholic and Protestant Dissenters with two *Declarations of Indulgence*; they failed to produce any substantial support. In the end what clinched James' downfall was the birth of a Catholic son to succeed him. In 1688 the Tories sent a letter to William of Orange, the husband of Charles II's daughter Mary, inviting him to come and take the crown. James, having lost all influence, fled the country, and William sailed into London unhindered; he and Mary became King and Queen of England.

Parliament passed the *Act of Toleration* in 1689 which broke the Church of England's monopoly on English religion, and allowed Dissenters to meet, preach within licensed buildings, and worship without hindrance.[19]

---

[16] Pennington, *Seventeenth Century*, p. 410.
[17] Hill, *Century*, p. 205.
[18] *Ibid.*, p. 206.
[19] For a brief history and theology including a copy of the Act see Gerald Bray, ed., *Documents of the English Reformation* (Minneapolis, 1994), pp. 570-577.

The Theological Context

This study is predicated on a proper understanding of the term "orthodoxy" during the period of 1640 to 1660. The charges of heterodoxy levelled against Knollys are based on his contemporary polemicists' assumptions of orthodoxy. In order for us to understand the charges we must have some knowledge of the assumed standard of "orthodoxy" in the Revolutionary period.[20] These charges of Anabaptism, Antinomianism and Fifth Monarchism which were made against Knollys, came from the Reformed community of Presbyterians, Church of England divines and, to a lesser extent, Independents.[21] Consequently, the standard of "orthodoxy" was the Reformed teaching of these groups. In order to ascertain this standard we will use their Confessions of Faith, and so be able to understand the assumptions upon which Knollys' antagonists charged him with heterodoxy. The three *Confession*s we will use in order to understand the orthodoxy of this period are the *Thirty-Nine Articles* (Church of England), the *Westminster Confession of Faith* (Presbyterian), and the *Savoy Declaration* (Independents-Congregationalists). Our discussion of these Reformed communities' meaning of orthodoxy will only deal with those areas of theology that are pertinent to the charges made against Knollys. As we mentioned in the introduction the standard of orthodoxy against which hyper-Calvinism will be measured is John Calvin's writings.

All three of these Reformed communities believed that God is Triune, that the three persons of the Godhead, the Father, the Son, and the Holy Spirit, are one substance, power and eternity. This

---

[20]   This section will only give us a general understanding of the theological context against which Knolly was charged with heterodoxy. The specific context of each charge will be given in the following chapters where the charge is discussed.

[21]   "Reformed" is that heritage of the Protestant Reformation which came out of Zurich (Ulrich Zwingli, Heinrich Bullinger) and Geneva (John Calvin). In the 1520s and 30s Lutheranism was the dominant influence upon the English Church. During the Edwardian years the Reformed teaching began to dominate. During the Elizabethan years Reformed teaching was clearly the dominant teaching in the English Church. For example, many of the Marian exiles were influenced by Reformed doctrine during their stay on the Continent in Zurich, Geneva, and other cities. Moreover, the Geneva Bible became the Bible of choice for many of the clergy, and Bullinger's *Decades* became the Homilies for the English clergy to preach to their congregations. In addition, this influence is seen in the theology of the *Thirty-Nine Articles* which received its final form in these years. And the two most influential theologians for the seventeenth century, William Perkins and William Ames, based their theology upon Reformed teaching.

meant that the Son is eternally begotten of the Father, being very and eternal God, and equal with the Father. In the fulness of time the Son took upon himself human nature, and consequently, his Godhead and manhood became inseparably joined together in one person without conversion, composition, or confusion.[22] In addition, these *Confessions* espoused the Reformed teaching of predestination and election. They teach that God, before the foundation of the world, decreed by his secret counsel to deliver from damnation those whom He had chosen out of humanity in Christ, and to bring them by Christ to everlasting life.[23]

All three *Confessions* affirm the inability of humans "to will" the spiritual good because of their fallen state in sin. In this state they cannot turn and prepare themselves for faith and good works. God must convert the sinner and translate her into a state of grace, freeing her from her natural bondage under sin, and enabling her to will and to do that which is spiritually good.[24]

Justification for this Reformed community meant that God accounted and accepted the believer in Christ as righteous on account of Christ's righteousness. This justification is applied to the sinner when she believes in Christ for her salvation.[25] Faith is, therefore, a condition of justification.[26] Every person that is justified is also sanctified and, consequently, will bear the fruit of a sanctified life. This fruit is an evidence of a living, saving faith.[27] Therefore, assurance is not only based on the promise of salvation in the gospel, the testimony of the Holy Spirit, but also the inward and outward evidence of grace in the believer's life.[28] This sanctification is not perfect in this life, but only in heaven.[29] Consequently, the *Westminster* and *Savoy* teach that believers, because of their sins, may fall under God's displeasure.[30] However, the sinner, who is elect and called by God to salvation through the Spirit, will persevere to heaven and

---

[22] *Thirty-Nine Articles* (TNA) I, II; *Westminster* (WC) II:3, VIII:2; *Savoy* (SD) II:3, VII:2.
[23] TNA XVII; WC III:1-8; SD III:1-8.
[24] TNA X; WC IX:3,4; SD IX:3,4. All three Confessions hold to original sin TNA IX; WC VI:1-6; SD VI:1-6.
[25] TNA XI; WC XI:1,2,4; SD XI:1,2,4.
[26] TNA XI; WC XI:1,2; SD XI:1,2.
[27] TNA XII, XVII; WC XI:2, XVIII:1,2; SD XI:2, XVIII:1,2.
[28] TNA XVII; WC XI:2, XIV:2, XVIII:1,2; SD XI:2, XIV:2, XVIII:1,2.
[29] TNA XV; WC VI:5, XIII:2; SD VI:5, XIII:2.
[30] TNA XV; WC XI:5; SD XI:5.

cannot fall away.[31] The *Westminster* and *Savoy* state that the believer at conversion is quickened and renewed by the Holy Spirit, her mind is enlightened, her heart is changed, and her will renewed.[32] The Holy Spirit is an actual influence who works in believers to will and to do of His good pleasure.[33] For this Reformed community the moral law of God is binding on all persons. For the regenerate, the law serves as a rule of life informing them of the will of God and their duty, directing and binding them to walk accordingly.[34] The *Westminster* and *Savoy* maintain that Christians cannot live in sin but will grow in grace throughout their lives.[35]

All three *Confession*s declare that the baptism of infants is proper and most agreeable with the institution of Christ. This sacrament is to be administered by the ministry.[36] Moreover, baptism is rightly administered by sprinkling or pouring water upon the person.[37] The *Westminster* and *Savoy* state that baptism is only to be administered once to any person.[38] For these Reformed communities the visible Church is a congregation of faithful people where the Word of God is preached and the sacraments are properly administered.[39] The *Westminster* and *Savoy*, however, go further than the *Thirty-Nine Articles* in their concern for a purer visible church. All three *Confession*s teach that a duly called ministry is to minister the Word and administer the sacraments.[40] The Congregationalists also believed that others in the congregation, gifted to preach the Word, were permitted to do so.[41] The *Thirty-Nine Articles* and the *Westminster Confession* maintain that church government is hierarchical, either ruled through synods or bishops.[42] All three *Confession*s state that the mag-

---

[31] TNA XVII; WC XVII:1-3; SD XVII:1-3.

[32] WC X:1,2, XIII:1; SD X:1,2, XIII:1.

[33] WC XVI:3; SD XVI:3.

[34] TNA VII; WC XIX:5,6; SD XIX:5,6.

[35] WC XIII:1,3, XIV:3; SD XIII:1,3, XIV:3.

[36] TNA XXVII, XXIII, XXVI; WC XXVIII:4, XXVII:4; SD XXIX:4, XXVIII:4.

[37] Nothing about this is mentioned in the *Thirty-Nine Articles*. WC XXVIII:3; SD XIX:3.

[38] WC XXVIII:7; SD XXIX:7.

[39] TNA XIX; WC XXV:2, 4; SD XVI:2, *Platform* VIII.

[40] TNA XXIII; WC XXV:3, XXVII:4, see also "The Form of Presbyterial Church-Government"; SD *Platform* IX, XI, XVI.

[41] SD *Platform* XIII.

[42] Implied in TNA Introduction, and XXIII. Stated in WC XXXI:5. The Congregationalists believed that each church had authority under Christ to rule itself; and

istrate has a part to play in the welfare of the Church. Accordingly, the state has a responsibility, at the very least, to deal with those who subvert the faith, and to promote the true faith of Christ.[43] The *Thirty-Nine Articles* and the *Westminster Confession* go further, and maintain that the magistrate should make laws concerning the worship of God, and be involved in church affairs.[44]

All people are to pay respectful obedience to the civil authorities,[45] and Christians are permitted to serve as civil magistrates.[46] In addition, all three *Confessions* state that oaths are lawful for the Christian if the magistrate requires them;[47] and that the goods and property of Christians are not common but they have right, title and possession to these.[48]

Concerning eschatology the *Thirty-Nine Articles* give little attention to this subject. This confession simply acknowledges that Christ will return to judge all men at the last day.[49] The Episcopalian *Irish Articles* of 1615 do teach more about the Second Coming of Christ, speaking of the resurrection of the saints (living and dead), and the judgement of all people before the judgement seat of Christ.[50] The *Westminster* and *Savoy* elaborate on these themes of resurrection and judgement, as well as add that the Pope is Antichrist.[51] And the *Savoy* goes further, giving some details of the latter days, maintaining that "according to His promise, we expect that in the latter days, Antichrist being destroyed, the Jews called, and the adversaries of the kingdom of his dear Son broken, the churches of Christ being enlarged and edified through a free and plentiful communication of light and grace, shall enjoy in this world a more quiet,

---

Christ did not institute any other authority over each particular church (SD *Platform* IV-VI).

[43]   TNA XXXVII; WC XXIII:3; SD XXIV:3.

[44]   TNA XXI, XXXVI, XXXVII; WC XXIII:3. Congregationalists appear to be against the magistrate ordering set worship but are for him encouraging and promoting the profession of the gospel (SD XXIV:3).

[45]   TNA XXXVII; WC XXIII:4; SD XXIV:4

[46]   This is assumed in the TNA because a good churchman is also a good citizen. For example, Queen Elizabeth was considered both. WC XXIII:2; SD XXIV:2.

[47]   TNA XXXIX; WC XXII:1-7; SD XXIII:1-7.

[48]   TNA XXXVIII; WC XXVI:3; SD XXVII:3.

[49]   TNA IV.

[50]   *The Irish Articles of Religion* CIII, probably composed by one of the Westminster Divines James Ussher.

[51]   WC XXV:6; SD XXVI:4.

peaceable and glorious condition than they have enjoyed."[52] This *Confession* not only states some of the signs of the end, including the calling of the Jews, but also that there will be a literal millennial kingdom. It, however, does not say whether it will be premillennial or postmillennial.

The Historical Roots of Calvinistic Baptist Churches

In order to place the Calvinistic Baptists in context, we need to look briefly at their historical roots in England.[53]

In the twentieth century there has been an ongoing debate concerning the roots of English Baptist history. Scholars differ as to whether Puritanism, Separatism, Anabaptism or a combination of these is the source of Baptist beginnings. The prime area of debate concerns the place of Anabaptism in this history. For example, Winthrop Hudson[54], Hugh Wamble[55] and Lonnie Kliever[56] do not believe there was Anabaptist influence in English Baptist beginnings. On the other hand, Calvin Pater[57], Glen Stassen[58], William Estep[59], Robert Torbet[60], and Ernest Payne[61] contend there was.[62]

---

[52]   SD XXVI:5.

[53]   In this study the Calvinistic Baptists will at times be called "Particular Baptists". This was the name they later adopted; it distinguished them from the "General Baptists" who held the soteriological teaching of unlimited atonement.

[54]   Glen H. Stassen, "Anabaptist Influence in the Origin of The Particular Baptists," *Mennonite Quarterly Review*, 36 (1962), p. 324.

[55]   Hugh Wamble, "Inter-relations of Seventeenth Century English Baptists," *Review and Expositor*, 54 (1957), pp. 407-425.

[56]   Lonnie D. Kliever, "General Baptist Origins: The Question of Anabaptist Influence," *The Mennonite Quarterly Review*, 36 (1962), pp. 291-321.

[57]   Calvin Pater, *Karlstadt as the Father of the Baptist Movements: The Emergence of Lay Protestantism* (Toronto, 1984), pp. 253-278.

[58]   Stassen, "Anabaptist Influence," pp. 322-348.

[59]   William Estep, *The Anabaptist Story* (Nashville, 1963), pp. 200-222.

[60]   Robert Torbet, *A History of the Baptists* (Philadelphia, 1950), pp. 54-55. Torbet writes, "With respect to the relationship between Anabaptists and Baptists, it is safe to say that the latter are the spiritual descendants of *some* of the former. No historical continuity between the two groups can be proved" (*Ibid.*).

[61]   Ernest A. Payne, "Contacts Between Mennonites and Baptists," *Foundations* 4 (1961), pp. 39-55; and Payne, "Who were the Baptists?" *The Baptist Quarterly*, 26 (1956), pp. 339-342.

[62]   For an overview of the sources of Baptist beginnings see H. Leon McBeth, *The Baptist Heritage* (Nashville, 1987), p. 49-63. For more discussion of this subject see Appendix B.

It is difficult to know which position is correct on the basis of the extant evidence. Calvin Pater writes, "To what extent this Separatist tradition had been moulded not only by the inner logic of disestablished Calvinism but also by the presence of Dutch Baptists and Calvinists on English soil will probably remain a question of debate, in view of the lacunae that remain."[63] The roots of English Baptist history remain somewhat obscure.

We do know, however, a significant amount about Baptist beginnings despite our lack of knowledge concerning distinct roots.[64] We know that two distinct groups of Baptists emerged in the first half of the seventeenth century on English soil. The first group came to be known as General Baptists. They had their formation in 1609 under the leadership of John Smyth and Thomas Helwys. The second group, called the Particular Baptists, emerged a generation later in the 1630s under the leadership of John Spilsbury and later William Kiffin.[65]

---

[63]   Pater, "Karlstadt," p. 257. There is no doubt that both the General and Particular Baptists were in contact with Anabaptists. It may be assumed, therefore, that they were both influenced by them but the question is to what extent? For more on this see Appendix B.

[64]   One would think that the General Baptists (1610s) birthed or influenced the beginnings of the Particular Baptists (1630s). But there is no evidence of any direct connection between General Baptists and Particular Baptists. William Estep only speculates a connection from some changes made in the revised Particular Baptist Confession of 1646 ("On the Origins of English Baptists," *Baptist History and Heritage*, 22, No. 2, [1987], pp. 21-22). Glen Stassen states, "The General Baptists began in the first decade under the leadership of John Smyth and Thomas Helwys. The Particular Baptists began independently in 1638 or 1640 and were led by John Spilsbury and Richard Blunt.... We do not know whether the differing concepts [of baptism which gave birth to the Particular Baptists] were due to original thought, separatist Congregational influence, General Baptist influence, Mennonite influence, or some other theology present in London in the 1630's" ("Anabaptist Influence," pp. 322, 325; see also Hugh Wamble, "Inter-Relations," pp. 408-425). The Particular Baptists appear to have come to Baptist convictions without any contact with the General Baptists. Leon McBeth, speaking of the two British Baptist groups, writes, "These two groups did not 'divide'[because of their differing doctrines of the atonement]; instead, they had quite different origins, at different times and places, and with different leaders. The Particular group, emerging about a generation later, represent not just more Baptists, but Baptists of a significantly different kind" (*Baptist Heritage*, p. 39). It is possible, however, that both groups of English Baptists were influenced by the Anabaptists in some measure. The Anabaptist influence on the Particular Baptists is addressed in Appendix B.

[65]   William Kiffin was an important leader among the Particular Baptists but it is uncertain as to when he came to Baptist convictions. It was certainly by 1644. See B.R. White, "How did William Kiffin join the Baptists," *The Baptist Quarterly*, 23 (1970), pp. 201-207. For a different scenario see Murray Tolmie, *The Triumph of the Saints* (Cambridge, 1977), pp. 192-195. For Kiffin's life see B. R. White, "Kiffin, William (1616-

Before we look at each group in more detail, let us briefly trace each one's roots from the beginning of the English Reformation. The Reformation in England began in the first half of the sixteenth century and manifested itself in various ways. It began politically with Henry VIII and religiously with Edward VI.[66]

The movement that came to be known as Puritanism probably began during the reign of Mary Tudor (1553-58).[67] When Elizabeth ascended the throne in 1558 she followed the course of the "via media" regarding the Reformation. This was unsatisfactory to the Puritans who desired a purer form of church worship, like that of Calvin's Geneva. Some dissatisfied Puritans felt it was necessary to separate themselves from the Church of England and to practice what they believed to be biblical Christianity. Some of these Separatists hoped that their separation would be temporary until the state church reformed; others separated because they believed "the church ought to be free from government connection."[68] It was primarily from this latter group that the Baptists emerged.

In the 1560s and 1570s separatist congregations existed in London. But it was not until Robert Browne's publication of *A Treatise of reformation without tarrying for anie* in 1582 that Separatism became popular. He formed a church in Norwich in 1581 and two follow-

---

1701)," *Biographical Dictionary of British Radicals in the Seventeenth Century*, eds. Richard Greaves & Robert Zaller (Brighton, 1982-84), II, 155-157; and B. A. Ramsbottom, *Stranger than Fiction: The Life of William Kiffin* (Harpenden, Herts.: Gospel Standard Trust Publications, 1989).

    66   There are two schools of thought concerning the English Reformation. There is the traditional historiography of A.G. Dickens which holds that the Reformation in England essentially took place between 1525 and 1553. There is also the revisionist school of Christopher Haigh which sees the Reformation taking a much longer time even into the seventeenth century. For more on the historiography of the English Reformation and this recent debate see Rosemary O'Day, *The Debate on the English Reformation* (London, 1986). See also A.G. Dickens, *The English Reformation* (New York, 1964) and Christopher Haigh, *The English Reformations: Religion, Politics, and Society under the Tudors* (Oxford, 1993).

    67   Most scholars believe Puritanism began in the 1550s, and some believe it originated with Bishop John Hooper. Puritanism was surely born out of the Frankfurt controversy. See C.H. George, "Puritanism as History and Historiography," *Past and Present*, 41 (1968), pp. 77-104; and William M. Lamont, "Puritanism as History and Historigraphy: Some Further Thoughts," *Past and Present*, 44 (1969), pp. 133-146. See also Ronald J. Vander Molen, "Anglican against Puritan: Ideological Origins during the Marian Exile," *Church History*, 42 (1973), pp. 45-57, and W.M.S. West, "John Hooper and the Origins of Puritanism," *The Baptist Quarterly*, 15 (1953-54), pp. 346-368, and *Ibid.*, 16 (1955-1956), pp. 22-46, 67-88.

    68   McBeth, *Baptist Heritage*, p. 25.

ers, Henry Barrow and John Greenwood carried on his separatism in London. They were imprisoned in 1588 and executed in 1593. The Barrow-Greenwood congregation became a church in 1592 under the leadership of Francis Johnson. After the Barrow/Greenwood executions and the Conventicle Act of 1593 part of the church removed to Amsterdam to escape persecution.

Johnson was imprisoned prior to the exodus, and Henry Ainsworth eventually became the teacher of this church. The church put out an important confession called the *True Confession* in 1596 defining its beliefs. It, however, later split over the issue of church government. Johnson, having joined the group in Amsterdam after his release from prison, promoted a presbyterial form of church government; Ainsworth, on the other hand, held to a congregational form. Another separatist group led by John Robinson left Scrooby Manor, England, in 1608 and sailed to Amsterdam, shortly afterward settling down in Leyden. It was some of these church members who sailed on the Mayflower in 1620 to New England.[69]

The first of the English Baptists was John Smyth. He was born in the east of England, and studied theology at Cambridge, tutored by the would-be separatist, Francis Johnson. In 1602, after his ordination and brief lectureship at Lincoln Cathedral (1600), he was dismissed for "personal preaching" (1602). Several years later he joined a separatist church in Gainsborough (1606), and shortly afterwards became its pastor; in 1607 he removed this church to Amsterdam. A number of the members of this church lodged in the large bakehouse of a leading Amsterdam Mennonite, Jan Munter.[70] Most likely through the influence of these Waterlander Mennonites, Smyth came to the conviction that only believers, not infants, should be baptized. Smyth at this time did not agree with a number of Mennonite beliefs, and so kept his congregation separate from the Waterlanders.[71] Consequently, he was not baptized by them but instead baptized himself. Then he baptized Thomas Helwys and about forty others. It is believed that their mode of baptism was pouring, not immersion.

---

[69] William Bradford, *The History of Plymouth Colony — A Modern English Version with an Introduction by George F. Willison* (Roslyn, N.Y, 1948), pp. xiv-xix, 3-75.

[70] Payne, "Contacts," p. 42.

[71] *Ibid.*, p. 44. He gives some reasons why Smyth's church did not.

Not long after this Smyth rejected his self-baptism and encouraged the church to join the Mennonites. A number of the members refused to follow Smyth. With Helwys as their leader, they returned in 1611 to London where they established the first General Baptist Church on English soil.[72] By 1624 there were five General Baptist Churches in England. They became known as "General" Baptist churches because of their belief in the general atonement of Christ as opposed to the Calvinistic limited or particular atonement.[73]

The Historical Beginnings of Calvinistic Baptists In England

The Calvinistic (or Particular) Baptist churches had a distinct origin from that of the General Baptists. The historical evidence indicates that they were not an offshoot of this latter group.

The Particular Baptist churches trace their roots to Henry Jacob who was a Calvinist and a Puritan but not a Separatist of the ilk of John Smyth. He is considered a "moderate separatist" or semi-separatist.[74] He believed that the Church of England was a true church, and did not consider it a false one as the Separatists did.[75]

While calling for reforms in England he was put in prison; after his release in 1605, he went into exile in Holland. He pastored an independent church near Leyden and returned to England in 1616 to start a church in Southwark, London.[76] This church became

---

[72]   The people that joined with the Mennonites under Smyth were accepted as members in 1615. Smyth himself, however, died in 1612 before this took place.

[73]   For a detailed history of the first forty years of the General Baptists, see Murray Tolmie, "General and Particular Baptists in the Puritan Revolution," (unpublished Ph.D. dissertation, Harvard University, 1960), pp. 1-102.

[74]   McBeth, *Baptist Heritage*, p. 40.

[75]   *Ibid.*, p. 41. See also Stephen Brachlow, *The Communion of Saints: Radical Puritan and Separatist Ecclesiology 1570-1625* (Oxford, 1988), pp. 56-64, 101-106, 136-141, 185-193, 220-225, 256-262 for more on Jacob's ecclesiology. For a biographical account of Jacob see S. J. Brachlow, "Jacob, Henry (1563-1624)," *Biographical Dictionary of British Radicals*, II, 137-138.

[76]   We know that there were at least four illegal churches in London before 1620: some of Francis Johnson's congregation that did not go to the Netherlands in 1597; the General Baptists under Thomas Helwys; a Judaizing congregation under John Traske; and the congregation under Henry Jacob (B.R. White, "The Origins and Convictions of the First Calvinistic Baptists," *Baptist History and Heritage*, 24, No.4 [1990], pp. 40-42). For a history of the Jacob church see W.T. Whitley, "The Jacob-Jessey Church, 1616-1678," *Transactions of the Baptist Historical Society*, 1 (1910), pp. 246-256. For the church records of this church see W.T. Whitley, "Records of the Jacob-Lathorp-Jessey Church

known as the JLJ church (the initials standing for the first letter of the last name of the first three pastors, himself, John Lathrop and Henry Jessey).[77] In 1622 he left London for Virginia where he died in 1624.

In the 1630s baptism became an important topic of discussion in the church. Historians are unsure what precisely the discussion was about. The records state that some of the members in 1630 were "grieved against one that had his child then baptized in ye Common Assemblies, & desireing and urging a Renouncing of them."[78] This group under the leadership of Mr. Dupper took issue with the JLJ church's semi-separatist position, and broke away from it forming a new separatist church.[79] In 1633 another group of seventeen or eighteen people[80] under Samuel Eaton "desired dismission that they might become an Entire Church, & further ye Comunion of those Churches in Order amongst themselves, wch at last was granted to them."[81] The minutes of the church also state: "Mr. Eaton[82] with Some others receiving a furthur Baptism."[83]

This is where the confusion lies. Why did these two groups secede? Was it because some members became more separatist, believing the Church of England to be a false church, and therefore, its baptism null and void? Was this "further baptism", therefore a baptizing of its members in a "true church"? Or was this "further baptism" a baptizing of those only who confess faith, in other words "believer's baptism"?[84]

1616-1641," *Transactions of the Baptist Historical Society*, 1 (1910), pp. 203-225. For a brief biographical sketch on Lathrop see S. J. Brachlow, "Lathrop, (or Lothrop, Lathorp), John (1584-1653)," *Biographical Dictionary of British Radicals*, II, 173-174.

[77] For some of Jessey's involvement with the Particular Baptists in the 1630s and 1640s see B.R. White, "Henry Jessey in the Great Rebellion," in *Reformation Conformity and Dissent*, ed. R. Buick Knox (London, 1977), pp. 134-138. See also B. R. White, "Jessey, Henry (1601-1663)," *Biographical Dictionary of British Radicals*, II, 140-141.

[78] Champlin Burrage, *The Early English Dissenters* (Cambridge, 1912), II, 301, or Whitley, "Records," p. 225.

[79] See the "Jessey Memoranda" in Whitley, "Records," pp. 219-220.

[80] It is not clear as to how many people there were from the records. See Whitley, *Ibid.*, p. 220.

[81] *Ibid.*, p. 220. There were really two groups that broke away at different times.

[82] For more on Samuel Eaton, see B.R. White, "Samuel Eaton (d. 1639) Particular Baptist Pioneer," *The Baptist Quarterly*, 24 (1971,72), pp. 10-21.

[83] Burrage, *Dissenters*, II, 299, or Whitley, "Records," p. 220.

[84] B.R. White, one of the foremost scholars of Particular Baptist history, is not dogmatic but is inclined to believe "it could well have been Believer's Baptism" B.R.

After the 1633 departure of eighteen members of the JLJ church, six more left over the issue of baptism in 1638. This latter group joined a church whose leader was John Spilsbury.[85] This church could be Samuel Eaton's church which was now led by Spilsbury because of Eaton's imprisonment.[86] Tolmie does not agree with this conjecture.[87] He believes the Spilsbury church came out of the Dupper group that left the JLJ church in 1630.[88] Regardless of the details, it is clear that the Spilsbury church at this time believed that baptism should be administered only to those who were able to profess their own faith.[89] The Spilsbury church is considered the first Particular Baptist Church in England. By 1644 there were seven such churches in London.

Up until this time there is no clear evidence that the mode of baptism was anything other than pouring or effusion. In "the mid 1630s the records show several examples of individuals who advocated and/or practiced immersion, including Marke Lukar of the

---

White, "Baptist Beginnings and the Kiffin Manuscript," *Baptist History and Heritage*, 2, No.1 [1967], p. 35).

An interesting aside to this discussion of early Particular Baptist history concerns the son of the General Baptist leader John Murton (John Murton was the pastor of the first General Baptist Church after Thomas Helwys died in 1616). Leon McBeth suggests that the son had been a part of the JLJ church, and one of those who separated with Mr. Dupper in 1630. If this is so did he influence any of these people and groups of the JLJ church toward believer's baptism? Is there a connection between the General and Particular Baptists after all? As far as I know this possible connection has not been researched (McBeth, *Baptist Heritage*, p. 43).

[85]   See the "Kiffin Manuscript" in W.T. Whitley, "The Rise of the Particular Baptists in London, 1633-1644," *Transactions of the Baptist Historical Society*, 1 (1910), p. 231.

[86]   W.T. Whitley, "The Seven Churches of London," *The Review and Expositor*, 7 (1910), p. 386. Whitley believes that Spilsbury founded a church on or before 1633 and Samuel Eaton was one of his chief supporters. See White, "Baptist Beginnings," pp. 30-31, for the possible relationships between Spilsbury and Eaton. For Sam Eaton see D. B. Mock, "Eaton, Samuel (d. 1639)," *Biographical Dictionary of British Radicals*, I, 242-243. For John Spilsbury see R. L. Greaves, "Spilsbury (or Spilsbery), John (1593-c.1668)," *Biographical Dictionary of British Radicals*, III, 193-194, and James Renihan, "John Spilsbury (1593-c1662/1668)," in *The British Particular Baptists 1638-1910* (Springfield, Missouri, 1998), I, 21-37.

[87]   Neither does White, "Baptist Beginnings," p. 36.

[88]   Tolmie, *Triumph*, pp. 19-27.

[89]   B.R. White, *The English Baptists of the Seventeenth Century* (London, 1983), p. 59. Whitley believes that "as early as 1633 he (Spilsbury) was 'baptizing' on profession of belief," (Whitley, "Seven," p. 386). The Kiffin Manuscript reads, "1638 Mr. Tho: Wilson Mr Pen & H. Pen & 3 more being convinced that Baptism was not for Infants but professed Believers joyned with Mr Jo: Spilsbury ye Churches Favour being desired therein" (Whitley, "Rise", p. 231).

Eaton church."[90] By 1642, however, the mode of baptism for Particular Baptists had become immersion.

The "Kiffin Manuscript" gives details of the events surrounding their move to immersion as the mode of baptism.[91] By 1640 the JLJ church split: one group remained with Henry Jessey and the other group followed Praise-God Barebone.[92] Sometime after this, Henry Jessey and Richard Blunt[93] discussed the subject of the mode of baptism, and in light of Colossians 2:12 and Romans 6:4 they concluded that baptism "ought to be by diping ye Body into ye Water, resembling Burial & riseing again."[94] They believed that baptism was to be by immersion and not sprinkling. They heard that a group of Anabaptists in the Netherlands practised immersion, so they sent Dutch-speaking Blunt to Holland to receive advice from them on this subject.[95] This Anabaptist group was called the Rhynsburgers or Collegiants, a Dutch Mennonite group that originated out of the "controversies surrounding the Synod of Dort."[96]

When Blunt returned in 1641 the records tell us:

> They proceed on therein,viz, Those Persons yt ware persuaded Baptism should be by dipping ye Body had mett in two Companies, & did intend so to meet after this, all these agreed to proceed alike togeather. And then Manifesting (not by any formal Words a Covenant) wch word was scrupled by some of them, but by mutual desires & agreement each Testified.:

---

[90]   McBeth, *Baptist Heritage*, p. 45. Marke Lukar was a Greek who was known to advocate immersion before 1640. It would appear that as early as the mid-1630s he "advocated and / or practiced immersion." And by 1649 he was baptizing by immersion in Seekonk (*Ibid.*, pp. 43, 45, 141).

[91]   See Whitley, "Rise," pp. 232-235. Concerning the Kiffin Manuscript, B.R. White defends the plausibility of Kiffin's authorship contrary to Whitley's contention that it was authored by Henry Jessey (B.R. White, "Who really wrote the Kiffin Manuscript?" *Baptist History and Heritage*, 1, No.3 [1966], pp. 3-10,14).

[92]   For a brief biographical sketch of Barebone see, T. Liu, "Barebone, (or Barbon, Barbone), Praisegod (c. 1596-1679)," *Biographical Dictionary of British Radicals*, I, 37-38.

[93]   He was a part of the Samuel Eaton group.

[94]   Whitley, "Rise," p. 232. It should be noted that Henry Jessey, however, did not come to the conviction of believer's baptism until 1645. At that time he was baptised by Hanserd Knollys. From 1640 to 1645 he immersed infants.

[95]   Burrage, *Dissenters*, II, 302-303, or Whitley, "Rise," pp. 232-233.

[96]   Dirk Jellema, "Collegiants," *The New International Dictionary of the Christian Church*, revised ed. ed. J.D. Douglas, (Grand Rapids, 1974), pp. 237-238. Also see George H. Williams, *The Radical Reformation* (Philadelphia, 1962), pp. 412-413, 466-467, 591, 647, 654, 788, 803; and John P. Dever, "Schwenkfelders," *The New International Dictionary of the Christian Church*, ed. J. D. Douglas (Grand Rapids, 1974), pp. 888-889.

> Those two Companyes did set apart one to Baptize the rest; So it was sol-
> emnly performed by them.
> Mr Blunt Baptized Mr Blacklock yt was a Teacher amongst them, & Mr
> Blunt being Baptized, he and Mr Blacklock Baptized ye rest of their friends
> that ware so minded, & many being added to them they increased much.[97]

It is uncertain whether Mr. Blunt was baptized in Holland or whether he was baptized by Mr. Blacklock after he had baptized Mr. Blacklock. Burrage gives some strong original evidence for the latter position.[98] There was some concern about historic succession of baptism, and so some Particular Baptists felt Blunt needed to be baptized by someone who had already been baptized. Spilsbury, however, did not agree, believing there was no need for succession. He said: "Where there is a beginning, some one must be first."[99]

Whether baptism by immersion for Baptists began with Mr. Blunt being baptised by the Collegiants in Holland, or with Mr. Blacklock by an unbaptised Mr. Blunt in England, immersion became the mode of baptism for Particular Baptists by 1642.[100]

It should be noted that neither the General Baptists nor the Particular Baptists used the name "Baptist" until the mid-1650s. They used the names, "Brethren", "Baptized Churches" or "Churches of the Baptized Way".[101]

---

[97] Whitley, "Rise," pp. 233-234. Fifty-three people were baptised at this time in January 1642.

[98] Champlin Burrage, "The Restoration of Immersion by the English Anabaptists and Baptists (1640-1700)," *The American Journal of Theology*, 16 (1912), pp. 70-79. His reasons include: 1) the Kiffin Manuscript does not explicitly state that Blunt was baptized by Batten; and 2) Praise-God Barebone, Francis Bamfield, Nathaniel Homes and Henry Jessey state that these Baptists began by baptizing themselves. White agrees with him, "Baptist Beginnings," p. 36.

[99] McBeth, *Baptist Heritage*, p. 47.

[100] Burrage, "Restoration," pp. 70-89. For further information on the history, the administrator, and the mode of baptism for Particular Baptists from some original documents see this article.

[101] McBeth, *Baptist Heritage*, p. 48. See also Robert B. Hannen, "Historical Notes on the Name 'Baptist'," *Foundations*, 8 (1965), pp. 62-71.

History of the Calvinistic Baptists from 1640 – 1689

1640 to 1660 was a period of revolution and change for all Englishmen. Not least among those greatly affected was the newly organized fellowship of Calvinistic Baptist churches. For this new group of churches, politically, it was a time of liberty; theologically, it was a time of apology; and denominationally, it was a time of growth. Politically, throughout the Interregnum, the Particular Baptists benefited and used the freedoms and privileges accorded to them, but as a group remained free from political involvement. It is quite true that many Particular Baptists were involved in the political leadership of the day but as a group of churches they did not identify themselves with any government or movement. They saw their purpose for existence in spiritual things, not in political or earthly things. For example, in the 1640s numerous Baptists were sympathetic to the Leveller movement with some involved in it; but as a whole they opposed it.[102] Again, in the 1650s some Baptists were involved in the Fifth Monarchy movement to one degree or another but as a group they did not associate with it, particularly, its political side.[103] In addition, Antinomianism, Ranterism, Quakerism and Seekerism troubled Baptist churches of the 1640s and 1650s.[104] Concerning Cromwell's New Model Army and the Commonwealth/Protectorate government, the Particular Baptists were strong supporters.[105] Many of them were members of both the government and the Army with some in places of leadership.[106]

Although Particular Baptists were involved in the politics of the day, their influence from 1640 to 1660, politically, was minimal.[107]

---

[102] See Tolmie, *Triumph*, pp. 161-169. See also Tolmie, "General," pp. 258-297, for a fuller look at the involvement of Baptists with the Levellers.

[103] A.C. Underwood, *A History of the English Baptists* (London, 1947), p. 84. See Tolmie, "General," pp. 539-591, on Baptists and their involvement with the Fifth Monarchists.

[104] J.F McGregor, "The Baptists: The Fount of all Heresy," in *Radical Religion in the English Revolution*, eds. J.F McGregor & B. Reay (Oxford, 1984), pp. 58-62, 124-125.

[105] One of the reasons they supported Cromwell was his commitment to religious liberty.

[106] See Underwood, *English Baptists*, pp. 74-77 for Particular Baptists in the Army, and pp. 77-80 for Particular Baptists in the Government. See also Tolmie, *Triumph*, pp. 155-161; Torbet, *History of the Baptists*, pp. 75-79; and Whitley, *A History of British Baptists* (London, 1923), pp. 73-81. See also Tolmie, "General," pp. 237-258 for the years 1647-49, and pp. 591-636 for the 1650s.

[107] B.R. White states, "What is fairly clear about Particular Baptist political views

As J. F. MacGregor has said, "The Baptists [Arminian and Calvin-
istic] played a minor role in the political events of the English Revolution."[108] Among the reasons, he cites two of great importance:
the "Baptists' attitude to the world which inhibited them from effective political action;" and "[their] predominantly theocratic
temperment." He goes on to say that, "the sectarian sense that the
saints were apart from the world, exacerbated by popular notions
of Anabaptism, encouraged a passive response to the events of the
Revolution."[109] The Particular Baptists' main political concern was
the guarantee of their religious liberty so that they might freely
worship the Lord and preach the gospel.

Theologically, during the 1640s and 50s, the Particular Baptists
along with other sectarian groups were accorded a measure of religious freedom. However, this did not prevent these Baptists from
being charged by the Reformed ecclesiastical community with various heresies. In the 1640s they had to defend themselves against
charges of Anabaptism[110], Arminianism[111], Antinomianism[112], and

during the Great Rebellion is that most of them loathed and abominated tithes." Some
Particular Baptists were not against state support but most were. For example, in 1657
when the Hereford church looked to London for some answers to this question of tithes,
it was asserted by Kiffin and others that "every church of Christ is bound to take general care that such as minister to them be sufficiently and comfortably supplied in all
good things for themselves and families and, in case of real insufficiency in any church,
that that church ought to apply themselves to other churches for assistance." The London leaders went on to say that if their minister persisted in receiving state support they
should deal with him according to Matthew 18:15-17. They should "withdraw from
him as [a] disorderly person," if he does not listen to the church (B. R. White, "The
English Particular Baptists and the Great Rebellion," *Baptist History and Heritage*, 9, No.
1 [1974], pp. 28-29).

[108]   J.F. MacGregor, "The Baptists: Fount of All Heresy," in *Radical Religion in the
English Revolution*, eds. J.F. McGregor & B. Reay (New York, 1988), p. 56. The Baptists,
however, were influential in Ireland under Henry Cromwell during the revolutionary
period.

[109]   *Ibid.*

[110]   Paul Gritz, "Samuel Richardson and the Religious and Political Controversies
Confronting the London Particular Baptists, 1643 to 1658," (unpublished Ph.D. dissertation, Southwestern Baptist Theological Seminary, 1987), p. 126ff.

[111]   Featley's book *The Dippers dipt.* (1645), pp. 219-220 asserts that the Particular
Baptists held Arminian errors.

[112]   Those considered Antinomians include Tobias Crisp, John Saltmarsh, John
Eaton, Henry Denne, and Paul Hobson. For a history of Antinomianism at this time
see Gertrude Huehns, *Antinomianism in English History* (London, 1951), pp. 55-88. For a
doctrinal exposition of this teaching see *Ibid.*, pp. 37-54. See also Ernest Kevan, *The
Grace of Law* (n.d.; rpt. Ligonier, PA, 1993), pp. 22-36, 146-148, 167-172. See chapter
three for the teachings of English antinomianism. See Gritz, "Samuel Richardson," p.

Socinianism[113]. By the early 1650s these charges of heresy had waned. Nevertheless, in these years, the Particular Baptists were found defending themselves against such things as the millennial radicalism of the Fifth Monarchy Men[114], the infiltration of the heretical teachings of the Quakers in their ranks[115], and the teachings of the Seventh-Day Baptists[116]. In addition, during the 1640s

---

245. Gritz says, "The Antinomians focused on an intimate relationship of oneness or union with Christ, which the Holy Spirit revealed to the person in an immediate experience of faith" (*Ibid.*, p. 241).

[113] Socinianism taught that Jesus was a created person who only had a human nature; the Spirit is God's power; salvation is by works; and the wicked are annihilated. For Socinianism in England see H. John McLachlan, *Socinianism in Seventeenth Century England* (Oxford, 1951). It was through Baillie's book *Anabaptism* that Particular Baptists were associated with Socinianism.

[114] White, *English Baptists*, pp. 82-86.

[115] As the Quakers grew they took members from both General and Particular Baptist Churches (though it was more of a problem for the former than the latter). The Particular Baptist Churches of Hexham, Newcastle, Kensworth, Oxford, and Newbury lost members to the Quakers (B.R. White, ed., *Association Records of the Particular Baptists of England, Wales and Ireland to 1660* (London, n.d.), pp. 192, 194, 204). The Tiverton Church warned against those "who lay aside Christ, Scripture, and obedience all at once, subjecting themselves to a suggestion or voice within them more than to the mind of God written in the holy scriptures" (quoted in Geoffrey Nuttall, "The Baptist Western Association 1653-1658," *Journal of Ecclesiastical History*, 11 [1960], p. 217). At Kent the Particular Baptist Luke Howard became a leader in the Quaker movement (Craig W. Horle, "Quakers and Baptists 1547-1660," *The Baptist Quarterly*, 26 [1975,76], p. 347). In 1650 the Particular Baptist leaders published a pamphlet against the Ranters and Quakers entitled, *Heart bleedings for Professors' Abominations*. It was signed by Spilsbury, Kiffin and fourteen others. The Quaker movement was of such a concern that this pamphlet was reprinted with the 1651 and 1652 edition of the 1644 *Confession*. The pamphlet warned against the teaching that the Cross of Christ was a "mere history and shadow", that the Scriptures were but a letter, that the ordinances were but fleshly forms, and that the traditional standards of holy living were no longer applicable (White, *English Baptists*, p. 78). Paul Hobson and Henry Jessey also reported and spoke against the Quakers (Horle, "Quakers," p. 349).

[116] A minor problem for the Particular Baptists was the issue of the Seventh Day Sabbath. A number of churches were Seventh-Day Baptists in the 1650s (Thomas Tillam became a Seventh Day Baptist in 1657; see Michael J. Novak, "'Thy Will Be Done' The Theology of the English Particular Baptists, 1638-1660" [unpublished Ph.D. dissertation, Harvard University, 1979], pp. 410-411). The Watford church of Hertfordshire lost some members to the Seventh-Day men. The Abingdon Association discussed the subject in 1659. They concluded: "It was desired by diverse of the messengers yt in case nothing else should be found amisse but the bare observing of the 7th Day Sabbath, then the saying of the Apostle in Rom. 14:1-5f; might be well minded" (White, *Association Records*, p. 195). It appears that this never became a major issue with the Particular Baptists and, consequently, did not cause any significant problems for them. For more on Seventh Day Baptists see Bryan W. Ball, *The Seventh-Day Men: Sabbatarians and Sabbatarianism in England and Wales, 1660-1800* (Oxford, 1994).

the Particular Baptists promoted religious toleration or liberty beyond the limits acceptable to the majority of people in the England
of their day. They believed that the civil government had no authority in spiritual matters.[117] The Parliament of the 1640s, dominated by Presbyterians, however, opposed religious toleration.[118]
When the reigns of power changed in the 1650s, the Particular
Baptists continued to champion the cause of religious toleration,
supporting Cromwell and his government which, in principle, advocated such toleration.

Denominationally, the Particular Baptist Churches grew significantly during the 1640s and 50s. The founding seven churches of
London which subscribed to the 1644 *Confession* came into being
not only because of their theological convictions but also because
of the political climate of the 1640s. The Particular Baptists along
with other Dissenters were permitted to worship openly as they
thought best and to propagate their beliefs freely through print and
debate.[119] This was unprecedented in English history. In these early
years, their missionary efforts extended only to the surrounding
counties of London. After the Civil War and the victories of the
Parliamentary Armies of 1644 and 1645, the Particular Baptists
took their message beyond London. Army and civilian evangelists
preached the gospel and set up Baptist Churches all over England.[120] The main strength of the Particular Baptists lay in the
south, west, and the Midlands. By 1660 they were well established
in the countryside[121] including Wales and Ireland. Leon McBeth
writes:

> The Baptists experienced vast growth during the years 1648-1660. Taking
> advantage of the relative liberty of the times and the public favor toward

---

[117]   Gritz, "Samuel Richardson," pp. 296-301.
[118]   *Ibid.*, p. 294.
[119]   Concerning pamphlets during the Revolution see Reay, "Radical Religion,"
in *Radical Religion*, p. 13. From Arthur S. Langley's article "Seventeenth Century Baptist
Disputations," *Transactions Of Baptist Historical Society*, 6 (1919), pp. 216-243, we see that
there were at least 79 disputations between Baptists and others during the years 1641-
1660. Kiffin, Tombes, Jessey, and Blackwood are a few of the Particular Baptists that
took part. The greatest number of disputations was on the subjects of baptism and
Quakerism.
[120]   See Tolmie, "General," pp. 298-347, for details of the stability, organization,
and expansion of the Particular Baptists from 1649-1657.
[121]   MacGregor, "Baptists," p. 36.

evangelical Protestantism, they preached publicly, formed new churches, linked them into associations, issued confessions of faith and published their views in a steady stream of tracts and books.[122]

One of the keys to their success was the close association between the country churches and the London churches.[123] In the 1650s five associations of churches were born, scattered throughout England, Wales and Ireland.[124] The five associations were: the Western Association[125], the South Wales Association[126], the Abingdon Asso-

---

[122]   McBeth, *Baptist Heritage*, p. 111.

[123]   The central Association of the Particular Baptist group of churches was the London Association. This group committed themselves to one another in their like precious faith, united upon the 1644 *Confession*. The leadership of the London Particular Baptist Churches included Paul Hobson, Thomas Patient, John Spilsbury, Thomas Kilcop, Samuel Richardson, Hanserd Knollys, Benjamin Cox, Edward Harrison, John Miles, John Pendaveres, and Christopher Blackwood (B.R. White, "The London Calvinistic Baptist Leadership 1644-1660," *The Baptist Quarterly*, 32 [1987,88], pp. 36-40).

Why were the London churches so important to the Particular Baptist church movement? B.R. White states that the London Baptist community appeared to have fulfilled several important functions for the whole group: 1) they provided the doctrinal standards for all the churches in the country at large by means of the 1644 *Confession* and its later editions; 2) they provided a clearinghouse for ideas and a center for consultation for those churches; 3) they initiated evangelistic missions in various parts of the British Isles (*Ibid.*, pp. 43-44).

[124]   Churches also associated in the north of England through the commissioning of the London church in Swan Alley. But these churches did not become an association in these early years because of conflict over the subject of the laying on of hands and open communion (B.R. White, "The Organization of the Particular Baptists 1644-1660," *Journal of Ecclesiastical History*, 17 [1966], pp. 214-216). For an account of Tillam's career, see E.A. Payne, "Thomas Tillam," *The Baptist Quarterly*, 17 (1957,58). For a history of one of those North England churches, see W.T. Whitley, "Hill Cliff in England Parts 1 & 2," *Review and Expositor*, 6 (1909), pp. 274-284, 424-435.

[125]   The Western Association was probably founded through the work of Thomas Collier, and had a close association with the London leaders and their theology. This Association's activities include: days spent in waiting upon God; the resolution of queries submitted by the churches of the Association; and the issuing of circular letters of exhortation to the churches (Nuttall, "Baptist Western," pp. 213ff). For a brief sketch of Collier see M. A. Hartman, "Collier (or Collyer), Thomas (fl. 1634?-1691)," *Biographical Dictionary of British Radicals*, I, 162-163.

[126]   The first provincial Association traced its beginnings to John Miles who in 1649 was sent from London to South Wales along with Thomas Proud. There they founded a church in Ilston in Glamorgan in October of the same year. Another Church was started in Llanigon in early 1650. And a third church began that summer in Llanharan in East Glamorgan (B.R. White, "Organisation," p. 210). A fourth church (1651) and a fifth (1652) were founded in Carmarthen and in Abergavenny, respectively. These churches were all formed upon the doctrine of closed communion.

ciation[127], the English Midlands Association[128], and the Irish[129] Association.[130] These Associations were started as a result of missionary endeavors from London.[131] B.R. White, in his study of the Particular Baptist associational organization in the period of 1644-1660, concludes several things: 1) that the London leadership and theology were important to these Associations; 2) that the "general meeting" of messengers was the characteristic unit of the organization; 3) that the local associations kept close touch with each other by personal visitation and by sharing reports of their meetings[132]; and 4) that the cement of the nation-wide organization was the

---

[127]   In October 1652 representatives from Reading, Abingdon, and Henly met together and formed the Abingdon Association. In October 1652 representatives from the churches met together and agreed upon matters requiring intercongregational collaboration, and decided they would meet for mutual advice, financial support, and the carrying out of the work of God. Two other churches joined them from Kensworth and Eversholt. In March 1653 all five churches met together and signed *The Agreement of the Churches* which stated their purpose for meeting together. It was made clear that any recommendations at the associational level needed individual church approval before being returned for confirmation at the next Association meeting. A major concern for this association was to remain in close contact with the London Churches. This Association continued to grow adding to its number in 1655 the churches of Wantage, Wallington, Kingston, Hoddenham and Pyrton. In 1656 Oxford, Hemel Hempstead, and North Warnborough joined the Association (White, "Organisation," pp. 216-217).

[128]   The Midland Association had its beginning in June 1655 uniting upon the basis of a *Confession of Faith in Sixteen Articles* and an *Agreement* of the churches much like that of the Abingdon Association. Daniel King was probably the founder of some of the congregations that made up this Association. The first congregations of the Association were: Warwich, Moreton-in-the-Marsh, Bourton-on-the-Water, Tewkesbury, Hook Norton, Derby, and Alcester. The first meeting dealt with the lawfulness of state payment for the minister. The messengers voted against such payment. Other meetings dealt with the subjects of: closed communion; attending the preaching of national ministers; and the Fifth Monarchy. Concerning this latter issue it was made clear that violence and force were not to be used but to wait with patience and quietness for the time (White, "Organisation," pp. 223-225).

[129]   The Irish Association traced its beginnings to a letter, dated June 1653, sent from Waterford to the London churches. Ten congregations in Ireland, composed mainly of the Army men stationed there, had already met together at least once; and with this letter, among other things, they were calling other Calvinistic Baptists in England and Wales to special times of prayer and fasting. The London churches passed the Irish letter on to other congregations with which they were in contact (White, "Organisation," pp. 220-221).

[130]   This does not include the main association of London Churches.

[131]   R. Dwayne Conner gives five contributing factors for the forming of Baptist Associations: 1) security and fellowship; 2) demonstration of orthodoxy; 3) preservation of unity; 4) evangelism; and 5) expansion and institutionalization. He gives five aspects of associational life: 1) fellowship; 2) ordination; 3) discipline; 4) evangelism; and 5) benevolence ("Early English Baptist Associations," *Foundations*, 15 [1972], pp. 167-175).

[132]   See, for example, White, "Organisation," p. 222.

leadership of Benjamin Cox, John Miles, Thomas Patient, Thomas Collier, Daniel King, and Nathaniel Strange outside of London.[133]

Particular Baptist Churches grew rapidly during the period of 1640-1660, uniting together under a common *Confession*, supporting one another in their mission, and promoting their cause. It is estimated that there were 131 Particular Baptist Churches in the British Isles in 1660.[134] In their first twenty years these churches experienced tremendous growth.

The years 1660 to 1689 were quite different from the 1640s and 50s for the Particular Baptists and other Dissenters in Great Britain. For the Particular Baptist Churches, it was: politically, a time of repression; theologically, a time of internal and external polemics; and denominationally, a time of persecution and perseverance.

With the return of Charles II to the throne and his failure to bring about religious toleration, persecution of Dissenters, including Baptists,[135] followed. At this time Thomas Venner and other Fifth Monarchists led a rebellion in London.[136] Many were killed, and thirteen others including Venner were executed. The Baptists were strongly implicated in this rebellion, and in some ways they, in particular, were made a scapegoat for all the problems of church and state since 1640.[137]

In 1660 the Long Parliament was dissolved, and in the following year the Cavalier Parliament was elected. Consequently Presbyterians became Dissenters with Baptists and Quakers. The Cavalier

---

[133] *Ibid.*, p. 226. The churches who sent these men out held to the principle of closed communion.

[134] Underwood, *English Baptists*, p. 85. For a list of Particular and General Baptist Churches in England until 1660 see "Baptist Churches till 1660," *Transactions of the Baptist Historical Society*, 2 (1911), pp. 236-254.

[135] White, *English Baptists*, pp. 94-95.

[136] The Rebellion took place in January of 1661 and lasted four days. See B.S. Capp, *The Fifth Monarchy Men* (London, 1972), pp. 199-200.

[137] It was true that the Baptists had some connections with the Fifth Monarchy as has been noted earlier but they were almost all against violence and rebellion. For a study of the Baptists and the Fifth Monarchy movement see Louise Fargo Brown, *The Political Activities of the Baptists and Fifth Monarchy Men in England during the Interregnum* (Washington, 1912). To show their opposition to Venner's Rebellion and anything like it, several tracts were published by Baptists. One of those tracts was issued by William Kiffin and other Baptists, both General and Particular, entitled, *The Humble Apology of Some Commonly Called Anabaptists* (1661). The purpose of this tract was to distance themselves from the Fifth Monarchist radicals.

Parliament was quick to show its power over, and goals for, religion in the country. What came to be known as the *Clarendon Code*[138] was directed at those who dissented from the Church of England. It was primarily directed at the Presbyterians but it greatly affected the Baptists.[139] The *Conventicle Act* and *Five Mile Act* were effective in making Baptist meetings difficult to organize and sustain. The *Act of Uniformity* made sure that any Baptists who were supported by the State were ejected.[140] This Act had little effect on the Particular Baptists who generally opposed state support.[141] In total there were one thousand seven hundred and sixty Dissenting ministers ejected.[142] Approximately thirty Baptists retired or were ejected by 1662 and many of these came from Wales.[143] Some of the ejected Particular Baptists included Paul Hobson, John Skinner, Richard Harrison, William Kaye, John Tombes, John Miles, and Vavasor Powell.[144] All of these men practised open communion and open membership.

During the reign of Charles II persecution waxed and waned, with the pro-Church of England parliament continually seeking to stamp out dissent by passing various Acts.[145] In 1685 Charles died

---

[138]   The four Acts passed against dissent were: the *Coronation Act* (1661) which allowed only those who conformed to the state church to hold public office; the *Act of Uniformity* (1662) which permitted only ministers who believed the doctrines and worship of the Church of England to be serving in its pulpits; the *Conventicle Act* of 1664 which set severe penalties for holding unauthorized worship services with more than five people beyond the immediate family; and the *Five Mile Act* (1665) which forbade ejected ministers from preaching, teaching or residing within five miles of the town from which they had been ejected. The *Clarendon Code* made all religious dissent illegal. This made all Baptist meetings illegal, and opened the door to persecution.

[139]   See W.T. Whitley, "Militant Baptists 1660-1672," *Transactions of the Baptist Historical Society*, 1 (1909), pp. 148-155. This article shows the involvement of General and Particular Baptists in the planning of insurrections and plots.

[140]   See W.T. Whitley, "The Relation of Baptists to the Ejectment," in *The Enactment of 1662 and the Free Churches* (London, n.d.), pp. 75-96.

[141]   Only 90 Baptists (General and Particular) held posts in Cromwell's state church before the Restoration.

[142]   About 20% of the total clergy.

[143]   See W.T. Whitley, *A History of British Baptists* (London, 1923), p. 160.

[144]   Powell was involved with the Welsh Particular Baptists during the 1650s. Sometime in that decade he became a General Baptist. His doctrines after joining the latter group were written down and preserved. A copy of the manuscript was edited by Champlin Burrage, "Early Welsh Baptist Doctrines," *Transactions of the Baptist Historical Society*, 1 (1908), pp. 3-20.

[145]   E.g., *Conventicle Act* of 1670; and *Test Act* of 1673 (An Act for the preventing dangers which happen from popish recusants).

and James II ascended the throne. The fears of a return to Catholicism now became a reality. It was too much for some. In parts of the west country many Dissenters gathered around the illegitimate son of Charles, the Duke of Monmouth, in order to overthrow James and place the Duke on the throne. Some Particular Baptists were a part of this Rebellion, including Pastor Sampson Larke of Lyme, Abraham Holmes, Richard Rumbold, Henry Danvers, and two of William Kiffin's grandsons, Benjamin and William Hewling. When the Rebellion failed many of these Baptists were executed.[146] The Rebellion resulted in severe persecution of Baptists and other Dissenters. The "Bloody Assize" under Chief Justice Jeffreys followed the Rebellion in the Western circuit. Baptist Churches in Taunton, Lyme, Honiton and Dalwood suffered severely. As Whitley says, "For two years nothing could be done but barely exist."[147]

The persecution continued in England until April 1687 when, surprising as it may seem, James issued a *Declaration of Indulgence* which suspended all penal laws on ecclesiastical matters. The jails were emptied and chapels were built.[148] Unknown to the Baptists at that time, the years of persecution were over.[149] Shortly after the King issued a second *Indulgence*, the Tories invited William of Orange to invade their country and take the throne. William landed in Torbay in November of 1688 without a fight, and the King fled.[150]

In January of the following year, William Kiffin led a deputation of Baptists to present an address of welcome to the new ruler. He personally gave the new King five hundred pounds to help his government over the first six months of his reign. The Baptists as well as the Anglicans were pleased with the turn of events. Baptists were hopeful that William would provide toleration for their worship. And this he did in the next months by passing an Act concerning

---

[146] Danvers was at least one who escaped. He fled to Holland (White, *English Baptists*, pp. 133-134).

[147] Whitley, *British Baptists*, p. 149.

[148] For example, Henry Forty and church (White, *English Baptists*, p. 134).

[149] On Toleration and James II see S.H. Mayor, "James II and the Dissenters," *The Baptist Quarterly*, 34 (1991,92), pp. 80-90. See also Douglas C. Sparkes, "The Test Act of 1673 and its Aftermath," *The Baptist Quarterly*, 25 (1973,74), pp. 77-78.

[150] Christopher Hill gives some reasons for James' failure (*Century of Revolution 1603-1714* [London, 1974], pp. 205-209). Hill says, "His actions did everything to unite the propertied class against him and to heal the split between Whigs and Tories which had appeared to threaten civil war in 1681" (*Ibid.*, p. 205).

toleration through Parliament, entitled, *An Act of exempting their Majesties' Protestant Subjects Dissenting from the Church of England, from the Penalties of certain laws.*[151]

Times had not only changed politically for the Particular Baptists but they had also changed theologically. During the Interregnum the Particular Baptists were defending themselves against attacks from without. They were a new group of churches who needed to establish their orthodoxy before their fellow countrymen. They were not a heretical sect but fellow Calvinists with the Presbyterians and Independents.

By 1660 the Particular Baptists were well established in England, Wales and Ireland with over one hundred churches. The Presbyterians and Independents had become Dissenters along with the Baptists. Their common foe was the Church of England. Thus, the external polemics used to prove their orthodoxy to the Presbyterians and Independents during the Interregnum were unnecessary. Although the Particular Baptists still had to dispute with those outside

---

[151]   This *Act*, though a great blessing to Dissenters, did not give them full religious liberty, and it gave no liberty at all to Jews and Roman Catholics. It, however, did give Dissenters the right to worship separately from the Established church. The *Act* even made a special concession for Baptists that read: "And whereas some dissenting protestants scruple the baptizing of infants; be it enacted ... that every person in pretended holy orders, or pretending to holy orders, or preacher, or teacher, that shall subscribe the aforesaid articles of religion, except before excepted, and also except part of the seven and twentieth article touching infant baptism and shall take the said oaths, and make and subscribe the declaration aforesaid,... every such person shall enjoy all the privileges, benefits, and advantages, which any other dissenting minister, as aforesaid, might have or enjoy by virtue of this Act" (quoted in Sparkes, "Test Act," pp. 78-79).

This Act, as was mentioned above, did not give Baptists and other Dissenters full religious liberty. They still had to pay tithes to the Church of England, and register their meetings with the Church of England Bishops; their ministers were to subscribe to certain Church of England Articles (Art. 36 & 39), and if a Dissenter desired to hold public office he had to pass the Sacramental Test. Whatever were the motives behind the *Act of Toleration*, it accomplished two things: one, it brought about needed national unity and safety; and two, it gave Baptists and other Dissenters freedom to worship without fear of persecution. The thirty hard years of persecution for the Particular Baptists were over. They were very pleased with the measure of toleration they received. This can be seen in Benjamin Keach's response to William and Mary in his preface to *Distressed Zion Relieved* where he says,

And all the time in England you have been,
What strange amazing wonders have we seen?
A poor sick Land divided; by Christ's power
Made whole and all united in one hour
(quoted in McBeth, *Baptist Heritage*, p. 121).

their group such as the Quakers[152], Paedobaptists[153], and possibly Neonomists[154], their polemics were primarily internal. Their internal disputations concerned such things as Arminianism[155], hyper-

---

[152] The greatest external challenge to the Particular Baptists as in the 1650s continued to be the Quaker movement. During this period Particular and General Baptists wrote at least 27 works against the Quakers (White, *English Baptists*, p. 107). Particularily, the seven years after the *Declaration of Indulgence* of 1672 , "the feud between the Baptists and Quakers ... blazed forth" (Whitley, *British Baptists*, p. 127). Quakers continued to cause problems for Baptist Churches during the Restoration years, shattering some of them, taking ministers and members over to the Quaker teaching of the "Inner light."

[153] Particular Baptists had to defend their position against Paedobaptists. There were at least 28 works written by Baptists on the subject of Baptism during the Restoration period (White, *English Baptists*, p. 107). From 1674 Particular Baptists such as Henry Danvers, John Tombes, Hanserd Knollys, William Kiffin, and Benjamin Keach wrote polemically on the subject (W.T. Whitley, *A Baptist Bibliography* (London, 1916), pp. 105, 122, 123, 125). The issue of believer's baptism verses paedobaptism was not dead.

[154] This was a concern of all Calvinistic Dissenters including the Particular Baptists. They believed that Richard Baxter's doctrine of justification tended toward a salvation by works and legalism. Baxter's views were published in his *Aphorisms of Justification* (1649), *Richard Baxter's Confession of His Faith* (1655), and *Richard Baxter's Catholick Theologie* (1675). He was singled out as Amyraut's "only proselyte in England." Baxter believed that the true believer participated in his justification by obedience to the new law of grace.

Neonomianism and his doctrine of Justification were challenged by Isaac Chauncy, Robert Traill, Thomas Edwards, John Owen, William Eyre, and John Crandon. During these Restoration years he lived in Moorfields and in Acton (Middlesex). From these places his influences in writing and preaching on this issue must have disturbed the Calvinistic Baptists, particularily those who were High Calvinists. For more on neonomism see James I. Packer, "The Redemption and Restoration of Man in the Thought of Richard Baxter" (unpublished Ph.D dissertation, Oxford University, 1954), pp. 298-306; C.F. Allison, *The Rise of Moralism* (London, 1966), pp. 154-177; and Ernest F. Kevan, *The Grace of Law*, pp. 203-207.

[155] Just prior to the preparation of the 1677/89 *Confession*, Thomas Collier, a member of Kiffin's church and an evangelist of England's southwest, defected from the Particular Baptists. In 1674 he published a work entitled *A Body of Divinity* which: denied the Calvinistic doctrine of original sin; taught that Christ died for all men; and stated that Christ's humanity was eternal. Particular Baptist ministers including Kiffin and Nehemiah Coxe met with Collier to clear up the matter. The meeting failed to change or satisfactorily explain Collier's views, and Collier was accused of heresy. In 1677 Coxe responded to Collier's teaching with *Vindiciae Veritatis* in order to show non-Particular Baptists that Collier was not espousing Particular Baptist doctrine. His response was an extensive written rebuttal. See Michael Haykin, "The 1689 Confession: A Tercentennial Appreciation 1," *Reformation Canada*, 13, No. 4 (1990), p. 25; Joseph Ivimey, *History of the English Baptists* (London, 1811-1823), II, 403-407; and Richard D. Land, "Doctrinal Controversies of English Particular Baptists (1644-1691) as Illustrated by the Career and writings of Thomas Collier" (unpublished Ph.D dissertation, Oxford University, 1979), pp. 264-286.

Calvinism[156], Seventh-Day worship[157], singing[158], laying on of hands[159], Anti-trinitarianism[160], and mixed communion[161]. Most of these were minor issues for the group as a whole, but to certain Particular Baptist people and churches they were of great concern. Some of these issues were the reason for the writing of a new *Confession* in 1677.

---

[156]   An example of this teaching among Particular Baptists came from the southwest of England. Andrew Gifford Sr. (1642-1721), pastor of the Pithay Particular Baptist Church in Bristol, believed that "some ministers who were of the opinion that as none could pray acceptably without the influences of the Holy Spirit, and unconverted men being destitute of those influences, that therefore it was not their duty to pray, nor the duty of ministers to exhort them to seek spiritual blessings" (quoted in Ivimey, *English Baptists*, I, 416). Gifford wrote to the London Particular Baptists asking for their opinion on this matter. In January of 1675 William Kiffin and others responded saying, "Prayer is a part of that homage which everyman is obliged to give God ... [and] the want of the Spirit's immediate notions to, or its assistance in the duty, doth not take off the obligation to the duty.... If the obligation to this and other duties were suspended merely for want of such motions or assistance, then unconverted persons are so far from sinning in the omission of such duties, that it is their duty to omit them" (quoted in *Ibid.*, pp. 417-418).

[157]   In this period nine works were written by Baptists debating the Seventh Day Sabbath. We know that a certain Mr. Belcher, a bricklayer, of the Particular Baptists, practiced Seventh Day worship (Whitley, *British Baptists*, p. 102). The 1677/89 *Confession* does state that "from the resurrection of Christ, [the sabbath] was changed into the first day of the week, which is called the Lords Day" (XXII.7). Since the *Confession* was the basis of fellowship for Particular Baptists it appears that this issue was not much of a problem among them.

[158]   At the Horsleydown Church the pastor Benjamin Keach introduced hymn singing into the worship somewhere between 1673 and 1675. Keach faced opposition from a group within his own church as well as with some of the London Particular Baptist leaders. The printed debate began in 1690 with another Particular Baptist, Isaac Marlow. Keach had defended hymn-singing in two prior books entitled *Tropologia* (1681) and *Gold Refin'd* (1689). Hercules Collins also defended corporate singing in 1680. The 1677/89 *Confession* appears to endorse hymn singing when in Chapter 22 entitled, "Of Religious Worship and the Sabbath Day", it states, "Teaching and admonishing one another in Psalms, Hymns, and Spiritual songs ... are ... parts of Religious worship of *God*, to be performed in obedience to him" (XXII.5). This is an ambiguous endorsement, however, since it is simply quoting Scripture. This controversy did not really get underway until the 1690s, and so it was not formally a major issue during the Restoration years for Particular Baptists. See J. Barry Vaughn, "Public Worship and Practical Theology in the Work of Benjamin Keach (1640-1704)" (unpublished Ph.D. dissertation, University of St. Andrews, 1989), pp. 131-143 for the history of this controversy. For a brief biographical sketch of Keach see R. L. Greaves, "Keach (or Keeche), Benjamin (1640-1704)," *Biographical Dictionary of British Radicals*, II, 150-151.

Denominationally, Particular Baptist churches experienced freedom and growth during the Interregnum but in the Restoration period they experienced repression and persecution with little freedom for evangelism. Evangelism did take place but not nearly to the extent it had in the early years. We know that Henry Danvers, in the summer of 1672, after the *Declaration of Indulgence*, engaged in preaching tours in the country. We also know that at this time "churches revived and reorganised, new books were opened, new rolls of members were prepared, Associations and Assemblies began again

---

[159] In 1676 the Particular Baptist Henry Danvers wrote a tract on the ordinance of laying on of hands in a supplement to a revised edition of his *Treatise on Baptism*. The new Particular Baptist Benjamin Keach responded to him. Keach before he came to the Particular Baptists strongly defended the practice. See Vaughn, "Keach," pp. 67-75, and Whiting, *English Puritanism*, pp. 121-122. Also see J.K. Parrett on Keach and this subject in, "An Early Baptist on the Laying on of Hands," *The Baptist Quarterly*, 21 (1965,66), pp. 325-327, 320.

[160] A Particular Baptist pastor of Ashford in Kent in his work entitled, *The Veil Turned Aside* stated that most of the Baptists in Kent and Sussex: denied the doctrines of the Trinity, Christ's satisfaction, God's omnipresence; taught soul-sleep; and proclaimed that God has the form of a man. A hostile witness stated that "out of the multitude of Anabaptists [Baptists] that I have known, I cannot mind one that stopped there: They are Separatists, Arminians, Antinomians, Socinians, Libertines, Seekers, Familists" (quoted in Whiting, *English Puritanism*, p. 90). Socinianism was Anti-Trinitarian; it is possible that some Particular Baptists in Kent and Sussex were reading Sozzini's teachings.

[161] One of the most controversial issues that continued to haunt this Baptist group was that of open communion and open membership. For some of the history of this see E.P. Winter, "The Lord's Supper: admission and exclusion among the Baptists of the Seventeenth century," *The Baptist Quarterly*, 17 (1957,58), pp. 272-281 and B.R. White, "Open and Closed Membership among English and Welsh Baptists," *The Baptist Quarterly*, 24 (1971,72), pp. 330-334, 341. The Particular Baptist views on this issue were made clear in the *Appendix* to the 1646 revision of the 1644 *Confession*, saying, "We ... do not admit any to the use of the supper, nor communicate with any in the use of this ordinance, but disciples baptized, lest we should have fellowship with them in doing the contrary to order" (Article 20, quoted in E.B. Underhill, *Confessions of Faith* [London, 1854], p. 59). The communion issue was not resolved during the Restoration years but we should note that in the *Appendix* to the *Confession* of 1677/89 the Particular Baptists decided not to make this an issue in their agreement on "those important articles of the Christian religion." They acknowledged their differences on mixed communion but would not allow it to divide them on the fundamental issues.

to meet."[162] For the most part, however, the Restoration period was a time of perseverance and preservation for Particular Baptists.[163] The persecution for the thirty years ebbed and flowed[164] with some years worse than others, and with certain areas of Britain experiencing more persecution than others. Several very intense times of persecution took place from 1660-1667,[165] 1670-72, 1673-77,[166]

---

[162] Whitley, *British Baptists*, p. 128. We know that the Petty France church in London baptized 108 people from August 1675 to October 1684 (Tim Dowley, "A London Congregation During the Great Persecution," *The Baptist Quarterly*, 27 [1977,78], pp. 233-234).

[163] Baptists were even experiencing persecution before Charles II began to rule. Henry Jessey's book *The Lord's Loud Call to England* (1660) gave examples of persecution of the Baptists and Congregationalists.

[164] Whiting, *English Puritanism*, p. 113.

[165] During the first period of intense persecution, it is recorded at the end of 1662 in the Domestic State Papers that 289 Baptists were in Newgate Prison and 18 were in the Tower (Underwood, *English Baptists*, p. 97). Baptist meeting houses were raided and destroyed. For example, the church in Brick Lane near Whitechapel was raided six times: "the soldiers smashed the pulpit to pieces, and on July 27th a multitude of butchers out of Whitechapel, together with the bailiff's followers and a number of boys smashed the forms, windows, and doors" (Whiting, *English Puritanism*, p. 111). In addition, Baptist pastors were often put in prison. One such pastor was Bristol's Thomas Ewins in 1661. He was imprisoned for preaching, under the *Corporation Act*. Another pastor, Abraham Cheare of a Particular Baptist Church at Plymouth, was imprisoned for most of the time from 1660 to his death in 1668. During these years he published a book of his letters entitled *Words in Season* (1668) which reflected "a very clear theology of suffering under persecution and his concern for growth in holiness among his correspondents"(White, *English Baptists*, p. 113). By 1665 the fires of persecution were waning. In 1667 Clarendon fell from power.

[166] Persecution picked up again in the 1670s with the renewing of the *Conventicles Act*. We have an example of persecution during this period from the Broadmead Baptist Church in Bristol. In 1674 Guy Carleton, the Bishop of Bristol, Ralph Ollive (the Mayor), and John Hellier (a constable for the parish) made a determined attack upon the Dissenters of Bristol. Pastors were the main targets of the authorities; if they could imprison them or discourage them, the meetings might cease. Thomas Hardcastle, Broadmead's pastor, was imprisoned seven different times during these years but the church continued to meet. In order to arrest a pastor like Hardcastle the authorities would raid a Dissenting conventicle gathered in a private home. In July of 1675 the authorities fell upon a Bristol Baptist meeting but they "could not find ye Bro. that spake, for wee had conveyed him downe into a roome under, through a Trap made like a Biffet-Bench against ye Wall in a seate or pue enclosed" (Roger Hayden, ed., *The Records of a Church of Christ in Bristol, 1640-1687* [Printed for the Bristol Record Society, 1974], p. 170). In light of this danger these clandestine Baptist meetings were set up at different times and places. In addition, the Dissenting parishioners wore plain clothing to the meetings in order not to raise any suspicion. The *Records* tell us the people were "taking a great deal of Care in going and coming, ye Women wearing neither White aprons nor Pattens." Moreover, in case of a potential raid on a meeting in a home they agreed, to appoint some youth, or two of them, to be out at ye door every meeting, to Watch when...informers or officers were coming, and soe to come in, one of them, and

and 1680-1686,[167] ending only a year into James II's reign.[168]

give us notice thereof. Alsoe, some of ye hearers, women and Sisters, would Sitt and Crowde in ye Staires, when we did begin ye Meeting with any Exercise, that soe ye Informers might not too Suddainely come in upon us; by reason of which they were prevented divers times (Hayden, *Ibid.*, p. 149).

The Broadmead church not only had to watch out for sudden raids upon their meetings but also for informers *in* their meetings. One way to deal with this was to curtain off a section of the gathering where only the pastor and a few trusted members would sit. The curtain was closed while the preacher spoke. When the message was concluded the preacher sat down, the curtain was opened, and those sitting outside the curtain were not able to tell who had preached. The informer would not know whom to accuse. The Broadmead Particular Baptist Church went through hard times in these years. They described their plight in 1674 as follows: "Our Ministers being taken from us, one dead, and ye rest Imprissoned, and we feared their death likewise in such a Bad Prisson, and we being pursued closely every meeting, ... followed by ye Bishop's men.... For our Partes, at our Meeting, we presently made use of our ministering gifts in ye Church, (as we did in former persecutions, Contenting ourselves with meane gifts and coarse fare in ye want of Better). Wherefore we considered which way to Maintaine our Meetings, by preserving our Speakers" (*Ibid.*, p. 150). Such persecution took place in other places in Britain also.

[167]　In the 1680s the Baptists probably experienced the worst years of persecution since the Restoration. Fears concerning Charles Catholic brother James coming to the throne sparked persecution against all anti-Church of England people. From 1681 to 1686 persecution was fierce. One informer in 1682 claimed to have fifty men working for him to track down conventicles every Sunday (White, *English Baptists*, p. 130). Because of the intense persecution, the Broadmead church decided to stop meeting together publicly and break up into small groups in order to fall in line with the *Conventicle Act*.

The church at a later time had circular meetings at five different places with a lay leader preaching at each location. They would meet at different times. Within five weeks they would hear all the lay leaders and see all of its members even though only five of them met at each place. Before Pastor Fownes was imprisoned, the church would meet in the woods to avoid being caught under the *Conventicle Act*. The Church *Records* in 1681 read: "On Ld's day, ye 11th, Br. Fownes [the pastor], being come from London, but not daring to come into ye City because of ye Corporation Act, met with us and preacht in K's Wood, near Scruze Hole, under a Tree, and endured ye Rain" (Hayden, *Records*, p. 243).

A few days later, "Our Pastor preacht in another place in ye Wood" (*Ibid.*, p. 244). In 1686 James reversed his earlier policy and let Dissenters out of prison issuing his first *Declaration of Indulgence*. Although the Church of England adherents continued to harass them Dissenters never again experienced the persecution of the former years.

[168]　How did persecution affect the Particular Baptists? Did persecution cause their numbers to decrease? Generally speaking, the answer is no. Although persecution slowed down the growth of the Particular Baptists, growth still occurred with little loss through defection or excommunication. The Broadmead church, for example, grew from 100 members in 1671 to 166 members in 1679 with "only one case of a person excluded or refused membership for conformity to the established church" (Watts, *Dissenters*, I, 242).

Were there any benefits? Yes, the persecution brought the Dissenters together as never before in their common faith. In Bristol, the Presbyterians, General & Particular Baptists, and Congregationalists: formed a committee which sought for ways to legally

Freedom from persecution was secured in 1689, when the *Tolera-tion Act* was passed by Parliament. In the wake of their new-found liberty, the Particular Baptists of London sent out a July letter to all their churches in the country calling each to send two representatives to a General Assembly in September.[169]

---

resist persecution; united in prayer; and organized their individual meetings on different nights of the week (*Ibid.*, p. 243). In different places "Presbyterians and Anabaptists" were found worshipping together. Persecution also resulted in Particular Baptist teaching going beyond the borders of England and Wales. John Miles of Swansea and a large part of his church went to New England in the 1660s at first settling in Seekonk. Some people from Stead's church at Dartmouth and Kiffin's church at London went to the Boston area and won people to their views. In 1665 this group baptized people and constituted a church. Several Baptists from Somerton in Somersetshire first went to Maine and then to Carolina. Near Charlestown they met another group from England including the ardent Baptist, the widowed Lady Axtell, and her daughter. They were the first to erect a meeting-house in Charlestown. A third group joined them in 1686 and "thus the Church at Charlestown became strong" (Whitley, *British Baptists*, pp. 155-157).

Maybe the greatest benefit of persecution was the opportunity for spiritual growth it afforded the Dissenters. The Broadmead Church *Records* witness Pastor Thomas Hardcastle's view of the relationship between persecution and the church. From prison he wrote 22 letters to the congregation which were read to them on Sunday instead of the sermon. Roger Hayden writes: "Hardcastle understood the situation demanded a close look at the congregation's attitude to worship, and the inner drives which motivated the congregation. He believed it was good that persecutions should come because they would not only deepen faith and patience, but they would eventually bring about the conversion of many. Hardcastle did not see a quick end to the persecutions and said that greater trials and troubles would come; 'these are but the footmen you have been running with; these are but the little figures of Anti-Christ.'" This brought Hardcastle to a lengthy discussion of the nature of Christian faith at its deepest point. He talks of the precious gift of faith in God which purifies the heart of man. He sees such faith as a veritable shield in danger. This is the kind of faith by which the just shall be able to live: a faith which brings a deep and lasting joy. Such faith takes the warnings which God's judgments provide, looks upon life as a pilgrimage to God, and is capable of overcoming the world. When Christians are obedient to Christ, then despite all outward factors, they will enter into the very presence of God (Roger Hayden, *English Baptist History and Heritage* [n.p., 1990], p. 66).

During these days Particular Baptists were tried in their faith, and for the most part they persevered and grew in it.

[169]   The purpose of the meeting was to "giv[e] fit and proper encouragement for the raising up of an able and honourable ministry for the time to come" (Underwood, *English Baptists*, p. 129). More than a hundred churches from Wales and England attended the Assembly. In *A Narrative of the proceedings of the General Assembly* they declared the Assembly had no power over individual congregations and that "their intendment being to be helpers together of one another by way of counsel and advice" (Thomas Crosby, *The History of the English Baptists* [London, 1738], III, 246-258). This meeting decided several things: 1) to accept into membership churches which practiced open communion but not open membership; 2) to establish a fund to help weaker churches maintain their pastors; 3) to send preachers "where the Gospel hath or hath not yet

been preached, and to visit churches"; 4) to assist pastoral trainees in attaining a knowledge of Latin, Greek and Hebrew; 5) to suggest that smaller churches join together for
better support of their ministry and for edification; 6) to endorse the 1677 *Confession*; and
7) to agree to meet yearly as an Assembly (*Ibid.*)

CHAPTER TWO

THE LIFE AND WRITINGS OF HANSERD KNOLLYS

Hanserd Knollys was born at Cawkwell near Louth in Lincolnshire, England about the year 1599.[1] His father, Richard Knollys, was

---

[1]   For his life see his autobiography entitled, *The Life and Death of that Old Disciple of Jesus Christ, and Eminent Minister of the Gospel, Mr. Hanserd Knollys, who died in the Ninety-third Year of His Age written with his own hand to the year 1672, and continued in general, in an epistle by Mr William Kiffin*; "Knollys, Hanserd," *Dictionary of National Biography*, eds. Leslie Stephen & Sidney Lee (Oxford and London, 1921-22), XI, 279-281; J. Newton Brown, "Hanserd Knollys 1638-1641," in *Annals of the American Baptist Pulpit* (New York, 1860), pp. 1-7; William H. Brackney, *The Baptists* (Westport, CT, 1988), pp. 214-215; B.R. White, "Knollys, Hanserd (c.1599-1691)," in *Biographical Dictionary of British Radicals in the Seventeenth Century* (Brighton, 1982-84), II, 160-162; Walter Wilson, *The History and Antiquities of Dissenting Churches and Meeting Houses* (London, 1808), pp. 562-571; James Culross, *Hanserd Knollys: "A Minister and Witness of Jesus Christ" 1598-1691* (London, 1895); B.R. White, *Hanserd Knollys and Radical Dissent in the 17th Century* (London, 1977); Pope A. Duncan, *Hanserd Knollys: Seventeenth-Century Baptist* (Nashville, 1965); and Muriel James, *Religious Liberty on Trial: Hanserd Knollys — Early Baptist Hero* (Franklin, TN, 1997). Knollys' birthdate could be either 1598 or 1599. According to his autobiography he died on September 16, 1691 in his ninety-third year (*Life*, pp. 4, 7). Knollys' name was spelled in seventeenth-century documents variously including: Knollys, Knowles, Knolles, Knolies, Nowles, Noles, Knollis, Knowls and Knoles.
   Muriel James has studied the Parish records of Cawkwell and notes that Knollys was not baptized until November 13, 1609 (*Religious Liberty*, pp. 26-27). Muriel James has researched the Parish Records and State Papers and uncovered some previously unknown material concerning Hanserd Knollys. Unfortunately, she cannot always be trusted; I have found numerous technical and historical errors in her book, as well as statements without references. For example, she says without reference, "At the time of [Knollys'] birth, baptism issues were extremely controversial. In Lincolnshire a growing number were agreeing that baptism should be delayed until the person was old enough to understand its meaning and make a personal commitment" (p. 27). Is this so, or more likely, were some people (Separatists) questioning whether their Church of England baptism was a true baptism? Another example of no reference is that Knollys considered Charles II the "Beast of the Apocalypse" (p. 120). This may be so but I do not know of this. She makes a technical error when she says that Knollys learned much from an elderly Brownist woman in Gainsborough (p. 42). Knollys says it was "a godly old widow in Gainsborough ... who told me of one called a Brownist, who used to pray and expound scriptures in his family, whom I went sometimes to hear, and with whom I had conference and very good counsel" (*Life*, p. 12). An example of an historical error is when she says that Robert Brown "did not urge separation from the Church of England but wanted to change the structure" (p. 57). Brown is considered one of the first Separatists. Other errors include wrong dates (his resignation from the Church of Eng-

probably "the resident clergy man of the parish," a God-fearing man.[2] At the age of ten Hanserd was tutored at home, and later briefly attended Grimsby free school.[3] When he was fourteen years old his father was appointed the Church of England rector of Scartho near Market Grimsby; consequently, the family moved to Scartho, only a short distance from Cawkwell.[4] Sometime afterwards he studied at Puritan Cambridge and, in particular, St. Katherine's Hall College[5] where such Puritans as William Strong,

---

land was not 1636, p. 67, but at least two or three years earlier; the time he prayed for John Lilburne was not between 1647 and 1650, p. 133, but 1645; his *Song of Solomon* was not printed in 1653, p. 137, but in 1656), wrong details (John Cotton did not want Wheelwright with him at the Boston Church, p. 86, on the contrary he wanted him; Knollys did not mention the death of his child that occurred on their voyage to New England, p. 93, but he did [*Life*, pp. 26-27]; Knollys said it is not the duty of unbelievers to pray, p. 132, on the contrary he said they should [see chapter four]; Knollys was not imprisoned a fourth time, p. 183, but only three times, this last reference is part of his third imprisonment), and wrong titles (Knollys did not print *An Exposition of the Book of Revelation* in 1679, p. 178, but *An Exposition of the Eleventh Chapter of the Revelation*, he published *An Exposition of the whole Book of the Revelation* in 1688/89).

[2] Culross, *Hanserd Knollys*, pp. 2-3, 9. For more on Richard Knollys' wife's family see James, *Religious Liberty*, pp. 38-40. We do not know her given name but her maiden name is Hanserd, daughter of Richard Hanserd Jr. and Christobel Sutcliffe. Richard matriculated at Trinity College, Cambridge in 1581, then went over to Peterhouse in 1582 and received his B.A. in 1585-86 (*Ibid.*, p. 54). G. Lipscomb maintains that Richard Knollys served briefly in Mentmore as vicar in 1597 (*History and Antiquities of the County of Buckingham* [London, 1847] cited in James, *Religious Liberty*, p. 48). Culross states that there is no evidence that Richard was a Puritan while Hanserd was a child (Culross, *Hanserd Knollys*, p. 9); but it is possible that by 1635 he was. The *Calendar of State Papers* reads on October 15, 1635, "Richard Knowles, clerk, Rector of Scartho, co. Lincoln. Appeared and took oath to answer articles; and was monished to be examined before next court day." On Oct 22 he, "Appeared and was ordered to be examined before next court day under pain of contempt." On the 29th, "If he be not examined by next court day, he is to be attached." On November 12, "He is examined. Proofs to be completed by the third session from the present" (*Calendar of State Papers, Domestic Series, of the Reign of Charles I*, ed. John Bruce [London, 1866], pp. 90, 95, 102, 110).

[3] *Life*, p. 9.

[4] Culross, *Hanserd Knollys*, p. 9. The Record Office has recorded "Ricūs Knolles R. 17 Feb., 11° Jacobi. Yearly value £40." He appears to have remained rector of St. Giles until at least 1641. His name is recorded in the *Liber Cleri* for a visitation in 1634, and he signed the *Oath of Protestation* pledging allegiance to the King in 1641 (James, *Religious Liberty*, p. 64).

[5] St. Katherine's Hall College, Cambridge University, was founded in 1473, becoming Protestant after the English Reformation of the sixteenth century. The fervently Protestant Edwin Sandys was Master from 1547-1554, and John Bradford, the Marian martyr, was educated there in 1548. In the seventeenth century under the Mastership of the Puritan Richard Sibbes (1626-1635) the College became a Puritan stronghold with five Puritan Fellows — Thomas Goodwin, John Arrowsmith, William Strong, William Spurstow and John Bond (W.H.S. Jones, *The Story of St. Catherine's College*

John Arrowsmith and Thomas Goodwin, his contemporaries, also attended.[6]

During these early years Knollys experienced several significant events that were to mark his life. One occurred at the age of six when he was rescued from drowning by his father.[7] Another had to do with his father's counsel against strong drink and making vows.[8] A third involved a fight with his brother after which he felt convicted of sin before God and his father.[9] A fourth occurred after hearing several sermons at Cambridge on a particular Lord's day when he became quite convinced of his sinful state. He tells us,

> I was much more convinced of my sinful condition, and that I was a child of wrath, without Christ, and grace, &c. which work of conviction remained upon me above one year; under which I was filled with great horror, fears of hell, sore buffettings and temptations of the devil, and made to possess the sins of my youth: but yet I prayed daily, heard all the godly ministers I could, read and searched the holy scriptures, read good books, got acquainted with gracious christians then called Puritans, kept several days of fasting and prayer alone, wherein I did humble my soul for my sin, and begged pardon and grace of God for Christ's sake; grew strict in performing holy duties and in reformation of my own life, examining myself every night, confessing my sins and mourning for them, and had a great zeal for God, and indignation against actual sins, both committed by myself and others.[10]

After completing his course at Cambridge he was appointed Master of Gainsborough Free school. While in Gainsborough he became aquainted with an elderly, pious widow who helped him in the Christian walk and put him in touch with a Brownist who held a

---

Cambridge [Cambridge, 1951], p. 42). These men were influential during the Revolutionary years. It was during his time at St. Katherine's Hall that Knollys says he "got aquainted with gracious christians then called Puritans" (*Life*, p. 11). Comparatively, St. Katherine's was small for Cambridge. In 1621 it and Trinity Hall had the fewest number of fellows and students with 56 (St. John's had 370 and Trinity had 440). In 1641 St. Katherine's increased their number to 102, the eighth largest enrolment of the sixteen Cambridge colleges (John Twigg, *The University of Cambridge and the English Revolution* [Cambridge, 1990], p. 289).

   6 I do not know the exact years that each attended the College; Arrowsmith was born in 1602 and was a Fellow at the College; Goodwin was born in 1600 and was a Fellow there; and Strong was educated and became a Fellow there.

   7 *Life*, p. 8.
   8 *Ibid.*, pp. 8-9.
   9 *Ibid.*, pp. 9-10.
   10 *Ibid.*, pp. 10-11.

conventicle in his own house. Knollys often attended the meetings and spent time with this man.[11] After a few years Knollys left Gainsborough and, on March 30th, 1629, he became a pensioner at St. Katherine's Hall, Cambridge with a view to ordination in the Church of England.[12] During his time at St. Katherine's he was under the Mastership of the Puritan Richard Sibbes.[13] After only three months Knollys was ordained a Deacon and the following day ordained Presbyter of the Church of England by the bishop of Peterborough, Dr. Dove.[14]

Two years later, on August 24th, the bishop of Lincoln, John Williams, gave Knollys a small living at Humberstone, near his father's parish in Scartho.[15] During his time at Humberstone he saw the unusual working of God in the life of a widow who was expected to die. She had lain speechless for two or three days when Knollys went to her home. While he was there he tells us, "The devil set upon me with a violent suggestion, that the scriptures are not the word of God." He responded,

Satan, thou art a liar, a deceiver, and a false accuser. The holy scriptures are the word of God, and the scriptures of truth; and seeing thou hast often tempted me in this kind, and now dost assault me again, that I may for ever silence thee thou wicked and lying devil, I will trust in God, and act faith in the name of Christ in that very word of his truth which thou hast now suggested.[16]

Knollys then went to her bedside and prayed for her healing in order that the devil be found a liar. While he was praying she began

---

[11]   *Ibid.*, p. 12; Culross, *Hanserd Knollys*, pp. 12-13.

[12]   Muriel James maintains that according to the college's annual audit accounts Hanserd Knollys matriculated on Michaelmas 1627 (*Religious Liberty*, p. 55). According to his autobiography he attended Cambridge at the free school in Gainsborough prior to his ordination in June 1629. It is possible he attended Cambridge twice, once for his Bachelor's degree and once for his Master's degree.

[13]   Culross, *Hanserd Knollys*, p. 13. Sibbes became Master in 1625 and remained there until his death.

[14]   *Life*, p. 11; Culross, *Hanserd Knollys*, p. 13. He writes, "[I] preached above sixteen sermons before I was ordained, by way of trial of my ability for that great work of the ministry" (*Life*, pp. 11-12). He was ordained Deacon on June 29th. It should be noted that by his own admission he was as yet to experience the salvation of God in his life.

[15]   *Ibid.*, p. 12. He preached twice on Sunday and once every holy-day.

[16]   *Ibid.*, pp. 13-14.

to recover and eventually became well. He was never tempted by the devil on that issue again.

In 1631 Knollys married Anne Cheney, a woman ten years younger than himself, the daughter of John Cheney Esq. of Bennington. He tells us she "was a holy, discreet woman, and a meet help for me in the ways of her household, and also in the way of holiness."[17] Shortly after his marriage Knollys became convinced that some of the practices of the Church, including the wearing of the surplice, the signing of the cross in baptism, and the admitting of wicked persons to the Lord's Supper were sinful. Consequently, he resigned his living sometime after March 1633 but was permitted for several years to continue preaching.[18] About 1635 or 1636 he became convinced that his ordination was false and that he "had not received any seal from Christ of [his] ministry; for though many had been reformed and moralized, yet [he] knew not that [he] had been instrumental to convert any souls to God." He resolved not to preach anymore "until [he] had a clear call and commission from Christ to preach the gospel."[19] Consequently, he began to pray "day and night" for several weeks asking "that Christ would count me worthy, and put me into the ministry."

One day after praying in the woods at Anderby in Lincolnshire his prayers were answered while he was walking home and meditating. Not hearing any voice, nor seeing any vision but only those words which were "plainly and articulately spoken" into his "ears and understanding" Knollys was told to "go to Mr. Wheelwright, and he shall tell thee, and shew thee how to glorify God in the ministry."[20] The next morning he went to see Wheelwright who, unbe

---

[17]   Culross, *Hanserd Knollys*, p. 14; *Life*, p. 16; Anne's ancestry is briefly examined by James, *Religious Liberty*, p. 58.

[18]   The Parish records show that as a minister of the Church of England Hanserd Knollys baptized his son John on March 11, 1633 at Goulceby, Lincolnshire (Parish Records Goulceby FHL 432506, taken from James, *Religious Liberty*, p. 105). The bishop who permitted Hanserd to preach was Dr. John Williams who was educated at St. John's College, Cambridge. He was bishop of Lincoln from 1621-1641. He then was appointed Archbishop of York by the Long Parliament (Culross, *Hanserd Knollys*, pp. 17-18). He was a friend to Puritans.

[19]   *Ibid.*, p. 17.

[20]   John Wheelwright was born c. 1592, was ordained in 1619, and was vicar of Bilsby, Lincs 1623-1633. He was silenced for his nonconformity and lived privately in Lincoln for three years. He then moved to Boston, Mass. arriving in May 1636. A year and a half later (November 1637) he was banished from Massachusetts for antinomianism. His second wife was the sister to Anne Hutchinson's husband. Hutchinson was the

known to Knollys, had just moved to a village three miles from Humberstone. He told Wheelwright of his case, and that the Lord had sent him. After some conversation together Wheelwright told Knollys that the latter could not glorify God in the ministry because he was building his "soul upon a covenant of works, and was a stranger to the covenant of grace." Wheelwright then explained to him the covenant of free grace. Upon hearing this, Knollys tells us, he considered himself "a stranger to [free grace] in great measure, having [been] only under legal convictions and a spirit of bondage." He went on to confess, "And though I had some discoveries of my want of Christ, yet I had sought righteousness as it were by the works of the law, and got my peace by performing duties, and rested on them." Knollys then went home and prayed and "begged of God to teach [him] the covenant of grace." He searched the Scriptures and one day, hearing a message by a Mr. How on Galatians 2:20, he came to understand that he had lived a "life of works, not of faith." Now he began "to see the necessity of believing in Christ for pardon and salvation." How had explained that "Christ was the author, root, and only foundation of saving faith, and that God did give the faith of evidence, Heb. xi. 1, in some new covenant promise, Gal. iii. 14; and that those promises were given of God, 2 Pet. i 4." For that night and the next day he prayed that God would give him such a promise. The following day he locked himself in the church and while he was praying "mourning and bemoaning" himself and his "soul's condition, fearing ... that God would leave" him and "forsake" him, he was given the promise "I will never leave thee, nor forsake thee." He then confessed,

Lord who am I! I am a vile sinful sinner, the chief of sinners, most unworthy of pardon and salvation! How, Lord! never leave thee nor forsake thee? Oh, infinite mercy! Oh free grace! who am I? I have been a graceless soul, a formal professor, a legal performer of holy duties, and have gone about to establish mine own righteousness, which I now see is but filthy rags.

---

key figure in the antinomian controversy in New England in the 1630s; Wheelwright became embroiled in it. He, however, was reconciled in May 1644 and became minister at Hampton, New Hampshire and Salisbury until he died in 1679 (White, *Knollys*, pp. 7, 25).

Then God gave him two promises from Isaiah 43:22-25 and 54:9-10, assuring him of the forgiveness of his sins, and of his place in the covenant of peace. He records that he experienced "joy and peace in believing."[21]

The next day he saw Wheelwright who told him he was now "somewhat prepared to preach Jesus Christ and the gospel of free grace to others, having been taught it of God." He instructed Knollys to wait upon God, and the Holy Spirit through the word would teach him how to preach. He went home and began to pray for this. One day, while he was praying, these words were spoken to his heart by the Spirit, "I have appeared unto thee for this purpose, to make thee a minister and a witness both of those things which thou hast seen, and of those things in the which I will appear unto thee."[22] Upon hearing these words from the Lord he felt called and commissioned to preach the gospel.[23] For the next three or four years Knollys experienced the blessing of the Lord on his

---

[21]   This was Knollys' conversion by Puritan standards. I, therefore, disagree with Muriel James who considers his conversion experience to have taken place when at Cambridge (*Religious Liberty*, pp. 55-56).

[22]   This is a quote from Acts 26:16.

[23]   *Life*, pp. 17-24. In the early 1670s he writes about his call, "God was pleased to confirm my call unto that great work [preaching]. 1, By the conversion of many sinners, who having declared the dealings of God with their souls, testified God did convince them, convert them, and establish many of them by my ministry, through the powerful and effectual operation of his holy Spirit, and word, preached by me unto them. 2, By some healing power of God put forth upon the sick and infirm bodies of several persons, who were suddenly restored to health immediately in time of prayer with them, or by and through faith in Jesus Christ, especially in this City of London; and of the sickness called the plague, both in former years and in the year 1665. Not to me, but to God, be given the glory and praise, for in his name, through faith in his name, they were healed. 3, By enabling me, standing by me, and strengthening me, by his Holy Spirit and sanctifying grace, to preach the gospel, in season and out of season, with all boldness; neither being ashamed, nor afraid to bear my testimony for Christ, his gospel, churches, ministry, worship, and ordinances, against the antichristian powers, ministers, worshippers, and traditions of the beast, the great mystical whore, and the false prophet. Nor have I been terrified by the adversary, by virtue of the Acts of Parliament, touching private meetings and conventicles, commencing May 10, 1670" (*Ibid.*, pp. 42-44). Knollys was involved in the healing of Benjamin Keach in 1689. Thomas Crosby writes, "But the reverend Mr. *Hanserd Knollis* seeing his then dying friend, and brother in the Gospel, near, to all appearance, expiring, betook himself to prayer, and in an earnest and very extraordinary manner begged, that God would spare him, and add unto his days, the time he granted to his servant *Hezekiah*; and as soon as he ended his prayer, he said, Brother *Keach* I shall be in heaven before you, and quickly after left him" (Crosby, *History of the English Baptists*, II, 307-308). Knollys died in 1691 and Keach died in 1704 fifteen years after Knollys prayed, the same years given to Hezekiah.

preaching "whereby very many sinners were converted and many believers were established in the faith."[24]

In 1633 the situation worsened for the Puritans in England with the elevation of William Laud to the Archbishopric of Canterbury. Laud aggressively pursued a policy of uniformity of worship for all citizens. He left no room for dissent and persecuted those who rebelled. This policy had its effect upon the newly converted Puritan, Hanserd Knollys. While he was preaching in Lincolnshire in 1636 he was arrested on a warrant from the Court of High Commission. He convinced the man who issued the warrant to let him go. Knollys and his family then went to London for a time. From there they set off for Boston, Massachusetts on a twelve-week voyage during which they suffered much hardship including the loss of their only child.[25] They probably reached Boston in the summer of 1638. Meanwhile, Knollys' former mentor, John Wheelwright, who had earlier made his way over to New England, had become involved in the antinomian controversy of Mrs. Hutchinson, and was consequently banished from the plantation for antinomianism.[26] On Knollys' arrival the magistrates were told by the ministers that Knollys was an antinomian.[27] But before any action was taken against him he was asked to come to Piscattuah (now Dover, New Hampshire) to preach.[28] He formed a church and ministered there until September 1641. It appears that he left Piscattuah and settled in Long Island for several months.[29] In December he was called

---

[24] *Life*, p. 26. During these years he preached at Anderby, at Fulleby on the Hill, and at Wainfleet.

[25] Knollys had to leave his books behind in England. They were apparently inventoried by the authorities and were found to be mostly theological; but he owned two suspicious works entitled, *Sir Walter Raleigh's Advice to his Son* and *A brief relation of certain special and most material passages and speeches in the Star Chameber at the censure of the three worthy gentlemen, Bastwick, Burton, and Prynne* (Culross, *Hanserd Knollys*, p. 28).

[26] *Life*, pp. 26-27; White, *Knollys*, p. 6. Wheelwright was banished in November 1637 and Hutchinson was excommunicated in March 1638. For a historical account of this controversy see David D. Hall, *The Antinomian Controversy, 1636-1638: A Documentary History* (Middletown, CT, 1968). For a detailed theological account of this controversy see William K.B. Stoever, *A Faire and Easie Way to Heaven* (Middletown, CT, 1978). See also chapter three of this study.

[27] John Winthrop tells us he was rejected "for holding some of Mrs Hutchinson's opinions" (*Winthrop's Journal "History of New England" 1630-1649*, ed. James K. Hosmer [New York, 1908], I, 295).

[28] For some of the history of Dover see James, *Religious Liberty*, pp. 94-97; and for Knollys' involvement there see *Ibid.*, pp. 96-102.

[29] It is likely that Knollys moved because Dover was about to be annexed by

back to England by his aged father.[30] Knollys, his wife and their
three year old child arrived in London on December 24, 1641 in
the midst of the struggle between King and Parliament that led to
Civil War the following year. It was around this time that the London Particular Baptist group of churches was forming.[31] Between
the years 1638 and 1644 seven churches joined together to form a
fellowship of Calvinistic Baptist churches; and in 1644 they declared their orthodoxy and Baptist convictions in a *Confession of
Faith*.[32] About this time Knollys came to Baptist convictions, and
joined this young group of churches as one of its pastors.

Massachusetts (Oct. 9, 1641). He sold his land for thirty pounds (Nathaniel Bolton,
Documents and Records of the Province of New Hampshire: 1623-1686 [Concord, 1867], I, 197,
cited in James, *Religious Liberty*, p. 101).

[30] Upon his arrival at Piscattuah a Captain Burdet usurped the government and
forbid Knollys to preach. In September 1638 Burdet was removed and Captain John
Underhill, a follower of Wheelwright, became the governor. In 1639 through Underhill
Knollys gathered "some of the best minded into a church, and became their Pastor."
This was probably the second Congregationalist church in New Hampshire (John
Wheelwright's in Exeter was the first). After about two years of peaceful ministry
Knollys experienced some difficulties in Piscattuah. He had a dispute with another
minister Thomas Larkham. Larkham had Knollys removed and became the pastor.
Larkham admitted "men notoriously scandalous and ignorant" into the church. He fell
into contention with the people because of it and sought to rule them, even the magistrates. The people eventually restored Knollys and excommunicated Larkham. The
group with Larkham raised a riot in April, 1641. Requested by Larkham's company,
some armed men from Portsmouth assumed control, sat as a Court, and pronounced
sentence against Knollys fining him £100 and ordered him to depart the plantation
(Winthrop, *Journal*, I, 295, 309, 328, and II, 27-28; Brown, "Knollys," pp. 3-4).
    Moreover, Knollys at this time of censure was accused of moral misconduct.
Winthrop's *Journal* states that Knollys "was discovered to be an unclean person, and to
have solicited the chastity of two maids, his servants, and to have used filthy dalliance
with them, which he acknowledged before the church there, and so was dismissed, and
removed from Pascataquack" (Winthrop, *Journal*, II, 28; Raymond P. Stearns, *The Strenuous Puritan: Hugh Peter 1598-1660* [Urbana, 1954], pp. 144-148). Was this report accurate? Against its accuracy we need to remember the colony's and Winthrop's prejudice
against Knollys and his alleged antinomianism. In addition, we need to remember he
was considered by contemporaries and the historian Cotton Mather as an upright and
godly man. Moreover, the Judicial Records of New Hampshire for 1641 show that
Knollys was entered as plaintiff in an action of slander. Although it was not prosecuted
on account of his return to England, this action by Knollys suggests that he believed he
was wrongfully accused. Furthermore, if this accusation was true, as far as we know
Knollys never fell into such inappropriate behaviour again in his life (Brown, "Knollys,"
p. 5). For a brief biographical sketch of Larkham see N. F. Collins, "Larkham, Thomas
(1602-1669)," *Biographical Dictionary of British Radicals*, II, 171-172.

[31] See Murray Tolmie, *The Triumph of the Saints* (Cambridge, 1977).

[32] This *Confession* is found in W.L. Lumpkin, *Baptist Confessions of Faith* (Philadelphia,
1959), pp. 153-171.

Soon after Knollys returned to England from the New World, he took up teaching at Great Tower Hill in order to provide for his family, and later became master of Mary-Axe free school.[33] When the Civil War began, his sympathies being with the Parliament, he left his school and joined the army, preaching to the common soldiers. Unhappy with the commanders who "sought their own things, more than the cause of God and his people, breaking their vows and solemn engagements," he eventually quit the army.[34] Consequently, he returned to London to continue his teaching.

By this time Knollys had become a member of Henry Jessey's Independent congregation.[35] It was during this time that Knollys

---

[33]   *Life*, p. 30. At the latter school he taught 140 students and sixteen boarders.

[34]   *Ibid.*, p. 30. Thomas Edwards says Knollys "did a great deal of mischief" in the army (*Gangraena* (1646), I, pt. 2, p. 39).

[35]   This church is the Henry Jacob church which at the time was pastored by Jessey. The Stinton manuscript, transcript 4, records Hanserd Knollys as a brother who asks a question concerning baptism for church discussion (W.T. Whitley, "Debate on Infant Baptism, 1643," *Transactions of the Baptist Historical Society*, 1 [1910], p. 240). Prior to his involvement in Jessey's church he preached in various places. There is some evidence that Knollys held the cure of Dallinghoo in Suffolk in 1645 (Additional MSS 15,669, Folio 92: June 21, 1645, cited in Ashley J. Klaiber, *The Story of the Suffolk Baptists* [London, 1931]). In 1645 he was preaching in the Bow Church when the Committee for Plundered Ministers sent a warrant to the keeper of Ely House to apprehend him and bring him to them. They asked by what authority he preached. He answered that the churchwardens asked him to preach. He explained to the committee what he had preached that day from Isaiah 58. Thirty of the Assembly of Divines heard him and let him go. Shortly after this he was brought before the Committee for Examinations on the charge of stirring up trouble in Suffolk. After giving an account of his activities to the committee they made their report to the House of Commons. Satisfied with Knollys' account they ordered that he might preach in any part of Suffolk when the minister of that place did not preach. Following this he was summoned before another Committee at Westminster "for preaching without holy orders." The Minutes of the Assembly state, "Information against Mr. Knowles, his preaching in private, and venting his Antimonian opinions. *Ordered* — Dr. Burgess, Mr. Vines, Mr. Seaman, Mr. Ley, Mr. Ward, Mr. Calamy, [Mr. Tuckney], Mr. Spurstow, Mr. Walker, — a Committee to consider of this complaint, and of all other disorders formerly complained of" (*Minutes of the Sessions of the Westminster Assembly of Divines*, eds. Alex Mitchell & John Struthers [Edinburgh & London, 1874], p. 96, May 20th, 1645). Knollys explained that he "was ordained ... in a church of God according to the order of the gospel of Christ." The committee commanded him to preach no more; however, he told them he would preach because "it was more equal to obey Christ who had commanded me, than them who forbid me." This latter occurrence took place when he was pastor of the Baptist church at Great St. Helens and Finsbury Hills (*Life*, pp. 31-34).

It should be noted that on May 16, 1645 he published two sermons that he had preached in Suffolk from Col. 3:11 and Eph. 1:4 entitled, *Christ Exalted in a sermon* with a preface to the "Honourable Committee of Examinations." This was later published under the title, *Christ Exalted: a lost sinner sought and saved* with an additional sermon from

seriously began to question infant baptism and consider that only
believers were the proper recipients of this ordinance.[36] In January
1643/44 he told Jessey that he was not prepared to have his child
baptized and requested that some meetings take place that "they
[the church] might satisfye him, or he rectify them if amiss herein."[37] The discussions were carried on for two months at which time
sixteen members felt it was wrong to have their infants baptized
and had removed themselves "not satisfyed we ware [sic] baptized
as a true Church."[38] At the same time, some of those who held to
believer's baptism scrupled over the adminstrator of baptism. Anne
Knollys, with eight others, became "satisfiyed in their scruple &
judged yt Such Disciples as are gifted to teach & Evangelize may
also baptize &c & ware baptized."[39] Some of these people joined
the church that Knollys had apparently gathered and some joined
the church led by William Kiffin.[40]

Knollys' congregation in 1645 met next door to Great St. He-
len's Church where it was reported by some neighbours that as
many as a thousand attended his services.[41] He was eventually
turned out of there by his landlord and moved to Finsbury Fields.[42]
During his years as pastor of the church he says,

Luke 19:10. After preaching the Col. 3:11 text he reports that he "was stoned out of the
pulpit; prosecuted at a privy Session; fetched out of the country sixty miles up to London; and was constrained to bring up four or five witnesses of good repute and credit,
to prove and vindicate [himself] from false accusations" (*Life*, p. 33).

[36] J. Newton Brown believes that Knollys became a Baptist before he came to
America because: Dr. Belknap calls him an Anabaptist at the time of his arrival; Baptist
views were gaining ground in London prior to 1638; that he took Baptist ground in the
dispute with Thomas Larkham in Piscattuah; there is no account of his baptism after
his return to England; and the reason he was never accused of being an Anabaptist in
America was due to the Boston clergy's claim to have "tolerated peaceable Anabaptists"
("Knollys," p. 7).

[37] Whitley, "Debate on Infant Baptism, 1643," p. 240.

[38] *Ibid.*, p. 243.

[39] *Ibid.*, p. 244.

[40] *Ibid.*, pp. 244-245. This church would have been founded sometime after March
17, 1643/44. It should also be noted that the Westminster Assembly in an August 1644
report to the Commons stated that Knollys "did preach against the baptizing of children" (S.W. Carruthers, *The Everyday Work of the Westminster Assembly* [Philadelphia,
1943], p. 96). He, therefore, came to Baptist convictions prior to August 1644. He,
however, did not sign the *First London Confession of Faith* published in October of that
same year.

[41] Edwards, *Gangraena*, I, pt. 2, p. 40. This number could be an exaggeration coming from a hostile source.

[42] Edwards, *Gangraena*, I, pt. 2, p. 39.

I received from the church always according to their ability, most of the members of the church being poor; but I coveted no man's gold nor silver, but chose rather to labour, knowing, 'It is more blessed to give than to receive:' nor did I neglect the whole of my duty as a pastor, but preached two or three times in the week, and visited the members of the church from house to house, especially when they were sick.[43]

There is also some evidence to suggest that Knollys was the vicar of the church in Scartho (his father's parish) in 1648, dividing his time between this church and the London one.[44]

During the year 1645, Knollys published three works.[45] On July 17, 1645 he answered John Bastwick's *Independency not God's Ordinance* with *A Moderate Answer unto Dr Bastwicks book*. In this work he denied Bastwick's assertion that Scripture taught a presbyterian, synodical church government, and asserted that it taught an independent one. In addition, *A Moderate Answer* taught that membership into the local church was based upon profession of faith, repentance, and baptism as in the Apostles' days. In December of the same year Knollys published another book with Benjamin Cox and William Kiffin entitled *A Declaration concerning the public dispute*. A debate had been arranged between the three Baptists and some Presbyterians, including Edmund Calamy, for December third on the issue of baptism. However, it was cancelled by the Lord Mayor for fear of violence. The Baptists, therefore, stated their position in this book.[46]

---

[43] *Life*, pp. 34-35.

[44] Culross, *Hanserd Knollys*, p. 66, and James, *Religious Liberty*, p. 64. James gives no reference for this but her book indicates she has investigated the St. Giles Parish, Scartho records. Maybe Knollys' father was ill or had died, and Hanserd wanted to help his home church. If his father was a nonconformist then his church would have been sympathetic to Hanserd's Puritanism, and he to them. As confirmation of his involvement with St. Giles the *State Papers* of May 15, 1656 state: "Petition of Hanserd Knollys [patron of the church] for the inhabitants of Scartho, co. Lincoln, to the Protector and Council. Our parish church is much decayed, and the spire ready to fall. We beg your order to Thos. Clayton and 5 other inhabitants to take down the spire, and in 3 years' time to repair the south aisle and other parts of the church (*Calendar of State Papers, Domestic Series, 1655-56*, ed., Mary Anne E. Green [London, 1882] Vol. 127, No. 31, p. 319).
Hanserd's son, Cheney, according to James, pastored St. Giles for several years in the early 1660s (James, *Religious Liberty*, pp. 64, 136).

[45] The first was noted above entitled, *Christ Exalted in a sermon* published on May 16. He also wrote the "Epistle to the Reader" of Thomas Collier's *The exaltation of Christ in the days of the Gospel* which taught among other things the nature of the true church.

[46] Knollys and William Kiffin entered into a formal disputation on baptism with

In 1646 Knollys contributed two more works in defence of the
Baptist cause.[47] The first was the second edition of the *First London
Confession of Faith*. This second edition contained a few changes
made to the first as a result of some criticisms made by the Presbyterian Daniel Featley.[48] Later that year *An Appendix to a Confession of
Faith* was published. The author of the *Appendix* was Benjamin Cox
but the internal evidence shows that the whole group who signed
the revised *Confession*, including Knollys, agreed with it.[49] It espoused a High Calvinist soteriology and a closed communion ecclesiology. The other work Knollys published in this year was *The Shining of a flaming fire in Zion*, a response to John Saltmarsh's *The smoke
in the temple*, which denied the need for ordinances at all.[50] In this
work Knollys argued that the church, after the apostles, was to continue practicing the ordinances of Christ. In it he also maintained
that only those who had the gifts of the Spirit to preach the gospel,
and so tested by the church, were permitted to administer the ordinances of Baptism and the Lord's Supper.

In 1648 Knollys published his first Ecclesiatical language grammar entitled, *The rudiments of Hebrew grammar in English*, in order to
help friends understand the original Hebrew of the Bible.[51] Over
the course of the next years he produced seven more language
study works to help his former students, now teachers themselves,

---

John Bryan, the vicar of Trinity parish church Coventry and Obadiah Grew, vicar of
the nearby parish of St. Michael's. Crosby says, "It was managed with good temper,
and great moderation; both sides claiming the victory, and parted good friends. All
granted that the *Baptists* came off with great reputation" (Crosby, *English Baptists*, III,
5; John Ley, *A Discourse of Disputations* [1648], pp. 74-75). For Benjamin Coxe see B. R.
White, "Cox, Benjamin (1595-c. 1664)," *Biographical Dictionary of British Radicals*, I, 184-
185.

[47]   During this year he was also imprisoned in Ipswich (White, *Knollys*, p. 13) and
wrote an Epistle "To the Churches" for Robert Garner's *Mysteries Unvailed*. Garner's
work attacked Arminian teaching, and espoused a High Calvinistic soteriology. Garner
was probably a member of Knollys' congregation (Tolmie, "General," p. 145).

[48]   See W.L. Lumpkin, *Baptist Confessions of Faith* (Philadelphia, 1959), pp. 147-148,
156-171, particularly, pp. 165, 166, 167.

[49]   For this *Appendix* see E. B. Underhill, *Confessions of Faith and other Public Documents
illustrative of the history of Baptist Churches of England in the 17th Century* (London, 1854), pp.
49-60.

[50]   Saltmarsh, though not a Seeker, took the position of a Seeker in his argument
against the Baptists.

[51]   In the *Dictionary of National Biography* (1921-22), we are told, "He learned Hebrew
from Christian Ravy [Ravis] Berlinas, 'Hebrew professor' in London" (XI, 280).

review what they were taught especially for reading the Scriptures in the originals.[52]

In the 1640s and 1650s, the Particular Baptists were to experience tremendous growth as they spread their message beyond London. Knollys was quite involved in this expansion.[53] For example, in 1649 Kiffin and Knollys were authorized by Parliament to go to Ipswich to preach.[54] And in the early 1650s he went to Wales as an evangelist probably appointed by the London churches.[55] And in

---

[52] *Grammaticae Graecae compendium* (1664), *Grammaticae Latinae compendium* (1664), *Grammaticae Latinae, Graecae, & Hebaicae* (1665), *Linguae Hebricae delineatio* (1664), *Rhetoricae adumbratio* (1663), *Radices simplicium vocum* (1664), and *Radices Hebraicae omnes* (1664). In the General Assembly of Particular Baptists of 1689 a central fund was to be collected for three purposes. One of the purposes was to assist "those members that shall be found in any of the aforesaid churches that are disposed for study have an inviting gift, and are sound in fundamentals, in attaining to the knowledge and understanding of the languages, *Latin, Greek* and *Hebrew*" (Crosby, *English Baptists*, III, 252). In addition, at the 1691 Assembly Knollys signed an epistle to the churches recommending the institution of a Freewill offering. One of the reasons given in the *Narrative of the Proceedings of the Assembly* for this offering was "that godly young men whom God hath gifted, and who are approved of, may be instructed in the tongues wherein the Holy Scriptures were written" (Culross, *Hanserd Knollys*, p. 106). Knollys not only would have supported such statements but probably was one of those who initiated them.

[53] Moreover, in 1648 Knollys was appointed Rector of Scartho (*Institutions and Composition Books*. Record Office, cited in Culross, *Hanserd Knollys*, p. 66). As noted above, on May 15, 1656 Knollys presented a petition to the Protector and his council "with a memorial from the inhabitants of Scartho, showing that the parish church was so much decayed as to be dangerous, the broach or steeple being like to fall, as also the south aisle." The inhabitants of the parish asked Knollys, partron of the church, to petition Cromwell and the Council on their behalf (*Ibid.*, p. 76).

[54] *Ibid.*, p. 67, and White, *Knollys*, p. 14. In a letter to Oliver Cromwell the citizens of Ipswich wrote: "We cannot sufficiently express our thankfulness to the honourable house, and your honour for the great favour wch out of yr sense of our present condition you were pleased to shew unto us, that there is liberty granted to Mr. Knollys and Mr. Kiffin according to our desire to come among us, whose labours (through God's blessing) are like to bee not only very comfortable to us in particular but very profitable to the state in generall; yet as there is noe good Action but finds opposition, soe we have heard that this much opposed by some, who (as wee are informed) doe labour to hinder it. Now if any such should be, who are thus contrary minded, our humble and earnest desire is, that your honour; would be pleased to continue your former favour unto us, that we may not be deprived of this great good that is coming unto us" (Tenison MSS, Lambeth Palace Library quoted in James, *Religious Liberty*, p. 144).

In this same year Army records list Knollys as a chaplain of E. Whally's Regiment of Horse (Anne Laurence, *Parliamentary Army Chaplains 1642-1651* [A Royal Historical Society Publication, Suffolk, 1990], pp. 58, 143, cited in James, *Religious Liberty*, p. 126). During this chaplaincy the regiment mutinied supporting Lilburne and the Levellers. Consequently, an anti-Leveller declaration was written up which Knollys signed (Laurence, *Parliamentary*, pp. 58, 143, cited in James, *Religious Liberty*, p. 126).

[55] White tells us that Knollys worked in Radnor and Breconshire sometime during

1654 or 1655 Knollys might have helped settle and organize a
church in Cornwall.[56] In addition to his pastoral and evangelistic
duties in the 1650s Knollys was involved in civil affairs. During the
Commonwealth years, Knollys held the office of the examiner of
the Customs and Excise under the Commonwealth at a salary of
120 pounds a year but resigned on March 1653 "by reason of more
beneficial employment calling him away."[57] During the Protectorate he was Clerk of the Check, keeping a register of the men em-
ployed on board ships of the navy, and the navy artificers, in the
port of London.[58] Knollys also engaged in politics when he felt it
was necessary. In 1657, when Cromwell was offered the crown,
Knollys, along with the Independent John Goodwin and Calvinistic
Baptists John Spilsbury, Henry Jessey and others, petitioned him
with *Address of the Anabaptist Ministers in London, To the Lord Protector*
encouraging him to refuse it.[59] These petitioners did not want a
return to monarchial government, but desired for the sake of the
cause of God that it remain a republican one.

Knollys did little writing in the 1650s. He published only one
work in 1656, namely, *An Exposition of the first chapter of the Song of*

1650-52 and appeared to have no qualms about receiving state pay for his ministry
(White, *Knollys*, p. 15). Interestingly, Knollys petitioned Parliament for the abolition of
tithes in 1647 and 1652, and signed the document entitled, *A Declaration of divers elders and
brethren of congregational societies* (1651) (*Transactions of the Baptist Historical Society*, IV, 206,
cited in *Ibid.*, p. 14).

During the late 1640s and the 1650s the Particular Baptist group grew throughout
England, Wales, and Ireland. This evangelism was spearheaded by the London
churches. As was noted in chapter one there were over a hundred Particular Baptist
churches in the United Kingdom by 1660.

By 1652 Knollys' congregation was meeting in Coleman Street, London.

[56]   Folger Shakespeare Library, Washington, US. Additional MS 667, cited in
White, *Knollys*, pp. 16-17. Abraham Cheare of the Plymouth church wrote to Robert
Bennet about someone coming to Cornwall to do this work, and suggested Hanserd
Knollys for it. Bennet was to talk to Kiffin about it. We do not know what resulted from
this letter.

[57]   *Calendar of State Papers* states, "Hansard Knowles, examiner at the customs and
excise, at a salary of 120*l.*, having resigned for more beneficial employment, ..." (*Domestic Series, 1652-1653*, ed., Mary Anne Everett Green [London, 1878], Vol. 34, No. 102,
p. 40, March 29, 1653).

[58]   The State Papers show that, "Another clerk of the check has been appointed in
place of Mr. Knowles [Knollys], who is troubled by them about the money he received
for sick and wounded men; he handed it to the surgeon before the ship came out, and
it is laid out in necessaries for the men" ("Letters and Papers relating to the Navy,"
[*Domestic Series, 1655-56*, May 23, 1655, p. 484], quoted in James, *Religious Liberty*, p.
150).

[59]   Underhill, *Confessions of Faith*, pp. 335-338.

Solomon. The book was formed from some messages he gave at the household of Lord Willoughby of Parham near Gainsborough. These studies were probably given by Knollys in the 1640s prior to Willoughby's 1647 imprisonment and later escape to Holland.[60] The *Exposition*'s chief concern was the communion between Christ and the church. But it also touched on such things as the Lord's Supper and the Christian's relationship to the civil government. Concerning the latter he clearly teaches that the saints are only to use spiritual weapons in their warfare against the enemy. He also had a treatise published under his name entitled, *Redemption by Jesus Christ* (1653). Except for the title page and the preface this is the same treatise as Robert Garner's *Mysteries Unvailed* (1646) in which Knollys wrote an "Epistle to the Reader". Knollys probably agreed with much of its content but it is definitely the work of Garner.[61]

In 1660, after Cromwell died and his son Richard retired from leadership, the crown was restored to Charles II. A number of Fifth Monarchists, led by the Baptist Thomas Venner, believing the Lord's Coming was at hand, attempted an insurrection in London. It failed miserably and resulted in the arrest of four hundred people suspected of taking part in the uprising. Knollys was one of those people imprisoned in Newgate for eighteen weeks because he "refused to take the oaths of allegiance and supremacy." Many, however, were pardoned at the time of the King's coronation.[62] The Restoration of the crown began twenty-eight years of persecution for all Dissenters.[63] The pro-Church of England Parliament passed four Acts which sought to eliminate dissent in the country. These

---

[60] James, *Religious Liberty*, pp. 121-124.

[61] We do not know how this work came to be published under Knollys' name. The internal evidence is inconclusive. The Title page could be read in such a way that the author is anonymous, with the "Epistle to the Churches" written by Knollys; this hypothesis, however, is very gratuitous. It should also be noted that it was published by Giles Calvert, a publisher of many sectarian works, as was Garner's treatise. Is it possible that it was published without Knollys' knowledge? Or maybe Calvert considered Knollys more popular than Garner; under his name it would have a wider readership. For Calvert see H.T. Blethen, "Cavert, Giles (d.1663)," *Biographical Dictionary of British Radicals*, I, 119-120.

[62] *Life*, pp. 35-36.

[63] The Dissenters included Independents (Congregationalists), Baptists, Quakers and, after the election of the Cavalier Parliament, the Presbyterians. For a study of these Dissenters and their struggles during the Restoration years see Michael R. Watts, *The Dissenters: From the Reformation to the French Revolution* (Oxford, 1978), pp. 221-262.

Acts came to be known as the *Clarendon Code*.[64] Knollys was one of
many who experienced the trials of persecution during these years.
After he was released from Newgate prison he preached with
millenarians Henry Jessey and John Simpson at All Hallows
church,[65] and then shortly after, went to Holland,[66] and then to
Germany with his wife and two children.[67] After two or three years
he and his family returned to London, having sold all their goods

---

[64] These Acts were the *Coronation Act* (1661), the *Act of Uniformity* (1662), the *Conventicle Act* (1664), and the *Five Mile Act* (1665). Persecution during the Restoration years was sporadic, and depended on time and location.

[65] The *Calendar of State Papers* show that, "Knowles, Jesse and John Simpson are the persons who preached at Great All-Hallows, Mr. Braggs church, at a Fast on August 24, and that they preach there every Monday and Thursday, where they may best be apprehended. Those that preach there are bred to it at a conventicle in Anchor Lane, where two pulpits are put up for prophesying" (*Domestic Series, of the Reign of Charles II, 1661-1662*, ed. Mary Anne Everett Green [London, 1861], Vol. 41, No. 39, p. 87, Sept. 11, 1661).

[66] The *Calendar of State Papers* states, "Mr. Knowles and others, who were in Newgate, are sent into Holland, where they are in good condition, but act their business more secretly than here; they only wait an opportunity" (*Domestic series, of the Reign of Charles II*, Vol. 42, No. 38, p. 98, Sept. 26, 1661).

[67] *Life*, pp. 36-37. Knollys was probably able to purchase this because he was a beneficiary of Thomas Taylor's will which was proven in January 10, 1658 (Henry Waters, *Geneological Gleanings in England* [Boston, 1901], II, 974, cited in James, *Religious Liberty*, pp. 161-162). While absent the estate he had purchased from the Artillary Company of London was seized at a worth of £760. We understand that later he petitioned for reimboursement. The *Calendar of State Papers* records, "Hansard Knollys to the King. Petition stating that the petitioner bought for 300*l*. the old Armoury house in the Artillary Ground near Spitalfields from the Artillary Company and spent 460*l*. more in repairs and building there and fitting the premises for his schoolhouse and dwellinghouse, which he inhabited and enjoyed about two years, that Col. Legge deceased, Lieutenant of the Ordnance [*sic*], under pretence of his patent by force and violence took away all the said premises from the petitioner and kept them during his life, that David Walter, the present Lieutenant, finding the premises in Col. Legge's possession when he died, keeps the same from the petitioner, and that the poor and aged petitioner has for above ten years been kept out of his right to the impoverishing of himself and his poor family, he having borrowed a great part of the said sums, and praying his Majesty to appoint some one to examine and report on this petition, that, if his Majesty see cause, he may require the Artillary Company, Legge's executors and David Walter to repay the said 760*l*. to the petitioner or may grant him lease of the premises for 99 years" (*Domestic Series, of the Reign of Charles II*, December, 1673, p. 66). The *Calendar* goes on to show that two reports were made to Sir H. Finch, Lord Keeper concerning this petition; the second report recommends that Knollys be reimbursed (*Ibid.*, pp. 66-67). For details concerning his attempts to recover his loss see James, *Religious Liberty*, pp. 175-177.

During the Restoration Knollys took frequent trading trips to Holland and accumulated some wealth (W.T. Whitley, "London Churches in 1682," *The Baptist Quarterly*, 1 [1922], p. 86).

to make the trip.[68] He then took up teaching again to provide for his family. We know little of his activities in the 1660s. We do know that during the London Plague of 1665 Knollys remained in the city and ministered to the suffering and bereaved.[69] We also know that on June 28, 1666 he and Edward Harrison were involved in the setting apart of the elder Thomas Patient and two deacons in William Kiffin's congregation. And when Patient died, Knollys was involved in the setting apart of Daniel Dyke in the same church to replace Patient.[70] In addition, we know that it was during these years that he published the first of six eschatological works. This first book, written in 1667, was *Apocalyptical Mysteries*. In it, he expounded the historicist view of the Book of Revelation in three parts discussing the seven trumpets, the seven vials, and the kingdom of Christ to come.[71]

We know a little more of Knollys' activities in the 1670s. On May 10, 1670, shortly after the passing of the Second Conventicle Act he was apprehended at a meeting in George Yard and then taken to the Compter in Bishopsgate. He was permitted there to preach twice a day to the prisoners. Soon after he was discharged

---

[68]   In his autobiography he acknowledges the Lord's provision in a couple of ways on this trip. The first had to do with the ship's skipper who cheated him out of some money. While at a harbour on the Rhine River the chief of the toll-masters learned of the Knollys family's situation and had the skipper pay Knollys back. The second occured in Rotterdam when two catholics prevailed with Prince Dewit to send Knollys 160 Dix dollars for a house he had built in the Prince's country, but couldn't sell. He received the money in Rotterdam (*Life*, pp. 37-38).

[69]   Culross, *Hanserd Knollys*, p. 92.

[70]   White, *Knollys*, p. 19.

[71]   In addition, Knollys wrote the preface for Benjamin Keach's *The childs instructor; or, a new and easy primer*. It was used for English instruction, and it contained a children's catechism. I am unsure in which addition(s) his preface is contained. The first edition was published in 1664; the fifth in 1679.

It should also be noted that an eschatological treatise entitled, *A Glimpse of Syons Glory* (1641) has been attributed to Hanserd Knollys by A.S.P. Woodhouse (*Puritanism and Liberty: Being the Army Debates (1647-49) From the Clarke Manuscripts* [1938; rpt. London & Rutland, VT, 1992], p. 233) and others. It has been shown not to be Knollys' work but most likely that of either Thomas Goodwin (John F. Wilson, "A Glimpse of Syons Glory," *Church History*, 31 [1962], pp. 66-73, and A.R. Dallison, "The Authorship of the 'Glimpse of Syons Glory'," in *Puritans, The Millennium & The Future of Israel*, ed. Peter Toon [Cambridge & London, 1970], pp. 131-136) or Jeremiah Burroughs (Paul Christianson, *Reformers and Babylon: English apocalyptic visions from the reformation to the eve of the civil war* [Toronto, 1978], pp. 251-252).

at a session of Old Bailey.[72] During the early 1670s his wife,[73] one grand-child, three sons,[74] and possibly another grandchild and a daughter-in-law, all died.[75] Moreover, he thought he was about to die as well. However, believing the Lord could heal him, he called for Kiffin and Vavasor Powell to pray over him and anoint him with oil according to James 5:14,15. As a result of this and the prayers of others, he recovered.[76] His wife, however, did not recover from her illness and died in 1671 in her sixty-third year, after forty years of marriage.[77] We also know that in the year 1672 he officiated at the marriage of Benjamin Keach and Susannah Partridge.[78]

In 1674 Knollys wrote his second eschatological work, *The Parable of the Kingdom of God Expounded*. In it, he sought to encourage Chris-

---

[72] *Life*, p. 44.

[73] She died after forty years of marriage on April 30, 1671 (*Ibid.*, p. 48). We understand that she was 63 years old and had given birth to seven sons and three daughters (Culross, *Hanserd Knollys*, p. 95).

[74] From Knollys' autobiography it appears that three died in 1670-71 of which one was Issac (*Life*, pp. 46, 51-52). Isaac died on November 15, 1671; he was converted during this time of sickness (*Ibid.*, pp. 51-52).

[75] *Ibid.*, p. 46. These last two were "likely to die" but Knollys does not tell us if they did. In addition, one of Knollys' children had a still born birth (*Ibid.*, p. 46). For more details on Knollys' children see James, *Religious Liberty*, pp. 104-109.

[76] *Life*, pp. 47-48.

[77] She was buried in Bunhill Fields. On her grave stone were written these words:

> Here lyeth the body of Mrs. Anne Knollys,
> Daughter of John Cheney, Esq., and wife
> of Hanserd Knollys (Minister of the Gospel),
> by whom he had issue of 7 sons and 3 daughters;
> who dyed April 30th, 1671, and in the 63rd
> year of her age.

> My only wife, that in her life
> Lived forty years with me,
> Lyes now in rest, for ever blest
> With immortality.

> My dear is gone — left me alone
> For Christ to do and dye,
> Who dyed for me, and dyed to be
> My Saviour-God Most High.

(Preserved in the Heralds' College, London, quoted from Culross, *Hanserd Knollys*, p. 95). After his wife died his granddaughter moved into his home, and took care of the house for which he was truely thankful.

[78] On April 22 (White, *Knollys*, p. 20).

tian professors and sinners to be ready for the Coming of the Lord which he believed was to be very soon. In this work he also clearly taught a postmillennial eschatology where Christ will come at the beginning of the millennium, spiritually and powerfully, and at the end, physically and personally. Five years later, after the Popish Plot scare, he published two more eschatological works, *Mystical Babylon Unvailed* and *An Exposition of the Eleventh Chapter of Revelation*. Both of these works boldly taught that Papal Rome was the great enemy of God's people. At the end of the former treatise he calls people to come out of Papal Rome, and in the latter he states that he believes the end will occur around 1688.

In 1675 Knollys joined with Kiffin, Daniel Dyke, John Gosnold, Henry Forty and Thomas Delaune to answer Obediah Wills' criticism of Henry Danvers' works on baptism including Danvers' *Treatise on Baptism* (1673).[79] Knollys, along with others, also signed a letter to Andrew Gifford concerning the issue of believers praying with unbelievers. Gifford had asked the London ministers for their advice. The London pastors assured him that "prayer is a part of that homage which everyman is obliged to give to God."[80] In addition to the above works of the 1670s, Knollys and the London Particular Baptist churches anonymously published a new *Confession of Faith* in 1677. It was made public in 1689 when William and Mary came to the throne and a measure of toleration was given to Dissenters under the *Act of Toleration*. At that time Knollys, with thirty-six others, signed this *Confession* which was a Baptist revision of the *Westminster Confession* and *Savoy Declaration*.[81] No doubt Knollys and others would have signed this *Confession* in 1677 but refrained from doing so because of persecution. In 1689 Kiffin and Knollys were the only Particular Baptists who had been a part of the movement

---

[79]   Henry Danvers and Obed Wills exchanged pamphlets in debate over baptism. The order of treatises was as follows: 1) Danvers, *A Treatise of Infant-Baptism asserted & vindicated* (1673, 1674); 2) Wills, *Infant-Baptism asserted & vindicated ... in answer to a treatise on baptism lately published by Mr. Henry D'Anvers* (1674); 3) Danvers, *Innocency and Truth Vindicated: or, A Sober reply to Mr. Will's* (1675); 4) Wills, *Vindiciae Vindiciarum* (1675); and 5) Danvers, *A Rejoynder to Mr. Wills his Vindiciae* (1675). In *Vindiciae* Will's appealed to the Baptists against Mr. Danvers. The Baptists including Knollys answered him in *The Baptists Answer to Mr. Obed Wills, His Appeal against Mr. H. Danvers*. On Danvers see R. L. Greaves, "Danvers, Henry (c. 1622-1687)," *Biographical Dictionary of British Radicals*, I, 210-212.

[80]   Joseph Ivimey, *A History of the English Baptists* (London, 1811), I, 417.

[81]   It is now entitled, *The Second London Baptist Confession of Faith*, and is transcribed with a history in Lumpkin, *Baptist Confessions*, pp. 235-295.

in its early years, and signatories to this *Confession*; and they were the
only two to sign both the *First* and *Second London Confessions.*[82]

There is little record of the life of Knollys in the 1680s. According to Thomas Harrison, Knollys was still effectively ministering in
his declining years.[83] In a sermon he preached at the time of
Knollys' death he states that Knollys

> had a *great deal of work to do for God in his declining Age*, which is evident from
> the many *Seals which God gave to his Ministry, even towards the close of it.* When
> he had, as it were, *one foot in the Grave*, he was *Instrumental* to the *Resurrection
> of many Dead Souls to a Spiritual Life.* God put an end to his *Ministerial Work* but
> a very little time before he *call'd him to receive his Crown*, which was a singular
> favour granted to this *Venerable Old Man.*[84]

We also know that Knollys signed a foreward with Kiffin, Dyke,
Cox, William Collins, and John Harris for John Russell's book entitled, *A brief narrative of some considerable passages concerning the first gathering and further progress of a church of Christ in Gospel-order in Boston in New*

---

[82]   Knollys and other Particular Baptists also became involved in a controversy
between the Baptist Thomas Hicks, and the leaders of the Quakers, William Penn and
G. Whitehead. Hicks had written two works against the Quakers' teachings using quotes
from Quaker books. G. Whitehead called the first work "a malitious Forgery." William
Penn answered Hicks' first two works with his own book. And Hicks responded with a
third work in which William Penn charged Hicks with "*vile Forgeries, and black slanders,
&c.*" The Quakers asked that the Baptists censor Hicks for his forgeries. The Baptists
had a public meeting to see if Hicks' quotations, taken from the Quakers, were accurate
or not. After the meeting the Baptists agreed that Hicks' quotes were correct and they
signed a statement to that effect. Knollys was one of the signatories. The whole affair
from the Baptists point of view was recorded and added to Hick's later work, *The Quakers Appeal Answered or a full relation of the Occasion, Progress, and Issue of the meeting held in Barbican, the 28th of August last past* (London, 1674). For Hicks see T. L. Underwood, "Hicks,
Thomas (d.c. 1688)," *Biographical Dictionary of British Radicals*, II, 87-88.

[83]   There is some evidence of Knollys' importance and influence in his latter years.
In Roger Morrice's (c. 1626-1702) political diary entitled, *Entring Book* (March 1677-
April 1691) he states that Edward Hyde, the Earl of Clarendon, sought Knollys' support for the King's proposed changes to the penal codes (Morrice, *Entring Book*, cited in
James, *Religious Liberty*, p. 166). This is probably what Ivimey was referring to when he
stated, "It was credibly reported that a little time before [Knollys] was imprisoned [in
1684], a lord came to him from the court, and asked him whether he and his friends of
his persuasion would accept of a toleration gladly. The excellent man replied, 'I am old,
and know but few men's minds.' Being further pressed for an answer, he said, "I am of
opinion that no liberty but what came by act of parliament would be very acceptable,
because that would be stable, firm, and certain" (Ivimey, *English Baptists*, I, 411; Culross,
Hanserd Knollys, p. 110).

[84]   Thomas Harrison, *A Sermon on the Decease of Mr. Hanserd Knollis Minister of the Gospel. Preached at Pinners Hall Octob. 4. 1691*, p. 39.

England. In this foreward the authors were encouraging toleration for the Baptists of Boston.[85] In 1681 Knollys wrote his fifth eschatological work, *The World that now is and the World that is to Come.* This treatise is divided into two parts dealing with the two Comings of Christ. The first part teaches that the first Coming of Christ was to save sinners, to build up the church of God, and to institute the gospel ordinances for his people to worship the Lord in spirit and truth. The second part deals with the millennial kingdom, the Second Coming of Christ, the resurrection of the dead, and the eternal judgement.

Dissenters in general experienced difficult persecution from 1682 until 1688.[86] During the Spring of 1684, Knollys was imprisoned in Newgate for breaking the Conventicle Act.[87] He was eighty-six at the time and remained there for sixteen months.[88] Again while in prison he preached daily to the prisoners "the things that concern the kingdom of God."[89] Four years later Knollys published his last and crowning work on eschatology, his *Exposition of the Book of the Revelation.* It was formed from the messages he preached to his congregation in past years. In it he also gives an invitation to the people of God to come out of Papal Rome and again suggests the time of the end to be around 1688. In the next year Knollys, Kiffin and others wrote a commendation for the book, *The gospel minister's maintenance vindicated.*[90] That same year Knollys and other London Particular Baptist leaders sent out a letter calling for a general assembly of the churches to gather in September. Two of the reasons given for calling this meeting were to address: "the great neglect of the present ministry"; and the "raising up of an honourable minis-

---

[85]   Knollys, Hanserd, *et al,* "Christian Reader," in John Russel, *A Brief Narrative of some Considerable Passages Concerning the First Gathering and further Progress of a Church of Christ in Gospel Order, in BOSTON.....IN NEW.....ENGLAND. Commonly (though falsely) called by the Name of ANABAPTISTS: For the clearing their innocency from the Scandalous things laid to their charge.* 1680, in Nathan E. Wood, *The History of the First Baptist Church of Boston (1665-1899).* (Philadelphia, 1899), pp. 149-172. See White, *Knollys,* pp. 21, 29. This book was the first Baptist title published in North America.

[86]   The period from 1672-1682 was relatively free from persecution.

[87]   Regardless of the persecution Knollys would not cease his meetings. The *Calendar of State Papers* records in a letter from James Warner to Mrs. Jane Harvey, "Meetings here are suppressed generally, though, when I am with Mr. Knowles, we keep our public meetings" (*Domestic Series, of the Reign of Charles II,* July 24,1683, London, p. 196).

[88]   *Life,* p. 59.

[89]   Culross, *Hanserd Knollys,* p. 100.

[90]   It is believed that Benjamin Keach wrote this book.

try for the time to come."[91] More than one hundred churches were represented with over one hundred and fifty messengers.[92]

In his final years Knollys was embroiled in a controversy over the congregational singing of Psalms and hymns. Knollys' involvement in this issue, however, began years before. In 1663 he wrote a foreward to Katherine Sutton's *A Christian Womans Experiences of the glorious working of God's free grace.*[93] In this foreward he commends the singing of Psalms, hymns and spirtual songs as an ordinance of God's worship whether performed privately or publicly. For the next years he contended for the singing of hymns and Psalms in the public worship of his congregation. And in 1691 he wrote *An Answer to I.[saac] M.[arlow] "A brief discourse concerning singing in the public worship of God in the Gospel-Church"* and *A small piece in defence of Singing ye Praises of God.*[94] Both of these works defended this practice.[95] In addition to this controversy Knollys was involved in one over antinomianism when he and eleven other ministers appended their signatures to a publication of the complete sermons of Tobias Crisp. Crisp had been accused of antinomianism in the 1640s and had long since died. In 1690, however, his son, Samuel Crisp, decided to republish his sermons.[96] Knollys died in the midst of the controversy.

During the last two years of his life, Knollys was limited in what

---

[91]   Ivimey, *English Baptists*, I, 478-480.

[92]   Crosby, *English Baptists*, III, 249. At this time Knollys' congregation was meeting at Broken Wharf (Thames Street) in London with Robert Steed as co-pastor. In 1691 the congregation moved to Bagnio Court, Newgate Street, and later to Currier's Hall, Cripplegate.

[93]   This work by Sutton was published in Rotterdam (1663) around the time that Knollys was on the continent with his family. Near the end of his two or three year sojourn Knollys was in Rotterdam for a brief time (*Life*, p. 37-38). Could he have written the preface then?

[94]   The former is extant, the latter is not.

[95]   Interestingly, Robert Steed co-pastor with Knollys opposed congregational singing as a "gospel ordinance." It appears that those who were against congregational singing believed: 1) that congregational singing meant the use of set prayers; and 2) that it encouraged fellowship in prayer with unbelievers (White, *Knollys*, p. 23; see also Murdina MacDonald, "London Calvinistic Baptists after 1688" [unpublished Ph.D dissertation, Oxford University, 1979]).

[96]   Their commendation of Crisp's sermons was viewed as support for antinomianism. After Knollys died the ministers who signed the commendation made it known that their signatures were intended primarily to certify that the editor, Samuel Crisp, had correctly transcribed eight previously unpublished sermons (White, "Knollys," pp. 23-24).

he could do; he, however, did attend the 1690 and 1691 General Assemblies of the Particular Baptists.[97] And sometime after the 1691 Assembly on September 19, he died in his ninety-third year.[98] He was buried in Bunhill Fields.[99]

We conclude this section of our study of Knollys with two testimonies, one from himself and another from his friend, Thomas Harrison, which reflect something of Knollys' spiritual life. The first comes from his own pen. Knollys had experienced the faithfulness of God throughout his life, and he acknowledged it in his autobiography. In 1671 he wrote:

> In these removings [to New England, Wales, Holland, etc.] I gained great experiences of God's faithfulness, goodness, and truth, in his great and precious promises; and I have gained some experiences of my own heart's deceitfulness, and the power of my own corruptions; the reigning of Christ, and his captivating and subduing my sins; making conquests of the devil, world, and sin, and then giving me the victory, and causing me to triumph, and to bless his most holy name. Three things made my latter sufferings very easy to be endured; 1, The former straits and hardships which I had undergone with patience. 2, The present lively acts and exercise of grace, especially faith and hope, under those latter and greater trials. 3, The light of God's countenance, and the full assurance of his love, and of eternal life. I would not want those experiences and teachings that my soul hath enjoyed, for all that ever I suffered.
>
> My wilderness-mercies, sea-mercies, city-mercies, and prison-mercies, afforded me very many and strong consolations. The spiritual sights of the glory of God, the divine sweetness of the spiritual and providential presence of my Lord Jesus Christ, and the joys and comforts of the Holy and Eternal Spirit, communicated to my soul; together with suitable and seasonable scriptures of truth; have so often, and so powerfully revived, refreshed, and strengthened my heart in the days of my pilgrimage, trials and sufferings, that the sense, yea the life and sweetness thereof abides still upon my heart, and hath engaged my soul to live by faith, to walk humbly, and

---

[97] *Ibid.*, p. 23.

[98] A year earlier in October Knollys, William Collins and Hercules Collins appointed Richard Adams to be an elder with William Kiffin at Devonshire Square. In March 1690 Knollys was involved in the ordination of Joseph Stennet; he "spoke some words of exhortation" (Ivimey, *English Baptists*, II, 485).

[99] It should be noted that Knollys read widely, including Ecclesiastical histories (e.g., Eusebius, Socrates), Biblical commentaries, the church Fathers (e.g., Jerome, Ambrose, Chrysostom, Augustine), Aquinas, the Reformers (Calvin, Luther, Zwingli, Beza), ancient histories (Pliny, Josephus), ancient writers (Ovid, Virgil, Aristotle), numerous Roman Catholic authors (e.g., Bellarmine), and Puritans (e.g. Owen, Reynolds). See Appendix A for a list of the authors he cites or quotes in his works.

to desire and endeavour to excel in holiness, to God's glory and the example of others.[100]

The second testimony comes from Thomas Harrison's funeral sermon for Knollys at Pinner's Hall on October 4. The sermon contained these commendable words about Knollys as a person,

> He walked with that caution, that his greatest Enemies had nothing against him, save only on the matter of his God; That holy Life which he lived, did command Reverence even from those who were Enemies to the holy Doctrine which he preached. He was a *Preacher out of the Pulpit as well as in it.... He had a great respect to Christ's New Commandment, which he gave to his Disciples, to love one another.* He *loved the Image of God wheresoever he saw it.* He was not a man of a narrow and private, but of *a large and publick spirit. The difference of his fellow Christians Opinions from his, did not alienate his affections from them.* He lov'd all *his fellow Travellers, tho' they did not walk in the same particular path with himself....* He chearfully went about suffering as well as preaching work. He was not *unwilling to take up his cross and follow his Lord and Master in the Thorny road of Tribulation.*[101]

---

[100]   *Life*, pp. 40-41.

[101]   Harrison, *Sermon*, pp. 56-57, 57-58, 60. The funeral sermon preached to Knollys' own congregation was preached by someone else. Harrison's sermon was preached at the "*morning Lecture* at Pinners-Hall, *which was first erected by him* [Knollys]" (*Ibid.*, Epistle to the Reader). In this sermon Harrison calls his hearers to imitate the excellencies of deceased ministers like Knollys. Then he points out some of Knollys' excellencies worthy of imitation: 1) "His accurate and circumspect walking ... with that caution, that his greatest Enemies had nothing against him, save only in matters of his God"; 2) "His *universal love to Christians....* He was a not a man of narrow and private, but of *a large and publick spirit. The difference of his fellow Christians Opinions from his did not alienate his affections from them.* He *lov'd all his fellow travellers, tho they did not walk in the same particular path with himself*"; 3) "His meekness and humility. He was not of a proud and lofty Temper"; 4) "His *laboriousness in that work which he was engaged in....* He was *willing to spend and to be spent in the service of his Lord, and for the good of poor souls*"; and 5) "*His couragious and chearful suffering for his Masters and the Gospels sake*" (*Ibid.*, pp. 56-60).

CHAPTER THREE

ANTINOMIANISM[1]

From their beginnings and throughout the century the Calvinistic Baptists in general, and Hanserd Knollys in particular, were accused of Antinomianism. Antinomianism had existed in various forms throughout the history of the church but did not manifest itself in England in any significant degree until the Revolutionary years of the 1640s.[2] It was during these years that the Presbyterians in particular brought this heresy to the attention of Parliament and country.[3] This heresy reached its peak from 1645 to 1649 in the

---

[1] Antinomianism literally means "against the law." Broadly defined in the Christian context, it is the teaching that the moral law is not relevant to the believer's life. Since the believer is under grace and not law, she is not bound by the law as a rule of life. The Church has feared this teaching because it allows or encourages professing Christians to live immoral lives. For more on a general definition and history of Antinomianism see Hugh J. Blair, "Antinomianism," *The New International Dictionary of the Christian Church*, revised ed., ed. J.D. Douglas (Grand Rapids, 1974), p. 48; A.H. Newman, "Antinomianism and Antinomian Controversies," *The New Schaff-Herzog Encyclopedia* 15 vols., ed. Samuel M. Jackson (n.d.; rpt. Grand Rapids, 1977), I, 196-201; John Henry Blunt, "Antinomianism," *Dictionary of Doctrinal and Historical Theology*, (London, 1892), pp. 30-31; and J. MacBride Sterrett, "Antinomianism," *Encyclopedia of Religion and Ethics*, 13 vols., ed. James Hastings (Edinburgh & New York, 1980), I, 581-582.

[2] See Gertrude Huehns, *Antinomianism in English History* (London, 1951), pp. 25-36.

[3] Some of the tracts and books written against Antinomianism include [Nathaniel Holmes], *An Antidote against Antinomianisme. Penned for the regaining of our mistaken brother H.D., by D.H.* (1644); [Thomas Gataker], *The Triumph of Faith by T.G., the Second Impression* (n.d.); John Sedgwick, *Antinomians Anatomized; or, a Glasse for the Lawlesse* (1643); Samuel Rutherford, *A Survey of the Spiritual Antichrist. Opening the secrets of Familisme and Antinomianisme in the Antichristian doctrines of John Saltmarsh and Will. Dell, and of Robert Towne, Tob. Crisp and others* (1647); Thomas Edwards, *Gangraena; or, a Catalogue of many Errours, Heresies and pernicious Practices of the Sectaries of our Time*, 3rd ed. (1646); Ephraim Pagitt, *Heresiography; or, A Description of the Heretics and Sectaries of these Latter times* (1645); Thomas Gataker, *God's Eye on his Israel; or numb. 23.21 expounded and cleared from Antinomian abuse* (1644); William Prynne, *A Fresh Discovery of some prodigious new Wandering-Blasing-Stars and Firebrands, stiling themselves New-Lights, firing our Church and state into new Combustions* (1645); Anthony Burgess, *The true Doctrine of Justification asserted and vindicated from the errors of Papists, Arminians, Socinians, and more especially Antinomians* (1648); Stephen Geree, *The Doctrine of the Antinomians by Evidence of Gods truth, Plainely Confuted* (1644); and Thomas Hotchkiss, *An Exercitation concerning the Nature of Forgiveness of Sin. Intended as an antidote for preventing the danger of Antimnomian doctrine* (1655).

New Model Army which had become so influential and powerful.[4]
The charges of Antinomianism were levelled at the Particular Bap-
tist churches both implicitly and explicitly. For example, Robert
Baillie considered the seven Baptist churches that signed the 1644
Confession, "the most of them are exceeding farre from making these
Articles the rule of their belief." He went on to accuse them of be-
ing Brownists, Antipaedobaptists, Arminians, Antinomians, Arians
and Familists.[5] He later states,

> The Confession of their seven-Churches does not so flatly contradict these
> errours [of Antinomianism] as the former of Arminianisme, but rather
> countenances them; it sets down such a justification as acquits us before
> God of all sin past, present, and to come: The second Edition omits that
> sentence of past, present, and to come, (I wish this correction did proceed
> from a dislike of the conclusions which the Antinomians draw from the
> words omitted) but in both Editions they expressly exclude the necessity of
> the Laws Ministery to bring the soul to any repentance before or in the
> time of its calling and conversion to Christ.[6]

In 1646 Hanserd Knollys signed this *Confession* which would have
identified him with the heresy of Antinomianism in the minds of
the orthodox. Moreover, several Particular Baptists including
Knollys were specifically accused of Antinomianism.[7] It, however,

---

4   Huehns, *Antinomianism*, pp. 71-124.
5   Robert Baillie, *Anabaptism, The True Fountain of Independency, Antinomy, Brownisme and Familisme, And the most of the other Errours, which for the time doe trouble the Church of England, Unsealed* (1647), pp. 49.
6   *Anabaptism*, p. 96. Daniel Featley in his *Dippers dipt* (1645) appears to be concerned about the Antinomianism of Article 31 which states, "Whatsoever the saints, any of them doe enjoy of God in this life, is onely by faith." The implication being that only saints have a right to own property which opens the door to civil and legal disorder (p. 221).
7   Other Calvinistic Baptists accused of Antinomianism include John Simpson, Paul Hobson, Samuel Richardson and Thomas Collier. For John Simpson see Richard Greaves, "Simpson, John (d. 1662)," *Biographical Dictionary of British Radicals*, eds. Richard Greaves & Robert Zaller (Brighton, 1982-1984), III, 176-177, and Richard L. Greaves, *Saints and Rebels: Seven Nonconformists in Stuart England* (Macon, GA, 1985), pp. 99-132. He is considered an Antinomian by Thomas Edwards (*Gangraena* 3rd ed. [1646], I, pt. 2, p. 39). For Paul Hobson see Richard Greaves, "Hobson, Paul (d. 1666)," *Biographical Dictionary of British Radicals*, II, 95-97, and Greaves, *Saints and Rebels*, pp. 133-156. Hobson is called an Antinomian by Robert Baillie (*Anabaptism*, p. 95), by Richard Baxter (*Reliquiae Baxterianae: or, Mr. Richard Baxter's Narrative of the Most Memorable Passages of His Life and Times* [1696], p. 111); and by Thomas Edwards (*Gangraena* 3rd ed. [1646], I, pt. 2, pp. 33, 34). For Samuel Richardson see Richard Greaves & B. R. White, "Richardson, Samuel (fl. 1637-1658)," *Biographical Dictionary of British Radicals*, III, 93-95.

was in New England in the 1630s that Knollys was first branded an Antinomian, and it was most likely the initial reason he was accused of being one in England. When Knollys arrived in Massachusetts the governor John Winthrop, in 1638, states he was "rejected by us for holding some of Mrs. Hutchinson's opinions."[8] In March of that year just prior to Knollys' arrival, Mrs. Hutchinson had been excommunicated for her Antinomianism. The Antinomian Controversy raged in Massachusetts from 1636 to 1638.[9] Its central figures allegedly espousing Antinomianism were Anne Hutchinson, John Cotton and John Wheelwright.[10] It was probably because of Knollys' association with John Wheelwright that he was labeled an Antinomian. In his autobiography Knollys acknowledged that it was through Wheelwright that he came into the Covenant of Grace. Knollys stated that prior to meeting with Wheelwright he was "a stranger to [free grace] in great measure, having [been] only under legal convictions and a spirit of bondage." He had "sought righteousness as it were by the works of the law, and got [his] peace by performing duties, and rested on them." He prayed and "begged God to teach [him] the covenant of grace." Sometime after this Knollys heard a certain Mr. How[11] preach that "God did give the faith of evidence...in some covenant promise." Knollys

---

Paul Linton Gritz shows that Richardson held Antinomian tenets in his, "Samuel Richardson and the Religious and Political Controversies Confronting the London Particular Baptists, 1643 to 1658" (unpublished Ph.D dissertation, Southwestern Baptist Theological Seminary, 1987), pp. 263-290. For Thomas Collier's Antinomianism see Huehns, *Antinomianism*, pp. 53, 99, 130.

[8]   Winthrop, *Journal*, I, 295. He also writes in February 1640, "One Mr. Hanserd Knolles, a minister in England, who came over the last summer in the company of our familistical opinionists, and so suspected and examined, and found inclining that way, was denied residence in the Massachusetts" (*Journal*, I, 328). Familism was in a number of ways similar to Antinomianism. For more on this sect see R.E.D. Clark, "Familists," *The New International Dictionary of the Christian Church*, ed. J.D. Douglas (Grand Rapids, 1974), pp. 368-369. It is not unlikely that Mrs. Hutchinson was influenced by this teaching prior to her coming to Boston (Iain H. Murray, "Antinomianism: New England's First Controversy," *The Banner of Truth*, 179-180 [1978], pp. 36-39).

[9]   For more on this controversy see Emery Battis, *Saints and Sectaries: Anne Hutchinson and the Antinomian Controversy in the Massachusetts Bay Colony* (Chapel Hill, 1962); David D. Hall, *The Antinomian Controversy, 1636-1638: A Documentary History* (Durham and London, 1990); and Murray, "Antinomianism," pp. 1-75.

[10]   For some details concerning Wheelwright's life and his involvement in this controversy see Battis, *Saints and Sectaries*, pp. 110-124, and Hall, *Antinomian*, pp. 152-172.

[11]   This was probably Samuel How, the Baptist Cobbler who wrote *The Sufficiencie of the Spirits Teaching, without Humane Learning* (1640). See J. F. Maclear, "How, Samuel (fl. 1632-1640)," *Biographical Dictionary of British Radicals*, II, 114-115.

prayed for this promise. The next day as he was praying God gave him several promises concerning the forgiveness of his sins and his place in the covenant of peace. Consequently, he states he experienced "joy and peace in believing." The following day Knollys told Wheelwright of his experience and the latter told him he was now "somewhat prepared to preach Jesus Christ and the gospel of free grace to others, having been taught it of God."[12] Knollys would have felt a deep affection for both Wheelwright and his teaching on salvation and free grace. Although Wheelwright was not present when Knollys arrived in Boston, having been banished from the plantation the year before, Knollys' association with, and affection for Wheelwright were known by the Massachusetts authorities. Consequently, he was accused of being an Antinomian shortly after his arrival in Boston.

Knollys' association with Antinomianism continued through Wheelwright and the Governor of New Hampshire, Captain Underhill (Wheelwright's friend), when Knollys became the pastor of the church in Piscattuah.[13] Moreover, the evidence for Knollys' Antinomianism was probably strengthened in the minds of the Boston authorities when both Underhill and Knollys were accused of illicit sexual involvement while in New England.[14]

After his return to England Knollys was accused of Antinomianism in several places during the 1640s. In 1645, after Knollys had preached in Suffolk, the *Minutes of the Assembly of the Westminster Divines* state,

> Upon information against Mr. Knowles, his preaching in private, and venting his Antinomian opinions.
> Ordered — Dr. Burgess, Mr. Vines, Mr. Seaman, Mr. Ley, Mr. Ward, Mr. Callamy, [Mr. Tuckney], Mr Spurstow, Mr. Walker, — a Committee to

---

[12]   Knollys, *Life*, pp. 17-24.
[13]   Winthrop, *Journal*, I, 295; Jeremy Belknap, *The History of New Hampshire* (Boston, 1813), I, 32-53; Brown, "Knollys," pp. 1-7. This was the second church of New Hampshire. The first was pastored by Wheelwright himself.
[14]   Winthrop, *Journal*, I, 328-329; II, 28. As has already been noted in chapter two, the evidence concerning Knollys' sexual dalliance is inconclusive. Regardless, Winthrop was all the more willing to believe the charge because he considered Knollys an Antinomian; he states, "And it is very observable how God gave up these two [Knollys & Capt. Underhill], and some others who had held with Mrs. Hutchinson, in crying down all evidence from sanctification, etc., to fall into these unclean courses, whereby themselves and their erroneous opinions were laid open to the world" (*Ibid.*).

consider this complaint, and of all other disorders formerly complained of, or fit to be complained of, to be of the like nature.[15]

Most likely this committee met with Knollys in 1646 with some of the details given by Thomas Edwards in his *Gangraena*. Edwards states that Knollys, a little after returning to Old England,

> discovered himself to be an Antinomian, and was in a Brotherly way delt with by some Ministers meeting at Mr. *Calamies*; and after some reasoning and debate ... he and Mr. *Simpson* the Antinomian, set their hands to a Paper drawn up of some Propositions, concerning the *Moral Law* and the *Ten Commandments* delivered by *Moses*; and yet after that complaints were made to the Ministers by some godly Christians of either one or both, preaching against those points they had subscribed.[16]

Knollys was again charged with Antinomianism at the end of his life. Knollys had signed the republication of Tobias Crisp's sermons entitled, *Christ alone exalted, being the compleat works of Tobias Crisp, D.D.* (1690) edited by his son Samuel Crisp. In the 1640s Tobias Crisp was considered one of the chief proponents of Antinomianism along with William Dell, Paul Hobson, John Eaton, and John Saltmarsh.[17] There were fifty-two sermons in this edition of his *Works*, of which eight were previously unpublished. In order to certify the authenticity of these eight sermons Knollys and eleven other ministers signed a certificate which was placed in the volume stating that they had "been faithfully transcribed from [Crisp's] own notes."[18] Richard Baxter, who despised Antinomianism,

---

[15]   *Minutes of the Sessions of the Westminster Assembly of Divines*, p. 96. Crosby states that, "[Knollys] went into Suffolk, where he preached in several places, as he had opportunity and was desired by his friends; but he being counted an *Antinomian*, and an *Anabaptist*, this was looked upon to be *sedition* and *faction*, and the rabble being encouraged by the high-constable, set themselves zealously to oppose him" (Crosby, *English Baptists*, I, 228).

[16]   Edwards, *Gangraena*, 3rd ed. (1646), I, pt. 2, p. 39.

[17]   For more on Tobias Crisp see J. F. Maclear, "Crisp, Tobias (1600-1643)," *Biographical Dictionary of British Radicals*, I, 191-192, and Christopher Hill, *The Collected Essays of Christopher Hill: Religion and Politics in 17th Century England*, vol. 2 (Amherst, 1986), pp. 141-161. For John Eaton see J. F. H. New, "Eaton, John (c. 1575-1642)," *Biographical Dictionary of British Radicals*, I, 242. For William Dell see N. T. Burns, "Dell, William (c. 1607-1669)," *Biographical Dictionary of British Radicals*, I, 221-223. For John Saltmarsh see N. T. Burns, "Saltmarsh, John (c. 1612-1647)," *Biographical Dictionary of British Radicals*, III, 136-137, and "Saltmarsh, John," *Dictionary of National Biography*, eds. Leslie Stephen & Sidney Lee (Oxford and London, 1921-22), XVII, 709-711.

[18]   Peter Toon, *The Emergence of Hyper-Calvinism in English Nonconformity 1689-1765*

responded to this republication, and to the twelve ministers who signed it. In a sermon at Pinner's Hall on January 28, 1690 he accused the minsters of "hanging up a sign to show where Jezebel dwelt."[19] John Howe, one of the signatories, defended himself in a pamphlet entitled, *Some considerations of a certificate* (1690). A year later seven of the twelve ministers published an explanatory letter in John Flavell's book, *Planelogia; A succinct and seasonable discourse* (1691).[20] They explained that they had signed the certificate only to certify that Samuel Crisp had correctly copied the eight additional sermons for this new edition. Only seven of the original twelve signed this explanatory letter; Knollys was not one of them because he had died that same year. Once again, Knollys was accused of Antinomianism.

Today scholars still see Knollys as an Antinomian based on the accusations made against him in the 1630s and 1640s. For example, Philip Gura maintains that in England in the 1640s "[Knollys] continued to be attacked for his antinomian views, which in his case he genuinely held."[21]

The question remains, however, was Knollys *in fact* an Antinomian according to seventeenth-century English Reformed orthodoxy? In order to answer this question, we will begin by exploring the meaning of Antinomianism in the seventeenth-century context of both England and New England where Knollys was accused of this heresy. Our aim will be to understand the proper meaning of

---

(London, 1967), pp. 49-50. Some others who signed include John Howe (Pres.), Vincent Alsop (Pres.), Isaac Chauncy (Ind.), Increase Mather (Ind.), and George Cokayn (Ind.). Six Presbyterians and five Independents signed; Knollys was the only Baptist to sign.

19   Quoted in Toon, *Hyper-Calvinism*, p. 50.

20   Part of this book attacked doctrinal Antinomianism.

21   Philip F. Gura, *A Glimpse of Sion's Glory: Puritan Radicalism in New England, 1620-1660* (Middletown, 1984), p. 67. Also in his chapter on 'Dissent in New Hampshire, 1640-1792,' William G. McLoughlin writes, "When the Antinomians were driven out of Boston in 1638 they thought at first that the New Hampshire frontier would provide haven for them. Two men who later became prominent Baptists (Hanserd Knollys and John Clarke) spent some time trying to establish themselves here at that time. Clarke left for Rhode Island after one cold winter and Knollys returned to England in 1641 after a division in his church at Dover. The same year (1639) that John Wheelwright and the Antinomians were setting up a church in Exeter and Knollys was establishing one in Dover, a group of Anglicans formed a church in Portsmouth and a group of orthodox Puritans settled in Hampton and three other New Hampshire towns" (*New England Dissent 1630-1883* [Cambridge, 1971], II, 834). McLoughlin language is ambiguous. Is he saying that Knollys was an Antinomian? Even if this is not what he is saying, the reader could be left with the impression that Knollys was.

this teaching *from the contexts in which Knollys was accused* in order to assess better this charge made against him. The meaning of Antinomianism in New England will be examined first because it was there that Knollys was initially charged with it. Then a synthesis of the Antinomian tenets held in the two places will be given. Finally, Knollys' writings will be compared with the Antinomian tenets of his contemporaries to test whether this charge is in fact valid. We will also see something of Knollys' teaching on such subjects as justification by faith, sanctification, and the relation of the law and sin to the believer.

The New England Antinomian Controversy: Its History

The Antinomian Controversy took place between 1636-1638. The alleged principal Antinomians were Anne Hutchinson, John Wheelwright and John Cotton. Cotton was an ordained minister of the Church of England, a graduate of Emmanuel College, Cambridge, who, in 1612, at the age of twenty-seven became the minister of Boston, Lincolnshire. Twenty-one years later Cotton, one of the leading Puritans in England, left his homeland for New England to avoid imprisonment for his nonconformity. Shortly after his arrival in Massachusetts he became the preacher of the Boston church.[22] Anne Hutchinson had been a long-time admirer of Cotton's ministry in England and felt she " 'could not be at rest' until she followed her beloved minister across the sea."[23] Consequently, the Hutchinson family sailed to New England in 1634 and became quite involved in the Boston church. Hutchinson became a spiritual advisor to other women in the congregation. This began with her visiting women who were in childbirth and later she had meetings in her own home to repeat and discuss Cotton's previous week's sermons as well as other minister's messages from other towns near Boston. These meetings became very popular, attracting more than sixty people to her home.[24] Hutchinson began to teach that, with the exception of Cotton, all the other ministers were legalists. In the

---

[22] For a history of Cotton's role in the Antinomian Controversy see Larzer Ziff, *The Career of John Cotton: Puritanism and the American Experience* (Princeton, 1962), pp. 106-148.
[23] Hall, *Antinomian*, p. 5.
[24] Men were also attending these meetings.

spring of 1636 these other ministers "warned Cotton of the strange opinions circulating among his parishoners."[25] They also wondered if Hutchinson's opinions were coming from Cotton himself. It was about this time that John Wheelwright arrived in Boston from England. Upon his arrival he was warmly received and proffered Anne Hutchinson's assurance that he was "a sealed and able minister of the Gospel."[26]

In October a conference between the ministers[27] and Cotton, Hutchinson and Wheelwright took place to see where the latter group stood on the subjects of sanctification and its relationship to justification. Winthrop states that Cotton "gave satisfaction to them, so as he agreed with them all in the point of sanctification, and so did Mr. Wheelwright; so as they all did hold, that sanctification did help to evidence justification."[28] Following this conference a majority of the Boston congregation proposed Wheelwright as a teacher in the Boston church. The minority of the church including John Winthrop opposed this election which was meant to insult and re-

---

[25]   Hall, *Antinomian*, p. 6. About this time letters were exchanged between Thomas Shepard and John Cotton concerning Cotton's views. They disagreed on three points: 1) the relationship between the Word and the Spirit; 2) the activity of a sinner before he received the Holy Spirit; and 3) the life of righteousness as evidence of justification (*Ibid.*, pp. 24-33). Also about mid-year Cotton and Peter Bulkeley exchanged views on union with Christ. They debated over whether faith is *antecedent* or *consequent* to union with Christ and justification (*Ibid.*, pp. 34-42).

[26]   Battis, *Saints and Sectaries*, p. 114. John Wheelwright was born in 1592 near Alford, Lincolnshire. In 1611 he matriculated at Sidney Sussex College, Cambridge admitted as a sizar. His master was the Puritan Samuel Ward. Seven years later he received the Master of Arts degree and began his probationary term as deacon at the cathedral in Peterborough. In 1621 Wheelwright married Marie Storre, the daughter of Bilsby's vicar, near Alford, and shortly afterwards became the vicar of Bilsby, serving for nine years in this ministry. At this time Wheelwright was moving closer to Puritan principles and somewhat beyond them, emphasizing "man's utter dependence on God's free grace, and rejected any hint that man could strive on his own or that his work bore any merit in God's eyes." During his years at Bilsby his wife Marie died in childbirth, and soon after he married Mary Hutchinson of Alford. Mary was the sister-in-law to Anne Hutchinson. In 1632 the Bilsby benefice was turned over to the Crown through the irregularity of simony. Probably this was used by the authorities to get rid of him for his Puritan teachings. It was during this time that Hanserd Knollys met with Wheelwright for counsel. Many of Wheelwright's friends and relations had already settled in Massachusetts including his brothers-in-law William and Edward Hutchinson in 1634. In the spring of 1636 Wheelwright and his family set sail for New England (*Ibid.*, pp. 110-114).

[27]   We assume these to be Thomas Weld and John Eliot of Roxbury, Zachariah Symmes of Charlestown, and Thomas Shepard of Newtown.

[28]   Winthrop, *Journal*, I, 196.

place the second minister of the Boston church, John Wilson. Consequently, there was great tension in the Boston church.

Two months later the ministers met again with Hutchinson and Cotton but this time they did not come to any agreement.[29] Cotton feared that if sanctification were understood incorrectly it could lead a person to trust in "works" rather than "grace." Hutchinson told the ministers they were preaching "works" not "grace." In December, the General Court became involved in the controversy and found itself as divided on this issue as the colony and church. The Court called for a general Fast on January 19 in order that peace might be restored.

At this Fast, Cotton invited John Wheelwright to preach. Winthrop states that in his sermon Wheelwright "inveighed against all that walked in a covenant of works, as he described it to be, viz., such as maintain sanctification as an evidence of justification, etc. and called them antichrists, and stirred up the people against them with much bitterness and vehemency."[30] In the weeks that followed, the Antinomian party put "public questions" to the other ministers during the lectures and church services in order to expose them as preaching a "covenant of works" and not a "covenant of grace." In March (1637) Wheelwright and others of his party were brought before the Court. Wheelwright was adjuged to be guilty of "sedition, and ... contempt" for his divisive actions on the Fast day. The minority in the Court and the Boston church tendered a protestation and a petition respectively. The petition from the Church "justif[ied] Mr. Wheelwright's sermon."[31]

In May the "general court of elections" took place in Newtown (Cambridge). The majority elected John Winthrop governor in place of the Antinomian supporter, Henry Vane, Jr.. This new

---

[29] The ministers had written up a list of sixteen questions that they asked Cotton to answer. These questions and Cotton's answers are given in Hall, *Antinomian*, pp. 43-59. Cotton's answers were probably given in January. Soon after Cotton gave his answers the Elder's replied with the *Elders Reply* also given in *Ibid.*, pp. 60-77. The two main points in their reply were: 1) to defend the use of sanctification as an evidence of justification; and 2) to vindicate their orthodoxy on free grace. Cotton responded with a *Rejoinder to the Elder's Reply* which is given in *Ibid.*, pp. 78-151. Here Cotton teaches that in the order of causes the Spirit comes first then faith; in addition, works were not the grounds and causes of our first assurance.

[30] Winthrop, *Journal*, I, 211. Wheelwright's Fast-Day sermon is given in Hall, *Antinomian*, pp. 152-172.

[31] Winthrop, *Journal*, I, 211.

Court tightened its grip against the Antinomians. It passed a law that "no 'strangers' could be received in the colony for longer than three weeks without permission of the Court."[32] The purpose of this law, according to Winthrop, was to keep Antinomians from settling in the colony and building up their numbers. At the same time that the elections were taking place, the ministers were meeting with Cotton and coming to agreement with him on the doctrine of sanctification.[33] But there were still other doctrines in dispute, consequently, they called a synod which met in August. The synod identified and refuted eighty-two errors of the Antinomians[34] and warned against two matters of church order: the liberty to question the minister, and the liberty to hold private meetings.[35] The synod adjourned in September having dealt a heavy blow against the Antinomians. The Antinomians, however, "persisted in their opinions, and were as busy in nourishing contentions... as before."[36] Consequently, Winthrop and the Court, which met in November, "agreed to send away some of the principal" Antinomians for the sake of the colony. The leaders, including Wheelwright, were disenfranchized and banished from the colony. Their followers were given lesser penalties. After this Hutchinson was brought before the Court and banished primarily for her "receiving revelations from God."[37] She was tried also by the Boston church and excommunicated in March, 1638.[38] Six days later she left for Rhode Island never again to return to Massachusetts.[39]

---

[32] Hall, *Antinomian*, p. 9.

[33] Winthrop, *Journal*, I, 216-217.

[34] These eighty-two errors are given in John Winthrop's *A Short Story of the Rise, reign, and ruine of the Antinomians, Familists & Libertines*, found in Hall, *Antinomian*, pp. 219-243.

[35] Winthrop, *Journal*, I, 232-235. Either at the time of this synod or sometime earlier (May – August) Cotton had a conference with the elders touching upon three questions. They were: "1. *Touching gracious conditions, or qualifications, wrought in the soule before faith*"; "2. *Touching the gathering of our first evident assurance of our faith from sanctification*"; and "3. *Touching the active power of faith, and other spirituall gifts of grace in a Christian conversation*" (Hall, *Antinomian*, p. 175). These answers are given in *Ibid.*, pp. 175-198.

[36] Winthrop, *Journal*, I, 239.

[37] This examination is given in detail in Hall, *Antinomian*, pp. 311-348.

[38] This trial is also given in *Ibid.*, pp. 349-388.

[39] The months between the Court meeting (Nov., 1637) and the Church meeting (March, 1638) found the churches disciplining members who were involved with the Antinomians.

The New England Antinomian Controversy: Its Theology

The key issue around which the Antinomian crisis revolved was that of assurance. How could a person know if he or she were of the elect and in the covenant of grace? Reformed and Puritan theology had at least two answers. Both Calvin and Ames had taught that assurance came by the witness of the Spirit and by evidence of sanctification in a person's life.[40] And it is these answers that came into tension in the Antinomian crisis in New England. Assurance became an important issue in 1636 in New England for two reasons: one, the spiritual revival of 1633 had passed; and two, church membership required the candidate to testify to her conversion. John Cotton began to preach in 1636 that "'sanctification' could amount to no more than a 'righteousness of one's own,'" and that "reformation is no assurance that God hath made an everlasting Covenant with us."[41] What was at stake for Cotton, Hutchinson and Wheelwright was the gospel of the free grace of God in the covenant of grace. The elders, according to Mrs. Huchinson, were "legal" preachers who declared a covenant of works which was no salvation at all. They were encouraging people to look to their sanctification for evidence of their place in the covenant of grace. For the Hutchinsonians this was contrary to the gospel. Out of this key issue the Antinomian errors flowed. The Antinomian charges laid against Cotton, Hutchinson and Wheelwright were given on several different occasions. In December 1636 the Bay Colony elders asked Cotton to answer sixteen questions concerning his teaching entitled, *Sixteene Questions of Serious and Necessary Consequence.* John Winthrop

---

[40] For Calvin see Joel R. Beeke, *Assurance of Faith: Calvin, English Puritanism, and the Dutch Second Reformation* (New York, 1991), pp. 47-78. See for Calvin on immediate witness of the Spirit his *Institutes* III. 11. 4; III. 2. 6-7; III. 2. 14-16, and on the role of sanctification for assurance see *Ibid.*, III. 14. 18-20; III. 24. 1-6; III. 2.8; and comments on 2 Peter 1:10 and 1 John 2:3; 4:17 in John Calvin, *Calvin's New Testament Commentaries*, eds. David W. Torrance & Thomas F. Torrance (Grand Rapids, 1974). For Ames see Michael Schuldiner, *Gifts and Works: The Post-Conversion Paradigm and Spiritual Controversy in Seventeenth-Century Massachusetts* (Macon, 1991), pp. 67-69. For assurance through the testimony of the Holy Spirit see Ames' *Marrow*, I. 28. 22-24; and for assurance through sanctification see *Ibid.*, I. 30. 10-20. For Calvin the immediate witness of the Spirit is based on the promises of salvation in Christ, never divorced from the Word of God. For him the primary emphasis is on this means of assurance.

[41] Hall, *Antinomian*, 16. For Cotton's theology in this controversy see Everett Emerson, *John Cotton*, revised edition (Boston, 1990), pp. 85-96, and Murray, *Antinomianism*, pp. 53-68.

also laid out what he saw to be twenty-nine errors of the Hutchinsonians in his *A Short Story of the Rise, reign, and ruine of the Antinomians, Familists & Libertines.*[42] In addition, this latter book lists eighty-two errors of the Hutchinsonians with confutations in "A Catalogue of such erroneous opinions as were found to have beene brought into *New-England*, and spread under-hand there, as they were condemned by an Assembly of the Churches, at *New Town, Aug.* 30.1." Some of the more radical charges against Hutchinson herself are given in *A Report of a Trial of Mrs Anne Hutchinson before the Church of Boston* whose trial took place in March 1638.

When these charges and their answers by the Hutchinsonians are examined, several points of Antinomian doctrine in New England come to the fore. The first has to do with the relation between justification and sanctification. Cotton and the Hutchinsonians believed that sanctification is no evidence of justification. The thirteenth question of the *Sixteen Questions* given to Cotton stated, "*Whether evidencing Iustification by Sanctification, be a building my Iustification on Sanctification: or a going on in a* Covenant of Workes." He answered,

> To give my Sanctification for an evident ground, [and] cause, or matter of my Iustification, is to build my Iustification upon my Sanctification, and to go on in a Covenant of Works. [This is the foundation of Popery, and will be the ruine and destruction of it.].... To give my sanctification for an evident ground or cause of my Faith, whereby I am justified, as when I doe not, or dare not depend upon Christ for my *Iustification*, till I evidently see my *Sanctification*, this is also to build my Iustification on my sanctification, and to go on in a Covenant of works.... To give my Sanctification for an evident cause and ground of my faith (not whereby I am justified, but) whereby I beleeve my selfe to be justified (which they call the faith of assurance) this may be a building my Iustification on my Sanctification, or a going on in a Covenant of works two wayes: 1. If the Soul have no Evidence of his Dependance upon Christ for Righteousnesse, nor no Evidence of His Effectuall Calling unto Christ, and unto faith in Christ ... but onely seeth an evident change [wrought] in himselfe, from a prophane [or] civill course to a sanctified Conversation; [This is still a building of Justification upon Sanctification].[43]

---

[42]   In Hall, *Antinomian*, pp.199-310.
[43]   *Ibid.*, pp. 52-53.

For Cotton sanctification on its own could not be sufficient evidence of justification.[44]

John Wheelwright concurred with Cotton. In his Fast Day sermon of January 1637 he stated,

> If men thinke to be saved, because they see some worke of sanctification in them, as hungring and thirsting and the like: if they be saved, they are saved without the Gospell. No, no this is a covenant of works, for in the covenant of grace, nothing is revealed but Christ for our righteousness; and so for the knowledge of our justification by faith, nothing is revealed to the soule but only Christ and his righteousness freely given.[45]

As Winthrop correctly observed of the Antinomians' rhetoric, "Here is a great stirre about graces and looking to hearts, but give mee Christ, I seeke not for graces, but for Christ, I seeke not for promises, but for Christ, I seeke not for sanctification, but for Christ, tell not mee of meditation and duties, but tell mee of Christ."[46] In the Catalogue of erroneous errors given by the Assembly of the Churches in August 1637, Error 67 states, "A man cannot evidence his justification by his sanctification, but he must needs build upon his sanctification, and trust to it."[47] And again at Mrs. Hutchinson's trial in the Boston church in March 1638 one of the charges laid against her was "That Sanctification could be no Evidence of a good Estate at all."[48] The Hutchinsonians clearly wanted to separate sanctification from justification when it came to assurance of salvation.

The second point of Antinomian doctrine taught by the Hutchinsonians had to do with the primary evidence of a person's justification. They strongly claimed that it must be the direct testimony of the Holy Spirit to the heart. In answer to Question 13 of the *Sixteene Questions* Cotton states, "But now if the Spirit of God

---

[44] For more on Cotton's views on this subject see his answer to Question Two in *A Conference ... Held at Boston (Ibid.*, pp. 177-192). Cotton did believe that sanctification was an evidence but not on its own.

[45] *Ibid.*, p. 161.

[46] *Ibid.*, pp. 17-18.

[47] *Ibid.*, p. 237. Error 72 also maintains, "It is a fundamentall and soule-damning errour to make sanctification an evidence of justification"; and Error 81 states, "Where faith is held forth by the Ministery, as the condition of the covenant of grace on mans part, as also evidencing justification by sanctification, and the activity of faith, in that Church there is not sufficient bread" (*Ibid.*, pp. 239, 242).

[48] *Ibid.*, p. 375.

[himselfe] do shed abroad his Light into such a Soule, and give him a cleare sight of his estate in a free Promise of grace in Christ; such a one evidently discerneth both his *Justification* and his *Sanctification*."[49] Wheelwright fully agrees with Cotton, stating in his Fast Day sermon, "Truly both in poynt of justification, and the knowledg [*sic*] of this our justification by faith, there must be nothing in the world revealed but Christ Jesus, none other doctrine under heaven is able to justify any, but merely the revelation of the Lord Jesus Christ."[50] According to the Assembly of Churches this was a false teaching; Error 40 states, "There is a testimony of the Spirit, and voyce unto the Soule, meerely immediate, without any respect unto, or concurrence with the word."[51] At Hutchinson's trial one of the charges laid against her stated, "That Sanctification cant be an Evidence but as it flowes from Christ and is witnessed to us by the Spirit."[52] Contrary to the Bay Colony elders, the Hutchinsonians believed the only sure evidence of justification was the direct witness of the Holy Spirit. Works or sanctification could be hypocritical and, therefore, false evidence.

A third point of Antinomian doctrine taught by Cotton and the others was that faith was an after effect, a consequence of justification, not a condition or active instrument for receiving grace. The Colony elders believed that the conditions for entrance into the covenant of grace were faith and repentance.[53] The Hutchinsonians disagreed. For them this would mean that the elect's salvation was based on a human work and not free grace. Cotton states, "In this union the soule Receyveth Christ, as an empty vessell receyveth oyle: but this recyving is not active but passive.... Faith in union is also Effectuall, though not as an Efficient Cause to Effect the union,

---

[49]   *Ibid.*, p. 57. And again in answer to Question 15 he states, "Nevertheless a good Conscience will not satisfie [it] selfe in this way [by practical reasoning], till it be established by the Witnesse of the Spirit [it selfe]" (*Ibid.*, p. 58).

[50]   *Ibid.*, p. 161.

[51]   *Ibid.*, pp. 230. Error 47 charges, "The seale of the Spirit is limited onely to the immediate witnesse of the Spirit, and doth never witnesse to any worke of grace, or to any conclusion by a Syllogisme"; Error 71 states, "The immediate revelation of my good estate, without respect to the Scriptures, is as cleare to me, as the voyce of God from Heaven to *Paul*"; and Error 75 maintains, "The Spirit giveth such full and cleare evidence of my good estate, that I have no need to be tried by the fruits of sanctification, this were to light a candle to the Sun" (*Ibid.*, pp. 232, 238, 239).

[52]   *Ibid.*, p. 376.

[53]   See the exchange between Cotton and Bulkeley in *Ibid.*, pp. 34–42, and Confutation 38 in *A Short Story* in *Ibid.*, p. 229.

yet as a Formal cause to constitute the union."[54] Wheelwright agreed with Cotton, proclaiming,

> And so for the knowledge of our justification by faith, nothing is revealed to the soule but only Christ and his righteousnes freely given, it was the very grace of God that appeared, that same apparition whereby the soule cometh to know that he is justified, the object of it is Christ freely given, when the loving kindnes of Christ appeared 3 Titus 5. Not by the works of righteousnes, they are layd aside, and the Lord revealth only to them the righteousnes of himselfe given freely to the soule.[55]

The logical implication of this teaching for the Bay Colony Assembly was that "to be justified by [our] faith is to be justified by workes."[56] The Assembly understood the Hutchinsonians to be saying that

> to affirme there must be faith on mans part to receive the Covenant; is to undermine Christ ... [and] We are compleatly united to Christ, before, or without any faith wrought in us by the Spirit ... [and] There can be no closing with Christ in a promise that hath a qualification or condition expressed.[57]

This was anathema to the elders. At Hutchinson's church trial she was charged with teaching "that union to Christ Jesus is not by Fayth."[58] Cotton, Wheelwright and Hutchinson clearly taught that union with Christ preceeded faith because faith was a grace that could only flow out of that union. The believer's faith was a revealing by the Spirit *of* justification. Faith is the effect not the cause of justification.

The fourth Antinomian teaching of the Hutchinsonians had to do with increated grace as opposed to created grace. William

---

[54] *Ibid.*, pp. 37-38. Again in his *Rejoynder* he states, "In case of Justification when the Spirit doth witness, and apply and seal that unto the Soul, it witnesseth without sight of any work of ours foregoing as any way preparing us thereunto: yea the witness thereof upon the only sight of Christs righteousnes imputed to us (not upon sight or work of any righteousnes of ours) is the cause of our faith, and the good works that follow it, not they of it" (*Ibid.*, p. 87). See also his answer to the third question in the *Boston Conference* in *Ibid.*, pp. 192-198.

[55] Fast Day Sermon in *Ibid.*, p. 161.

[56] *Ibid.*, p. 224.

[57] *Ibid.*, pp. 226, 228, 229. Also Error 68 states, "Faith justifies an unbeleever, that is, that faith that is in Christ, justifieth me that have no faith in my selfe" (*Ibid.*, p. 237).

[58] *Ibid.*, p. 375.

Stoever believes this was the more basic issue in the whole controversy.[59] This was certainly the underlying theological issue but the
prime pastoral concern for Cotton and the Bay elders remained
that of assurance of salvation for the professing community of
faith.[60] Nevertheless Stoever is right to point out the importance of
this theological issue. Is a person's salvation so totally of Christ that
the Spirit in effect overrides human participation? Or as the Bay
elders taught, does God not grace the soul (regeneration) in order
to enable the heart, will and mind of the elect to believe and repent? For the latter, the elect person truly responds to the call of
salvation by exercising his faith. As Stoever states, the Hutchinsonians claimed that "in accomplishing and in revealing regeneration, ... the Spirit operates directly upon the individual's mind and
will; [and] they strongly implied that regeneration does not consist
in gifts of grace empowering the mind to new insight and the will
to new obedience, but in the indwelling in the believer of divine
being itself."[61] John Wheelwright in his Fast Day Sermon states,

> The Gospell is such a doctrine as doth hold forth Jesus Christ and nothing
> but Christ, when such a doctrine is holden forth as doth reveale Jesus
> Christ to be our wisdome, our righteousnes, our sanctification and our
> redemption 1 Corinthians 1.30. When all is taken away from the creature,
> and all given to Christ, so that neither before our conversion nor after, we
> are able to put forth from the Lord Jesus Christ, with whom we are made
> one; and such a doctrine holden forth declares, that we are not able to do
> any worke of sanctification, further then we are acted by the Lord, nor able
> to procure our justification, but it must be the Lord Jesus Christ that must

---

[59]   William K.B. Stoever, 'A Faire and Easie Way to Heaven': Covenant Theology and Antinomianism in Early Massachusetts (Middletowm, CT, 1978), p. 170.

[60]   It should also be noted that many have followed Perry Miller who believes that
New England Antinomianism was a reaction to the growing emphasis on "preparation"
for salvation (The New England Mind: From Colony to Province [Cambridge, 1953], pp. 59-
60; Norman Petitt, The Heart Prepared: Grace and Conversion in Puritan Spiritual Life [1966;
rpt. Middletown, CT, 1989], pp. 125-157; Edmund Morgan, The Puritan Dilemma: The
Story of John Winthrop [Boston & Toronto, 1958], pp. 136-137). There is no doubt, as we
have already observed, that the Antinomians believed that sanctification for the Bay
Colony Elders played too confident a role in assessing one's election; however, their
concern was not to attack preparationism but to encourage what they considered to be
a proper assurance, and to keep salvation centred on free grace and not works. See
Hall, Antinomian, pp. 12ff; Stoever, Faire and Easie, pp. 192-199; and Dewey Wallace,
Puritans and Predestination: Grace in English Protestant Theology, 1525-1695 (Chapel Hill,
1982), p. 114.

[61]   Stoever, Faire and Easie, p. 172.

apply himselfe and his righteousness to us; and we are not able to redeem our selves from the least evill, but he is our redemption, when Christ is thus holden forth to be all in all, all in the roote, all in the branch, all in all, this is the Gospell, this is that fountayne open for the inhabitants of Judah and Jerusalem for sinne and uncleanes.

And later in the sermon he says plainly, "we know (through the mercy of God) assoone [*sic*] as Christ cometh into the soule, he maketh the creature nothing."[62] The Bay Colony Assembly understood this to mean that "in the conversion of a sinner, which is saving and gracious, the faculties of the soule, and workings thereof, in things partaining to God, are destroyed and made to cease.... In stead of them, the Holy Ghost doth come and take place, and doth all the works of those natures, as the faculties of the human nature of Christ do."[63] The charges laid against Hutchinson at her Boston trial stated that she taught, "That thear [*sic*] is no created graces in Belevers after Union. Before Union ther is, but after Union Christ takes them out of us into himselfe....That thear [*sic*] is no created Graces." In answer to the first of these charges she states, "For no Graces beinge in beleevers I desier [*sic*] that to be understood that thay are *not in us but as thay flow from Christ*."[64] The Hutchinsonians had so wanted to magnify the free grace of God in salvation that they left no room for human participation in salvation. All was of Christ or there was no salvation.

In conclusion, the Bay Colony elders believed that the drift and direction of these Hutchinsonian teachings implicitly, if not explicitly, taught the heresy of Antinomianism. The Assembly stated in Error 4, 5, "That those that bee in Christ are not under the Law and commands of the word, as the rule of life. *Alias*, that the will of God in the Word, or directions thereof, are not the rule whereunto Christians are bound to conforme themselves, to live thereafter." Was Cotton not encouraging Antinomianism in his *Rejoynder* when he stated that, "Though a Christians comfort and sense of it will be darkned and shaken by falling into any gross sin; yet the assurance

---

[62] *Ibid.*, pp. 160, 164.
[63] Errors 1 and 2 in *Ibid.*, pp. 219, 220. In addition, Error 15 states, "There is no inherent righteousnes in the Saints, or grace, and graces are not in the soules of beleevers, but in Christ only," and again Error 44, "No created worke can bee a manifest signe of Gods love" (*Ibid.*, pp. 223, 231).
[64] *Ibid.*, pp. 374, 375.

of his justification may be still maintained to him, even when the frame of his Spirit and course is grown much degenerate Isaiah 63.16.17."[65] And was not Wheelwright doing the same when he preached,

> If a beleever had power in him selfe to worke, it killeth the spirit of God's children, put any worke of sanctification in a legall frame and it killeth him, the Law killeth, but it is the spirit that quickens, that is the Gospell in which the spiritt of God is convayed, when God speaketh he speaketh the words of eternall life:... Therefore ought no works of sanctification to be urged upon the servants of God, so as if they had a power to do them, it will kill the soule of a man, and it oppresseth the poore souls of the saynts of God.[66]

For the Bay Colony elders, Antinomianism, with its attendant teachings, was a heresy that had to be removed. Cotton reformed, Hutchinson and Wheelwright were banished. The Colony was saved from the Antinomian heresy.[67] The New England Controversy of the 1630s became a warning and encouragement to the English church of the 1640s when it faced the same heresy. The next sections of this chapter will examine the history and theology of Antinomianism in 1640s England, the second context in which Knollys was accused of it.

Antinomianism in England: Its History

English Antinomianism has its roots in the person of John Eaton.[68] Eaton was accused of "libertinism" by Peter Gunter as early as

---

[65] *Ibid.*, p. 88.

[66] *Ibid.*, p. 162.

[67] Murray believes, and I think rightly, that Hutchinson and her followers went far beyond Cotton and Wheelwright. Cotton only recognized this in 1637. The difference between Cotton and the other New England ministers was not a fundamental one but one of emphasis (Murray, *Antinomianism*, pp. 30-35, 53-68).

[68] Many of his contemporaries considered him the father of the movement. See Thomas Gataker, *God's Eye*, "To the Reader," p. 2; Stephen Geree, *Plain Confutation* (1644), p. 5; Ephraim Pagitt, *Heresiography*, p. 89; and Ernest F. Kevan, *Grace of Law: A Study in Puritan Theology* (1976; rpt. Ligonier, 1993), p. 26. This should be qualified: We know that Antinomianism existed in various forms in England before Eaton. For example, in 1607 Thomas Rogers was dealing with Antinomians in his *The Faith, Doctrine and Religion, Professed and Protected in the Realm of England* (1681 edition), pp. 38-39. But Eaton is undoubtedly the father of the English Antinomianism of the 1640's as will be seen.

1615 while ministering at Wickham Market, Suffolk. Gunter believed that Eaton taught Familism and Anabaptism because Eaton maintained that after justification God no longer saw the sin of the justified. Gunter attacked Eaton in a sermon he preached and published entitled, *A Sermon Preached in the Countie of Suffolk, before the Clergie and Laytie, for the discoverie and confutation of certain strange, pernicious, and Heretical Positions, ... by a certain factious Preacher of Wickam Market....* In 1619 Eaton was deprived of his living because he was "an incorrigible divulger of errors and false opinions."[69]

In 1617, the Grindleton congregation of Roger Brearley was accused of holding that "the Christian assured can never commit gross sin," and that it is sinful to ask forgiveness of God or to believe the Bible "without a motion of the spirit."[70] Another man who held to Antinomian teachings was John Traske. He was alleged to have believed that a converted person was "as free from sin as Jesus Christ."[71] In the 1630s there were some Antinomian rumblings and charges.[72] In 1631 Samuel Pretty was brought before the High Commission charged with Antinomianism, and a year later the case of a certain vicar, John Etsall, was brought before Archbishop Abbot to face the same charge.[73] At the latter's

Eaton was "influenced by the work of John Everard, who translated into English in 1628 the famous, *Theologia Germanica*, a mystical religious work published by Luther" (Leo F. Solt, *Saints in Arms* [Stanford, 1959]), p. 27.

[69] *Calendar of State Papers, Domestic Series, of the Reign of James I. 1619-1623*, ed. Mary Anne Everett Green (London, 1858), Vol. 108, No. 84, April 29, 1619, p. 41.

[70] Christopher Hill, *The World Turned Upside Down* (1975; rpt. Harmondsworth, 1991), pp. 81-85; Christopher Hill, *The Collected Essays of Christopher Hill* (Amherst, 1986), II, 163.

[71] B.R.White, "John Traske (1585-1636) and London Puritanism," *Baptist Quarterly*, 20 (1968), pp. 223-233. John Sedgwick puts John Traske's name first in his list of Antinomians in *Antinomianisme Anatomized* (1643), p. 1. See also R. L. Greaves, "Traske (or Trask), John (1585-1636)," *Biographical Dictionary of British Radicals*, III, 251-252.

[72] See Henry Burton's *The Law and the Gospell Reconciled* (1631), pp. 3-7, 20-22, 68; also Stoever, *Faire and Easie*, pp. 164, 172, 236n.

[73] Pretty was charged with affirming "that a christian or a believer ought not to be sorrowful for his sinnes nor be grieved for anything, noe, though he sinne foulely, ... that a believer is as righteous as the law itselfe," and "that justification and salvation differ not and that this is the doctrine of the Church of England." Pretty at his trial affirmed these beliefs but not the phrase, "Noe, though he sinne and that foulely" (Samuel R. Gardiner, ed., *Reports of Cases in the Courts of Star Chamber and High Commission* [Westminster, 1886], pp. 181-185). John Etsall was charged with holding that "God seeth noe sinne in his children." Etsall's response to this charge was, "It is God's mercy to sinners, that though they are borne in sinne, and cursed by the law, yet through Christ Jesus every beleiver [*sic*], as the whole Church is said to be, is without spott or wrinkle in

trial Thomas Townes[74], Samuel Pretty and John Etsall were accused of holding "the same opinions," and of being followers of
John Eaton's teaching.[75] In 1631 Richard Lane was accused of
Antinomian teachings. The High Commission charged that he and
his wife held that a Christian in this world is as "absolutely perfect
as Christ Jesus himselfe."[76] Again in 1632 the Commission charged
Henry Mudford, Henry Ferman, and Francis Bridges with holding,

> 1. That to the believer all things are pure, and that David when he commit-
> ted adultery pleased God as well as when he danced before the Arke. 2.
> That justifyed persons cannott displease God. 3. That the morall law doth
> not binde the conscience nor accuse the believer. 4. That those that lived
> before Christ, and looked for his comming and did believe it were actuallie
> justifyed. 5. That believers are justifyed before they have faith actuallie.[77]

In 1634 the anti-sectarian Commissioners for Ecclesiastical
Causes stated that "in divers parts of the kingdom" there were,
"sundry sorts of separatists and novalists [sic], and sectaries, as
namely — Brownists, Anabaptists, Arians, Traskites, Familists and
some other sorts;" and in 1636 the Commissioners enumerate that
"at present in London and many other parts, [there are] sundry
sorts of separatists and sectaries, as namely Brownists, Anabaptists,
Arians, Thraskists, Familists, Sensualists, Antinomians and oth-

---

God's sight, and accordinge to the second article of our Church and the booke of common prayer, and the Creed calleth the Church the holie Catholique Church not
inherentlie holy of it selfe, but imputatively holie, and in this sense he beleiveth [sic] this
article to be true and noe otherwise." This was perceived as Antinomianism by the
Puritan Archbishop John Abbot; he comments, "If God seeth not sinne in his children,
then they may take upon them to committ sinne without feare: We know how far this
is gone"(*Ibid.*, pp. 316-321).

   [74]   This is not Robert Towne who wrote, The *Assurance of Grace* (1644) and stated in
it, "I am a sinner and no sinner. Daily I fall in myself and stand in Christ for ever. My
works fail, his never can, and they are also mine," and "to faith there is no sin, nor any
unclean heart" (pp. 40, 71)?

   [75]   Gardiner, *Reports*, p. 317.

   [76]   *Ibid.*, p. 191. In response Lane stated, "The beleiver [sic] is not soe righteous and
perfect in himself, but is soe accepted for perfect by God through Christ Jesus." Lane
was also accused of saying, "[He is] as perfect as Christ and to prove it have brought
this place 1 John 4. 17. and that all beleivers [sic] are soe and therfore [sic] they cannot
sinne" (*Ibid.*, pp. 191-192). See also *Ibid.*, pp. 188-189. Later Lane was "sent to
Bridewell againe for falling into speeches as badd as his former" (*Ibid.*, p. 269).

   [77]   *Ibid.*, pp. 270, 313.

ers."[78] Huehns rightly calculates that "it was during this time [Charles personal rule] that [Antinomianism] first took shape as a definitely recognizable movement."[79] Be that as it may, Antinomianism before the 1640s was localized and "[was] almost all situated in the counties bordering London to the north and south."[80] It wasn't until the 1640s that this teaching became a major concern among the orthodox Puritans. Many historians believe the occasion for Antinomianism lies "in the political, social and spiritual ferment of the times."[81]

By 1643 Antinomianism was a concern to the orthodox. Robert Baillie, one of the Scottish delegates sitting in the Westminster Assembly, stated "the Independent partie growes but the Anabaptists more; and the Antinomians most."[82] On August 10, 1643 the Assembly presented a petition against the Antinomians to the House of Commons. The Antinomian books mentioned included those of Henry Denne, John Eaton and Tobias Crisp.[83] Two months later the Assembly was concerned enough about the heresy that they brought one of the Antinomian party into the Star Chamber for questioning. John Lightfoot, one of the divines of the Assembly, wrote in his *Journal* "[The assembly] went into the star-chamber, where Mr. *Lancaster* was to make his answer, for putting out a book of Dr. *Crisps*, called, 'Christ alone exalted;' another of Mr. *Eaton*,

---

[78]   *Calendar of State Papers, Domestic series, of the Reign of Charles I, 1633-1634*, ed. John Bruce (London, 1863), Vol. 265, No. 6, April 1, 1634, Lambeth, p. 8; Vol. 314, No. 34, Feb. 20, 1635-36, pp. 242-243.

[79]   Huehns, *Antinomianism*, p. 66.

[80]   *Ibid.*, p. 71. Mrs. Hutchinson and John Cotton were from Lincolnshire. Samuel Groton came from Lancashire.

[81]   Kevan, *Grace of Law*, p. 23; W.S. Carruthers, *Everyday Work of the Westminster Assembly* (Philadelphia, 1943), pp. 86-89; and A.S.P. Woodhouse, ed., *Puritanism and Liberty: Being the Army Debates (1647-49) From the Clarke Manuscripts*, revised edition (London, 1992), pp. [11-100]. Richard Baxter stated, "*Antinomianism* rose among us from our obscure Preaching of Evangelical Grace, and insisting too much on tears and terrors" (*An Apology for the Nonconformists Ministry*, [1681], p. 226).

[82]   Robert Baillie, *The Letters and Journals of Robert Baillie*, ed. David Laing (Edinburgh, 1841-42), II, 117. In addition, there were numerous references made against Antinomianism in the sermons to the House of Commons in 1643 (Hill, *Essays*, II, 150).

[83]   John Lightfoot, *The Journal of the Proceedings of the Assembly of Divines* (London, 1824), p. 9. Also the following names were mentioned: Mr. Randall, Mr. Batte, Mr. Lancaster, Mr. Symeon, Mr. Heydon, Mr. Emmerson, Mr. Erbury, Mr. Towne, and Mr. Pen. For a sketch of Henry Denne's life see B. R. White, "Denne, Henry (fl. 1621-1661)," *Biographical Dictionary of British Radicals*, I, 223-224. For Eaton see J. F. H. New, "Eaton, John (c. 1575-1642)," *Biographical Dictionary of British Radicals*, I, 242.

called, 'The Honey Comb;' both replenished with abundance of
erroneous and abominable doctrines."[84] The chief protaganists of
Antinomianism were Tobias Crisp, John Eaton, Paul Hobson,
Henry Denne, William Dell, Robert Towne, Robert Lancaster,
Giles Randall, and John Simpson. These Antinomians are considered "moderate" because they in no way espoused sinful living but
emphasized the free grace of God and the Spirit's work apart from
the Law for both justification and sanctification; this was motivated
by their concern for Christ's glory in the work of salvation. The
chief opponents of Antinomianism were Thomas Gataker, Richard
Baxter, Samuel Rutherford, John Ball, John Sedgwick, Anthony
Burgess, Thomas Taylor and Edward Elton.[85]

In 1642 the first Antinomian pamphlet of the revolutionary period was published by John Eaton entitled, *The Honey-combe of Free
Justification by Christ Alone.*[86] A year later Tobias Crisp's sermons enti-
tled, *Christ Alone Exalted* were made available to the public at the
same time as was Henry Denne's *The Doctrine and Conversation of John
Baptist.* In the following year, Robert Towne's *The Assertion of Grace*
was published. In 1645 four more were printed: John Saltmarsh's
Free grace: or, the Flowing of Christs Blood freely to Sinners; William Dell's
Power from on High: or the Power of the Holy Ghost; Henry Denne's *The
Man of Sinne Discovered*; and the anonymous *The Fountain of Free Grace
Opened by Questions and Answers.* In 1643, the Westminster Assembly
sent a petition with the names of the Antinomian leaders to the
House of Commons, and the first anti-Antinomian work was published by John Sedgwick entitled, *Antinomianisme Anatomized.* In the
following year an anonymous tract entitled, *Declaration against the
Antinomians and their Doctrine of Liberty* was published as well as two of
Stephen Geree's works, *A Plaine Confutation of Diverse dangerous positions
in...Dr Crispe's 14 sermons entitled Christ Alone Exalted* and *The Doctrine
of the Antinomians*, and Thomas Bakewell's *The Antinomians Christ Con-
founded and the Lords Christ Exalted.* That same year Thomas Welde's
A Short Story of the Rise, reigne, and ruine of the Antinomians, and Thomas
Gataker's *God's Eye on Isreal* also appeared. The next year two more

---

84   *Ibid.*, pp. 12-13.
85   Kevan, *Grace of Law*, pp. 25, 28.
86   Solt maintains that Eaton's views were supported by those of Giles Randall, and
that they "grew stronger as the English nation took up arms to resolve the quarrels
between King and Parliament" (*Saints in Arms*, p. 27).

anti-Antinomian works were enlisted in the battle: Ephraim Pagitt's *Heresiography: or, a description of the Heretickes and Sectaries of these latter times*, and Thomas Edwards', *Gangraena*. In the following years several other important works in the controversy were published including: Thomas Bedford, *An Examination of the chief Points of Antinomianism* (1646), Paul Hobson, *Practicall Divinity* (1646), and Samuel Rutherford, *A Survey of the Spirituall Antichrist, Part I and Part II* (1648).

It was primarily in the New Model Army that Antinomianism flourished, particularly under the chaplaincies of John Saltmarsh and William Dell.[87] As Huehns rightly states, "The New Model army [was] a most fertile breeding-ground of political and other ideas."[88] After the Battle of Nasby in 1645 Richard Baxter maintained that, "Independency and Anabaptistry were most prevelent: Antinomianism and Arminianism were equally distributed." And later in his *Reliquiae* he observed that Antinomianism was the "predominent Infection."[89] And again we see how widespread Antinomianism was when "Mr. Martiall informed the House that many Ministers and Gentry, in the several counties have desired to petition the House to prevent the spreading opinions of Antinomianism with that Turbulency, that it touch to a Division among them that join in the Owning of this great Cause."[90] Why did Antinomianism flourish in the Army? Huehns is correct in saying, "The inner assurance it gave of the rightness and righteousness of one's decisions, made it especially welcome to the troopers in their search after 'England's Freedom and Soldiers Rights.' "[91] Huehns concludes,

> The army was saturated with antinomian tendencies, and followed willingly the lead of its chaplains in that direction. Thus antinomianism found the sword at its service in the England of the seventeenth century. It could even with its help reach beyond the strictly military circle. For 'the People admiring the conquering army, were ready to receive whatever they commanded them: and it was the way of the Faction to speake what they spake as the sense of the army'. Every faction did this and antinomianism proved no exception.[92]

---

[87] *Ibid.*, p. 8.
[88] Huehns, *Antinomianism*, p. 78.
[89] Baxter, *Reliquiae*, pp. 50, 111.
[90] *Commons' Journal*, III, 584, Aug. 9, 1646 quoted in Huehns, *Antinomianism*, p. 82.
[91] *Ibid.*, p. 85.
[92] *Ibid.*, p. 88. The internal quote is from Baxter's *Reliquiae*, p. 56.

After 1646 Antinomianism in the army declined and was surpassed by political concerns.[93] It was at this time the Leveller doctrine of political liberty came to the fore in the army and, in fact, was "the effect and the cause of the decline of antinomianism."[94]

Fifty years later in the early 1690s Antinomianism became an issue again.[95] It was a rehashing of the same concerns of the 1640s. A certain Mr. Marshall wrote to Samuel Crisp, the son of Tobias Crisp, suggesting that he republish his father's sermons. Consequently, in 1690 Samuel had published *Christ alone exalted, being the compleat works of Tobias Crisp, D.D.* In addition to the fifty sermons that had been published in the 1640s there were eight more added from Tobias Crisp's manuscripts. In order to authenticate the additional sermons twelve London Ministers signed and placed in the 1690s edition a certificate which stated that the sermons had "been faithfully transcribed from [Crisp's] own notes."[96] In the preface Samuel Crisp attacked Baxter's theology and stirred up a controversy that had its roots in a 1670s Calvinist-Arminian debate among Nonconformists.[97] The Antinomian antagonist, Richard Baxter, responded to this republication, attacking Crisp's doctrine of the imputation of sin to Christ in the Pinner's Hall lecture on January 29th, 1690. In addition, he accused the twelve ministers of "hanging up a sign to show where Jezebel dwelt."[98] The ministers made at least three replys to Baxter. The first came from John Howe in a work entitled, *Some considerations of a certificate* (1690).[99]

---

[93]   Of the seventeen Antinomian tracts in the Thomason catalogue twelve were written before 1647 and none before 1644 (Huehns, *Antinomianism*, p. 107).

[94]   *Ibid.*, p. 109. Both the Antinomian and the Leveller sought personal freedom; the former a religious freedom, and the latter a political freedom. Both also saw a levelling of the classes; the Antinomian before God, and the Leveller in the earthly political realm. See *Ibid.*, pp. 114-115, 121-124.

[95]   The seeds of this renewing of the controversy really began to sprout in 1674 when Baxter was being accused of Arminianism by the orthodox Calvinists both Independents and Presbyterians (Bolam, *The English Presbyterians*, p. 105).

[96]   The twelve were: Presbyterians Vincent Alsop, Richard Bures, John Gammon, John Howe, Thomas Powell, John Turner; Independents Isaac Chauncy, George Cokayn, George Griffith, Increase Mather, Nathaniel Mather; and the Baptist Hanserd Knollys.

[97]   *Ibid.*, p. 107.

[98]   Toon, *Hyper-Calvinism*, p. 50. Shortly after his lecture Baxter published *The Scripture Gospel defended ... against libertines.*

[99]   In this work he "disavowed any share in the elder Crisp's distinctive notions in the most handsome and forthright terms, but added that it might be right to suppose that the elder Crisp, good saintly man, could not really have meant anything so wicked

The second came from seven of the twelve in an explanatory letter attached to John Flavell's book, *Planelogia; a succinct and seasonable discourse* (1691). In this latter document "the ministers explained that they had signed only to vouch for the integrity of Samuel Crisp as a copyist."[100] The third came from Samuel Crisp in his *Christ made sin* (1691) showing that his father's doctrine of imputation was Biblical and orthodox.[101] By 1694 this Antinomian controversy caused the break up of the "Happy Union" between the Presbyterians and Congregationalists which had been established in 1691.[102] In 1713, Robert Nelson assessed the influence of Crisp's book and stated that, "by means of Crisp's book the poison of antinomianism soon spread, not only in the country but infected London too."[103] The orthodox in the 1690s, as in the 1640s, were still concerned that this teaching would cut "the sinews of all the duties and exercises of Christianity."[104]

Antinomianism in England: Its Theology

The chief literary protagonists of moderate Antinomianism in the early 1640s were Tobias Crisp and John Eaton.[105] As the decade

---

as his words could be taken to mean" (Bolam, *The English Presbyterians*, p. 108).

[100] They also stated, "The difference between him and other good men seems to lie not so much in the things which the one or the other of them believe as about their order and reference to one another" (quoted in Peter Toon, *Puritans and Calvinism*, [Swengal, PA, 1973], p. 89). In this book Flavel was quite critical of Crisp; in its second appendix entiled, *A Synopsis of Ancient and Modern Antinomian Errors*, he condemned ten errors, of which all to some degree were to be found in Crisp's sermons (*Ibid.*).

[101] Toon, *Hyper-Calvinism*, p. 50.

[102] Bolam, *et al*, rightly see Baxter's rationalism as an important factor in the later departure of Presbyterianism from orthodoxy (*The English Presbyterians*, pp. 108-112). As J. I. Packer has somewhere said, Baxter was a great pastor but a poor theologian.

[103] Robert Nelson, *The Life of Dr George Bull, Late Lord Bishop of St Davids* (1713), p. 260, quoted in Hill, *Essays*, II, 155.

[104] Anonymous, *Crispianism Unmask'd* (1693), 54, 61.

[105] By "moderate" is meant those Antinomians who were by no means practical Antinomians. John Sedgwick in his *Antinomians Anatomized* spoke of doctrinal and practical Antinomianism (p. 30). Men like Crisp, Denne, Eaton, Hobson were moderate or doctrinal Antinomians; their writings clearly indicate they abhorred the concept of a true Christian willingly living in sin. Moreover, their opponents also knew and stated that these "moderate" Antinomians were men who lived godly lives. One could designate the Ranters of the latter 1640s practical Antinomians but certainly not the men that were the primary concern of the orthodox in the early 1640s. Their concern was that doctrinal Antinomianism would lead people into practical Antinomianism.

progressed others of considerable importance such as Henry
Denne, Robert Towne, William Dell, John Saltmarsh and Paul
Hobson carried the torch. It is from the writings of these men, and
those who wrote against them, that we can assertain the meaning
of Antinomianism in 1640s England.

Dewey Wallace is certainly correct in saying that the issue of Antinomianism in England was primarily concerned with assurance
of salvation, as it was in New England.[106] But it is also clear that for
the Antinomians it was an issue of giving Christ his proper due in
the work of salvation. For them salvation was all of Christ and to
credit humans with any part in their salvation was to take away
from Christ. For example, John Eaton's concern in his *Honey-Combe*
was to separate grace from all legalism in justification. For him
sanctification could show a person's justification to the world but to
rely on sanctification for assurance of justification was to confuse
law and grace.[107] He did not want the legalism of conditions and
qualifications to be mixed with the free grace of God in the gospel.[108] For Eaton, assurance for the believer comes from believing
that the imputed righteousness of Christ had replaced sin, apart
from works. The law's purpose before salvation is to move the sinner to see his need of Christ, and after conversion it is not needed
because the believer serves Christ spontaneously and thankfully.[109]
Eaton also believed that Christ was made a sinner on the cross and
suffered the curse of God against sinners and not just the punishment due the elect for their sins.[110] Furthermore, Eaton taught that
Christ so covered the believer with his righteousness that God sees
no sin in him/her, even in his/her imperfect sanctification.[111] This
left him open to the charge of Antinomianism. In addition, Eaton
also embraced the notion that the believer had an inner knowledge

---

[106] Wallace, *Puritans and Predestination*, p. 135. This was certainly a concern for
Thomas Gataker, *Mistake or Misconstruction removed* (1646), pp. 37-38.

[107] John Eaton, *The Honey-Combe of Free Justification by Christ Alone* (1642), pp. 150-
151,185-188, 212, 235, 241-249, 286-287, 307-312.

[108] *Ibid.*, pp. 85-86.

[109] *Ibid.*, pp. 121-123, 142, 145. See also Wallace, *Puritans and Predestination*, pp. 115-
116.

[110] *Honey-Combe*, pp. 38, 68, 362, 365. He wrote, "That as Christ by Gods imputation was made, not an imaginary sinner, but really a true sinner for us, and so truly and
really suffered the curse of God, and true rending and tearing upon the Crosse, even
unto true and reall death for true sinne that God saw truly upon him" (p. 362).

[111] *Ibid.*, pp. 47-48, 137-138, 257, 321, 343, 371-373.

of his justification which "opens unto us the very closets of heaven."[112] Moreover, he used incautious language concerning the believer's union with Christ.[113] Yet this is but one man's Antinomianism. In the next pages we will note eight tenets of the English moderate Antinomians, taken from their writings and those of their antagonists.

The first Antinomian tenet was that sanctification is no evidence of justification. Ephraim Pagitt believed the Antinomians taught "that it is a foul damning errour to make Sanctification an evidence of Justification, contrary to *Romans*. 8.1. *John*. 3.10."[114] Thomas Edwards understood the Antininomians to be saying that "sanctification is not an evidence of Justification, and all notes and signes of a Christians estate [were] legall and unlawfull."[115] The Antinomian Tobias Crisp preached a sermon entitled, "Inherent Qualifications are doubtfull Evidences for Heaven," and in it he states in conclusion, "Let me tell you, who ever you are, that goe by signes and marks drawne from sanctification, you shall be puzzled, if you deal faithfully with your own spirits, though you attain to never so great a height of sanctification"; and in a sermon on "The Revealing Evidence of the Spirit of Christ", he denies that the believer "walks by such a rule [of the law] for his peace ..." because "the best sanctification, in regard of the imperfections of it, is not able to speake peace to the soul, because it pronounces directly a curse."[116] Henry Denne counselled the sick man, "Works indeed are an evidence of faith among men ... But faith is an evidence of our works in the Court of Conscience, and judgement of certainty."[117] The believer should not interpret the evidence of good

---

[112]   *Ibid.*, p. 406.

[113]   *Ibid.*, pp. 430-435. Citing Zanchius approvingly Eaton writes, "The Union of us with Christ, and of Christ with us, is essentiall, and substantiall, true and reall. First substantiall (saith he) because the substances themselves of the flesh of Christ, and of our flesh, both of the person of Christ, and of our persons, are united together; and so not the fruit and graces only of Christ are received, seeing they cannot bee received, but by partaking to the substance it selfe of Christ. Secondly, I call it true and reall, (saith hee) because we are not in bare imagination, but *reipsa* in very deed, united into Christ; and being united, (although *non Physico, sed spirituali & supernaturali modo*, not by a naturall, but a spirituall and supernaturall manner,) wee grow more and more into one body with Christ" (*Ibid.*, pp. 430-431).

[114]   Pagitt, *Heresiography*, p. 109.

[115]   Edwards, *Gangraena*, 3rd ed. (1646), I, pt. 1, p. 20.

[116]   Tobias Crisp, *Christ alone exalted* (1643), II, 428, 463.

[117]   Henry Denne, *A Conference Between a Sick Man, and a Minister* (1643), pp. 8-14.

works in his life because he can so easily be self-deceived.[118] According to Paul Gritz, the Calvinistic Baptist, Samuel Richardson, "considered that seeking comfort in one's personal sanctification or inward feelings was completely misguided and futile. Relief from doubts about one's election came only through God's Word and the work of his Spirit."[119]

A second Antinomian tenet stated that the believer obtains assurance through the witness of the Spirit. Paul Gritz writes that "assurance of salvation in Richardson's view ultimately resulted from the Holy Spirit's enabling the person to apprehend God's love in Christ by revealing and applying it to his heart."[120] Henry Pinnell concurs,

> But (in the second *Adam*) God doth betroth his people to himself, in Mercy, Righteousnesse, and Truth,whereby they shall *KNOW* the Lord: their Espousals are for ever, and such as whereby they have a true spiritual knowledge of God. The Lord doth unite his people to himself in Christ, by a New Covenant, the Covenant of Grace; such a Matrimoniall engagement that cannot admit of a divorce; such sweet enjoyments have they from Him, such Conjugall and Spiritual Communion with Him, that they increase and multiply in their Joyes, Peace, Comfort, rest, &c.[121]

Crisp agrees: "The revealing evidence of interest in the priviledges of Christ, which will put an end to all objections, is the voyce of the Spirit of God to a mans own spirit: This is the great evidence indeed, and the evidence which at last doth determine the ques-

---

[118]   Kevan, *Grace of Law*, p. 211.

[119]   Gritz, "Richardson," p. 284. Gritz is basing this on Richardson's treatise entitled, *Divine Consolations or the Teachings of God in Three Parts* (1649), 2:237, 244, 250. Another Antinomian John Saltmarsh in his *Free grace*, says, "And for establishing souls upon any works of their own, as a way, means, or ground of assurance, as that upon such a measure of repentance or obedience, they may beleeve [*sic*] by, I dare not deal in any such way of our own *righteousnesse*, because I finde no *infallible mark* in any thing of our own *sanctification*, save in a lower way of perswasion, or motive" (*Free Grace: or, the Flowings of Christs Blood freely to Sinners* [1645], p. 31. See also pp. 32, 34, 54-55, 62, 85, 128; and John Eaton, *The Discovery of the most dangerous Dead Faith and Abrahams Steps of Faith* [1642], pp. 6-14).

[120]   Gritz, "Richardson," p. 283. Gritz is basing this on Richardson's treatise entitled, *Divine Consolations* (1649), 1:5; 2:236.

[121]   Henry Pinnell, *A word of Prophesy concerning the Parliament, Generall and the Army* (1648), p. 35. For Pinnell's life see M. B. Endy, "Pinnell (or Pinnel), b.c. 1613)," *Biographical Dictionary of British Radicals*, III, 44-45.

tion."[122] Saltmarsh, implying the Spirit's work, states, "That *faith* in the *beleever* doth nothing, no not *instrumentally* as to *justification*, but as by way of *revelation* and *manifestation* of that *justification*."[123] In *Free Grace*, he encouraged the troubled person to believe in "Christ in the Word and Promise."[124] And again, in the same work he writes, "This is the *Scripture-assurance* for a *childe of God* or *beleever*, to see every thing in *himselfe as* nothing, *and* himselfe *everything in* Christ.... All other *assurances* are rotten conclusions for the *Word*; and such things as true *legal Teachers* have invented not understanding the mystery of *the Kingdom of Christ*."[125]

A third tenet the English Antinomians taught was that faith follows justification. Henry Denne stated that Christ's righteousness is made ours by God's imputation "before the act of our Faith, and therefore necessarily without it."[126] Faith was not a condition of justification as the orthodox taught but a consequence of it. He maintained that "the act of our faith is a consequent of our justification, and not an intercedent is plain ... we must be ingrafted into Christ Jesus before we can believe. Therefore, we must be justified before we can believe."[127] This tenet assumes the Calvinistic concept of union with Christ. Denne said, "We must be ingrafted into Christ Jesus before we can believe."[128] Saltmarsh concurs:

> [The elect] look not on *justification* as flowing from *Christ* acted upon by the *faith* of a beleever first, and so a consequent of *beleeving* or of *faith*, but an *antecedent* or going before *faith*; they hold Jesus Christ to be *righteousness* and *justification* to a *sinner*, and that all are *justified* before they beleeve or *repent*;

---

[122] Crisp, *Christ alone exalted* (1643), II, 465.

[123] John Saltmarsh, *Sparkles of Glory, or, Some Beams of the Morning Star* (1647), pp. 191-192.

[124] Saltmarsh, *Free Grace*, p. 32.

[125] *Ibid.*, pp. 85. And again, "*A Soul is then properly, actually, or expressly in* Covenant *with* God, *when* God *hath come to it in the* promise, *and then when it feels it self under the power of the* promise, *it begins onely to know it is in* Covenant" (*Ibid.*, p. 129).

[126] Henry Denne, *The Doctrine and Conversation of John Baptist* (1644), p. 25.

[127] Denne, *Conference*, pp. 14-15. And again he states, "Remission of sins is even as ancient as satisfaction *for sin* & at what time Christ Iesus taketh our sins upon himself, at the same time are the persons of God's elect just before the Tribunall of Almighty God" (*Ibid.*, p.14). See also Crisp, *Christ alone exalted* (1643), pp. 43, 58, 60, and Denne, *John Baptist*, p. 25.

[128] Denne, *Conference*, p. 15. See also Samuel Richardson, *Saints Desire; or a Cordiall for a Fainting Soule* (1647), p. 12, and Gritz, "Richardson," pp. 276-277.

and faith, repentence, are fruits of *righteousness* or *justification*, Christ being given to open the *eyes of the blind, and to bring the prisoners out of prison, &c.*[129]

A fourth Antinomian tenet, contrary to the Orthodox Puritan teaching, taught that the sinner could not prepare for salvation by obedience and good works. For the Antinomian these things were not causes of salvation. There were no conditions to be fullfilled by the sinner to enter into the Covenant of Grace because only Christ and free grace could fulfill these conditions. Commenting on this, Richardson states that "faith is a fruit of the Covenant ... but not a condition on our part to perform."[130] If one preaches covenant conditions, such preaching "ingendereth unto bondage, it leaves the conscience in feare, it robs it of peace, joy and consolation."[131] John Saltmarsh makes the same point when he says, "We *beleeve, repent, love, and obey...* not that we may be *saved,* but because we are *saved.*"[132] Again, he says, "If you suppose that God takes in any part of your *faith, repentance* or new obedience, or *sanctification* as a ground upon which he *justifies* or *forgives* you, you are clear against the *Word.*"[133] Again, he says, "God takes us into *Covenant,* not upon any *condition* in us before; he brings with him *Christ,* and in him all the *conditions,* and *makes* us as he would *have* us."[134] John Eaton stated,

> When there is any morall work commanded to be done upon paine of pun-
> ishment, or upon promise of any reward either temporall or eternall; there
> is to be understood the voyce of the Law. Contrarywise, where the promise
> of life, favour, salvation, or any other blessings and benefits are offered
> unto us freely, without all our deservings, and simply without any condition
> annexed to them of any Law, either naturall, ceremoniall, or morall, all

---

[129]   Saltmarsh, *Sparkles of Glory*, pp. 190-191.

[130]   Samuel Richardson, *Justification by Christ Alone, a Fountain of Life and Comfort, Declaring that the Whole Worke of Mans Salvation Was Acomplished by Jesus Christ upon the Crosse, in that He Took Away & Healed All His, from All Sinnes, And Presented Them to God Holy without Fault in His Sight* (1647), p. 46.

[131]   Samuel Richardson, *Divine Consolations*, 3:95, quoted in Gritz, "Richardson," p. 283.

[132]   Saltmarsh, *Sparkles of Glory*, p. 192.

[133]   Saltmarsh, *Free Grace*, pp. 82-83.

[134]   *Ibid.*, p. 127, see also p. 129. Henry Denne states, "Some *Protestants* ... do say that Christ is made ours ... by Faith alone: Christ being the garment, our faith the hand that putteth this garment on; yet me thinks that there is Christ set forth, upon some conditions, and not freely given: I must here profess my ignorance, that I cannot con-ceive, how faith should put on Christ, apply Christ, or make Christ ours *in the sight of God*" (*John Baptist*, p. 25).

those places, whether they be read in the old Testament, or in the new, are to be referred to the voice and doctrine of the Gospel.[135]

A fifth tenet of the Antinomians was that God doesn't see any sin in any of his justified children. For example, John Eaton stated, "All our works ... are made perfectly holy."[136] How? By the perfection of justification, which "presents all their works and holy walking, *to bee perfectly holy and righteous in the sight of God freely*, and by this meanes are made continually acceptable and pleasing in the sight of God,"[137] even, for example, when Abraham lied.[138] Tobias Crisp states,

> Let me speake freely to you, and in so doing, tell you that the Lord hath no more to lay to the charge of an elect person, yet in the heighth of iniquity, and in the excess of riot, and committing all abominations that can be committed, I say, even then, when an elect person runs such a course the Lord hath no more to lay to that persons charge than God hath to lay to the charge of a beleever, nay God hath no more to lay to the charge of such a person, then he hath to lay to the charge of a Saint triumphant in glory.[139]

Robert Towne maintains that to be made a new creature was to be "made personally, perfectly, and everlastingly righteous."[140] Samuel Rutherford interpreted Towne's teaching to mean that "a justified person cannot sinne, ... because Faith maketh him worthy; and if so, the way of Grace is a wanton merry way; the justified are freed from the Law, and from any danger of sinning."[141] He also

---

[135] Eaton, *Honey-Combe*, pp. 85, 86.

[136] Eaton, *Honey-Combe*, p. 321, see also *Ibid.*, pp. 76-78. See also *Ibid.*, pp. 106-109, where he teaches that we are under the third dispensation, the time of the Gospel. Consequently, when Jesus said, "It is finished," sin, guilt and punishment "by the full exhibiting of the wedding-garment, by this infinite meanes of his owne death upon the crosse, are so utterly and infinitely abolished, and such an everlasting righteousnesse is so fully brought in upon Gods children" (p. 106).

[137] *Ibid.*, pp. 322-323; see also p. 41.

[138] *Ibid.*, pp. 79-80.

[139] Crisp, *Christ alone exalted* (1643), II, 272. And again he states that the transference of sin to Christ means that, "Thou ceasest to be a Transgressor from that time they were laid upon Christ, to the last hour of thy life.... Mark it well, Christ himselfe is not so compleatly righteous, but we are as righteous as He was" (*Ibid.*, I, 89).

[140] Robert Towne, *The Assertion of Grace, or a defence of the doctrine of free Justification* (1644), p. 9.

[141] Samuel Rutherford, *The Tryal and Triumph of Faith* (1645), pp. 24-25.

states "*Antinomians* have not to this day explained in their writings, whether the justified can sin or no; but in practise they say they may, lye, whore, sweare, cousen; *God* seeth no such sinnes in them."[142] Samuel Richardson incautiously wrote, "The state of the believer in Christ, as considered in him, is an estate of perfection."[143]

Fast on the heels of this last tenet is a sixth Antinomian tenet that Christians can live in sin. None of the moderate Antinomians held this. Some of the radicals, however, did.[144] Nevertheless, some of the language of the moderates was incautious. Pagitt noted that the modern Antinomians teach "that if a man know himselfe to be in the state of grace, though he be drunke or commit murther, God sees no sin in him."[145] Again, he believed Eaton to teach "since *Christ* groaned out his bloud and life upon the Crosse, by which sin it selfe, and guilt, and punishment are so utterly and infinitely abolished, that there is no sin in the *Church* of God, and that now God sees no sin in us: and whosoever beleeveth not this poynt is undoubtedly damed."[146] Tobias Crisp states,

> As soon as ever [the believer] hath committed this sinne of his, he hath *the Lamb of God* in his eye, *that takes away the sinnes of the world*, that hath already taken away this very sinne, that at this very instant he now committed.... If therefore all be done by Christ, that is to be done, to make *perfect the*

<hr/>

[142] Rutherford, *Survey of the Spiritual Antichrist*, I, 3. The moderate Antinomian Saltmarsh states, "They suppose they cannot *sin* as they do, and not be *accountable*; and they cannot but be *sinners* in *Gods* sight as well as their own" (*Free grace*, p. 174. See also Eaton, *Honey-Combe*, pp. 7, 30, 32, 41, 47, 76-78, 79, 138, 142, 293, 321-323, 325, 343, 371). William Dell taught that, "By being crucified with Christ, *we are freed of sin*. For one of the chief ends of the indwelling of the Word & Spirit in Believers, is to free them, and save them from *sin*: and though *sin* hath its ful power in our own *humane* life, yet it hath no power over *Christs* life in us, which we live through Faith. Wherefore saith *Paul*, Rom. 6.6.... And in *verse* 12. saith he, *Let not sin therefore reign ... in your mortal or dead body*; which he cals *dead*, not in reference to the *common mortality* of the world, but in reference to our *crucifying with* Christ; and in the body that is crucified with Christ, *sin is not to reign*. And so you see, that through our *crucifying* with Christ, we are *dead* to *sin* also.... For it is impossible that *Christ* and *sin* should live together in *strength*, in the same flesh; but if *sin* live in our *flesh*, it will crucifie us to *Christ*; and if *Christ* live in our *flesh*, he will crucifie us to *sin*" (*The Crucified and quicknd Christian*, pp. 316-318, 327-389, quoted in Humphrey Chambers, *Animadversions on Mr. William Dells Book intituled The Crucified and Quickned Christian* [1652], p. 29).
[143] Richardson, *Newes from Heaven*, p. 13.
[144] See Hill, *Essays*, II, 170-1.
[145] Pagitt, *Heresiography*, pp. 105-106.
[146] *Ibid.*, p. 105.

commers unto him, and *to save them to the uttermost;* then all the sinnes that beleevers commit, that beleevers shall hereafter commit; nay, all the sins that all the beleevers to the end of the world commit, they are all already laid upon Christ, he hath nailed them all to the crosse.[147]

Eaton wrote, "Let the godly learn therefore, that the Law and Christ are two contrary things, ... when Christ is present, the Law may in no case rule, but must depart out of the conscience."[148] This is the most blatant reason the moderates were charged with Antinomianism. Robert Towne responds to Thomas Taylor, *"You say, Christ was the end of Morall Law, because he obeyed the Law &c.* And what Christ performed for us we are freed from, now you are with us, that is, Christ hath freed us from subjection to the Morall Law."[149] Saltmarsh states, "They interpret every *curse* in the *Law* and *new Testament* for *sin*, their own, if it be against their sin."[150] Towne proclaims, "Thus I am a sinner, and no sinner; Daily I fall in myself, and stand in Christ forever."[151]

A seventh tenet the Antinomians were charged with teaching was that Christ was as sinful as we are. This tenet was espoused more by Tobias Crisp than by any other individual. In order to magnify the work of Christ and the grace of God in the believer's salvation, Crisp emphasized that "God doth really pass over sin upon [Christ] ... so that ... in respect of transgression, in respect of conveyance, in respect of passing accounts from one head to another, in respect of that, there is reality of making of Christ to be sin."[152] When Christ took death upon himself he took away the actual sins of the be-

---

[147] Crisp, *Christ alone exalted* (1643), I, 146-147.

[148] Eaton, *Honey-Combe* (1642), p. 449, quoted in Kevan, *Grace of Law*, p. 147.

[149] Towne, *Assertion of Grace*, p. 140.

[150] Saltmarsh, *Free Grace*, p. 174.

[151] Towne, *Assertion of Grace*, p. 40. See Crisp's disclaimer that he teaches that the believer can live in sin in Hill, *Essays*, II, 148.

[152] Crisp, *Christ alone exalted* (1643), I, 283. He goes on to say, "When one man becomes a Debtor in another Man's room, legally and by consent, this Surety that doth become the Debtor, he is not barely supposed to be the Debtor, but by undertaking of it, and legally having it past upon him, he is as really and truly the Debtor, as he was that was the principal before, I say, as really and truly the Debtor: So that there is an absolute truth and reality of God's Act in passing over sins upon Christ, and laying sins upon Christ.... As I said before, there must of necessity be a present desert upon a Person, before the Judge can inflict any thing upon such a Person. A fault must be found upon a Man, before he may be executed legally and justly: Therefore the fault must be found really upon Christ himself, before there can be an act of God's justice in wounding Christ" (*Ibid.*).

liever. In stating this, his language was incautious and he opened himself to misinterpretation. For example, in one place he proclaimed, "Mark it well, we are not so compleatly righteous, but we are as righteous as he was; nor wee so compleatly sinfull, but Christ became, being made sin, as compleatly sinful as we ... that very sinfulnes that we were, Christ is made that very sinfulnes before God."[153] Similarly, in another place he writes:

> Indeed, let us not make God so childish: if he laid iniquity on Christ, he past this real act upon him, and the thing is thus really, as he diposes of it; and therefore, in brief, this laying iniquity upon him, is such a translation of sin from those whose iniquity he lays upon him, that by it he now becomes, or did become, when they were laid, as really and truly the person that had all these sins, as those who did commit them really and truly had them themselves: it is true, as I said before, Christ never sinned in all his life; "He did no violence, neither was any deceit in his mouth"; but this hinders not, but that there may be on him an absolute transaction; so that by laying iniquity on him, he becomes the sole person in the behalf of all the elect, that truly hath iniquity upon him.[154]

Finally the English Antinomians taught that there ought to be no preaching of the terrors of the Law and Hell. For most this meant there was no use for the Law of God after conversion.[155] John Sedgwick quotes the Antinomians as saying, *"Away with Moses, Out of doors with Moses, we beleevers can no longer abide his voice; the Law is no fit Doctrine to be taught or heard, to be beleeved or obeyed."*[156] He also quotes the accusation of the Antinomians against the orthodox saying,

> I must tell you that your Ministers are a company of Scribes and Pharisees, even such who with a shew of Phylosophie and vain Learning, do set up *Moses* and cry down Christ; advance Dutie, and cast down Free Grace; nay they make it their work by Preaching the Law to terrifie peoples consciences, that thereby they may suck no finall advantage to themselves.[157]

---

[153] *Ibid.*, I, 89, 146-7.
[154] *Ibid.*, I, 283.
[155] For some it meant no use before conversion as well as after (Kevan, *Grace of Law*, pp. 85,87).
[156] John Sedgwick, *Antinomianisme Anatomized. Or, A Glasse for the Lawless: Who deny the Ruling use of the Morall Law unto Christians under the Gospel* (1643), p. 4.
[157] *Ibid.*, p. 2.

Pagitt believed that Antinominians taught that "the Moral Law is of no use at all to a Beleever, nor a rule for him to walke in, nor to examine his life by, and that Christians are free from the mandatory power of it: whence one of them cryed out in the *Pulpit, Away with the Law which cuts off a mans legs, and then bids him walke.*"[158] The Antinomian William Dell agrees:

> We are *freed from the Law*.... For as the *humanity* of Christ being crucified by the *Word* and *Spirit*, by this means became *dead to the Law*, and the Law lost all its power over him; ... so all the faithful that are thus *crucified* with him, are through this *crucifying* set free from the Law; for their own life being extinguished by the *living Word* and *Spirit*, and they living in *that* word and spirit, a life not their *own*, but *Christs*, are as truly freed from the *Law* as Christ himself was.... And this *Paul* doth plainly teach us, *Rom.* 7.1. saying, *that the Law hath Lordship over a man all the time he lives*, and no longer. But when he is once *crucified* with Christ, and *dead* with Christ, the *Law* hath no more *Dominion* over him. So then as long as we live our *own life*, the *Law* hath *power* over us; but when we are *dead* to our selves through the *Life* of Christ, we are set quite without the reach of the Law, and the *Law* hath no more to do with us the *Members*, then with Christ the *Head*.[159]

John Eaton concurs, saying, "Christ living in me, I am [now] dead to the Law, that is He abolisheth the law to me."[160] In addition, Eaton saw no use of chastening for believers by the law:

> This Doctrine, that God sees sinne in his justified children, to whip, correct, and punish them for the same, is the very instrument and Engine that confounds the New Testament (in respect of the legall government of the morall Law) with the old, that is finished, *Heb. 8,9,13.* by bringing back ... the full-grown Heire, to be again ... the Heire in his non-age: it brings back again the full growne Heire to bee whipped againe under the School-master.[161]

---

[158] Pagitt, *Heresiography*, p. 105. The Antinomian Robert Towne somewhat confirms these accusations of the orthodox, when he writes, "To faith, or in the state or things of faith, there is no obligation, nor use of the law" (*A Re-Assertion of Grace* [1654], p. 118). As does also John Saltmarsh when he says, "The Gospel is ... a perfect *law* of life and righteousnesse ... and therefore I wonder at any that should contend for the *ministery* of the *Law* or *Ten Commandments* under *Moses*" (*Free Grace*, p. 146).

[159] Dell, *The Crucified and quicknd Christian*, quoted in Humphrey Chambers, *Animadversions*, p. 29.

[160] Eaton, *Honey-Combe*, p. 443.

[161] *Ibid.*, pp. 143-144, Eaton again states, "Not feeling how powerful the treasures of the Gospel alone are, both to abolish all sin from before God, and by joy and zeale thereof to mortifie all sin in our selves, they goe to borrow helpe by feare from the

Summary of Antinomian Tenets

The Antinomian tenets of New England in the 1630s included the following: sanctification was no evidence of justification; the primary evidence of justification is the direct testimony of the Spirit; faith is a consequence of justification; and grace is increated. The chief tenets held in England in the 1640s were: sanctification is no evidence of justification; assurance is through the witness of the Spirit; faith follows justification; the sinner could not prepare for salvation by obedience and good works; God does not see any sin in his justified children; Christians can live in sin; Christ was as sinful as we are; and there is no use for the law before or after conversion. When we bring the Antinomian tenets of England and New England together we come up with a synthesis of seven. They are:

1. A prime evidence of justification is the testimony of the Holy Spirit and not sanctification.
2. Faith is not a condition of justification but a consequence.
3. The sinner cannot prepare for salvation by good works, etc.. No conditions prepare the way.
4. Increated grace — Christ does not simply renew the created human faculties in conversion but he overrides them so that all is of Christ.
5. God does not see any sin in his justified children.
6. Christians can live in sin.
7. The law of God is not necessary in leading to conversion, nor for living after conversion.[162]

---

whippings of the Law; as if the Gospel that kils the old man, and makes us alive, and raiseth us up from spiritual death to life, were not able to encrease that life begun, and sufficient to bury the old man utterly, except it borrowed helpe of the whippings of the Law" (*Ibid.*, pp. 136-137). For more on the Antinomian views of the uselessness of the law prior to conversion see Kevan, *Grace of Law*, pp. 89-90. Not all Antinomians held this, e.g., Crisp and Eaton, *Ibid.*, pp. 85, 87.

[162] In this summary we do not include Tobias Crisp's unique teaching that Christ was as sinful as we are. He was the only one to espouse this teaching in the 1640s, and nowhere does Knollys teach this.

Hanserd Knollys and Antinomianism

In the final section of this chapter we will examine Knollys' writings against the seven summary tenets we have gleaned from our study of New England and England Antinomianism of the 1630s and 1640s.

The first point of Antinomianism was directly concerned with assurance. As both Antinomians and orthodox were concerned with assurance so was Knollys. Knollys firmly believed that a sinner could not be saved unless the Holy Spirit had effectually worked in his/her heart. For him it is the Holy Spirit and the Word that convince the sinner of sin, righteousness and judgement, that enlighten his understanding to see and know that there is a Saviour Jesus Christ who came to save sinners and that whosoever shall believe in Him shall be saved, and that convert the sinner and change him into the image of Jesus Christ. In the *Parable of the Kingdom of God Expounded* he writes,

> True Grace is the incorruptible seed of the New Birth, I *Pet.* 1. 23. and of the Kingdom of God in the hearts of Believers, *Mat.* 13. 31, 32. which Kingdom of God within us, *Luke* 17. 21 is not in Word only, but in power and in the holy Spirit, I *Cor.* 4. 20. & I *Thes.* 1. 4, 5.... The Gospel must come to professors not in word only, but also in power and in the holy Spirit, ... before they can come to Christ or attain to the power of Godliness.[163]

Moreover, according to his own conversion experience Knollys maintained that sinners are unable to believe until "the day of Gods exceeding great power come[s] upon [him] and set[s] home a promise of free grace by his Spirit, with divine light and mighty

---

[163] *Christ Exalted*, pp. 17-21; *Parable*, pp. 29, 50. See also *World*, pt. 1, p. 33; 1644/46 *Confession*, XXII; and 1677/89 *Confession* on "Assurance of Grace and Salvation," XVIII, 2-4. It states that, "This certainty [that they are in a state of grace] is ... grounded upon ... an infallible assurance of faith, founded ... upon the inward evidence of those graces of the Spirit unto which promises are made, and on the testimony of the Spirit of adoption, witnessing with our Spirits that we are the children of God" (XVIII, 2). In the next paragraph, however, the *Confession* goes on to say, "This infallible assurance doth not so belong to the essence of faith, but that a true Believer, may wait long and conflict with many difficulties before he be partaker of it (XVIII, 3). Though paragraph two leans in an Antinomian direction, paragraph three places it in an orthodox context. All quotes from the 1677/89 *Confession* are taken from William L. Lumpkin, *Baptist Confessions of Faith* (Philadelphia, 1959), pp. 235-295.

power upon [his] heart."[164] Concerning his conversion experience Knollys testified that in the early 1630s the New England Antinomian John Wheelwright counselled him on the covenant of free grace. Sometime afterwards he heard a message by Mr. How who taught that "Christ was the author, root, and only foundation of saving faith, and that God did give the faith of evidence, Heb. xi. 1, in some new covenant promise, Gal. iii. 14; and that those promises were given of God, 2 Pet. i 4." According to Knollys he prayed that night and the next day that God would give him such a promise. The following day, while locked in the church and praying, he was given the promise from the Lord, "I will never leave thee, nor forsake thee." God gave him two more promises from Isaiah 43:22-25 and 54:9-10, assuring him of the forgiveness of his sins, and of his place in the covenant of peace. He records that he experienced "joy and peace in believing."[165] It is evident that Knollys did hold this Antinomian tenet with Cotton and Wheelwright. He, however, did not espouse the Spirit's witness apart from the promise or Word as did Mrs. Hutchinson and other antinomians.

Even though Knollys did agree in part with the antinomians on the witness of the Holy Spirit, he did not believe it was the *only* evidence of assurance for the believer. Contrary to the teaching of the Antinomians, Knollys believed that assurance *was* based on one's sanctification. In 1646 he states,

> Therefore make sure that Christ is yours. Some would ask this question, How shall I so examine, that I may know assuredly that I have Christ? I answer, you must bring your hearts to the touchstone of the Word of God, and cast them into the balance of the Sanctuary and weigh them there. And to this purpose, I shall propound one Scripture of truth for your examination and tryall, to wit, 2 Cor. 5.17.... To wit; first he is made a new man.... Secondly, he hath a new heart [new will, affections, judgment, and

---

[164] *Christ Exalted*, p. 28. See his *Life*, pp. 21-23. Knollys also endorsed Katherine Sutton's *A Christian Woman's Experiences of the glorious working of Gods free grace* (1663) with a Preface. Her testimony speaks of assurance through the witness of the Spirit and a promise to the heart (pp. 8-9). Knollys often himself used the term "free grace" (e.g., *Revelation*, p. 136; *Eleventh*, pp. 19-20; *Parable*, p. 113). See also 1644/46 *Confession* where it says, "All beleevers through the knowledge of that justification of life given by the Father, and brought forth by the bloud of Christ, have this as their great priviledge of that new covenant, peace with God, and reconciliation" (XXX).

[165] This was Knollys' conversion by Puritan standards. I, therefore, disagree with Muriel James who considers his conversion experience to have taken place when at Cambridge (*Religious Liberty*, pp. 55-56).

understanding].... Thirdly he walks in newness of life ...That is, the conversation of a new creature should be such as becomes the Gospel ...To wit, humble, harmlesse, and holy.... Examine your selves, Are you a new creature? Such of you as have not put off the old man, but still have your old hearts, and your old sins, and walk in your old wayes, and fulfill the old lusts of your sinful natures, are not a new creature, you are not in Christ, nor Christ in you.[166]

Concerning the James 2:24 text which teaches that a man is justified by works, Knollys maintained in his 1679 work that, "a mans Person is justified by faith before God, and works justifie his Faith before Men ... And so Peter Martyr and other of the Ancients used to Distinguish; Faith (saith [Martyr]) justifies our Persons, and good Works justifie our Faith."[167] Again, in his *Parable of the Kingdom of God Expounded*, Knollys answers how wise virgins may know they have attained the power of godliness and not just the form. He exhorted the wise virgins to examine their lives: 1) by the victory they have attained over the world, Satan and their sins; 2) by the lively acts and constant exercise of grace; and 3) by their holy conversation in the world.[168] Knollys asks the wise virgins among his readers, "Art thou an Isrealite indeed? Dost thou worship God in spirit and Truth? Hast thou both the form and power of Godliness? Then be of good Comfort. For ... Christ is thine.... God is thy Father, Grace is thy portion, and Heaven is thine Inheritance, Holiness is thy way, and Happiness will be thine end."[169] This evidence contradicts Paul Gritz's statement that Knollys "rejected the idea that following the moral law ... could serve as a source of assurance of salvation", and by inference associating him with Antinomianism.[170] From these examples, taken from different periods of his life, it is clear that Knollys believed that a Christian's assurance was primarily based on a changed heart and life, that is, on his sanctification.[171] Con-

---

[166] *Christ Exalted*, pp. 7-8.
[167] *Mystical Babylon*, pp. 23-24.
[168] *Parable*, pp. 51-52.
[169] *Ibid.*, p. 47.
[170] Gritz, "Richardson," p. 263.
[171] Knollys did, however, recognize that a person could gain a false asssurance from his duties when he says, "The poore sinner prayes still, reads the Scriptures, heares the Word, is both constant, and conscionable [*sic*] in the performance of holy duties, but now he cannot ... raise his hopes of salvation[,] gather his comforts in promises, nor conclude his assurance of eternall life from his duties done, because he knows not

cerning the subject of assurance and this first point of Antinomianism Knollys did agree with the Antinomians that the Spirit gives assurance of salvation in a promise of free grace to the heart at conversion, but also with the orthodox that it comes by the evidence of sanctification in the believer's life.[172]

Since Calvin the Reformed teaching of union with Christ as the means by which the believer partakes of the grace of God in justification has been fundamental. The Antinomians differed from the orthodox by positing that faith was not a condition of justification but a consequence. Knollys clearly agreed with Calvin that a believer's justification was based on union with Christ. The 1644/46 *Confession* which Knollys signed states that, "All beleevers are by Christ, united to God, by which union, God is one with them, and they are one with him; and that all believers are the Sons of God, and joynt heires with Christ, to whom belong all the promises of this life, and that which is to come."[173] Again, in 1681, when discussing the subject of the sinner's conversion Knollys teaches that the soul is united to Christ at this time. He states, "This Faith Jesus Christ is the Author of, and will be the finisher of it, *Heb.* 12. 2. and therefore called the faith of the son of God, *Gal.* 2. 20. by which faith the Soul in its Conversion is united unto Christ, and kept through it by the Power of God unto salvation."[174]

But when was the sinner's conversion for Knollys? Was the sinner's union with Christ prior to faith, and thus merely a recognition of this union as the Antinomians taught? Knollys was no Antinomian on this point. He taught in numerous places that this union with Christ is by faith. In *Christ Exalted* in the heat of the 1640s he states, "Thus being by the Spirit and Faith united with Christ, we are made a new creature, or creation,... have a new heart,... and walk in newnesse of life." And in the same work he teaches concerning the conversion of the sinner, "The Lord ... doth enable the poore soul so ... to receive ... Jesus Christ, and by faith to rest on

---

whether Christ be his or no, and whether or no he performs those duties from the spirit of life in Christ" (*Christ Exalted*, p. 18).

172   As noted above Knollys did not speak of the Spirit's witness apart from the promise/Word as some antinomians did.

173   1644/46 *Confession*, XXVII.

174   *World*, pt. 1, p. 35. See also *Song of Solomon*, pp. 47, 64-65, 7, where Knollys teaches that every saint is joined and ingrafted or set into Christ, and also united and knit together unto the Church as members of Christ's mystical body.

him for wisedome, righteousnesse, sanctification and redemption: which Christ being given to the sinner, of the Father, is of God made all this to him.... And now the sinner is drawne to Christ, and is sought and saved by Christ."[175] For Knollys the sinner's salvation takes place at the time he receives Christ by faith. Again, in 1681, when speaking about "the work of faith with power" as one of the works of God in the Christian he proclaims that "we are justified, adopted and sanctified by this faith."[176] He states in *Song of Solomon*,

Our union by Faith, the Pardon of sin, our Reconciliation with God, the sanctification of our hearts and lives, our peace of conscience, and the Salvation of our Souls, are the Benefits of our Redemption by Christ, I Cor. 1. 30. these are as a Cluster of Camphire, full of divine virtue, and spiritual sweetnesse unto beleevers, when they can apply these benefits unto themselves by Faith.[177]

Another area of conflict between the Antinomians and orthodox, as we have noted above, has to do with preparation for salvation. The Antinomians believed that a person could not really prepare himself for salvation because it was purely a matter of God sovereignly working by grace without respect to the person's prior actions. On the other hand, the orthodox following the federal-experimental morphology of conversion believed that a person could prepare himself for salvation by performing certain religious acts. Knollys sits somewhere between the two. He believed that conver-

---

[175] *Christ Exalted*, pp. 1-2, 21.
[176] *World*, pt. 1, p. 36.
[177] *Song of Solomon*, pp. 64-65. See also 1677/89 *Confession* which Knollys signed. Concerning God's Covenant the *Confession* states, "It pleased the *Lord* to make a *Covenant* of *Grace* wherein he freely offereth unto *Sinners*, Life and Salvation by *Jesus Christ*, requiring of them Faith in him, that they may be saved" (VII.2). And again, "Faith thus receiving and resting on Christ, and his Righteousness, is the alone instrument of Justification" (XI.2). Similarly, "The Grace of *Faith*, whereby the Elect are enabled to believe to the saving of their souls, is the work of the *Spirit* of *Christ* in their hearts" (XIV.1). And finally, "All *Saints* that are united to Jesus Christ their *Head* by his Spirit, and Faith ... have fellowship in his Graces, sufferings, death, resurrection, and glory" (XXVII.1). See also 1644/46 *Confession*, Article XXVIII where it states, "Those that have union with Christ, are justified from all their sins by the bloud of Christ.... And this [justification] applied (in the manifestation of it) through faith." Could this be interpreted in an Antinomian way? Even if it could, Knollys' other works firmly teach that the believer's union with Christ and his justification occur not prior to faith but when he exercises faith in Christ.

sion took place when the sinner simply trusted in the promise of God for salvation. In a 1646 sermon he gives his own testimony of conversion to help "the poore sinner" who thinks that it is a "hard thing to believe in Jesus Christ,"

> When that promise came, it was so sutable [sic] to my present condition, my heart objections were so answered by it, and it pleased God so cleerly to reveale his rich and free love in Christ Jesus to my soul in it, that I could not but with teares and much heart breakings admire the infinite goodness of God to to [sic] me, & I was so self-ashamed & abased, as that I saw my selfe the chief of sinners, which promise of the spirit I received by faith, applyed to my self, and in the believing that Christ was mine and I his, I was filled with joy unspeakable.[178]

Not only did Knollys believe that conversion took place when the sinner simply trusted in the promise of God for salvation, but he also denied that we can save ourselves by our religious performances. Concerning some professors touching their salvation, he states, "They thinke to save themselves by seeking, praying, mourning, reforming &c. And considers [sic] not, that Christ must seek and save them. They will take the work out of his hand, and thinke to do it themselves, by their humiliations, duties, &c." Is Knollys taking a swipe at the federal-experimental teaching on preparation for salvation, or is he attacking formal Christianity? Probably the latter because he goes on to say that these "look not to Christ who must save them, but to themselves."[179] In addition, he made clear that sinners cannot bargain for salvation upon the old Covenant of Works. Knollys states,

> For as it was a great sin in *Simon Magus* to offer money, and to think that the gifts of the Holy Ghost might be bought for material money, so it is a very great sin in any Minister to sell this Mystical Oyle [the Unction of the Holy Spirit and the saving, sanctifying Grace of God] for Material Silver or

---

[178]   *Christ Exalted*, p. 28.

[179]   *Ibid.*, p. 26. But I do think he is taking a swipe at the orthodox when he says, "Consider this you who will not believe, unless you could see your selves so holy, so humble; except you can first have such a sinne subdued, you will not beleeve any of your sinnes are pardoned, untill you find & feel in your selves a soft heart, a praying spirit, a mourning spirit, you cry out you are not justified.... Thus most professors would bring in (if not their own righteousnesse) some grace or work of God in them, to joyn with Christ in their justification, not considering that God justifies the ungodly,... and that Christ is all; and in all in the justification of sinners" (*Ibid.*, p. 10).

Gold, or any price or earthly commodity. And it is a very great mistake in foolish Professors, to think they may buy *that is*, bargain with God for Christ and Grace upon the terms of the old Covenant of works, and their own Righteousness, which is as menstruous raggs.[180]

On the other hand, contrary to the Antinomians, Knollys maintained that we are to use *means* in order to bring about our conversion. He states,

Gods gracious and free promises doe not exclude the meanes he hath appointed to attaine the mercies therein promised. It pleaseth him to tye his creatures to the use of meanes, when he affords it them, though he will sometimes worke without it. Now the ordinarie meanes which God hath in his infinite wisedome appointed to convert sinners ... is the Word preached.[181]

In addition, he speaks of receiving Christ on Gospel-terms which implies that certain conditions must be fulfilled before a sinner can be saved. These gospel terms consist of: 1) a recognition that "Christ is the only necessary, meanes of Salvation"; 2) a recognition that "God doth offer Christ to lost sinners without respect to price or person"; and 3) a requirement "that those who do receive him shall depart from iniquity.... Live soberly, righteously and Godly in this present world ... And that they shall sell all, lose all, and hate all for the sake of Christ, and take up the Crosse and follow him."[182] For Knollys the conditions for salvation were faith and repentance as they were for the orthodox. Moreover, in the *Parable of the Kingdom of God Expounded* Knollys declared how a sinner buys the oil necessary for salvation:

---

[180] *Parable*, p. 108. Knollys endorsed the work by Robert Garner, *Mysteries Unvialed, Redemption by Jesus Christ, unto lost sinners*, with a preface. In this work Garner reveals his Antinomianism when he proclaims, "[Those who preach] repentance as relating to the Law, as a legal work or duty, as a condition of righteousness, life and salvation, as a preparation or qualification to Christ, or as something to be done by us before we can have Christ, or believe in him unto the remission of sins; Such doe not preach repentance and remission of sins in the Name of Christ, they rather seek to drive men from Christ, and bottom them upon some other foundation than Jesus Christ" (p. 185, quoted in Pope Duncan, *Hanserd Knollys*). Knollys' endorsement of the book does not necessarily imply he agreed with everything in it.

[181] *Christ Exalted*, p. 12. See also *Ibid.*, pp. 13, 14. Preaching to sinners he says, "And you ought to wait on God in the diligent use of meanes untill the day of his power come upon you, and then you shall be a willing, a beleeving people" (p. 13).

[182] *Christ Exalted*, p. 13; see also *Ibid.*, p. 32 and *Parable*, p. 113.

1. A sense of want and need of it, which the foolish Virgins ... had [when the bridegroom had come at midnight]. 2. Attending upon the Ministry of the word and Administrations of the Gospel to obtain it or get some of this Oyle, having their heart and hand open and willing to receive it, Acts 16. 14.... 3. a willingness to have it upon Christs own terms of free Grace, without money and without price, Isa. 55. 1, 2, 3. & Rev. 21.6. 22. 7.[183]

In addition, Knollys held his own morphology of salvation by teaching that a sinner comes to salvation first through conviction, then through spiritual illumination in the saving knowledge of Jesus Christ, and finally, following conversion, through sanctification. Knollys believed that the work of conviction brings the sinner through several stages: 1) he sees and is convicted of his sinful nature, original corruption, actual sins; 2) he begins to have fears of Hell, death and damnation; 3) he sets upon reformation, performing holy duties; and 4) he sees himself as an unbeliever and so cannot be saved until he believes.[184] Knollys was certainly not a thorough going federal-experimental preparationist, but he certainly did not hold the Antinomian tenet that there were no conditions to be met for salvation, or that a sinner could do nothing prior to conversion to prepare for it. His theology on this score was well within the spectrum of Calvinistic orthodoxy.

Another Antinomian tenet had to do with increated grace as opposed to created grace. Knollys firmly believed that in our salvation Christ is everything. In 1646, when preaching from the Colossians 3:11 text that Christ is all, and in all in the new man, he writes:

We have nothing but what we have received, and we have received all from his fulnesse.... He is the Alpha and Omega, the beginning and ending, of all those graces, gifts and fruits of the Spirit, which are in the New man.... Thus Christ is all in all, in the New man. He is the Authour, Preserver, and finisher of all; He purchased all, He is the Donour of all, He is the beauty of all, the summe of all, the perfection of all in the New man.[185]

---

[183]   *Parable*, pp. 108-109.

[184]   *World*, pt. 1, pp. 10-34. He considered this work of conviction very important because, for him, a lack of a thorough work of conviction was the cause of the lack of a sound and saving work of conversion (*Ibid.*, p. 22).

[185]   *Christ Exalted*, pp. 2, 4. Knollys' exaltation of Christ in the work of salvation is also evident in his devotional treatise, *Song of Solomon*.

Knollys' language could be interpreted in an Antinomian sense but
even the Westminster Divines used the same kind of language in
their *Confession* when they taught that "[the believer's] ability to do
good works is not at all of themselves, but wholly from the Spirit of
Christ."[186] Knollys did not adhere to increated grace as is evident
from the same sermon quoted above where he teaches that Christ
is the *foundation* of the new man, that is, the source of the sinner's
new man not something overriding it. He states:

> Christ is the foundation of all that faith, repentance, love, and other graces,
> gifts and fruits of the Spirit, which are in every true believer.... All those
> spiritual breathings of the hunger-thirsting soul, after the enjoyment of
> God in any of his holy Ordinances are from Christ; and from him are all
> those quickening, all that life we have in prayer, preaching, conference, and
> other spiritual duties. In a word, the spirit of life himself, who so sweetly
> refresheth the weary soul, comforts the sorrowful heart, and quickens the
> sanctified affections, is from Christ.[187]

For Knollys, the work of Christ in sanctification is a "renovation or
renewing of the minde" and a "changing [of] their hearts in[to] the
Image of Christ."[188] Christ does not override the created human
faculties but changes them. Knollys did not agree with the Antinomian teaching of increated grace.

Antinomians have been charged by the orthodox for holding
heretical teachings on the believer's relation to sin and the law,
both before and after conversion. The last three tenets of our study
of seventeenth-century Antinomianism have to do with these teachings. As will become evident, Knollys espoused none of them. First,
is the Antinomian belief that God doesn't see any sin in his justified
children. As was stated earlier, the moderate Antinomians did not
teach that a child of God is sinless in a practical sense, but some of
their statements could have been interpreted this way. Knollys in
no way uses unwise language in this respect. What we do find in
Knollys is a realistic and healthy recognition of the problem of sin
in the believer. For example, in 1674, after explaining what takes

---

[186]   *Westminster Confession of Faith*, XVI.3, quoting from *Westminster Confession of Faith*
(Inverness, 1976). This statement is identical to the one found in the 1677/89 *Baptist
Confession* on 'Good Works' that Knollys signed.
[187]   *Christ Exalted*, p. 2.
[188]   *Ibid.*, p. 32.

place in a person's life before and at conversion, he goes on to describe what the believer's experience will be like after conversion. He taught that God works in the Christian's life "gradually" until he is complete in Christ which only takes place at death. He then speaks of the "work of mortification" during the believer's life; the believer seeks to oppose and subdue the power of indwelling sin that remains in him after regeneration.

Also there is a positive "work of sanctification of heart and life" taking place which consists in the truth of grace and in the growth of grace. For Knollys the "truth of grace" produces the spiritual fruit of the gospel, and the "growth of grace" progresses through three stages — babes, young men, fathers. The "perfection of grace" does not occur until the believer reaches heaven.[189] Throughout his works Knollys recognizes the fallability of professing Christians and is constantly calling them to grow in grace. In *World that now is* he says,

> I do exhort sanctified Believers to prepare themselves to leave the world, and to enjoy the world to come. Noah did prepare himself, *all the time he was building the Ark*, by being a just and perfect man, and walking with God, *Gen.* 6. 9. for the Ending Time of this world draws near: and the End of our *natural* life is *to us* the End of this World: And that we may be prepared, we ought to dye daily to sin, to self, and to this *evil* world; And we must live to God, live in Christ Jesus, *Titus* 2. 11, 12, 13, 14.[190]

And again in *Parable of the Kingdom of God Expounded* he writes,

> Saints, you ought to prepare and be ready to meet Christ *the Churches Bridegroom*, when he cometh, and therefore consider what you have to do ere you and Jesus Christ meet in his Marriage Kingdom. O gracious and precious Saints, have you not something to do ere you dye?... Again consider Saints, are you *prepared* as a Bride adorned for her Husband? *Rev.* 21. 2, 3. Are you cloathed in fine Linnen, white and clean, *Rev.* 19. 8. and so made *Ready* for the Marriage of the Lamb? *Rev.* 19.7. Or do not some of you stand in need to wash your *Robes* and make them white in the blood of the Lamb, *Rev.* 7. 14, 15. before you can put on your *beautiful* garments, *Isa.* 52. 1, 2.... O beloved and blessed Virgin Saints, how much cleaning, purging, sanctifying work is there yet to be done in your souls by the spirit, and word

---

[189] *Parable*, pp. 34-41.
[190] *World*, pt. 1, pp. 103-104.

of God in the lively and powerful applications of the precious blood of Jesus Christ.[191]

Consequently, Knollys is no advocate of perfectionism of which some Antinomians were accused. For example, when speaking of the believer's possession of the glorious liberties of God's Spirit as a motive to prize Christ, he cautions that this is "not any carnall liberty to sin, and to fulfill the lusts of the Flesh,... but Spiritual liberty, and freedome from sin. I mean not a perfect and totall freedome from all sin, as if the people of God could never sin after conversion." And again later in the same treatise when speaking of salvation from the pollution of sin, he makes clear that "the Saints have sin, and do sin."[192] Moreover, in a sermon concerned with the believer's holiness, Knollys exhorts them saying,

> Then may this doctrine occasion a deep Humiliation, and godly sorrow in believers for their unholinesse, carnalnesse, and sinfulnesse in heart or life. O beloved, let you and I commune with our owne hearts, how much unbelief, hypocrisie [,] self-filthinesse, formality and wickednesse, shall we upon diligent examination finde remaining in us? What vanity of minde and carnality is in our hearts? How many hard thoughts of God have we still?[193]

And this is only a brief part of his exhortation. Knollys understood the power of remaining sin in the believer. When it came to denying sin in the believer's experience and any form of perfectionism, he was no Antinomian.[194]

The second Antinomian tenet having to do with sin was that Christians may live in sin. This was the primary reason the orthodox opposed Antinomianism. They believed that the teachings of

---

[191]   *Parable*, pp. 121-123. See also *Ibid.*, pp. 56-57, 58-60, 131-132; and *World*, pt. 2, pp. 44-45.

[192]   *Christ Exalted*, pp. 6, 22.

[193]   *Ibid.*, pp. 34-35. See also *Ibid.*, p. 23 where he espouses the classic Reformed interpretation of Romans 7:14-25.

[194]   It should also be noted that both the 1644/46 and 1677/89 *Confessions* teach that sin is a reality in the life of the believer. See 1677/89 *Confession* XI.5 where it states that there is no perfection after conversion; XVIII.4 where it speaks of a loss of assurance because of sin; and XIX.6 where it teaches that the law reveals "the sinfull pollutions of [the believer's] Natures, Hearts and Lives." It is also interesting that in Article XXVIII when speaking on the believer's justification from "all sinnes", the 1646 edition removed the objectionable addition of "past, present and to come" from the 1644 *Confession*. Knollys signed the former but not the latter.

even the moderate Antinomians would encourage professing Christians either to take indwelling sin less seriously or be totally indifferent to it. The orthodox realized that it was only some radical Antinomians that really condoned believers living in sin.[195] Knollys was so far from believing this tenet that it is hard to know where to begin. Every one of his treatises that dealt with salvation and the believer's life taught and exhorted Christians to repent of sin and pursue holiness. For example, in a 1646 printed sermon, entitled, 'That We Should Be holy,' he states, "Those people, that are ungodly, unsanctified, are not the people of God, such may boast of their justification, but they deceive themselves, for God hath not justified unsanctified people." He then continues to describe false Christians as "legall", "formall" or "carnall Professors."[196]

In 1656, when addressing the subject of Christ's Lordship over the believer, Knollys maintained that sin and grace cannot reign together in one and the same heart; the saints are not to serve their lusts.[197] In 1674, in His work on the *Parable of the Kingdom of God Expounded* he makes a clear distinction between true and false professors in Christ; the latter have only the form of godliness while the former have the power as well. The power of godliness consists in: 1) the truth of grace evidenced in a new birth demonstrated in denying all ungodliness, living soberly, righteously and godly in this present evil world, hating sin and loving holiness; 2) the lively acts and exercise of grace exemplified in the labour of fervent love, in constant exercise of patience, humility, meekness and self denial, taking up the cross daily; and 3) growth and perfection of grace consisting in a life of holiness and righteousness, demonstrated in a holy conversation.[198] He exhorts the foolish virgins, who have a form of godliness but not the power, to become wise virgins and to buy the oil that is necessary for their salvation. He writes:

> I exhort such to consider seriously whether seeming to be Religious, and saying Lord, Lord, will save your immortal souls, Matth. 7. 21, 22, 23.... Remember Professors that the foolish Virgins had their lamps lighted, and they shined in the form of Godliness, but they found the Door of the Kingdom of Heaven shut against them.... Do not rest in a form, without the

---

[195]   See Hill, *Essays*, II, 170-171.
[196]   *Christ Exalted*, pp. 33-34.
[197]   *Song of Solomon*, p. 15.
[198]   *Parable*, pp. 25-33.

power of Godliness, lest you sitting down in any Church of Saints and under the sacred Ordinances of God without Christ, come short of Heaven, for without Holiness no man shall see the Lord, *Heb.* 12. 14.

For Knollys, "the spiritual Oyle is the Unction of the Holy one,... the saving, sanctifying Grace of God, the gifts and the fruits of the holy Spirit."[199]

And again, in 1681, Knollys taught that the believer's life after conversion is a life of mortification of sin, seeking to oppose and subdue the power of indwelling sin, and a life of sanctification of heart and life. He states:

> This part of God's *Workmanship* called *Mortification*, is begun in *Evangelical* Repentance, and godly sorrow for sin; whereby a sanctified Believer is made to loath, abhor and hate his sins 2 *Cor.* 7. 9, 10. and by the Grace of God to deny ungodliness, and worldy lusts: And to live soberly, righteously, and godly in this evil world, *Tit.* 2. 11, 12. Now his heart being out of love with sin, the *Young* Convert doth by the Assistance of the holy Spirit, and Grace of God, labour and endeavour the mortification of every corruption, and the power of the *indwelling* Spirit in every *sanctified Believer* opposeth and subdueth the power of *indwelling* sin, that remains in him after *Regeneration*, *Gal.* 5. 17.[200]

He also maintained that the congregations of Christ are to walk by the same rule of the written Word of God, and the church is to excommunicate those members that live in gross and scandalous sins. Knollys writes:

> This one Church, and all the Congregations of Saints, that are Members thereof, walk by one and the same Rule *of the written Word of God*, being ordered and guided by their Bishops, Pastors, Teachers, Presbyters, or Elders, according to the *Royal* Laws of God's House *(called the perfect Law of Liberty*, *Jam.* 1. 25.) submitting themselves unto those Guides whom God hath made *Overseers.*[201]

In addition, Knollys called virgin professors to prepare for Christ's Coming by taking heed that they do not fall asleep while the Bridegroom tarries, seeking their own things more than those of Christ;

---

[199] *Ibid.*, pp. 48-52. See also *Ibid.*, pp. 23, 38, 41-43, 82-83, 89, 93, 96, 120-121.
[200] *World*, pt. 1, pp. 38-39.
[201] *Ibid.*, pp. 51-52.

and they are to consider what manner of persons they ought to be in all holy conversation and godliness as they look and wait for the glory of Christ, His saints and Church in the world to come.[202] And in Knollys' last work, a commentary on the Book of Revelation which he completed in 1688, he instructs pastors

> to inspect them that Worship, and to take care before persons be admitted unto the visible Churches of Saints, to partake of all the sacred Ordinances of God, that they be found in the Faith, and holy in their Life.... And after they be added to the Church, the Ministers ought to oversee them, that they do not walk disorderly, to the dishonour of God, and scandal of the Church.[203]

In this work also he calls people to be ready for Christ's return by "Keeping our Gospel Profession unspotted of the world... [and] Keeping the faith.... *Keep thy self pure*; white, and clean; which is the righteousness of saints." And at the last judgment in agreement with the text of Revelation 20:12, Knollys states, "The Righteous shall receive their reward of Grace, as God hath promised them, according to their good Deeds."[204] Knollys was by no means a practical Antinomian, not only in agreement with the moderate Antinomians on this score, but also with the orthodox Puritans.[205]

The last Antinomian tenet that has to do with the believer's life is the use of the Law before and after conversion. The moderate Antinomians recognized a limited use of the law before and after conversion but in their writings they played down its function. Knollys agreed with the orthodox that, at conversion, the believer was freed from the guilt and condemnation of the Law, but he taught in his works, that the "moral law" was useful not only before conversion as a means of bringing conviction but also after conversion as a revelation of the will of God for the believer to walk by. For example, when considering the use of the law prior to conversion, Knollys encourages ministers "to labour in the Word and Doctrine on a thorough Gospel conviction." He calls this "law-

---

[202] *World*, pt. 2, pp. 44-45.
[203] *Revelation*, p. 124.
[204] *Ibid.*, pp. 198, 226.
[205] The two *Confessions* that Knollys signed also clearly teach that the believer's life is to be one of holiness. See 1644/46 *Confession*, XXIX, and 1677/89 *Confession*, XI.1,3; XV.4,5; XVI.1-7; XXI.3; and XXVI.2,5.

work." In another place he states, "God doth by his spirit and Word convince the soul of sin, righteousnesse and Judgement,... First, of sin, to wit, sins not only against the Law, as drunkennesse, uncleanesse, covetousnesse, &c. But also sins against the Gospel, because they believe not in Christ." He goes on to say that "the effect of this conviction [of being a sinner] usually is much trouble of conscience, feare of Hell, and sensible apprehensions of the wrath of God, and such like."[206] From this it would appear that Knollys agreed with the preaching of the terrors of the Law in order to bring about conviction.[207]

Knollys not only saw a use for the law before conversion but agreed with the Calvinistic teaching on the third use of the law, to rule and guide the believer. In 1646 after explaining that the believer is delivered from the ceremonies of the law, from under the penalties of the law, from the schoolmastership of the law, from the Old Covenant of the law (the Ten Commandments) as a means of salvation, he then states, "and yet we do not hereby make voide the Law, but establish it.... For we say that we ought to yeeld obedience of Faith, in newnesse of spirit, and to fulfill the Royal law according to the Scripture.... Neither are we without Law to God, but under Law to Christ."[208] In his commentary on Revelation he similarly states that the elect are saved, "From the Law, not from evangelical obedience unto the moral part of the Law,... but from the Ceremonial part of the Law,... and from the curse of the Law."[209]

In addition, Knollys taught that Christ is the Lawgiver of the Church and that the Church is to conform to the Word of God and

---

[206] *World*, pt. 1, pp. 23-24. *Christ Exalted*, p. 17. See also *Ibid.*, p. 27.

[207] The 1644/46 *Confession* would seem to contradict this position when it states, "The preaching of the Gospel to the conversion of sinners, is absolutely free; no way requiring as absolutely necessary, any qualifications, preparations, or terrors of the Law, or preceding ministry of the Law; but onely and alone the naked soule, a sinner and ungodly to receive Christ" (XXV). But we must realize: 1) Knollys' own conversion experience was evidence that this statement was true; and 2) from his other writings we know that he believed the law was useful prior to conversion. Therefore, 3) he could agree with this Article as long as the words "absolutely necessary" were not removed from the statement, "no way requiring as absolutely necessary, any ... terrors of the Law, or preceding ministry of the Law."

[208] *Christ Exalted*, pp. 23-25.

[209] *Revelation*, pp. 93-94. When commenting on the Blessed who do God's commandments and so have a right to the tree of life, Revelation 22:14, he says, "By the Commandments of God, we are to understand the moral Law which Christ came not to destroy but fulfil" (*Ibid.*, p. 241).

that pastors are to govern according to Christ's Laws and Ordinances. Commenting on the phrase "Thy neck with Chains of Gold" in verse ten of chapter one of *Song of Solomon*, he counsels,

> The neck is that part of the body next to the head, about which men and women did use to wear chains of Gold, for honour and for ornament, Gen. 41. 42. and so are the Saints adorned, Ezek. 16. 11.... By chains of gold you may understand, first, the spiritual Laws of Christ, which are called his Yoke, Mat. 11. 29, 30. unto which the Saints are to submit their neck, and account it their dignity, as well as their duty, their privilege, as well as their Allegiance, to be found obedient to all Christs commandments, and observing of all his holy Ordinances.[210]

And again in *Parable of the Kingdom of God Expounded* he writes,

> Christ the King of his Church, is their Law-giver, *Isa.* 33. 22. The Lord is our statute-maker, and the Bible is his Sacred-Book wherein are published all the Laws of Gods house, *Ezek.* 43. 10, 11. according to which Laws the Church of saints are [sic] to be governed by their Elders whom Christ hath set over them to Rule and Govern them, *Heb.* 13 7, 17. according to the Laws of his house.... The Churches of saints shall be ruled and Governed by the holy, Righteous and good Laws of the Lord Jesus Christ ... who is the Son over the house of God, Heb. 3. 1, 6.... Christ is the Legislator, the Law-giver, the Bible is his and his Churches Statute Book, and all the Churches, Ministers and Saints of God are to be governed by his Royal Law of Liberty, in obeying and keeping whereof there is a Blessing promised, *James* 1. 25.[211]

And again concerning worship in *Parable* Knollys states,

> In the *form* of Godliness there must be a Conformity unto the Revealed will of God in his word, especially in the External part of the Instituted worship of God in the Gospel.
> Uniformity in Worship in any Nation or Congregation without Conformity unto the *Rule* or *Canon* of the holy Scripture, is but superstition and a worshipping God after the Inventions and Traditions of men, which the apostle reproved in the Colossians, and calls *Will-worship, Col.* 2. 20, 21, 22, 23.
> The Temple, the Altar and they that worship, *(that is, the Church*, the *worship of God and the worshippers of God)* are to be measured by the Reed or Rod of the Sanctuary, that is, the written word of God, *Rev.* 11. 1.[212]

---

[210] *Song of Solomon*, p. 48. *See also Eleventh*, pp. 4-6; and *Revelation*, p. 106.
[211] *Parable*, pp. 6, 11-12.
[212] *Ibid.*, pp. 42-43.

Knollys was no Antinomian when it came to the use of the law either before or after a person's conversion.[213]

Conclusion

Knollys was accused of Antinomianism primarily because of his association with the Antinomian John Wheelwright in the 1630s, and later in the 1640s because of his association with the Anabaptists. In England the latter group was feared because of the anarchy and immorality of the Munsterites and John of Leyden. In addition, this appellation made the report of Knollys' "filthy dalliance" by John Winthrop all the more believable. Moreover, it is clear that Knollys believed that at the time of conversion, assurance of salvation came by the witness of the Spirit to a promise of salvation. This is in part similar to one of the tenets held by the Antinomians in both New England and England.

Nevertheless, our study of his writings puts into question this charge against him. Except on the subject of assurance Knollys does not hold any of the other Antinomian tenets. And even on the subject of assurance Knollys did not espouse the Spirit's witness apart from the promise or Word as did some Antinomians like Mrs Hutchinson; and he believed, along with the orthodox, that the primary evidence of assurance throughout the believer's life is sanctification. He also taught that a sinner enters into union with Christ by faith. Therefore, faith is a condition of justification not a consequence (although this faith was the work of the Holy Spirit) as the orthodox taught; consequently, conversion takes place when the sinner trusts in the promise of God for salvation. In addition, concerning preparation for salvation he encouraged people to use *means* (particularly the Word preached) in order to bring about conversion, but that they must not rely on religious performances. He also taught his own morphology of salvation: conviction (of sin, fears of

---

[213] See 1644/46 *Confession* where it says that the believer "presseth after a heavenly and Evangelical obedience to all the commands which Christ as Head and King in his new covenant hath prescribed to them" (XXIX; see also XLIX). See 1677/89 *Confession* XIV.2 which states that the believer yields obedience to the commands, trembling at the threatenings, and embracing the promises of God; and XIX.5-6 which deals with the moral law of God as binding upon the believer to the obedience thereof, as a Rule of Life, and even brings threatenings.

Hell and death, reformation of life, self-perception as an unbeliever), spiritual illumination, and sanctification. Furthermore,
Knollys maintained that Christ was everything in salvation but did
not hold to the Antinomian notion of increated grace. Moreover,
he did not hold any of the Antinomian teachings on the believer's
relationship to sin and the law. Knollys knew that believers continued to be plagued by sin in this life, and that perfection was only
possible in heaven. Nevertheless, he also taught that Christians
ought to live holy lives. If a professing Christian lived in sin then he
was a false Christian. Moreover, he saw a use for the law before
and after a person was converted.

After comparing Knollys' writings with the seven Antinomian
tenets, it is understandable how Knollys could have been perceived
as an Antinomian on the important issue of assurance. On the
other hand, Knollys did not hold any of the other tenets of seventeenth-century England and New England Antinomianism but espoused Reformed orthodoxy, especially concerning the key issues
of the believer's relationship to the law and sin. Contrary to his
contemporaries John Winthrop, Thomas Edwards, and the Assembly of Divines, and his twentieth-century interpreters, Philip Gura
and Paul Gritz, Knollys cannot properly be categorized as an Antinomian.

CHAPTER FOUR

HYPER-CALVINISM

Rooted in the teaching of Joseph Hussey in the early 1700s, hyper-Calvinism became an influential teaching in Particular Baptist churches in the eighteenth century. It has been suggested by Michael Haykin and indirectly by Peter Toon that Knollys' soteriology encouraged this development in the Particular Baptist denomination.[1] What kind of a Calvinist was Knollys? Was he a High Calvinist like John Owen or did he go beyond High Calvinism and espouse hyper-Calvinism? The charge has some merit because the father of Calvinistic Baptist hyper-Calvinism according to Curt Daniel and Edward Seymour is John Skepp who claimed in *Divine Energy*, his only published work, to be building upon the foundation of teaching which Knollys had laid.[2] Were Skepp's and Knollys' Calvinism similar? In addition, two nineteenth-century Baptist historians, Joseph Ivimey and James Culross, felt it necessary to defend Knollys against this charge.[3] For these reasons the question of Knollys' Calvinism/hyper-Calvinism should more comprehensively be examined.

In this chapter we will begin by taking note of the evidence for, and charges made of hyper-Calvinism against Knollys. Then we will set out the history and theology of both High Calvinism in its seventeenth-century context, and hyper-Calvinism in the context of the late seventeenth and eighteenth centuries. In this latter context the works of John Gill and John Brine, the premier Baptist

---

[1]   The references will be given below.

[2]   Curt Daniel, "Hyper-Calvinism and John Gill" (unpublished Ph.D. dissertation, University of Edinburgh, 1983), pp. 6, 366; Robert Edward Seymour, "John Gill, Baptist Theologian (1697-1771)" (unpublished Ph.D. dissertation, University of Edinburgh, 1954), pp. 54-55; and John Skepp, *Divine Energy or the Efficacious Operations of the Spirit of God upon the Soul of Man, in his Effectual Calling and Conversion, stated, Prov'd and Vindicated Wherein the real Weakness and Insufficiency of Moral Suasion ... for Faith and Conversion to God are fully evinced, Being an Antidote against the Pelagian Plague* (1722), "To the Church of Christ", pp. A5-A7.

[3]   Ivimey, *English Baptists*, III, 364-365, and Culross, *Hanserd Knollys*, pp. 36-37.

hyper-Calvinists of the eighteenth-century, will be examined. The
theologies of seventeenth-century English High Calvinism and
eighteenth-century Baptist hyper-Calvinism will be measured
against the writings of John Calvin (his theology is the standard of
orthodoxy on this particular charge). The aim of this chapter is to
compare Knollys' writings with the theological tenets of seventeenth-century English High Calvinism, and with those tenets of
hyper-Calvinism espoused by Gill and Brine in order to determine
whether Knollys was a High Calvinist and/or a hyper-Calvinist.[4]
In this fashion we will be able to judge more adequately whether
the charge of hyper-Calvinism against Knollys is valid, as well as
discern something of his thought on such doctrinal themes as evangelism, the work of the Holy Spirit in salvation, and election.

Hanserd Knollys and the seventeenth-century Particular Baptists
have been accused of incipient hyper-Calvinism by modern historians. Peter Toon maintains in *Puritans and Calvinism* that the Calvinism of the *Westminster Confession of Faith* was strengthened in the
Congregationalist *Savoy Declaration*, and consequently, in the *Second
London Confession of Faith* (1677/89) which Knollys signed. The latter
two *Confessions* put a greater emphasis on the sovereignty of God
and removed the emphasis on human responsibility in the chapters
on repentance, saving faith, and assurance of grace. Moreover, the
additional chapter on the Gospel (found in the *Savoy* and *London
Confessions* but not in *Westminster*), has nothing on human responsibility to respond to the Gospel but is totally concerned with the
sovereignty of God. And finally, there is a strengthening of federal
theology in these *Confessions*. For example, the terms "Covenant of
Works" and "Covenant of Grace" are more liberally, and frequently used in them as compared to *Westminster*.[5] Toon concludes,
"Perhaps this imbalance [emphasis on sovereignty of God in *Savoy*
and consequently in *London*] may be seen as one root of that hyper-

---

[4]   Those studies that have touched on the hyper-Calvinism of these three men
together include W.T. Whitley, *Calvinism and Evangelism in England especially in Baptist Circles*
(London, n.d.); Peter Toon, *The Emergence of Hyper-Calvinism in English Nonconformity* (London, 1967); and R. Philip Roberts, *Continuity and Change: London Calvinistic Baptists and the
Evangelical Revival 1760-1820* (Wheaton, 1989).

[5]   Peter Toon, *Puritans and Calvinism* (Swengal, PA, 1973), pp. 77-83. In addition, in
chapter 8 of the *Savoy* and *London Confessions* on "Christ the Mediator" when speaking
on God ordaining the Lord Jesus to be Mediator, they add "according to a Covenant
made between them."

Calvinism which infected both Congregational and Baptist churches in the early eighteenth century."[6]

Another historian, Michael Haykin, believes that Knollys' "high Calvinist soteriology [was] developed by many of his eighteenth century heirs into a hyper-Calvinism that all but paralyzed evangelism." Haykin knows that Knollys was "an irrepressible evangelist" but his comment implies an incipient hyper-Calvinism in him.[7] Though Haykin does not say so, this is confirmed by Knollys signature on the 1677/89 *London Baptist Confession* that Toon considers a possible precursor to eighteenth-century hyper-Calvinism. In addition, there are some traces of early hyper-Calvinism among seventeenth-century Baptists. For example, in 1675 Andrew Gifford of Pithay Baptist Church, Bristol, wrote to the ministers of the London Calvinistic Baptist churches for their opinion on the obligations of the unconverted to pray. Some of the ministers of Bristol were of the opinion "that as none could pray acceptably without the influences of the Holy Spirit, and unconverted men being destitute of those influences, that therefore it was not their duty to pray, nor the duty of ministers to exhort them to seek for spiritual blessings."[8]

The most damning evidence of hyper-Calvinism, however, against Knollys, in particular, is found in John Skepp's treatise entitled, *Divine Energy*. Skepp, the third pastor to follow after Knollys as pastor of his congregation, was the eighteenth-century Particular Baptist father of hyper-Calvinism. In his 'Dedication' to the church he implicates Knollys in his theology when he writes,

> I thought it my Duty; yea, my Honour to hold forth this Doctrine ministerially amongst You [his congregation]. Not so much for Your Information, as for Your Encouragement, Consolation and Stability; and for the Publick Advantage of Others. I say, not so much for Your Information, for the Nature and Power of the *Divine Energy* You have already known and

---

[6]   *Ibid.*, p. 83.
[7]   Michael Haykin, "Hanserd Knollys (ca. 1599-1691) on the Gifts of the Spirit," *Westminster Theological Journal*, 54 (1992), p. 100.
[8]   Ivimey, *English Baptists*, I, 416. Gifford was probably not of this opinion. The same incipient hyper-Calvinism may also have existed in the Midlands Association. In its association meeting of 1657, a question was asked, "Whether it be lawfull for a Christian to joyne or make a shew of joyning with a visible unbeliever when hee makes a shew of speaking in prayer, either in saying of grace, as they call it, or otherwise." The answer was, "wee judg it not lawfull considering that the sacrifices of the wicked are abomination to the Lord, Prov. 15.8, therefore his prayers also, Prov. 28.9" (B.R. White, ed., *Association Records*, p. 31).

believ'd, having known and receiv'd the Grace of God in Truth. Nor have I thro' Grace, as yet found you wavering or unsettled, nor that You needed to have the Foundation laid again, as tho' the first was faulty, or You gone off from it. I both hope and pray, that none will ever be permitted, by God, or You, nor Your Survivors so much as to attempt, to lay among You, *any other Foundation than that which is already laid, which is Jesus Christ*: Nor to be left to build *Wood, Hay and Stubble* upon such a Bottom. Your Foundation, as to Gospel Order, was skilfully and successfully laid, in the very beginning of the Troublesome Times, by the indefatigable Pains and Care of that eminent Servant and Sufferer for Christ, Mr. *Hanserd Knollis.* And Your Walls were not only rear'd, but beautified, by the Labours and Success of that Evangelick Son of Consolation, Mr. *Robert Steed.* These Two were the chief Master Builders, by whose blessed Ministry You were built, and continued, upon the Foundation of the *Prophets and Apostles, Jesus Christ himself being the Chief Corner Stone.*

And now seeing Christ and You have done me the Honour to call and fix me in the Pastoral Charge, I look upon it my Duty, to take heed what I build; that it is agreeable to, (tho' full short, thro' my Weakness and Insufficiency, of) what You once sat under. Now, that I may be kept faithful, serviceable and acceptable in my Ministry, and successful in my Labours amongst you, in Christ's Gospel, is what I most earnestly desire; and hope I shall always labour after: And that I may attain the same, and an everlasting Crown of Glory with You, and Your aforesaid Pastors, with Christ above.[9]

Skepp's preface clearly links Knollys, whose teaching he seeks to emulate, with the eighteenth-century Baptist hyper-Calvinists. As mentioned above, two nineteenth-century Baptist historians felt it necessary to defend Knollys against this charge because of the lingering influence of eighteenth-century Baptist hyper-Calvinism. In a biographical sketch on Skepp, Joseph Ivimey quotes from Skepp's *Divine Energy* where Skepp writes about building on the "foundation, as to gospel order, ... laid ... by... Mr. Hanserd Knollys." Then in a long footnote Ivimey defends Knollys against any association with Skepp's hyper-Calvinism. In part of that footnote he states,

> If Mr. Skepp meant to intimate that Mr. Knollys was of the sentiments propagated in the work on "Divine Energy," respecting the non-invitations of the gospel to the unconverted, nothing could have been more erroneous.

---

[9]   John Skepp, *Divine Energy or the Efficacious Operations of the Spirit of God upon the Soul of Man, in his Effectual Calling and Conversion, stated, Prov'd and Vindicated Wherein the real Weakness and Insufficiency of Moral Suasion ... for Faith and Conversion to God are fully evinced, Being an Antidote against the Pelagian Plague* (1722), "To the Church of Christ", pp. A5-A7.

Mr. Knollys was one of those ministers who, as Mr. Skepp expresses it, used an Arminian dialect in addressing the unconverted.[10]

Ivimey then concludes with several quotes from Knollys' work entitled, *The World that now is, and the World this is to come*, where Knollys called the unconverted to Christ.

James Culross in his biography of Knollys also defends him against this charge. He writes about the seventeenth century: "There was then a question which troubled many minds, known almost to our own times as 'the modern question' — whether it is right to appeal directly to the unconverted, and urge them to repentance and faith. Though a decided Calvinist (like the late Mr. Spurgeon), Knollys had no doubt or hesitation." He then quotes from Knollys' *The World that now is*, as Ivimey did, illustrating his evangelical ministry.[11] For all these reasons the question of Knollys' hyper-Calvinism needs to be more thoroughly examined from his writings. Was Knollys a hyper-Calvinist of the seventeenth century or a possible proto-hyper-Calvinist holding some hyper-Calvinist tenets?

It is undoubtedly true that a good portion of eighteenth-century Particular Baptists of London and of southeastern England went beyond High Calvinism into hyper-Calvinism.[12] But is it also true that Knollys was a hyper-Calvinist? In order to discover whether he was, the next sections of this chapter will examine the history and theology of High Calvinism and hyper-Calvinism, and compare Knollys' writings with them to see if he was a High Calvinist, and if he was, is there any indication that he went beyond it espousing hyper-Calvinism.

---

[10] Ivimey, *English Baptists*, III, 364-365.
[11] Culross, *Hanserd Knollys*, pp. 36-37.
[12] This is supported by such historians as Henry C. Vedder, *A Short History of the Baptists* (Philadelphia, 1907), pp. 239-241; W.T. Whitley, *A History of the British Baptists* (London, 1923), pp. 231-232; A.C. Underwood, *A History of the English Baptists* (London, 1947), pp. 134-135; Michael Watts, *The Dissenters*, I, 456-460; J. Ryland, *The Work of Faith, the Labour of Love, and the Patience of Hope, illustrated; in the Life and Death of the Rev. Andrew Fuller* (London, 1818), pp. 4-6; Peter Toon, *The Emergence of Hyper-Calvinism in English Nonconformity* (London, 1967), pp. 70-127; Raymond Brown, *The English Baptists of the 18th Century* (London, 1986), pp. 72-76; Alan P.F. Sell, *The Great Debate: Calvinism, Arminianism, and Salvation* (Grand Rapids, 1983), pp. 83-84; H. Leon McBeth, *The Baptist Heritage* (Nashville, Broadman Press, 1987), pp. 171-178; and Robert Edward Seymour, "John Gill, Baptist Theologian (1697-1771)" (unpublished Ph.D. dissertation, University of Edinburgh, 1954), pp. 25-27.

High Calvinism: Its History

The Reformed tradition has its roots in the teachings of Ulrich Zwingli and Heinrich Bullinger in Zurich, and John Calvin in Geneva, as well as in those of some lesser known Reformers such as Martin Bucer, Peter Vermigli, and Oecolampadius. Although the English Reformed community was influenced to a certain extent by all of these Reformers, Calvin's name and possibly his thought have most dominated English Reformed thought after the mid-sixteenth century and into the seventeenth century.[13] Calvin's theology, principally found in his *Institutes of the Christian Religion*, became foundational for future Reformed thought, including seventeenth-century English Puritan theology. Although there is debate as to what extent Calvin's thought developed in the Reformed community after his death, there is little doubt that it did develop.[14] This development of Calvin's theology began with his friend and successor in Geneva, Theodore Beza, and was popularized in England by the Cambridge theologian/preacher William Perkins and his disciple William Ames. Ames and Perkins were widely read throughout the seventeenth century in both England and New England, their works having gone through numerous printings.

Also influential on the English church at this time were the *Canons of Dort* which came out of the Synod of Dort of 1617. This Synod brought together Reformed theologians from different parts of Europe in order to answer the teachings of the Dutch Remonstrants who had articulated, in five points, the teachings of James Arminius. These *Canons* are the developed expression of what has come to be called High Calvinism.[15] By the Revolutionary years,

---

[13]   We recognize that this is up for debate. For example, Bullinger was very influential in England during Elizabeth's reign, e.g., his *Decades* were used as Homilies for the Church; and his correspondence with numerous leaders in the English church.

[14]   Those who see a distortion of Calvinism after Calvin include R.T. Kendall, *Calvin and English Calvinism to 1649* (New York, 1979) and Basil Hall, "Calvin against the Calvinists" in *John Calvin*, ed. G.E. Duffield (Appleford, 1966), pp. 19-37; and those that see a logical development of Calvinism implicit in Calvin include Paul Helm, *Calvin and the Calvinists* (Edinburgh, 1982), Richard Muller, *Christ and the Decrees: Christology and Predestination in Reformed Theology from Calvin to Perkins* (Grand Rapids, 1985), and Joel Beeke, *Assurance of Faith: Calvin, English Puritanism, and the Dutch Second Reformation* (New York, 1991).

[15]   For a discussion of High Calvinism on the Continent, and in Perkins in England, see Charles Robert Munson, "William Perkins Theologian of Transition" (unpublished Ph.D. dissertation, Case Western Reserve University, 1971), pp. 63-115.

many Puritans had embraced this Dortian High Calvinism. One of the more influential High Calvinists who most clearly articulated its theology was the Independent theologian/pastor John Owen.[16] He was one of the High Calvinists who had a hand in the production of the *Savoy Declaration* which served as the basis for the *London Baptist Confession* of 1677/89. Both documents are examples of High Calvinistic theology.

The Theology of High Calvinism and Hanserd Knollys

There are numerous reasons for the rise of High Calvinism. One in particular was a desire by those who immediately followed Calvin to systematize the Reformed faith as it developed. After Calvin, the Reformed faith was well established in places like Switzerland and England. How could it best be transmitted to the next generation? Would it not be logical to organize it and systematize it for easy learning? This is certainly what Beza and Perkins did. Furthermore, if the enemy of salvation by God's grace alone was Roman Catholic Pelagianism, would it not be wise to develop a system that guarded this truth? Would it not be wise to show that a person's salvation is totally of God by focusing on predestination and election which guards soteriology from any form of Pelagianism? In addition, the Reformed faith had to deal with heresies such as Socinianism, Arminianism, moralism and Baxterianism. These heresies helped Reformed theologians like Owen and Thomas Goodwin to sharpen and further develop their theology.[17] By mid-seventeenth century High Calvinism was well established.

What then was the theology of High Calvinism at this time? There are at least seven theological tenets or emphases that mark off High Calvinism from the Calvinism of that espoused by John Calvin. In this section of the chapter we will compare Knollys' writings with the seven tenets of High Calvinism to see if he is one. The first tenet of High Calvinism has to do with the placement of the doctrine of predestination. Calvin placed it in his *Institutes* in his section on salvation. The High Calvinists placed it under the doc-

---

[16]   See Wallace, *Puritans and Predestination*, pp. 144-157. Other important English High Calvinists of the seventeenth century include Thomas Goodwin and William Twisse.

[17]   Wallace, *Puritans and Presdestination*, pp. 144-157.

trine of God and His Providence at the beginning of their theologies. This is evident in Beza's *Tractationes Theologiae*, Jerome Zanchi's *Absolute Predestination*, William Perkins' *Golden Chain*, the *Irish Articles of Religion* of 1615, the *Westminster Confession of Faith*, and the *Savoy Declaration*. For example, the *Westminster Confession* in its third chapter (following the chapters on Holy Scripture and God the Trinity) entitled "Of God's Eternal Decree" states, "By the decree of God, for the manifestation of his glory, some men and angels are predestinated unto everlasting life, and others foreordained to everlasting death."[18] This same emphasis is also evident in the supralapsarian position of numerous men like Samuel Rutherford, William Twisse, Beza and Perkins who ordered the decrees in such a way that God's first decree is the decree to manifest justice and mercy in the salvation of some humans and the reprobation of others. According to this schema the decrees of the Creation and the Fall follow this one.

Knollys espoused this Puritan doctrine of predestination and election. Contrary to Calvin he believed that the doctrine of predestination should be placed under the doctrine of God instead of under the doctrine of salvation. This is evident from the 1644/46 *Confession* and the 1677/89 *Confession* both of which he signed. In the 1644/46 *Confession* the doctrine of predestination is located in the third article on the decrees of God (following a brief description of the Godhead in the first two articles). The third Article states,

> God hath decreed in himselfe before the world was concerning all things, whether necessary, accidentall or voluntary, with all circumstances of them, to worke, dispose, and bring about all things according to the counsell of his own will, to his glory (yet without being the Author of sin, or having fellowship with any, therein) in which appeares his wisdome in disposing all things, unchangeablenesse, power, and faithfulnesse in accomplishing his decree: and God hath before the foundation of the world, foreordained some men to eternall life, through Jesus Christ, to the praise and glory of his grace, leaving the rest in their sinne to their just condemnation, to the praise of his justice.[19]

In the 1677/89 *Confession* again in the third chapter on the decrees following the first two articles on the Scriptures and the Godhead, Knollys and others maintain,

---

[18] *Westminster Confession of Faith*, III.3.
[19] 1644/46 *Confession*, Article III.

By the *decree* of God, for the manifestation of his glory some men and Angels are predestinated, or fore-ordained to Eternal Life, through Jesus
Christ, to the praise of his glorious grace; others being left to act in their sin
to their just condemnation, to the praise of his glorious justice.... These
Angels and Men thus predestinated, and fore-ordained, are particularly,
and unchangeably designed, and their number so certain, and definite, that
it cannot be either increased, or diminished.... Those of mankind that are
predestinated to life, God, before the foundation of the world was laid,
according to his eternal and immutable purpose, and the secret Councel
and good pleasure of his will, hath chosen in Christ unto everlasting glory,
out of his meer free grace and love; without any other thing in the creature
as a condition or cause moving him thereunto.[20]

Predestination, under the subject of God's decrees, also appears in
his exposition of the book of Revelation. In it he writes, "By [*the
book of life*] is meant, *First,* The Decree of Gods Election, Phil. 4.3.
Whose Names are in the book of life, that is, in the Record or Decree of
Election.... This *Jesus* was the *Lamb* slain before the foundation of
the world ... in Gods Purpose and Decree of the Salvation of his
Elect, chosen in Christ before the foundation of the world."[21]
Knollys certainly espoused this High Calvinistic tenet.

The second mark of High Calvinism concerns the imputation of
Adam's guilt to every descendent within the framework of a Reformed federal theology. Calvin had not developed a federal theology but others did including Olevanius, Perkins, Ames and Owen.[22]
This federal theology taught that God made a "covenant of works"
with Adam at the time of his creation. If Adam fulfilled the re-

---

[20]   In William L. Lumpkin, *Baptist Confessions of Faith* (Philadelphia, 1959), pp. 254-
255. In other places Knollys mentions the Covenant of Grace with believers (*Christ
Exalted*, p. 36), and Election (*Ibid.*, p. 30); but none of these explicitly places the subject
in the context of God's decrees.
[21]   *Revelation*, pp. 49, 93.
[22]   Bullinger's covenant theology was somewhat different from Calvin's. Calvin
followed the Augustinian line of two covenants: a spiritual one or gospel (the New Testament) and a carnal one or law (the Old Testament). In addition, Calvin's emphasis
was on the unilateral unconditionality of the new covenant that ran from Adam's time
to the present. Bullinger also spoke of the one gospel covenant made with Adam but
emphasized the bilateral conditional nature of it. Although all the explicit elements of
federal theology are not present in Bullinger, they are there in embryo. See Charles S.
McCoy and J. Wayne Baker, *Fountainhead of Federalism: Heinrich Bullinger and the Covenantal
Tradition* (Louisville, 1991), pp. 22-26. Consequently, as a forerunner or fountainhead
of federal covenant theology he could be added to our list of federal covenant theologians. But we have refrained from doing so because we are concerned with the explicit
federal theology espoused by the early High Calvinists.

quirements of this covenant by perfect obedience he would have been granted eternal life with God. Adam, therefore, was made the representative or federal head of the human race. His innocence or guilt would be passed on to the rest of humanity depending on how he performed in the "covenant of works". When Adam failed to fulfill the "covenant of works" because of his disobedience and sin, all of humanity inherited Adam's guilt before God; Adam's guilt was imputed to all his posterity. This was clearly emphasized and taught by the High Calvinists. Calvin, on the other hand, taught that the morally depraved nature of Adam was transmitted from one generation to the next with very little emphasis on the imputation of Adam's guilt.[23] Owen states that Adam's failure to keep the conditions of the "covenant of works" brought "the guilt of condemnation upon all them in whose room he was a public person (being the head and natural fountain of them all, they all being wrapped up in the same condition with him by divine institution)."[24] The *Westminster Confession* agrees: "[Adam and Eve] being the root of all mankind, the guilt of this sin [the eating of the forbidden fruit] was imputed."[25] The Puritan, Matthew Poole, commenting on Romans 5:14 states, "Though infants did not sin like Adam, yet they sinned in Adam; the guilt of his sin was imputed to them."[26]

Knollys agreed with the High Calvinists and taught that God imputed Adam's guilt to every one of his descendents. This is clearly stated in the 1677/89 *Confession*:

> [Our first parents] being the root and by *Gods* appointment, standing in the room, and stead of all mankind; the guilt of the *Sin* was imputed, and *corrupted* nature conveyed, to all their posterity descending from them by ordinary generation, being now conceived in *Sin*, and by nature children of

---

[23] See his chapters on Original Sin in his *Institutes of the Christian Religion*, ed. John T. McNeill & trans. by Ford Lewis Battles (Philadelphia, 1977), and especially II.i.6. See also T.H.L. Parker, *Calvin: An Introduction to His Thought* (London, 1995), pp. 51-52.

[24] John Owen, *The Works of John Owen*, 16 vols, ed. William H. Goold (Edinburgh, 1968), X, 354.

[25] *Westminster Confession of Faith*, VI.3. See also the answer to the Larger Catechism's Question 25: "The sinfulness of that estate whereinto man fell consisteth in the guilt of Adam's first sin."

[26] Matthew Poole, *A Commentary on the Holy Bible* (McLean, VA, n.d.), III, 495. Also see Francis Turretin, *Institutes of Elenctic Theology*, ed. James T. Dennison, Jr. (Phillipsburg, 1992), I, 620. Commenting on 1 Cor. 15:22 he maintains that, '"In Adam all die" ..., that is, incur the guilt of death and condemnation. Therefore in the same one they also sinned and are held in a common blameworthiness with him."

wrath, the servants of *Sin*, the subjects of *death* and all other miseries, spiritual, temporary and eternal, unless the *Lord Jesus* set them free.[27]

In *Christ Exalted*, Knollys, without mentioning Adam, states, "The Scriptures of truth do testifie, that Jesus Christ having sought lost sinners doth save them; First, Christ doth save them from sinne,... That is to say, First, from the guilt and Imputation of sinne; For all have sinned ... and all the world is become guilty before God."[28]

The third distinguishing mark of High Calvinism was its emphasis on irresistible grace. Calvin did not use this term but did teach that a sinner will only come to Christ if drawn by the Holy Spirit.[29] However, this teaching was given a greater emphasis by the High Calvinists. For example, Owen, speaking on the work of the Holy Spirit in a person's regeneration, states, "This *internal efficiency* of the Holy Spirit on the minds of men, as to the event, is *infallible*, victorious, irresistible, or always efficacious.... As to that end whereunto of God it is designed, it is always prevalent or effectual, and cannot be resisted, or it will effectually work what God designs it to work."[30] The *Westminster Confession* under the title "Effectual Calling" states,

> All those whom God hath predestinated unto life, and those only, he is pleased, in his appointed and accepted time, effectually to call, by his word and Spirit, out of that state of sin and death ... to grace and salvation by Jesus Christ.... This effectual call is of God's free and special grace alone, not from any thing at all foreseen in man; who is altogether passive therein, until, being quickened and renewed by the Holy Spirit, he is thereby enabled to answer this call, and to embrace the grace offered and conveyed in it.[31]

---

[27]   In Lumpkin, *Baptist Confessions*, pp. 258-259.
[28]   *Christ Exalted*, p. 21.
[29]   For example, *Institute* III.ii.33-35. Calvin does not use the term "irresistible grace". See also Francois Wendel, *Calvin: Origins and Development of His Religious Thought*, trans. Philip Mairet (1963; Durham, NC, 1987), pp. 233-263. Calvin emphasizes both human responsibility and God's sovereignty in a person's salvation. The difference between Calvin and the High Calvinists is one of emphasis. The High Calvinists were prone to emphasize irresistible grace and pay less attention to human responsibility. See for example, *Savoy Declaration* XX:1-4, "Of the Gospel, and of the Extent of the Grace thereof.".
[30]   Owen, *Works*, III, 317-318.
[31]   *Westminster Confession of Faith*, X.1-2.

The *Canons of Dort* under the Third and Fourth Heads of Doctrine, Article XII state, "Regeneration ... is evidently a supernatural work, most powerful ... so that all in whose hearts God works in this marvelous manner are certainly, infallibly, and effectually regenerated, and do actually believe."[32]

Concerning this third tenet of High Calvinism, Knollys firmly taught irresistible grace and the effectual work of the Holy Spirit in salvation. This is evident in the 1644/46 *Confession* where it states in Article XXII, "Faith is the gift of God, wrought in the hearts of the Elect by the Spirit of God; by which faith they come to know and believe the truth of the Scriptures,... and ... are inabled to cast their soules upon this truth thus believed." And again in Article XXIV: "Faith is ordinarily begotten by the preaching of the Gospel, or word of Christ, without respect to any power or agency in the creature; but it being wholly passive, and dead in trespasses and sins, doth believe and is converted by no lesse power, then that which raised Christ from the dead."[33] In his sermons he explicitly tells his hearers that only God can convert them:

> You will say to me, Alas, here is my miserie, to wit,... I have no power of my selfe to receive Christ, to beleeve in him, and accept of him[.] True, it is not ... in him that willeth, nor him that runneth but in God, who sheweth mercy?... It is the exceeding greatnesse of his power to us-wards, who beleeve, which must be put forth in your hearts, to make you beleeve also, according to the working of his mighty power, which he wrought in Christ, when he raised him from the dead.... It is the meer mercy and free grace of God to drive you to Christ, which nothing but his everlasting love can move him to doe, Ier, 31.3.[34]

In the *Song of Solomon* Knollys teaches that the Spirit and power of grace are necessary in order for people to follow Christ. People need to be drawn by the Spirit because they have: 1) no active power in themselves to come to Christ; 2) no subjective power of themselves to submit to Christ; 3) a resisting power in their will to refuse the offers of grace; and 4) a contradicting power opposing the offers of grace in the preaching of the Gospel.[35] For Knollys

---

32   Philip Schaff, *The Creeds of Christendom* (1931; rpt. Grand Rapids, 1990), III, 590.
33   1644/46 *Confession.*
34   *Christ Exalted*, pp. 13-14. See also *Ibid.*, pp. 21, 32-33.
35   *Song of Solomon*, p. 13.

conversion was not something humans can achieve, it can only be accomplished by the grace of God and the power of the Holy Spirit effectually drawing the sinner to Christ.

The fourth tenet of High Calvinism teaches that Christ died for the elect only. This is never stated explicitly by Calvin but it was by his followers.[36] Calvin taught in his commentary on John 3:16 that God, out of his love, gave His only begotten Son for the "whole world".[37] And in 1 John 2:2 he agreed with the statement of the schoolmen that "Christ suffered sufficiently for the whole world but effectively only for the elect."[38] Some High Calvinists maintained this teaching but emphasized the latter aspect in their soteriology. For example, Owen taught the former in *Display of Arminianism* that,

[Christ's] death was of sufficient dignity to have been made a ransom for all the sins of every one in the world. And on this internal sufficiency of his death and passion is grounded the universality of evangelical promises;

---

[36]   This is a highly debated subject. The sheer volume of material debating the issue should indicate that Calvin's position is not easy to determine. I agree with Roger Nicole's statement in his review of the debate that "it is often stated – and with considerable propriety – that Calvin did not write an explicit treatment concerning the extent of the atonement, in fact did not deal with this precise issue in the terms to which Reformed theology had been accustomed.... [A] full discussion of the scope of the atonement is not found in Calvin's writings, and the assessment of his position in this area has been varied" ("John Calvin's View of the Extent of the Atonement," *Westminster Theological Journal*, 47 [1985], pp. 197-198). Nicole goes on to argue that Calvin did in fact hold to a definite atonement; and though I agree with Nicole I still maintain that Calvin's position is not as explicit as that of the High Calvinists. Paul Helm, in agreement with Nicole, states, "Bearing in mind what has so far been learned about Calvin [in Helm's book], it might be argued that he was committed to definite or limited atonement even though he was not committed himself, in express terms to such a view.... Calvin, not being a universalist, could be said to *be committed to* definite atonement, even though he does not *commit himself to* definite atonement. And, it could be added, there is sound reason for this. There was no occasion for Calvin to enter into argument about the matter, for before the Arminian controversy the extent of the atonement had not been debated expressly within the Reformed churches.... There are passages in Calvin which show that he held the doctrine of limited atonement, even though the doctrine does not gain the prominence in his writings that it did during later controversies" (*Calvin and the Calvinists*, pp. 17-18). Jonathan Rainbow discusses this question as well in his *The Will of God and The Cross*. In his chapter on Calvin's view of 'Christ's Death for the Elect', Rainbow cites numerous passages where Calvin taught that Christ redeemed the elect or was sacrificed for them. However, Calvin never states explicitly that Christ died for the elect only as later High Calvinists did ([Allison Park, PA, 1990], pp.110-116). This is why I say limited atonement is implicit in Calvin, but explicit in the High Calvinists.

[37]   John Calvin, *Calvin's New Testament Commentaries*, eds. David W. Torrance & Thomas F. Torrance (Grand Rapids, 1974), IV, 74-75.

[38]   *Calvin's New Testament Commentaries*, V, 244.

which have no such restriction in their own nature as that they should not
be made to all and every one, though the promulgation and knowledge of
them are tied only to the good pleasure of God's special providence.

However, this aspect received little attention in Owen. His major
emphasis was on the effectiveness of Christ's death. In the same
treatise he states, "The death of Christ is in divers places of the
Scriptures restrained to his 'people,' and 'elect,' his 'church,' and
'sheep'.... Christ died for them whom God gave unto him to be
saved.... He layeth down his life for the sheep committed to his
charge, [John]. X. 11. But all are not the sheep of Christ, all are
not given unto him of God to be brought to glory."[39] Owen even
maintained that the "world" in John 3:16 and I John 2:2 is the elect
only.[40] This High Calvinist doctrine has come to be known as "limited atonement" or "particular redemption" whereby Christ's
atonement on the cross was only on behalf of those whom the Father had given Him in the covenant of redemption based on the
decree of predestination. The *Westminster Confession* states, "The
Lord Jesus, by his perfect obedience and sacrifice of himself, which
he through the eternal Spirit once offered up unto God, hath fully
satisfied the justice of his Father; and purchased not only reconciliation, but an everlasting inheritance in the kingdom of heaven, for
all those whom the Father hath given unto him." And again, "God
did, from all eternity, decree to justify all the elect; and Christ did,
in the fulness of time, die for their sins."[41] Under the Second Head
of Doctrine of the *Canons of Dort*, Article VIII states,

> For this was the sovereign counsel and most gracious will and purpose of
> God the Father, that the quickening and saving efficacy of the most pre-
> cious death of his Son should extend to all the elect, for bestowing upon
> them alone the gift of justifying faith, thereby to bring them infallibly to
> salvation: that is it was the will of God, that by the blood of the cross ...
> [Christ] should effectually redeem out of every people, tribe, nation, and
> language, all those, and those only, who were from eternity chosen to salva-
> tion, and given to him by the Father.[42]

---

[39]   Owen, *Works*, X, 89, 91, 92.
[40]   *Ibid.*, X, 316-329 (John 3:16) and 330-338 (1 John 2:2). In the latter verse Owen
states "the whole world" signifies believers only.
[41]   *Westminster Confession of Faith*, VII.5; XI.4. See also XXIV.2 and the answer to
Question 44 of the *Larger Catechism*.
[42]   Schaff, *Creeds*, III, 587.

In his *Institutes* Francis Turretin uses much ink affirming the latter part of the question, "Did Christ die for each and every man universally or only for the elect?" In one place he states, "Christ was given and died for no others than those who were given to him by the Father."[43]

Knollys also held this High Calvinist teaching of particular redemption. Both of the *Confessions* which Knollys signed clearly taught that Christ died only for the elect. For example, in the 1644/46 *Confession* it states in Article XVII, "Concerning his Priesthood, Christ having sanctified himselfe, hath appeared once to put away sinne by that one offering of himselfe a sacrifice for sinne, by which he hath fully finished and suffered all things God required for the salvation of his elect." And again in Article XXI: "Jesus Christ by his death did purchase salvation for the Elect that God gave unto him: These onely have interest in him, and fellowship with him."[44] The same is affirmed in several places in the 1677/89 *Confession*; Chapter XI states, "God did from all eternity decree to justifie all the Elect, and Christ did in the fulness of time die for their sins, and rise again for their Justification."[45] In 1646 in *Christ Exalted* Knollys preached,

> Faith looks at Christ as a Saviour made sinne, made a Curse and crucified to redeem his Elect from the Curse due to sinne; What punishment the Law and justice of God could exact or require of sinners, that the Lord Jesus Christ suffered, & he hath fully satisfied his fathers justice for all the sinnes of all his people, Christ is therefore called our Surety.[46]

And again at the end of his life commenting on the reason the Lamb in Rev. 5:9 is "worthy to take the Book, and to open the seals thereof," he states, "*First*, Because [*thou wast slain*;] that is Crucified for the Sins of thy people, *Phil.* 2. 6-9. and *Heb.* 12. 2. *Secondly*, because thou [*hast Redeemed us to God by thy blood*;] that is, Christ by his

---

[43]   Turretin, *Institutes*, II, 463. In the Dennison edition Turretin writes 27 pages to answer this one question. On no other question in his *Institutes* does he spend as much time.

[44]   1644/46 *Confession*.

[45]   In Lumpkin, *Baptist Confessions*, p. 266. See also 1677/89 *Confession*, Chapters III.6 and XXX.2.

[46]   *Christ Exalted*, p. 23.

precious blood obtained *eternal* Redemption for us, (not for all,) *Heb.*
9. 12. for Gods elect; *that is*, Christ bought them."[47]

The fifth tenet of High Calvinism has to do with the distinction
between the active and passive righteousness of Christ with an emphasis on the imputation of Christ's righteousness. Dewey Wallace
states, "Insistence on the importance of the imputation of Christ's
righteousness came to be characteristic of high Calvinism." Calvin
did speak of a person's justification consisting in "the remission of
sins and the imputation of Christ's righteousness."[48] However, this
concept of justification was developed by later Reformed theologians into the active and passive righteousness of Christ. The active
righteousness of Christ consists in his perfect obedience to God's
law as the Incarnate Son of God on earth; the passive righteousness
is his submission to death on the cross. The former provides the
elect with his righteousness as fulfilling God's law, and the latter
provides for the remission of their sins; both are necessary for their
acceptance with God. This distinction that became commonplace
among High Calvinists of the seventeenth century began in Reformed circles with Theodore Beza.[49] Toon states, "Beza adopted
this distinction and taught that justification consists not only in the
forgiveness of sins through Christ's death, but also the imputation
of the righteousness of Christ founded upon His active obedience
to the law of God."[50] William Ames in his *Marrow of Theology* in the
chapter on Justification gives a prominent place to the "obedience
of Christ [as] that ... righteousness ... in the name of which the
grace of God justifies us." He goes on to say, "Therefore, the righteousness of Christ is imputed to believers in justification." And
again, "This righteousness ... arises ... with remission of sins, out of
Christ's total obedience."[51] The *Westminster Confession* in its chapter
on Justification states, "Those whom God effectually calleth he also
freely justifieth ... by pardoning their sins, and by accounting and

---

47   *Revelation*, p. 76. In addition, in *The World that now is* he taught that Christ is an
all-sufficient Saviour having made full satisfaction for the sins of all whom the Father
gave him to redeem (*World*, pt. 1, pp. 6-7).
48   Calvin, *Institutes*, III.xi.2. See also III.xi.3.
49   Theodore Beza, *Tractationes Theologiae*, III, 248ff, cited in Toon, *Hyper-Calvinism*,
p. 16. It probably originated with the Lutheran Flavius Illycricus and the Dane Nicolaus
Hemmingius.
50   Toon, *Hyper-Calvinism*, p. 16.
51   William Ames, *The Marrow of Theology*. Trans. By John Dykstra Eusden. (1968;
rpt. Durham, NC, 1983), pp. 162, 164.

accepting their persons as righteous ... by imputing the obedience and satisfaction of Christ unto them."[52] The *Savoy* is more explicit, "Those whom God effectually calleth he also freely justifieth ... by pardoning their sins, and by accounting and accepting their persons as righteous by imputing Christ's active obedience unto the whole law, and passive obedience in his death, for their whole and sole righteousness."[53] John Owen, one of the chief architects of the *Savoy*, in his work entitled, *Communion with God*, states,

> We may be not sinners, and yet not be so far righteous as to have a right to the kingdom of heaven. Adam had no right to life because he was innocent; he must, moreover, "do this," and then he shall "live." He must not only have a *negative* righteousness, — he was not guilty of any thing; but also a *positive* righteousness, he must do all things.... These two things, then, complete our grace of acceptation. Sin being removed, and righteousness bestowed, we have peace with God.... In remission of sin and imputation of righteousness doth it consist; from the death of Christ, as a price, sacrifice, and a punishment, — from the life of Christ spent in obedience to the law, doth it arise.[54]

With other High Calvinists Knollys also made a distinction between the active and passive righteousness of Christ with an emphasis on the imputation of Christ's righteousness. In this Knollys was at one with the High Calvinists. It was clearly taught in the 1677/89 *Confession*, Chapter XI:

> Those whom God effectually calleth, he also freely justifieth, not by infusing Righteousness in them, but by pardoning their sins, and by accounting, and accepting their Persons as Righteous; not for any thing wrought in them, or done by them, but for Christ's sake alone, not by imputing faith it self, the act of believing, or any other evangelical obedience to them as their Righteousness; but by imputing Christ's active obedience unto the whole Law, and passive obedience in his death, for their whole and sole Righteousness, they receiving, and resting on him and his Righteousness, by Faith; which faith they have not of themselves, it is the gift of *God*.[55]

---

[52]   *Westminster Confession of Faith*, XI.1.
[53]   *Savoy Declaration*, XI.1, in Williston Walker, *The Creeds and Platforms of Congregationalism* (New York, 1893).
[54]   Owen, *Works*, II, 170.
[55]   In Lumpkin, *Baptist Confessions*, pp. 265-266.

In *Christ Exalted* he states, "This righteousnesse of Christ must be imputed to him to Iustification of life, Rom. 5. 18. 19.... It is not [the sinner's] inherent qualifications, but the righteousnesse of Christ, whereby he must be justified before God."[56]

A sixth tenet which the High Calvinists taught was that the sufferings of Christ were the exact penalty due for the sins of the elect. This was a peculiarly Puritan tenet which "maximized the sufferings of Christ in order to exalt the extent of God's grace."[57] They spoke of Christ literally suffering the exact pains of the elect. This became a part of what came to be known as the *pietas crucis*. Calvin, however, did not speak in such terms. All that he would say in commenting on Isa 53:5 is that, "By these words [Isaiah's] means that Christ was put in place of evildoers as surety and pledge — submitting himself even as the accused — to bear and suffer all the punishments that they ought to have sustained."[58] This was not so for many Puritans.[59] For example, in response to Richard Baxter, John Owen writes,

> Christ paid the same thing that was in the obligation; as if, in things real, a friend should pay twenty pounds for him that owed so much, and not any thing in another kind.... I affirm that he paid *idem*, that is, the *same thing* that was in the obligation, and not *tantundem, something equivalent* thereunto, in another kind.... A commutation of persons is allowed, Christ undergoing the penalty of the offence; though he were not the person offending, I cannot but still suppose that he paid the *idem* of the obligation.... That the punishment which our Saviour underwent was the same that the law required of us, God relaxing his law to the person suffering, but not as to the penalty suffered.... There is a sameness in Christ's sufferings with that in the obligation in respect of essence, and equivalency in respect of attendancies.... In the meeting of our iniquities upon Christ, Isa. liii. 6, and his being thereby made sin for us, 2 Cor. V. 21, lay the very punishment of our sin, as to us

---

[56]   *Christ Exalted*, p. 18. Knollys in *The World that now is* stated that sinners must be covered with the robe of Christ's righteousness, and the garments of his salvation (*World*, pt. 1, p. 20).

[57]   Wallace, *Puritans and Predestination*, p. 153.

[58]   Calvin, *Institutes*, II.xvi.10.

[59]   Others include Henry Jacob, *A Treatise of the Sufferings and Victory, in the work of our Redemption* (1598), pp. 4, 7, 16-17, 22, 33-34, 36, 37-38 47, 73, 77-78; Christopher Shutte, *Compendious forme and summe of Christian doctrine* (1584), sig. C6; *Lectures of I.B. upon the XII Articles of our Christian Faith, briefly set forth for the comfort of the godly*, sig. Fviii, cited in Wallace, *Puritans and Predestination*, pp. 48-49, 212.

threatened, upon him.... It was no less than the weight of the wrath of God and the whole punishment due to sin that he wrestled under.[60]

Knollys espoused this sixth High Calvinist tenet that the sufferings of Christ are the exact penalty due for the sins of the elect. This is taught in the 1677/89 *Confession*, Chapter XI states,

> Christ by his obedience, and death, did fully discharge the debt of all those that are justified; and did by the sacrifice of himself, in the blood of the cross, undergoing in their stead, the penalty due unto them: make a proper, real, and full satisfaction to Gods justice in their behalf; yet in asmuch as he was given by the Father for them, and his Obedience and Satisfaction accepted in their stead, and both freely, not for anything in them; their Justification is only of Free Grace, that both the exact justice and rich Grace of God, might be glorified in the Justification of sinners.[61]

Moreover, in *The World that now is*, Knollys stated that Christ had made "full satisfaction" for the sins of all them whom the Father had given him.[62]

A seventh tenet was that assurance of salvation was based mainly upon one's sanctification, using the practical syllogism. As was evident in the third chapter, both England and New England Puritans believed sanctification to be the primary means of assurance for the believer. The believer, therefore, was to examine herself to see if the fruits of sanctification were present. If they were present, then she could be assured that she was one of the elect. This way of determining assurance was motivated by predestinarian theology. People would ask, "How do I know I am one of the elect?" Calvin would answer, "Have you trusted in Christ as your Saviour?"[63] The Puritans, on the other hand, were more prone to ask, "Is there any evidence of saving faith in your life?"[64] Joel Beeke has rightly shown

---

[60]   Owen, *Of the Death of Christ* in *Works*, X, 438, 443, 447, 448, 449.

[61]   In Lumpkin, *Baptist Confessions*, p. 266. See also Article VIII.4 in *Ibid.*, pp. 261-262.

[62]   *World*, pt. 1, pp. 6-7.

[63]   Calvin taught that assurance was of the very essence of faith. He defined faith as "a firm and certain knowledge of God's benevolence toward us, founded upon the truth of the freely given promise in Christ, both revealed to our minds and sealed upon our hearts by the Holy Spirit" (*Institutes*, III.ii.7).

[64]   For more on this see William Chalker, "Calvin and Some Seventeenth Century Calvinists" (unpublished Ph.D. dissertation, Duke University, 1961), pp. 61-66; Wilhelm Niesel, *The Theology of Calvin* (London, 1956), pp. 169-181; and R.M. Hawkes, "The

that assurance for Calvin, Beza, Perkins, the Westmister Divines and John Owen included: 1) the believer's trust in the promise of salvation in Christ; 2) the inner testimony of the Holy Spirit; and 3) the *Syllogismus Practicus.* But it is also clear that Calvin was more prone to emphasize the first and second, while the Puritans and High Calvinists the third. For example, William Perkins taught that a person can determine whether he has justifying faith by examining his own life, for he says,

> Now if any man would know, whether his faith be sound, and sauing, or no; it is knowne by this: If it purifie the heart.... If then thy faith doe not purifie thy heart, and cleanse thy life, and cause thee to abound in good workes, it is no sound nor sauing faith, it is but a generall faith, it is but an historical knowledge, & cannot saue the soule: he therefore that vpon examination of his heart and life, findeth his faith to bee such, let him not content himselfe, but turne his generall *faith* into a sauing faith, which in this world will *purifie his heart*, and at the last day will *saue his soule.* And this must euery man rather doe, because what knowledge, or what other gifts of God soeuer any man hath, without *faith* in Christ all are nothing: for it is faith that seasoneth them all, and makes both them and the person himselfe to please God.[65]

As a corollary to this emphasis on sanctification as a means of assurance, there followed the theology of preparationism which has

---

Logic of Assurance in English Puritan theology," *Westminster Theological Journal,* 52 (1990), pp. 247-261. Hawkes acknowledges that, "the Puritans distinguish a simple saving faith from a developed assurance" which was not so prevelant in the Reformers. John Owen believed that the early reformers sometimes '"place[d] the *essence* of faith in the *highest acting* of it,' confusing a necessary initial trusting in Christ with an assurance of salvation based on a continuing life in Christ" (*Ibid.,* p. 250). Richard Sibbes maintained, "The most familiar way of knowledge about our estates is from the effects to gather the cause" (Quoted in *Ibid.,* p. 255). Hawkes concludes, "The believer's assurance revolves around the foci of a fixed, completed salvation in Christ, a daily obedience, and an evaluation to see the work of God in the believer, establishing a closer conformity to God's immutable will, a deeper knowledge of his infinite goodness. Thus does the believer grow into a full realization of the greatness of the salvation that is his from eternity. This is the very hopeful message of the Puritans' doctine of assurance" (*Ibid.,* pp. 260-261). Joel Beeke also notes the change of emphasis on sanctification for assurance between the Puritans and Calvin when he states, "By raising the secondary grounds of assurance [the syllogisms and the witness of the Spirit] to a 'mainline' from the 'sideline' they occupied in Calvin's thought, the post-Reformers were only enlarging for fresh pastoral reasons" (*Assurance,* p. 365).

   65   William Perkins, *A Clovvd of Faithful Witnesses, Leading to the heavenly Canaan: Or, A commentarie upon the 11. Chapter to the Hebrews* (1609; rpt. New York, 1991), pp. 26-27.

been well examined by Baird Tipson and Norman Petitt.[66] This was first articulated by Perkins in England but developed by both New England and England Puritans. Perkins taught that a person with saving but weak faith could look at his life to see if the evidences of faith were present.[67] These evidences were articulated as steps prior to, through, and after conversion. These steps in Puritan circles became a means by which a person could determine whether she had justifying/saving faith, and consequently, whether she was one of the elect or not.[68] Through Perkins and Ames this emphasis on sanctification as an evidence of assurance became a major part of the fabric of Puritan practical theology. This is evident in the *Westminster Confession* in Chapter 18 on Assurance; the Divines speak of assurance in the first two paragraphs as consisting in trust in the divine promises of salvation in Christ, the testimony of the Holy Spirit, and the inward evidence of saving graces. However, in paragraph three they state that "this infallible assurance doth not so belong to the essence of faith, but that a true believer may wait long, and conflict with many difficulties, before he be partaker of it." This is quite contrary to Calvin.[69] In the same chapter on Assurance the *Savoy Declaration* is in total agreement with *Westminster*.

Another important Puritan work that emphasizes sanctification as a means of assurance for the believer is the popular *Marrow of Modern Divinity* by E.F. Written in the 1640s the work is a polemic against Antinomianism and Arminianism. In it, the author spends much time explaining how a believer can "attain to assurance," as well as presenting "marks and evidences of true faith," and "marks

---

[66] Norman Pettit, *The Heart Prepared: Grace and Conversion in Puritan Spiritual Life* (Middletown, CT, 1989); Tipson, "The Development of a Puritan Understanding of Conversion" (unpublished Ph.D. dissertation, Yale University, 1972).

[67] On Perkins see Beeke, *Assurance*, pp. 105-118.

[68] Ames in his *Conscience with the Power and Cases Thereof* (1639) gives eight signs by which a person can discern if he is in a state of sin or if sin reigns in him; moreover, he explains how a sinner ought to prepare himself for conversion by outlining steps like Perkins does; in addition, he outlines four signs by which the believer can determine whether he has been effectually called, and how a weak faith may be discerned to be a true faith (II. 4-16).

[69] See note above on Calvin's definition of faith. It is true that the Puritans emphasis on sanctification as a means of assurance was pastoral (Sinclair Ferguson, *John Owen on the Christian Life* [Edinburgh, 1987], pp. 99-100) and not primarily theological. But Calvin was also a pastor and his *Institutes* were not written devoid of a pastor's heart. Calvin's definition of faith and assurance is based on pastoral experience as well as theological exactness.

and signs of union with Christ." In answer to the question, "How may I be assured that I have faith in Christ?" E.F. answers, "The next way [the first way was the direct act of faith] to find out and know this is to look back and reflect upon your own heart, and consider what actions have passed through there." For E.F. these include: past conviction that you are a sinful person and, consequently, fear of the Lord's wrath and Hell; recognition of helplessness in yourself to acquire this condition; realisation that Christ is your only help; realisation that He is willing to receive you; a consenting to take Christ and to give yourself unto Him; a sensing in your heart that Christ loves you, and you love Him; and a manifestation of this love in "an unfeigned desire to be obedient and subject to his will in all things, and never to displease him in anything." E.F. concludes, "[If you have them in some measure] then I tell you truly, you have a sure ground to lay your believing that you have believed upon." He further gives three other evidences of believing: 1) love for the Word of God and a right use of it; 2) love for the children of God; and 3) love for your enemies.[70] E.F. spends far more time on the evidence of sanctification for assurance than on the exercise of faith in the promise of salvation in Christ. E.F.'s emphasis on evidences for assurance is representative of most Puritans of the seventeenth century.[71] Moreover, John von Rohr has shown the close connection between the Puritan understanding of the covenant in its relation to the individual and assurance. He states, "The problem for each individual was one of knowing whether the covenant had actually been extended to him. Thus Puritan thought turned time and again to the question of evidences, and the evidences themselves were found largely in experience."[72] This, however, did not entail semi-pelagianism for the Puritans because they firmly believed that faith, repentance, and all the fruit of the

---

[70]   E.F., *Marrow of Modern Divinity* (n.d.; reprint Edmonton, 1991), pp. 235-239.

[71]   See Hawkes, "Logic of Assurance," pp. 247-261; John Von Rohr, "Covenant and Assurance in Early English Puritanism," *Church History*, 34 (1965), pp. 195-203; John Von Rohr, *The Covenant of Grace in Puritan Thought* (Atlanta, 1986), pp. 155-191; and Beeke, *Assurance*, pp. 158-169, 361-382.

[72]   Von Rohr, "Covenant," pp. 196-197. He goes on to say, "Thus the motion [the stirring of spiritual life in a true believer] of God's covenant working is to be seen most clearly in the impulses and actions of a new life. Sanctification is the test of justification, and even as Jacob's ladder reached from earth to heaven, we can ascend in assurance by starting at the bottom rung of awareness of God's sanctifying gifts and then by moving upward until at the height our calling and election become fully sure" (p. 198).

Spirit (e.g., the evidences of salvation) were given by God's grace.

As we discovered in chapter three Knollys agreed with the High Calvinists that assurance was based on one's sanctification. In 1646 he states,

> Therefore make sure that Christ is yours. Some would ask this question, How shall I so examine, that I may know assuredly that I have Christ? I answer, you must bring your hearts to the touchstone of the Word of God, and cast them into the balance of the Sanctuary and weigh them there. And to this purpose, I shall propound one Scripture of truth for your examination and tryall, to wit, 2 Cor. 5.17.... To wit; first he is made a new man.... Secondly, he hath a new heart [new will, affections, judgment, and understanding].... Thirdly he walks in newness of life ... That is, the conversation of a new creature should be such as becomes the Gospel ... To wit, humble, harmlesse, and holy.... Examine your selves, Are you a new creature? Such of you as have not put off the old man, but still have your old hearts, and your old sins, and walk in your old wayes, and fulfill the old lusts of your sinful natures, are not a new creature, you are not in Christ, nor Christ in you.[73]

Again, in his *Parable of the Kingdom of God Expounded*, Knollys answers how wise virgins may know they have attained the power of godliness and not just the form. He exhorted the wise virgins to examine their lives: 1) by the victory they have attained over the world, Satan and their sins; 2) by the lively acts and constant exercise of grace; and 3) by their holy conversation in the world.[74] Knollys asks the wise virgins among his readers, "Art thou an Isrealite indeed? Dost thou worship God in spirit and Truth? Hast thou both the form and power of Godliness? Then be of good Comfort. For ... Christ is thine.... God is thy Father, Grace is thy portion, and Heaven is thine Inheritance, Holiness is thy way, and Happiness will be thine end."[75] It is clear that Knollys believed that a Christian's assurance was based on his sanctification.[76]

---

[73] *Christ Exalted*, pp. 7-8.

[74] *Parable*, pp. 51-52.

[75] *Ibid.*, p. 47.

[76] Knollys did, however, recognize that a person could gain a false asssurance from his duties when he says, "The poore sinner prayes still, reads the Scriptures, heares the Word, is both constant, and conscionable [*sic*] in the performance of holy duties, but now he cannot ... raise his hopes of salvation[,] gather his comforts in promises, nor conclude his assurance of eternall life from his duties done, because he knows not whether Christ be his or no, and whether or no he performs those duties from the spirit

With regard to preparationism we also saw in the last chapter that to a certain extent Knollys believed a person could prepare herself for salvation. He, however, denied that we can save our-selves by our religious performances. He stated in *Christ Exalted*, "They thinke to save themselves by seeking, praying, mourning, reforming &c. And considers [*sic*] not, that Christ must seek and save them. They will take the work out of his hand, and thinke to do it themselves, by their humiliations, duties, &c."

On the other hand, as we saw in the previous chapter, Knollys also maintained that the sinner is to use *means* in order to bring about her conversion. He states,

> Gods gracious and free promises doe not exclude the meanes he hath ap-pointed to attaine the mercies therein promised. It pleaseth him to tye his creatures to the use of meanes, when he affords it them, though he will sometimes worke without it. Now the ordinarie meanes which God hath in his infinite wisedome appointed to convert sinners ... is the Word preached.[77]

Furthermore, in the *Parable of the Kingdom of God Expounded* Knollys shows how a sinner buys the oil necessary for salvation:

> 1. A sense of want and need of it, which the foolish Virgins ... had [when the bridegroom had come at midnight]. 2. Attending upon the Ministry of the word and Administrations of the Gospel to obtain it or get some of this Oyle, having their heart and hand open and willing to receive it, Acts 16. 14.... 3. a willingness to have it upon Christs own terms of free Grace, with-out money and without price, Isa. 55. 1, 2, 3. & Rev. 21.6. 22. 7.[78]

Is this not a brand of preparationism presented here by Knollys? In another place Knollys outlined his own morphology of salvation by teaching that a sinner comes to salvation first through conviction, then through spiritual illumination in the saving knowledge of Jesus Christ, and finally, following conversion, through sanctification. Knollys believed that the work of conviction brings the sinner through several stages: 1) he sees and is convicted of his sinful na-

---

of life in Christ" (*Christ Exalted*, p. 18).

[77] *Christ Exalted*, p. 12. See also *Ibid.*, pp. 13, 14. Preaching to sinners he says, "And you ought to wait on God in the diligent use of meanes untill the day of his power come upon you, and then you shall be a willing, a beleeving people" (p. 13).

[78] *Parable*, pp. 108-109.

ture, original corruption, actual sins; 2) he begins to have fears of Hell, death and damnation; 3) he sets upon reformation, performing holy duties; 4) he sees himself as an unbeliever and so cannot be saved until he believes.[79]

Knollys did hold this seventh High Calvinist tenet of sanctification as a means of assurance, and of preparation for salvation. It is evident from this brief study of Knollys' soteriology that he was a High Calvinist. In addition, it should be noted that he endorsed two High Calvinist treatises in the 1640s, Robert Garner's *Mysteries Unvailed wherein the Doctrine of Redemption by Jesus Christ, flowing from the glorious Grace, and everlasting Love of God, the very fountain of Life and Salvation unto lost Sinners, is handled* (1646), and Thomas Collier's *The Exaltation of Christ in the dayes of the gospel: as the alone High Priest, Prophet, and King, of Saints*.[80] Concerning the former treatise Knollys states in the "Epistle,"

[In this treatise] the most usuall Scriptures (which are alledged by after *Den. Thomas Moore, Thomas Lambe* [General Baptists], and others to prove the Universality of the Death of Christ, extended to all persons) are explanted, and freed from the corrupt sense, and unfounded interpretations, which are put upon them: And the most weighty Reasons urged by them in defence of that their Opinion are fully and clearly answered.[81]

Knollys not only taught High Calvinism but also sought to encourage its dissemination through these treatises in order to help his Particular Baptist brethren counter Arminian arguments. The question remains, did he go beyond High Calvinism and espouse hyper-Calvinism? In the next section we will look at the history of hyper-Calvinism with special emphasis upon the eighteenth-century Calvinistic Baptists, and in particular, John Skepp, and then exam-

---

[79] *World*, pt. 1, pp. 10-34. He considered this work of conviction very important because, for him, a lack of a thorough work of conviction was the cause of the lack of a sound and saving work of conversion (*Ibid.*, p. 22).

[80] That these are High Calvinist treatises, see Pope Duncan, *Hanserd Knollys*, pp. 16-18, and Richard D. Land , "Doctrinal Controversies of English Baptists (1644-1691) as Illustrated by the Career and Writings of Thomas Collier" (unpublished Ph.D. dissertation, Oxford University, 1979), pp. 306-311. Collier was a High Calvinist in his early career. Knollys wrote "Epistles" for both of these works.

[81] "The Epistle Dedicatory to the Churches of God in London and elsewhere in all places with the Bishops and Deacons", in Robert Garner, *Mysteries Unvailed*.

ine the theology of its foremost Baptist proponents, John Gill and John Brine, comparing their writings with Knollys'.

Hyper-Calvinism: Its History

Hyper-Calvinism grew out of High Calvinism in the early eighteenth century.[82] It was preceeded by the Antinomian Controversy of the 1690s out of which a rigid Calvinism and a moderate Calvinism were clearly distinguished. This Controversy began with the republication of sermons of the alleged antinomian Tobias Crisp, entitled, *Christ alone exalted, being the compleat works of Tobias Crisp* (1689-90). Shortly after its appearance, Richard Baxter, the self-appointed anti-antinomian, condemned the republication and its antinomian contents, particularly its teaching on the imputation of sin to Christ. Samuel Crisp defended his father's doctrine as Biblical and orthodox in *Christ made sin* (1691). In this same year the "Happy Union" between Presbyterians and Independents ministers was formed. This Union was born out of weekly lectures in which both Dissenting groups had taken part at Pinner's Hall since 1673.[83] They called themselves the "United Ministers" and agreed to hold regular assemblies together, and to assent to certain articles of Faith and Order. Within four years the Happy Union was dissolved because of infighting over antinomianism. The main contenders were the Independents Thomas Cole and Nathaniel Mather, espousing Crispianism, against the Presbyterian Daniel Williams, a moderate Calvinist who carried the torch after Baxter died in 1691. In 1694 the subscribers of the Pinner's Hall lectureship expelled Williams. Consequently, the three other Presbyterian lecturers left with Williams to form a new lectureship at Salter's Hall. The two parties separated primarily for doctrinal reasons and in the following years were unable to be reunited.[84]

---

[82]   Concerning the name hyper-Calvinist and its history see Daniel, "John Gill," pp. 746ff. It appears that Andrew Fuller is the first to use the term (*Ibid.*, p. 751). However, as Daniel notes the *Oxford English Dictionary* does quote a Hickman as having used it in 1674.

[83]   These lectures were funded by the merchants, and given at the Glass House in Old Broad Street, later renamed Pinner's Hall.

[84]   The things upon which they differed included justification by grace and the power of synods (Toon, *Hyper-Calvinism*, p. 51). In addition, the division was exacer-

In 1692 Williams published his anti-antinomian work entitled, *Gospel-Truth Stated and Vindicated wherein some of Dr. Crisp's opinions are considered*. Sixteen Presbyterian ministers signed a preface stating their agreement with Williams' assessment of Crisp's teaching. Many Congregationalists and Particular Baptists, though not fully in agreement with Crisp on all points, felt it better to side with Crisp erring on the side of exalting God's free grace as opposed to Williams quasi-grace and works-salvation. Until the end of the century this dispute persisted with pamphlets being exchanged between the two groups.[85]

The main points of controversy included the doctrines of justification, Christ's satisfaction, and eternal justification as well as practical issues such as the conditionality of the covenant of grace, neonomianism, assurance, and the preaching of the Gospel.[86] This controversy between the two groups made it virtually impossible to restore the Happy Union. And even when the fighting ceased in 1700 the Union was never restored. Peter Toon concludes, "The controversy served to harden each side in its respective theological position."[87] This prepared the way for further development of doctrine on both sides of the dispute: the High Calvinists became more rigid with some espousing what came to be called ultra-Calvinism or hyper-Calvinism; and the moderate Calvinists became more liberal with some eventually espousing Unitarianism. From the time of the dispute to the early eighteenth century, a more rigid Calvinism spread throughout England in three ways: through Crisp's re-published sermons and the pamphlets of his defenders, in particular, through the many influential writings of Isaac Chauncey; through the theological academies where young men were trained for ministry; and through the preaching of Richard Davis and his lay-preachers.[88]

---

bated by the preaching ministry of the Northhamptonshire Independent pastor, Richard Davis. He was an antinomian of the Crispian mould, and was consequently attacked by Williams in 1692. The assembly of the United Ministers sought to deal with Davis' alleged errors but no decision was made. The assembly failed to handle this problem successfully, encouraging its subsequent demise.

[85] For more on this controversy and the disputants see *Ibid.*, p. 52-54.

[86] For the doctrinal differences between the moderate and rigid Calvinists in this dispute see *Ibid.*, pp. 54-65. See also Wallace, *Puritans and Predestination*, pp. 181-182.

[87] Toon, *Hyper-Calvinism*, p. 65.

[88] *Ibid.*, p. 66.

It was in 1706 and 1707 that hyper-Calvinism was born in the person and writings of Joseph Hussey (b. 1660). In these two years he published two works entitled, *The Glory of Christ Unveil'd or the excellency of Christ Vindicated* (1706) and *God's Operations of Grace but No Offers of His Grace* (1707). Hussey had been a pastor to a Presbyterian Church in Cambridge since 1688 and was, therefore, certainly aware of, and to some degree involved in, the disputes between the moderate and rigid Calvinists. From the years 1694-1705 Hussey comprehensively studied the writings of many past and present theologians including Athanasius, Augustine, Aquinas, Arminius, Calvin, Beza, Amyraldus, Luther and Socinus.[89] Thus in *Glory of Christ* he wrote,

> I declare, therefore, that wherein I go contrary to many Good Men, I do it after an *examining* of their writings, and weighing books at the *Sanctuary Scales* (a labour that hath been now upon my hands more than *Ten* Years past) and good reason, to go by God's *Word* and *Spirit* at last having been carried away with much *Deceit* in many *other writings*, and by too many of some of our good men who have found more Goodness to mean well, than judgement to open all well they have undertook.[90]

He believed that after this study he had landed on true doctrine even to the point of criticising his own publication of 1693 entitled, *The Gospel Feast Opened* in which he openly presented the Gospel and freely invited his readers to trust in Christ. In his 1706 and 1707 books Hussey expounded his new found theology. At least four of his teachings are important for our discussion. First, he held a supralapsarian position on predestination. Second, he believed that justification is eternal. Third, he argued that assurance is based on the testimony of the Holy Spirit whispering "you are elect". And fourth, he asserted that the gospel should not be offered to sinners indiscriminately because it will not help them become Christians (only the irresistible grace of God can make a sinner a Christian).

Concerning the last doctrine, he could find no support from any previous theologians.[91] He, however, gave three reasons for adopt-

---

[89] *Ibid.*, pp. 73-74. See also his list of theologians consulted in *God's Operations*, "The Epistle to the Ministers," p. III.

[90] Quoted in Toon, *Hyper-Calvinism*, p. 74. Similar quote in *God's Operations*, "The Epistle to the Ministers," pp. II-IV.

[91] Toon, *Hyper-Calvinism*, pp. 74-82; Hussey, *God's Operations*, pp. 61-63.

ing his position. One, he distinguished between "preaching" and "offering Christ". Noah and Paul preached Christ openly but the Scriptures do not teach that they offered Christ openly. Second, logically it is of no use to offer salvation to sinners unless they are irresistibly drawn. Only irresistible grace will make them Christians. Third, the gifts of eternal life and the Holy Spirit are only intended for the elect whom the Father has given to the Son before the world began. For Hussey this meant that ministers ought to preach Christ to all but not offer salvation to all.[92] In *God's Operations* he gave twenty propositions answering the question, "How must we preach the Gospel to sinners, if we do not offer the Gospel to 'em?" They are:

1. We must *Preach* the Gospel, as it always stands with the *Reconciliation* of Sinners to God, through *the Gift by Grace*, in the Imputation of the Righteousness of God in Christ to them....

2. We must Preach the Gospel, as the Gospel is the Way or Means of God's bestowing the *Holy Spirit* on the Elect, and the Way and Means of our *Exalting* the Gift of God herein. It's God's Gift of the Spirit [that] must be exalted: But an *Offer* exalts not the Gift of God's Spirit. The Gift bestowed....

3. We must Preach the Gospel as it is most fitted unto *Effectual Grace*. And where is He that will *Presume* to talk of an Effectual *Offer*? God saith, *Thou shalt not steal*.... Yet He who dares give the Attributes of *the Gospel of God* ... to his *own Offers* ... Steals from God to dress up his *own Idol*....

4. We must Preach the Gospel so Evangelically, as, it's no ways fitted to glory in the Creature ... *we Preach not our selves but Christ Jesus the Lord*....

5. We must Preach the Gospel so as it's fitted, under the exalted Operations of the Spirit, to beat down the Practical *Arminianism* of all our Natures.... *Arminianism* is the Universal *Nature* of Mankind....

6. We ought to Preach the Gospel *accountably*, so as to be in some good Measure able in the Light of the Lord to determine and clear the Matter, *when* Christ and Salvation are effectually given, and *where*, and in *whose Hands* the Gift of Salvation lies....

7. We must so Preach the Gospel as to take a special Care that we clear the *Spirit's Work* in all the *Creature's Acts*, and in the most *Applicative* and Practical Truths we Preach....

8. We ought to Preach the Gospel in the Way of an *Institution* of Christ. The Command runs to Preaching the Word, 2 *Tim*. 4. 2.... But there is no Command for *Offers*....

---

[92] *Ibid.*, pp. 36-38, 60-61, 112-113, 204-207; Toon, *Hyper-Calvinism*, pp. 80-81.

9. We ought to Preach the Gospel as it lies under a special [Promise] of Success....

10. We should Preach the Gospel so as the Gospel will boldly *justify its self.* For the Gospel in all the Parts of it being of one Piece of Grace is *fitted* so to do....

11. We should Preach the Gospel as Certain in its *Individuations*, or Particular Interests for *Me*, for *Thee*. But *Offers* are all *Indeterminate* to any Body, and so indeed are fix'd upon no Body.

12. We should Preach the Gospel as it's *discover'd* to be an admirable *Contrivance of Way and Means* to effect Salvation....

13. We ought to Preach the Gospel so as it riseth higher than any *Natural*, Unconverted, *Notional* Man in the World can either *receive* it by a *Practical* closing with it, or carry it in the *Pulpit* towards such a Reception of it in the *Pews* before a Change....

14. We should Preach the Gospel *Singularly*, as the greatest Part of Professing Ministers do *not* Preach it....

15. You ought to Preach the Gospel *indeed*, and that will be so as not to give this open *Scandal*, and Offence *to such as are most led by God the Spirit* into His own Work. *Offers*, contrary to the Preaching of the Gospel, *offend* such as are most led into the *Spirit*'s Work....

16. You ought to Preach the Gospel in the *Encouragements* of it unto Salvation. But Offers are no Encouragements to Salvation....

17. We should Preach the Gospel so Spiritually and *discerningly* that the more our Preaching is *examined*, cavill'd at, despised, struck at and hated, the more it should be still seen both from the *Pulpit* and the *Press*, how sweetly it accords with the *Spirit*'s Work. But *Offers* the more they are examin'd, struck at, oppos'd and *argued down*, the more injurious they are still found to the *Spirit*'s Work....

18. We must Preach the Gospel so as Christ may *see* in it *of the Travel of his Soul and be satisfy'd*....

19. We should Preach the Gospel so as Satan *doth* not, *cannot* Preach in his Temptations and Allurements, *That is*, we should exalt what has from God an *Irresistible* Influence to *over-power* our Corruptions, and free our Wills of Slavery and Bondage to Sin.... Offers are Satan's way of *Pleasure*, *Profit* and *Worldly Friendship* to [damn] the Non-Elect....

20. We must Preach the Gospel with a Humble *Confidence* and a Holy Cautionary Fear, that we do not lean with too much *Stress* upon the *Creature*, but express the *Whole* of our Confidence as to the Success of our Preaching, in the *Lord alone*. But *Offers* are *Presumptuous*....[93]

---

[93]   *God's Operations*, pp. 155, 162, 165, 193, 198, 210, 216, 217, 218, 222, 223, 225-6, 233, 237, 241, 243, 243-244, 255, 256-257, 257.

Hussey's immediate influence fell upon three men, Samuel Stockell, William Bentley and John Skepp.[94] The one who is most important for this study is John Skepp.[95] Skepp had been a member of Hussey's church, imbibing his teaching.[96] In August 1714 he left the Cambridge church and became pastor of the Particular Baptist Church that met in Currier's Hall, Cripplegate.[97] Skepp only wrote one work, published posthumously, entitled, *Divine Energy or the Operations of the Spirit of God upon the soul of man in his effectual calling and conversion, stated, proved, and vindicated ... being an antidote against the Pelagian error* (1722). The title's similarity to Hussey's 1707 book is significant. Skepp's influence was felt by Particular Baptists in London and Cambridgeshire. In particular, he had an enormous influence upon two London Baptist ministers, John Gill and John Brine. Skepp took part in Gill's ordination, and encouraged him in Hebrew studies; and when Skepp died in 1722 Gill purchased many of his books.[98] Brine became the pastor of Skepp's church in the 1730s.[99] Murdina MacDonald in her study of early eighteenth-century London Baptists makes this comment on Skepp's theological influence:

---

[94] Stockell was a member of Hussey's church, and later became a pastor of an Independent church at Red Cross Street from 1730 to 1753. He developed a Supralasarian Christology and propagated a *no-offer* preaching of the Gospel (Toon, *Hyper-Calvinism*, pp. 44, 46). Bentley was a minister of a Congregational church in the 1730s which met at Crispin Street, Southwark.

[95] Curt Daniel states that the most important hyper-Calvinists of the period between 1690 and 1720 were Davis, Hussey and Skepp ("John Gill," p. 9).

[96] MacDonald, "London Calvinistic Baptists 1689-1727: Tensions within a Dissenting Community Under Toleration" (unpublished Ph.D. dissertation, Oxford University, 1982), p. 120; Ivimey, *English Baptists*, III, 363. Curt Daniel states that Skepp agreed with Hussey on "all essential points at the time of his [conversion]" ("John Gill," p. 6). Robert Seymour ("Gill," p. 54), and Walter Wilson (*The History and Antiquities of Dissenting Churches and Meeting Houses in London, Westminster and Southwark* [London, 1808], II, 572) agree with Daniel. Daniel and Seymour also state that Skepp was the first Baptist hyper-Calvinist to not offer the gospel (Daniel, "John Gill," pp. 6, 366; Seymour, "Gill," pp. 54-55).

[97] MacDonald, "Calvinistic", p. 120.

[98] Gill edited Skepp's *Divine Energy* in 1751, and in it wrote, "Mr. John Skepp was a man of singular talents and abilites; of very quick, strong, natural parts; of great diligence and industry in acquiring useful knowledge; a warm and lively preacher of the gospel; a zealous defender of the special and peculiar doctrines of it: whose ministry was blessed to many souls, for the conversion of some, and for the edification of others." In addition, Gill mentions his relationship and influence on him and others with these words, "Being personally and intimately known by [Gill], and whose memory was precious to [Gill] and to many Christians now living" (Quoted in Ivimey, *English Baptists*, III, 364).

[99] Sell, *Great Debate*, p. 78.

The enemy he fought was not simply Arminianism, though it was that as well, but Rationalism, and he did so by the presentation of an exaggerated form of Calvinism. Between the solution offered by Edward Wallin and that offered by John Skepp to the problems of religious decline and hetero-doxy, it would be Skepp's and not Wallin's that would prevail among London Calvinistic Baptists of the eighteenth century.[100]

There is little doubt that Skepp is "the connecting link between Hussey and the Hyper-Calvinism of many Particular Baptists throughout the eighteenth century."[101] Moreover, it was during the time of Skepp's ministry that theology or orthodoxy became more of an issue among the London Calvinistic Baptists.[102]

Skepp's legacy to hyper-Calvinism is found in his work *Divine Energy* which addresses the subject of conversion.[103] Toon sees

---

[100]   MacDonald, "Calvinistic," p. 130. Wallin saw the solution to the spiritual prob-lems of the day in practical terms, e.g., no labour on the Lord's Day; but Skepp saw the problem in spiritual terms (*Ibid.*, pp. 129-130).

[101]   Toon, *Hyper-Calvinism*, pp. 88-89.

[102]   MacDonald, "Calvinistic," pp. 282-283. MacDonald has shown that from 1706 to 1717 there was a struggle between a moderate and a rigorist Calvinism among Lon-don Particular Baptists. By 1717 the rigorist party had won out (*Ibid.*, p. 371).

[103]   The following is Skepp's outline for this work:

" *I. First*, I shall shew you wherein Conversion and true Faith do consist.

II. Secondly, Lay open, and demonstrate the real Weakness and Insufficiency of Moral Suasion to effect so great a Change, as that of true Conversion to God, and saving Faith in the Lord Jesus Christ, from any remaining Power or Ability in fallen Man.

III. Thirdly, I shall make it evident, that in true Conversion, and saving Faith, as they are the Effects of the Divine Power, and Omnipotence, working effectually and irresistibly upon the Heart by the Word, the Will of Man is not forced, nor its natural Liberty in the least infring'd; but, on the other Hand, that noble Faculty is, by renewing Grace, made truly, and spiritually free.

IV. Fourthly, I will in several Instances manifest, that a Person, in a true and proper Sense, may be said to be Passive, in some Part of the Holy Spirit's Work upon the Heart, both in, and after Conversion.

V. Fifthly, I shall demonstrate from the Doctrine and Evidence of the Holy Scriptures, that there is an absolute Necessity for the exceeding Greatness of God's Almighty Power to be irresistibly and efficaciously put forth upon the Heart and Soul of Man, to effect his Conversion, and bring him to saving Faith in Christ.

VI. Sixthly, I will shew you out of the Holy Scriptures, that the Spirit of God has a pecu-liar Work and Office under the New Testament Administration, as he is given of the Father, and sent forth by Christ, to accompany the Word of the Gospel in its publick Ministration in the World; and also, that in Respect of the Church of Christ, and its particular Members, he hath divers peculiar Epithets given him, and much Work to do upon their Souls, in beginning, carrying on, and compleating the whole *Work of Faith with Power*; thereby bringing them into a State of Grace; and fitting them for Glory.

VII. *Seventhly*, and *Lastly*, I shall close the whole with some Inferences, practical Uses, and Directions" (*Divine Energy*, pp. 9-10).

Skepp teaching three important things in this work: 1) that true conversion is not improvement in biblical knowledge, effort to live a religious life, becoming a defender of the Christian faith, changing from a loose morality to strict religious observance, or being born into a Christian home, but that it certainly included belief in sound Biblical doctrines; 2) that humans were totally impotent to accept the Gospel in their natural, rebellious selves, and that preachers were powerless to persuade; in fact, for him moral suasion was Pelagian; and 3) that the Holy Spirit, the Divine Energy, is absolutely necessary in conversion (the elect person was passive in regeneration, enunciating the experiential steps through which the elect person passes to regeneration, paying no attention to the human response).[104] Toon is correct in his analysis of Skepp's *Divine Energy*, particularly concerning the last two points.[105] However, the last point should be emphasized for this study. Skepp emphasized that only God's divine energy of efficacious grace, imparted to the sinner by the work of His Spirit brings a person to faith in Christ. For example, commenting on Psalm 110:3 he says,

This Day of a Mediator's Power, is the Gospel Day of efficatious Grace upon the Hearts of his chosen People, who are *his* by Donation and Purchase as to Right; before they are *his* by Conquest, and the Marriage Con-

---

[104]   Toon, *Hyper-Calvinism*, pp.85-88.

[105]   Skepp states, "There are such Lets and Hindrances, (both within and without) that stand in the Way of a Sinner's Conversion to God, as render it wholly impracticable, and impossible; without the Concurrance of his efficacious Grace and Omnipotence. And these may be consider'd under four general Heads; I*st.* Impotency, through a spiritual Death, that has seiz'd all Mankind in the Fall. 2*dly.* Inbred Enmity and Rebellion, as seated in the Heart and Will. 3*dly* The present reigning Power, Prevelancy, and Dominion of Sin. 4*thly.* The fast Hold, and firm Possession, that *Satan* has of every natural unregenerate Man; together with his present reigning Power in, and Influence over the Heart" (*Divine Energy*, p. 54). And again, "As for Ability and Will, [the poor miserable sinner] has none, and *Moral Suasion* is but of little Use to such a dead , or disabled soul, since all it can say, and do, amounts to no more, than a dead and helpless Exhortation" (*Ibid.*, p. 56). Concerning human passivity in conversion he says, "Man is really and truly Passive in his Receiving of the Holy Spirit, as the Spirit of all effectual Conviction and Saving Grace.... The soul is really Passive in its receiving Vital Union with Christ, as the Head and Root of all Life and spiritual Strength and Fruitfulness.... A Man is really Passive in the great Work of Regeneaation [*sic*] or the New Birth as it is effected by the Spirit and the Word.... There is a real Passiveness of soul in the first Beginnings of all spiritual Motions of Grace in order for the repeated Acts and Exercise thereof" (*Ibid.*, pp. 142-143). And again, "We are sure we are as passive in our being quickned by, and from our Life-giving Head and Spiritual *Adam* as we were in our first Union to, and quickning in our natural Parent" (*Ibid.*, p. 165).

tract at the time of effectual Calling: The Gospel-Ministry is the instituted
Means that God hath ordain'd (being accompany'd by the Spirit) to make
the same powerfull and efficatious to the Hearts of his Elect, both for Renovation and Salvation.[106]

The essence of Skepp's *Divine Energy* can be seen in this passage
where he begins by quoting a preacher who is calling his hearers to
come to Christ:

'Come *Man*; why dost Thou lie thus? endeavour to get up, and go about
your immediate Work and Business: Don't lie here to be starv'd with Cold
and Hunger; rise up, do your best, and God will assist you.' This is the Im-
port and genuine Language of *Moral Suasion*; and as far as it can go, and yet
this is Helpless, Lifeless Way of Preaching, and Reasoning now in *vogue*
with our high and mighty *Rationalists*, and Doctors of *Free-will*: and I heartily wish it were not be found among some others, who profess to know
better, and to have experienced something more than those, who set themselves to oppose the Spirit's efficatious and irrestistable work upon the Soul
in Regeneration; without which, their lifeless Motives, and spiritless Exhortations and Offers are as ineffectual as the Prophet's Staff in *Gehazi*'s Hand:
(for Spiritual Gospel Duties, and Moral Duties too, require more Ability
and Skill than most Men seem to be aware of:) forasmuch as all Mankind
sustained such a Loss in the Fall of *Adam*, and received such a deadly Blow,
and mortal Wound (in a Moral and Scripture Sense) as can never be made
up to them, but by the Gift of Grace, and Righteousness through Christ
Jesus; together with the Spirit of Life, and Strength, communicated from
him, as the *Second Adam*, and New Covenant Head, in such a Manner as to
quicken their Souls, and renew their Hearts; thereby working in them a
Principle to will, and also an Ability suited for the Performance of all sorts
of Duties, whether Moral or Evangelical.[107]

From these passages Skepp's hyper-Calvinism is evident, particularly because of his emphasis on the exceeding greatness of God's
efficacious grace to convert the sinner as well as the sinner's impotence to accept the Gospel and the preacher's impotence to per-

---

[106] *Ibid.*, p. 134. In another place he states, "That true Conversion to God, and
saving Faith in our Lord Jesus Christ, are the Effects of an exceeding Greatness of
God's mighty Power, working in, and upon the Soul; and are not to be effected by *Moral
Suasion*, or any Ability in the Creature" (*Ibid.*, p. 8). And again, "And the better to open,
confirm, and vindicate this sacred Truth, *i.e.* the Necessity of the internal Operation of
the Divine Power upon the Heart in effectual Calling and Conversion; thereby to discover and lay open Man's real Impotency and Inability, and the Insufficiency of Moral
Suasion to effect so great a Change" (*Ibid.*, pp. 8-9).
[107] *Ibid.*, pp. 56-57.

suade the sinner to receive Christ as Saviour.[108] Irresistible grace was a tenet of High Calvinism, but Skepp's emphasis on it far exceeds that of the High Calvinists.

Hussey's and Skepp's hyper-Calvinism was disseminated in Particular Baptist circles by John Gill (b.1697)[109] and John Brine (b.1703).[110] Gill was raised in the Kettering Baptist Church (called the Little Meeting) which had been under the influence of the doctrinal antinomian Richard Davis.[111] In his early years Gill studied Latin and Greek, and read many of the continental divines. In 1717 he was assistant to John Davis, the minister of the Baptist church in Higham Ferrers, Northamptonshire. It was through John Davis that Gill came to have associations with Cambridge and Hussey's ministry.[112] In 1719 he became the pastor of the Particular Baptist Church at Horsleydown, Southwark, succeeding Benjamin Stinton. He pastored this church until his death in 1771. His influence can be seen in the numerous ordinations and funerals in which he took part, as well as in his weekly message at the Wednesday Lecture in Great Eastcheap from 1729 to 1756. These lectures sometimes became the basis of books he later published. Gill saw himself, and was viewed by other Particular Baptists, as the protector and defender of Reformed orthodoxy.[113] He defended such doctrines as the Trinity, the Deity of Christ, eternal justification,

---

[108] Daniel and Seymour also state that Skepp was the first Baptist not to "offer" the gospel (Daniel, "John Gill," pp. 6, 366, 420; Seymour, "Gill," p. 55).

[109] On Gill's life and thought see John Rippon, *A Brief Memoir of the Life and Writings of the Rev. John Gill D.D.* (N.d.; rpt., Harrisonburg, VA, 1992); Michael A.G. Haykin, *The Life and Thought of John Gill (1697-1771) A Tercentennial Appreciation* (Leiden, 1997); Robert W. Oliver, "John Gill," in *British Particular Baptists*, I, 145-165; and Daniel, "John Gill."

[110] Geoffrey Nuttall, "Northamptonshire and the Modern Question: A Turning-Point in Eighteenth Century Dissent," *Journal of Theological Studies*, N.S., 16 (1965), p. 117. Murdina MacDonald believes that the institutional seedbed for the triumph of the exaggerated Calvinism of Gill and Brine came from: 1) a troubled religious scene; 2) an ordering impulse; and 3) the heightened interest in theological issues since 1717 ("Calvinistic," p. 381).

[111] Gill wrote a preface to Richard Davis' *Hymns* in 1748. In addition, we see his influence on Gill when the latter wrote in the preface, "His memory has always been precious to me partly on account of his great regard both for my Education, for which he was heartily concerned, and also for my spiritual and eternal welfare" (Quoted in Nuttall, "Modern," p. 116).

[112] Nuttall, "Modern," p. 116. Davis became pastor to the Baptist church in Cambridge that seceded from Hussey's Congregational church in 1721 after Hussey moved to London. Gill was involved with Cambridge Baptists long after Davis had died.

[113] MacDonald, "Calvinistic," p. 368.

predestination, perseverance of the saints, election, and baptism. Gill was not only influenced by Richard Davis and John Skepp[114] but also by the doctrinal antinomian Tobias Crisp whose *Works* he edited in 1755. Toon well sums up the effect of these influences on Gill by stating, "The High Calvinism of Richard Davis, hardened by controversy with Baxterianism and Arminianism, modified through the assimilation of Crispian doctrines, and severely conditioned by the influence of Hussey's 'no offers of grace' theology, was the theological environment in which Gill was nurtured."[115] Concerning Hussey and Crisp Gill wrote in *Truth Defended* (1736), "They were both, in their day and generation, men of great piety and learning, of long standing and much usefulness in the Church of Christ; whose name and memory will be dear and precious to the saints, when this writer [Job Burt] and his pamphlet will be remembered no more."[116]

John Brine was also raised in the Kettering Little Meeting church.[117] It was under the preaching of John Gill and while still living in Kettering that Brine was converted. Although uneducated prior to his conversion, he afterwards vigorously studied the ancient languages under the tutelage of his pastor Thomas Wallis and Gill. The Kettering church, seeing he possessed the preaching gifts, called him into the ministry of the Word. In 1726 he succeeded his father-in-law John Moore in the Particular Baptist Church in Jordan Well, Coventry. In 1729 he was called to pastor Knollys' and Skepp's church in London which was then meeting in Currier's Hall, Cripplegate. Brine, like Gill, defended the Reformed faith against heresies such as Deism, Arianism and Baxterianism.[118] He also was quite active in the Particular Baptist Churches, preaching at ordinations and funerals. Moreover, he was one of the lecturers to follow Gill at the Wednesday Lecture in Great Eastcheap, and he often preached at the Sunday evening lecture at Devonshire

---

[114]   Further evidence of Skepp's influence on Gill is seen in the latter's republishing of Skepp's *Divine Energy* (1751) with a preface.

[115]   Toon, *Hyper-Calvinism*, p. 99. See also Curt Daniel, "John Gill and Calvinistic Antinomianism" in *The Life and Thought of John Gill*, pp. 180-187.

[116]   John Gill, *Truth Defended* in *Sermons and Tracts, by the late Reverend and Learned John Gill, D.D. A New Edition* (1814; rpt. Streamwood, IL, 1981), III, 427.

[117]   For some of the details of his life see *Dictionary of National Biography* (Oxford and London, 1921-22), II, 1253-1255.

[118]   Toon,. *Hyper-Calvinism*, p. 101.

Square. Gill and Brine had "cultivated a particular friendship" in London and enjoyed "a perfect congeniality of views upon religious subjects." Brine died in 1765 with Gill preaching his funeral sermon.[119]

The hyper-Calvinism of Gill, Brine and the Particular Baptists becomes most evident when the controversy concerning the "Modern question" took place in Northamptonshire in the 1730s. The initial battle occured between Matthias Maurice at Rothwell and Lewis Wayman of Kimbolton. The "modern question" was whether it was the duty of sinners to repent and believe the Gospel. Maurice affirmed the question with a tract entitled, *A modern question modestly answer'd* (1637).[120] What made this tract so stunning was that Maurice was a High Calvinist of the Crispian/Davis mould.[121] Hoping for Lewis Wayman's support, Maurice encouraged some of his friends to pass on a copy to him. Unfortunately, the tract was met with protestation, and in 1738 Wayman published, *A further enquiry after truth, wherein is shewn, what faith is required of unregenerate persons; what the faith of God's elect is, which is a blessing of the covenant of grace; occasion'd by a pamphlet, entitled, A modern question modestly answer'd.* In this work Wayman stated that this "modern question" was not modern at all. It had been answered by Joseph Hussey thirty years earlier in *God's operations of grace: but no offers of his grace*; and that Davis had learned such from Hussey, and now with others he mourned the loss of their clear teaching in Rothwell, Cambridge, Kimbolton, etc..[122] Maurice followed up this treatise with *The modern question*

---

[119]   Nuttall, "Modern," p. 117. Brine had a deep respect for Hussey. In his *Remarks upon a pamphlet, intitled, Some Doctrines in the Superlapsarian Scheme impartially examin'd by the Word of God* (1736) he calls him, "The learned and great Mr. *Hussey*" (p. 16). Gill was Brine's closest friend (John Gill, *A Collection of Sermons and Tracts: In Two Volumes* [London, 1773], II, 591-592; Daniel, "John Gill," p. 7).

[120]   Nuttall, "Modern," p. 102.

[121]   For Maurice's High Calvinism see *Ibid.*, pp. 108-110.

[122]   *Ibid.*, p. 111. Actually Davis believed that the Gospel should be preached to all indiscriminately. In *Truth and innocency* (1692) he taught that "the Ministers of the Gospel must offer the grace of the Gospel to all that hear them universally without exceptions, because they know not who the Elect are" (Quoted in *Ibid.*, 113). However, in the following years Davis came closer to Hussey on this matter, and John Gill later wrote in the preface of the reprint of Davis' *Hymns*, "I can affirm, upon good and sufficient testimony, that Mr. Davis, before his death, changed his mind in this matter, and disused the phrase [offering Christ and grace], as being improper, and being too bold and free for a minister of Christ to make use of" (Richard Davis, *Hymns composed on several subjects* [1694; rpt. 1833], "Recommendatory Preface").

affirm'd and prov'd: viz. That the eternal God does by his word make it the duty of poor unconverted sinners, who hear the gospel preach'd or publish'd to believe in Jesus Christ (1739). In it was a commendatory preface by the eminent Congregational minister, Thomas Bradbury, as well as a printed "Testimony of the Church of Christ at Rowel, against the pernicious New Opinion, at their Meeting, August 31, 1737," signed by fifty-one members and Maurice.[123] The preface by Bradbury brought London into the controversy.[124] Dr. Abraham Taylor[125], a London Congregational minister and theological tutor, in the same year wrote *Address to young students in divinity, by way of caution against some paradoxes, which lead to doctrinal antinomianism* in which he stated, "This odd fancy [that Christ must not be offered to sinners] was started above thirty years since, by a gentleman [Hussey] of a great deal of rambling learning, but of a confused head."[126] John Gill replied to this *Address* with *The necessity of good works unto salvation considered: occasion'd by some reflections and misrepresentations of Mr. (Alias Dr.) Abraham Taylor in a pamphlet of his lately published, called, An Address to young students....*[127] Three years later in response Taylor anonymously wrote, *The modern question ... examined.* This was answered by John Brine in *A refutation of Arminian principles, delivered in a pamphlet, intitled, The modern question concerning repentance and faith, examined with candour* (1743).

It wasn't until the latter part of the century that hyper-Calvinism's hold on Calvinistic Baptists was released by Andrew Fuller who was called to the pastorate of the Little Meeting in Kettering in 1782. It was his treatise, entitled, *The gospel worthy of all acceptation* (1785) that returned these Baptists to a more evangelical High Calvinism.

---

[123] Nuttall, "Modern," p. 114.
[124] According to W.T. Whitley, the controversy spread also to North-West England in Barnoldswick. (*Baptists of North-West England*, pp. 83ff., cited in Toon, *Hyper-Calvinism*, pp. 131, 139).
[125] For Abraham Taylor see *Dictionary of National Biography* (Oxford and London, 1921-22), XIX, 402.
[126] Quoted in Nuttall, "Modern," p. 115.
[127] It should also be noted that between the years 1735 and 1738 Gill wrote his important High Calvinistic treatise against Arminianism and Pelagianism entitled, *The Cause of God and Truth in Four Parts*. In this treatise he maintains that a saving faith is not required of the unregenerate but only an historical faith ([1855; rpt. Edmonton, n.d.], pp. 31-32).

However, between the 1730s and 1780s Gill and Brine continued to influence the Baptist churches on the subject in Northamptonshire, Cambridge, and London.[128]

The Theology of Hyper-Calvinism and Hanserd Knollys

This section will examine the theology of hyper-Calvinism from the
writings of its most important Baptist expositors, John Gill and
John Brine, and compare their writings with Knollys' in order to
see if he espoused hyper-Calvinism or elements of it.[129] Hyper-Calvinism is one step beyond that of the High Calvinism of the seventeenth century. Consequently, the two primary distinctives of
hyper-Calvinism are: that the gospel is not to be offered indiscriminately to all people; and secondly, its corollary, that it is the duty
only of the elect to exercise saving faith and evangelical repentance.[130] Three secondary distinctives include: eternal justification;
an eternal covenant of grace; and an excessive emphasis on irresistible grace and the passivity of the elect in their salvation.[131] There

---

[128]   We know that there were many West Country Baptists who were not hyper-
Calvinists, e.g., A. Gifford, B. Francis. Others also include D. Crossley, J. Thomas, B.
Beddome, John Ash, Hugh and Caleb Evans. In addition, Bristol Baptist Academy was
not hyper-Calvinist (R. Philip Roberts, *Continuity and Change: London Calvinistic Baptists and
the Evangelical Revival 1760-1820* [Wheaton, 1989], pp. 41-43).
[129]   Daniel sees Gill as the leader of hyper-Calvinism not only among Particular
Baptists but in all circles; it found "its cohesion in [him]" (Daniel, "John Gill," p. 9).
[130]   Daniel sees these as the main tenets of hyper-Calvinism (*Ibid.*, p. x). He, however, unites these tenets into one.
[131]   See Toon, *Hyper-Calvinism*, pp. 108-138. For a complete definition of hyper-
Calvinism by those who have done the most work in this area see *Ibid.*, pp. 144-145,
and Daniel, "John Gill," p. 767. Daniel states: "Hyper-Calvinism is that school of supralapsarian 'Five Point' Calvinism which so stresses the sovereignty of God by over-
emphasizing the secret over the revealed will and eternity over time, that it minimizes
the responsibility of Man, notably with respect to the denial of the word 'offer' in relation to the preaching of the Gospel of a finished and limited atonement, thus determining the universal duty of sinners to believe savingly with the assurance that the Lord
Jesus Christ died for them, with the result that presumption is overly warned of, intro-
spection is over-encouraged, and a view of sanctification akin to doctrinal antinomianism is often approached." He then summarizes it even further, "It is the rejection of the
word 'offer' in connection with evangelism for supposedly Calvinistic reasons. In all our
researches, the only real tangible thing which differentiates the Hyper from the High
Calvinists is the word offer." I particularly agree with this last definition but with one
qualification: duty-faith logically follows the no-offer theology and is also a distinctive,
and therefore, also marks a person off as a hyper-Calvinist and not simply a High Calvinist.

is no doubt that Brine and Gill were High Calvinists but it is also evident from their writings that they went a step further holding to, and emphasizing, the above hyper-Calvinistic distinctives.[132] We will examine these distinctives held by Gill and Brine comparing them with Knollys' writings.

The first hyper-Calvinist distinctive that Gill and Brine held was that the gospel or grace or Christ ought not to be offered to all people indiscriminately but only to those who are the elect.[133] This was not the teaching of Calvin. In his comment on Acts 2:21 where the Apostle Peter preached, "Whosoever shall call upon the name of the Lord shall be saved," Calvin writes, "We must also observe the universal word, 'whosoever'. For God admits all men to Himself without exception and by this means invites them to salvation, even as Paul deduces in Rom. 10." And again commenting on Romans 1:16 he states,

> The Gospel is indeed offered to all for their salvation, but its power is not universally manifest.... When, therefore, the Gospel invites all to partake of salvation without any difference, it is rightly termed the doctrine of salvation. For Christ is there offered, whose proper office is to save that which is lost, and those who refuse to be saved by Him shall find Him their Judge.[134]

John Gill disagrees with Calvin. He states in *The Cause of God and Truth* in reference to Isaiah 55:1:

---

[132]   Most Baptist historians consider these men to be hyper-Calvinists (see Thomas J. Nettles, *By His Grace and for His Glory: A Historical, Theological and Practical Study of the Doctrines of Grace in Baptist Life* [Grand Rapids, 1986], pp. 84-89). In addition, the most recent assessments including Alan Sell, *Great Debate*; Robert Oliver, "John Gill (1697-1771) His Life and Ministry," in *The Life and Thought of John Gill*; and Curt Daniel, "John Gill," consider these men to be hyper-Calvinists. Nettles, however, disagrees and defends Gill (*By His Grace*, pp. 89-107; it, however, should be noted that in a recent essay Nettles has modified his view seeing some hyper-Calvinistic elements in Gill [Nettles, "John Gill and the Evangelical Awakening," in *The Life and Thought of John Gill*, pp. 131-170]).

[133]   The hyper-Calvinists do not reject such words as: God holds forth, stretches out, extends, reveals, shows, directs, bestows, imparts, communicates and encourages. Preachers may: call, preach, proclaim, declare, publish, speak and teach. But they are not to use the word "offer" because they cannot "offer" Christ, only God can.

[134]   Calvin, *NT Commentaries*, VI, 62; VIII, 27. See also his comments on John 3:16 and 2 Cor. 2:15.

These words are no call, invitation, or offer of grace to dead sinners, since they are spoken to such who were *thirsty*, that is, who, in a spiritual sense, were thirsting after pardon of sin, a justifying righteousness, and salvation by Christ; after a greater knowledge of him, communion with him, conformity to him, and the enjoyment of him in his ordinances, which supposes them to be spiritually alive.... The persons here encouraged are such, who not only have no money, but know they have none; which are *poor in spirit*, and sensible of their spiritual poverty; which sense arises from the quickening influences of the Spirit of God upon their souls.[135]

Again he states,

I know of no exhortations to dead sinners, to return and live, in a spiritual manner. Those referred to in Ezex. [*sic*] xviii., I have often observed, respect civil and temporal, and not spiritual and eternal things; we may, and should indeed, encourage and exhort sensible sinners to believe in Christ, and testify their repentance, by bringing forth fruits meet for the same.[136]

In some places Gill gives the impression that the gospel ought not to be offered to anyone whether elect or not:

Salvation is not offered at all by God, upon any condition whatsoever, to any of the sons of men, no not to the elect: they are *chosen* to it, Christ has procured it for them, the gospel publishes and reveals it, and the Spirit of God applies it to them; much less to the non-elect, or to all mankind; and consequently this doctrine, or God according to it, is not chargeable with *delusion* and *insult*.[137]

---

[135]   Gill, *Cause of God* , pp. 19-20.

[136]   *Ibid.*, p. 172. See also *Ibid.*, pp. 19-20, 87-88, 102, 152-153, 155, 156, 164, 167, 172, 181, 184, 209, 210, 211. Moreover, see his "Recommendatory Preface" to Richard Davis' *Hymns composed on several subjects* where he explains why Davis used the phrases of offering Christ or grace, and assures the reader that at the end of Davis' life he "changed his mind in this matter, and disused the phrase, as being improper, and being to bold and free for the minister of Christ to make use of" (p. 64). In his *Body of Divinity* Gill states, "Nor is the gospel ministry an offer of Christ, and of his grace and salvation by him, which are not in the power of the ministers of it to give, nor of carnal men to receive" (*Body of Divinity* [1839; 2nd. reprint Atlanta, 1957], p. 539).

[137]   John Gill, *An Answer to the Birmingham Dialogue-Writer*, in *Sermons and Tracts* (1773), II, 119; see also p. 146. See also *Cause of God*, pp. 103, 156; and *The Doctrine of Predestination stated and set in the Scripture Light* (1752) in *Sermons and Tracts* (1814), III, 118.

Again in his tract *The Doctrine of Predestination, Stated*, Gill writes,

> That there are universal offers of grace and salvation I utterly deny; nay,
> I deny they are made to any; no, not to God's elect; grace and salvation are
> provided for them in the everlasting covenant, procured for them by
> Christ, published and revealed in the gospel, and applied by the Spirit;
> much less are they made to others.... Let the patrons of universal offers
> defend themselves ... I have nothing to do with it.[138]

This, however, did not mean that the gospel should not be preached to all. He states,

> The ministers of the gospel are sent to *preach the gospel to every creature*; that is,
> not to offer, but to preach Christ, and salvation by him; to publish peace
> and pardon as things already obtained by him. The ministers are ... *criers* or
> *heralds*; their business is ... to *proclaim* aloud, to publish facts, to declare
> things that are done, and not to offer them to be done on conditions; as
> when a peace is concluded and finished, the herald's business, and in which
> he is employed, is to proclaim the peace, and not to offer it; of this nature
> is the gospel, and the whole system of it; which preaches, not offers peace
> by Christ, who is Lord of all.[139]

John Brine concurred with Gill that the gospel or grace was not to
be offered. In *A Refutation of Arminian Principles*, Brine's response to
Matthias Maurice's pamphlet *A Modern Question*, he challenges Mau-
rices' contention that it is the duty of all people to exercise saving
faith and evangelical repentance. This is the logical progression of
the "no offers of grace" teaching, and is one step beyond it. However, in a work entitled, *The Certain Efficacy of the Death of Christ* published in the same year as *A Refutation* he clearly states his disap-
proval of offering grace to all:

> But I am of opinion, that an Offer or Proposal for acceptance of New Cov-
> enant Blessings, is not made to Men, whilst they are under the old Cove-
> nant, or Law of Works, which are all men 'till regenerated, or so long as
> they are under the Dominion of Sin. *Offers* of grace as I conceive, are not

---

[138]   *Ibid.*

[139]   John Gill, *An Answer to the Birmingham Diologue-Writer's Second Part*, in *Sermons and
Tracts* (1771), II, 146-147. In *The Cause of God and Truth* he states, "The ministers of the
Gospel, though they ought not to offer and tender salvation to any, for which they have
no commission, yet they may preach the gospel to all men, and declare, that *whosoever
believes shall be saved*" (p. 164; see also, p. 88; and *Body of Divinity*, p. 539).

made to those who are not under grace, nor interested in the Covenant of Grace, which many are not, to whom the Gospel is preached.[140]

Moreover, in *A Refutation* when considering passages of Scripture where repentance and faith are exhorted he states, "It evidently appears, that the Persons addressed were the happy Subjects of a Conviction of their Misery by Nature, and therefore not to be considered in a State of Unregeneracy."[141]

Did Knollys espouse this hyper-Calvinist tenet? Along with the hyper-Calvinists Knollys believed that the gospel should be preached to all.[142] But contrary to this first hyper-Calvinist tenet he believed the gospel should be *offered* to all. When preaching on Colossians 3:11 that "Christ is all, and in all", he says, "Let me tell you God offers you Christ upon Gospel-termes,... God doth offer Christ to lost sinners without respect to price or person. He invites them, that have no money, to come, and buy Wine, and milk (that is to say, Christ) without price."

And, again, when preaching on Luke 19:10 where Jesus said, "For the Son of Man is come to seek and to save that which is lost", Knollys proclaims, "The Lord having propounded or offered Jesus Christ to lost sinners, outwardly and in generall by the word, and inwardly and perticular to this or that lost sinner by the Spirit, accompanying that word of the Gospel with divine light and power to the heart of the sinner, doth enable the poore soul so to assent unto what is propounded."[143] In 1688 commenting on Revelation 22:17 where "The Spirit and bride say, Come", Knollys writes, "The Church of God, and the holy Spirit of God, and all converted persons, do invite all sorts of sinners, *especially*, thirsty sinners, without exception against any Persons, that are willing, and without any price, to take Christ freely."[144] Notice that Knollys says that the church of God is to invite not only thirsty sinners but "all sorts of sinners." Gill had said that the offer of Isaiah 55:1 was *only* to

---

[140]   John Brine, *The Certain Efficacy* (1743), p. 75, quoted in Toon, *Hyper-Calvinism*, p. 129.

[141]   John Brine, *A Refutation of Arminian Principles, Delivered in a intitled, the Modern Question Concerning Repentance and Faith, examined with Candour, & In a Letter to a Friend* (1743), p. 11.

[142]   See 1677/89 *Confession* X.4; *Christ Exalted*, p. 12; *Parable*, pp. 50-51; and *Revelation*, pp. 241-242.

[143]   *Christ Exalted*, pp. 13, 21.

[144]   *Revelation*, pp. 241-242.

thirsty sinners. In the *Parable of the Kingdom* he writes, "These that sell this Mystical and Spiritual Oyle are Christ and His Ministers, and Servants.... Ordinarily and commonly Christ authorizes and commands his faithful Servants (the Ministers of the Gospel) whom he appoints, commissions and sends to offer this spiritual Oyle to sale, and to sell it unto whomsoever will buy it." And again in the same treatise he calls sinners "to open the door of your hearts to Christ."[145]

At the end of the first part of his treatise, *The World that now is*, he calls unbelievers to believe and repent, exhorting them "to come to Christ because there is salvation in no other."[146] In the second part of the same treatise he closes with another exhortation to "profane sinners" calling them to get into a state of salvation before Christ comes from heaven to judge the quick and the dead, and before they die. He goes on to counsel them to consider: that they are dead in trespasses and sins and are without Christ; that they are in need of Jesus Christ; and that God offers Christ to poor, lost, miserable sinners upon gospel-terms of free grace (everyone who is willing may come to Christ and have Christ freely). He then exhorts them to suffer Jesus to come into their hearts by his Spirit and Word, and open their hearts to Christ when he knocks at the door of their souls and let him come in (if the sinner be willing to open the door of his heart, Christ will come in by his Holy Spirit).[147] It is evident that from the beginning of his Baptist ministry to the end, Knollys believed the gospel should be offered to all, and that the minister should offer the gospel to all. Knollys' extant writings make it quite clear that he had a passionate concern for lost sinners and that he called them to seek Christ, repent, come to him upon "Gospel-terms", and to attend the "means" of salvation in order that they might be converted.[148] Knollys did not hold this first important hyper-Calvinist tenet.

The second important tenet of hyper-Calvinism held by Gill and Brine is akin to the first but a logical step beyond it. Since Calvin believed in the free offer of the gospel to all men it logically meant for him that all had a duty to believe the gospel. This is implied in

---

[145] *Parable*, pp. 107-108, 120.
[146] *World*, pt. 1, pp. 100-103.
[147] *World*, pt. 2, pp. 32-35. See also *Parable*, pp. 47, 112.
[148] See *Christ Exalted*, pp. 12-13.

his comment of 2 Cor. 2:15, where he writes, "But the question arises how this can be consistent with the nature of the Gospel which he defines a little later as the 'ministry'. The answer is easy: the Gospel is preached unto salvation, for that is its real purpose, but only believers share in this salvation; for unbelievers it is an occasion of condemnation, but is they who make it so."[149] The hyper-Calvinists, however, believed that only the elect were obliged to exercise saving faith and evangelical repentance. To put it negatively, it was not the duty of the non-elect to exercise these graces because they did not have the ability to do so, only the elect did. This was called the "modern question" which both John Brine and John Gill affirmed.[150] It is true that Gill did not directly enter into

---

[149] Calvin, *NT Commentaries*, X, 35.

[150] One can see a hint of this tenet in Skepp when he says, "Conversion Work is not so easy and common, as the Generality of Persons imagine, who think they want only to be told their Duties, and if they will attend, they may perform all that is told them; for this corrupt Notion hath got footing in the Hearts of Men, that God will require no more than they are able to perform; but I have shown, that the Law of God requires more then the Creature is able to give; for otherwise Righteousness would be by the Law, and Christ would have died in vain" (*Divine Energy*, p. 208). And again, "Without [the Spirit's efficatious and irresistible work upon the soul in regeneration], [the preachers'] lifeless Motives, and spiritless Exhortations and Offers are as ineffectual as the Prophet's Staff in *Gehazi*'s Hand: (for Spiritual Gospel Duties, and Moral Duties too, require more Ability and Skill than most Men seem to be aware of:) forasmuch as all Mankind sustained such a Loss in the Fall of *Adam*, and received such a deadly blow, and mortal Wound (in a Moral and Scripture Sense) as can never be made up to them, but by the Gift of Grace, and Righteousness through Christ Jesus; together with the Spirit of Life, and Strength, communicated from him, as the *Second Adam*, and New Covenant Head, in such a Manner as to quicken their Souls, and renew their Hearts; thereby working in them a Principle to will, and also an Ability suited for the Performance of all sorts of Duties, whether Moral or Evangelical" (*Ibid.*, p. 57). Again, "And out of this Part of the Spirit's supernatural and efficacious Work upon the Hearts of God's Elect in effectual Calling, it is, that Faith and every other Grace, Spiritual Duty and Performance do arise" (*Ibid.*, p. 169). Again, "Now Faith is to be consider'd *first* as a Moral Duty, and so the Law requireth Faith (as well as Mercy and Justice, as our Lord declares) as one of the weighty Matters and of the greatest Moment: Thus, as a necessary Moral Duty *He that cometh to God* in an Act of Worship, *must believe that he is, and that he is a Rewarder of those who diligently seek him.* But this is not enough, for there must also to this be added a Gospel justifying saving Faith.... The Soul, thereby is convinced now, that his Work and Duty is not to work for Life, Righteousness, and Acceptance with God, but to believe for Righteousness by laying hold of it as in another, being of meer Grace provided for him" (*Ibid.*, pp. 153-4). Again, "'Tis therefore only Men's Ignorance makes them to think or talk of Faith as some easy Thing; and as if it was no more than a Moral Duty and Act of the rational Creature, assenting and consenting to this and the other revealed Truth and Proposition laid down or to be evidenced and demonstrated from the Word; whereas 'tis, as I have shew'd under the first Head, a new created Principle of the new Creature, and is to be found only in the Souls of the New-born who

the debate but his words in many places leave us in little doubt where he stood on the issue.[151] For example, Gill maintains in *The Cause of God and Truth*,

> However there are many things which many be believed and done by reprobates, and therefore they may be justly required to believe and obey; it is true, they are not able to believe in Christ to the saving of their souls, or to perform spiritual and evangelical obedience, but then it will be difficult to prove that God requires these things of them, and should that appear, yet the impossiblity of doing them, arises from the corruption of their hearts.[152]

And again he states,

> God never calls persons to evangelical repentance, or requires them to believe in Christ to the saving of their souls, but he gives that special grace, and puts forth that divine energy which enables them to believe and repent. God does not require all men to believe in Christ, and where he does, it is according to the revelation he makes of him. He does not require the heathens, who are without an external revelation of Christ, to believe in him at all; and those who only have the outward ministry of the word, unattended with the special illuminations of the Spirit of God, are obliged to believe no further than that external revelation they enjoy, reaches; as that Jesus is the Son of God, the Messiah, &c., not to believe these things is the sin of all that are under the gospel dispensation, as it was with the Jews.[153]

---

are born from above.... Faith is not of ourselves, but is *the Gift of God*, and must be wrought in the Soul by the Energy or Operation of God" (*Ibid.*, p. 157). And again, "There is more of the Spirit of God, as to his Efficiency and Energy, and kind Assistances in every gracious Act and Spiritual Duty, than some are aware off, or care to own" (*Ibid.*, pp. 174-5). And again, "I have from the Holy Scriptures and the Saints Experience, endeavour'd to evince something of the passive Work of the Spirit of God upon the Hearts of his Elect, both in and after effectual Calling and Conversion, as the first in all that is Good, in which it appeareth Man is wrought upon, and moved, before ever he can move, so as to perform one Spiritual Act or Duty" (*Ibid.*, pp. 176-7).

[151]   Even Tom Nettles believes that Gill held this tenet. He states: "Although I think the judgment should still be surrounded with cautions and caveats, there may be compelling evidence that Gill held to [this] distinctive Hyper-Calvinist tenet" ("John Gill and the Evangelical Awakening," p. 153).

[152]   Gill, *Cause of God*, p. 158.

[153]   *Ibid.*, p. 166. See also *Ibid.*, pp. 31-32, 115, 170, and 208.

In another place he writes,

> The things spiritually good which man cannot do, have been instanced in; as to convert and regenerate himself, to believe in Christ, and to repent of sin in an evangelical manner; and these are things which he is not obliged to do of himself, and will not be damned for not performing of them. There are indeed things which man is obliged to, which he now cannot do, as to keep the whole law; which impotency of his is owing to his sin and fall.[154]

Though Gill did not directly enter into the debate concerning the modern question, his friend, John Brine did. In 1743 he responded to Maurice's pamphlet on the modern question with *A Refutation of Arminian Principles*. In it he affirmed that only the elect have a duty to exercise saving faith and evangelical repentance. He states, "With respect to special Faith in Christ, it seems to me, that the Powers of Man in his perfect State were not fitted and disposed to that Act." The reason for this, he contends, is that "this Act necessarily supposes a Dependence on Christ for Salvation, as Creatures lost and miserable in ourselves; but 'till Man was fallen and become miserable, he could not exercise such a Trust in Christ, as a Redeemer." He goes on to say that "special Faith in Christ, belongs to the new Creation, of which he as Mediator between God and his People, is the Author; and therefore, I apprehend, that a Power of acting this special Faith in him, was not given to Man, by, or according to the Law of his first Creation." For Brine, this ability comes only to the elect. Again, after examing the subject of repentance in the Old Covenant to the Jews he concludes that "Evangelical Repentance and special Faith, are Duties only of such Persons, to whom God reveals himself in his word, as their Redeemer through Christ." In this place Brine contends that the interpreter needs to distinguish between "natural and evangelical Repentance" and of "historical and special Faith." Only natural repentance and historical faith are required of all humans.[155] And so he can say,

---

[154] Gill, *Answer to Birmingham ... Second Part*, in *Sermons and Tracts* (1773), II, 153. See also *Ibid.*, II, 154. In addition, see his *Body of Divinity*, where he answers the questions, "Whether faith is a duty of the moral law, or is to be referred to the gospel?" and "Whether repentance is a doctrine of the law or the gospel?" (p. 376).

[155] Brine, *Refutation*, pp. 4-8.

But special Faith in those heavenly Mysteries, the Powers of Man in a State of Innocence, it is apprehended were not disposed to, and fitted for, by his Creation Principles, and therefore it is concluded, that special Faith becomes a Duty, only upon the Supposition of the Infusion of super-Creation-Principles, into the Souls of Men.[156]

In other words special faith only becomes a duty for the elect who are given the power to exercise it.

Did Knollys espouse this second important hyper-Calvinist tenet, that it is not the duty of the non-elect to exercise evangelical repentance and saving faith in Christ? Or, to put it positively, that it is only the duty of the elect to exercise these things? It would appear from our study of Knollys' teaching concerning "the offering of the gospel" that he implicitly believed it was the duty of all people to come to Christ. This, however, is not only implicitly but also explicitly stated in at least one place in his writings. In his 1674 treatise *The Parable of the Kingdom of God Expounded* he writes,

> It's the duty of every person, that sees their need and want of Christ, his holy Spirit, and sanctifying Grace to attend upon the Ministry of the Gospel and Administrations of the holy Ordinances of God, and to accept and receive Christ and Grace offered freely, without money or price.... And as it is their Duty to hear, so it is their Duty to believe, 1 *Joh*. 3. 23. and by faith to accept and receive Jesus Christ offered to them upon Gospel terms of free Grace.[157]

It is also explicit from his answer to the Pithay Baptist Church question concerning prayer with unbelievers. Knollys along with several other London Particular Baptists wrote back to the church stating,

> Prayer is a part of that homage which every man is obliged to give to God; 'tis a duty belonging to natural, and not only instituted religion.... It cannot be supposed that man being such a creature as he is should not be obliged to love, fear, and obey God.... If hereunto it be objected, that such persons have not the Spirit, therefore ought not to pray; this objection is not cogent, forasmuch as neither the want of the Spirit's immediate motions to, or its assistance in duty, doth not take off the obligation of duty. If it would, then also from every other duty; and consequently all religion be cashiered. If

---

[156] *Ibid.*, p. 26. See also *Ibid.*, pp. 19, 29, 44.

[157] *Parable*, pp. 112-113. The phrase "that sees their need and want of Christ" is not spoken in a hyper-Calvinist sense because the context is concerned with offering the "spiritual Oyle unto whomsoever will buy it."

the obligations to this and other duties were suspended merely for want of such motions and assistance, then unconverted persons are so far from sinning in the omission of such duties, that it is their duty to omit them. 'Tis certain no man can, without the assistance of the Holy Spirit, either repent or believe; yet it will not therefore follow, that impenitency and unbelief are not sins; if these be sins, then the contrary must be their duty. It cannot be their sin to cry to God for the assistance of his Spirit to enable them thereunto. If a duty be no duty to us, except we be immediately moved to it; then whether sin doth not cease to be a sin, if the Spirit do not immediately hinder us from it; and thus by the same reason we may omit a duty, we may likewise commit a sin; and hereby that great rule of duty God hath given unto men to walk by, is wholly made void, or at least allowed to be but a rule only at some certain times, *viz.* when the Spirit immediately moves us to the observance of it; till then it hath no authority to oblige us: and so every man is sinless, whatever sin be committed, or whatever duty be neglected, if the Spirit do not immediately hinder us from the one and move us to the other.

Moreover the design of the objection doth as effectually discourage such as are under doubts and desertions, from this duty, as any other person; and thus it would be as that great enemy to the souls of men would have it, namely, that there would be but very few in the world to acknowledge God in this solemn part of his worship: whereas all men are obliged to acknowledge him as the fountain of all goodness; and themselves to be dependant creatures on him, and therefore to supplicate him for those blessings whereof they stand in need: or otherwise it must follow, that they have no wants, and are not dependant on him, but are all-sufficient: or if they be under the sense of wants and of their dependance upon the supreme goodness, yet they must not (at least in the way of prayer) acknowledge those wants, and that dependance, by seeking unto God for the bettering their conditions: but they be obliged hereunto, not only from those innate notions they have of God in their minds, but by the express revelations of the Divine will in the holy scriptures. Christianity improves and rectifies, but it doth not abolish our reason; it helps to better mediums and motives to perform our service to God, but it doth not in any wise make void that which was a duty before.

If yet it be objected, that an unregenerate person fails in the due manner of the performance of this duty, therefore he ought not to pray; not to be joined with in prayer; We answer — the defect in the manner (though a sin) doth not discharge the person from the obligation; for still it is his duty to pray: 'tis true there are such directions given in the holy scriptures as to the right performance of this duty, which the mere light of nature could not give; yet the duty itself of invocating God is so agreeable to the universal reason and sentiments of mankind, that there is nothing spoken of this in the scriptures but what doth suppose it previously to be a duty: therefore, unless we suppose that the law of nature is totally obliterated, we must conclude that mankind are under an obligation to this duty. But if a failure in the manner doth take off this obligation, then every unconverted person is sinless, if he totally neglect this and *every other duty.* Yea, every Christian, when under deadness and distractions is discouraged from this duty; and thus a door would be opened to all manner of wickedness and irreligion in the world. Again, as the aforesaid defect doth not discharge the person himself from the duty, neither are we so far concerned therein, as thereby to derive guilt and pollution to ourselves, in case we should join in prayer with such a person; for if it would, then may we not communicate in duty with any person of whose sincerity we are not assured. But where such an assurance is made necessary to our discharge to those duties which jointly are to be performed with others we know not: much more might have been added, but we consider what herein is said may suffice.[158]

Knollys believed it was the duty of unbelievers to pray, and consequently, to offer to God all that is due Him from the creature. It is evident that Knollys did not hold this hyper-Calvinistic tenet of "no duty faith" but would have affirmed the "modern question" of the eighteenth century.

The third tenet of the hyper-Calvinists was a carry-over from antinomianism. Gill and Brine believed that the elect are justified eternally, and not simply at the moment they exercise faith.[159] Calvin, on the other hand, only spoke of justification by faith. When examining the subject of the Holy Spirit's uniting us to Christ, he writes,

---

[158]   Ivimey, *English Baptists*, I, 417-420. The other signitories were William Kiffin, Daniel Dyke, Laurence Wise, Henry Forty, William Collins, Nehemiah Coxe, James Jones, Thomas Hicks, Joseph Morton, James Hycrigg, Robert Snelling and Thomas Hopgood. Moreover, it should be noted that the 1677/89 *Confession* similarly states in Chapter XXII.1,3, "THE light of Nature shews that there is a God, who hath Lordship, and Soveraigntye over all; is just, good, and doth good unto all; and is therefore to be feared, loved, praised, called upon, trusted in, and served, with all the Heart, and all the Soul, and with all the Might.... Prayer with thanksgiving, being one special part of natural worship, is by *God* required of all men" (In Lumpkin, *Baptist Confessions*, pp. 280-281).,

[159]   John Skepp held the antinomian tenet of the elect's salvation prior to faith: "And here we are to distinguish between a spiritual vital Union, which is the Spirit's Act upon the Soul; and this conjugal Union which is effected only by Faith. And so likewise, as to a new Covenant Interest, the first Part of the Title arises out of that Grace, that was settled upon all the Elect, by Way of Covenant, as, *Grace was given us in Christ before the world began*; and the purchased Title, which Christ, by his Death, procur'd for all his; these also are distinct and prior to this Marriage, Interest, and Title" (*Divine Energy*, pp. 37-38).

We must understand that as long as Christ remains outside of us, and we are separated from him, all that he has suffered and done for the salvation of the human race remains useless and of no value for us. Therefore, to share with us what he has received from the Father, he had to become ours and to dwell within us.... We also, in turn, are said to be "engrafted into him" [Rom. 11:17], and to "put on Christ" [Gal. 3:27]; for as I have said, all that he possesses is nothing to us until we obtain this by faith.[160]

The Baptist hyper-Calvinists went beyond this in their understanding of justification. For example, John Gill taught that justification should be "distinguished into active and passive justification." The latter is the "act of God, terminating on the conscience of the believer." The former is an "act internal and eternal, taken up in the divine mind from eternity, and is an imminent, abiding one in it." He goes on to say, "It does not begin to take place in time, or at believing, but is antecedent to any act of faith."[161] He later states, "Nor is [faith] the *causa sine qua non*, or that without which a man cannot be justified in the sight of God. For, I hope, I have already proved, that all God's elect are justified in his sight, and in his account, before faith; and if before faith, then without it."[162] And so in his *Body of Divinity* he writes,

If God's elect, as such, can have nothing laid to their charge; but are by God acquitted, discharged, and justified; and if they bore this character of elect from eternity, or were chosen in Christ before the world began; then they must be acquitted, discharged and justified so early, so as nothing could be laid to their charge ... for *there is no condemnation to them which are in Christ*, Rom. viii. 1 and therefore must be considered as righteous, and so justified.[163]

John Brine concurs with Gill on eternal justification. In 1732 he wrote a treatise defending the doctrine entitled, *A Defence of Eternal Justification*. In it he writes,

As God put the elect into Christ, or united them to him in eternal election, He views and considers them in Him, and so justifies them, and takes infi-

---

[160] Calvin, *Institute* III.i.1. See also *Ibid.*, III.xi.2,3.
[161] Gill, *Body of Divinity*, p. 203; *The Doctrine of Justification*, in *Sermons and Tracts* (1814), II, 459-460, 482-483, 491-492, 502. See his arguments for it, and his defence against objections in *Body of Divinity*, pp. 203-209.
[162] Gill, *Doctrine of Justification*, in *Sermons and Tracts* (1814), II, 491-492.
[163] Gill, *Body of Divinity*, p. 205.

nite pleasure in their persons as members of the Mediator, in whom He always had the fullest satisfaction and delight; though they are under a sentence of condemnation by the law, as violators of it, while in unbelief.[164]

In the same treatise Brine argues, "[Justification] is the imputation of Christ's righteousness to us, which is an act in God's mind, and effects no real change in us; therefore our existence is not necessary to our Justification before God."[165] In other words, not only are the elect justified before they exercise faith in Christ but before their very existence. In his *Remarks Upon a Pamphlet Intitled, Some Doctrines in the Superlapsarian Scheme impartially examin'd by the Word of God* where he responds to an objection to eternal justification made by the anonymous author "that we no where read of being justified before faith," he answers, "Though we do not read this syllabically, or in such Terms expressly; yet we read that which is equivalent to it." He goes on to state that "God eternally willed not to impute Sin to his Chosen.... And therefore, their Pardon is as ancient as God's Decrees."[166]

Knollys did not espouse the teaching of eternal justification. When he spoke of justification he only spoke of it in relation to faith. Knollys believed, as we saw in chapter three, that a person's justification was based on union with Christ. The 1644/46 *Confession* which Knollys signed states that, "All beleevers are by Christ, united to God, by which union, God is one with them, and they are one with him; and that all believers are the Sons of God, and joynt heires with Christ, to whom belong all the promises of this life, and that which is to come."[167] This union was effectual by faith: "This Faith Jesus Christ is the Author of, and will be the finisher of it, *Heb.* 12. 2. and therefore called the faith of the son of God, *Gal.* 2. 20. by which faith the Soul in its Conversion is united unto Christ,

---

[164]   John Brine, *A Defence of the Doctrine of Eternal Justification, from some Exceptions made to it by Mr. Bragge, and others* (1732; rpt. Paris, Arkansas, 1978), p. 62; Peter Naylor, *Picking up a Pin for the Lord: English Particular Baptists from 1688 to the Early Nineteenth Century* (London, 1992), p. 179.

[165]   Brine, *Defence*, p. 23; Roberts, *Continuity and Change*, p. 41.

[166]   Brine, *Remarks*, pp. 9-11. This treatise essentially defends the doctrine of eternal justification.

[167]   1644/46 *Confession*, XXVII.

and kept through it by the Power of God unto salvation."[168] And again in *Christ Exalted*, he states, "Thus being by the Spirit and Faith united with Christ, we are made a new creature, or creation,... have a new heart,... and walk in newnesse of life." And in the same work he teaches concerning the conversion of the sinner, "The Lord ... doth enable the poore soul so ... to receive ... Jesus Christ, and by faith to rest on him for wisedome, righteousnesse, sanctification and redemption: which Christ being given to the sinner, of the Father, is of God made all this to him.... And now the sinner is drawne to Christ, and is sought and saved by Christ."[169] For Knollys the sinner's salvation takes place at the time he receives Christ by faith. In *The World that now is*, he proclaims that "we are justified, adopted and sanctified by this faith."[170] He states in *Song of Solomon*,

> Our union by Faith, the Pardon of sin, our Reconciliation with God, the sanctification of our hearts and lives, our peace of conscience, and the Salvation of our Souls, are the Benefits of our Redemption by Christ, I Cor. 1. 30. these are as a Cluster of Camphire, full of divine virtue, and spiritual sweetnesse unto beleevers, when they can apply these benefits unto themselves by Faith.[171]

Knollys never spoke of eternal justification only of justification by faith.

---

[168] *World*, pt. 1, p. 35. See also *Song of Solomon*, pp. 47, 64-65, 7, where Knollys teaches that every saint is joined and ingrafted or set into Christ, and also united and knit together unto the Church as members of Christ's mystical body.

[169] *Christ Exalted*, pp. 1-2, 21.

[170] *World*, pt. 1, p. 36.

[171] *Song of Solomon*, pp. 64-65. See also 1677/89 *Confession* which Knollys signed. Concerning God's Covenant the *Confession* states, "It pleased the *Lord* to make a *Covenant* of *Grace* wherein he freely offereth unto *Sinners*, Life and Salvation by *Jesus Christ*, requiring of them Faith in him, that they may be saved" (VII.2). And again, "Faith thus receiving and resting on Christ, and his Righteousness, is the alone instrument of Justification" (XI.2). Similarly, "The Grace of *Faith*, whereby the Elect are enabled to believe to the saving of their souls, is the work of the *Spirit* of *Christ* in their hearts" (XIV.1). And finally, "All *Saints* that are united to Jesus Christ their *Head* by his Spirit, and Faith ... have fellowship in his Graces, sufferings, death, resurrection, and glory" (XXVII.1). See also 1644/46 *Confession*, Article XXVIII where it states, "Those that have union with Christ, are justified from all their sins by the bloud of Christ.... And this [justification] applied (in the manifestation of it) through faith." Could this be interpreted in an antinomian way? Even if it could, Knollys' other works firmly teach that the believer's union with Christ and his justification occur not prior to faith but when he exercises faith in Christ.

A fourth hyper-Calvinistic tenet logically follows upon eternal justification; that is, the elect are eternally members of the covenant of grace. The Baptist hyper-Calvinists speculated about the eternal internal acts of God whereby the Persons of the Trinity deliberated about the salvation of humans. Calvin did not speculate concerning these internal acts in the Godhead.[172] On the other hand, the High Calvinists did, and the hyper-Calvinists emphasized it even more. For example, Gill has a whole section in his *Body of Divinity* on the internal acts and works of God. In one place he writes,

> That there has been such a transaction between the Father and the Son, which, with propriety enough, may be called the *counsel of peace*, we have sufficient warrant from 2 Cor. V. 19... by the *world* is meant the elect of God, he so loved, as to send his Son to be the Saviour of, and for the life of whom Christ gave his flesh, John iii. 16. And vi. 51. And about the peace and reconciliation of those, or in what way to make peace and atonement for them, God was in Christ, or with Christ, consulting, contriving, and planning the scheme of it; which was this, not to impute their sins unto them, but to Christ, now called to be the Saviour of them; and this contains the sum of what we mean by the counsel of peace.[173]

In another place he writes,

> In the covenant of grace it was eternally settled who should be the saved ones, or partake of this great salvation; namely, those the Lord had a design of grace and mercy towards: and a love for; whom he determined to show mercy unto, even the vessels of mercy, afore appointed unto glory.... Even the whole Israel of God shall be saved in the Lord, with an everlasting salvation; consisting of Jews and Gentiles, the whole election of grace throughout the whole world who are the *all men* God would have to be saved, and come to the knowledge of the truth.[174]

In another place he states, "It is an *eternal* covenant; not merely as to duration, being what will continue to eternity, and so is called an everlasting covenant, but as to the original of it; it was made in

---

172   See his section on election in his *Institute* III.xxi.7. He spoke of a covenant of life that extended from Old Testament times based on Christ to the present. He also taught that election was determined by God before the foundation of the world, but warned against speculation into this subject. See also Niesel, *Theology of Calvin*, pp. 92-93.

173   Gill, *Body of Divinity*, pp. 211-212.

174   Gill, *The Covenant of Grace, A Believer's Support in Trouble* in *Sermons and Tracts* (1814), II, 99.

eternity, and commenced and bears date from eternity."[175] He goes on to say, "The blessings of the covenant were put into the hands of Christ so early, and the elect were blessed with them in him, as they were chosen in him before the foundation of the world, and are the *grace* given to them in him, *before the world began*."[176] And again, "God hath loved his people with an everlasting love; not only with a love, which shall abide forever; but with a love which was from all eternity." Consequently, "notwithstanding all that is done by, or done unto, these covenant ones, God will not break his covenant, nor alter the thing that is gone out of his lips. Though they sin, and he chastises them for their sins; yet his loving-kindness he will not utterly take from them, nor suffer his faithfulness, in keeping the covenant, to fail."[177]

John Brine is in total agreement with Gill. In several places in his writings Brine spoke of the internal acts of God in the Covenant of Grace. For example, in his funeral sermon for Margaret Busfield entitled, *The Covenant of grace Open'd*, he writes,

> This Covenant is most wisely ordered for the Honour of God. The Glory of the Father as the Contriver of our Redemption, is greatly displayed in this Compact. He is to be considered as the first Mover in this weighty Affair: He drew the Plan and Model of it, and concerted the best Methods to accomplish it. The Honour of the Mediator is herein highly advanced, his Glory is great in our Salvation. It was agreed on, that he should perform the Work of our Redemption, in every Branch of it, that all the Glory arising from thence might be attributed to him. Nor is the Honour of the divine Spirit less secured by this Covenant; for as the Father projected the way of our Recovery, and the Son compleated the Work of our Redemption, agreeable to his Word and Promise in this great Transaction, the Holy Ghost discovers and applies what the Father and Son have done for us. Wherefore the three divine Persons equally divide the Glory of our Salvation, according to everlasting agreement.[178]

After elaborating on the internal acts of God in his *The Proper Eternity of the Divine Decrees*, he concludes, "These *distinct* and *mutual*

---

[175]   Gill, *Body of Divinity*, p. 247.

[176]   *Ibid.*, p. 247.

[177]   Gill, *The Covenant of Grace*, in *Sermons and Tracts* (1814), II, 94, 95. In addition, see his treatise entitled, *The Doctrines of God's Everlasting Love To His Elect, and Their Eternal Union with Christ*, where he defends the eternal union of the elect with Christ (*Sermons and Tracts* [1814], III, 1-62; especially 15, 25-27).

[178]   Brine, *Grace*, pp. 24-25. See also *Doctrines of the Imputation* (1757), pp. 9-10.

Actings of the divine Persons, between themselves, are the Covenant of Grace, wherein the Method of our Salvation was fixed, and that gracious Design effectually secured."[179] Brine writes in another place about the eternity of this Covenant, "[The Covenant of Grace] is called an everlasting Covenant ... not only because of the benefits of it will eternally continue, but also on the Account of its being actually entered into, before Time began." He goes on to say, "Grace was given to the Elect in Christ before the World was formed.... All Grace and Glory were granted to Christ as the fœderal Head and Representative of his People, in the Covenant of Grace; since therefore this was done before the Commencement of Time, it may be justly concluded, that this Covenant is eternal."[180] And concerning its benefits eternally secured before time began, he states,

> The everlasting Covenant was made with [Christ], considered as the Church's Head.... And, therefore, all Blessings promised and granted, in the Covenant, were given to us in him. *We were blessed with all spiritual Blessings, in heavenly places in Christ.* And that Grace according to which, we are saved and called with an holy Calling, *was given us in Christ, before the World began.* Which necessarily supposes the subsistence of a real Union between Christ as Head, and us, as Members of him.[181]

Did Knollys speculate on the internal acts of the Godhead concerning the covenant of grace? He does mention the covenant of grace when giving a reason that Christ Jesus must seek and save lost sinners; he says, "Because (the Father having exalted him to be a Prince, and a Saviour, and promised in his everlasting covenant of grace, that all Israel shall be saved, Rom. 11. 26 27.) There is no other name under heaven given among men, whereby we must be saved." And again when encouraging believers to be holy, he states, "That God hath made with thee an everlasting Covenant of Grace and Holinesse, wherein he hath given thee many great and precious

---

[179] Brine, *The Proper Eternity of the Divine Decrees and of the Mediatorial Office, of Jesus Christ: Asserted and Proved* (London, 1754), pp. 19-21. Brine does not agree with the Reformed distinction between the Covenant of Redemption (made by God the Father with Christ) and the Covenant of Grace (made by God with believers through Christ). For him these two are the one Covenant of Grace (*Grace*, pp. 16-24).

[180] John Brine, *The Covenant of Grace Open'd* (1734), pp. 22, 23.

[181] John Brine, *The Doctrines of the Imputation of Sin to Christ, and the Imputation of his Righteousness to his People: Clearly stated, explained, and improved ...* (1757), p. 22.

promises, to pardon sin, to subdue iniquity, and to put his Law in thy minde, and write it in thy heart."[182] In both these passages, however, Knollys is not concerned with delving into the intricacies of the eternal salvation of the elect.[183] He does allude to the covenant of redemption between the Father and the Son in a 1646 sermon where he states,

> This was the good pleasure of the Fathers will, that all fulnesse, all sufficiency, all spiritualnesse, should dwell in Christ, and should by Christ be communicated to his people, that in all things Christ might have the preheminence, Col. I 18, 19. And thus God will have it done to the Man Christ Jesus, whom he delighted to honour, for the service Christ did unto his Father in the Redemption of his people.[184]

However, this is no less than what a High Calvinist would have said concerning the covenant. Knollys did not emphasize this hyper-Calvinist tenet as did Gill and Brine.

A fifth Baptist hyper-Calvinist tenet is an excessive emphasis on irresistible grace and the passivity of the elect. As noted above this tenet was implicit in Calvin[185] but became quite explicit in the High Calvinists, and even more by the hyper-Calvinists. This is so patently obvious in Gill's and Brine's writings that it is hard to know which passages to present. Gill's *The Cause of God and Truth* is a case in point. The whole work emphasizes the irresistible grace of God in salvation and human passivity. For example, he writes, "Man has neither will nor power to act of himself in things spiritually good, or in such as relate to his spiritual and eternal welfare; as conversion, regeneration, faith, repentance, and the like." Commenting on Romans 2:29 Gill states, "Circumcision of the flesh was typical of that of the spirit, and fitly expresses the passiveness of men

---

[182]   *Christ Exalted*, pp. 25, 36.
[183]   In all of his writings Knollys does little to no theologizing on this subject or any subject beyond what the Scriptures clearly state, save eschatology.
[184]   *Christ Exalted*, p. 4.
[185]   For example, *Institute* II.ii.6. Calvin does not use the term "irresistible grace". See also Francois Wendel, *Calvin: Origins and Development of His Religious Thought*, trans. Philip Mairet (1963; Durham, NC, 1987), pp. 233-263. Calvin emphasizes both human responsibility and God's sovereignty in a person's salvation. The difference between Calvin and the High Calvinists is one of emphasis. The High Calvinists were prone to emphasize irresistible grace and pay less attention to human responsibility. See for example, *Savoy Declaration* XX:1-4, "Of the Gospel, and of the Extent of the Grace thereof.".

in it; for as the infant was entierly passive and not active in circumcision, so is man in regeneration and first conversion."[186] And again
commenting on John 6:37 he writes,

> The doctrine of efficacious grace in conversion is strongly asserted in these
> words; for such who are given in eternal election, and in the everlasting
> covenant of grace to Christ, *shall* in time *come unto* him, that is, believe in
> him. Which is not to be ascribed to any power and will in them, but to the
> power and grace of God; for there is not in them naturally any will, desire,
> or inclination to come to Christ for life; they had rather go any where else,
> than to him for it.[187]

In another place he states, "No man is or can be truly converted
unto God, but by his powerful, efficacious and irresistible grace."[188]
And in his *Declaration of the Faith* he writes, "We believe, That the
work of regeneration, conversion, sanctification, and faith, is not an
act of man's free will and power, but of the mighty, efficacious, and
irresistible grace of God."[189]

John Brine was just as convinced of the irresistible grace of God
and passivity of humans in salvation as was Gill. He writes in *A
Refutation*, "As the Implantation of spiritual Principles in the Mind
is Regeneration, the Soul is passive in it, and it is instantaneous or
wrought at once."[190] In *Grace, proved to be at the sovereign Disposal of
God*, he declares, "In our depraved Nature, there is nothing but a
mere passive Capacity to receive a holy, spiritual Principle from
God, in a way of Creation, or Infusion. That is all which we can
with Truth, say of ourselves, as we are carnal and corrupt. The Will
of the Flesh does not, it cannot co-operate with the Grace of God,

---

[186]   Gill, *Cause of God*, pp. 10, 22.

[187]   *Ibid.*, p. 89. Further on he states, "Supposing the exhortations [to come to
Christ] ... respect the internal work of faith and conversion, they may be attended with
that power from God, who makes use of them, so as to produce such principles of life
and grace, in which men are purely passive.... We conclude that [a being born again]
is wrought by the omnipotent and unfrustrable grace of God, in which man is as passive
as an infant is in its natural generation and birth" (*Ibid.*, pp. 105, 107). These last two
quotes are taken from one of two sections in this work that examines the efficacious
grace of God in the salvation of sinners (*Ibid.*, 104-121, 178-183). For more on this
subject see *Ibid.*, pp. 10, 15, 21, 70, 112, 114.

[188]   Gill, *Answer to Birmingham*, in *Sermons and Tracts* (1773), p. 124.

[189]   *A Declaration of the Faith and Practice of the Church of Christ, in Carter Lane, Southwark,
under the Pastoral care of Dr. John Gill*, read and assented to at the Admission of Members
in *Sermons and Tracts* (1814), III, 559-560. See also his *Body of Divinity*, pp. 544, 548-550.

[190]   Brine, *Refutation*, p. 43.

in our Regeneration." Further on he says, "The Will is entirely passive, in the Infusion, or Creation of this [spiritual] Principle. It is not actively concerned therein. The Will holds itself absolutely inactive in the Infusion of this spiritual Principle. It neither chuses, nor refuses: Neither concurs, nor opposes, in this divine Work upon the Soul." And again, "The Will of Man, in Regeneration is wholly passive. It neither wills, nor nills." Consequently, "This holy, spiritual, and supernatural Principle, must be a divine Gift, in the most full, and absolute Sense. It is a new Life in the Soul, which was dead before. And it is as much the Gift of God, as Life is, which is communicated to a Man, who before, was dead naturally."[191] For Brine this grace is irresistible, therefore he can say, "to make a sinful Creature holy, by a Communication of Grace and Holiness, is a pure sovereign Act of God."[192]

Did Knollys place an excessive emphasis on irresistible grace? It has already been shown earlier in this chapter that Knollys did hold the teaching of irresistible grace. It is evident from the 1644/46 and 1677/89 *Confessions* and from his works. But he did not push it as far as Gill and Brine did, that is, to the point of not even offering the gospel or believing it was not the duty of the non-elect to savingly believe in Christ. Knollys would tell his auditor that no man "in his naturall condition can come to Christ, desire him, or seek to enjoy him, for none can come to Christ except the Father draw him." But he would also tell him,

God requiring poor sinners to use the meanes, he hath appointed, is pleased to make that means, effectuall for their conversion and salvation. For if God have purposed to shew mercy, and conferre his grace upon your soules, he will cause you to seeke unto him.... But albeit some of you see it is that which you ought to do, and that you had neede to do, to wit, to seeke the Lord; assenting to what you heard in the first use of the doctrine, that there is much worth, beauty, and excellency in Christ, and that poore lost undone sinners stand in neede of him.... Let me tell you, God offers you Christ upon Gospel-termes.... But having exhorted you to seeke him in the use of meanes, there I must leave you to waite on God for the moveing of his holy Spirit where you must lye and continue like the poore impotent man at the poole of Bethesda for healing: And though as he did, so you may see many a Lame, Blinde, Deaf, Dumb, Naked-leprous soule,

---

[191]   John Brine, *Grace, Proved to be at the Disposal of GOD: In a Discourse Preached July 19, 1760*, pp. 15, 21, 33, 17.
[192]   Brine, *Grace*, pp. 21, 19.

get healing and goe away rejoycing and praising God, and you remaine still so impotent, that you cannot get into the Fountain, set open for sin and for uncleannesse, nor have any that can helpe you in, that you may be cured: yet be not disheartned [*sic*], as Christ came sodainly [*sic*] and unexpectedly, and healed the impotent man after long waiting; so Christ will come according to his promise to your soules that seeke him, Malac. 3. 1. The Lord whom you seeke shall come, shall sodainly come, saith the Lord of Hosts.[193]

Even Knollys' emphasis on the need for the moving of the Spirit, qualified by his offer of Christ, concern for the sinner's soul, and the hope for God's working while waiting, is only found in his 1646 sermons. In his later works, as was evident under the first tenet, Knollys pleads with people to come to Christ with some emphasis on their inability and the necessity of God's work, but certainly not to the degree or quantity to which Gill and Brine did.

Conclusion

It is evident from our study that Knollys was a High Calvinist like his contemporary John Owen. But was he a hyper-Calvinist? Our study of Knollys' writings bears out Ivimey's and Culross' contention that he was not a hyper-Calvinist. Knollys did not hold the two primary tenets of hyper-Calvinism held by Gill and Brine. He believed and practiced that sinners should be offered the gospel, and that all people are under obligation before God to believe in Christ. He also did not teach eternal justification. The last two tenets are harder to assess because the difference between High Calvinism and hyper-Calvinism is a matter of emphasis. From his writings it is evident that Knollys did not discuss the internal acts of God in the covenant of grace to the degree that Gill and Brine did. It is true, however, that he did teach the inability of the sinner to come to Christ on his own, and therefore, the need for the Spirit's drawing of the sinner to Christ. But his writings do not emphasize this tenet to the degree that Skepp, Gill and Brine did. Consequently, in spite of Skepp's contention in his *Divine Energy*, the implied link between Knollys' and Skepp's Calvinism cannot be granted. And

---

[193]   *Christ Exalted*, pp. 12, 13, 14.

the suggestion by Haykin that Knollys was a forerunner of eighteenth-century hyper-Calvinism is highly questionable.

CHAPTER FIVE

ANABAPTISM

The strongest and most prolific heretical label attached to the Calvinistic Baptists during the revolutionary period was that of Anabaptist. After the recalling of the Long Parliament and consequently the breakdown of Laud's ecclesiastical control many sects sprang up in England. This proliferation of sects caused great consternation among the members of Parliament and the clergy. According to Thomas Edwards these sects included Independents, Brownists, Chiliasts, Antinomians, Anabaptists, Arminians, Libertines, Familists, Seekers, Perfectists, Enthusiasts, Socinians, Arians, and Antitrinitarians.[1] He also believed that their false teachings were intermingled, and in any one society there could be found many heresies; "Both the severall kinds of sects, and most persons of each kinde," he stated, "are compounded of many, yea, some of all: One and the same society of persons in our times, being both Anabaptisticall, Antinomian, Manifestarian [Arminian], Libertine, Socinian, Millenary, Independent, Enthusiasticall."[2]

According to Robert Baillie, Anabaptism was the worst of all the sects. It was the "True Fountaine of Independency, Antinomy, Brownisme, Familisme, and the most of the other Errors, which for the time doe trouble the Church of England."[3] Consequently, in the 1640s many tracts and treatises were written to counter this heresy. In 1642, two tracts were published anonymously to warn England against Anabaptism entitled, *A Short History of the Anabaptists of High and Low Germany*, and *A Warning for England Especially for London in the famous History of the Frantick Anabaptists Their wild Preachings*

---

[1]   Thomas Edwards, *The First and Second Part of Gangraena or a Catalogue or Discovery of many of the Errors, Heresies, Blasphemies and pernicious Practices of the Sectaries of this time, vented and acted in* England *in these four last yeers*, 3rd ed. (1646), I, pt. 2, p. 13.

[2]   *Ibid.*

[3]   Robert Baillie, *Anabaptism, The True Fountaine of Independency Antinomy, Brownisme, Familisme, and the most of the other Errors, which for the time doe trouble the Church of England* (1647), Title page.

& Practices. These were primarily histories of the Continental Anabaptist movement showing that Anabaptists were anarchists and
heretics. This same concern was evident in the House of Commons
and the Westminister Assembly. In March 1643/44 the Commons
instructed that an ordinance be prepared "for the suppressing the
unlawful assembling and meeting together of Antinomians and
Anabaptists, and the venting their erroneous and schismatical opinions in the counties as well as in London." Several months later,
Robert Baillie wrote in a letter that "a great many of our brethren
[in the Assembly] did complain of the great increase and insolency
in divers places of the Antinomian and Anabaptistical conventicles."[4] And in August he wrote that the Assembly's next work was
"to give advyce [to the Commons] what to doe for the suppressing
of Anabaptists, Antinomians, and other sectaries." In September,
after some discussion, the Assembly submitted to the Commons
"their conceptions for suppressing of Antinomianism and Anabaptism."[5] This concern over Anabaptism was expressed in some important treatises written to confute this heresy including Thomas
Shepard's *New Englands Lamentation for Old Englands present errours, and
divisions ... Occasioned by the increase of Anabaptists* (1644), Immanuel
Knutton's *Seven Questions about the Controversie between the Church of
England and the Separatists and Anabaptists* (1644), Anon., *A Declaration
Against Anabaptists* (1644), Thomas Edwards' *Gangraena* (1645),
Ephraim Pagitt's *Heresiography* (1645), Daniel Featley's *The Dippers
dipt* (1645), Anon., *The Anabaptists Catechisme* (1645), Anon., *A Letter
of the Ministers of the City of London, Presented ... to the Reverend Assembly
of Divines ..., Against Toleration* (1645), and Robert Baillie's *Anabaptism*
(1647).[6]

One of the sects labelled Anabaptist was the Calvinistic Baptist
group that formally confessed its faith in their 1644 *Confession* entitled, *A Confession of Faith of seven Congregations or Churches of Christ in
London, which are commonly (but unjustly) called Anabaptists* (1644). Its
primary purpose was to demonstrate its orthodoxy to its Calvinistic
brethren. It states in its preface,

---

[4]   Robert Baillie, *Letters and Journals of Mr. Robert Baillie*, ed. David Laing (Edinburgh,
1841), II, 215.
[5]   Baillie, *Letters and Journals*, II, 224, 218, 228; S.W. Carruthers, *The Everyday Work
of the Westminister Assembly* (Philadelphia, 1943), pp. 93, 98.
[6]   Gordon Kingsley, "Opposition to Early Baptists (1638-1645)," *The Baptist History
and Heritage*, 4 (1969), pp. 19-20.

Wee question not but that it will seeme strange to many men, that such as wee are fre-
quently termed to be, lying under that calumny and black brand of Heretickes, and sowers
of division as wee doo, should presume to appear so publickly as wee have done: But yet
not withstanding wee may well say, to give answer to such, what David *said to his*
brother, when the Lords battell was a fighting, I Sam. 29.30. *Is there not a cause?*
Surely, if ever people had cause to speake for the vindication of the truth of Christ *in their*
hands, wee have, that being indeed the maine wheele at this time that sets us aworke; for
had any thing by men been transacted against our persons onely, wee could quietly have
sitten still, and committed our Cause to him who is a righteous Judge, who will in the
great day judge the secrets of all mens hearts by Jesus Christ: But being it is not only us,
but the truth professed by us, wee cannot, wee dare not but speake; it is no strange thing
to any observing man, what sad charges are laid, not onely by the world, that know not
God, but also by those that thinke themselves much wronged, if they be not looked upon
as the chiefe Worthies of the Church of God, and Watchmen of the Citie: But it hath
fared with us from them, as from the poor Spouse seeking her Beloved, Cant. 5. 6, 7.
They finding us out of that common road-way themselves walke, have smote us and taken
away our vaile, that so wee may by them be recommended odious in the eyes of all that
behold us, and in the hearts of all that thinke upon us, which they have done both in
Pulpit and Print, charging us with holding Free-will, Falling away from grace, denying
Originall sinne, disclaiming of Magistracy, denying to assist them either in persons or
purse in any of their lawfull Commands, doing acts unseemly in the dispensing the Ordi-
nance of Baptism, not to be named amongst Christians: All which Charges wee disclaime
as notoriously untrue, though by reason of these calumnies cast upon us, many that feare
God are discouraged and forestalled in harbouring a good thought, either of us or what
wee professe; and many that know not God incouraged, if they can finde the place of our
meeting, to get together in Clusters to stone us, as looking upon us as people holding such
things, as that wee are not worthy to live: Wee have therefore for the cleering of the truth
we professe, that it may be at libertie, though wee be in bonds, briefly published a Confes-
sion of our Faith, as desiring all that feare God, seriously to consider whether ... men have
not with their tongues in Pulpit, and pens in Print, both spoken and written things that
are contrary to truth.[7]

In spite of the group's *Confession* this heretical epithet continued to
plague this small group of Calvinistic Baptist Churches in the following years. As noted above, important clergymen like Featley,
Pagitt, and Baillie wrote treatises accusing these churches of
Anabaptism.[8] One of the first works that came out against the Lon-

---

[7]   *The Confession of Faith* (1644) in W.L. Lumpkin, *Baptist Confessions of Faith*
(Philadelphia, 1959), pp. 154-155.
[8]   The *Confession* was also mentioned in the Commons on January 29, 1644/45.
They referred the "Confession of Faith of the seven Anabaptist Churches in London"
to the Committee of Plundered Ministers. There is no evidence that the Committee
discussed the *Confession* or reported back to the Commons (Carruthers, *Everyday Work*,
pp. 103-104).

don Baptists after they published their *Confession* was *The Dippers dipt. Or, The Anabaptists Duck'd and Plung'd over Head and Eares, at a Disputation in Southwark* by the Church of England clergyman and controversialist Daniel Featley. This work was his most popular, going through six editions in the same number of years. He believed that "of all the Heretiques and Schismatiques the Anabaptists in three regards ought to be most carefully looked unto, and severely punished, if not utterly exterminated and banished out of the Church and Kingdome." His three concerns were: 1) "their affinity with many other damnable Heretiques, both ancient and later"; 2) "their audacious attempts upon Church and State"; and 3) "the peculiar malignity this heresie hath to Magistracie; other heresies are stricken by Authority, this strikes at Authority itselfe."[9] In this work Featley gives an account of his disputation in Southwark in 1642 with some "Anabaptists". One of the disputants was the Calvinistic Baptist William Kiffin. In a marginal note of *Dippers dipt.* Featley writes, "This Cufin [Kiffin] is said to be one of the first that subscribed the Anabaptists confession printed 1644. London."[10] The rest of the treatise looks at the history and doctrine of the Continental Anabaptists with a final chapter identifying the London Calvinistic Baptists with them. In this last chapter he censures the Baptist *Confession* of 1644 saying,

> *They offer to the unlearned their faire cup full of venome, anointing the brim with the honey of sweet and holy words, they thrust in store of true positions, that together with them they may juggle in the venome of their falshood:* they cover a little ratsbane in a great quantity of sugar that it may not be discerned. For among the fifty three Articles of their confession, there are not above six but may passe with a faire construction: and in those six none of the foulest and most odious positions wherewith that Sect is aspersed are expressed.

He goes on to say that if it appears that the English Anabaptists are not teaching the same things as their Continental brethren, "it seems to me that these Anabaptists are but *in fieri* (as the Schooles speak) not *in facto esse*; like the fish and Serpents in the mud of *Nilus*, not fully shaped: like a statue in the Stone-cutters shop, not fin-

---

   [9]   "Epistle", quoted in W.J. McGlothlin, "Dr. Daniel Featley and the First Calvinistic Baptist Confession," *The Review and Expositor*, 6 (1909), pp. 580-581.
   [10]   *Dippers dipt.*, p. 4.

ished: they are Anabaptists but in part, not in whole."[11] He concludes the treatise with a critique of several of the *Confession*'s articles.[12]

Another attack in 1645 upon the Calvinistic Baptists and their
Confession identifying them with Anabaptism came from the pen of
Thomas Edwards in his *Gangraena*. In the first Part of *Gangraena* he
writes,

> There is a Book lately printed, and that with license, (as the Title of the
> Booke expresses, and now the time is come, that all of kind Errors are
> Printed *cum privilegio*) call'd a *Confession of faith, of seven Churches of Christ in*
> London, which are commonly (but unjustly) call'd Anabaptists, Dedicated
> to the High Court of Parliament.... There are many dangerous opinions
> and practices, which to my knowledge by Books in Print, and discourses of
> theirs, some of those whose hands are subscrib'd to the *Confession of Faith*,
> hold, but are concealed, other points of their confession express'd gener-
> ally, and doubtfully, not holding them as the Reformed Churches do.[13]

In addition, Edwards considered the Calvinistic Baptists William
Kiffin and Paul Hobson to be Anabaptists, and identified them with
the 1644 Baptist *Confession*. He states,

> *Will. Kiffin*, sometimes servant to a Brewer ... this mans man is now become
> a pretended Preacher, and to that end hath by his inticing words, seduced
> and gathered a Schismatical rabble of deluded children, servants and peo-
> ple without either Parents or Masters consent.... For a further manifestation
> of him in a Pamphlet called, *The Confession of faith of the seven Anabaptistical*
> *Churches*, there he is underwritten first, as Metropolitan of that Fraternity.

Later, in *Gangraena* Edwards writes, "This *Paul Hobson* is one of
those whose hand is subscribed to the *Confession of Faith of the Anabap-*
tists, set forth last winter.... He hath also lately Printed a Discourse
against Baptizing of Children, upon occasion of that Disputation

---

[11]   *Dippers dipt.*, p. 220. Featley also identifies the Calvinistic Baptists of London with
the Continental Anabaptists in the second last chapter. He states, "In their Confession
printed this year, they finde themselves agrieved with the name of Anabaptist, saying,
they are falsly so called: yet it is well knowne they all of them either rebaptize or are rebaptized.... They have hitherto been known in generall by no other names then of
Anabaptists, or Catabaptists, and *never a barrell better herring*" (*Ibid.*, pp. 203-204).
[12]   For an analysis of Featley's critique of the 1644 Baptist *Confession* see
McGlothlin, "Dr. Daniel Featley," pp. 579-589.
[13]   Edwards, *Gangraena* (1646), I, pt. 2, pp. 108-109.

that should have been between Mr. *Calamy* and some of the Anabaptists."[14]

In the same year another important work identifying the Calvinistic Baptists with the Continental Anabaptist heretics was written by Ephraim Pagitt. Entitled, *Heresiography*, it also traced the history and identified the false teachings of the Continental Anabaptists. In this work he states that these Anabaptists now "lift up their heads" in England. One of the examples he gives of the presence of Anabaptism in England was the disputation that Dr. Featley had with some Baptists in Southwark, the same debate that Dr. Featley "hath given the World an account." He continues,

> Would to God our religious Patriots assembled in Parliament would at length take care (as they have done of the Romish Emissaries) to suppresse these, that the name of God be not blasphemed: that they may not infect the simple people with their abhominable Errours.... The plague of Heresie is among us, and wee have no power to keep the sick from the whole.[15]

In the next two pages he identifies the 1644 Baptist *Confession* with Anabaptism critiquing several of its articles.[16]

Two years later in 1647 another treatise against the Anabaptists was authored by the Scottish Presbyterian minister Robert Baillie entitled, *Anabaptism, The True Fountaine of Independency, Antinomy, Brownisme, Familisme, and the most of the other Errours*. In the first two chapters of the work he sought to demonstrate "That the younger Anabaptists who now trouble the Church of England, are nothing inferiour to their Fathers in the art of erring." In chapter three he addresses the modern tenets of the Anabaptists in England, and in so doing identifies the churches who signed the 1644 *Confession of Faith* as Anabaptist. He states,

> How ever the tenets which the most of them are likely to acknowledge, be these which seven of their best Churches did offer in print to the Parliament, as their common sense: We wish that all these who go under the name of Anabaptists in *England*, were resolved to stand to the articles of

---

[14] *Ibid.*, I, pt. 2, p. 6; I, pt. 2, pp. 33-34. For more on Kiffin see *Ibid.*, I, pt. 2, pp. 35-36; II, 83-84. He also identifies Thomas Patience as an Anabaptist preacher (*Ibid.*, II, 37). All three of these men signed the 1644 Baptist *Confession*.

[15] Ephraim Pagitt, *Heresiography: or, A description of the Heretickes and Sectaries of these latter times* (1647), p. 37.

[16] *Ibid.*, pp. 38-39.

that confession without any further progresse in errour: but how farre the
very prime Subscribers are from any such resolution, it will appear anon.
As for the *Members* whether of these seven, or of their other thirty nine
Congregations [these are other churches identified as Anabaptist but not
Calvinistic] ... the most of them are exceeding farre from making these
Articles the rule of their belief.[17]

Baillie's assessment of these English Anabaptists was based on the
testimony of Stephen Marshall and Thomas Blake. In his *A Defence
of infant baptism; in answer to two treatises by Mr. Tombes* Marshall states,
"The Confession [of 1644] is such a one as I beleeve thousands of
our new Anabaptists will be far from owning, as any man may be
able to say without a spirit of divination, knowing that their received and usuall doctrines do much more agree with the Anabaptists in Germany, then with this handfull who made this Confession in London."[18] Marshall and Baillie were far from certain that
these Anabaptists or any others in England truly espoused the tenets of the 1644 *Confession.* Baillie goes on to identify the heresies of
Brownism, Antipaedobaptism, Arminianism, Antinomianism, and
Antitrinitarianism with the London Calvinistic Baptists using their
1644 *Confession* or the works of those who signed it such as Paul
Hobson, Benjamin Coxe, William Kiffin, John Spilsbury, and Samuel Richardson.[19] In addition, the last chapter of *Anabaptism* addresses the nine arguments given by the Calvinistic Baptists Benjamin Coxe, Hanserd Knollys and William Kiffin against infant baptism in their *A Declaration concerning the Publike Dispute ... concerning
Infant Baptism* (1645).[20]

There was little doubt among the Presbyterian and Church of
England clergy that the churches of the 1644 *Confession* were Anabaptist and heretical. Moreover, among those associated with these
churches, Hanserd Knollys was also accused of Anabaptism. As
early as August 1644 a report was sent to the Commons from the
Assembly concerning Knollys,

---

[17] Baillie, *Anabaptism*, pp. 48-49.
[18] Quoted in *Ibid.*, p. 66.
[19] *Ibid.*, pp. 49-128. All but Coxe signed the 1644 edition of the *Confession.* Coxe
signed the revised edition of 1646.
[20] *Ibid.*, p. 163. Baillie's answers to the nine arguments are given in *Ibid.*, pp. 163-
179.

But now we see those men [Antinomian and Anabaptistical] have cast off all affection, and are so embittered that it is high time to suppress them; and we can forbear no longer, but petition this House to think of some such way for the stopping of them as you, in your wisdom, shall think fit. Some things of late done are come to our knowledge; one Mr. Knollys, in a church in Cornhill, did openly preach against the baptising of children, and on the last Fast Day did preach that the baptizing of children was one of the greatest sins of the land.[21]

In the following year the anonymous anti-Anabaptist work entitled, *The Anabaptists Catechisme* named Knollys as one of its preachers. In answer to the catechism's question, "Who are your Preachers, and what are they?", it says, "There are divers: *viz*. Mr. *Patience*, an honest Glover; Mr. *Griffin*, a reverend Taylor; Mr. *Knowles*, a learned Schollar; Mr. *Spilsbey* [Spilsbury], a renowned Cobler; Mr. *Barber*, a Button-maker, and divers others, most gallant teachers, well grounded in their opinions." In the same year Edwards in his *Gangraena* implicitly identifies Knollys as an Anabaptist sectary saying,

This *Knowls* went into the army which was under the command of the Earl of *Manchester*, where he did a great deal of mischief; and afterwards coming to *London*, Preached at *Bow* in *Cheapside* openly against Childrens baptism, which then gave great offence, that he was complained of to the Parliament for that Doctrine.... *Knowls* is one of them who dares keep publike Disputations (though it is well known he is a weak man, and sorry Disputant) with Ministers of the City against Paedo-Baptism, and is one of them whose hand is subscribed to the Declaration lately put forth concerning the publike Dispute which should have been concerning *Infants baptism*.[22]

Later in *Gangraena* Edwards explicitly identifies Knollys with the Anabaptists and their 1644 *Confession*. He states,

Whereas they [Anabaptists in England] plead a peaceable and quiet carriage, I can prove a tumultuous disorderly managing their opinions, as in Mr. *Knols*, and *Paul Hobson*, besides of many other Anabaptists in the Kingdom, which particulars I thought briefly to hint, as an Antidote against that

---

[21] Quoted in Carruthers, *Everyday Work*, p. 96. While writing about the sufferings of Knollys in the 1640s, and in particular his suffering in Suffolk Crosby states that Knollys was counted "an *Antinomian*, and an *Anabaptist*" by his persecutors (*History of the English Baptists*, I, 228).

[22] Edwards, *Gangraena*, I, pt. 2, pp. 39-40.

Book for the present, intending suddenly a more full discovery of the fraud and fallaciousnesse of this *Confession of Faith of seven Churches.*[23]

Edwards identifies Knollys with the London Calvinistic Baptists even before he signed the revision of their 1644 *Confession* in 1646 as a pastor in one of their seven churches. Even as late as 1661 Knollys was being accused of Anabaptism. In the anonymous work entitled, *The Traytors Unvail'd, or A Brief and true account of that horrrid and bloody designe intended by those Rebellious People, known by the names of Anabaptists and Fifth Monarchy,* Knollys was identified as "a Prisoner speaker to the Anabaptists."[24]

It is evident from this brief look at the London Calvinistic Baptists and Hanserd Knollys, one of their pastors and signatories of their 1644/46 *Confession,* that rightly or wrongly they were accused of the heterodoxy of Continental Anabaptism.[25] The question remains, did Knollys espouse the teachings with which he and his Baptist confessors were being charged? In order to determine whether he did, first we will identify of which Continental Anabaptist doctrines he and his Baptist brethren were being accused by their contemporaries. We are not concerned here with the meaning of Anabaptism in general but with the meaning of Anabaptism in the minds of Knollys' antagonists.[26] This will enable us to see if *their* charges of Anabaptism are valid against Knollys. The writings of such antagonists of English Anabaptism as Robert Baillie, Thomas Edwards, Ephraim Pagitt and Daniel Featley will be examined in order to ascertain what they believed were the *specific* Anabaptist teachings that Knollys and the Calvinistic Baptists held in the 1640s.[27] This study of the literature of these English Anabaptist

---

[23]   *Ibid.,* I, pt. 2, p. 109.

[24]   *The Traytors Unvail'd* (1661), p. 5. Knollys is also mentioned as an Anabaptist by John Lightfoot in his *Journal of the Proceedings of the Westminster Assembly* in *The Whole Works of the Rev. John Lightfoot, Master of Catherine Hall, Cambridge,* ed. John Rogers Pitman (London, 1824), XIII, 302.

[25]   As mentioned in chapter two Knollys was preaching against infant baptism in the summer of 1644 even though he did not sign the first edition of the 1644 *Confession* published in October.

[26]   For a history of Continental Anabaptism see William Estep, *The Anabaptist Story* (Nashville, 1963), and George H. Williams, *The Radical Reformation* (Philadelphia, 1962).

[27]   It should be noted that Featley's *Dipper's dipt.* went through six printings between 1645 and 1660. Pagitt's *Heresiography* went through eight printings between 1645 and 1662. Edward's *Gangraena* was published in several parts at different times in 1645 and 1646.

antagonists *specifically* made against the Calvinistic Baptists of the 1640s, has not, to my knowledge, been undertaken to-date.[28] Consequently, by looking at these important writings we will be able to more accurately understand and assess the charge of Anabaptism made against Knollys. Finally, Knollys' writings will be examined in the relevant areas that address Anabaptism to see whether this charge is in fact valid. As a result, this chapter will present Knollys' thought on ecclesiological issues.

The Alleged Anabaptist Teachings of Knollys and the Calvinistic Baptists

The most formidable English Anabaptist antagonists of the 1640s were undoubtedly Daniel Featley, Ephraim Pagitt, Robert Baillie and Thomas Edwards. Each of them identified the Calvinistic London Baptists and their *Confession* with Anabaptism. Most, if not all, of the heretical teachings of the Continental Anabaptists were considered by them and their readers to be those espoused by these Calvinistic Baptists. It was guilt by association. For example, at the end of Featley's *Dippers dipt.* he makes these following observations concerning Anabaptists: they are "an Illiterate, and Sottish Sect"; "a lying and blasphemous sect, falsly pretending to divine Visions and Revelations"; "an impure and carnall Sect"; "a cruel and bloody Sect"; and "a profane and sacrilegious sect."[29] Then, following these observations, he censures the Calvinistic Baptists' 1644 *Confession* saying, "[With this Confession] they cover a little ratsbane in a great quantity of sugar that it may not be discerned. For among the fifty three Articles of their confession, there are not above six but may passe with a faire construction."[30] He then goes on to address several of those articles showing their heresy, so ending the book. It would be, therefore, obvious to the reader that the heresies of the Continental Anabaptists, given earlier in the treatise,

---

[28]   Gordon Kingsley has examined over fifty tracts written against "all" English Baptists from 1638-1646 ("Opposition to Early Baptists [1638-1645]," *Baptist History and Heritiage*, 4 [1969], pp. 18-30, 66). Consequently, his work is a broader study than this one. Our study is more specific. Our aim is to find out specifically what Anabaptist tenets the Calvinistic Baptists and Knollys, one of its signatories, were charged with.

[29]   Featley, *Dippers dipt.*, pp. 199-217.

[30]   *Ibid.*, p. 220.

were those also of the English Anabaptists, that is, the London Calvinistic Baptists.

Featley's earlier list of Anabaptist heresies is divided into three
parts: ecclesiastical, political, and economical errors. The ecclesiastical errors are: 1) "that Christ took not flesh from the Virgin Mary,
but that he past through her as the sun beams do through glasse, or
rain through a spout"; 2) "that there is no originall sin"; 3) "that
children ought not to be baptized"; 4) "that such as have been baptized in their infancie ought to be rebaptized when they come to
years of discretion"; 5) "that Lay-people may preach and administer the sacraments"; 6) "that men have freewill, not only in naturall
and morall, but also in spirituall actions"; 7) "that absolution and
the church-peace ought to be denied to such who are fallen into
any grievous sin; yea, though they repent of it"; and 8) "that *Luthers*
doctrine is worse then [*sic*] the Popes." The political errors are: 1)
"that the people may depose their magistrates and chief rulers"; 2)
"that a Christian with a good conscience may not take upon him,
or bear the office of a magistrate, or keep any court of Justice"; 3)
"that none may administer an oath to another"; and 4) "that no
malefactors ought to be put to death." And the economical errors
are: 1) "that no man hath a proprietie in his goods, but that all
things ought to be held in common"; 2) "that it is lawfull to have
more wives then one at once"; and 3) "that a man may put away
his wife, if she differ from him in point of religion, and be not of
their sect."[31] He goes on to add a few more errors that "are peculiar to their sect" of which we will only name two that were not
named in the above list: 1) "that none are rightly baptized but those
who are dipt"; and 2) "that there ought to be no set forme of
Liturgie or prayer by the book, but only by the Spirit."[32]

Although all of these "heretical errors" of the Anabaptists are
attributed to the Calvinistic Baptists in the above work as well as in
the works of Edwards, Pagitt and Baillie, we will only present the
errors that they *explicitly* identified with the London Calvinistic Baptists, or those that are addressed by the 1644 *Confession* and by Samuel Richardson in his *Brief Considerations* wherein is contained the

---

[31] *Ibid.*, pp. 28-29.
[32] *Ibid.*, pp. 30, 32. Pagitt in *Heresiography* gives a similar list (pp. 11-25).

official Calvinistic Baptist response to Featley's book.[33] In total there are eleven errors of which these Baptists, including Knollys, were accused.

The first six Anabaptist errors shall be classified as Ecclesiastical.[34] The first is that of believers' baptism or anti-paedobaptism. In response to the thirty-ninth article of the Baptist *Confession* which states that baptism is "an ordinance of the new Testament, given by Christ to be dispensed only upon persons professing Faith, or that are disciples, or taught, who upon profession of Faith ought to be baptized," Featley states,

> Here they lispe not, but speak out plaine their Anabaptisticall doctrine; whereby they exclude all the children of the faithfull from the sacrament of entrance into the Church, and the only outward meanes of their salvation in that state.... This heretical assertion [that only those who profess faith in Christ] is at large refuted by manifold Arguments drawne from Scripture, Fathers and reason, and all their cavils and evasions exploded.[35]

Pagitt, in response to this article, says much the same: "By this Article most cruely they exclude all Infants baptisme from the sacrament of entrance into the Church, being the onely outward meanes of their saluation."[36] Consequently, Baillie writes,

> They exclude all infants from any interest in the Covenant of grace; they grant that the Jewish infants had interest in some earthly priviledges, which

---

[33] Those Anabaptist errors Richardson addresses in *Brief Considerations* are: disloyalty to the state, anarchy, antitrinitarianism, schismatic, believer's baptism, revelations by the Spirit, an ignorant & uneducated ministry, and lay-preaching. In the 1644 revised edition of the Baptist *Confession* (1646) the reader is encouraged to read Richardson's treatise for "satisfaction to the answers [whereof wee are accused]" (*A Confession of Faith of seven Congregations or Churches of Christ in London, which are commonly (but unjustly) called Anabaptists*, second Impression corrected and enlarged [1646], "To the Judicious and Impartiall Reader", p. 3). For more on *Brief Considerations* see Gritz, "Samuel Richardson," pp. 141-155.

[34] We are following Featley's categorisation of Anabaptist errors (Featley, *Dippers dipt.*, pp. 28-29).

[35] *Ibid.*, pp. 222-223.

[36] Pagitt, *Heresiography*, p. 38. In answer to the question, "What be the opinions of the Anabaptists?" the anonymous writer of *The Anabaptists Catechisme* states, "The Anabaptists ... are of the opinion that infants are not fit to be baptized, nor received into Communion and brotherly fellowship, till they be of bignesse fit to accompany with" (pp. 2-3). In addition, Edwards mentions in his "Catalogue of the many Errors of the Sectaries," that the Calvinistic Baptist Paul Hobson "hath also lately Printed a Discourse against Baptizing of Children" (*Gangraena*, I, pt. 2, p. 34).

Circumcision did seal unto them; but they deny that any children whether of Jews or Gentiles have any promise of grace made to them till they come to age and beleeve: so they will not have Circumcision a seal of the Covenant of grace to any of the children of Abraham while they are infants, but only of temporal benefits.[37]

On account of this belief, the Calvinistic Baptists were also accused of denying children's salvation and the Old Testament.[38] In addition, to this error of anti-paedobaptism Featley accuses them of a new Anabaptist error, that of dipping or immersing the person being baptized. In response to the Baptist *Confession*'s fortieth article he writes,

> This article is wholly sowred with the new leaven of Anabaptisme, I say the *new leaven*, for it cannot be proved that any of the ancient Anabaptists maintained as such position, there being three ways of baptizing, either by dipping, or washing, or sprinkling, to which the Scripture alludeth in sundry places.... It is true, *Iohn* baptized Christ in *Iordan*, and *Philip* baptized the Eunuch in the river: but the Text saith not that either the Eunuch, or Christ himselfe, or any baptized by *Iohn*, or his Disciples, or any of Christs Disciples, were *dipped*, *plunged*, or *dowsed* over head and eares, as this Article implyeth, and our Anabaptists now practice.[39]

Clearly, for these writers, the Calvinistic Baptist teaching on baptism was an Anabaptist heresy.

A second Anabaptist error with which these English Baptists were charged had to do with their ecclesiology. They were accused of Brownism, that is, they taught that each church was autonomous and independent without any synodical oversight. Baillie writes,

> Concerning the government of the Church, what ever their Fathers of old did teach the Brownists, they are perfect disciples therein to the Brownists, this day: for they acknowledge no Nationall Church, nor any Church visible, but a Congregationall, which they make absolutely Independent and uncontrollable by any Superiour Synod. Though they should break out in never so many the grossest heresies and schisms, yet they have no remedy against them, none on earth must pretend any Jurisdiction, any power to

---

[37] Baillie, *Anabaptism*, pp. 89-90.
[38] *A Confession of Faith* (1644/46), "To the judicious and impartiall Reader," p. 3.
[39] Featley, *Dippers dipt.*, pp. 223-224. Pagitt responds to this Article similarly, "In the 40. they making dipping necessary, which Christ never commanded" (*Heresiography*, p. 39).

inflict the least Ecclesiastick censure upon their Congregation or any member thereof, though guilty of all imaginable blasphemies.[40]

Along with this teaching these English Anabaptists taught that the authority over the church belonged to the congregation and not the leaders. The author of *The Anabaptists Catechisme* in response to the question, "What is it that is in the power of the Congregation?" answered, "Whatsoever is done, is confirmed by the approbation of them, for against their consent the Pastor and Deacon hath not power to do any thing."

Baillie also charged them with teaching that church membership was to be pure and regenerate:

> The chiefe singularities of Brownism are about the constitution and government of the Church, they say the Church is made up only of members who are really and convincingly holy, of such who do evidence the truth of their regeneration to the satisfaction of the whole or the greater part of the Church. Hereupon they do ground their separation from the rest of the reformed.... They will have all their members to be reall Saints, and they separate from all other Churches who neglect to presse the necessity of such a qualification.... They avow all their members to be holy and elect.[41]

These Baptists believed that it was only upon profession of faith giving a "sufficient testimony before the Congregation," followed by baptism that one became a member of the church.[42]

Closely associated with an Anabaptist ecclesiology, the Calvinistic Baptists were charged with a third error, an Anabaptist ministry.

---

[40]   Baillie, *Anabaptism*, p. 52. The Brownists were the followers of Robert Brown, an Elizabethan radical Puritan/Separatist, who gathered an independent church in Norwich. For more on Brown see B.R. White, *The English Separatist Tradition* (Oxford, 1971), pp. 44-66. In his Catalogue of errors, citing Paul Hobson, Edwards writes, "That the Presbytery and Presbyteriall Government, are the false Prophet, and the Beast spoken of in the *Revelations*: Presbytery is a third part of the City of *Rome*, yea that Beast, in *Revel*. 11. That ascends, and shall kill the two Witnesses, namely the Independents" (*Gangraena*, I, pt. 1, p. 28). Baillie also considered these London Anabaptists schismatical, he writes, "In this separation [from the reformed churches as taught by Kiffin] they run on so rashly that themselves know not where to stop it; for first with the Separatists they divide from all other Protestants, thereafter they shake off the Separatists: for the most intelligent and zealous among them refuse to remain in any Congregation either of the Independents or Brownists" (*Anabaptism*, p. 51). These Baptists were also purported to have taught that those people who were not of their group were damned (*Confession of Faith* [1644/46], p. 3).

[41]   Baillie, *Anabaptism*, pp. 49-51.

[42]   *Anabaptists Catechisme*, pp. 10-11.

Featley believed they taught that there were no distinctions between the clergy and laity. In response to the Baptists' *Confession* Article forty-one which states that, "The persons designed by Christ to dispence this ordinance [baptism], the Scriptures hold forth to be a preaching disciple, it being no where tyed to a particular Church, Officer, or Person," Featley writes:

> If the eye be darknesse, how great is that darknesse? If there be confusion in order it selfe, how great must the confusion needs be? if all be Pastours, where are their flocks? if all be teachers, where are their Scolars [*sic*]? a preaching Disciple sounds as harshly as a Scholar-Master, or Lecturing hearer.... But this error of the Anabaptists, whereby they overthrow all order in the Church, and confound shepheards and flocks, Masters and scholars, Clergy and Laity, I have professedly impugned.[43]

Along with this, these Baptists believed that not only Ministers were to preach but also lay-people who were so gifted. Concerning the Baptist *Confession*'s Article forty-two endorsing lay-preaching, Pagitt writes:

> When *Muncer*, a seditious *Anabaptist*, began first to preach, Luther advised the Senate of *Mulbus*, to demand of him what calling hee had: and if hee should avouch God to be his Author, then they should require him to prove his extraordinary calling by some evident signe. For whensoever it pleaseth God to change the ordinary course, and to call any man to any office extraordinary, he declareth that his good will and pleasure by some evident signe: If the *Anabaptisticall* Calling be ordinary, let them prove it by Scripture; if extraordinary, let them prove it by Miracles.[44]

Baillie concurs with Featley's assessment of the London Baptists' ministry: "With the power of censure they joyn the power of preaching, all their members who finde themselves gifted are per-

---

[43]   Featley, *Dippers dipt.*, pp. 224-225.

[44]   Pagitt, *Heresiography*, p. 39, (Featley debates this point with the Baptists including Kiffin at Southwark in 1642 [*Dippers dipt.*, pp. 12-13]).Consequently, Featley believed that their ministry was illegitimate because, "None may take upon him the cure of soules without Commission; nor divide the word, and dispence the Sacraments without ordination, and imposition of hands: none *may preach except he be sent, none may assume the honour of the Priesthood, except hee bee called as was* Aaron: none may open and shut the Kingdome of heaven, except they have received the *keyes* from Christ; neither a calling without gifts, nor gifts without a calling, makes a *man of God*." Furthermore, he maintained that without lawfully called pastors the Baptist churches were no true churches (*Ibid.*, pp. 225, 8).

mitted to prophecy in the face of the Congregation."[45] Not only could they preach but according to their *Confession* anyone could administer the sacraments. Baillie again states:

> Unto their members out of office they ascribe not only the power of censure and of preaching the word, but also of celebrating the Sacraments: this is clear of baptism, for they require in a baptizer not only no office, but not so much as baptism it selfe, all of them avowing the lawfulnesse for a person not bapitized to baptize, and as it seems to celebrate the Lords Supper.[46]

This lay-preaching and ministry included an uneducated, untrained ministry in the Anabaptist churches. Featley, responding to the *Confession*'s forty-fifth Article which states, "That such to whom God hath given gifts, being tryed in the Church, may and ought by the appointment of the congregation to prophecie," saying,

> For rude and illiterate Mechanicks, without calling, without knowledge of Arts, or Tongues, upon a Scripture read in the Congregation to give their suddain judgements, and interpretations thereof, as is the manner of the Anabaptists: we hold it an intolerable presumption in them, and unsufferable abuse in the Church. For those extraordinary revelations they pretend unto, together with the miraculous gift of tongues and healing, for many hundred yeares agoe: have failed in the Church.[47]

These London Anabaptists were of the same ilk as their Continental counterparts holding and practicing a false ministry.

The opponents found a fourth Ecclesiastical error in the English Anabaptists understanding of Christ and the Trinity. In the

---

[45] Baillie, *Anabaptism*, p. 52.

[46] *Ibid.*, p. 53. Edwards concurs citing Article forty-one of the Baptist *Confession*, stating in his Catalogue, "That baptizing belongs not to Ministers onely, all gifted and preaching Disciples (though no Ministers) may baptize" (*Gangraena*, I, pt. 1, p. 24).

[47] Featley, *Dippers dipt.*, p. 227. In his discussion of Continental Anabaptists his first observation is that they are "an Illiterate, and a Sottish sect" (*Ibid.*, p. 199). In his debate with the Baptists in Southwark he states, "None ought to take upon them the office of a pastour, or minister of the word, who are not able to reprove and convince Hereticks, and all gain-sayers: but your lay and unlettered men are not able to convince Hereticks, and stop the mouths of gain-sayers, because they can alledge no scripture but that which is translated in their mother-tongue, in which there may be and are some errors" (*Ibid.*, p. 14).

William Kiffin did practice healing on at least one occasion following the teaching of James 5:13-16 where the elders are instructed to anoint the sick with oil and pray over them (Edwards, *Gangraena*, I, pt. 2, pp. 44-45).

Southwark disputation Featley asked the Baptists a question concerning John 17:3, that if each of the three Persons of the Trinity is God why then does Christ say that the Father is the only true God. The Baptist answer given was that "the Father is said to be the only God in respect of Essence." Featley responded that "this Answer containes in it Blasphemy; for if the Father bee onely true God, in respect of Essence, then is not the Son or Holy Ghost God in respect of Essence; but that is false and blasphemous, for then the three persons should not be one God in Essence; or in respect of Essence."[48] It appears that these Baptist disputers denied the Deity of Christ. Baillie concurs with Featley; when referring to the English Anabaptists he states,

> They do ... joyn with him [Paul Beasts] to preach down the Divinity of Jesus Christ and the Person of the holy Ghost, as their old Father the Anabaptist *Servetus* does lead them the way. It is very suspicious that their seven Churches in their Confession make no mention at all of the Trinity, nor expresse any thing of the Person either of Christ or of the holy Ghost, when they have pregnant occasion so to do. What they speak in their second Article of the Father, Word, and Spirit, as being all three one God, is expounded by some of their followers not of the Trinity of Persons, but of three offices onely of one and the same Person.... It cannot but give offence that in their twenty second Article where they speak of that which Scripture holds out, and we accordingly are to beleeve of Jesus Christ and the holy Ghost, they mention in both their Editions [of their *Confession*] onely the nature and offices of Christ, the power and fulnesse of the Spirit in his works and operations, but speak not a syllable of the Persons either of the Son, or of the Spirit; and to Christ they give but one nature, while as all Divines since his Incarnation give him two.[49]

Baillie accuses these English Anabaptists not only of error concerning the Trinity but also concerning their Christology.

These English Anabaptists also were accused of Arminianism. This included denying original Sin, election, and teaching freewill and falling from grace.[50] For example, concerning election Baillie writes,

---

[48]   Featley, *Dippers dipt.*, pp. 3, 22.
[49]   Baillie, *Anabaptism*, pp. 97-98. The "follower" who spoke "of the three offices onely of one and the same Person", is an unnamed Lieutenant in the army (Edwards, *Gangraena*, II, 5-6).
[50]   *Confession of Faith* (1644/46), "To the judicious and impartiall Reader," p. 3.

It is true, the late Confession of the seven Churches seem [*sic*] to reject clearly enough all the five Articles of the Arminians; but as our former witnesses testifie, thousands of them care not for that Confession; yea, I professe I cannot conjecture at the reason, why the second Edition of this Confession which alone was offered to Parliament, does change so many materiall passages of the first, which point-blank did militate against Arminianism, unlesse it be their farther declination to Arminianism at the penning of the second Edition.

For instance, the seventeenth Article in the first Edition stood thus, *He hath fully performed all these things by which God might reconcile his elect only*; In the second the word only is put away; as if Christ by his sacrifice had reconciled to God all mankinde as well as the elect. This our suspicion is increased by finding the same alteration acted over again in the Article twenty first, where the first Edition reads it thus, *Christ by his death did bring forth salvation and reconciliation only for the elect*; in the Second Edition the words *reconciliation only* are omitted. Also in the nineteenth Article these words, *which are the reprobate*, in the second Edition are scraped out: and in that same Article, The execution of Gods determinate counsell whereby he delivers up his enemies to a reprobate minde to be kept unto judgement, are scraped out in the second Edition.

And concerning falling from grace and perseverance he states,

Likewise in that same Article I finde two more alterations; In the first among the fruits which the elect have of Christs Priesthood are set down their justification, adoption, regeneration, and sanctification; all those are omitted in the latter Edition. In the first Edition it is said of the Spirit that he is never taken away when once given, but doth still abide begetting and nourishing faith unto immortality; this is omitted in the latter Edition. I grant it is put in the 23 Article, which is clear enough against the Arminian errour of perseverance, had not the addition of one little word cast it all loose: for in the former Edition the 23 Article did run thus, *Those that have this precious faith can never totally nor finally fall away*; but in the latter, *all*, is added, *all these cannot fall away, etc.* which is very true, if some few persevere, albeit many and the most part of these who have justifying faith should fall away totally and finally.[51]

Not only were these English Baptists accused of Arminianism but also of Antinomianism; in fact the two were seen to go hand in hand. In answer to the question, "What be the opinions of the Anabaptists?", the *Anabaptist Catechisme* states, "The Anabaptists are of the opinion that they may do what they will if conscience moves

---

[51] Baillie, *Anabaptism*, pp. 93-94.

them to it.... Also that what the conscience approves of, cannot be ill, and that all men and women who are not of this minde, are the prophane of the world, who have not any power at all to command us to any thing against our conscience." And again in answer to the question, "If you cast off all order, by what Discipline do you walke?" the *Catechisme* answers, "Discipline! do you talke to us of Discipline? What doe you thinke we cannot walke without Discipline: alas! alas! We have a liberty (which the rest of the world are ignorant of) there is never a one of us but may follow what Discipline he thinks in his own conscience is best and thats a pleasant Discipline." Further in answer to the question "What Customes have you in your meetings? have you no lawes?" the *Catechisme* states, "Customes, oh fie upon them, they are Popish, we hate the very name of superstitious Customes and lawes are a burden that we cannot beare."[52] The *Catechisme* goes on to state ten of their privileges as Anabaptists which include sexual libertinism. The seventh states, "No man is to lye with his brothers wife, whilst her husband is in presence, except hee be fast asleep, or dead drunk"; and the tenth maintains, "None of the Fellowship is to keep his house, his table, his wife, his servant, his estate, or any thing he hath, for himselfe; but is to let any member of the Congregation partake with him of all things in common." The next question asks, "What use do you make of these priviledges?", and is answered, "Wee have two special benefits by them; first, in having a share in the Brethrens goods; and secondly, in having a right in the Sisters affections."[53]

Featley agreed with this assessment of the English Anabaptists. He called the Anabaptists in general "an impure and carnall Sect". And writing about their practice of baptism he maintains,

> They strip themselves stark naked, not onely when they flock in great multitudes, men and women together, to their *Iordans* to be dipt; but also upon other occasions, when the season permits:and when they are questioned for it, they shelter this their shamelesse act, with the proverb, *Veritas nuda ist*, the *truth is naked*, and desires no *vail*, *masque*, or guise ... for as the proverb is *Veritas nuda est*, Truth is naked, which warranteth them, as they conceive,

---

[52] *Anabaptist Catechisme*, pp. 2-3, 3-4, 4.
[53] *Ibid.*, pp. 5-6

to throw off their clothes; so also there is a proverb, *Veritas non queris angelos, truth seekes no corners*, nor innocencie starting holes, yet they doe. [54]

In addition to this practical antinomianism Baillie exposes the English Anabaptists' doctrinal antinomianism through the writings of Paul Hobson. Baillie writes, "M. *Hobson* proclaims all his wonted religious exercises to be but legall duties which he professes to give over."[55]

These first six Anabaptist errors that were associated with the London Calvinistic Baptists would be classed under Featley's "Ecclesiastical errors." These were not the only errors attributed to the London Baptists. They were also accused of several "political" errors. First, they believed that the state should not compel or force people to church duties. Kiffin in his dispute with Featley is purported to have said, "*You say your church is a true church; that cannot be: for the true church compells none to come to church, or punishes him for his conscience, as the church of England doth.*"[56] Baillie concurs,

All this Independent Doctrine is brought from the Anabaptists schools, it is one of the articles of their faith offered to the present Parliament, that no laws ought to be made by any men upon earth about any things which concern the worship of God; That who ever makes any rules for the service of God does charge Christ with want of wisdom or faithfulnesse, or both, in not making Laws anew for his house; That the great Law for matters of Religion is this, Let every man be fully perswaded in his own minde of the truth of what he beleeves without any controll from any upon earth; That it is the Magistrates duty to protect every man in his just liberty of conscience, without which all other liberties are unworthy the naming.[57]

Consequently, these Baptists believed that tithes should not be forced from the people by the state; each church should support its own minister by voluntary tithes. Featley, in response to the Baptist *Confession*'s thirty-eighth article which stated that "the due maintenance of the officers aforesaid should be the free, and voluntary

54 Featley, *Dippers dipt.*, pp. 207, 203.
55 Baillie, *Anabaptism*, p. 95. Edwards also mentions Hobson as an antinomian and one of the signatories of the Anabaptist *Confession* of 1644 (*Gangraena*, I, pt. 2, pp. 33-34). He writes, "Besides these, there are many strains of Antinomianism, Libertinism, and unwholesome words which are not according to godlinesse, in that Treatise of [Paul Hobson's] *Discovery of Truth*, pag. 63, 65, 66" (*Ibid.* I, pt. 2, p. 34).
56 Featley, *Dippers dipt.*, p. 5.
57 Baillie, *Anabaptism*, p. 55.

communication of the church, and not by constraint to be compelled from the people by a forced Law," answered,

> If their meaning be, that the maintenance ought to depend upon the volun-
> tary contribution of their parishoners, and that in case the flock should
> deny their Shepherds either part of their milke or fleece, that the Pastours
> should have no assistance of Law to recover them: this their opinion is
> most impious and sacrilegious, and directly repugnant to the Law of God,
> which assigneth tithes for the maintenance of the Priests; and that Law of
> God in the old Testament is not abrogated in the new, but rather con-
> firmed, at least in the equity thereof.[58]

A second Anabaptist "political" error of which these Calvinistic
Baptists were accused concerned the assertion that a Christian
could not take the office of civil magistrate. Featley wrote: "They
teach that the office of civill Magistrate cannot consist with Christian perfection, yet they themselves in Munster and elsewhere had
a *Consul*, and *Senatours*, and a *Headsman* of their own, yea, and a
King also, *Iohn Leiden* the Tayler, who *stitched up a Kingdome* in one
yeer, and *ravelled it out* the next."[59]

Thirdly, they held the Anabaptist error of denying the taking of
oaths. In answer to *The Anabaptists Catechisme*'s question concerning
their privileges, they say that "wee are free from all oaths and covenants, either with the King, Parliament, or People, so we keep
promise amongst ourselves."[60]

A fourth "political" Anabaptist error the Calvinistic Baptists
were accused of was anarchy. *The Anabaptists Catechisme* alludes to
this when it gives two of the Anabaptist's privileges: "That wee are
free from bowing down under the yoke of mans Law, and Rule,
and all obedience, and subjection whatsoever....That wee are free
from all oaths and covenants, either with the King, Parliament, or
People, so we keep promise amongst ourselves. "[61] One of the rea-

---

[58]   Featley, *Dippers dipt.*, pp. 221-222. Pagitt agrees with Featley saying, "In the 38.
Article, that the due maintanence of the Officers, (*viz.* The Ministers) should be free, &c.
their meaning being, that their maintenance should depend upon the voluntary contribution of their people: this their opinion is most impious and sacriligious, and directly
repugnant to Gods Law" (*Heresiography*, p. 38). Baillie similarly states, "All tythes to them
are an abomination" (*Anabaptism*, p. 53).

[59]   Featley, *Dippers dipt.*, p. 203.

[60]   *Anabaptists Catechisme*, p. 5.

[61]   *Ibid.*, p. 5. See also Kingsley, "Opposition to Early Baptists," pp. 25-27.

sons for cancelling the public debate on baptism between the Calvinistic Baptists and some Presbyterians which was supposed to have taken place in 1645, was violence. Knollys, Coxe and Kiffin who sought to find out from Mr. Callamy why the meeting was cancelled, were told,

> *That it was reported at the Lord Mayors table by some body (he knew not whom) that an Anabaptist, but he knew not who [sic], said that he would bring his sword with him to the Dispute, or he would not come without his sword*; or words to that purpose: And Mr. *Callamy* also told us, *That a woman told him, that some (no body knows who [sic]) should say, That if the publique Dispute held, Mr.* Callamy *would scarce escape with his life*: and other strange reports are whispered touching that Dispute, as if we were the cause of the Lord Mayors forbidding it.... As concerning those two Reports before mentioned, we do adhorre the thoughts of such a thing; as to mannage our Dispute with any other sword, then with the sword of the Spirit.[62]

Finally, not only are they accused of "ecclesiastical" and "political" errors but also of one "economical" error. It has to do with communism and the denial of private property. The 1644 revised edition of the Baptist *Confession* (1646) mentions in its preface the false charge against them that "both in Pulpit and Print ... [they] charge us, with ... denying ... mens proprietie in their estates."[63] Featley writes that "they [Anabaptists] inveigh against covetousnesse, and to extirpate that *root of all evill*, teach men to renounce all proprietie in their goods, and to have all things in common." Featley, in response to the thirty-first Article of the Baptist *Confession* which states, "*Whatsoever the Saints any of them doe possesse or enjoy of God in this life, is by Faith*," writes, "This passage favours ranke of that errour or heresie ... imputed to *Armacanus*, who is said to have taught that the right of all possessions and goods or temporall blessings is founded in grace and not in nature; and that we hold them by no legall tenure, but Evangelical promises."[64] *The Anabaptist Catechisme* concurs when addressing what are their privileges, they answer, "That all the goods, husband, wife, and all things whatsoever, any of the Congregation have is in common to all ... [and] whosoever

---

[62] Benjamin Coxe, Hanserd Knollys, William Kiffin, &c. *A Declaration Concerning The Public Dispute* (1645), p. 5.
[63] *Confession of Faith*, "To the judicious and impartiall Reader," p. 3.
[64] Featley, *Dippers dipt.*, pp. 203, 221

desires to live without taking paines, to get his living by his trade and calling hee may go from house to house, to be releeved with all that he can get."[65]

As an apt conclusion to this section of our chapter, a dialogue between an Anabaptist and an Independent in *The Anabaptist Catechisme* is recorded; in answer to the Anabaptist's question, "But I pray you tell mee why you do charge us so high, for what cause do you do it?" the Independent answers,

> You do not only teach to your owne disciples, but print, and publish blasphemies, and profane, scurrilous, and naughtie things, and the generallitie of the people take us and you to be all one, and so wee are hardly thought on for your sakes, though wee abhor, and do utterly disclaime your wretched and horrible impietie therein.[66]

Even if we acknowledge this Independent writer's overstated apologetic to dissociate himself from the English Anabaptists, his words (those from one whose ecclesiology is closest to that of the Anabaptist) surely give us a sense of the utter hatred most English Protestants had for Anabaptists, whether Continental or English.

Knollys' Teachings Relevant to the Charges of Anabaptism

Did Hanserd Knollys espouse any of the eleven Anabaptist teachings with which he and his Baptist brethren were identified? In order to discover whether or not he did, we will examine the relevant areas of his work including his doctrine of God, baptism, ecclesiology, ministry, his Christology, and his teaching on the relationship of church and state.[67] From this examination we will be able to understand more adequately where Knollys stood on this charge of Anabaptism.

---

[65] *Anabaptists Catechisme*, p. 5.
[66] *Ibid.*, p. 14.
[67] For those teachings of Anabaptism which involve Arminian and Antinomian tendancies, Knollys' thought on these issues was examined in the last two chapters.

Knollys' Doctrine of Baptism

For the first forty-five years of Knollys' life he was a paedobaptist, first as a minister of the Church of England and then as an Independent in New England and England. Why did he change his views? Perhaps an answer can be found in his writings. The most important tract dealing with this subject was his coauthored, *A Declaration concerning the Public Dispute ... Concerning Infants-Baptisme* (1645). William Kiffin, Benjamin Coxe and Knollys were scheduled to debate the subject of infant baptism with some Presbyterians at Alderman-Bury. The meeting was cancelled by the Mayor who feared that violence would erupt at the event. The three Baptists, consequently, put forth their arguments against infant baptism in this tract. All nine of their arguments will be noted that we might better understand Knollys' doctrine of baptism.

Their first argument was that John the Baptist, Christ's disciples, and apostles administered baptism only to those people who repented and believed. Moreover, the commission of Christ in Matt. 28:19 and Mark 16:15,16 taught that disciples, i.e. believers, are to be baptised.[68] Argument two had to do with the administration of the sacrament. Knollys argued that the administration of baptism differs from the doctrine of baptism with regard to both subject matter, and form. The subject matter for paedobaptists is "infants borne in sin, and children of wrath, who neither do actually beleeve nor repent, whom you say must be baptized, though there be no warrant in the word of God for such an administration." The form for paedobaptists is "administred after the invention of men, by sprinkling their faces with water, not dipping or washing their bodies in water." For

the forme or manner of Baptisme, according to the doctrine of Christ, his Disciples, and Apostles, is such a dipping, or washing of the person baptized in or with water, as holdeth forth their communion with Christ in his Death, Buriall, and Resurrection, as appears by these Scriptures, Matth. 28.19. Acts 8 38. Heb. 10.22. Rom. 6.3,4. Col. 2.12. I Cor. 15.29.[69]

---

[68] Coxe, Knollys, Kiffin, *Public Dispute*, pp. 7-8.
[69] *Ibid.*, pp. 8, 9.

Knollys' third argument was that infant baptism is "Will-worship, and unlawfull" because a proper act of religious worship must be exemplified or commanded in Scripture, either in the Old or New Testaments.[70] For a fourth argument he stated that infant baptism denies Christ has come in the flesh. By basing infant baptism on the Old Testament (i.e. circumcision to all in the covenant including children) the paedobaptists undervalue Christ's prophetical office, and make Moses greater than Christ. This implies that the Old Testament expounds the New. On the contrary, Knollys believed the New Testament expounds the Old. In addition, he maintained that infant baptism also undervalues Christ's kingly office. The laws of Christ are greater than Moses'. Consequently, the Christian ought to follow Christ's laws, e.g., believer's baptism.[71]

Fifth, infant baptism was no part of righteousness because, "Neither in the person or practice of Jesus Christ, is the baptizing of Infants seen or held forth.[72] Sixthly, only those who are of the seed of Abraham "either of the flesh, or according to the Faith" ought to be baptized. But the children of believing Gentiles are neither; consequently, they should not be baptized. God made a covenant of works with Abraham's physical seed (Gen. 17:7 concerns only the Jews) but He made an everlasting covenant of grace with Abraham and his spiritual seed. According to the New Testament (Gal. 4) Abraham's spiritual seed are those born after the Spirit.[73] His seventh argument stated that "it is not lawfull, to apply or administer any Ordinance of Christ other wise then according to the Rule of the Word." Since infant baptism is not according to the Rule of the Word, it is unlawful. It is unlawful because Scripture teaches that all will-worship is condemned; adding to it is forbidden. We are not to follow the commandments of men and we are not to be the doers of things God did not command. If we were, we would not be faithful to Christ. Knollys also maintained that if infant baptism is lawful otherwise than according to Scripture then the ordinances of Christ could be applied to both Jews and Turks.[74] The eighth argument stated that, "If Christ commanded not his Apostles to

---

[70] *Ibid.*, pp. 10-13.
[71] *Ibid.*, pp. 13-14.
[72] *Ibid.*, p. 15.
[73] *Ibid.*, pp. 15-18.
[74] *Ibid.*, pp. 18-19.

practice or teach the baptizing of Infants, then Infants ought not to be baptized." Knollys concludes that since Christ did not command them to do such then infants ought not to be baptized. And lastly, infants ought not to be baptized because it "is no part of the revealed counsell of God, as appears by the Apostles not declaring it."[75]

It is evident from this debate that Knollys and his Baptist coauthors were staunch defenders of believer's baptism by immersion. This is confirmed in other places. Both the *Confessions* of 1644/46 and 1677/89 affirm believer's baptism. The 1644/46 *Confession*, Article XXXIX states, "Baptisme is an ordinance of the new Testament, given by Christ, to be dispensed upon persons professing faith, or that are made Disciples; who upon profession of faith, ought to be baptized, and after to partake of the Lords Supper." The 1677/89 *Confession* changes the *Westminster*'s and *Savoy*'s chapter on baptism stating, "Those who do actually profess repentance towards *God*, faith in, and obedience, to our Lord Jesus, are the only proper subjects of this ordinance."[76] Knollys writes in *A Declaration of a Public Dispute* that "the onely written Commission to Baptize (which is in Matth. 28.19) directeth us to baptize Disciples onely ... for this is the onely construction and interpretation that the Greek word can there beare; and Infants cannot be made Disciples, because they cannot learne."[77] Similarly in *The World that now is* Knollys maintains that those fit for baptism are those who have received the Holy Spirit, believed in Christ, confessed their sins, and repented.[78] And in case some might think that "any such Ordinance [as baptism] of Jesus Christ ... [dispensed by] one that is not distinctly, spiritually, powerfully, enabled as the first dispensers" ought not to administer it, Knollys answers: "We are as powerfully inabled as the first Dispenser of Baptism: And we having received

---

[75]   *Ibid.*, p. 20.

[76]   The 1646 revised edition of the 1644 *Confession* will be identified as 1644/46 *Confession*. All quotes are taken from the revised edition referenced by Article (no page numbers were given in this edition). *Confession of Faith* (1677/89), 29.2. All quotations of the 1677/89 *Confession* are taken from Lumpkin, *Baptist Confessions of Faith*, pp. 241-295.

[77]   Coxe, Knollys, Kiffin, *Public Dispute*, p. 19.

[78]   *World*, pt. 1, p. 73.

Authority from Jesus Christ in that Commission given to Christs Disciples."[79]

Both *Confessions* also affirm baptism by immersion. The 1644/46 *Confession*, Article XL, taught that

> The way and manner of the dispensing this ordinance, is dipping or plung-
> ing the body under water, it being a signe, must answer the things signified,
> which is, that interest the Saints have in the death, burial, and resurrection
> of Christ. And that as certainly as the body is buried under water, and risen
> again, so certainly shall the bodies of the Saints bee raised by the power of
> Christ, in the day of the resurrection, to reigne with Christ.

The 1677/89 *Confession* states similarly, "Immersion, or dipping of the person in water, is necessary to the due administration of this ordinance."[80] Knollys' proof for immersion is that, "The Greek word Βαπτίζω, signifieth to dip, or wash, but never to sprinkl [*sic*]." He goes on to say, "Our Reasons why Baptisme ought to be thus administred by dipping or washing the body in water are these, to wit, 1. *Because*, It was administred in much water; Joh, 3. 23. 2. *Because*, It must represent a death, buriall, and resurrection; Rom.6.34. I Cor.15.29. Col.2.12. 3. *Because*, The Parties baptized are to go into the water; Matth. 3. 13.16. and Acts 8. 38. 39."[81] It should also be noted that in response to the accusation of baptizing believers naked, the 1644/46 *Confession* states in the margin of its Article on immersion, "The word Βαπτίζω signifies to dip or plunge, (Yet so as convenient garments be both upon the Adminis-trator and subject with all modesty.)"[82]

It is evident that Knollys' arguments against paedobaptism and in favour of believer's baptism, particularly in *A Declaration of the Public Dispute*, are based on a New Testament hermeneutic, that is, the New Testament takes precedence over the Old Testament. This is apparent from his fourth argument that states that Christ's Pro-phetical and Kingly offices supercede those of Moses, and that Gen. 17:7 refers to Abraham's seed after the flesh, and Gal. 4 to Abraham's seed after the Spirit. In fact, all of his arguments are based on the precedence of the New Testament over the Old Testa-

---

79 *The Shining of a Flaming fire in Zion* (1646), p. 14.
80 *Confession of Faith* (1677/89), 29.4.
81 Coxe, Knollys, Kiffin, *Public Dispute*, pp. 9-10. See also *World*, pt. 1, p. 74.
82 *Confession of Faith* (1644/46), Article XL.

ment. Michael Novak has shown that this New Testament hermeneutic is the basis upon which the Calvinistic Baptists as a whole
interpreted their doctrine of baptism.[83]

Knollys' Ecclesiology

Knollys taught that the Church is the "Spouse of Christ" and a
"Mystical Body" consisting of many spiritual members. These
members are all the Churches of the Saints and every individual
believer compacted and joined together in love and faith. For him
Christ is the object of the saints' joy in his Churches, ordinances
and holy administration.[84] In his exposition of *Song of Solomon* 1:5 he
maintained that "Jerusalem" symbolized "the Church of God on
Earth", and its "daughters" were "all the Churches of the saints."
From these references Knollys alludes to the existence of the invisible, universal church. The 1677/89 Confession which Knollys
signed similarly states, "The Catholick or universal Church, which
(with respect to internal work of the Spirit, and truth of grace) may
be called invisible, consists of the whole number of the Elect, that
have been, are, or shall be gathered into one, under Christ the head
thereof; and is the spouse, the body, the fulness of him that filleth
all in all."[85] For Knollys this was one of the meanings of the word
ecclesia in the New Testament. He also believed that *ecclesia* signified
a true visible constituted Church of Christ, a congregation of saints
called out of the world, separated from idolaters and idol temples,
and from all legal observations, assembled together in one place.[86]
The 1644/46 *Confession* which Knollys signed, states,

> Jesus Christ hath on earth a spiritual kingdom, which is his Church, whom
> he hath purchased and redeemed to himselfe as a peculiar inheritance;
> which Church is a company of visible Saints, called and separated from the
> world by the word and spirit of God, to the visible profession of faith of the

---

[83] Michael J. Novak, "'Thy Will Be Done' The Theology of the English Particular
Baptists, 1638-1660" (unpublished Ph.D. dissertation, Harvard University, 1979), pp.
262-277. In fact, Novak shows that this hermeneutic is the foundation upon which the
Calvinistic Baptists interpreted Scripture. The Old Covenant was superceded by the
New; obedience to Christ supercedes that obedience to any of the Old Testament
prophets (*Ibid.*, pp. 192-241).

[84] *Song of Solomon*, p. 17.

[85] *Confession of Faith* (1677/89), 26.1.

[86] *Parable*, p. 5; *World*, pt. 1, p. 44.

gospel, being baptized into that faith, and joyned to the Lord, and each to other, by mutuall agreement in a practical enjoyment of the ordinances commanded by Christ their Head and King.[87]

And again in his commentary on John's Revelation he makes several comments concerning the "*Churches* of God in these *latter* days:"

> *First*, The *fit* matter of a true visible Church of God under the Gospel, is a company of sanctified, Baptized Believers.... *Secondly*, The *essential* form of a true visible Church of God, is *right* joining and *orderly* compacting of those sanctified Believers together into one *mystical* body, by the Ministers of Christ, according to the constitution of the Gospel.... *Thirdly*, The end why the Church is so planted, builded, and formed, is that they may meet together in *ONE* to *Worship* God *publickly* in Spirit and Truth in all his *sacred* Gospel Ordinances, to the Glory of God, and for the mutual Edification of that *mystical* body of Christ.... *Fourthly*, It is not lawful for any Member of a true Church to separate himself from it, nor forsake the assembling of himself with it.... *Fifthly*, The Ministers and Members of a Church may keep themselves from being *partakers* of other Mens Sins, and from being *defiled* with them, by bearing their Testimony and Witness *orderly* in the Church, against them that hold any unsound Doctrine, or any corrupt manners, or any false Worship.[88]

Interestingly, Knollys wrote in his *The World that now is* that the Jerusalem church, according to the account in the Book of Acts, was a particular congregation of sanctified believers baptized with water in the name of the Father, Son and Holy Spirit, but with several congregations or churches making up the one church in that city. Knollys writes,

> The Church at Jerusalem was the first of all those Gospel-Churches ... Which Church was at its first Constitution a particular Congregation of sanctified Believers baptized with Water ... And although the number of the Disciples were multiplied from one hundred and twenty ... to three thousand ... yea to five thousand.... So that the Apostles had their own distinct Companies, Societies, or Congregations in Jerusalem [Acts. 4.13, 19, 23 ....] Yet they all being one heart, and of one soul, were but one church ... And so were all the particular Congregations in every City denominated and called.

---

[87]   *Confession of Faith* (1644/46), Article XXXIV.
[88]   *Revelation*, pp. 61-63.

And when addressing the wellbeing of the particular church Knollys goes on to say, "Gospel-Oneness which maketh very much for the Well-being of a particular Church is threefold: First, that there be but ONE Church in one City; and that all the Congregations of Saints in that City (called Churches) bear that one Name."[89]

Again when commenting on the seven churches of Asia Minor in chapters two and three of John's Revelation, Knollys writes:

> Each church contained and comprehended, the whole number of them that believed in Jesus Christ ... had the Denomination of that City, and was called the Church of God in that City.... Although the Church in any City, at the beginning and first Planting of it, was but *one* Congregation, and assembled themselves together in one place ... yet when the number of the Disciples was multiplied ... then the Church was necessitated, for the Edification of the Multitude, and great number of the Members thereof, to assemble themselves together in particular Congregations, and became distinct Companies, ... each Company or Congregation had their Elders and Deacons ... and are called Churches.[90]

From these quotes it appears that Knollys is looking for an ideal church structure. Did Knollys believe that this ideal structure existed in the Baptist churches of London? Probably not. He, however, conceivably expected this church structure to exist just prior to the coming of Christ as the Bridegroom, and on into the millennium when the church would be restored to its primitive purity as in the days of the Apostles. Nevertheless, for Knollys churches were particular congregations of believers in Jesus Christ. They were not national churches as in England or on the Continent.[91]

Moreover, Knollys believed that these particular churches were autonomous, independent churches, accountable to Christ, and they received their authority directly from Him. As the 1644/46 *Confession*, Article XXXVI, maintains, "Being thus joyned, every Church hath power given them from Christ, for their wel-being to chuse among themselves meet persons for Elders and Deacons."

---

[89] *World*, pt. 1, pp.44-45, 50-51.
[90] *Revelation*, pp. 8-9. Knollys also states that "Church is a *Homogenial* Word ... so the Assembly or Congregation of Sanctified Believers in the *general* Assembly, is called the Church ... and the *particular* Assemblies or Congregations in any City is called the Church ... so in any Village or Town ... yea, in any House"(*Ibid.*, p. 9).
[91] *World*, pt. 1, p. 45; *Apocalyptical Mysteries*, I, 6; *Revelation*, p. 200.

Similarly, in his commentary on Revelation, Knollys states, "The Churches of Saints have Power and Authority from Christ to try the Calling, Gifts, Doctrine and Conversation of their teachers."[92] This implies not only that each congregation receives its authority directly from Christ but that each one governs itself without any national or synodical hierarchy ruling over it. This is affirmed in the 1644/46 *Confession* when it addresses the subject of excommunication; Article XLII states, "Christ hath likewise given power to his Church to receive in, and cast out, any member that deserves it; and this power is given to every Congregation, and not to one particular person, either member or officer, but in relation to the whole body, in reference to their faith and fellowship."[93]

Consequently, what sort of leadership did the church have according to Knollys? What was the position of the elders and pastors in Calvinistic Baptist church government? Knollys was committed to a Presbyterian style of church government within each church. In his commentary on Revelation Knollys explains that by the "angel" of each church, "We are to understand the Episcopacy, Presbytery, and Ministery in each *particular* Church, unto whom the charge, oversight, care and government thereof was committed by the holy Spirit." He believed that the pastors and elders were given "the care and charge of the flock" by Christ "to feed them," who also have "the Rule over the Members of the Church ... to govern them by the Laws of the Lord Jesus Christ."[94] The pastors and elders do have authority in the local church but only in so far as they follow Christ's laws. According to Knollys Jesus has delegated church government to the pastors and teachers according to Ephesians 4:11,12 which involved church censures of admonition, supervision or withdrawal from a disorderly member or brother, and excommunication of those members that live in gross and scandal-

---

[92]   *Revelation*, p. 22. In *A Moderate Answer unto Dr. Bastwicks Book Called, Independency not Gods Ordinance* Knollys' contention with Bastwick has to do with whether the church is independent or not. Knollys uses almost three quarters of the book to challenge Bastwick's argument that the New Testament church in any one place consisting of several congregations was governed under one synodical government; and consequently, that each congregation was dependent and not independent (pp. 1-14).

[93]   *Confession of Faith* (1644/46), XLII. See also *Confession of Faith* (1677/89), 26.9.

[94]   *Revelation*, pp. 19, 66. See also the 1644/46 *Confession*, Article XLIV, where it says, "Christ for the keeping of his Church in holy and orderly communion, placeth some special men over the Church, who by their office, are to governe, oversee, visite, watch." See also *Parable*, pp. 6-7, and *World*, pt. 1, pp. 55-57.

ous sins.[95] In *Song of Solomon* Knollys maintained that Christ had given authority and power to his ministers and churches to rule, govern, and order the saints, and that the saints ought to be subject to the elders.[96] Knollys also believed that there was a preeminence and priority among the ministers in the Church. However, this pre-eminence among ministers had to do with his concept of one Church with several congregations in one city, and not with each particular church. Consequently, the presbytery of the one Church had its president or chief who was chosen by the rest of the elders, pastors and teachers from the particular churches that made up the one Church. This president acts, guides, and rules with the other elders consent, suffrage and assistance according to the laws of Christ. Knollys writes,

> [This president is] set over them as *Chief* Bishop or Presbyter of the Church in any City and Villages adjacent, who for Order sake in Gospel-Government, hath priority, Pre-emminence, and Authority above the rest of the same Church, not alone, *nor without them*, but when *convened* with them, to Act, Rule, Guide, Order and Govern with their Consent, Suffrage and assistance, according to the Laws of the Lord Jesus Christ.[97]

Knollys' argument with Bastwick in *A Moderate Answer* had not to do with Presbyterian church government in an individual church but over many churches. He disagreed with Presbyterian synodical church government. Knollys states, "*That the Brethren on both sides, that the Government of the church is Presbyterian-Government, both acknowledging a Presbyterie.* But whether it be Dependent, or Independent is the maine thing in the question." And later in agreement with Bastwick he writes, "But the Presbyters had the care and oversight of some one Church onely, as Ephesus Acts 20. 28. or Philippi, Phil. I.I. and this the Dr. often asserts in his Book. That all the Churches we read of in the new Testament (though they were Presbyterially governed) were dependent upon their severall Presbyters."[98]

Thus far we have shown that Knollys believed the local church to be an autonomous, independent, and congregationally-governed

---

[95] *World*, pt. 1, pp. 53-54.
[96] *Song of Solomon*, p. 38.
[97] *World*, pt. 1, p. 68. This was an important concept for Knollys. He spends about twelve pages (pp. 57-69) proving the presidency of bishops.
[98] *Moderate Answer*, pp. 2, 13.

institution, but what did he maintain concerning the constitution of this church? Knollys unamibiguously believed that each particular church was to be constituted of visibly professing believers who had separated themselves from the corruption of the world. This is confirmed in his writings where he addresses the qualifications for admission into the church. For example, in his *Exposition of the Eleventh Chapter of the Revelation* Knollys taught that "[Pastors] ought to Inspect them that worship, and to take care before persons be Admitted into the visible Churches of Saints, to partake of all the Sacred Ordinances of God, that they may be found in the faith, and holy in their life."[99] In Knollys' *Moderate Answer* he states, "The condition which those [New Testament] Preachers both publickly and privately propounded to the people, unto whom they Preached, upon which they were to be admitted into the Church was Faith, Repentance, and Baptisme; and none other."[100] Knollys' commitment to a visibly professing church is also confirmed by his comment on the meaning of the "candlesticks" in John's Revelation. The churches are called "candlesticks"

> for their visibility.... First, from the purity of the worship of God administered in the Churches of Saints ... according to Christs Institutions .... Secondly, From the Holiness of the Ministers and Members in the Churches of God, upon whom was written Holiness to the Lord, and therefore called the Churches of Saints.... Thirdly, From the purging Power, and purifying Efficacy of Church Censures, to wit, Admonition of offending unruly Persons, Suspension of those that walked disorderly, and Excommunication of wicked, ungodly, and obstinate Sinners.[101]

This, however, did not mean for Knollys or the London Calvinistic Baptists that they should physically separate themselves from the world (as will be seen below under the subject of the relation between church and state). Nor did it mean that he believed that the church would be without mixture and error, or that the church should schismatically separate whenever there were errors in it. In

---

[99] *Eleventh*, p. 6.

[100] *Moderate Answer*, pp. 19-20. See also *World*, pt. 1, pp. 44, 46. It should be noted that contrary to his paedobaptist Independent brethren Knollys believed that no covenant should be made in order to become a member. For him baptism was the act of initiation into the church (*Moderate Answer*, pp. 19, 20).

[101] *Revelation*, pp. 9-10.

The World that now is, he addressed the subject of separation. He recognized that there would be a mixture of wheat and tares in the church, and consequently true believers ought not to separate themselves from the true churches of God and of his saints. Even the most pure churches are subject to mixture of false brethren, false teachers, men of corrupt minds and manners, and errors in doctrine and in conversation. A person may eventually need to separate but only after he has: 1) faithfully and orderly born his testimony against the offenders; 2) humbly entreated the church and the ministers to reform those things that are amiss; and 3) waited until the church and ministers refuse to reform those things. According to Knollys, he ought to bear and have patience, to wait upon Christ and the church until the offense is dealt with or else until the candlestick is removed; then separate.[102]

Moreover, the London Calvinistic Baptists denied being schismatical in both of their *Confessions*.[103] This, however, did not mean they ought not separate from false worship. In the same context of separation he states that the believing Gentiles are to be separated from idolaters and unbelievers, and to have no fellowship with them in any false worship. Separation is imperative where false worship is involved, I.e., from the Church of England or the Papacy.[104] The importance of true worship for Knollys is evident when he gives counsel to "virgin professors" in his *Parable of the Kingdom of Heaven Expounded*. He mentions three necessary things for a person to possess a true form of godliness: 1) the knowledge of the revealed will of God in the Scriptures touching ordinances and Christs constitution of worship; 2) there must be a conformity unto the revealed will of God in His Word because uniformity in worship in any nation or congregation without conformity to the rule of Scripture is but superstition; and 3) there ought to be a uniformity among all the churches of God in every nation, city and vil-

---

[102] *World*, pt. 1, pp. 96-99. See also *Song of Solomon*, pp. 21-23; and *Confession of Faith* (1677/89), 26.3

[103] *Confession of Faith* (1644/46), "To the ... Reader", XLVI; *Confession of Faith* (1677/89), 26.13.

[104] *World*, pt. 1, p. 95. In *Song of Solomon* he taught that the first step towards true worship is to forsake the assemblies of false worship and to separate from them. False worship is to worship the true God in a false manner (pp. 36, 33).

lage.[105] For Knollys, Scripture ought to be our guide for worship, and not the traditions of men.[106] He maintained that

> The worshippers of God in his Churches of saints ought to be Measured by the Reed of God's written Word, as well as the Temple, and the Alter of God: that thereby it may appear, they are the true worshippers of God in his House, and worship him in Spirit and Truth.... All things in the Church and worship of God ought to be done according to the Rule of the written Word of God.... There is but one Rule for all the Churches, Worship, and Worshippers of God to be framed, measured, and Ordered by.[107]

True worship and a pure church were important to Knollys because he believed that in the time just prior to the Second Coming of Christ the churches will be restored to such a state and will exist as such in the millennium. In *Apocalyptical Mysteries* when dealing with Revelation 15:5-7 he exhorts, "Let Christians consider, that *none* of the seven *Vials* are to be poured out until the temple be opened, *that is to say,* until the Church of God on Earth be restored in some measure unto its Apostolical Constitutions, and primitive Purity, which is not yet done [in 1667]."[108]

According to Knollys the church's true worship entailed a proper use of the ordinances of God. He taught that the Lord came into the world at his First Coming for three purposes: 1) the salvation of sinners; 2) the edification of the church of God through the gospel ministry; and 3) the institution of gospel ordinances. It is this last purpose that concerns us here. Knollys taught that these gospel ordinances included: 1) prayers in the Spirit by the elders; 2) the reading, expounding and interpreting of the written Word by the teacher that the people might know the will and mind of God; 3) the preaching of the gospel, and the exhorting of the people to repent and believe the gospel, and to be holy and walk in the commandments and ordinances of the Lord; 4) the baptizing of those who believe the gospel; 5) the partaking of the Lord's Supper; and

---

[105] *Parable*, pp. 41-43.

[106] *Song of Solomon*, pp. 37, 15.

[107] *Eleventh*, pp. 4-5.

[108] *Apocalyptical Mysteries*, II, 37. In *Eleventh* written in 1679 he stated, "That the Ministers of Jesus Christ ... ought to Measure the Patern [*sic*] of the Churches, Worship, and Worshippers of God in the Daies [*sic*] of Christ and his Appostles [*sic*], and to See that the Churches, Worship, and Worshippers of God *now* in these *latter* Daies [*sic*] be in all things, as they were *then*, and to Reform those things, that are amiss" (p. 4).

6) the singing of the Word of God in psalms, hymns and spiritual songs.[109] The fulfilment of these ordinances would constitute proper worship according to the Word of God, and would ensure the church's well-being.

Not only did the church's well-being consist in proper administration of the ordinances according to Knollys, but also in three other things: 1) Oneness — one church in one city though there be numerous congregations or churches who all walk by the same rule of the written Word being ordered and judged by their pastors, elders; 2) Order — the bishops and elders are to set in order the things that are lacking, making sure that all things are done decently and in order, and to make sure the order of the gospel is carefully observed and kept in the Administration of the ordinances, in the Admission of members, in the ordination of church officers, and in withdrawing from a disorderly brother; and 3) Government — Christ has given church government to the pastors, elders, not as a coercive power over men's consciences but as a stewardship of the mysteries of God which consists in church censures of admonition, supervision or withdrawing from a member or brother that has and does walk disorderly, and excommunication of those members that live in gross and scandalous sins.[110]

Knollys' Doctrine of the Ministry

One of the Anabaptist charges against the Calvinistic Baptists had to do with a denial of any division between the clergy and laity.

---

[109] *World*, pt. 1, pp. 70-78. The importance of the ordinances is a constant refrain in Knollys' *Song of Solomon*. For example, he teaches that: the church is not to be negligent in keeping the ordinances of God; Christ gave his holy ordinances for the feeding, nourishing, strengthening and establishing of the saints; Christ and his saints do enjoy mutual communion and spiritual fellowship one with another at the Lord's Supper and in all other of his ordinances; the believer is to go to the holy ordinances where by the hand of faith she may receive spiritual gifts and fruits from Christ and enjoy abundance of sweet communion with Him; and the conversing with Christ in his ordinances makes a spring of graces, comforts, experiences, and all other spiritual fruits in the hearts of believers (pp. 25, 38, 57, 66, 78).

[110] *World*, pt. 1, pp. 50-54. Knollys strongly affirmed and encouraged the church's unity in Christ: "Every saint is joyned and ingrafted or set into Christ ... and also united and knit together unto the Church as members of Christs mystical body.... The union of the saints in Christ is the unity of faith ... [and] their union with the church is the unity of love ... [and] the unity of their gifts and graces is the unity of the Spirit.... The whole believer is united to whole Christ, our faith is faith in Christ, and our love is love in Christ ... and this is the saints beauty and spiritual glory" (*Song of Solomon*, pp. 47-48).

This was simply not true as we have already seen above in our section on Knollys' ecclesiology. Knollys believed that God had given special gifts for leadership in the church. There were two types of officers in the church, pastors/elders/bishops and deacons for the administration of the churches spiritual and physical affairs. In particular the pastors were called by God to rule, feed and guide the flock of God in His ways. In the 1644/46 *Confession*, Articles XXXVI and XXXVII state,

> Being thus joyned, every Church hath power given them from Christ, for their wel-being to chuse among themselves meet persons for Elders and Deacons, being qualified according to the Word, as those which Christ hath appointed in his Testament, for feeding, governing, serving, and building up of his Church, and that none have any power to impose on them either these or any other....
> That the ministers lawfully called, as aforesaid, ought to continue in their calling and place, according to Gods ordinance, and carefull to feed the flock of God committed to them, not for filthy lucre, but of a ready mind.

The 1677/89 *Confession* is even stronger,

> A particular Church gathered, and compleatly Organized, according to the mind of *Christ*, consists of Officers, and Members; And the Officers appointed by Christ to be chosen and set apart by the Church (so called and gathered) for the peculiar Administration of Ordinances, and Execution of Power, Or Duty, which he intrusts them with, or calls them to, to be continued to the end of the World, are Bishops or Elders and Deacons.[111]

This division between the clergy and laity is evident in Knollys' commentary on John's Revelation. In chapter five where Christ is standing in the midst of the four living creatures and the twenty-four elders, he states, "[This] doth signify his gracious presence in the Church,... with his Ministers, (called Pastors, Teachers, and Elders, *Eph.* 4. 11,12,13. *Act.* 20. 17.) to present their Persons, Prayers, and all their Spiritual Services and Sacrifices at the throne of Grace, with his *Incense* unto the Father with *Acceptance*."[112] Fur-

---

[111]   *Confession of Faith* (1677/89), 26.8.
[112]   *Revelation*, p. 74. In *A Moderate Answer* Knollys agrees with Bastwick that the church is to have a Presbyterial government. And in *The World that now is* he maintains that the Lord has ordained and appointed a preceding ministry to be workers together with Him in building up the house of God (pt. 1, pp. 43-45, 52).

thermore, Knollys considers pastors to be guides in the truth along with the Word and Spirit, thus highlighting the importance of the ministry. He states,

> Now God hath in great Mercy unto the Souls of his People out of the exceeding Riches of his free Grace, and marvelous loving Kindness towards them, *(That they might not be led away with the Errors of the wicked)*, appointed them a threefold Guide, which God hath plainly declared in the holy Scripture of Truth to direct, lead and guide his People in the WAY of TRUTH until they come to Heaven: *namely*, I. His holy Spirit, 2. His written Word, and 3. His faithful Ministers.[113]

And again, "The Churches of Christ can no more stand, and continue sound in the faith, pure in Administration, and holy in Conversation without able and faithful Ministers, than the Temple could have stood without Pillars and Beams of Cedar."[114]

Did this separation between clergy and laity mean that only the clergy could preach the Word of God? No, Knollys believed that if some lay person was gifted by God for preaching, he should exercise his gift for the good of the church. The 1644/46 *Confession*, Article XLV, maintained that "Such to whom God hath given gifts in the Church, may and ought to Prophecie, according to the proportion of faith, & so to teach publickly the Word of God, for the edification, exhortation, and comfort of the Church." And again, in the 1677/89 *Confession* the Calvinistic Baptists state, "Although it be incumbent on the Bishops or Pastors of the Churches to be instant in Preaching the Word, by way of Office; yet the work of Preaching the Word, is not so peculiarly confined to them; but that others also gifted, and fitted by the Holy *Spirit* for it, and approved, and called by the *Church*, may and ought to perform it."[115]

This also appears to be the case concerning the administration of the Lord's Supper and baptism in the group's early years. In the 1644/46 *Confession*, Article, XLI, they state, "The person designed by Christ to dispence Baptisme, the Scripture holds to be a Disciple, it being no where tied to a particular Church officer, or person extraordinarily sent, the Commission injoyning the administration,

---

[113] *Mystical Babylon*, pp. 28-29. See also *Song of Solomon*, p. 72, and *World*, pt. 1, p. 57. The church is to submit unto these Ministers (*Ibid.*, p. 51).

[114] *Song of Solomon*, p. 82.

[115] *Confession of Faith* (1677/89), 26.11.

being given to them as considered Disciples, being men able to preach." For Knollys this did not mean that "any Brother" could "baptize, or ... administer other Ordinances; unless he have received such gifts of the Spirit, as fitteth, or inableth him to preach the Gospel. And those guifts [*sic*] being first tried by, and known to the Church, such a Brother is chosen, and appointed thereunto by the Suffrage of the Church."[116] This teaching was tightened up by both Knollys and his fellow Baptists in later years. The 1677/89 *Confession* states in its chapter on the ordinances, "These holy appointments are to be administered by those onely, who are qualified and thereunto called according to the commission of Christ."[117] From Knollys' writings this appears to be the elders of the church. In *The Parable of the Kingdom of Heaven Expounded* (1674) Knollys writes, "There is the Door of Grace, and that is all opportunities and seasons that the Ministers of Christ have and improve to preach ... also to administer and partake of the holy Ordinances of God in any place, and at any time, called an open Door."[118] In *The World that now is* he teaches that the ministers are to baptize, and they are to consecrate the cup and bread for the Lord's Supper and give it to the people.[119]

What were the duties of the elders/pastors? In his last work Knollys delineates the duties of a pastor. Generally, the Ministers of Christ "ought to measure, frame, and order all things in the Churches and Worship of God by the same Rule [of the written Word of God]." Specifically this meant four things:

> *First*, The Ministers ought to take care, and inspection of the Church of God, and see (for they are called Seers and Overseers ...) That the Church be builded upon the Foundation Doctrines.... *Secondly*, They are to take care, that the Pillars ... in Gods house ... be not only Trees of Righteousnesse, the planting of the Lord, that he may be glorified, but that they also be able Ministers of the New Testament, both of the letter, and also of the spirit.... *Thirdly*, They ought to take care, or heed, that the whole Worship of God, and all the sacred Ordinances of the Lord be Administred according to the Gospel Institutions, Commandments, and Examples of Christ and his holy Apostles; and not after the rudiments of the World, nor after the commandments of Men.... *Fourthly*, They ought to

---

[116] *Shining*, p. 9.
[117] *Confession of Faith* (1677/89), 28.2.
[118] *Parable*, p. 118.
[119] *World*, pt. 1, pp. 72, 75-76.

inspect them that Worship, and to take care before persons be admitted unto the visible Churches of Saints, to partake of all the sacred Ordinances of God, that they be found in the Faith, and holy in Life.... And after they be added to the Church, the Ministers ought to oversee them, that they do not walk disorderly, to the dishonour of God, and scandal of the Church.[120]

In *Song of Solomon* Knollys teaches that Christ feeds his flocks by his faithful ministers, and elders of the churches whose work is to convert, feed, comfort, strengthen, confirm, establish, and save souls. They are to bear up them that are weak and to strengthen the weak hands and feeble hearts of the poor doubting, tempted and afflicted members of the Church of God. The apostles, prophets and evangelists are used of God for the gathering of the saints one by one, and planting them together; the pastors and teachers are for the edification of the body.[121] In addition, Knollys believed that the work of the ministry must be done in sincerity, with zeal to God's glory and with affection to the souls of the people. Pastors should improve "all their Ministerial Gifts, graces, and abilities to the utmost; making full proof of their Ministery for the Conversion of Sinners unto Christ, the Edification of the saints in Faith, Love, and good Works; and the feeding, and ruling the Church according to the Word of God."[122] For Knollys preaching was of vital importance to the well-being of the church. Ministers must preach Christ in the demonstration of the Spirit and in power. According to Knollys the plain and powerful preaching of the gospel is the ordinary means whereby God draws sinners with the cords of love to Christ and makes the ministry of the word powerful and effectual to call, convert, sanctify and save sinners. Similarly in the same treatise he writes,

They that sell this Mystical Oyle [the Unction of the Holy One, the saving, sanctifying grace of God, the gifts and the fruits of the Holy Spirit] are Christ and His Ministers, and Servants.... Ordinarily and commonly Christ authorizes and commands his faithful Servants (the Ministers of the Gospel)

---

[120] *Revelation*, pp. 123-124; *Eleventh*, pp. 4-6; *World*, pt. 1, pp. 23-24, 55-69.
[121] *Song of Solomon*, pp. 29-30, 81-82.
[122] *Revelation*, pp. 44-45.

whom he appoints, commissions and sends to offer this spiritual Oyle to sale, and to sell it unto whomsoever will buy it.[123]

If these Pastors were going to be effective in their ministry and preaching Knollys maintained that they should be educated. In his comment on Revelation he states, "The Pastors and Teachers in every Church (called *Presbyters*, that is Elders) that Rule well, I *Tim.* 5. 17. ought to be learned and holy Men, taught of God by his Holy Spirit, qualified with Spiritual and Ministerial Gifts and Graces; to wit, Knowledge, Wisdom, Meekness, amd a blameless Conversation, 2 *Tim.* 3.1-8. and *Tit.* I. 5-7."[124] Knollys' commitment to education for ministry is clear, not only from his own experience but in his commitment to train people in the languages of Hebrew, Greek and Latin with his own grammars and dictionaries. His *Rudiments of the Hebrew Grammar in English* was written "*for the benefit of some friends, who being ignorant of the Latine, are desirous to understand the Bible in the Originall TONGUE*".[125] If Knollys was concerned enough to write a Hebrew Grammar for the lay-people how much more must he have been for the pastors. Moreover, in his latter years Knollys was probably one of those who promoted the making of a fund for ministerial training. In the Baptists' General Assembly of 1689 a central fund was to be collected for three purposes. One of the purposes was to assist "those members that shall be found in any of the aforesaid churches that are disposed for study, have an inviting gift, and are sound in fundamentals, in attaining to the knowledge and understanding of the languages, *Latin, Greek* and *Hebrew.*"[126] And at the 1691 Assembly Knollys signed an epistle to the churches recommending the institution of a Freewill offering. One of the reasons given in the *Narrative of the Proceedings of the Assembly* for this offering was "that godly young men whom God hath gifted, and who are approved of, may be instructed in the tongues

---

[123]   *Parable*, pp. 50-51, 107-108.
[124]   *Revelation*, p. 123.
[125]   His eight works on language are: *The Rudiments of the Hebrew Grammar in English. Published for the benefit of some friends, who being ignorant of the Latine, are desirous to understand the Bible in the Originall TONGUE* (1648), *Grammaticae Graecae compendium* (1664), *Grammaticae Latinae compendium* (1664), *Grammaticae Latinae, Graecae, & Hebaicae* (1665), *Linguae Hebricae delineatio* (1664), *Rhetoricae adumbratio* (1663), *Radices simplicium vocum* (1664), and *Radices Hebraicae omnes* (1664).
[126]   Crosby, *History of the English Baptists*, III, 252.

wherein the Holy Scriptures were written."[127] Knollys not only
would have supported such statements but probably was one of
those who initiated them.

Knollys' Doctrine of the Trinity and of the Deity of Christ

The Calvinistic Baptists, as alleged Anabaptists, were also accused
of being anti-Trinitarian, and of not maintaining the deity of
Christ. This was simply not so. First, in both *Confessions* Knollys and
his fellow Baptists affirm that God is Triune. The 1644/46 *Confession*
states, "In this divine and infinite being, there is the Father, the
Word, and the holy Spirit, each having the whole divine essence
undivided; all infinite without any beginning, therefore but one
God, who is not to be divided in nature, and being, but distinguished by severall peculiar relative properties." The 1677/89 *Confession* similarly confesses,

> In this divine and infinite Being there are three subsistences, the Father, the
> Word (or Son) and the Holy Spirit, of one substance, power, and Eternity,
> each having the whole Divine Essence, yet the Essence undivided, the Fa-
> ther is of none neither begotten nor proceeding, the Son is Eternally begot-
> ten of the Father, the Holy Spirit proceeding from the Father and the Son,
> all infinite, without beginning, therefore but one God, who is not to be
> divided in nature and Being; but distinguished by several peculiar, relative
> properties, and personal relations; which doctrine of the Trinity is the foun-
> dation of all Communion with God, and comfortable dependence on
> him.[128]

In *Song of Solomon* Knollys states that "God the Father, Word and
holy Spirit are three divine Subsistences in one divine Essence." For
Him the "great mystery of the Trinity in Unity and Unity in the
Trinity is unveiled and revealed in the Face of Christ by the Spirit
of God and Word of the Scripture unto the hearts of believers....
In Christ we know the Trinity by Name, Image and Operations
and that in the unity of the divine nature."[129]

Secondly, not only was Knollys orthodox in his doctrine of the
Trinity but, consequently, also concerning Christ's deity. The

---

[127] Culross, *Knollys*, p. 106.
[128] *Confession of Faith* (1677/89), 2.3.
[129] *Song of Solomon*, pp. 50-51.

1644/46 *Confession*, Article XVI, teaches that "hee might be a Prophet every way compleat, it was necessary hee should be God." The 1677/89 *Confession* maintains the same: " The *Son* of *God*, the second Person in the *Holy Trinity*, being very and eternal *God*, the brightness of the Fathers glory, of one substance and equal with *him*."[130] In *Song of Solomon* Knollys taught that the "Name of Christ" means he is both God and human; as God he is the "second subsistence in the divine essence."[131] In *The World that now is* Knollys writes that Jesus Christ is the "God-Man", "True God and Eternal life."[132] And in his comment on Revelation 1:11 he states, "In this Verse, we have the former Description of Jesus Christ [from verse 8, as the Alpha and Omega], his Deity and Eternity repeated."[133]

Knollys' Teachings On Church and State Issues

Knollys and the Calvinistic Baptists believed it was their duty as citizens of the Commonwealth to submit to the civil magistrate. In the 1644/46 *Confession*, Article XLVIII, they taught,

> A civill Magistracy is an Ordinance of God, set up by him for the punishment of evill doers, and for the praise of them that doe well; and that in all lawfull things, commanded by them, subjection ought to be given by us in the Lord, not onely for wrath, but for conscience sake; and that we are to make supplications and prayers for Kings, and all that are in authoritie, that under them we may live a quiet and peaceable life, in all godlinesse and honesty.[134]

---

[130]   *Confession of Faith* (1677/89), 8.2.
[131]   *Song of Solomon*, p. 8. See also *Ibid.*, p. 74.
[132]   *World*, pt. 1, p. 4.
[133]   *Revelation*, p. 8.
[134]   In the margin they add, "The supreme Magistracy of this Kingdom wee acknowledge to be the King and Parliament (now established) freely chosen by the Kingdome, and that we are to maintaine and defend all civill Lawes and civill Officers made by them, which are for the good of the Commonwealth.... It is our dutie not to be wanting in nothing which is their honour and comfort and whatsoever is for the well-being of the Common-wealth wherein we live.... And if the Magistrate should require us to doe otherwise [to do things against our conscience], we are to yeeld our persons in a passive way to their power, as the Saints of old have done."
However, they also allude to a separation of church and state when they say, "And concerning the worship of God, there is but one Law-giver, which is able to save and destroy ... which is Jesus Christ, who hathe given Lawes and Rules sufficient in his Word for his worship.... Surely it is our wisdome, dutie, and priviledge, to observe Christs Lawes onely, ... so it is the Magistrates dutie to tender the libertie of mens consciences,... (which is the tenderest thing upon all conscientious men & most dear unto them, and

The 1677/89 *Confession* similarly teaches submission to the magistrate,

God the supream Lord, and King of all the World, hath ordained *Civil Magistrates* to be under him, over the people, for his own glory, and the publick good; and to this end hath armed them with the power of the Sword, for defence and encouragement of them that do good, and for the punishment of evil doers.... *Civil Magistrates* being set up by God, for the aforesaid; subjection in all things commanded by them, ought to be yielded by us, in the Lord; not only for wrath but for conscience sake; and we ought to make supplications and prayers for Kings, and all that are in Authority, that under them we may live a quiet and peaceable life, in all godliness and honesty. [135]

In this chapter of their *Confession* there is a silent commitment to separation of church and state. The statements on the use of the state's power in matters of religion which are found in the *Westminster* and *Savoy Confessions* are removed.[136] There is, therefore, an

---

without which all other liberties will not be worth the naming, much less injoying) and to protect all under them from wrong, injury, oppression and molestation; ... It is our dutie to do, and we beleeve it to be our expresse dutie, especially in matters of religion, to be fully perswaded in our minds of the lawfulnesse of what we doe, as knowing whatsoever is not of faith is sin; and as wee cannot doe any thing contrary to our understandings and consciences, so neither can we forbeare the doing of that which our understandings and consciences bind us to doe" (*Confession of Faith* (1644/46), margin to Article XLVIII).

[135]   *Confession of Faith* (1677/89), 24.1,3.

[136]   *Savoy* on this subject in Article three of Chapter twenty-four on the "Magistrate" states:

"Although the Magistrate is bound to incourage, promote, and protect the professor and profession of the Gospel, and to manage and order civil administrations in a due subserviency to the interest of Christ in the world, and to that end to take care that men of corrupt mindes and conversations do not licentiously publish and divulge Blasphemy and Errors in their own nature, subverting the faith, and inevitably destroying the souls of them that receive them: Yet in such differences about Doctrines of the Gospel, or ways of the worship of God, as may befall men exercising a good conscience, manifesting it in their conversation, and holding the foundation, not disturbing others in their ways or worship that differ from them; there is no warrant for the Magistrate under the Gospel to abridge them of their liberty" (Quoted in Williston Walker, *The Creeds and Platforms of Congregationalism* [New York, 1893], p. 393).

The *Westminster Confession* in Chapter twenty-three on the "Magistrate", Article three, similar to the *Savoy Confession*, states: "Yet he hath authority, and it is his duty, to take order, that unity and peace be preserved in the church, that the truth of God be kept pure and entire, that all blasphemies and heresies be suppressed, all corruptions and abuses in worship and discipline prevented or reformed, and all the ordinances of God duly settled, administered, and observed" (*The Confession of Faith* [Inverness, 1976], pp. 101-102).

implicit commitment among the Calvinistic Baptists to liberty of conscience in matters of religion. This is also implicit in Knollys' work *Song of Solomon* written in 1655, he writes,

> Soul-government solely belongeth to Jesus Christ. The Lord is our *Judge*, the Lord is our *Lawgiver*, the Lord is our *King*.... The government shall be upon His shoulder.... Saints must not be the servants of Men in the things of Christ.... They ought to obey God, rather then Men, Act. 5.29. and not worship God after Commandments, Traditions and Doctrines of Men.... It is a great sin, and of dangerous consequence, for the people of God to submit unto any impulsive or coercive power of the supreme Magistrate imposing or prescribing a false worship.[137]

What is implicit concerning the separation of church and state is made explicit in a document signed by Knollys in 1651 entitled, *A Declaration By Congregationalist Societies in, and about the City of LONDON.* The signatories write,

> The innate and intrinsical property of the powers and authorities of this world being terrene, and calculated only for the affaire thereof, we conceive they are not to act but within their own proper sphere; or if they shall attempt to do otherwise, misscarriage and disappointment in the undertaking is the best that can rationally be expected.
> And as it would be no less than a usurpation for a state ecclesiastical to impose laws upon a state civil, and to exercise a compulsive power therein, so likewise (not to say what the magistrate may do in recommending to the people the things of the gospel) it can be no less than an irregularity for a state civil to impose laws upon a state ecclesiastical and spiritual, so as to

---

See also Chapter twenty, Article four, of the *Westminster Confession* on "Christian Liberty and Liberty of Conscience" which states: "And because the powers which God hath ordained, and the liberty which Christ hath purchased, are not intended by God to destroy, but mutually to uphold and preserve one another; they who, upon pretence of Christian liberty, shall oppose any lawful power, or the lawful exercise of it, whether it be civil or ecclesiastical, resist the ordinance of God. And for their publishing of such opinions, or maintaining of such practices, as are contrary to the light of nature, or to the known principles of Christianity, whether concerning faith, worship, or conversation; or to the power of godliness; or such erroneous opinions or practices, as either in their own nature, or in the manner of publishing or maintaining them, are destructive to the external peace and order which Christ hath established in the church; they may lawfully be called to account, and proceeded against by the censures of the church, and by the power of the civil magistrate"(*Ibid.*, pp. 87-89). This article was removed from both the *Savoy Confession* and the Calvinistic Baptist *Confession* of 1677/89.

[137] *Song of Solomon*, pp. 15, 25.

exercise a coercive and worldly power therein, by inflicting a worldly and corporal punishment on men for a non-observation of them.[138]

Knollys also promotes submission to the magistrate in his writings. For example, in response to the cancelled disputation between the Presbyterians and Baptists for fear of violence he declares,

> Whereupon, we (who are falsely called Anabaptists) being as ready to obey our Civill Magistrates, as to professe our subjection to his Authority in all lawfull commands; [Whatever is preached or printed of us by any to the contrary; and whosoever have, or shall accuse us, either to the Magistrates, or the Common people, that we will not obey Authority, are false accusers of the Brethren; and we hope, that both the Magistrates, and the People have found them lyars, and will finde them so to be still, so often as just occasion shall be offered to manifest our willing and loyal subjection to the Magistrates Civill Authority] we were constrained in obedience to his Lord-ships lawfull power, to forbeare that intended and earnestly desired Disputation.[139]

Several other church and state issues that concern us include the freedom of Christians to serve in civil goverment, oath taking, compulsory tithing through the government, and private property. Concerning the first issue Knollys and his fellow Baptists believed a Christian was free to serve in government. The 1644/46 *Confession*, Article L, taught that, "It is lawfull for a Christian to be a Magistrate or Civill Officer." And the 1677/89 *Confession* maintained, "It is lawful for Christians to Accept, and Execute the Office of a Magistrate, when called thereunto."[140] Knollys himself served in government positions: in 1653 he held the office of the examiner of the Customs and Excise under the Commonwealth; and in 1655 he was the Clerk of the Check.[141] In addition, these Baptists believed, contrary to their accusers, that it was lawful for a Christian to take an oath. The 1644/46 *Confession*, Article L, states, "It is lawfull to take an Oath, so it be in truth, and in judgement, and in righteousnesse, for confirmation of truth, and ending of all strife." Moreover, the 1677/89 *Confession* similarly maintains, "A lawful Oath is a part of religious worship, wherein the person swearing in

---

[138] Quoted in Underhill, *Confessions of Faith*, p. 277.
[139] Coxe, Knollys, Kiffin, *Public Dispute*, p. 4.
[140] *Confession of Faith* (1677/89), 24.2.
[141] Culross, *Knollys*, p. 75.

Truth, Righteousness, and Judgment, solemnly calleth God to witness what he sweareth; and to judge him according to the Truth or falseness thereof."[142]

Knollys and the Calvinistic Baptists do not explicitly denounce government-enforced tithing in their *Confession*s, but they do positively endorse the voluntary support of their pastors. The 1644/46 *Confession*, Article XXXVIII, states that "the Ministers of Christ ought to have whatsoever they shall need, supplied freely by the Church that according to Christs ordinance they that preach the Gospel should live of the Gospel by the law of Christ." And again, the 1677/89 *Confession* teaches in its chapter on the church concerning pastors: "It is incumbent on the Churches to whom they Minister, not only to give them all due respect, but also to communicate to them of all their good things according to their ability, so as they may have a comfortable supply, without being themselves entangled in Secular Affairs."[143] And in his counsel to the church just prior to his death Knollys encourages them "to look out a Minister of Jesus Christ, whom he hath in some competent measure qualified with such ministerial gifts and graces, as may make him worthy of so great honour as is due to a Pastor, and Elder of the church; yea, of double honour, 1 Tim. v. 17; both of maintenance and obedience, Heb. xiii. 17."[144] In addition, there is some evidence that Knollys was against government-coerced tithing. Both he and Richard Wollaston are believed to have petitioned Parliament for the abolition of tithes in 1647 and again in 1652.[145]

Knollys and the Calvinistic Baptists also believed that all citizens had a right to private property. In the "To the ... Reader" of their 1644/46 *Confession* they disclaim the charge that they deny "*mens proprietie in their estates.*" And in their *Confession*, Article XXXV, they state that "[the saints] are to supply each others wants, inward and outward; (and although each person hath a propriety in his own

---

[142] *Confession of Faith* (1677/89), 23.1.

[143] *Ibid.*, 26.10.

[144] Knollys, *Life*, p. 67. In addition, Knollys endorsed Benjamin Keach's *The Gospel Minister's Maintenance Vindicated* (1689) as did other Calvinistic Baptists. Knollys and ten other leaders signed an epistle "To the Congregations of Baptized Believers in England and Wales, Grace, Mercy and Peace be multiplied through the saving Knowledge of our Lord Jesus Christ", and the title page reads, "*Recommended to the Baptized Congregations, by several Elders in and about the City of* London." The work is unsigned but has been attributed to Keach.

[145] White, *Hanserd Knollys*, p. 14.

estate, yet they are to supply each others wants, according as their necessities shall require." The 1677/89 *Confession* agrees, "[The saints] communion one with another as *Saints*, doth not take away or infringe the title or propriety, which each man hath in his goods and possessions."[146]

Knollys and Anabaptism: Conclusion

Having examined Knollys' writings against the charge of Ana-. baptism made by his Reformed contemporaries we see that he did not hold the Anabaptist errors of anti-Trinitarianism, an unedu-cated-unlearned ministry, taking oaths, no service as a magistrate, no submission to the state (anarchy), and communism.[147] Concern-ing the Anabaptist tenet of Arminianism, chapter four of our study showed that Knollys was a High Calvinist holding to the predesti-nation of the saints before the foundation of the world, Christ's death only for the elect, and irresistable grace; therefore, he was not theologically Arminian.[148] And concerning the Anabaptist error of Antinomianism, Knollys did have one "doctrinal antinomian" tendancy but certainly no "practical antinomian" ones as was evi-denced in chapter three. In addition, though he believed there was a distinction between the clergy and laity, he maintained with the Anabaptists that spiritually-gifted lay-people could preach. And he clearly held beliefs similar to the Anabaptists concerning believer's baptism, the gathered-independent-believing church, and separa-tion of church and state (including state-coerced tithing). Therefore, our study has shown that Knollys did hold some of the more basic Anabaptist tenets (e.g., lay-preaching, ecclesiology, believer's bap-tism, separation of church and state).[149] However, it also reveals

---

[146] *Confession of Faith* (1677/89), 27.2. That Knollys did not hold to a communism without the right of private property is also evident from the pamphlet entitled, *A Decla-ration By Congregational Societies* (1651) which he signed (in Underhill, *Confessions of Faith*, pp. 280-284).

[147] Not all Anabaptists held all of these teachings, e.g., many were not anti-Trinitarian or antinomian.

[148] Arminianism taught that predestination was based on the forseen faith of be-lievers, that Christ died for all people, and that grace could be resisted by a person.

[149] On the subject of Calvinistic Baptist derivation, as well as Knollys' derivation of these Anabaptist tenets see Appendix B.

that he did not hold the Anabaptist teachings that struck fear into the hearts and minds of the orthodox divines of England (e.g., anarchy, anti-magistracy, anti-private property), and those teachings that would harm the spiritual well-being of the people of God (e.g., falling from grace, denying original sin, espousing free will, living in sin).[150]

---

[150]   Our study has not addressed Knollys' thought on original sin or free will. However, we know that he espoused the reformed teaching on original sin as is evident from the two Confessions he signed (see 1644/46 *Confession*, Article IV, and 1677/89 *Confession* VII:1-5). Moreover Knollys did not believe the sinner could freely choose Christ on his own but that faith was wrought in her by the power of the Spirit (see 1644/46 *Confession*, Article XXII, XXIV, and 1677/89 *Confession* IX:1-5).

CHAPTER SIX

FIFTH MONARCHISM

Throughout the history of the church the subject of eschatology has held a place of importance in doctrinal discussion. In some eras it has had a place of prominence. One of those eras followed the Reformation. For example, in sixteenth-century England, the eschatological writings of John Foxe, John Napier and Thomas Brightman caught the imagination of the people. In the early seventeenth century, the works of such men as Johann Alsted and Joseph Mede were also being read on this subject. During these years there was a growing expectancy that Christ would return soon. However, with the revolution of the 1640s this expectancy turned into fervor with dates being set for the fulfilment of biblical prophecies, with the return of Christ itself taking place within the next sixty years.

One of the eschatologies that caught the imagination of numerous English people was Fifth Monarchism.[1] Many contemporaries considered this teaching a danger to England's stability, not to mention doctrinally false.[2] Members of this group came from various churches but most prominently from the ranks of the Independents and Baptists. In particular, many came from Calvinistic Baptist churches including some of its leaders Vavasor Powell, John Pendarves, John Simpson and Henry Jessey.[3] Consequently,

---

[1] One contemporary suggested there were 40,000 Fifth Monarchists. But this is probably exaggerated. Even if it were correct this would only be approximately 1% of the population (Bernard S. Capp, *The Fifth Monarchy Men: A Study in Seventeenth-century English Millenarianism* [London, 1972], pp. 81-82). They were considered fanatical in an anonymous tract entitled, *A True Discovery of a Bloody Plot Contrived by the Phanaticks against the Proceedings of the City of London* (1661).

[2] For some contemporary negative opinions of Fifth Monarchism including Thomas Hall and Nathaniel Stephens see Bryan W. Ball, *A Great Expectation: Eschatological Thought in English Protestantism to 1660* (Leiden, 1975), pp. 184-185.

[3] Capp, *Fifth Monarchy*, pp. 76-98. For Jessey see B.R. White, "Henry Jessey, a Pastor in Politics," *The Baptist Quarterly*, 25 (1973,74), pp. 3ff. For Powell see Alfred Cohen, "Two Roads to the Puritan Millennium," *Church History*, 32 (1963), pp. 329-338; R. T. Jones, "Powell, Vavasor (1617-1670)," *Biographical Dictionary of British Radicals*, III, 55-57; and Murray Tolmie, "General and Particular Baptists in the Puritan Revolu-

Calvinistic Baptists were accused of this false teaching.[4] In order to dissociate themselves from the movement after the 1661 Venner uprising, the Calvinistic Baptist churches wrote and signed *The Humble Apology of some commonly called Anabaptists* (1661).[5] Later that year Baptists were still being accused of Fifth Monarchism in a small tract entitled, *The Traytors Unvailed or A Brief and true account of that horrid and bloody designe intended by those Rebellious People, known by the names of Anabaptists and Fifth Monarchy* (1661).[6]

Not only were the Calvinistic Baptists as a whole accused of Fifth Monarchism but so also was one of their London leaders Hanserd Knollys. In response to Venner's uprising Knollys was accused of being one of the Fifth Monarchist leaders, and consequently arrested. In his autobiography he writes, "Upon Venner's rising, and others that with him made an insurrection in the city of London, myself and many other godly and peaceable persons, were taken out of their own dwelling houses, and brought to Wood-street Comptor; and many to Newgate and other prisons,... which time I suffered imprisonment eighteen weeks."[7] While in prison Knollys was also accused of giving leadership to another plot in April 14/15 by the anonymous author of *The Traytors Unvailed*.[8] In September the

---

tion" (unpublished Ph.D. dissertation, Harvard University, 1960), pp. 573-576. For Pendarves see B.R. White, "John Pendarves, the Calvinistic Baptists and the Fifth Monarchy," *The Baptist Quarterly*, 25 (1973,74), pp. 251-271, and Tolmie, "General," pp. 583-585; and B. R. White, "Pendarves (or Pendarvis), John (c. 1623-1656)," *Biographical Dictionary of British Radicals*, III, 20-21. For Simpson see Louise Fargo Brown, *The Political Activities of the Baptists and the Fifth Monarchy Men in England During the Interregnum* (Washington & London, 1912), pp. 22, 67, 97, and Tolmie, "General,", pp. 540-542, 571. For other Calvinistic Baptists who were involved in the movement see Brown, *Political Activities, passim*; and Tolmie, "General," pp. 540-542.

  [4] Louise Brown's work clearly shows that many Calvinistic Baptists were involved in the movement but none of their churches or the group as a whole supported it. See also Tolmie, "General," pp. 543-544.

  [5] For this document see Underhill, *Confessions of Faith*, pp. 343-352. This uprising was led by Thomas Venner. For more on him see B. S. Capp, "Venner, Thomas (c. 1608-1661)," *Biographical Dictionary of British Radicals*, III, 268-270.

  [6] This tract was written in response to a discovered plot against the King which was to take place on Sunday April 14 or 15, 1661. For more on this see Capp, *Fifth Monarchy*, p. 200.

  [7] Knollys, *Life*, p. 35. See also *Calendar of State Papers, Domestic Series, of the Reign of Charles II. 1661-1662*, ed. Mary Anne Everett Green (London, 1861), Vol. 42, No. 38, pp. 97-98, 1661-2.

  [8] The author writes, "Who was first acquainted with the business and the authority thereof was Mr. *Knolls*, a Prisoner speaker to the Anabaptists, who civilly requested to shew what Letters & Papers he had in his Custody" (*The Traytors Unvailed*, p. 5)

government still suspected him of Fifth Monarchism.[9] In addition, to these accusations there is much circumstancial evidence that ties him to Fifth Monarchism. First of all, his teaching, at least superficially, appears to be similar to that of Fifth Monarchism. For example, Knollys believed that the prophecies in the second chapter of Daniel taught that the fifth monarchy of Christ's millennial kingdom would follow the destruction of the fourth monarchy.[10] In addition, he taught that the Kingdoms of this world will become the Kingdom of Christ "by breaking the Kingdoms of this world to pieces, Dan. 2. 34, 35, 44." In another place he states that

> The Kingdoms of this WORLD shall be broken in pieces by the STONE, *to wit*, Christ and his Peoples falling upon them, *Matth.* 21. 44. *But whomsoever this STONE shall fall, it will grinde them to Powder*: and *Jer.* 51, 19, 20-24. *Thou art my Battle-AXE. And Weapons of WAR; for with thee will I break in pieces the Nations, and with thee will I destroy Kingdoms.*[11]

However, concerning the time of this "breaking" Knollys is quite vague.[12] Moreover, he held the rather novel belief, as did the Fifth

---

[9] *Calendar of State Papers, Domestic Series, of the Reign of Charles II. 1661-1662*, Vol. 41, No. 39, p. 87, Sept. 11, 1661. It states, "[The Fifth Monarchists] have bought a small ship to convey each other abroad. Mr. Knowles and others, who were in Newgate, are sent into Holland, where they are in good condition, but act their business more secretly than here; they only wait an opportunity."

[10] Knollys, *Apocalyptical Mysteries* (1667), III, 14-18. Knollys does not use the term "fifth monarchy" but calls it the "KINGDOM of our LORD." But in *An Exposition of the Eleventh Chapter of the Revelation* (1679) he calls the Kingdoms of the Roman Ceasars the Fourth Monarchy in which "*shall the God of Heaven set up a Kingdom, which shall never be Destroyed*, &c. that is the *fifth* monarchy, *viz.* the Kingdom of Christ" (*Eleventh*, p. 41; see also his *Parable of the Kingdom of Heaven Explained* (1674), p. 88, and *An Exposition of the whole Book of the Revelation* (1689), pp. 152-153).

[11] Knollys, *Apocalyptical Mysteries*, III, 10. He also states emphatically, "*That the Saints in this GENERATION ought not to Obey, nor to submit themselves unto the Roman-Antichristian-Politick and Ecclesiastick-POWER, Rule, Authority, Dominion, And Government of the BEAST, nor of the ten Kings or Kingdoms, who have given their POWER and Strength unto the Beast* (*Ibid.*, III, 9). At the time of writing (1667) this included the English Church. In addition, it should be noted that Knollys uses the Fifth Monarchist phrase "Generation Truth" but not "Generation Work" (*The World that now is, and the world that is to come* [1681], pt. 2, p. 141). The "Truth" was the preaching of the coming of Christ to set up his kingdom; the "Work" was the bringing in of this kingdom.

[12] Knollys, *Eleventh*, p. 42. In *Apocalyptical Mysteries* he states that the dominion and government of the Kingdom of Christ on earth shall be given to the saints who "shal be *Endued* with Courage, *Clad* with Zeal, and *Girded* with Strength and Truth, that they may binde Kings in *Chains*, and Nobles in *Fetters* of IRON, and *Execute* upon them the JUDGMENT written, *Luke* 19.27" (III, 16). However, in the context of *Apocalyptical*

Monarchist John Canne, that the vials of Revelation 16 had not yet
been poured out.[13]

Besides his teaching there is other circumstantial evidence that
implicates Knollys in Fifth Monarchism. For example, Knollys was
mentioned in a tract by Anna Trapnel, a Fifth Monarchist visionary
and opponent of the Protectorate, as one who visited her.[14] Moreover, fourteen members of Knollys' congregation signed the anti-
Protectorate Fifth Monarchist manifesto entitled, *A declaration of
several churches of Christ* (1654).[15] Other evidence that implicates him
in Fifth Monarchism includes his close friendship with Fifth Monarchists Henry Jessey and John Simpson[16], his opposition to Cromwell's acceptance of the crown in a letter of April 3, 1657[17], his not
signing of the anti-Fifth Monarchist Calvinistic Baptist *Humble Apology* which dissociated these Baptists from Venner's group[18], and his
continued preaching with John Simpson and Henry Jessey in 1661
at All Hallows church, which was the headquarters of millennial
enthusiasts[19].

Not only was Knollys considered a Fifth Monarchist by his contemporaries but he continues to be accused of being one by later
generations including present-day historians. For example, in 1823,
the Baptist historian Joseph Ivimey identified him with this teaching.[20] And in 1977 B.R. White thought it necessary to show that
Knollys was not a Fifth Monarchist in his Dr. Williams' Library

---

Mysteries this dominion and government of the saints does not take place until the millennium.

[13]   John Canne, *Truth with Time* (1656), "The Epistle Dedicatory." For Canne see
B. C. Weber, "Canne, John (c. 1590-c. 1667)," *Biographical Dictionary of British Radicals*,
I, 122-123.

[14]   Anna Trapnel, *The cry of a stone* (1654), pp. 3, 7. For Trapnel see A. Cohen,
"Trapnel, Anna (fl. 1642-1660)," *Biographical Dictionary of British Radicals*, III, 250-251.

[15]   *A Declaration of Several of the Churches of Christ ... Concerning The Kingly Interest of Christ
and The present Sufferings of His Cause and Saints in* England (1654), p. 22.

[16]   Knollys joined Jessey's congregation in the early 1640s, and on June 29, 1645
Knollys baptized him (E[dward] W[histon], *Life and Death of Mr. Henry Jessey* [1671], p.
83; White, *Hanserd Knollys*, p. 8). When Simpson was in trouble in his congregation over
Fifth Monarchist radicalism he sought help from Knollys (*Ibid.*, p. 17).

[17]   This was signed by Fifth Monarchists Henry Jessey and Edward Harrison
(Underhill, *Confessions of Faith*, pp. 335-8).

[18]   *Ibid.*, pp. 343-352.

[19]   *Calendar of State Papers, Domestic Series, of the Reign of Charles II. 1661-1662*, Vol. 41,
No. 39, p. 87, Sept. 11, 1661; Vol. 43, No. 57, p. 111, Oct. 13, 1661; Capp, *Fifth Monarchy*, p. 182; White, *Hanserd Knollys*, p. 19.

[20]   Ivimey, *English Baptists*, III, 360-1.

lecture entitled, *Hanserd Knollys and Radical Dissent*.[21] On the other hand, some twentieth-century Baptist historians have categorized him as a Fifth Monarchist. Commenting on Baptist involvement with Fifth Monarchism W.T. Whitley writes, "The politics of seven years from 1653 were influenced gravely by this party; among its leaders were both Pedobaptists and Baptists, of the latter may be mentioned Jessey, Knowles [Knollys], Simpson."[22] A.C. Underwood concurs, "[Knollys'] interest in the Apocalypse drew him ... into the Fifth Monarchy Movement.... Knollys died at a ripe old age, occupying his later years writing upon apocalyptic which had always interested him and infected his mind with Fifth Monarchy views."[23] In agreement with this interpretation in his recent history of Baptists Leon McBeth identifies Knollys as a "Fifth Monarchy Baptist."[24] And following this interpretation the New England historian Philip Gura accuses Knollys of Fifth Monarchism in his 1984 work entitled, *A Glimpse of Zion's Glory* on Puritan radicalism in early New England. He writes,

> Some, like Hanserd Knollys, accused of antinomian tendencies in New England, and upon his return to England the leader of a Particular Baptist congregation, were swept into Fifth Monarchist activity almost as an extension of their membership in radical congregations. Knollys's signature, along with those of William Kiffin, Henry Jessey, and other Baptists, frequently appeared on petitions criticizing Oliver Cromwell's regime and calling for further reformation. And, like New England's Hugh Peter, Knollys often was singled out as one of the main troublemakers among the radical sectarians.[25]

This chapter will see if these charges, old and new, of Knollys' participation in Fifth Monarchism can be substantiated. In order to accomplish this, first, we will briefly present a summary of Knollys' eschatology. Then we will examine seventeenth-century English eschatology in general, comparing Knollys' position with those of his contemporaries who were not Fifth Monarchists; this will enable us to see if his eschatology deviates from the mainstream, and so

---

[21]   White, *Hanserd Knollys*, pp. 17-19.
[22]   W.T. Whitley, *A History of British Baptists* (London, 1923), pp. 85-86.
[23]   A.C. Underwood, *A History of the English Baptists*. London, 1947), pp. 61, 110.
[24]   McBeth, *Baptist Heritage*, p. 94.
[25]   Philip F. Gura, *A Glimpse of Zion's Glory: Puritan Radicalism in New England 1620-1660* (Middletown, CT, 1984), p. 137.

place him on the fringe of seventeenth-century eschatological thought with the Fifth Monarchists. Finally, we will look at the history and distinctive teachings of the Fifth Monarchists of the 1650s, comparing them with Knollys' eschatology in order to see whether Knollys held any of their doctrines. This will enable us to evaluate more adequately the charge of Fifth Monarchism against him.

General Survey of Knollys' Eschatology

Knollys, like most preachers of his time believed that Christ's Second Coming was imminent.[26] The 1260 prophetic days of Revelation chapters eleven and twelve which signify 1260 literal years were almost at an end. These days began between 407 and 428 AD. At this time the beast arose out of the bottomless pit[27], and Mystical Babylon, Papal Rome came into existence.[28] This beast according to Knollys was the beast of the eighth head, the Popes of Rome.[29] The Pope is the man of sin, the Antichrist[30] who was declared universal bishop and head of the church in [606] AD by Emperor Phocas.[31] Later in the days of Henry IV the Pope obtained temporal sovereignty.[32] He is the seventh king with respect to his Imperial power and the eighth king regarding his Pontifical power.[33] According to Knollys the Church of Rome is the Great Whore because she leads people into spiritual adultery with its false worship and idolatry.[34] And the Roman Priests are the false prophet because of the false doctrines they teach and believe.[35]

During the 1260 year period of Papal Rome's rule the two wit-

---

[26]   Hanserd Knolles, *An Exposition of the Whole Book of the Revelation* (London, 1688), p. 61.

[27]   Ibid., p. 130; *Eleventh*, p. 13.

[28]   Knollys, *Revelation*, p. 137; *Mystical Babylon Unveiled* (1679), pp. 1-4.

[29]   Knollys, *Revelation*, p. 137; *Babylon*, pp. 5-13. Henceforth, all endnote titles where no author is given are Knollys' books.

[30]   *Revelation*, p. 178.

[31]   In Knollys' *Exposition on the Whole Book of Revelation*, page 175, instead of the year "606" he writes "426". This is either a typographical error made by Knollys or most likely the printer.

[32]   *Babylon*, p. 6-7; *Revelation*, p. 175.

[33]   *Babylon*, p. 9.

[34]   *Ibid.*, pp. 14-19.

[35]   *Ibid.*, pp. 22-24.

nesses of Revelation chapter eleven prophesy.[36] The two witnesses are the ministers and saints of Christ, the true church. In these days the two witnesses are to preach true doctrine, worship, and to proclaim Jesus as King. In addition, they are to preach against Papal Rome and its false teachings, its false worship, and its exaltation of the Pope.[37] Their preaching will continue until the gospel is preached in all the world.[38] Again during these 1260 years the woman clothed with the sun and travailing in childbirth (Revelation 12:1) flees into the wilderness.[39] This woman signifies the true church of Jesus Christ.[40] In these days the true church is persecuted by Papal Rome.[41] This persecution prior to the seventeenth century had been experienced by the true church represented by the Waldensians[42], the Wycliffites, Hussites, and Lollards, and was now being experienced by the true church in England during the Restoration.[43] Knollys believed the beast would rage more fiercely at the end of the 1260 days and make war against the witnesses because the witnesses' opposition would be more open and visible at this time.[44] According to Knollys this had already been fulfilled in the past and was being fulfilled in his day. This war had been experienced in the days of Charles V in the countries of Germany, France and Scotland, and in the days of Bloody Mary in England when the saints and ministers were persecuted.[45] And it was being experienced in Knollys' time during the Restoration period as the Beast raged against dissenting conventicles.[46]

Knollys believed when he wrote *Apocalyptical Mysteries* in 1667 that the end of the 1260 years was near;[47] they were living under the sixth trumpet.[48] In fact, he believed that the end would arrive in 1688 or thereabouts.[49] But according to Knollys before the end

---

[36] *Revelation*, p. 126.
[37] *Ibid.*, p. 136.
[38] *Ibid.*, p. 135.
[39] *Ibid.*, pp. 126, 162.
[40] *Ibid.*, p. 159.
[41] *Ibid.*, p. 162.
[42] Pope Alexander persecuted them (*Ibid.*, p. 138).
[43] *Ibid.*, p. 138.
[44] *Apocalyptical*, II, 18-19.
[45] *Ibid.*, p. 19.
[46] *Ibid.*, pp. 19-20; *Eleventh*, p. 22.
[47] *Apocalyptical*, I, 28.
[48] *Eleventh*, p. 39. This work was published in 1679.
[49] *Revelation*, p. 130.

of the 1260 years there must be the fulfillment of Revelation chapter eleven's 3 1/2 year period. At the beginning of this period the witnesses will be put to death by the beast of Rome. These witnesses will lie dead in the street of the great city of Babylon which according to Knollys was England and London.[50] Knollys saw a special place for England and London in the plan of God. He believed that later when the witnesses were raised the tenth part of the city, represented by England, Scotland and Ireland, would break away from Papal Rome and follow Christ.[51] During the 3 1/2 years the two witnesses who were dead and who represented the church would be deprived of civil liberty, the exercise of religion and even life. As a result the church would be diminished in various ways and become spiritually weak.[52] Knollys believed that during these 3 1/2 years there would be great tribulation for all,[53] a great apostasy from the true faith, and the church would be lukewarm and worldly.[54] At the end of the 3 1/2 years the witnesses would be raised and so the testimony of the Church restored. Knollys believed that the 3 1/2 year period had not yet begun when he wrote his final eschatological work in 1688 but that it was close to fulfillment. When the witnesses are restored the seventh trumpet will be sounded and the end will begin. The seven vials of God's wrath will begin to be poured out on Mystical Babylon (Papal Rome) and all those nations who align themselves against Christ.[55] During the pouring out of these vials the Islamic Turkish dominion will be destroyed[56] and the Jews will return to their own land.[57]

This is also the time of the Battle of Armageddon when Christ and His saints tread on Mystical Babylon, the beast and the false prophet and the Kings of the earth who follow the beast;[58] and where the Jews defeat the Pope and the Turk.[59] At the end of the

---

[50]   *Ibid.*, p. 140. Commenting on Revelation 16:18-19 Knollys interpreted the "cities of the nations" as the daughters of the great Whore, all national churches; and the "three parts of Mystical Babylon" as the national churches of the Papists, of the Lord Bishops, and of the Presbyterians (*Ibid.*, p. 200).

[51]   *Ibid.*, p. 148.

[52]   *Ibid.*, pp. 138-139; *Apocalyptical*, I, 20.

[53]   *Eleventh*, p. 30.

[54]   *Apocalyptical*, I, 28-29; *Revelation*, pp. 144-145.

[55]   *Apocalyptical*, III, 2-3.

[56]   *Apocalyptical*, II, 27.

[57]   *Ibid.*

[58]   *Ibid.*, p. 39.

seventh vial Christ's kingdom shall be set up in the new heavens and new earth and in the New Jerusalem; thus begins the latter day glory.[60] The false prophet and the beast are cast into the lake of fire, and the serpent, the devil, is bound for 1000 years.[61] This is the beginning of the 1000 year reign of Christ with His saints on earth.[62] It is important to note that Knollys believed in a spiritual return of Christ at this time. It takes place after the seventh trumpet and prior to the millennial reign and it is a virtual, spiritual, powerful, and glorious coming to earth but not a physical or visible one.[63]

During the reign of the 1000 years Christ is not physically present but reigns spiritually in and through His saints. In addition, the saints are given perfect bodies;[64] there will be no sufferings, sins, persecutions or pains;[65] and the saints will be kings and priests unto God. During this time the kingdoms of this world successively become the kingdoms of Christ.[66] This is accomplished by the preaching of the Gospel, by the pouring out of the Spirit, and by the breaking to pieces of the kingdoms of this world who oppose Christ.[67] In this millennial kingdom of Christ and His saints spiritual worship takes place in the New Jerusalem and the nations are converted by it.[68] The kingdom of Christ in the millennium is enlarged by the extraordinary conversion of Jews and Gentiles and by the pouring out of the Spirit on all flesh.[69] Those nations that do submit to Christ and His saints become the kingdom of Christ but those that do not are destroyed.[70] During this millennium the saints will be given the dominion and government of the kingdom of Christ; and they will rule by the laws of Christ.[71] They will be qualified for this work by being righteous, being spirited for government, and being clothed with humility. In addition, to being clothed with

---

[59] *Revelation*, pp. 198-199.
[60] *Apocalyptical*, II, 31; *Revelation*, p. 232.
[61] *Ibid.*, p. 230.
[62] *World*, pt. 2, p. 3; *Apocalyptical*, III, 15-16; *Eleventh*, p. 44.
[63] *Parable*, pp. 78-79.
[64] *World*, pt. 2, pp. 28-29.
[65] *Revelation*, pp. 229-330.
[66] *Apocalyptical*, III, 16-18; *Eleventh*, p. 14; *World*, pt. 2, p. 28.
[67] *Eleventh*, pp. 41-42.
[68] *World*, pt. 2, p. 8.
[69] *Ibid.*, p. 26.
[70] *Ibid.*, p. 28; *Apocalyptical*, III, 16-18.
[71] *Ibid.*, p. 16.

humility they will be endued with courage, clad with zeal, and girded with strength and truth so that they may be able to bind kings in chains, and nobles in fetters of iron, and execute judgement upon them.[72] Once the kingdom is established and the 1000 years are over Satan is loosed and defeated[73]; Christ returns and appears personally, certainly, suddenly, visibly and gloriously[74]; the dead will be raised; all people, righteous and wicked, will be judged; and the kingdom of Christ will be handed over to the Father.[75] Then the eternal kingdom will be ushered in.

Knollys and Seventeenth-Century Eschatology Compared

In this section of the chapter we will compare Knollys' eschatological writings with other seventeenth-century writers under ten different subject headings. Was Knollys' eschatology similar to, or radically different from other non-Fifth Monarchist eschatological writers?

Nearness of Christ's Return

From the beginning of the Reformation there was an expectancy that the end of the age was near and Christ would soon return.[76] In sixteenth-century England, Hugh Latimer, John Bradford, Edwin Sandys, George Joye, Thomas Rogers, and William Perkins were among those who believed in an imminent return of Christ.[77] The same could be said for many theologians and preachers of the seventeenth century. For example, Thomas Hall of Kings Norton wrote, "The days we live in, are the last dayes. Our times are the

---

72 *Ibid.*, p. 16.
73 *Revelation*, p. 225.
74 *World*, pt. 2, pp. 10-12.
75 *Ibid.*, pp. 28-30.
76 For example, Luther wrote, "This is my reply: A man should let lie what he cannot lift. If we can do no more, we must let our Lord Jesus Christ counsel and aid us by his coming, which cannot be far off. For the world has come to an end; the Roman Empire is almost gone; it is torn asunder; it is like the kingdom of the Jews when Christ's birth was near" (*Luther's Works*, ed. Robert C. Schultz [Philadelphia, 1967], XLVI, 199). For more on Luther, Melanchthon and Calvin see Ball, *Expectation*, pp. 15-16.
77 *Ibid.*, pp. 17-23.

last times.... This is the last hour ... and upon us the ends of the world are come."[78] Richard Baxter believed the day of Christ's return was "not far off", and it "comes apace, even he that comes will come, and will not tarry."[79] The Puritan Christopher Love stated, "The Scripture laies down some Prognosticks, whereby you may know that the day and hour is not farr off," and so "most Interpreters say 'tis near."[80] Richard Sibbes wrote, "Emanuell will appeare in our flesh ere long."[81] And Thomas Adams maintained that, "The end of the Apostles time was not farre off; now it must be very neere: if that were *ultima dies*, this is, *ultima hora*: or if that were *ultima hora*, the last houre, this is *ultimum horae*, the last minute."[82] Not only the clergy believed the end was near but so did laymen such as John Napier the mathematician, Sir Henry Finch the lawyer, and Samuel Hartlib the economist, as well as poets including Sir William Alexander, John Donne, John Milton and John Wither.[83]

Hanserd Knollys, though writing after the Revolutionary period, was of the same mind as his countrymen on this issue. In his *Apocalyptical Mysteries* written in 1667 he wrote in the preface,

> *The* dayes *wherein we live, being not onely the latter* Times *of the first Apostasie, prophesied of by the Apostle,* I Tim. 4.1,2,3. *but the last dayes of those perilous Times mentioned by him,* 2 Tim. 3.1,5. *I conceive, that the last part of God's revealed Will,* to wit, *the Book of the* Revelation, *hath in it those Truths, which more* peculiarly *belonged unto this Age wherein we live; which consideration hath made me willing ... to be searching them out.*[84]

---

[78]   Thomas Hall, *A Practical and Polemical Commentary or Exposition Upon The Third and Fourth Chapters of the latter Epistle of Saint Paul to Timothy* (1658), p. 7; Ball, *Expectation*, p. 41.

[79]   Baxter, *The Saints Everlasting Rest* (1650), pp. 49, 791; Ball, *Expectation*, p. 42.

[80]   Christopher Love, *Heavens Glory, Hells Terror. Or, Two Treatises; the one, Concerning the glory of the Saints with Jesus Christ, as a spur to Duty: the other, Of the Torments of the Damned, as a Preservative against Security* (1653), pp. 61-62.

[81]   Ball, *Expectation*, p. 93.

[82]   Thomas Adams, *A Commentary or Exposition upon the Divine Second Epistle Generall, written by the Blessed Apostle St. Peter* (1633), p. 1132.

[83]   Ball, *Expectation*, pp. 89-90. Other clergy and laypeople include Robert Maton, Bishop Brian Duppa, John Seagar, the Particular Baptist elder Robert Purnell, Edmund Calamy, Episcopalian Robert Gell, Joseph Mede and John Durant.

[84]   Knollys, *Apocalyptical*, I, preface.

And again twelve years later in the preface of his *Exposition of the Eleventh Chapter of the Revelation* he wrote,

> *My* intention *in the* Exposition *of this* Chapter *is, to* Explain *those things therein* Revealed, *which are not* Fulfilled: *but must shortly come to pass.... I earnestly desire the Reader diligently to search into the times of the forty two Months ... and the* three daies and an half *... by comparing the most* authentick *Histories with the Prophecies of this Book, whereby the judicious Reader may probably know how many of these* Prophetical *Months, and Daies are past, and so come to understand how near the* finishing *Time of the testimony of the* two Prophetical *Witnesses is, which must* shortly *come to pass, and be fulfilled.*[85]

In this work Knollys maintained that the end would occur in approximately ten years, citing 1688 or thereabouts.[86]

In his last work on eschatology, his crowning one, *An Exposition of the whole Book of the Revelation*, he wrote, "Both these Prophecies [that Christ shall be King of the earth, and that the kingdom and dominion shall be given to the saints], and that also, Rev. 11.15 [that the kingdoms of this world are become the kingdoms of our Lord and of His Christ] will shortly be fulfilled; even in the days of those Kings. Dan. 2.44,45 [the fourth monarchy]."[87] In this *Exposition*, licensed in 1688 and published in 1689, he predicts the time of the end to be 1688 or thereabouts.[88] Knollys, like his fellow apocalypticists, believed the time was at hand.

Nature of Christ's Return

Almost all those who believed in the Second Coming of Christ believed that His Return would be personal, visible-literal, and glorious. For example, Christopher Love stated, "Christ shal not only come *certainly*, but he shal come *personally* ... in his Body." In another sermon on Colossians 3:4 he wrote, "By Christs appearing here, is meant that glorious manifestation of Jesus Christ upon earth at the time, when he shall come at the last day."[89] John Seagar states,

---

[85] Knollys, *Eleventh*, pp. preface.
[86] *Ibid.*, p. 13.
[87] Knollys, *Revelation*, p. 61. Emphasis is Knollys'.
[88] *Ibid.*, pp. 130, 143-144.
[89] Christopher Love, *Penitant Pardoned ... Together with a discourse of Christ's Ascension in to Heaven, and of his coming again from Heaven. Wherein the opinion of the Chiliasts is considered, and solidly confuted* (1657), p. 175; Love, *Heavens Glory*, p. 32.

"That the second Coming of Christ in the Flesh shall be most sure and certain."[90] John Owen, commenting on Hebrew 9:28 where it says "and unto them that look for him shall he appear the second time," declares, "There shall be a public vision and sight of him."[91] And on the same verse he states that Christ's "second illustrious appearance shall fill the whole world with the beams of it."[92] And listen to Richard Baxter as he preaches,

> Methinks I see him coming in the clouds, with the attendants of his Angels in Majesty, and in Glory!... O then what a day will it be, when he will once more shake, not the Earth only, but the Heavens also, and remove the things that are shaken? when this Sun shall be taken out of the firmament, and be everlastingly darkened with the brightness of his Glory.[93]

Knollys also held to a personal, literal-visible, and glorious return of Christ. He states at the beginning of his commentary on Revelation that, "Christs Second coming will be visible, Act. 1.11. and Matt. 24.27. and Luk. 17.24."[94] And at the end of the same exposition he comments that, "This coming of Jesus Christ ... is his Second coming, called his appearing the second time ... which will be personal, *Act.* 1.11. visible, *Matt.* 24.30 and *Rev.* 1.7. and all his Saints with him, 1 *Thess.* 3.13."[95] And again in his book entitled, *The World that now is and the World that is to Come* he calls Christ's Return a "certain, sudden and visible appearing" and a "glorious manifestation."[96] There were few Christians who believed otherwise in the seventeenth century. The only ones who could have been accused of spiritualising the Second Coming of Christ were the Quakers.[97]

Book of Revelation Comparison

If a person were going to study eschatology it was imperative that he study the Prophecy of the Revelation written by the Apostle

---

[90] John Seagar, *A Discoverie of the World to Come* (1650), p. 77.
[91] John Owen, *An Exposition of the Epistle to the Hebrews*, ed. W. H. Goold (1855; rpt. Grand Rapids, 1980), VI, 414.
[92] *Ibid.*, p. 415.
[93] Baxter, *Saints Rest*, pp. 791, 777.
[94] Knollys, *Revelation*, p. 5.
[95] *Ibid.*, p. 239.
[96] Knollys, *World*, pt. 1, pp. 10, 12.
[97] Ball, *Expectation*, pp. 34, 201-210.

John. It was the most important book in the Bible for an understanding of future things. Between 1600 and 1660 many commentaries on the Revelation were written by scholars and laypeople
alike. Hanserd Knollys was, therefore, no different when he wrote
his comment on this Prophecy. Did, however, Knollys' commentary differ from that of his predecessors? We will compare his commentary with those who wrote prior to 1660 to find out the answer
to this question.[98]

In the years prior to 1660 many believed the Book of Revelation
ought to be studied and preached. The Puritan Arthur Dent in his
"Epistle to the Reader" of his work *The Ruine of Rome*, stated, "*I holde
that every Minister of the Gospell standeth bounde as much as in him lyeth, to
Preach the doctrine of the* Apocalyps *to his particular charge and congregation.*"[99] And Richard Sibbes wrote, "In all conditions of the
Church, the Church might have recourse into this Booke (The Revelation) to see what the issue of all would be." And again Thomas
Hall said:

> The Book of the *Revelations* is an excellent prophecie of the downfal of the
> Churches enemies, and of the great things which in the latter dayes God
> will do for his people, even to the end of the world; and therefore the Lord
> would have us attentively to consider, and humbly and accurately to weigh
> what is written there.[100]

Knollys agreed with these sentiments. In the preface to his commentary one of the reasons he gives for expounding it is,

> *That promised blessing,* Rev. 1. Vers. 3. *did incourage me to read, study, and expound
> this part of the holy Scripture, publickly in the course of my Ministry: And now (being
> aged) I have adventured to publish this my* Exposition *thereof* (such as it is) *for the
> benefit of them that shall read it, that they also may be partakers of* that *blessing.*[101]

In order to interpret or unlock the truths of the Book of Revelation,
certain principles of interpretation needed to be utilized. The majority of interpreters including the most eminent of the time,

---

[98] For a survey of Knollys' commentary on the Book of Revelation see Appendix
C.
[99] Arthur Dent, *The Ruine of Rome or an Exposition upon the whole Revelation* (1603),
Epistle to the Reader, *sig.* aalv. This work went through ten reprints before 1662.
[100] Hall, *A Practical and Polemical Commentary*, p. 5; Ball, *Expectation*, pp. 62.
[101] Knollys, *Revelation*, preface.

Napier[102], Dent, Brightman[103], and Mede[104], used the historicist and symbolic-figurative principles of interpretation. Richard Bernard wrote *Key of Knowledge for the Openning of the Secret Mysteries of St. Iohn's Mysticall Reuelation* which was primarily concerned with outlining the proper principles for the interpretation of the Revelation. Concerning the historicist principle he speaks for most seventeenth-century commentators when he states:

> The matter then of this prophecie is historicall, as it cometh to be fulfilled. It is therefore not a spirituall or allegoricall, but an historicall sense, which in this booke wee must attend vnto, from the beginning of the fourth chapter, to the end of the prophecie. For to *Iohn* was reuealed what things should come to passe here vpon earth, before the worlds end, as far as concerned the Church; and the same he here setteth forth to us, as to him it was reuealed. If we then doe loose the historicall sense, we loose the proper sense of this booke, what other spirituall vse soeuer we make of it.
>
> By this then we see what necessity there is to reade histories, into which wee must looke and search diligently ... according to the course of this prophetical narratiō.[105]

And concerning the figurative principle he says,

> The words are figurative, the whole prophecie full of Metaphors, and almost altogether Allegoricall; so we must take heede that we looke further then into the letter and naked relations of things, as they are set downe, otherwise the booke should be full of *absurdities, impossibilities, falsities, and flat contradictions* vnto other truthes of Scripture; all which are farre from the words of Gods holy spirit, which are euer holy and true. For who can beleeve a Lambe to haue seuen eyes, a mountaine burning to be cast into the sea, and this thereby in a third part to become blood, a starre to fall from heauen.... Therefore wee must not sticke in the letter, but search out

---

[102] John Napier published *A Plaine Discovery of the whole Reuelation of Saint Iohn* in 1593 with reprints in 1594, 1611, 1641, and 1645. It was also published twice in Dutch and four times in French.

[103] Thomas Brightman's commentary on Revelation entitled, *Revelation of the Revelation* appeared in Latin in 1609 and in English in 1611, 1615, 1616, and 1644.

[104] Joseph Mede's *Clavis Apocalyptica* was published three times in Latin and three times in English (as *The Key of the Revelation*) between 1627 and 1650. Three other prophetical books, *The Apostacy of the Latter Times* (1641, 1642, 1650, 1652), *Daniels Weeks* (1643) and *Diatribae* (1642) were published in his *Works* (1648, 1663-4, 1672, and 1677).

[105] Richard Bernard, *A Key of Knowledge for the Opening of the Secret Mysteries of St. Iohn's Mysticall Reuelation* (1617), p. 123; Ball, *Expectation*, p. 70.

an historicall sense, which is the truth intended, and so take the words typi-
cally, and not literally.[106]

For example, most expositors of the seventeenth century believed
a prophetical "day" in Revelation equaled a year in our time;
therefore, 1260 prophetical days equaled 1260 years. For many, the
prophetic "beast" symbolized earthly kingdoms or civil and spiritual rulers; prophetic "heads" and "horns" depicted secular and
ecclesiastical kinds of government; "sea" and "waters" symbolized
peoples or nations; a "woman" signified the church whether true
or false; and "angels" were preachers of truth.[107]

In all these points Knollys is in full agreement. Concerning the
historicist interpretation of the Revelation, he writes:

> *The* Historical *matter of this Book concerns the state of the Church of God, from the
> days of the Apostle* John *in the Isle of Patmos (about the year 96.) in the Reign of*
> Domitian *the Emperor unto the end of this World. And therefore, I would advise the*
> Reader *diligently to observe what is already past and fulfilled, what is now fulfilling
> in our days, and what is hereafter to be fulfilled. And to that end search the Scriptures,
> read Ecclesiastical Histories, and other* Expositions *of this Book, together with this*
> Exposition.[108]

Knollys believed that the seven seals depicted the first three hundred years of the church, the trumpets described the time from 300
AD to about 1688 AD, and the vials pictured the near future destruction of Papal Rome. Knollys agreed with the figurative-sym-
bolic principle of interpretation of several contemporaries. Like
Napier he believed that the prophetical "day" of Revelation
equalled a year of our time;[109] as Dent and Brightman he taught
that "the great Monarchs and Monarchies of this WORLD, have
been figured forth by wild beasts";[110] like Dent he maintained that
the "heads" and "horns" symbolize kinds of government;[111] as Bernard and John Cotton he held that the "waters" and "sea" symbol-

---

[106]   Bernard, *Key of Knowledge*, pp. 130-131.
[107]   Ball, *Expectation*, pp. 68-69. These examples are taken from Napier, Brightman,
Dent, Nathaniel Homes, Bernard, and Mede.
[108]   Knollys, *Revelation*, preface.
[109]   *Ibid.*, p. 163.
[110]   Knollys, *Apocalyptical*, II, 11; Knollys, *Revelation*, p. 169.
[111]   *Ibid.*, pp. 206-207.

ize people and nations;[112] like Mede he taught that the woman harlot riding the scarlet beast is the false church of Rome and that the
"woman clothed with the sun" is the true church;[113] and as Pareus
he believed that the "angels" are the ministers and messengers of
truth.[114]

Knollys followed the lead of his predecessors concerning the vi-
sions of Revelation which make up a significant part of the Book.
In agreement with Napier and Mede, but contrary to Dent and
Brightman, Knollys believed that the first three chapters of the
Prophecy dealt historically only with the seven churches of Asia.[115]
With Brightman and Dent he taught that the seals depicted the
Church under the persecution of the Roman Pagan Empire from
the sub-apostolic time to Constantine's reign.[116] Like Dent, Knollys
believed that the first four trumpets covered the period of time
from Constantine to about 606 AD when the church faced various
heresies.[117] He maintained as did Dent and Matthias Hoe that the
fifth trumpet symbolized the papacy's rise and growth, and the
sixth trumpet described the rise and growth of the Turks.[118] However, he disagreed with all of these men on the time of the seventh
trumpet. Knollys believed contrary to Mede that this trumpet began the pouring out of the vials of the wrath of God on the Papacy,
and that it had not yet been sounded.[119] Mede thought they began
to be poured out in the thirteenth century, and Brightman in 1560
under Queen Elizabeth.[120] Knollys believed, however, that they
would not begin to be poured out until the end of the 1260 year

---

[112]   *Ibid.*, p. 169.
[113]   *Ibid.*, pp. 203, 159.
[114]   *Ibid.*, pp. 19, 105.
[115]   Ball, *Expectation*, p. 81; L.E. Froom, *The Prophetic Faith of our Fathers: The Historical Development of Prophetic Interpretation* (Washington, 1946-1964), II, 530, 786; Knollys, *Revelation*, pp. 17-63.
[116]   Froom, *Prophetic Faith*, II, 530; Ball, *Expectation*, pp. 83-84; Knollys, *Revelation*, pp. 79-97.
[117]   Ball, *Expectation*, p. 82; Knollys, *Revelation*, pp. 97-105. Brightman believed the first three trumpets dealt with heresy, and the fourth trumpet depicted the invasion of Africa by the Vandals (Robert Clouse, "The Apocalyptic Interpretation of Thomas Brightman and Joseph Mede," *Bulletin of the Evangelical Theological Society*, 11 [1968], p. 184).
[118]   Ball, *Expectation*, p. 82; Froom, *Prophetic Faith*, II, 786; Knollys, *Revelation*, pp. 105-114.
[119]   Knollys believed that the sixth vial would be poured out on the Turks (*Revelation*, pp. 196-197).
[120]   Clouse, "Apocalyptic," pp. 185, 189.

period of the prophesying of the two witnesses (Rev. 11) which began around 428 AD. This meant that they would not be poured out
until 1688 or thereabouts.[121] He recognized this to be a novel interpretation but believed it was the correct one.[122] Consequently,
Knollys espoused contrary to most interpreters including Mede and
Thomas Goodwin that the seventh trumpet initiated the seven vials
of God's wrath.[123] It is also important to note that Knollys followed
Mede's first synchronization which the latter called "a noble qua-
ternion of prophecies." They believed that the three and a half
times, or 1260 days of the woman in the wilderness (12:6), the
forty-two months of the domination of the beast (13:5), the forty-
two months of the treading under foot of the court of the Gentiles
(11:2), and the 1260 days of the prophesying witnesses (11:3) began
and ended together.[124]

There are several other significant visions in the Revelation that
need to be examined including the two witnesses (chapter 11), the
war between Michael and the dragon (chapter 12), the beasts of
chapter thirteen, and Armageddon (chapter 19). The subjects of the
millennium (chapters 20, 21) and the harlot riding the scarlet beast
and Babylon the Great (chapters 17, 18) will be addressed under
other headings later in this section.

Knollys understood the two witnesses to be the ministers and the
saints of the true church.[125] This was essentially the same interpretation as Brightman who saw them as Christians, and the Fifth Monarchist John Tillinghast who saw them as the true church.[126] With
Mede he not only believed that the witnesses would prophecy dur-

---

[121]   Knollys, *Revelation*, pp. 143-144, 129ff, 149ff.

[122]   *Ibid.*, pp. 149ff. He writes, "Now, although I have a very honourable esteem for
those godly and learned Expositors of this Book of the *Revelation*, who have declared
their judgments, and some Reasons thereof; *viz.* That several of those Seven Vials have
been poured out upon mystical *Babylon*, and upon the Kingdom of the Beast; yet, not
withstanding all that they have said, I do humbly confess, that I am not of their minds,
but do rather think, that none of those Seven Vials are yet poured out" (*Ibid.*, pp. 149-
150). He then gives four Scripture grounds for his opinion. See also Knollys, *Apocalyptical*, II, 36-37, 40-41.

[123]   *Revelation*, 149ff; Joseph Mede, *The Key of the Revelation searched and demonstrated out
of the Naturall and proper Characters of the Visions*, trans. R. More (1643), pt. 2, pp. 112-121;
Clouse, "Apocalyptic," p. 189; and Thomas Goodwin, *Works of Thomas Goodwin*, DD
(Edinburgh, 1861), III, 84.

[124]   Clouse, "Apocalyptic," p. 187; Knollys, *Revelation*, p. 126.

[125]   *Ibid.*, pp. 127-128.

[126]   Froom, *Prophetic Faith*, II, 530, 786-787.

ing the activity of the beast who rose out of the bottomless pit but also that their death and resurrection would occur at the end of the sixth trumpet.[127] However, Knollys did not agree with Brightman that the witnesses were already dead and raised.[128] He believed the witnesses were still prophesying and that their being killed and raised would occur somewhere around 1688.[129]

In Revelation chapter twelve wherein is contained the vision of the great red dragon and the woman clothed with the sun, according to Knollys, the woman and her child are the true church during the first 300 hundred years of her existence. The dragon is metaphorically the Roman Pagan Emperors of the same time period. The war between Michael and the Dragon took place between Constantine and the other Christian Emperors, and the Roman Pagan priests and Emperors. These Roman Pagan leaders were defeated and cast out of their places of authority and dignity by Constantine and others.[130] This is essentially the same interpretation that Mede gave to this chapter.[131]

The two beasts of chapter thirteen according to Knollys depicted the Popedom or Kingdom of Papal Rome.[132] The ten horns are the ten Roman provinces and the seven heads are seven kingly governments, i.e., kings, consuls, decemvirs, tribunes, dictators, caesars, and popes.[133] The two horns of the second beast represent his politi-

---

[127]   Clouse, "Apocalyptic," p. 187; Knollys, *Revelation*, pp. 149-151.

[128]   *Ibid.*, pp. 143-146; Goodwin, *Works*, III, 153-158. Knollys writes, "The knowledge of this ending time is, that which many godly and learned Men have studiously searched, and laboured to understand, whose labours being published, have been profitable to the Lords people, and unto me, that have read their judgments, and have received much Light and Comfort in many things; but not being fully satisfied in their Interpretations and Expositions touching these two Witnesses and the time of their being killed, and raised again, I am willing to give my opinion also, and the grounds thereof" (*Revelation*, p. 143). Brightman believed the witnesses were killed when the Protestant party was overthrown in Germany in 1547 and when the Scriptures were condemned by the Council of Trent about the same time.

[129]   *Ibid.*, pp. 143-144. When Goodwin wrote his commentary in 1639 he agreed with Matthias Hoe and Joseph Mede that the two witnesses had not yet been killed and raised (Goodwin, *Works*, III, 154).

[130]   Knollys, *Revelation*, pp. 159-165.

[131]   Mede, *Clavis Apocalyptica*, II, 32, quoted in Ball, *Expectation*, p. 86. Pareus saw the dragon as pagan Rome, and Thomas Brightman saw the woman as the pure church. John Tillinghast and William Sherwin believed both (Froom, *Prophetic Faith*, II, 530-531, 786-787).

[132]   Knollys, *Revelation*, pp. 169, 174.

[133]   *Ibid.*, pp. 169, 206.

cal and ecclesiastical power. This interpretation was similar to that
of Joseph Mede. Mede maintained that the ten horns were the
Roman provinces, and that the the two beasts represented Papal
Rome. He, however, thought that the first beast signified the papal
secular power and the second, the religious power.[134] Moreover,
Knollys' interpretation of the beasts was also similar to that of John
Cotton. Cotton believed the two beasts were the Roman Catholic
visible church and the papacy, respectively. They were also in
agreement concerning the ten horns and the seven heads.[135] In addition, Knollys' interpretation of the two-horned beast signifying
the papal civil and ecclesiastical power was that of the Lutheran
theologian Johannes Gerhard.[136]

Before we leave chapter thirteen we should address the subject
of the number of the beast. Was Knollys' interpretation a novel
one? He believed that the 666 years were not to mark the end of
the Roman kingdom but the beginning. And so, if the beginning of
the Roman empire was around 60 BC, it therefore, ended around
606 AD. This was the time when Emperor Phocas declared the
bishop of Rome to be the Universal Head of the church.[137] Many
expositors believed the number of the beast was the sum total of
the numerical value of the letters of the word "Lateinos".[138]
Bullinger, John Bale, and the Geneva Bible, however, thought this
number also represented the time when the Antichrist or Pope began to be manifest in the world. Bale suggested a number of possible beginning dates from which time this number was to be
counted. One of those interpretations probably originating from
Luther was to date the 666 years from the time of Pompey's invasion of the Holy Land about 60 BC. Nathaniel Stephens also
agreed with this interpretation believing 60 BC was the time when
the church came under Roman domination.[139] Though Knollys
disagreed with Bale's and Stephens' reasons for the date of 60 BC

---

[134]   Clouse, "Apocalyptic," pp. 188-189.
[135]   Peter Toon, "The Latter-day Glory," in *Puritans, The Millennium, and the Future
of Israel*, ed. Peter Toon (Cambridge and London, 1970), p. 34.
[136]   Froom, *Prophetic Faith*, II, 604.
[137]   Knollys, *Revelation*, p. 179.
[138]   David Brady, "The Number of the Beast in Seventeenth- and Eighteenth-Century England," *The Evangelical Quarterly*, 45 (1973), pp. 220-221. Those who taught this
include Foxe, Brightman, Mede, Goodwin, Lightfoot, and the Geneva Bible.
[139]   *Ibid.*, pp. 223-225.

he agreed on the time. Knollys was not novel in his interpretation.

Knollys believed that the battle of Armegeddon, mentioned in chapter 19, would take place at the time of the pouring out of the sixth vial and just prior to the thousand year reign of the saints. At this battle the Turks and the Papacy would be defeated.[140] This is the same interpretation that Mede gives to this battle.[141] It, therefore, is evident that Knollys' overall interpretation of the Book of Revelation was similar to that of mainstream seventeenth-century interpreters.

Signs of the End

According to most interpreters the "last days" of Scripture referred generally to the whole period between the advents of Christ, and particularly to the final part of that time. This was sharpened by defining the "last times" of 1 Peter 1:20 as the time between the advents, and the "latter times" of 1 Timothy 4:1 as the latter part of the last time; and moreover, the "latter times" have their last times as depicted in 2 Timothy 3:1. Most English expositors of the seventeenth century believed they were living in the "latter times", and some in the last times of the "latter times".[142] Knollys concurred with this evaluation of the times. He wrote in 1667, "*The* dayes *wherein we live, being not onely the latter* Times *of the first Apostasie, prophesied of by the Apostle,* 1 Tim. 4. 1,2,3. *but the last dayes of those perilous Times mentioned by him,* 2 Tim. 3.1,5."[143]

If the end was near then it was believed that according to the Scriptures certain signs would follow. There were several signs that signalled the end. The most obvious one was the sinfulness of the age, particularly in England. Thomas Adams stated, "Now, like so many land-flouds from the mountaines, they meet in one chanell, and make a torrent of united wickednesse in these lower and latter dayes." And Thomas Hall referring to the list of sins of 2 Timothy 3 said, "I may truly call these 19. sins, *Englands Looking-glasse.*"[144]

Another sign was the apostasy of the church, a degeneration in

[140] Knollys, *Revelation*, pp. 196-199.
[141] Clouse, "Apocalyptic," p. 190.
[142] Ball, *Expectation*, pp. 93-96.
[143] Knollys, *Apocalyptical*, II, preface.
[144] Ball, *Expectation*, pp. 97; Hall, *A Practical and Polemical Commentary*, p. 13.

the life of the church and the clergy. When Thomas Hall referred to pride as the "Master-sin of this last and loose age," he asked,

> When did pride ever more abound in City and Country, in Body and Soule, in Heart, Head, Haire, Habit; In Gestures, Vestures, Words, Works? what Painting, Poudring, Patching, Spotting, and Blotting themselves? How are men loaded, and bedawbed with Variety of Ribbons, before and behind, above and beneath, with yellow, red black, blew; they have more colours then the Rain-bow, and are more like Morrice-dancers, then Professors.[145]

Along with apostasy in life there would be apostasy in doctrine. Thomas Hall believed, "The time ... [was] short" because "the Devill is broke loose, and now there appeare amongst us with open face; Arians, Arminians, Socinians, Anabaptists, Familists, Separatists, Mortalists, Perfectists, and (a *compendium* of all these in one) Quakers."[146]

A third sign of the end was the proclamation of the gospel to the whole world. For William Perkins this sign had already been accomplished by his day. He states, "If we consider the time since the Apostles days wee shall finde this to be true, that the Gospel hath beene preached to all the world, and therefore the first signe of Christs comming is already past and accomplished."[147] But he and many who followed him believed that the gospel to all nations included the Jews. And so a fourth sign of the end would be the conversion of the Jews. Christopher Love maintained that there would be an "eminent and general conversion" of the Jews and that it would be a sign that the end was "not farr off."[148]

A fifth sign would be hostility toward, and tribulation for, the church. William Strong wrote, "*The last attempts of the enemies shal be the fiercest, and ... the bitterest afflictions and the sharpest persecutions of the Church of God, are reserved for these last times.*"[149] These are a few of the

---

[145] Hall, *A Practical and Polemical Commentary*, p. 49.
[146] *Ibid.*, pp. 7-8.
[147] William Perkins, *An Exposition of the Apostles Creed* in *The Workes of That famous and Worthy Minister of Christ in the Universitie of Cambridge, M.W. Perkins* (1626-1631), I, 260. See also his *A Fruitful Dialogue,* in *Works*, III, 470.
[148] Love, *Heavens Glory*, p. 61.
[149] William Strong, *The Vengeance of the Temple* (1648), pp. 8, 9. For a sketch of Strong see T. Liu, "Strong, William (d. 1654)," *Biographical Dictionary of British Radicals*, III, 214-215.

more important signs that seventeenth-century expositors expected to take place prior to the end.[150]

In Knollys' work entitled, *The World that now is and the world that is to come*, he addresses the subject of the signs of the end. He saw three important signs. One sign would be the apostasy of professors and the Laodecian lukewarmness of ministers and members. Professors would be characterized by pride and covetousness, having a form of godliness but denying the power thereof. This apostasy includes that of doctrine and worship as well as that of life.[151] A second sign would be the abounding of iniquity among the profane of the world. Some of the sins he listed include adultery, false swearing, violence, drunkenness, robbery, bribery, and persecution of believers.[152] And a third sign of the end for him was a great tribulation. This tribulation will come upon the Jews, the Gentiles and the church of God.[153] In addition to the three signs mentioned in *The World that now is*, Knollys also taught in his commentary on Revelation that the gospel must be preached to all nations before the end would come. He writes, "The finishing Testimony of Christ's Two Prophetical Witnesses is the gospel of the Kingdom of our Lord Jesus Christ; which must be preached in all the World, for a Witness unto all Nations, Matt. 24. 14. and then the End shall be."[154] From these references we can see that he expected the same signs of the end that most seventeenth-century people were looking for.[155]

Date Setting

Setting a date for the end of the last times was not simply a phenomenon of the fringe expositors of the seventeenth century but

---

[150] Other signs include the gospel's progress among the Gentiles, wars among nations, and extreme phenomena such as comets, earthquakes, famine, storms, etc. (Ball, *Expectation*, pp. 108-114).

[151] Knollys, *World*, pt. 1, pp. 81ff; Knollys, *Revelation*, pp. 144-145; Knollys, *Eleventh*, p. 30. See also Knollys, *World*, pt. 2, pp. 13-20 and Knollys, *Eleventh*, p. 23. He also explains how apostasy occurs in the last days (Knollys, *Parable*, pp. 58-59).

[152] Knollys, *World*, pt. 1, pp. 92-93.

[153] *Ibid.*, pp. 93-94; Knollys, *Revelation*, p. 144; Knollys, *Eleventh*, p. 30. See also Knollys, *Revelation*, pp. 138-139 for a description of the Tribulation.

[154] *Ibid.*, pp. 135, 144; Knollys, *Eleventh*, p. 30.

[155] For the subject of the conversion of the Jews see below. It was not a sign of the end for Knollys but a part of the end.

also a practice of the mainstream. Most, if not all, believed that
only the Father knew the specific day of the end of the last times;
but they also believed that certain signs could tell us approximately
when the end would be. Moreover, the prophetic numbers given in
the Book of Revelation when placed in their proper historical context could yield an approximate date for the end. As a result there
was a tremendous propensity among seventeenth-century English
expositors to set dates for the end. For example, in 1593 John
Napier calculated that the 1335 years of Daniel 12:12 were to commence from the time of Julian the Apostate in 365 AD. This calcu-
lation yielded a final date of 1700 AD. In addition, he believed the
vision of the seven angels pouring out the vials of God's wrath began in 1541. The first three bowls were poured out consecutively,
49 years each, bringing the time to 1688. The last four bowls were
to be poured out simultaneously at the end of this time. So Napier
concluded from these calculations, "Wherefore, appearinglie betwixt this 1688. yeare, according to the *Reuelation*, and the 1700
yeare, according to Daniel, the said latter day should fall."[156]
Thomas Brightman not too long after Napier calculated a similar
date. He believed the 1260 years of Revelation chapter thirteen
related to the time of papal supremacy. This commenced around
the time of Constantine plus the 140 years approximately that the
beast was wounded by the Goth's kingdom. So he concludes, "The
last ende of Antichrist shall expire at the yeare 1686, or thereabouts."[157] A generation after Brightman, Joseph Mede made his
own calculations. For him the key was to get the right starting date
from which to commence them. He had to find the right date from
which to calculate the 1260 years, that is, the point of time from
whence Antichrist first appeared. He had three options: the death
of Julian the Apostate in 365 AD; the sack of Rome by Alaric in
410 AD; or the death of Valentinian in 455 AD. He believed,
therefore, that the end would come sometime between the years
1625 and 1715 AD.[158] During the Interregnum Thomas Goodwin
attempted to calculate the date of the end. He cautiously came up
with several possible dates which were dependent on his starting

---

[156]   Napier, *A Plaine Discovery*, pp. 15-21; Ball, *Expectation*, p. 116.
[157]   Thomas Brightman, *Revelation of the Revelation* (1615), pp. 451-452;.
[158]   Joseph Mede, *Remaines on Some Passages in the Apocalypse* (1650) in *The Works of ...
Joseph Mede, B.D.*, ed. J. Worthington (1672), pp. 654-662, 600; Ball, *Expectation*, p. 118.

point. He came up with the dates 1666/70, 1650/56, and 1690/1700 AD. His 1666 date was taken from 406 AD which was approximately the time the Goths took over the kingdom (410), the time of the succession of Innocent the bishop of Rome (404/6), and the excommunication of the eastern Emperor Arcadius (407).[159] Others who set dates include Johan Alsted (1694), Ephriam Huit (1695), Edmund Hall (1650), Thomas Parker (1649), and Nathaniel Homes (1670).[160]

When Knollys believed that the beginning of the latter day glory would be 1688 or thereabouts, he wasn't speaking from the fringes but along with mainstream expositors. Knollys believed along with Napier, Mede *et al* that the 1260 prophetic years of Revelation were significant. He also maintained with them that the commencing of the 1260 years was to be marked from somewhere between 407 – 428 AD. He writes,

> But yet I may say, that the best Ecclesiastical Historians, and the later Expositors of this Book of the Revelation, affirm, That these [thousand two hundred and threescore days] began about the Year of our Lord 407, 409, 410. or before 428.... And if these [thousand two hundred and threescore days] did begin about 428, then they will end about 1688, which a short time will manifest more certainly.[161]

He also agreed with those expositors like Goodwin who looked for historical events that signalled the rise to power of the papacy. For this reason he was particularly drawn to the year 428 AD because,

> The tyrannical power of the Papal Beast, according to the accompt of the best ecclesiastick Historians, began about the year of our Lord 428. in the reign of the Emperor *Theodosius* the Second, when Pope *Sixtus* the III. a *Roman*, who at the instance of the Empress *Eudoxias*, made a holy day for St. *Peter*'s Church.[162]

[159] Thomas Goodwin, *An Exposition of the Revelation* in *Works*, III, 195-198, 73-75.
[160] Ball, *Expectation*, pp. 119, 121-124.
[161] Knollys, *Revelation*, p. 130. Other places where he mentions the year 1688 include *Eleventh*, p. 13, and *Apocalytical*, II, 1, 10.
[162] Knollys, *Revelation*, pp. 143-144.

Even though Knollys and his fellow expositors of the seventeenth century worked out and published their calculations they also believed that "these ... [were] uncertain Conjectures."[163]

Papacy

Most historicist expositors of seventeenth-century England believed John's Revelation concentrated on the relationship of the fourth kingdom of Daniel's prophecy in addition to the kingdom of Christ. This fourth kingdom was both pagan and papal Rome. Revelation also dealt with the kingdom's relationship with Turkey and Mohammedism. After the demise of pagan Rome the vacuum was filled by the papacy in the West and the Turks in the East.[164] The prime focus, however, of the Revelation was on Papal Rome. Arthur Dent wrote,

> *The Church in the Apostles time had her conflicts. The ten great persecutions began euen then to be raised up. Heresies shortly after beganne to spring and sprout. Afterwards by degrees, the great Antichrist did approach towards his cursed seate. And after all this, S. Iohn foretelleth how hee should take possession of his abhominable and most execrable seate and sea of* Rome: *How hee should raigne and rule for a time as the Monarche of the world: How hee should preuaile against the Church, and make warre against the Saintes: How he should raigne but a short time and afterward come tumbling down as fast as euer he rose up, and decrease as fast as euer he increased.*[165]

Almost all expositors of the seventeenth century referred to the papal Antichrist.[166] The papacy took a prominent place in the interpretation of this Book. Dent could advise the reader, "Let men be studious and diligent in this booke, and they shall bee out of al doubt, that Rome is the great whoore of Babylon; that the Pope is Antichrist, and the Papacy the beast."[167]

Some examples of this interpretation will be given from a num-

---

[163] *Ibid.*, p. 130; Knollys, *Eleventh*, p. 13.

[164] Ball, *Expectation*, pp. 129-130.

[165] Dent, *The Ruine of Rome*, "Epistle to the Reader," p. aa. He believed the bulk of the two major visions of the Revelation related to the Antichrist (*Ibid.*, pp. 97-261). For another example, Goodwin believed that chapters thirteen to nineteen of Revelation dealt with the rise and ruin of the man of sin (*Revelation* in *Works*, III, 67-192).

[166] This is clear from Christopher Hill's *Antichrist in Seventeenth-Century England* (1971; revised London, 1990), and Paul Christianson's *Reformers and Babylon: English apocalyptic visions from the reformation to the eve of the civil war* (Toronto, 1978).

[167] Dent, *Ruine of Rome*, p. 243.

ber of the seventeenth-century expositors. We have already begun with Dent so we shall continue with him. Dent believed that the fifth trumpet of Revelation outlined the rise of Papal power beginning about 600 AD. The star who fell from heaven and who was given the key to the bottomless pit (9:1) was the Pope. The locusts (9:3) were the clergy, e.g., monks, priests, etc. The two beasts of chapter thirteen represented the Roman Empire and the Papacy; the second beast with two horns signified the civil and ecclesiastical papal authority. According to Dent chapters fourteen to twenty dealt with the decline of the fourth world empire and the papacy, the end of which would take place a little before Christ returns for judgement.[168] Differing with Dent Brightman along with Pareus, Cotton, and Goodwin saw both beasts of chapter thirteen as papal Rome. Brightman believed the ten horned beast with seven heads (13:1) was the Papacy in its civil role, and the two-horned beast (13:11) in its ecclesiastical role. Both roles began about 306 AD. The wound that was inflicted on the beast came by way of the Gothic invasions; and the completion of the healing of the wound took place in 606 AD under Phocas.[169] Napier believed that the seven heads on the beast of chapter seventeen represented seven successive forms of government. The first five had passed by the time John had written (Kings, Consuls, Tribunes, Decemvirs, and Dictators), the sixth head in John's day was the Emperors, and the seventh head was the rule of popes.[170] Concerning the harlot who rode the beast (Rev. 17:6) William Guild states,

> The summe then of the mystery of this woman is this, 1. This woman as a woman, is a Church. 2. As a harlot, is a false and idolatrous Church. 3. As inebriating the Kings and inhabitants of the earth with the wine of her fornications, is a pretended Catholick Church. 4. As a mother of harlots is a mother Church. And, 5. As Mystical Babylon ... is the *Roman* Church, all which being put toge[t]her makes up here by common consent the description of the Antichristian Church.[171]

---

[168] *Ibid.*, p. 195.
[169] Brightman, *Revelation*, pp. 429, 430, 431, 442, 452, 444; Ball, *Expectation*, p. 134.
[170] Napier, *Plaine Discovery*, p. 37.
[171] William Guild, *The Sealed Book Opened, or A cleer Explication of the Prophecies of the Revelation* (1656), pp. 251-252.

Mede agreed with Guild that the Roman church was an idolatrous one. He believed that the apostasy of the latter days was a revival of pagan worship-forms which deny worship to Christ alone. For Mede idolatry is "the very *soul*" of the antichristian apostasy; Antichrist is a *"Counter-Christ"*; and the Church (i.e., the papacy) after the days of Arianism was "wholly overshadowed with the thick darknesse of *Idolatrous Antichristianism*."[172] These forms were manifest in the Roman church, for he says,

> This Doctrine of Daemons comprehends in most express manner the whole Idolatry of the Mystery of iniquity, the Deifying and invocating of Saints and Angels, the bowing down to Images, the worshipping of Crosses as new-Idol columns, the adoring and templing of Reliques, the worshipping of any other Visible thing upon supposal of any Divinity therein.[173]

The Papacy not only corrupted true worship but also true doctrine; as William Strong wrote, "Popery ... is ... a mixture of Gods Ordinances, and carnal and heathenish superstitions." In addition, many believed the pope was the Antichrist, for as Archbishop James Ussher states,

> He is one who under the colour of being for Christ, and under title of his Vicegerent, exalteth himselfe above and against Christ, opposing himselfe against all his offices and ordinances both in Church and Common-wealth, bearing authority in the Church of God, ruling over that City with seven Hils, which did bear rule over Nations, and put our Lord to death; a Man of sinne, a Harlot, and a Mother of spirituall fornications to the Kings and people of the Nations, a childe of perdition, a destroyer establishing himselfe by lying miracles and false wonders: all which marks together, do agree with none but the Pope of Rome.[174]

With most of what Dent, Brightman, Mede and others had said about the papacy Knollys agreed. In his book entitled, *Mystical Babylon Unvailed* he addressed the subject of the papacy and its place in eschatology. In this work written in 1679 following the revelation

---

[172]   Joseph Mede, *The Apostacy of the Latter Times*, in *Works*, pp. 643, 647; *Diatribae ... as many discourses on divers texts of Scripture as there are Sundays in the Year*, in *Works*, p. 137.

[173]   Mede, *The Apostacy*, in *Works*, pp. 640.

[174]   William Strong, "One heart and one way," in *XXXI Select Sermons, Preached On Special Occasions* (1656), p. 473; James Ussher, *A Body of Divinitie, or the Summe and Substance of Christian Religion* (1645), p. 438; Ball, *Expectation*, p. 138.

of the Popish Plot he warned his countrymen concerning the papal church, and exhorted people to come out of her. In it he made four propositions concerning Mystical Babylon. The first was that the city of papal Rome is Mystical Babylon.[175] The second was that the Pope or papacy is the Beast who ascends out of the bottomless pit. He is the seventh head on the beast who was granted universal headship in 607 AD by Phocas. He exalts himself as God on earth and seeks to exercise both political and ecclesiastical power signified by his two horns. Moreover, according to Knollys the pope is the man of sin of Second Thessalonians chapter two.[176] The third proposition was that the Church of Rome is the Great Whore who rides the beast. She is a whore because she has caused the church to fall into false worship and idolatry. She teaches her people to pray to dead saints, and to worship images, the Host, and the cross. She also teaches false doctrines like transubstantiation. In addition, she shows herself to be this whore by her persecutions of the saints, e.g., by the Inquisition; by her persecution of the Waldensians, Albigensians, and Huguenots of recent centuries; by the Irish papists; by the Gunpowder plot of 1605; and by the 1678 Popish plot to murder the king. It should be noted that Knollys believed that all national churches like Germany, Spain, France, Italy, etc. were harlots with the Roman church.[177] The fourth proposition was that the Roman priests are the false prophet; this includes the pope, cardinals, Jesuits and all priests. They are the false prophet because of the false doctrines they believe and teach. Some of their false doctrines include the pope's supremacy, justification by works, and the false worship of God.[178] We could quote more material from Knollys' prophetic works on this subject but this is unnecessary.[179] What has been given sufficently shows that he was in essential

---

[175]   Knollys, *Mystical Babylon*, pp. 1-4.

[176]   *Ibid.*, pp. 5-13.

[177]   *Ibid.*, pp. 13-21. Is the "etc." in the last sentence an allusion to the English National church? Probably.

[178]   *Ibid.*, pp. 22-25.

[179]   He agrees with Dent's interpretation that the falling star is the Pope and the locusts are the clergy. He agrees with Goodwin, Brightman, and Cotton that the beasts of Revelation thirteen both depict papal Rome. He concurs with Napier that the seven heads of the beast are seven forms of government and that the seventh head is the papacy. As we have already seen in our study of Knollys' commentary on Revelation much of it is taken up with the subject of Papal Rome.

agreement with the expositors of the first half of the century concerning the place of the papacy in eschatology.

Turkey

Not only was the Papacy viewed as the Antichrist by seventeenth-century English expositors but so was the Mohammedan Turk. The successor to pagan Rome in the West was the papacy, and in the East, the Turk. Some viewed Daniel's "Little Horn" as the Turk in the East[180], the Papacy in the West[181] or a combination of the two.[182] Regardless of which view was taken the Turk was believed to play a significant role in the latter days.

The question of the Turk can be traced at least as far back as Luther. Since the fall of Constantinople in 1453 the Turk threatened Europe making his way to the Danube in fifty years. In the next thirty years Belgrade and Rhodes fell to the Turk, and the Magyars lost the battle of Mohács. Luther saw the same characteristics of the Antichrist in the Turk that lay in the papacy; he states, "Mohammed highly exalts and praises himself and boasts that he has talked with God and the angels.... Therefore the Turks think that their Mohammed is much higher and greater than Christ, for the office of Christ has come to an end and Mohammed's office is still in force". He goes on to say, "That the Roman empire is almost gone, Christ's coming is at the door, and the Turk is the empire's token of the end." And so he prays, "May our dear Lord Jesus Christ help, and come down from heaven with the Last Judgment, and strike down both Turk and pope."[183] Many English expositors followed Luther's assessment of the Turk, but not all did. For example, Edward Haughton did not believe that Turkey met all the requirements concerning the Antichrist. Although interpretations differed concerning the Turk most expositors believed he played a significant role in the final days. Both Mede and Dent believed Turkey to be an integral part of the fourth empire announced by the sixth trumpet of Revelation. They saw it running contemporaneously with the papacy until the seventh trumpet

---

[180]   For example, Henry Finch and Ephriam Huit.
[181]   For example, John Archer, Thomas Parker, and Nathaniel Stephens.
[182]   Ball, *Expectation*, p. 130. For example, Nathaniel Homes and David Pareus.
[183]   Luther, *Works*, XLVI, 176-177, 200, 205.

sounded. Both Goodwin and Brightman taught that the Turk reached his peak of power in 1300 AD; and since his number is an hour, a day, a month and a year which adds up to 396, his ending according to Goodwin would be around 1696 AD.[184]

Knollys also believed that the Turk played an important role in the latter days. He agreed with Mede and Dent that the sixth trumpet announced the loosing of the four angels from the river Euphrates which depicted the commanders of the Armies of the Turkish Emperor. They crossed over the river and destroyed a third part of the Roman Empire because God sent them to judge those "who had *Apostatized* from the *true Worship* of God." The Turk's time equaled 395 prophetic years or else "thereby is signified some certain time appointed of God."[185] During these wars with the Roman Empire, Knollys' says, "The *Turks* did not only kill the bodies of *many Apostate* Romans, but did also poison *many* of their Souls."[186]

At the same time according to Knollys the Turk was "aiding and assisting the *Beast*, and *Mystical* Babylon, against Christ and his *Zion*; for which Cause God will pour out this Vial [sixth] of his wrath upon both *Turk* and *Pope*, and upon all the peoples and Multitudes, who are the Waters of this great River."[187] The end of the Turk will come with the pouring out of the sixth vial.[188] At Armageddon both Pope and the Turk will be defeated and then the seventh vial will be poured out and "will diffuse and spread over all the Kingdoms of *Antichrist*, Pope and Turk, and all the enemies of God and his People."[189] With Brightman Knollys held that "Great Babylon" of Revelation 16:19 was Constantinople of the Turk and his kingdom which would be given "the cup of the wine of the fierceness of his wrath."[190] With the destruction of the Turk and the Papacy the setting up of the kingdom of Christ on earth for a thousand years begins. In conclusion, though Knollys was not concerned about the dates for the beginning and ending of the Turk he agreed with earlier expositors that the Turk was an Antichrist. Moreover, Knollys believed with others that he figured prominently in the latter days,

---

[184]   Ball, *Expectation*, p. 144.
[185]   Knollys, *Revelation*, pp. 112-113.
[186]   *Ibid.*, p. 114.
[187]   Knollys, *Apocalyptical*, II, 25.
[188]   Knollys, *Revelation*, pp. 196-197.
[189]   *Ibid.*, p. 198.
[190]   Knollys, *Apocalyptical*, II, 33-34.

being announced by the sixth trumpet and destroyed by the sixth and seventh vials just prior to the setting up of Christ's kingdom.

Jews

Jewish people also played a prominent role in the eschatology of the seventeenth-century English expositors.[191] Many expositors believed that in the latter days the Jews would be converted. Those among their number included Henry Finch, Joseph Mede, James Ussher, John Cotton, William Strong, Thomas Collier, and Thomas Adams.[192] Brightman wrote in 1609, "These men [Jews] beinge dispersed every where amonge all Nations, shalbe at last converted to the true faith, and shall mourne with an earnest sorrowe, both for theire forefathers horrible wickedness, as also for theire owne so longe obstinancy."[193] Some of those who believed in a conversion of the Jews also understood that they would be restored to their native land. Brightman, Huit and Robert Maton spoke of a restoration of the Jews in Palestine. Moreover, some thought that the kingdom of Christ would not appear before the kingdom of Israel had been restored, and that this would not occur until a number of the Jews had acknowledged Jesus as Messiah.[194] William Strong stated in a sermon, "With the calling of the Jews, the Kingdome of the God of heaven shall be set up." And so he exhorted, "Then suffer them to live among us, that they may have the Gospel preached to them, that's the way to their conversion, to bring them into our land."[195] Of Thomas Adam's six "precedent signes" of the imminent coming of Christ the last was "a new Troope," that is, the converted elect of Israel.[196] Henry Finch even believed that the fifth kingdom of Daniel chapter two was the kingdom of the Jews, and

---

[191]   Besides Ball's *A Great Expectation* (pp. 146-156) two articles that deal with the Jews in eschatological thought are Peter Toon, "The Question of Jewish Immigration," in *Puritans, The Millennium & the Future of Israel*, ed. Peter Toon (Cambridge, 1970), pp. 115-125, and Christopher Hill, "Till the Conversion of the Jews," in *Millenarianism and Messianism in English Literature and Thought 1650-1800*, ed. Richard H. Popkin (London, 1988), pp. 12-36.

[192]   Ball, *Expectation*, pp. 146-147.

[193]   Brightman, *Revelation*, p. 14; Ball, *Expectation*, p. 150.

[194]   *Ibid.*, p. 149.

[195]   William Strong, "The Doctrine of the Jews Vocation," in *XXXI Select Sermons, Preached On Special Occasions* (1656), pp. 287, 291.

[196]   Adams, *Commentary*, p. 1136; Ball, *Expectation*, p. 152.

John Cotton saw Revelation chapters twenty-one and twenty-two as applying to a Jewish Kingdom "here on earth."[197] For most expositors the destruction of Turkey and the Papacy was a prior necessity to the Jewish restoration. Finch and Huit maintained that the destruction of the Turks would take place as the Jews returned to their land; and Finch saw this as the final Armageddon.[198] Many including Goodwin believed that these things would take place somewhere between 1650 and 1700.[199]

Knollys would concur with much of what his contemporaries had stated concerning the Jews. He believed that one of the things that Christ will do when he comes at the end of this present world is gather together His elect which includes the conversion of the Jews.[200] At this time they will be called, gathered and united into one nation.[201] Knollys also believed that when the seventh trumpet is sounded the "mystery of God" should be finished. By the "mystery of God" he explained, "We may understand the Conversion of the *Jews* unto Jesus Christ, *Rom.* 11. 25, 26, 27. ... [and] the building and restoring of the Church of God unto its *primitive* purity of Worship and Ordinances." Knollys also taught that the "Kings of the earth," whose way will be prepared when the sixth vial is poured out, were the Jews. God had promised according to Zechariah 8:7-13 and Daniel 11:44f to save them from the East country.[202] According to Knollys this sixth vial will prepare the way for their conversion, and for the return to their land. He goes on to say,

> The *Papists* are a very great Stumbling-block unto the Conversion of the *Jews*; and the *Turks* are a great impediment unto their return unto their own Land, unto which God hath promised to bring them, ... and to that end God will have both these Stumbling-blocks removed out of the way of his Ancient People the *Jews.*[203]

The Jews will be involved, it appears, in the removing of these stumbling blocks. According to Knollys Armageddon is the name

---

[197] *Ibid.*, p. 150.
[198] *Ibid.*, p. 154.
[199] Goodwin, *Revelation* in *Works*, III, 195-198.
[200] Knollys, *World*, pt. 2, p. 20.
[201] *Ibid.*, p. 43.
[202] Knollys, *Revelation*, p. 197.
[203] Knollys, *Apocalyptical*, II, 26, 27.

given by the Jews to the place where the Turkish army will be destroyed "after they [Jews] have gotten the Victory (which God Almighty will give them) over their Enemies, both Turk and Pope."[204] This will occur just prior to the pouring out of the seventh vial after which the mystery of God will be finished. Knollys agreed with the main elements of the seventeenth-century English expositors' views concerning the Jews. He concurred with their interpretation that they would be converted near the end, that they would return to their land, and even that they would battle with the Turks just prior to the dawning of the kingdom of Christ on earth. And since Knollys believed that the end would take place around 1688 he agreed with Goodwin and many others that all these things would shortly take place. Though it is true as Christopher Hill maintains that "many of the sects with Fifth Monarchist tendencies interested themselves greatly in things Jewish" it would be incorrect to conclude that they were the only ones or even the main ones.[205]

The Millennium

The meaning of the "thousand years" of chapter twenty of John's Revelation has been debated throughout the history of the church.[206] The debate also continued in seventeenth-century England. As we noted earlier most expositors were neither preterist or futurist but historicist in their interpretation of Revelation. And of those who were historicist each one interpreted the thousand years essentially in one of three ways. The first and probably the largest group was amillennialist or modified Augustinian.[207] Many expositors including Hugh Broughton, Arthur Dent, David Pareus and Christopher Love fell into this group. They taught that the millennium encompassed the whole period between the two comings of Christ. When Christ comes a second time the resurrection of the dead, the eternal judgment, and the eternal kingdom will all occur

---

[204]   Knollys, *Revelation*, pp. 198-199.
[205]   Hill, *Puritanism and Revolution: Studies in Interpretation of the English Revolution of the 17th Century* (Harmondsworth, 1986), p. 142.
[206]   See D. H. Kromminga, *The Millennium in the Church* (Grand Rapids, 1945).
[207]   We recognize that "amillennialist" is an anachronism but it helps us categorize an interpretation. The same can be said for the other labels, "premillennialism" and "postmillennialism" that we will use below.

quickly.[208] Some expositors in this category like William Guild and Thomas Hall even believed that the millennium had already been fulfilled.[209] A second group of expositors was premillennialist. This group fell into two categories: some premillennialists like Goodwin, Mede, Alsted, Homes, and Archer believed that Christ would personally return at the beginning of the millennium, set up his kingdom, return to heaven, and reign spiritually for the thousand years through the saints;[210] other premillennialists including John Durant, William Hicks, John Tillinghast, and George Hammon taught that Christ would personally return to earth, set up his kingdom, and personally reign on earth for a thousand years.[211] Some of the premillennialists, like Nathaniel Homes, believed that the last two chapters of Revelation which contained the vision of the new heavens, the new earth, and the new Jerusalem, depicted the millennial state and not the eternal kingdom.[212] A third group which includes John Cotton, Nathaniel Stephens, Edward Haughton and Edmund Hall was postmillennialist. This group was similar to the first-category premillennialists except that they believed Christ would not return personally until the end of the thousand year reign. This view though popular in the 1640s and 1650s has its roots in the eschatology of Thomas Brightman. Brightman taught a spiritualized advent and John Cotton developed his teaching.[213] Cotton writes concerning the destruction of Antichrist in 2 Thess. 2:8,

> And though it be translated, ... The Lord shall destroy him with the brightnesse of his coming: yet the word is ἐν τη επιφανεια [sic] της παρουσιας αὐτου and παρουσια doth as well, and more firstly signify Presence, then comming. The Lord will destroy Antichrist with the brightnesse of his Presence in his sacred and Civill Ordinances, sundry ages before the brightnesse of his comming to Judgement.[214]

And what about Hanserd Knollys? We know that he was certainly a millenarian. Commenting on Revelation 20:3 where it teaches

---

[208] Ball, *Expectation*, p. 161.
[209] *Ibid.*, p. 162.
[210] *Ibid.*, pp. 164-166.
[211] *Ibid.*, pp. 166-168.
[212] *Ibid.*, p. 166.
[213] *Ibid.*, pp. 168-169.
[214] John Cotton, *Bloudy Tenent, washed, and made white in the bloud of the Lambe* (1647), p. 51.

that the Devil will be bound for a thousand years, Knollys states, "that [the thousand years] is, a certain definite time.... They are not any mystical or prophetical number, but literal."[215] He also taught with Nathaniel Homes that the new heavens, new earth, and the new Jerusalem were a vision of the millennial kingdom. He writes,

> The WORLD to COME is not that *eternal* State of God's Kingdom of GLORY in *Heaven*; but it is the *glorious* and *spiritual* State of the Kingdom of Christ on EARTH.... *That same* WORLD, *even* THAT, *that is to* COME; *to wit*, The inhabited WORLD to Come, wherein the PEOPLE of God shall build Houses, and inhabit them, according to Gods Promise, *in that day*, when he will *Create* New Heavens, and a new Earth.[216]

Though it is clear that Knollys was a millenarian, the question is, was he a premillennialist or a postmillennialist? In all of his eschatological works except for one his position appears unclear. It is only when we read his work entitled, *The Parable of the Kingdom of Heaven Expounded* written in 1674 that we clearly see that he was a postmillennialist.[217] According to Knollys this parable from Matthew 25:1-13 is concerned with the coming of Christ before the millennium. He called this coming a "virtual, spiritual, powerful and glorious appearance in his saints."[218] According to Knollys this spiritual coming is also taught in Revelation 11:15, 16, 17; 19:1, 4, 6, 7, 8, 9, 16; and 20:4-9. Following this coming Christ will reign spiritually for a thousand years in His saints who are alive when he comes. At the end of the millennium he will come visibly and personally for the second time (Heb. 9:28).[219] This is when he comes with all his saints, both resurrected and living (1 Thess. 4:13-18). At this time the eternal judgement will take place, the heavens and earth will be dissolved as the Apostle Peter taught (2 Peter 3:12),

---

[215]   Knollys, *Revelation*, p. 222.
[216]   Knollys, *Apocalyptical*, III, 15.
[217]   Though Knollys is explicit in the *Parable* about Christ's return he is not always so elsewhere. Sometimes he sounds like a premillennialist. For example in *World* (written seven years later) when making application to the churches of saints Knollys instructs them for their edification to receive this doctrine of Christ's *personal second* coming from heaven and believe: 1) when he comes he will glorify the house of his glory; 2) he will restore his holy ordinances unto their primitive power and purity, higher than the apostle's days; and 3) *he will presence himself with his people gloriously*, spiritually and *personally* (pp. 37-40).
[218]   Knollys, *Parable*, pp. 78-79.
[219]   *Ibid.*, pp. 75-77.

and the eternal kingdom will begin.[220] These were not unusual interpretations in the seventeenth century.

Practical Piety

Those who expounded on and wrote about the latter days were not primarily interested in theological speculation but in practical godliness and encouragement. Many were pastors who desired that their congregations and fellow countrymen be ready for the near coming of the Lord. Christians ought to be prepared for the Lord's coming as Richard Sibbes writes, "If we say this truly, *Come Lord Iesus*, undoubtedly it will have an influence into our lives, it will stirre up all graces in the soule; as Faith, to lay hold upon it; hope, to expect it; love, to embrace it; patience, to endure any thing for it; heavenly-mindednesse, to fit and prepare for it."[221] If the Christian was going to live eternally in the presence of the holy God of heaven then she must be prepared in holiness. Again Sibbes writes, "If a man hope for this comming of Christ, he will purifie himselfe for it, even as hee is pure, He will not appeare in his foule cloathes, but ... will fit himselfe as the Bride for the comming of the Bridegroome."[222] This holiness ultimately could only be found in God himself. Concerning the marriage supper of the Lamb that occurs when Christ comes, Sibbes exhorted, "Therefore above all, let us get the assurance of the grand point of justification, of being clothed with the righteousnesse of Christ." He went on to say,

> If wee be cloathed with the garments of Christs righteousnesse, wee may goe through the wrath of God: for, that alone is wrath-proofe; that will pacifie God, and pacifie the Conscience too. It is a righteousnesse of Gods owne providing.... Be sure that you understand it well; that you appeare not in your owne, but in his: and then may you thinke of that day with comfort.[223]

Consequently, the coming of Christ was a call to all those who profess faith in Christ, and to all sinners to repent and believe on Christ for their eternal welfare; as William Bridge exhorts, "Be wise

---

[220] *Ibid.*, p. 72.
[221] Richard Sibbes, *The Brides Longing for her Bridgroomes second comming* (1638), p. 79.
[222] Sibbes, *Brides Longing*, pp. 73, 74, quoted in Ball, *Expectation*, p. 215.
[223] Sibbes, *Brides Longing*, pp. 82-83.

now therefore, O ye Princes, Nobles, Rulers, Judges, Gentlemen, and others: Kisse the Son, lest ye perish in the way, for Christ is upon his way unto his kingdome."[224]

Not only was the doctrine of the coming of Christ a means to encourage holiness of life but it was also a means of comfort for the saints. William Hicks wrote,

> Is it not a blessing to know that the time of the woman in the Wilderness, and the witnesses mourning in sackcloth, the treading down the true Church of Christ and Professours thereof is but for 1260. dayes, which term is also neer expiring. Is it not a great blessing after all the troubles and afflictions of the Church and Saints here on earth to be assured, that Christ their head with Myriads of his Angels and Saints departed, will appear to the finall destroying of all their enemies[?][225]

All of Knollys' eschatological works were written to exhort and encourage saints and sinners regarding the day of the coming of the Lord. In particular his works *The World that now is and the World that is to Come* and *The Parable of the Kingdom of Heaven Expounded* were written to exhort his readers both professors and sinners to be prepared for the coming of the Lord. Knollys agreed with Sibbes that to be prepared meant that one be clothed with the righteousness of Christ. Expounding on the five wise virgins of the parable of Matthew 25:1-13, he writes,

> They that were ready had put off the filthy raggs of their own Righteousness and had put on the Robes of Christs Righteousness, *Rom.* 13.14. God had taken away their filthy garments and had cloathed them with change of raiment, *Zach.* 3.4.... And to be prepared for the Bridgrooms coming is

---

224 William Bridge, *Christs coming Opened in a Sermon Before the Honourable House of Commons in Margarets Westminster: May 17, 1648* (1648), p. 13.

225 William Hicks, ᾽ΑΠΟΚΑΛΥΨΙΣ ᾽ΑΠΟΚΑΛΥΨΕΩΣ *or, the Revelation Revealed: being a Practical Exposition on the Revelation of St. John* (1659), "The Preface." Consider also the comforting words of John Durant, "The bodies of *you that are alive are subject to sicknesses*, pains, weaknesses, death: And the bodies of the Saints departed, are subjected to corruption.... Well, but yet in that day, your bodies shall bee redeemed ... all your bodies shall then bee saved from sicknesses, weaknesse, yea, and *death*.... Now we groan under stones, and gouts, and feavors, and agues, and other distempers and paines; yea, and all the day long we are liable to death. But chear up ... in that day it shall not be so.... When Christ shall appear the second time, it shall be for salvation unto our bodies (*The Salvation of the Saints By the Appearances of Christ, 1. Now in Heaven, 2. Hereafter from Heaven* [1653], p. 225).

to be arrayed in fine Linnen, white and clean, which is the Righteousness of the saints.[226]

Knollys was concerned, however, that many who professed to be clothed with Christ's righteousness may not truly be so clothed. Consequently, he was concerned that many professors were not ready for Christ's coming. He believed that many had a form of godliness but lacked the power thereof. He exhorted professors in his *World that now is and the World that is to come* to get the power of godliness if they be lacking it. In this treatise he explained what this power was, and what it meant to deny this power. For Knollys the power of godliness consisted in the truth of grace, lively acts and experience of grace, and growth and perfection of grace.[227] The assurance of readiness was based on the professor's godliness.[228] Knollys believed that those who denied the power of godliness were those who did their religious duties out of the principle of self, of tradition, of legal fear, or of superstition.[229]

In addition, if the believer is to be ready for Christ's coming he should be "watching."[230] This watching means that the believer be awake, be in continual expectation of Christ's glorious appearance, and be looking out desirous of and longing for the coming and kingdom of Christ.[231] Moreover, since Christ was coming soon, Knollys, out of concern not only for the common reader but also for the rulers of England and London, exhorted the King, Nobles, Judges, and all magistrates to Kiss the Son.[232]

For Knollys the truth of the coming of Christ not only called for exhortation but also for encouragement. For the saints the coming of the Lord gives them great hope.[233] Therefore, according to Knollys the coming of Christ, this "generation truth", ought to be

---

[226] Knollys, *Parable*, pp. 114-115.
[227] *Ibid.*, pp. 29-30. He also explains how professors can attain the power of godliness (*Ibid.*, pp. 50-51), and how they might know they have it (*Ibid.*, pp. 51-52).
[228] *Ibid.*, pp. 46-47.
[229] *Ibid.*, pp. 26-28.
[230] *Ibid.*, pp. 130-132. Knollys explains what it means to watch. At the time of publication he believed that they were under the second of three watches which would end in about fifteen years. The third watch would begin with the death of the two witnesses. He also explains how to be ready in *Ibid.*, pp. 82-83, 89, 93, 96, 120-121.
[231] *Ibid.*, pp. 131-132.
[232] Knollys, *World*, pt. 2, pp. 45-46. He exhorts the profane in *Parable*, p. 47.
[233] Knollys, *World*, pt. 2, pp. 42-43.

preached for a warning to professors and profane, and for encouragement to the saints.[234]

It is evident from this comparison of Knollys with his contemporaries that his eschatology was essentially the same. In his works he mentions such expositors as Brightman, Mede, Pareus and Archer. He not only consulted with these but also with others like Dent and Cotton, to name a few, whose interpretations were similar to his. He was certainly not captive to any one man's interpretation of the end times or the Book of Revelation. In fact, we not only see his agreement with a variety of expositors on various points but also his venturing out with new interpretations in a couple of important places.

Before we close this section an important question should be answered, namely, why did Knollys write so many eschatological works at such a late time in his life, and when eschatological fervour had died down? There is no evidence that explicitly tells us why he did. We can only surmise an answer to this question from the external and internal evidence we possess. From our study one obvious reason he wrote these works is that he believed the end was near. In several of his works he taught that the end would occur around 1688. His first work was written in 1667 only twenty one years prior to 1688 and only a year after Goodwin's eschatological date of 1666. He probably felt compelled to warn people about the imminent coming of Christ at this crucial time. Writing "To all the Saints" in 1667 he states, "They that would serve God in their Generation ... ought to inquire diligently into the particular Truths of the Age they live in.... The days wherein we live, being ... the last dayes of those perilous Times mentioned by him [Apostle Paul], 2 Tim. 3. 1,5." He went on to state his purpose for writing this treatise,

> The late Apostacy of some, who have fallen in with the corrupt self-seeking interests of this sinful generation; and the Zeal of others, who have separated themselves from their Brethren, judging them to be defiled with the sins of the times, and therefore dare not have and hold Communion with them, though they hope they are Saints, and the dear Children of God, hath given me occasion to publish my Testimony at this time for the Kingdom of Christ, and against the Kingdom of Antichrist, wherein I have said

---

[234] *Ibid.*, p. 41.

some things that may, by the blessing of God, tend unto the recovery of backsliders, and to the rectifying of the Judgments of my zealous Brethren, and to the reducing of those Saints unto repentance, who have been defiled with any sins of this Age or Generation.

Some other reasons for Knollys eschatological writings appearing during the Restoration period include: 1) the date of 1666; 2) concern about the Papal antichrist; and 3) the lack of concern in the Church about Christ's Return.[235]

---

[235] Knollys, *Apocalyptical Mysteries*, I, preface. Expanding on the other reasons:

1) With the passing of the important date of 1666 Knollys may have felt people would either think Christ was not coming at all or not for a long time, and so not be prepared. Seven years later he wrote *The Parable of the Kingdom of Heaven Expounded* warning professors of the faith about lukewarmness because he believed they were not ready for Christ's coming (p. 57). Again in 1681 in *The World that now is and the World that is to Come* he gave words of counsel to virgin professors of the faith, and instructions to kings, nobles, magistrates, etc. in light of the coming of Christ (pt. 2, 44ff).

2) Knollys may have felt compelled to write at this time because the truth of Christ's Coming was not being taught. Christopher Hill has rightly taught that the discussion of a specific Antichrist had diminished after 1660 (Hill, *Antichrist*, pp. 154, 164). But this was not so for Knollys. He believed that the Antichristian beast was the papacy. For this reason he felt it was necessary to warn England and its people of their danger. In 1679 in the aftermath of the Popish Plot affair he wrote *Mystical Babylon Unvailed* to warn England against the Papists who Knollys believed were seeking in *"their Plots and Conspiracies,"*

the utter *destruction of the Protestants ... and the* Protestant-*Religion in* England especially, *and the* Re-establishment *of the* Popish-*Religion of the Church of* Rome *in this Kingdom; which End the Popish-Recusants in* England (in this Bloody and Traiterous design, that Damnable and Hellish Plot contrived and carried on by them for Assassinating and Murdering the King, Subverting the government, and Rooting out and Destroying the Protestant-Religion, as the King and Parliament have voted and declared) *are still endeavouring to effect, and bring to pass* (*Mystical Babylon*, preface).

In addition, Knollys ended this work and his commentary on Revelation with a call to those in Babylon to come out. Commenting on the words from Revelation 18:1, "Come out of her my people," he explains,

This *Call* is the Call of God our *Saviour* unto all his People in Mystical *Babylon* (*Papal Rome*) to come out of HER.... To come out of HER, is to Separate themselves from the Church of *Rome*, which is now a *false* Church, called *the great Whore, and Mother of Harlots.... Wherefore come out from among them, and be ye separate, saith the Lord* (*Revelation*, p. 243).

We must also remember that Knollys considered all national churches as daughters of the whore, the Roman papal church. He could say in 1688, "And is not *England* like *Egypt* for oppression, exaction, and other cruelties against the *Israel* of God?" (*Ibid.*, p. 140). And when commenting on the second vial of the wrath of God he believed that it would be poured out on "the See of *Rome*, the See of *Canterbury*, the See of *York* and

Thus far we have seen that Knollys held similar eschatological beliefs to other non-Fifth Monarchist writers, which would suggest that his thought was not on the eschatological fringe, like that of Fifth Monarchism. However, this is not enough to answer the charge of Fifth Monarchism made against him. In this next section we will examine the history and distinctive beliefs of this group, and compare those beliefs with Knollys' writings to see if he held any of them.

History of Fifth Monarchism

Dickens' phrase, "It was the best of times and the worst of times," could be said of seventeenth-century eschatological thought. It was the best of times because many Englishmen anticipated the final Coming of Christ to consummate his work and usher in the kingdom of God. It was the worst of times in that many people were reading the Book of Revelation and confidently predicting the time, place, and signs of the end. Most of the important English eschatological works were written before the Interregnum by such men as John Napier, Thomas Brightman, Arthur Dent, Joseph Mede, and Thomas Goodwin. During the Revolutionary period there was a ballooning of eschatological works because it appeared

---

all other *Ecclesiastical, Metropolitan,* and *Diocesan* Sees" (*Ibid.*, p. 194; see also *Ibid.*, p. 227). And again after the seventh vial was poured out in Revelation 16:19 where it is written, "The great city was divided into three parts. And the cities of the nations fell," Knollys interpreted the cities as National churches, and the three parts as "the National churches of the Papists, of the Lord Bishops [England], and of the Presbyterians" (*Ibid.*, p. 200). Remember that Knollys considered the true church to be that of the congregational churches. Remember also that he saw a significant future for England and London in the end as well as Scotland and Ireland (*Ibid.*, pp. 140, 148). In preparation for the end Knollys believed the British kingdom must be warned in these last days to choose Christ and so fulfil its destiny.

3) Maybe he also felt that many were not addressing this subject which he believed was so important for his generation. Therefore, he had to take up the task. Maybe he felt his eschatological efforts unnecessary prior to 1667 (there was enough preaching and writing to encourage English people to be prepared for Christ's coming, and enough hopeful expectation of the end among the people). But maybe he felt this was not so after 1666 when the date passed and the heavy persecution of the 1660s ended. But for Knollys Christ's coming was just around the corner; England needed to be warned and English people needed to be ready. And so for the last twenty-five years of his life Knollys preached and wrote about the coming of Christ, concerned for his fellow Christians, countrymen, and country.

that the end-time predictions of interpreters like Mede were coming true. It was during this time of end-times fascination that Fifth Monarchism came into existence. It was a part of what has been called "apocalyptic millennialism." Robert Clouse has suggested that seventeenth-century eschatological thought be divided into three streams: apocalyptic, academic, and enlightenment millennialism. Simply stated the "apocalyptic millennialists" anticipated a literal return of Christ and His literal reign on earth for a thousand years; the "academic millennialists" expected a literal return but a spiritual reign; and the "enlightenment millennialists" looked for a spiritual coming and spiritual reign.[236]

Although millennialism existed in the writings of such men as Alsted and Mede, "apocalyptic millennialism" was essentially unknown prior to the 1640s. Its immediate roots in the early 1640s can be traced to Robert Maton's work *Israel's Redemption* (1642), and to Henry Archer's *The Personal Reign of Christ on Earth* (1642).[237] Both of these works, though not teaching that Christ would be literally present during the millennium, taught that the saints will literally rule on the earth for a thousand years, "the saints militant rather than the saints spiritual."[238] Both of these works were popular with the Fifth Monarchy Men in the 1650s. This "apocalyptic millennialism" was most prevalent in the New Model Army of the late

---

[236] See Robert Clouse, "The Millennium that Survived the Fifth Monarchy Men," in *Sixteenth Century Essays and Studies* 8, ed. Jerome Friedman (Kirksville, MI: Sixteenth Century Journal Publishers, 1987), pp. 19-29. Clouse gives William Sherwin as an example of the apocalyptic, Nathaniel Homes as an academic, and the Cambridge Platonist Henry More as an enlightenment millennialist. Another suggested breakdown of seventeenth-century millennialism is that of Murray Tolmie — the religious/spiritual and the prophetic/political ("General," pp. 531-532). The Fifth Monarchy Men fit into the later category. It should be noted that less than 50% of the writers of eschatology who were published during the Interregnum were millenarian — that is, those who believed in a coming thousand year reign of the church on earth prior to the last judgement (Ball, *Expectation*, p. 181). For Homes see R. G. Clouse, "Holmes (or Homes), Nathaniel (1599-1678)," *Biographical Dictionary of British Radicals*, II, 108-109.

[237] In 1644 Alexander Petrie responded to Maton's work with *Chiliasto-mastix*. Two years later Maton answered with *Israel's Redemption Redeemed*. This later work was republished in 1652 as *Christ's Personall Reign on Earth One Thousand Yeares with His Saints*, and again in 1655 as *A Treatise of the Fifth Monarchy*. The Fifth Monarchists obviously considered him a friend whether he liked it or not (Maton died in 1653) (Ball, *Expectation*, p. 167). For Archer see K. L. Sprunger, "Archer, John (fl. 1627-1642)," *Biographical Dictionary of British Radicals*, I, 18.

[238] Tolmie, "General," p. 534. For a brief discussion of these writings see *Ibid.*, pp. 533-534.

1640s which was composed of many Baptists in the ranks and leadership.[239]

In 1649 with the beheading of King Charles the way was clear for the Rule of King Jesus for the more militant of the godly. Consequently, some Norfolk millenarians presented to the army leaders some proposals entitled, *Certain Quaeries Humbly presented in the way of Petition, by many Christian people, dispersed abroad through the County of Norfolk and the City of Norwich.*[240] In this document several proposals were presented for the reorganization of the government which included the abandonment of England's worldly government, and the "monarchy of Christ set up by the immediate transfer of the civil power to the saints, both Independent and Presbyterian, through whom Christ could begin his rule."[241] They stated that "[the kingdom of Christ is to be administered] by such laws and officers as Jesus Christ our Mediator hath appointed in his kingdom" and it is to "put down all worldly rule and authority (so far as relates to the worldly constitution thereof), though in the hands of Christians," and it "is to be expected about this time we live in."[242] This administration will take place when more and more people become Christians and are organized in churches. Norfolk and London became the strongholds of this new movement. In December 1651 the Fifth Monarchists of London were organized around regular meetings at All Hallows the Great, Thames Street, in response to the cold shoulder given by Cromwell to Chrisopher Feake and others including some from the Army who were urging "him to do something for Christ's cause."[243] On their first meeting

---

[239] For more on the millennial roots of Fifth Monarchism see Capp, *Fifth Monarchy*, pp. 23-49.

[240] This is reprinted in A.S.P. Woodhouse, ed., *Puritanism and Liberty: Being the Army Debates (1647-49) from the Clarke Manuscripts* (1974; rpt. Rutland, VA & London, 1992), pp. 241-247.

[241] Tolmie, "General," p. 539.

[242] *Certain Quaeries* in Woodhouse, *Puritanism and Liberty*, pp. 244-245. See also Brown, *Political Activities*, pp. 17-18; Tolmie, "General," p. 539; Capp, "Extreme Millenarianism," in *Puritans, the Millennium and the Future of Israel*, ed. Peter Toon (Cambridge & London, 1970), p. 79.

[243] Capp, "Extreme," p. 79. In these meetings with Cromwell they urged him to "press forward in promoting that *glorious Cause* ... and particularly, to quicken the *Parliament* to do some *honest and honourable works*" (Christopher Feake, *Beam of Light, shining in the midst of much Darkness* [1659], p. 39; see also Brown, *Political Activities*, pp. 19-22; and Capp, *Fifth Monarchy*, pp.58-59). For more on Feake see B. S. Capp, "Feake, Christopher (1612-c. 1683)," *Biographical Dictionary of British Radicals*, I, 270-271.

these millenarians agreed on six points of prayer which included: the exaltation of the Kingdom of Christ in Britain and all the earth and that "whatsoever stood in the way" of Christ's kingdom "might be utterly pulled down, and brought to nothing"; seeking the removal of ungodly magistrates and ministers; ceasing of divisions among the godly; the fulfilment of the promises of Parliament, Churches and Army; and the Lord's providential intervention in the English-Dutch negotiations that nothing would hinder the cause of Christ in Britain.[244]

For the next two years the Fifth Monarchists continued to meet, pray, preach and write. Then in 1653 with the downfall of the Rump Parliament and the election of the Nominated Parliament of the saints their hopes for the dawning of the millennium appeared to be coming to pass. They petitioned Parliament to implement bills for the abolition of Chancery, for law reform, and for the abolition of tithes and Church patronage. But unfortunately none of these were carried forward in the months that followed. This turned such leaders as Peter Chamberlen, and John Spittlehouse against Cromwell. Cromwell dissolved the Parliament of saints in December 1653, and became Lord Protector of the realm with the support of the Army. In this role "radical reforms and preparation for the millennium were abandoned."[245] Bernard Capp explains, "With the fall of the Barebones [Nominated Parliament], the Fifth Monarchists went into permanent and unwavering opposition. They reviled Cromwell for accepting the resignation of the assembly and so disrupting the reign of the saints."[246]

On the eve of the first Protectorate Parliament the London Fifth Monarchists published their manifesto entitled, *A Declaration of several churches of Christ , and Godly People in and about the Citie of London; Concerning the Kingly Interest of Christ, and the Present Sufferings of his Cause and Saints in England*. The manifesto was "a violent attack upon the Government, and upon the Army for betraying its former principles, although the authors were careful to say that they were against 'all Carnall Plots, Devilish Designes, or ungodly Combinations of

---

[244]   Feake, *Beam of Light*, pp. 41-42; Capp, *Fifth Monarchy*, p. 59; Capp, "Extreme," p. 79.

[245]   Capp, "Extreme," p. 81. For more on the Nominated Parliament and its failure see Capp, *Fifth Monarchy*, pp. 66-75, and Brown, *Political Activities*, pp. 28-43.

[246]   Capp, *Fifth Monarchy*, p. 75.

men whatsoever.' "[247] Appended to this tract were 150 signatures grouped according to ten congregations; two of the congregations were those of Feake and Rogers, four were Congregationalist, and four were Baptist, three of which were Calvinistic (Knollys', Simpson's, and Jessey's). Only one Baptist church signed as a group, the General Baptist church of Peter Chamberlen.[248] This manifesto was followed by tracts from Fifth Monarchists John Spittlehouse and Thomas Aspinwall, members of Chamberlen's congregation.[249]

In response, and speaking on behalf of the Calvinistic Baptists, Samuel Richardson countered these anti-government denunciations in his *Apology for the Present Government* (October 1654) revealing their commitment to the Cromwellian government.[250] Other millenarian groups also accepted Cromwell's rule but the Fifth Monarchists were obstinately opposed. Some Fifth Monarchists saw Cromwell as the "Little Horn" of Daniel's prophecy, and the new government as a part of the Fourth anti-Christian Monarchy which needed to be opposed.[251] As private citizens and saints they believed it was their duty "to act as God's instruments in preparing the way for His kingdom." Most millenarians were repulsed by this anarchistic rhetoric.[252] Feake, Simpson, John Rogers and Anna Trapnel were arrested, Powell fled to Wales, and Major General Thomas Harrison was deprived of his commission.[253] In early 1655

---

[247]   Tolmie, "General," p. 563.

[248]   Half of the 150 people who signed the document were Baptists with 35 of them from the Calvinistic Baptist churches (Tolmie, "General," pp. 563-564).

[249]   Spittlehouse wrote *Certain Queries Propounded To the most serious Consideration of those Persons Now in Power* (September 1654), and *An Answer to one part of the Lord Protectors Speech: or a Vindication of the Fifth Monarchy Men* (September, 1654). Aspinwall published *A Premonition of Sundry Sad Calamities Yet to Come* (November 1654). For Aspinwall see J. F. Maclear, "Aspinwall, William (fl. 1630-1657)," *Biographical Dictionary of British Radicals*, I, 25-26. For Spittlehouse see S. J. Stearns, "Spittlehouse, John (fl. 1643-1656)," *Biographical Dictionary of British Radicals*, III, 194-195.

[250]   For Richardson's views on this issue see Gritz, "Samuel Richardson," pp. 368-374.

[251]   Capp, *Fifth Monarchy*, p. 101; Capp, "Extreme," p. 81-82; Tolmie, "General," p. 553; Brown, *Politicial Activities*, p. 45. On the Fifth Monarchists and the Protectorate see *Ibid.*, pp. 44-75.

[252]   Capp, "Extreme," p. 81.

[253]   The other Fifth Monarchist army officers like Nathaniel Rich, Robert Overton and William Allen did not stir up resistence against Cromwell. For John Rogers see R. M. Gibson, "Rogers, John (1627-c. 1665)," *Biographical Dictionary of British Radicals*, III, 107-110.

Harrison, Nathaniel Rich, John Carew and Hugh Courtney were arrested for denying the legality of the government and promoting the lawfulness of opposing it. In this same year several Fifth Monarchist tracts appeared, including, *A Short Discovery of His Highness's Intentions concerning Anabaptists in the Army, The Protector (So called,) In Part Unvailed,* and *A Ground Voice, or some Discoveries offered to the view ... of the whole Army,* and *A Word from God.*[254] These tracts accused Cromwell, called the Army back to its principles, accused Baptists of deserting the Good Old Cause, and tried to rally support against the Protectorate.

During the years of 1655 and 1656 Fifth Monarchists were causing trouble in Wales[255], Norfolk[256] and the Midlands. It was in the latter area that a major stir of Fifth Monarchist activity concerned the government in 1656. Numerous Fifth Monarchists gathered at the funeral of the young Calvinistic Baptist preacher and Fifth Monarchist John Pendarves. Fearing that this gathering would be the occasion of an armed uprising the government intervened.[257] Consequently, nothing came of the event but the government's crackdown increased the government's unpopularity in the minds of these millenarians.[258] Nevertheless, Calvinistic Baptist support for Fifth Monarchism was diminishing including the defection of two of its leaders, John Simpson and Henry Jessey (numbers of

---

[254] The first three tracts were anonymous; the last one was a Welsh manifesto authored by Vavasor Powell. For more on Powell's *A Word from God* see Capp, *Fifth Monarchy,* pp. 110-112. The Calvinistic Baptist response to this work was by Samuel Richardson entitled, *Plain Dealing: or The unvailing of the opposers of the Present Government* (January 1656). The argument in *Plain Dealing* is similar to his earlier work *Apology* (October 1654) supporting the Cromwellian government.

[255] For Fifth Monarchism in Wales see Capp, *Fifth Monarchy,* pp. 61-65, 76-79, 109-113, and Tolmie, "General," pp. 573-577.

[256] For Fifth Monarchist agitation in Norfolk see Tolmie, "General," pp. 579-583.

[257] There is some factual basis for the government's concern. Probably some of the extreme members of the group were preparing to use the funeral as an occasion for a rebellion. This accounts for the large number of Londoners at the funeral including one of the central plotters, John Portman. They were probably hoping to convince other dissatisfied Baptists to join in the uprising (*Ibid.,* pp. 586-587). See also Capp, *Fifth Monarchy,* for other Fifth Monarchist activity surrounding this event (p. 116). For Portman see J. W. Spurgeon, "Portman, John (fl. 1652-1667)," *Biographical Dictionary of British Radicals,* III, 54.

[258] For more on this see White, "John Pendarves," pp. 251-271, and Tolmie, "General," pp. 583-587. The London Baptists expressed their displeasure in *The Complaining Testimony of some ... of Sion's Children ... occasioned at their Meeting to seek the Lord at Abingdon* (1656).

Fifth Monarchists in general had greatly decreased since 1653). These defections essentially nullified what existed of any serious support from Calvinistic Baptists.

These events, however, did not stop Thomas Venner, one of the extreme Fifth Monarchists, from planning an uprising in 1657 under the manifesto *A Standard Set Up.* Their plan was to assemble in Storeditch and march to East Anglia in order to rally support. The government discovered their plans, arrested them as they gathered, and put Venner and two of his lieutenants in the Tower until 1659. Many Fifth Monarchists like Harrision, Rich and Rogers opposed the Venner plan because they were not "prepared to stir up violence unless providence showed that this was God's will."[259]

Nevertheless, many Fifth Monarchists were unhappy with the reestablishment of the monarchy under King Cromwell and not King Jesus. They also believed, inspite of Venner's failure, that the 3 ½ years in which the two witnesses were to lie dead were to be completed in 1657 (Revelation 11:2-11). Their hopes were raised when Cromwell died in September 1658. The Army leaders were able to overpower the new Protector, Richard Cromwell, forcing him to dissolve Parliament and eventually causing the collapse of the Protectorate. Now with power in their hands the Fifth Monarchists sought the best course to restore the Good Old Cause. But they were divided among themselves over how this might be accomplished. Some desired a new Nominated Parliament, and others were for a restored Rump. The latter won out but did not fulfil the hopes of its Fifth Monarchist members, failing to reform the law or the church. Overton, Powell, Allen and others called for a purge of those members who had supported the Protectorate. Other Army officers were not pleased with the Rump, and in October they ousted the Parliament by force. No agreement could be made for a government, and consequently the Rump was recalled in December. In February of the following year General Monck marched to London from Scotland, reestablished the Long Parliament, and Charles Stuart was asked to return to England as King.[260]

The hopes of the Fifth Monarchists had not been fulfilled, and

---

[259] Capp, "Extreme," p. 84; Capp, *Fifth Monarchy*, pp. 117-118.
[260] For more details on the opposition of the Fifth Monarchists from 1653-1660 see Capp, *Fifth Monarchy*, pp. 99-130, and Brown, *Political Activities*, pp. 44-75.

by 1660 their expectations for the immediate millennial reign of Christ appeared to have been crushed. Harrison and Carew were executed as regicides; Rich, Overton, Portman and Powell were arrested and imprisoned for years. The movement split in two directions. The majority of Fifth Monarchists continued to preach against the government but moved away from violence. The minority, however, went the opposite direction encouraging violence. In January 1661 Venner gathered about fifty people marching through London seeking to set up the kingdom of God by force. The determined band fought for several days; twenty six were killed and twenty arrested. Venner and twelve others were executed.[261] Other attempts of lesser violence followed in the next twenty-five years but without success. For example, in the 1660s John Belcher and Nathaniel Strange separately plotted uprisings against the government but both attempts amounted to nothing. Years later both the Rye House Plot (1683) and Monmouth's Rebellion (1685) included a number of Fifth Monarchists. After these failures the cause was all but dead. Although the movement survived 1660 by a quarter of a century Capp suggests that its demise was partly the "gradual advance of rationalism and scepticism", and more importantly the uniting of the landed classes "to enforce order and discipline."[262]

The Doctrine of the Fifth Monarchists and Hanserd Knollys

Was Knollys a Fifth Monarchist? In order to help answer this question we will compare the distinctive tenets of Fifth Monarchism with Knollys' writings. Bernard Capp, the premier historian of Fifth Monarchism, noted three teachings that distinguished the Fifth Monarchists from other millenarians. First, they taught that the saints will be actively involved in the removal of the anti-Christian Fourth Monarchy using force if necessary, not leaving this to

---

[261] Champlin Burrage, "The Fifth Monarchy Insurrections," *English Historical Review*, 25 (1910), pp. 739-745.

[262] Capp, "Extreme," p. 89. The Fifth Monarchists alienated almost all of the gentry, merchants and clergy, and were made up mainly of the lower classes (Capp, *Fifth Monarchy*, pp. 76-98). However, in one list of 233 Fifth Monarchists there were 20 gentry, and 48 beneficed ministers (*Ibid.*, pp. 83-85).

God alone.[263] Secondly, they believed that many of the prophetic symbols of Scripture referred to contemporary English political events and people. And thirdly, they gave a greater detailed description of the political, social, and economic structure of the millennium than other groups.[264]

The Fifth Monarchists believed that they were to take an active part in bringing in the Fifth Monarchy. It is true that only God could establish the kingdom but for these millenarians this establishment would be accomplished through the saints. This was the clear meaning of Jeremiah 51:20, "Thou art my battle axe and weapons of war: for with thee will I break in pieces the nations, and with thee will I destroy kingdoms." Tillinghast believed that though only God could bring in the kingdom this was no excuse "for us ... to sit still and do nothing ... to the effecting these glorious things." He maintained that the God-given duty of his generation was "TO BRING DOWNE LOFTY MEN, TO LAY LOW, AND TO THROWE DOWN ANTICHRIST." An anonymous Fifth Monarchist wrote: "A Sword is as really the appointment of Christ, as any other Ordinance in the Church.... And a man may as well go into the harvest without his Sickle as to this work without ... his Sword." According to some Fifth Monarchists this action would prepare the way for the millennium.[265] Major-General Harrison, seeking to convince the sceptical Ludlow of this cause, quoted Daniel 7:22, "the saints shall *take* the kingdom."[266] According to Tillinghast the kingdom of God has a twofold nature — the first part is the establishment of the kingdom by the saints by force, and the second part concerns Christ's appearing at the time of perfection.[267]

While others had forsaken the cause of God these millennialists believed they were upholding what God had begun in the early

---

[263] Ball agrees with Capp that this was a mark of Fifth Monarchism (*Expectation*, p. 181).

[264] Capp, "Extreme, " p. 68. For more detail on the beliefs of the Fifth Monarchists see Capp, *Fifth Monarchy*, pp. 131-156, 172-194.

[265] John Tillinghast, *Mr. Tillinghast's Eight Last Sermons* (1655), p. 219; anon, *A Witness to the Saints* (1657), p. 6. For a brief look at Tillinghast see R. L. Greaves, "Tillinghast, John (1604-1655)," *Biographical Dictionary of British Radicals*, III, 241-242.

[266] E. Ludlow, *Memoirs*, ed. C.H. Firth (Oxford, 1894), II, 7-8 (emphasis added); Capp, *Fifth Monarchy*, p. 131.

[267] John Tillinghast, *Knowledge of the Times* (1654), *passim*; John Tillinghast, *Mr. Tillinghhasts Eight Last Sermons* (1655), pp. 61-62.

1640s, that is, the destruction of the anti-Christian Fourth Monarchy and the incoming of the millennium.[268] The Fifth Monarchist Manifesto of 1654 declared,

> We are fully perswaded in our souls, that [Christ] who hath hitherto most eminently appeared, and plainly owned this *blessed Cause* (which the *Apostates* of the times have cast aside, and we yet cleave unto) ... will *yet appear* and that more eminently, (and terribly too) to save, then ever, and witness to the *righteousness* of his *own Cause*.[269]

It should be understood that some Fifth Monarchists like Thomas Venner believed that the millennium would begin when the saints took military action. One of John Rogers followers who joined Venner in his exploits stated, "Wee did not live in an age to expect miracles; that Babilon cannot bee destroyed, nor the fainte at Windsor be released, by only faith and prayer; but you must bee of courage, and make use of materiall instruments, and proceed by force." And in 1661, "William James, the preacher, prayed that God would deliver them from the scarlet whore, who bathed herself in the blood of the saints, and that the people might be willing to lay down trade or estate to do God's work."[270] This path became more pronounced as time passed but most Fifth Monarchists maintained that they must wait for God's signal before acting. John Rogers declares, "Come sirs! prepare your *companies* for *King Jesus*, his *Mount Zion Musterday* is at hand, his *Magazine* and *Artillery*, yea his most excellent *mortar-peices* [sic] and *batteries* be ready, we wait only for the *Word* from on high to *fal on*."[271] Most denied any insurrection, as John Canne stated, they "*do abhor all secret Designes and Plots.... And below their Principles, to provide Pikes and Muskets.*" Thus the saints were to "*remain in their* chambers" waiting for God's call.[272] In the meantime, however, they were "to denounce the wrath of God

---

[268] Feake, *A Beam of Light*, pp. 39-46; Capp, *Fifth Monarchy*, pp. 131-132.

[269] *A Declaration of Several of the Churches of Christ, ... Concerning The Kingly Interest of Christ and the present Sufferings of His Cause and Saints in* England (1654), pp. 7-8.

[270] John Thurloe, *A Collection of the State Papers of John Thurloe, Esq. &c.*, ed. T. Birch (1742), III, 136; *Calendar of State Papers, Domestic Series, of the Reign of Charles II. 1661-1662*, Vol. 43, No. 46, p. 110, Oct. 11, 1661.

[271] John Rogers, *Jegar-Sahadutha: An Oyled Pillar: Set up for Posterity* (1657), p. 140.

[272] John Canne, *Truth with Time: or, certaine Reasons proving, that none of the seven last Plagues, or Vials, are yet poured out* (1656), *sig.* B1v, B2; John Canne, *The Time of the End* (1657), p. 206; John Canne, *The Time of Finding* (1658), *sig.* A2v-A3.

against *Rulers*, for their Apostacies and abhominable hypocrisies;
yea, and to deale particularly with them, laying the finger on the
sore, pointing out the Abhominations by name, denouncing the
vengeance of God upon them."[273] Tillinghast stated that because
it was the hour of fulfilment, "of necessity must the Witnesses of
Christ in this Age bear forth such a testimony of truth as may lay
a foundation in the hearts of Gods people for such a work [as] ...
the regaining that kingdom."[274] And in 1654 John Spittlehouse,
though not calling for armed revolt, called for the present implementation of the rule of Christ desiring that *"God the Father of our
Lord Jesus Christ would cast down all those earthly, carnal, cruel, political
combinations of men ... who would not have [Christ] reign ever [sic] us but set
up themselves and their corrupt interests in the room of that scepter of
righteousnesse which he hath given into the hands of his dear Son."*[275]

It is evident that though not all Fifth Monarchists believed that
the Fifth Monarchy should be brought in by force, all expected that
when the time was right, force and violence would be used. When
King Jesus gave the signal they would go to arms and bring in the
kingdom. However, as the movement aged in the 1650s the rhetoric of establishing the kingdom by force became more pronounced
in some circles, and in the minds of some it became a mark of the
movement.

Did Knollys espouse this Fifth Monarchist teaching? In his writings Knollys never speaks of the use of force in order to bring in the
millennium. For example, in 1688 in his commentary on Revelation concerning the prophecy of the two witnesses which continues
just prior to the coming of Christ, he tells his readers that the "Ecclesiastical Power ordained by Christ and given to his Ministers, is
not Magisterial, but Ministerial; not the Power of the Sword but of
the Word."[276] When commenting on Revelation 11:5 that from the
two witnesses "fire proceedeth out of their mouth, and devoureth
their enemies," Knollys states,

---

[273]   W. Llanvaedonon, *A Brief Exposition upon the Second Psalme* (1655), p. 23.
[274]   John Tillinghast, *Knowledge of the Times* (1654), p. 345.
[275]   John Spittlehouse, *An Answer to One Part of the Lord Protector's Speech: or a Vindication
of the Fifth Monarchy Men* (1654), pp. 5-6. For more examples of the encouragement of
violence by Fifth Monarchists see Ball, *Expectation*, pp. 187-191.
[276]   *Revelation*, p. 129.

Christ's Ministers and his Churches of Saints [the two witnesses], when they are injured, wronged, and hurt by Persecution, Oppression, Imprisonment, Banishment, &c. ought not to betake themselves to their material Arms, but to their spiritual Prayers; their fire which devoureth and kills their enemies, must not proceed out of their Guns, their brass or iron Canons, &c. but out of their Mouth; *viz.* their Prophecy and Testimony of *Jesus*.... The faithful Ministers of Christ, and the Churches of the Saints, have spiritual weapons; and especially the Sword of the Spirit, which is the Word of God.[277]

In *Apocalyptical Mysteries* Knollys explains how the kingdom of Christ is to be set up, that is, by the breaking in pieces of the kingdoms of this world; this will be accomplished by: 1) the conversion of sinners; 2) by the pouring out of the Spirit upon all flesh; 3) by the union of all the saints; and 4) the restitution of all things.[278] There is no mention of physical force to set up the kingdom. Kings will only be bound physically when the saints and Christ reign on earth, and Christ will be the one who will bring in the Fifth Monarchy and its rule.[279] Knollys writes that in this age,

Let the Churches, Ministers, and all the Saints know, and Consider *seriously*, That though they ought to pray for Kings, and all that are in Authority,... to obey Magistrates, and be subject to Principalities, and Powers, being God's Ordinance.... Yet in Case the Powers of this World shall command them to do any thing, which God hath forbidden, or shall forbid them to do any thing, which God hath Commanded, they ought to obey God rather then Men.[280]

---

[277] *Ibid.*, p. 134. This was exactly what he said ten years earlier in 1679 in *The Exposition of the Eleventh Chapter of Revelation* (p. 17). In the margin of *Eleventh* when discussing the two witnesses (the Congregational churches and the ministers of Christ) exercising not "*Magisterial*-Power" but "*Ministerial--Prophetical* – Power" Knollys states, "Though the Ministers of the Gospel may declare the righteous Judgments of God against Men, according to his written word, yet They ought not to sit in Judgment and pass Sentence of Corporal punishment upon any Man" (p. 11).

[278] Knollys, *Apocalyptical Mysteries*, III, 11-12. He also states here that the kingdom of Christ is not of this world, nor "of a *Worldly* constitution; but it is a spiritual and *heavenly* Kingdom" (p. 12). All subsequent references without authors are to Knollys' works.

[279] *Apocalyptical Mysteries*, III, 16; *Revelation*, pp. 153-154.

[280] *Eleventh*, p. 43. Knollys believed with other Baptist brethren that submission was due the magistrate. In his co-authored work entitled, *A Declaration concerning the Public Dispute* Knollys maintained that they (the Baptist disputers) were "ready to obey our Civill Magistrates, as to professe our subjection to his Authority in all lawfull commands" (p. 4). See also the 1644/46 *Confession of Faith*, articles XLVIII and XLIX.

More importantly, in the midst of the Fifth Monarchist activity in 1655, in his treatise entitled, *An Exposition of the first chapter of the Song of Solomon*, Knollys makes some comments that clearly contradict this tenet of Fifth Monarchist teaching. Concerning the saints involvement when Christ and His enemies come into final conflict, he writes:

> The spirit of faith in prayers and prophecyings of the Saints, will certainly effect the ruin and utter destruction of all their Enemies Zac. 4.6,7.... O ye Saints! Pray in faith, and prophecie in faith by the Spirit of the Lord, and your Enemies will fall; ye shall not need to fight, for Christs Enemies and yours will every one help to destroy another.... The worm *Jacob* is Christs Battle-Axe, Jer. 51.20. whereby he will destroy kingdomes, his praying Saints, and prophesying Servants, are the Lords company of Horses, though now in *Pharoahs* Chariot, under the powers of the Earth, who lord it over the Lords Heritage.[281]

Knollys believed that the saints were *only* to use spiritual weapons in this conflict with the enemy. Yet, it is understandable how contemporaries and historians could have perceived Knollys as a Fifth Monarchist on this point of force and violence. He does speak of the saints using force in the millennium, but not prior to it. On the other hand, we have seen that there are places in his works where he clearly speaks against force to bring in the millennium, even teaching that prayer and preaching will be the spiritual weapons used in the final conflict.

The second mark of the Fifth Monarchists was their propensity to see events of, and people in the 1640s and 50s fulfilling prophecy. For example, Tillinghast believed that the second vial of Revelation 16 was the destruction of the anti-christian English episcopacy by the Long Parliament, and the third vial included the fall of Charles I and the Long Parliament (after it apostasized).[282] Various dates were said to be apocalyptically important as 1641, 1645, 1648, 1649, 1650, 1655-57, 1656/7, 1660, and 1665 with the most important date being 1666 adding up to the mark of the beast (Revelation 13:18). John Canne believed that important apocalyptic

---

[281] *Song of Solomon*, pp. 44-45. Note that he refers to Jer. 51:20 which states, "The worm *Jacob* is Christs Battle-Axe," whereby God will destroy kingdoms. This was an important verse for Fifth Monarchists. Knollys, however, believed that it was to be interpreted spiritually.

[282] Capp, "Extreme," p. 69.

events had taken place in 1656/7 but were unnoticed by the ungodly.[283]

When it came to the "Little Horn" of Daniel 7:8 Aspinwall, Rogers, Mary Cary, John More, and the authors of *A Ground Voice* and *Faithful Narrative* began to identify it with Charles I or a series of English kings, or after 1653 with the Lord Protector Cromwell. For John More Cromwell was the number of the Beast 666 by adding up the title "Rex Oliver Lord Protector" (discounting the letter 'L').[284] Vavasor Powell did not see Charles I as the "Little Horn" but the "King of the North" whose fall was prophesied in Daniel 11:15-19. Cromwell was the one who would follow and be overthrown with ease (Daniel 11:20).[285]

In 1655, while under examination by Cromwell John Rogers boldly proclaimed "the remnant of the woman's seed Rev. 12:17 must be at it when they have the Call. For I beseech you, my Lord, consider how neer it is to the End of the Beast's dominion, the 42 months (of the profanation of the Holy Temple by the Gentiles, Rev. 11:2) and what time of day it is with us now."[286] In 1651 Mary Cary saw the "Little Horn's" doom and downfall during the reigns of James I and Charles I; and John Canne believed that the Jews and Turks would do battle from 1655 to 1700 with the Jews getting the victory.[287] This propensity to prophetically afix names to contemporary events and people was beyond what most millenarians of the Revolutionary period were willing to do.

Was Knollys prone to identifying contemporary events and people with prophecy? On the contrary, in comparison with his Fifth Monarchist contemporaries, he was quite restrained. In *Apocalyptical Mysteries* published a year after the important eschatological year of 1666 Knollys identified events and people no more than moderate eschatological writers had. For example, he identifies the "Roman Politick and Ecclesiastical State" as the man of sin, and states that

---

[283] Canne, *The Time of Finding*, pp. 273-279. See also anon, *A Door of Hope: or, A Call ... unto the Standard of our Lord, King Jesus* (1661), pp. 12-13; Capp, *Fifth Monarchy*, p. 193.

[284] Capp, *Fifth Monarchy*, p. 194; Capp, "Extreme," pp. 70-71.

[285] Capp, "Extreme," p. 71.

[286] Anon., *The Faithful Narrative of the Late Testimony* (1655), p. 35, quoted in Capp, "Extreme," p. 71.

[287] Mary Cary, *The Little Horns Doom & Downfall: or a Scripture Prophesie of King James, and King Charles* (1651); John Canne, *A Voice in the Temple* (1653), pp. 27-29; Capp, "Extreme," p. 72; Capp, *Fifth Monarchy*, pp. 190-191. For Mary Cary see A. Cohen, "Cary (or Rande), Mary (fl. 1636-1653)," *Biographical Dictionary of British Radicals*, I, 127-128.

the Jews will return to their land without giving any date for this event. In addition, like other moderate expositors he identifies prophecy with past historical events, e.g., at the end of the 42 months the beast begins to rage as he did against Charles V in Germany, France, Scotland, etc., and in Queen Mary's days in England. Moreover, he maintained that the vials had yet to be poured out, countering some Fifth Monarchists who believed that one of the vials had fallen on the Long Parliament. As with many others he maintained that the fourth monarchy was the Roman kingdom, and that the end of this monarchy was near.[288]

Fifteen years later in *The World that now is and the World that is to come* Knollys makes no contemporary identifications with prophecy. When expounding on the signs of the end, he does however, say that there is more iniquity in England in 1681 than in former ages. Moreover, at the end of the treatise he calls England and London to "Kiss the son"; and to the magistrates and inhabitants of London he exhorts them to consider that God has already visited the city with pestilence and fire but they have not responded, and God threatens a famine of bread and of the Word if they do not repent and amend their ways.[289]

In *An Exposition of the Eleventh Chapter of the Revelation* written during the hysteria of the Popish Plot Knollys has much to say about the time of the end but again makes little contemporary identification of prophecy. As with many others he identifies the Pope with the man of sin, and Roman-papal-dominion as Babylon. And as in *Apocalyptical Mysteries* he identifies past historical events with prophecy, e.g., the 1260 prophetical days began about the year 407, 409, 410 or before 428, and so should end about 1688. In addition, in line with a tradition since John Foxe he gives England a special place in the end times; he identifies England, Scotland and Ireland as the "tenth part of the city" (Rev. 11:13) which will "fall off *totally* and *finally* from the Pope, and Church of Rome"; and states that the "street of the city" (Rev. 11:8) is England, "some very eminent and famous *Kingdom*, where these two-Witnesses have most eminently born their *Testimony* for Christ against the Beast," and this

---

[288]   *Apocalyptical Mysteries*, II, 21; II, 27; I, 19; II, 40-41; I, 12; I, 28. Also in his interpretation of Daniel two and seven he does not make any contemporary identification (III, 9-18).

[289]   *World*, pt.1 , p. 93; pt. 2, pp. 45-48.

testimony "hath been, yet is, and will be born by Christs faithful Ministers, and his Churches of Saints ... here in England ... in London." [290]

In the same year as *Eleventh* he wrote *Mystical Babylon* and again identified the Pope with the man of sin, and identified past historical events with prophecy, e.g., the pope became the Beast of the eighth head in 607 AD, and had temporal sovereignty in Henry IV's time. However, in light of the Popish plot he identified the events (persecutions) in England in 1588 (Spanish Armada), 1605 (Gun-Powder Plot) and 1678 (Popish Plot) as coming from the Great Whore, the Church of Rome. In addition, he feared the coming of the Papists into England; he believed their goal was "*the utter Destruction of the Protestants ... and the Protestant-Religion in England especially, and the Re-establishment of the Popish-Religion of the Church of Rome in this Kingdom.*"[291]

In his commentary on Revelation he again identifies the pope as the Antichrist, past events with prophetic Scriptures, and the kingdom of England as the "tenth part of the city" (Rev. 11:13) and the "street of the city" (Rev. 11:8). And as in *Eleventh* he states that the "end" will come in about the year 1688.[292]

In conclusion, one can see that Knollys made few contemporary identifications with prophetic Scripture, and those which he did, fall within those of the mainstream seventeenth-century eschatological writers, millenarian or not. Even during the heyday of Fifth Monarchism when discussing the enemies of Christ prior to his millennial reign, Knollys states that one of his enemies will be a mighty man who shall arise in the fourth monarchy (Daniel 7:23-27), but does not identify him.[293]

The third mark of the Fifth Monarchists was their detailed description of the political, social, economic, and ecclesiastical structure of the millennium. Most millennialists left this issue unaddressed because such a description was not clearly given in the Scriptures. But this was not so for the Fifth Monarchists. Concerning the presence of Christ there was much disagreement among them. Mary Cary, the Baptist Thomas Tillam and John Rogers

---

[290] *Eleventh*, "Epistle to the Reader," pp. 24, 13, 35, 24-25.
[291] *Mystical Babylon*, pp. 11, *passim*, 7, 20-21, "Epistle to the Reader."
[292] *Revelation*, pp. 178, *passim*, 148, 140.
[293] *Song of Solomon*, p. 56.

maintained that he would be present, while Aspinwall and Danvers said he would not.[294] If Christ was present the government would be monarchical but if he were in heaven then the saints would reign according to the Old Testament Mosaic judicial and moral laws, and penalties; either way Christ's will and rule prevailed.[295] They believed that no profane men would be a part of the government. The rulers should be wise, godly, well-known, just, and haters of covetousness.[296] In 1656 some of the Fifth Monarchist groups did vow to execute vengeance against "Nations, Provinces, Universities, Corporations, Cities, Towns, Kings, Rulers, Chief Captains", etc. during the millennium. In addition, John Simpson maintained that the "wicked, ungodly and unbelieving men shall be raised as slaves, and vassels, and be brought forth in chaines and fetters, before the dreadfull tribunall."[297] It was to be a new hierarchical society, a "new built arrastocracy [sic]", the wicked unregenerate (poor and wealthy) would be ruled by the saints. The saints would appear as kings, nobles, and princes.[298] Even the dress of the saints would be "rich apparel."[299] Moreover, the saints would live long lives, be immune to sickness, have peace, plenty and prosperity without hard work.[300] These things will be the "glory and happines of the Saints under the fifth Monarchy, in relation to civil Government."[301]

Most Fifth Monarchist writers who addressed the issue of the

---

[294]   Cary, *Little Horns Doom*, pp. 212-213; John Rogers, אהל *Ohel or Beth-shemesh. A Tabernacle for the Sun* (1653), p. 24; Thomas Tillam, *The Two Witnesses* (1651), pp. 109-110; William Aspinwall, *A Brief Description of the Fifth Monarchy* (1653), p. 4; Capp, *Fifth Monarchy*, p. 137. For a sketch of Tillam see B. R. White, "Tillam, Thomas (fl. 1637-1668)," *Biographical Dictionary of British Radicals*, III, 240-241.

[295]   Aspinwall, *Brief Description*, pp. 8, 9; anon., *Door of Hope*, pp. 4-5. For more on Fifth Monarchist teachings on the law see Capp, *Fifth Monarchy*, pp. 162-168.

[296]   Capp, *Fifth Monarchy*, p. 137. In *To his Excellency the Lord General Cromwell. A few Proposals, relating to Civil Government* (1653) John Rogers gives Cromwell some proposals for the government of the Commonwealth. One of the proposals outlines the qualifications for leadership in preparation for the setting up of the kingdom; for Rogers those who should presently be in leadership should be men who fear God, love truth and justice, hate bribes and covetousness, are active in the things of God, and hear & help the oppressed (p. 1).

[297]   John Simpson, *The Great Joy of Saints* (1654), p. 118, quoted in Capp, *Fifth Monarchy*, p. 143; Capp, "Extreme," p. 73

[298]   Capp, "Extreme," pp. 72-75.

[299]   Cary, *Little Horns Doom*, pp. 268-269.

[300]   Aspinwall, *Brief Description*, p. 13; Cary, *Little Horns Doom*, p. 71; Capp, *Fifth Monarchy*, p. 155.

[301]   Aspinwall, *Brief Description*, p. 13.

economic program of the millennium stated that beggars would be put to work by the state, resulting in a mutual benefit. Chamberlen believed that royal and episcopal lands, and disused commons and mines, could be used to give work to the poor. This could lead to the abolition of taxes.[302] According to the Venner 1661 manifesto there would be a ban on such things as the export of fuller's earth used in the cleaning of cloth in the kingdom of Christ.[303] In addition, there would be a redistribution of private property bringing about equality of ownership among the saints as well as the abolition of land tenures. Christopher Feake preached that in the millennium there would be "no difference betwixt high and low, the greatest, and the poorest beggar."[304]

Ecclesiastically the national church would be removed and the true church would be made up only of saints in voluntary gatherings. There would be no tithes to support the ministry; ministers would support themselves or be provided for by voluntary offerings. Preaching and praying would be the main fare in the churches with the total abandonment of prescribed services. In the millennium, both baptism and the Lord's Supper would be abolished.[305]

Was Knollys prone to elaborate on the details of millennial life, giving a rather earthly description of the millennium in his writings? Compared to Fifth Monarchist millenarians Knollys said very little about the millennium. For example in his commentary on the Revelation, in chapters twenty to twenty-two Knollys only tells his readers that it will be "a sorrowless time and condition to the Church and People of God.... They shall have no sufferings ... no sins ... no enemies to hurt them, to persecute them, nor to destroy them.... The Church of God hath rest, peace and glory. Now the Lords redeemed ones are made unto God Kings and Priests, and shall reign on earth." He says further that Christ "will restore all things to their original purity and perfection." And in these latter days, "The Church of God, his Worship, Ordinances, and Worshippers, will all be according unto the Golden Rule of the written Word of God." When commenting on the New Jerusalem described in chapter twenty-one and twenty-two, with little comment

---

[302] Capp, "Extreme," pp. 75-76.
[303] Anon., *Door of Hope*, p. 5.
[304] Thurloe, V, 755.
[305] Cary, *Little Horns Doom*, pp. 255-260; Capp, "Extreme," p. 76.

he interprets them mystically not physically, e.g., the precious stones are the living stones which shall be built up a spiritual house — the saints; the fruits from the tree of life are the fruits of the Holy Spirit.[306]

In his other eschatological works he is also quite restrained about the millennium. For example, in *The Parable of the Kingdom of Heaven Expounded* he teaches that the judgement shall be given to the saints, and they shall possess the kingdom and govern the nations by Christ's Laws and in his Name, and by his Commission with his Holy Spirit and power in great glory. During this time Christ will put down all rule by his saints.[307] In *The World that now is and the World that is to come* he maintains that the new creation of the millennium will bear some resemblance to the first creation in respect of "matter, manners, parts and end thereof." There will be a new frame of government on the earth at this time which Jesus will constitute, and command his Saints to execute over all the earth. The kingdom will be enlarged by conversion of sinners both Jews and Gentiles, by the pouring out of the Spirit upon all flesh, and by the qualifying and spiriting of the saints for government to bind kings and to execute upon them judgement. In addition, there will be set up a pure worship in the New Jerusalem where Christ will restore his holy ordinances unto their primitive power and purity, higher than the Apostles' days. The saints will be in a sinless state, and there will be a confluence of all spiritual comforts to the church — the performance of all promises, the pouring out of the Spirit, and the unity of the Spirit to a perfect man.[308]

In *Apocalyptical Mysteries* (1667), Knollys taught that the dominion and government of the kingdom in the millennium will be given to the saints who will rule by the laws of God. The saints shall be righteous and do no iniquity. This kingdom is not "of a *Worldly* Constitution; but it is a spiritual and *heavenly* Kingdom ... and will be a *glorious* state,... of a NEW *Heaven*, and of a NEW *Earth*, wherein dwells righteousness." In it "the PEOPLE of God shall build Houses, and inhabit them." During this time the Gospel shall be preached in all the world; those nations who submit shall be ruled

---

[306] *Revelation*, pp. 229-230, 234, 235, 238.
[307] *Parable*, pp. 74-75, 85.
[308] *World*, pt. 2, pp. 5, 7, 26-28, 8, 37-40, 42-43.

by the saints according to the laws of the Lord, and those who reject the witness "shall be utterly Wasted, and Destroyed."[309]

In comparison with the third mark of Fifth Monarchism it is evident that Knollys is quite mild and restrained. He focusses on the
spiritual (restitution of all things, righteousness on the earth, pure
worship in the churches, Gospel preached, pouring out of the
Spirit), not the physical elements of the millennium. In the places
where he does mention the physical aspects his comments have to
do with the rule of Christ (government by the saints, by Christ's
laws, destroying those who do not submit), freedom (from sin) and
comfort of the saints (inhabit houses, be sorrowless, have rest and
peace); but even these comments are not expanded upon.

Conclusion

Was Knollys a Fifth Monarchist? Our comparison of Knollys' eschatology with other mainstream eschatologies like those of Napier,
Mede, Brightman, Goodwin, Homes, etc. has shown that Knollys
was not unusual in what he taught, nor with the attention he gave
the subject. And even in those areas that he was novel in his interpretation (e.g., the death and resurrection of the two witnesses not
yet having taken place, and the seven vials poured out at the seventh trumpet also having not yet taken place) his teachings were
certainly not peculiarly Fifth Monarchist even though some like
John Canne also espoused such things.[310] Moreover, when Knollys'
writings are compared with the three major tenets of Fifth Monarchism there is little evidence of it in, at least, two of them; compared with Fifth Monarchist writers he gives little description of the
millennium, and attaches few prophetic references to contemporary
events. However, as we noted earlier, Knollys does speak of force
in his works which could have been interpreted by contemporaries
and historians as Fifth Monarchism. But in their context we have
noted that he is referring to events *in* the millennium. Moreover, as

---

[309] *Apocalyptical Mysteries*, III, 16, 13, 12-13, 15, 17-18.
[310] For example, in 1653, 54 John Tillinghast believed that three vials had already
been poured out, two or three years prior to the publication of Canne's *Truth with Time*
(Capp, "Extreme," p. 69).

we have seen he speaks against force, encouraging the use of spiritual weapons *only* to bring in the kingdom.

In addition, we have seen that he taught that the Fifth Monarchy would begin in the Fourth, and that England played an important part in the end time. For this reason he also could have been perceived as a Fifth Monarchist by his contemporaries. But as Bryan Ball has shown this did not necessarily make him a Fifth Monarchist.[311] Knollys also used the term "Generation-Truth" as did the Fifth Monarchist Tillinghast, but he never spoke of "Generation-Worke" which to some degree meant the inbringing of the millennium by force.[312]

In conclusion, it is true that the circumstantial evidence of Knollys' involvement with the Fifth Monarchists is weighty, as well as his adherence to Daniel's prophecy of a fifth monarchy, a literal millennial reign of Christ through the saints, and his use of force in the millennium. Knollys was obviously sympathetic to the movement with which some of his close friends were associated. It is understandable that contemporaries suspected him of Fifth Monarchism. On the other hand, our study of Knollys' writings indicate he was not sympathetic to its distinctive teachings. In addition, there is circumstancial evidence against his involvement with the group. For example, he did not sign the 1654 Fifth Monarchist Manifesto *A Declaration* even though several of his congregation did. If he was a Fifth Monarchist why didn't he sign this document? Moreover, he makes no claim to Fifth Monarchism in his treatises or his autobiography. In fact, he denies it; for example, when writing about his imprisonment after Venner's rising, he states, "Myself and many other godly and peaceable persons, were taken out of their own dwelling houses, and brought to Wood-street Comptor; and many to Newgate and other prisons, though we were innocent, and knew not of their design."[313] If Knollys was a Fifth Monarchist why didn't he say so? He certainly wasn't afraid to align himself with other unpopular movements, i.e., Baptists?

---

[311] For the issue of the Fifth Monarchy beginning in the Fourth see Ball, *Expectation*, pp. 168, 182-183. For the issue of England's important part in the end time see *Ibid.*, p. 184.

[312] Tillinghast, *Generation Work*, pt. 1, p. 6; Ball, *Expectation*, p. 188.

[313] Knollys, *Life*, p. 35.

In conclusion, we believe that though Knollys certainly shared some affinities with the Fifth Monarchists, his eschatological writings tip the balance against labelling him as one, as his contemporaries and later historians have.

CONCLUSION

In this study we have sought to cast more light on the question of Hanserd Knollys' orthodoxy in the seventeenth-century English context. After examining Knollys writings against the four charges levelled against him, one would be hard-pressed to say that he was a thorough-going Antinomian, Anabaptist, or a Fifth Monarchist according to the seventeenth-century English context of these charges; or that he was a hyper-Calvinist according to eighteenth-century Baptist hyper-Calvinism. On the other hand, we have seen that certain elements of his teaching/theology *were* Antinomian, Anabaptist and Fifth Monarchist. For example, Knollys held the important Anabaptist teachings of believer's baptism, the gathered-independent church, and the separation of church and state. Moreover, with the Antinomians he believed that the Spirit bears witness to a sinner's conversion in a promise of salvation (though he did not espouse the Spirit's witness apart from the promise or Word). And with the Fifth Monarchists he believed in a literal millennium, called the Fifth Monarchy, *in* which force would be used to bring people in submission to Christ. Consequently, one can understand why these charges were made against Knollys, particularly the charge of Anabaptism. However, in my opinion, one would be going beyond the evidence to say that he was an Antinomian, Fifth Monarchist, or even an Anabaptist according to seventeenth-century Reformed orthodoxy. And the same could be said for the charge of hyper-Calvinism made against him, or his association with it after the seventeenth century.

This study has also provided us with a more comprehensive understanding of Knollys' theology which, heretofore, has not been available in the secondary literature, and which furthers our understanding of seventeenth-century Calvinistic Baptist thought. Therefore, we will conclude our study by briefly summarizing his theology, particularly his soteriology, ecclesiology, and eschatology.

A few preliminary remarks about Knollys' theology are in order.

Knollys wrote no theological works during his lifetime. Though he was a university educated scholar Knollys wrote as a pastor seeking to minister the gospel to his own congregation, to the broader Calvinistic Baptist community, and to whomever else might read his work. He published commentaries (usually former sermons to his congregation), devotionals, sermons, instructions on church polity, and polemical works (on baptism, on the church, against Rome). He wrote with passion for the salvation of sinners and professors of religion, and for the edification of believers. His writings are filled with Scripture quotations and references. Maybe it was partly because most Baptists were less educated that he did not write on the level of a Goodwin or an Owen? Since Knollys did not write a systematic work on soteriology, ecclesiology or eschatology our understanding of these subjects must necessarily be drawn from things he says in various places, and then gathered together. This we will do below. But before we move to our exposition of Knollys' theology it should also be noted that during the forty-five years in which he published his works, his theology changed very little. In part this is due to his coming to Baptist convictions so much later in life (age forty-five). Between twenty-five and thirty-five years of age he came to Puritan convictions and then to Independency; and from thirty-five to forty-five he came to Baptist convictions. By that time his Puritan/Calvinistic/Independent convictions were firmly in place. This may be the reason for so little evolution in his thought.

Having made these preliminary remarks we will now proceed to explicate Knollys' theology from his writings. Chapters three and four of our study dealt with soteriological issues. What was Knollys' soteriology? Most importantly he believed that God was the source of the whole scheme of salvation. Predestination and election were foundational in this scheme. God decreed, before the foundation of the world, the foreordination of the elect to eternal life, and left the rest in their sin to their condemnation. The elect were chosen in Christ, not on the basis of any condition or cause seen in them, but upon the secret counsel of God. Knollys maintained that in eternity God entered into an eternal covenant of grace with his elect.

For Knollys God's plan of salvation through Jesus Christ was necessary for the salvation of the elect. It was necessary because Adam sinned against God and fell from his perfect state, and in consequence, all of his posterity inherited his guilt and his depraved nature. The only way of salvation for the elect was, therefore, through God's Son, Jesus Christ. This salvation was accomplished through Christ's active obedience, obeying the whole law, and through His passive obedience in His death. At the time of the believer's conversion Christ's active and passive obedience is imputed to him, and is his whole and soul righteousness before God.

Knollys believed that this salvation is not effective for the elect until they are united to Christ by faith. Their justification, pardon, adoption, reconciliation, and sanctification take place only when they receive Christ by faith. Even this faith is a result of their union with Christ, along with repentance, love, and the gifts and fruit of the Spirit; for Knollys Christ is all in all in the believer's salvation. When the sinner is united to Christ she is converted and regenerated by the Spirit and the Word. Prior to conversion God uses various means, especially the Word preached, to draw the sinner to Himself. Moreover, He uses the law to convict the sinner of sin and judgement. This conviction includes a troubling of conscience, a fear of Hell, and a sensible apprehension of God's wrath. Then the Spirit and Word enlighten the sinner to see and know Jesus as Saviour, followed by her conversion and regeneration into the image of Christ. At this time the believer is sanctified, made holy in the sight of God. However, in practice she is not perfect, and will not be so until she reaches heaven. In the meantime she is to grow in holiness, negatively by subduing the power of indwelling sin (mortification), and positively by following the law of Christ. She will persevere unto the end, being kept by the power of God unto salvation. The believer's means of assurance at conversion is the Spirit's witness to a promise of salvation. However, the primary means of assurance throughout the believer's life is her sanctification.

Chapter five of our study examined ecclesiological issues. We found that Knollys believed that the word *ecclesia* in the New Testament had at least two meanings. It signified the universal, invisible church of God which is the Mystical Body of Christ; it includes all of God's people, past, present and future. It also signified a true visible constituted Church of Christ, a congregation of saints called out of the world assembled together in one place. These saints are a company of baptized and sanctified believers who are to gather together to worship God publicly in Spirit and Truth in all his sacred Gospel ordinances, for the glory of God, and the mutual edification of the body of Christ. Knollys believed that properly constituted worship according to the Word of God was necessary, and would be the way of the church in the millennium. This meant a proper use of the ordinances which included: prayers in the Spirit by the elders; reading, expounding and interpreting of the Word; the preaching of the gospel and exhortation to people to believe and repent; baptism of those who believe the gospel; partaking of the Lord's Supper; and the singing of Psalms, hymns and spiritual songs. The well-being of the church comes by keeping these ordinances as well as by unity in the Word, by order of the church kept in the gospel, and by proper government of the church by the elders.

The believers who make up the local church are to be "found in the faith and holy in their life." They are to be admitted into membership upon faith, repentance and baptism, "and none other". This baptism was not for infants but for believers who profess faith in Jesus Christ. Knollys firmly believed that only believers ought to be baptized because the New Testament took precedence over the Old. In the former John the Baptist, Christ's disciples and apostles administered baptism only to those who repented and believed. In addition, infant baptism, based on the Old Testament, denied that Christ had come in the flesh, making Moses greater than Christ. Knollys also believed that the only proper mode of baptism was immersion. He reasoned that the Greek word Βαπτίζω never signified to sprinkle, but to dip or wash, and that the parties baptized go into water. More importantly, he maintained that this mode held forth the believer's communion with Christ in his death, burial, and resurrection. A person is fit for believer's baptism when she has received the Holy Spirit, believed in Christ, confessed her sins, and repented.

Although Knollys' requirements for membership were quite strict, it did not mean that the saints were without sin, and lived perfect lives. Nor did he deny the teaching that there would be a mixture of wheat and tares in the church until Christ comes. Consequently, true believers ought not to separate from true churches and saints. However, if a church maintains false worship, then the believer is to separate.

Knollys believed that the church was independent and autonomous, accountable only to Christ. He encouraged a presbyterial form of church government at the congregational level; each church should choose elders and deacons from among themselves to guide, govern, oversee and care for the church under the headship and laws of Christ. These elders were to teach, and feed the flock, as well as carry out church censures of admonition, supervision or withdrawal from disorderly members, and excommunication of members who live in scandalous sins. Although he maintained that the saints ought to be subject to the elders, he also taught that the congregation had the final authority in matters such as receiving or excommunicating members.

Although there was a difference in roles and giftedness between the laity and the clergy, Knollys maintained that the gifts of teaching and preaching were given to members other than the elders in the congregation. These members were permitted, if found to be so gifted, to share in the ministry of the Word. Nevertheless this did not take away from the importance of the ministry for Knollys. In order for the church to stand and continue sound in the faith, it cannot be without able and faithful ministers. They are so important that Knollys considered them to be one of the guides in the way of truth, along with the Spirit and the Word. These pastors are to take care that the doctrine, the ministers, the worship, and the people are kept in accordance with the will of Christ. Their work is to convert, feed, comfort, strengthen, confirm, establish, and save souls. Preaching was a vital function of the pastor; for this was the ordinary means of the conversion of sinners, as well as an important means whereby the saints are edified. In addition, Knollys believed that the pastor should be supported by the voluntary offerings of the church.

Knollys maintained that the Church should be separate from the state. For him the state has no power over it, and therefore, the civil state is not to impose laws upon the Church; "soul-government" belongs to Jesus Christ alone. Consequently, the saints are not to submit to the magistrate who imposes false worship. However, the saints are to submit to the magistrate in all civil matters because he has been ordained by God to defend and encourage those that do good, and to punish evildoers. Moreover, Knollys maintained that a Christian could serve in the office of a magistrate.

Several of Knollys' works were either wholly or partly concerned with eschatological matters which formed an important part of his theology. It was important because he believed that his generation was living in the last days of the latter times; for him the end of the age was near, predicting that it would take place in 1688 or thereabouts. He came to this position through his understanding of the Book of Revelation which allegorically outlined the history of the

Church of God between the two Comings of Christ. The Revelation primarily outlined the history of the Church under the domination of Daniel's antichristian fourth monarchy which included pagan and papal Rome. From the seventh to the seventeenth century the Antichrist had been the Papacy, and the Scarlet Whore riding the Beast was the Roman church which leads the people into false worship and idolatry. The Pope was the man of lawlessness, and the priests were the false prophets. Along with the papacy, the Antichrist also included the Mohammedan Turk.

Knollys believed that certain signs would indicate the nearness of the end. These signs included: apostasy and lukewarmness in the church; abounding of iniquity of the world; a great tribulation upon the whole world; and the gospel preached to the whole world. He believed that the first two signs were evident in England in his day.

Like some of his contemporaries Knollys was a millennialist, maintaining that Christ would rule over the world for a literal thousand years. He was, however, a postmillennialist believing that the Scriptures taught three comings of Christ. The middle coming was his coming as a Bridegroom for his bride. This coming will not be personal as the first and last, but a virtual, spiritual and powerful appearance *in* his saints. Consequently, Christ would reign on earth through his saints in the millennium. Certain events, however, must take place before the millennial reign of the saints could begin. The Turk and the Papacy must be destroyed, the Jews must be converted and return to their land, and the Battle of Armageddon completed. At the dawn of the millennium Christ will restore all things to their original purity and perfection. During it the saints will reign by the laws of Christ, the Church will worship according to the Word of God, sinners will be converted, and the nations will be brought under subjection to Christ. At the end of the thousand years Christ will return personally, visibly, literally, and gloriously for a second time. He will return with both his resurrected and living saints; the eternal judgement, the dissolution of the heavens and earth, and the eternal kingdom will follow.

In light of the time Knollys warned the professors of faith as well as sinners to be prepared for Christ's Coming. He encouraged professors to be clothed with Christ's righteousness, and to be looking and longing for His Coming.

APPENDICES

AUTHORS CITED OR QUOTED IN KNOLLYS' WORKS

Christ Exalted – Hierome.

An Answer to a Discourse – Beza, Screvilius (Greek lexicographer) Hill (Greek lexicographer), Owen.

Declaration concerning a publicke dispute – Calamy, Stephen Marshall, Blake, Tombes.

Exposition of the Whole Book of the Revelation – Augustine, Calvin, Sympson (Ecc. Historian), Fox, Eusebius (Ecc. Historian), Hierom, Alsted, Helvicus, Plessaeus, Socrates (Ecc. Hist.), Gregory, Franciscus Claudius, Rhemists, Platina (R.C.), Martinus (R.C.), Unaphrius (R.C.), Bellarmine (R.C.), Magdel., Prideaux, Archer, Mede, Durham, *Decretum Martini*, the School-men.

Exposition of the Eleventh Chapter of the Book of Revelation – Socrates, Sympson, Helvicus, Magdeb..

Preface to Thomas Collier's *Exaltation of Christ* – Aristotle.

Mystical Babylon Unvailed – Propertius, Virgil, Ovid, Cornel. à Lap., Bellarmine, Viegas, Suarez, Ribera, Cardinal Poole, Isadorus Musconius, Abraham Bzovius, Celsus Mancinus, R. Caron, Irenaeus, Tertullian, Joan. Viguer, Nich. Sander., Hionne Bestiam, Dionys. Halicarnass, Ambrose, Cyril, Theophylact, Crysostom, Pridaeux, Richard Bernard, Council of Trent, Roman Catechism, Aquinas, Guliel Malmsbur, Vasquez (Jesuit).

Apocalyptical Mysteries – Sympson, Socrates, Helvicus, Magdeb..

The World that now is and the World that is to come – Walo (Salmasius), Hierom, Ambrose, Primasius, Gregory the Great, Beza, Scultetus,

Luther, Moulin, Tossanus, Zwingli, Calvin, Dr. Gerard, Dr. Reynolds, Dr. Scultetus, Marlorat, Smectymnuus, Ignatius, Eusebius Hegesippus (Ecc. Hist.), Clement, Irenaeus, Origin, Cyril, Justin, Jerome, *A Looking-glass for the ARMY*, Army Remonstrance 1648.

Song of Solomon – Josephus, Pliny.

APPENDIX B

THE QUESTION OF DERIVATION OF ANABAPTIST TEACHINGS: DID KNOLLYS AND THE CALVINISTIC BAPTISTS DERIVE THEIR TEACHINGS FROM THE CONTINENTAL ANABAPTISTS?

The Calvinistic Baptists claimed that they were not Anabaptists. They denied it in both their *Confessions* as well as in the Calvinistic Baptist endorsed treatise by Samuel Richardson entitled, *Some Brief Considerations On Doctor* Featley *his Book, intituled, The Dipper Dipt, Wherein In some measure is discovered his many great and false accusations of divers persons, commonly called* Anabaptists, *with an Answer to them.*[1] In addition, Knollys, in the "Postscript" of his *The Shining of a Flaming-fire in Zion* (1646) writes to the courteous reader, "*Thou mayest think it strange, that I have said nothing unto those 6. Or 7. particulars mentioned pag. 14. which we (who are scandalously called Anabaptists) are said to hold: Unto which I give this Answer, We have once, and a second time published in Print to all the World, a Confession of our Faith, wherein thou mayest see at large, what we hold.*"[2] Knollys and his fellow Calvinistic Baptists strongly denied any adherence to Anabaptism. Why then did they have similar beliefs concerning the church, baptism and the state? Did they learn these from Anabaptists or their writings? Certainly Anabaptists lived in England, and their writings were readily available. In fact, we know that Knollys taught school in Gainsborough prior to 1629 where both the General Baptist John Smyth and the Separatist John Robinson lived before they left for the Continent. Could he have been influenced by some who knew these men ? Is there any evidence that Knollys or the Calvinistic Baptists were influenced by Anabaptists? Or did they derive these teachings on baptism, the church and the state from some other source(s) or from their own study of the Scriptures? This appendix will examine the secondary literature in search of answers to these questions.

---

[1]   In one of the sections in this work Richardson addresses Featley's "false Accusations against the Anabaptists" (*Brief Considerations*, title page).
[2]   *Shining*, p. 16.

First, is there any known link between Knollys & the Calvinistic
Baptists and the Continental Anabaptists in their ecclesiology? The
Anabaptists and the English Baptists both believed that the true
church consisted of those who professed faith in Jesus Christ. However, there is no extant evidence that the English Baptists derived
this teaching from the Anabaptists. B.R. White in his study on English Separatism states,

> The type of Churchmanship characteristic of the Anabaptists was certainly
> close enough to that of the English Separatists to warrant raising the ques-
> tion of their relationship, but unfortunately evidence of anything approach-
> ing direct influence from Anabaptism upon English Separatists before John
> Smyth arrived in Amsterdam appears to be lacking.[3]

But there is plenty of evidence connecting the Calvinistic Baptist
ecclesiology with Puritan-Separatism.[4] B.R. White has shown that
those who organized and joined the first Calvinistic Baptist
churches in London were formerly members of separated Calvinistic churches, and Murray Tolmie has said the same for the counties.[5] Scholars believe that the ecclesiology of the Calvinistic Bap-

---

[3] B.R. White, *English Separatist*, p. 162. Smyth was a General Baptist who became
a Mennonite in Holland. Some of his followers including Thomas Helwys split off from
Smyth at this time, returned to England, and established the first Baptist church on
English soil. As noted in chapter one the Calvinistic and General Baptists were two
distinct groups in England with historically unrelated beginnings. In fact, during the
Revolutionary years they had no relations with each other (Timothy George, "Between
Pacifism and Coercion: The English Baptist Doctrine of Religious Toleration," *The
Mennonite Quarterly Review*, 58 (1984), p. 46n; Tolmie, *Triumph*, p. 72). The Calvinists
would have considered the General Baptists Arminian heretics; and the Arminian General Baptists refused to see their fellow Baptists as Christians (*Ibid.*).

[4] White states that the subjects of church organization, the use of discipline as in
Matthew 18:15-17, congregational autonomy, and the authority of the risen Christ over
each church can be found in the Calvinist/Puritan/Separatist tradition (*English Separatist*, pp. 162-163).

[5] B.R. White, "The Doctrine of the Church in the Particular Baptist Confession
of 1644," *The Journal of Theological Studies*, N.S., 19 (1968), pp. 571-574; Murray Tolmie,
"General," pp. 118-121; see also Novak, "Thy Will," p. 5. All of the Calvinistic Baptists
in Novak's study, where evidence survives, were exposed to "the radical Calvinism of
separated worship before [their] adoption of the Particular Baptist position" (*Ibid.*)
Those Novak studied include Hanserd Knollys, Andrew Ritor, Benjamin Cox, Robert
Garner, Henry Jessey, Christopher Blackwood, Thomas Patience, Thomas Tillam, John
Pendarves, Henry Lawrence, William Kiffin, Samuel Richardson, Robert Purnell, John
Spilsbury, Paul Hobson, Edward Drapes, Thomas Kilcop, Thomas Collier, and Daniel
King. These men had widely diverse backgrounds, social standing and education (*Ibid,.*,
pp. 62-63).

tists can be traced to Henry Jacob (the pastor of the semi-separatist church that was founded in Southwark in 1616, the parent church of the Calvinistic Baptist churches) and from him back to Puritan-Separatism. For example, Slayden Yarborough has shown that the Calvinistic Baptist congregational ecclesiology came from Jacob who encouraged the " 'free consent' of the people in discussing, and deciding matters of importance to the church." Moreover, the autonomy of the local church and the concept of interchurch fellowship and counsel found in the 1644 Baptist *Confession* can be traced to Jacob. Yarborough concludes, "[Henry Jacob's] influence was obvious. He provided a theory of independent congregationalism on the one hand and voluntary congregational cooperation on the other. While Jacob's theory of inter-church cooperation was not fully developed, it did provide a foundation upon which the Particular Baptists could build."[6] Moreover, Murray Tolmie has shown that Jacob's encouragement of lay-preaching in his church resulted in many of the daughter churches (of the 1630s and early 1640s) having self-supporting lay ministries.[7] This is probably the basis upon which the Calvinistic Baptists encouraged lay-preaching by a gifted disciple and not just a minister.

Not only is there evidence of an ecclesiological connection between the Calvinistic Baptists and the Jacob church but also from the Jacob Church to Puritan-Separatism. B.R. White, Stephen Brachlow, and John Von Rohr have shown the undeniable connection of Jacob's ecclesiology to that of Puritan-Separatism.[8] White shows the historical/theological connections of early Separatism from the Marian martyrs to Robert Browne to Henry Barrow and John Greenwood to Francis Johnson to Henry Jacob. He gives evidence that Jacob was influenced by the Separatists Francis Johnson and John Robinson; and from them that Jacob learned such concepts as: 1) the church is a fellowship of believers separated from

---

[6]   Slayden Yarborough, "The Origin of Baptist Associations Among the English Baptists," *Baptist History and Heritage*, 23, No. 2 (1988), pp. 15-18, 17, 21, 22. The Calvinistic Baptist concept of associationism derived from Jacob is also taught by B. R. White, "Doctrine of the Church in the Particular Baptist Confession of 1644," *Journal of Theological Studies*, N.S., 19 (1968), pp. 586-587.

[7]   Tolmie, *Triumph*, pp. 14-16, 21, 37-38.

[8]   John Von Rohr, "Extra Ecclesiam Nulla Salus: An Early Congregational Version," *Church History*, 36 (1967), pp. 107-121; Stephen Brachlow, *The Communion of the Saints: Radical Puritan and Separatist Ecclesiology 1570-1625* (Oxford, 1988); and White, *English Separatist*.

the ungodly and uncommitted; 2) the taking of a covenant promise at the foundation of their Congregation; 3) the church is independent with only Christ as its head; 4) and the power of the church to appoint and dismiss its ministers.[9] Moreover, he outlines the similarites between the Separatist Johnson-Ainsworth *True Confession* and the Calvinistic Baptist *Confession* of 1644. It is quite clear that the 1644 Baptist *Confession* was based on the *True Confession*; twenty-six of the fifty two articles were borrowed from the *True Confession*. Concerning the doctrine of the church, White states: "There is ... wide area of agreement between the two *Confessions*." There points of agreement include: 1) "Christ hath here on earth a spirituall Kingdome" in which he requires all those who acknowledge Him as Saviour "be enrolled amongst his household servants"; 2) Christ has entrusted power to his whole church and to every congregation of it "to receive in and cast out ... any member", which power is given to no individual but to the whole body; 3) Christ places men in the congregation "who by their office are to governe, oversee, visit, watch"; 4) this ministry includes "Pastors, Teachers, Elders, Deacons" which the church itself chooses; 5) each truly constituted church has faults and corruptions but the members should not withdraw from membership "untill they have in due order sought redresse thereof"; and 6) individual churches were all "to walk by one and the same Rule, and by all means convenient to have counsell and help one another."[10]

In addition to White's research, Stephen Brachlow convincingly demonstrates that the ecclesiologies of Radical Puritans such as John Foxe, Thomas Cartwright and Walter Travers, and those of

---

[9]   White, *English Separatist*, pp. 165-166.

[10]   White, "Doctrine of the Church," pp. 577-578. These similarities are found in Articles XXXIII-XXXV (1644)/ 17-19 (1596), XLII-XLIV (1644)/ 24-26 (1596), and XLVI, XLVII (1644)/ 36, 38 (1596). The differences in ecclesiology are attributed to the circumstances and motives for writing (*Ibid.*, p. 579). The Baptists refrained from calling the Established church a false one because of their roots in Henry Jacob's semi-separatism. As well their *Confession* was not delineating their reasons for separation as the *True Confession* was, but its purpose was to declare their orthodoxy to the Presbyterians and Calvinistic members of the Church of England.

Stanley Nelson has also suggested that some of the ecclesiology of the Baptist 1644 *Confession* could have come from William Ames' *Marrow of Theology*. Ames taught that one of the marks of a visible church was a personal profession of orthodox faith (*Marrow* I, XXXII/ 1644 *Confession*, XXI-XXXII; Stanley A. Nelson, "Reflecting on Baptist Origins: The London Confession of Faith of 1644," *Baptist History and Heritage*, 29, No. 2 [1994], pp. 39-40).

Separatists Robert Browne, Henry Barrow, Francis Johnson, John Robinson and Henry Jacob, are quite similar. For example, Brachlow states,

> [The Elizabethan and Jacobean Radicals and Separatists] all agreed that the membership of gathered churches should be confined to the visibly elect and faithful. The two criteria required for membership — sound doctrine and good conduct — were, in the context of puritan soteriology, considered the 'infallible marks' of election. For separatists and radical puritans alike, entrance into church fellowship through a profession of faith, therefore offered a public affirmation that would have been reinforced in the continuing, weekly life of the congregation by the tightly disciplined communities that were the ideal of left-wing puritan and separatist congregationalist polity.

In addition, Brachlow says there was similarity among these Radical Puritans and Separatists on the issue of ministerial authority for the government of the gathered church:

> While wanting to grant genuine power to the people, by which they intended only adult male members of the congregation, they nevertheless fully intended to preserve the special status and authority of the reformed ministry. The result was a complex, sometimes equivocal paradigm of the power structure for individual churches that left the issue of authority in the gathered congregation poised between the two organizational models of aristocracy and democracy.[11]

This dilemma is evident in the writings and confessions of Knollys and the Calvinistic Baptists.

Consequently, what can one conclude concerning the derivation of Calvinistic Baptist ecclesiology? Undoubtedly there is much evidence to support the claim that their ecclesiological heritage began with the Elizabethan Radical Puritans and Separatists through Henry Jacob, and not from Anabaptism. We might also add three more things that weaken the claim of Anabaptist ecclesiological derivation. First, both Horton Davies and Ernest Payne note that the Calvinistic Baptist form of worship is unlike that of the General Baptists or the Anabaptists, and therefore, it ought not be linked to either of them. For example, the Calvinistic Baptists made use of the Psalms in their singing where the General Baptists did not. In

---

[11]   Brachlow, *Communion*, pp. 269-270, 270.

addition, the General Baptists and Anabaptists thought the sermon in the worship should be by the Spirit laying aside all books; this was not so for the Calvinistic Baptists.[12] Davies states that apart from baptism "it would be difficult to distinguish their [Calvinistic Baptists] worship from that of the Independents, for the latter were Calvinists in doctrine, demanded Scriptural warrants for all their ordinances, believed in extemporaneous prayer, and insisted upon the local autonomy of each gathered church."[13]

Secondly, it has been shown by B.R. White that the innovations of these Calvinistic Baptists did not compromise their Calvinistic thought.[14] And thirdly, Michael Novak has shown in his comprehensive dissertation on early Calvinistic Baptist thought that their ecclesiology was based firmly on three things: Scripture, their hermeneutical assumptions, and Puritan ecclesiology. Concerning the Calvinistic Baptist connection with Puritan ecclesiology he states,

> The component elements of their system had already been professed and publicized in various forms by two generations of English Calvinists in the Puritan movement. They break no new ground when they justify their ecclesiological position by reference to the idea that the church of Christ must be built solely upon the blueprint which He established once and for all in the ordinances of His New Testament. Puritans from Cartwright to the divines at Westminster and from Browne to Owen rested their own cases on the same authority. Nor does their insistence that true Christians are distinguished by the work of grace in their hearts set the Particular Baptist authors apart from their predecessors and contemporaries. Puritans who had no intention of separation from the established church had said much the same with regard to participation in the Lord's Supper and conversion, while Separatists to whom believer's baptism constituted irredeemable heresy had called for more rigorous discipline precisely in order to purge the manifestly unfaithful from the church fellowship.[15]

---

[12]   Ernest Payne, *Fellowship of Believers: Baptist Thought and Practice Yesterday and Today, Enlarged edition* (London, 1952), p. 93.

[13]   Horton Davies, *Worship and Theology in England From Cranmer to Baxter and Fox, 1534-1690* (1975; rpt. Grand Rapids, 1996), II, 507.

[14]   B.R. White, "The English Particular Baptists and the Great Rebellion," *Baptist History and Heritage*, 9 (1974), pp. 17-22.

[15]   Novak, "Thy Will," p. 345. He goes on to say that their notions of an autonomous-congregational-voluntary church, of a regenerate church membership, and that the state has no authority to alter the laws of Christ for the church, were all part of the Elizabethan Puritan church, Separatist or otherwise (*Ibid.*, p. 346).

Novak has also clearly shown that the various aspects of their ecclesiology, whether taken from their Puritan predecessors or not, were firmly based on Scripture. Novak writes,

> Their most basic argument for the believers' church is that in the authoritative accounts of the New Testament none but those who have heard the Word, been converted and professed faith are ever admitted to church fellowship.... By their own account the Particular Baptist authors have separated from the established church to render personal obedience to the revealed will of God.[16]

The Calvinistic Baptists held firmly to their ecclesiology because of their commitment of strict obedience to the will of God in Scripture. According to Novak this obedience, like all other Calvinists, was based on certain hermeneutical assumptions. Though all Calvinists would have generally agreed with the assumptions of the Calvinistic Baptists, they would not have taken them as far as the Baptists. Novak has shown that these assumptions were two in number: the Mission of Christ in His First Coming, and the New Covenant. The Calvinistic Baptists believed that Christ came to enable people to give true spiritual worship which could not occur under the Old Covenant. Therefore, it was imperative for them to obey the laws of Christ strictly when it came to true worship (Christ's laws concerning the Church supercede those of the Old Dispensation; no mixing of the two Dispensations). In addition, they maintained that only in the New Covenant inaugurated by Christ's work on the cross could a people serve Him truly in spirit. This is the ultimate purpose of God's design. Consequently, only those people whom God has remade in faith ought to have membership in the church. Novak sums up their belief: "Those who wish to see His will be done must then recognize that under the New Covenant God's design now prescribes new inward principles of obedience as well as new outward forms." On the basis of these assumptions these Baptists not only held to a gathered independent, autonomous church but also to believer's baptism, and separation of church and state.[17]

---

[16] *Ibid.*, pp. 244-45.
[17] *Ibid.*, pp. 245-249, 234. Novak's whole thesis demonstrates that these assumptions undergird their hermeneutic and Baptist distinctives that went beyond Independency and Separatism.

For all of the above reasons there is much evidence to support the claim that the Calvinistic Baptists derived their ecclesiology from their English Puritan/Separatist heritage and not from Anabaptism. As for Knollys, there is no evidence of any Anabaptist influence on him but there is much to suggest he derived his ecclesiology from Puritan-Separatism. This is not surprising since Knollys was educated at the Puritan St. Katherine's College, Cambridge under Richard Sibbes and, after his ordination, was influenced by a Brownist "who used to pray and expound scriptures in his family, whom [he] went sometimes to hear, and with whom [he] had conference and very good counsel."[18] Moreover, he was probably influenced by the Separatist/Independent Samuel How, and certainly by the Independent John Wheelwright in the 1630s; and while in New England he was surrounded by the Congregationalist polity of its citizens, and even pastored an independent church in New Hampshire. Furthermore, when he returned to England, he joined the independent church that Henry Jessey pastored (the Jacob-Lathrop-Jessey church), and it was in this context that he came to espouse believer's baptism. In conclusion, there is little or no evidence for an ecclesiological connection to Anabaptism for the Calvinistic Baptists but much to commend a Puritan-Separatist one.

But what about the issue of baptism? Calvinistic Baptist ecclesiology may have been derived from Puritan-Separatism but not baptism. Did it not come from the Anabaptists? It is quite clear that both the Calvinistic Baptists and the Anabaptists shared the notion that baptism was for believers only and not for infants. Did the Calvinistic Baptists derive their teaching on baptism from them? Is there any evidence to support such derivation? Yes, there is some circumstancial evidence that could link them to the Continental Anabaptists. The first has to do with Richard Blunt and his visit to Holland in 1641 to find out more about the practice of immersion for believer's baptism. Believer's baptism among those who signed the 1644 *Confession* was possibly being practiced by 1633 but certainly by 1638; the mode, however, in 1638 was effusion not immersion. In 1640 Richard Blunt

> being convinced of Baptism yt also it ought to be by diping ye Body into ye Water, resembling Burial & riseing again. 2 Col: 2. 12. Rom: 6. 4. had

---

[18]   Knollys, *Life*, p. 12.

sober conferance about in ye Church.... And after Prayer & conferance about their so enjoying it, none haveing then so so [*sic*] practised in England to professed Believers, & hearing that some in ye Nether Lands had so practised they agreed & sent over Mr Rich. Blunt (who understood Dutch) wth Letters of Comendation, who was kindly accepted there, & returned wth Letters from them Jo: Batte a Teacher there, & from that Church to such as sent him.[19]

Blunt visited John Batte [Batten] who taught an Anabaptist congregation known as the Collegiants or Rynsburgers of Holland where immersion was practised. When Blunt returned from Holland at the end of 1641, two groups from the Jessey church "did set apart one to baptize the rest; So it was solemnly performed by them. Mr Blunt Baptized Mr Blacklock yt was a Teacher amongst them, & Mr Blunt being Baptized, he & Mr Blacklock Baptized ye rest of their friends that ware so minded, & many being added to them they increased much." From this evidence there is no doubt that the Calvinistic Baptists had contact with the Anabaptists.[20] But the influence, if any, seems minimal. First, the Baptists already were practicing believer's baptism. It is more likely that the Blunt group came to its conviction through its contact with the Spilsbury church. Secondly, Blunt appears to have become convinced of immersion before his trip and makes no mention of coming to this conviction through these Anabaptists. Thirdly, he either went to Holland seeking, 1) succession, or 2) knowledge concerning immersion (the how to) or both.[21] If it is either one of these or even both, the influence is minimal; there is certainly no evidence that these Calvinistic Baptists came to a conviction of believer's baptism or immersion through this contact.

A second piece of circumstancial evidence of Anabaptist influ-

---

[19] "Kiffin Manuscript" in "Rise of the Particular Baptists in London, 1633-1644," *Transactions of the Baptist Historical Society*, 1 (1910), pp. 232-233. For a brief sketch of Blunt see R. L. Greaves, "Blunt, Richard (fl. 1633-1642)," *Biographical Dictionary of British Radicals*, I, 78.

[20] Ernest Payne sees Anabaptist influence on this point. He believes that Blunt most likely was "already aware that this was the practice of the Dutch Collegiants" ("Contacts Between Mennonites and Baptists," *Foundations*, 4 [1961], p. 48).

[21] White and Champlin Burrage do not believe he went over to be baptized for purposes of succession (White, "Baptist Beginnings and Kiffin Manuscript," *Baptist History and Heritage*, 2, No. 1 [1967], p. 36; Champlin Burrage, "The Restoration of Immersion by the English Anabaptists and Baptists [1640-1700]," *American Journal of Theology*, 16, No. 1, pp. 70-71).

ence concerning believer's baptism has been suggested by Glen
Stassen. He posits that the source for the phrase "death , buriall,
and resurrection" in Article XL describing the signification of baptism is taken from Menno Simons' *Foundation Book*. Stassen states,
"Such imagery comes from another source than that of the Baptists, who saw the power of God not so much in the spotless obedience and sacrifice of Christ as in the mercy and power by which
Christ died, was buried, and was raised again."[22] It is quite possible
that this is the source for this phrase. The Kiffin manuscript, however, simply gives us the impression that these Baptists held this
position based on the Scripture texts Colossians 2:12 and Romans
6:4. In addition, there is another possible source closer to their Cal-
vinistic-Puritan tradition. John Calvin in his *Institutes* speaks of baptism as "a sign of our forgiveness, of our participation in Christ's
death and resurrection.... 'we have been baptized into his death,'
'buried with him into death,... that we may walk in newness of
life'."[23] In this section he uses the same passages the Baptists use,
Romans 6:3,4 and Col. 2:11-12. The Baptists, having had prior
knowledge of these passages on baptism from their Reformed tradition, saw that immersion was a perfect picture of what Christ's
death, burial and resurrection signified in the believer upon their
conversion. This would not have been a stretch for them given their
Reformed tradition on baptism using the above Scriptures, and
their belief in believer's baptism.[24]

---

[22]   Glen Stassen, "Anabaptist Influence in the Origin of the Particular Baptists," *The
Mennonite Quarterly Review*, 36 (1962), p. 330.

[23]   John Calvin, *Institutes of the Christian Religion*, ed. John McNeil, trans. Ford Lewis
Battles (Philadelphia, 1977), IV.xv.1-6.

[24]   Stassen in a later article states that his first article on this subject in 1962 gives
"conclusive evidence that Menno Simons's most widely distributed book, *The Foundation
of Christian Doctrine*, ... laid the foundation of the Particular Baptist origin" ("*Opening
Menno Simons's* Foundation-Book *and Finding the Father of Baptist Origins Alongside the Mother
– Calvinist Congregationalism*," *Baptist History and Heritage* 33, No. 1 [1998], p. 34). In this
later article he seeks to show the textual parallels of the *Foundation Book* and the Baptist
1644 *Confession*. However, what he sees as the *source of the distinctive Baptist phrases* in their
Confession could also be attributed to Calvin and to the Scriptures as we have noted
above. Did not Menno get his wording from Scripture. Why, then, might not some
other people committed to Scripture also come up with similar wording years later?
Without any external evidence supporting Stassen's thesis it remains pure conjecture,
and therefore *not* "conclusive."

For more against Stassen's thesis see B.R. White, "The English Particular Baptists
and the Great Rebellion," *Baptist History and Heritage*, 9, No. 1 (1974), pp. 18-19; Kenneth Ross Manley, "Origins of the Baptists: The Case for Development from Puritan-

Consequently, without more substantive evidence the two suggestions of Anabaptist influence posited above are either minimal (concerning Blunt) or wanting (concerning the baptismal signification of death, burial and resurrection).

In addition, there are other reasons to deny Anabaptist influence on the Calvinistic Baptists' doctrine of baptism. The first concerns immersion. If, as the Kiffin Manuscript suggests, the Calvinistic Baptists came to their conviction of immersion before Blunt went to Holland, then where did it come from? It certainly did not come through the General Baptists or through Menno Simons' *Foundation Book* or followers, because neither of these practiced it. It could have come from some other Anabaptist group like the Dutch Collegiants that Blunt later visited, but there is no evidence to this effect. In the Kiffin Manuscript they simply give Scripture as the reason for their belief. Is it not possible that they came to this conviction through their own study of the Scriptures given their New Testament hermeneutic. They certainly knew about Anabaptists and that some of them practiced immersion as is evident in the Kiffin manuscript. This could have prompted them to consider it but certainly would not have been the decisive factor in advocating it.

These Baptists loathed the Anabaptist appellation placed upon them by their Calvinistic contemporaries. If they did not believe that believer's baptism by immersion was clearly taught in the Scriptures they would certainly not have espoused it. White, Tolmie and Novak insist that believer's baptism was a result of their own study of the Scriptures: "the most critical factor in [the Baptists] adoption of believer's baptism was their own independent examination of the New Testament precedents."[25] This is evident when one reads their works or their *Confessions* on the subject of baptism.[26] Furthermore, as with their ecclesiology so with their doctrine of baptism, they apply their New Testament hermeneutic in their interpretation. Novak writes:

Separatism," *Baptist History and Heritage*, 22, No. 4 (1987), pp. 42-43; Nelson, "Reflecting on Baptist Origins," pp. 40-41.

[25] Novak, "Thy Will," p. 9, 262-277; Tolmie, *Triumph*, pp. 50-51; Tolmie, "General," p. 128; White, "Church," pp. 583-584; White, "How did William Kiffin Join the Baptists," *The Baptist Quarterly*, 23 (1970), pp. 204-206.

[26] Novak, "Thy Will," pp. 263-266.

On both issues [believer's church and believer's baptism] the common
Calvinistic insistence on the literal authority of the New Testament precedents is central to their approach. Yet even more clearly on the question of
the proper subject of baptism it is the special theological emphases of these
authors which distinguish them from their fellow Calvinists and enhance
their certainty of the model which they derive. Once again their insistence
that through the work of Christ the New Covenant breaks completely from
the Old both in form and in nature proves decisive. Acting upon this imperative they assess the apostolic precedents without analogy to the Old
Covenant practice of circumcision. These precedents themselves they interpret exclusively in the light of their assumption that in the New Covenant
God will accept only true spiritual service which none but the regenerate
can offer Him.[27]

Hence, for the Calvinistic Baptists, baptism ought to be for believers only. Given this hermeneutic one can see how they came to
hold believer's baptism, particularly since their Separatist/Inde-
pendent heritage had already used this hermeneutic in order to
support their belief in an independent/gathered church. Novak has
shown that the logic of the gathered church naturally leads to believer's baptism. Novak states:

As in their defense of the believers' church their certainty [of believer's
baptism] derives in large part from their distinctive understanding of the
mission of Christ and of the relation of His Covenant to that which it re-
places. Especially important is their belief that God sent His Son to call and
enable who would in the New Covenant offer Him only the true spiritual
service which His plan requires. In this context the baptism of unregenerate infants raises a number of major contradictions.[28]

These Baptists believed that baptizing infants would lead those so
baptized to believe that their membership in the New Covenant
was certain. Furthermore, they believed that paedobaptism failed
"to fulfill the greater purposes which God Himself appended to the
ordinance" that is, a spiritual people to offer spiritual worship.[29]
Novak continues:

To justify their separation [from the Established church these Baptists]
have already proposed that in matters of worship and polity the literal

---

[27] *Ibid.*, pp. 262-263.
[28] *Ibid.*, p. 271. See also *Ibid.*, pp. 274-276.
[29] *Ibid.*, pp. 271-272, 274.

model of the New Testament must hold absolute authority over the faithful. They have also pointed out that because in the New Covenant God will accept only the services of the regenerate both the Lord's Supper and church membership must be limited to believers. Beyond this they have asserted that any society not built solely upon the true apostolic forms and upon the true matter of spiritual saints cannot expect divine sanction as a true church of Christ. With these ideas constantly before them the practice of baptizing infants obviously incapable of faith and service would seem a glaring contradiction of their own terms of fellowship.[30]

The second reason to question any Anabaptist influence on the Calvinistic Baptists teaching concerning baptism is the latter's theology of baptism. In a recent thesis Stanley Fowler has shown that these seventeenth-century Baptists espoused a sacramentalist concept of baptism.[31] They held with the Reformed tradition since Calvin that baptism was a means of grace. For example, Robert Garner in his *A Treatise of Baptism* (1645) states, "In this Ordinance, the Lord Jesus by his Spirit acting in a believers heart, doth more richly seal up or confirm to him the free and full remission of all his sinnes, through the blood of Christ."[32] Henry Laurence in his *Of Baptism* (1659) also maintains, "[The Word and Sacraments] are both instruments in the hands of the holy Spirit for edification and salvation, the word is a dead letter without the Spirit, and so also is Baptism, it speaks no more than it is bid."[33] The General Baptists and the Anabaptists were more Zwinglian and nonsacramentalist in their interpretation of the ordinances of baptism and the Lord's Supper.[34]

For these reasons we believe the sources of the Calvinistic Baptists' teaching on baptism are their own study of Scripture and the Reformed tradition. As for Knollys there is no evidence that he had any contact with Anabaptists on this subject. As was mentioned above he was influenced by the Reformed tradition from College,

---

[30] *Ibid.*, pp. 275-276.

[31] Stanley Fowler, "Baptism as a Sacrament in 20th-Century British Baptist Theology" (unpublished Th.D. thesis, Wycliffe College, University of Toronto, 1998), pp. 7-31.

[32] Robert Garner, *A Treatise on Baptism* (1645), p. 24.

[33] Henry Lawrence, *Of Baptism* (1659), pp. 46,47.

[34] For the Anabaptists see William R. Estep, *The Anabaptist Story* (Nashville, 1963), pp. 145-173. For the General Baptists see E.P. Winter, "Calvinist and Zwinglian Views of the Lord's Supper among the Baptists of the Seventeenth Century," *The Baptist Quarterly*, 15 (1953,54), pp. 323-329.

and later probably by the Calvinistic Separatist Samuel How and certainly by the Calvinistic Separatist John Wheelwright. Upon his return to England he became a member of Henry Jessey's open communion/membership church in the early 1640's. In early 1644 Knollys was unclear concerning infant baptism and desired a conference by the church "that they might satisfye him, or he rectify them if amiss herein." In this conference the answer given by Kiffin in support of believer's baptism was that in Gospel times we must not go to Moses but to the New Testament for our answer on this subject. There is no mention of Anabaptist influence, only debate about the Scriptures. At the end of the debate some who "searched ye Scriptures" were convinced that paedobaptism was wrong.[35] At some point after this Knollys himself came to the conviction of believer's baptism (in the summer he was preaching against infant baptism from a church in Cornhill).[36] We do not know anything about his own baptism which must have occured sometime in 1644. His views on baptism show no Anabaptist influence but influence from his Reformed tradition and his own study of the Bible.

But what about the issue of the separation of church and state, liberty of conscience, and religious toleration? Did these not come from the Anabaptists? It is quite clear that both the Calvinistic Baptists and the Anabaptists shared the notion of the separation of church and state. However, as with ecclesiology there is no evidence that links these Baptists with Anabaptism on this issue other than their similarity of belief. Leon McBeth in the conclusion to his study on seventeenth-century Baptist religious liberty writes, "While Mennonite influence was clearly formative for General Baptists, religious liberty among Baptists was possible without such influence as is clear from Particular Baptists."[37] Not only is there no evidence for an Anabaptist connection for their espousal of religious liberty but several scholars posit a Puritan-Separatist influence for it. Looking at such Calvinistic-Separatists like Robert Harrison, Robert Browne, Francis Johnson, John Robinson, and Roger Williams who from Calvin onwards used the notion of the

---

[35]   W.T. Whitley, "Debate on Infant Baptism, 1643," *Transactions of the Baptist Historical Society*, 1 (1910), pp. 239-245.

[36]   Carruthers, *Everyday Work*, p. 96.

[37]   H. Leon McBeth, *English Baptist Literature on Religious Liberty to 1689* (New York, 1980), p. 283.

covenant as a conceptual tool for interpretation, George Selement concludes:

> Separatists took the covenant interpretation of the Bible in a direction that implicitly and eventually explicitly had revolutionary implication, regarding not only the nature of the church but the relationship of church and state. The crux of the matter involved the radical division that Separatists made between the Abrahamic covenant, which they asserted no longer applied to Christians, and the covenant of the New Testament. Christ, in short, made the Jewish system of theocracy obsolete. Such an interpretation of the Scriptures led Separatists to repudiation of national covenants, their own peculiar typological interpretation of Israel, and eventually to a denial of the magistrate's right to interfere in religious matters.[38]

And again Ken Manley in his study of Baptist origins believes "a reasonable case for tracing [religious toleration] can be found within Separatism. The inviolability of conscience was a Puritan concern."[39] In his study of Radical Puritan and Separatist ecclesiology from Cartwright to Jacob, Stephen Brachlow has shown that they all "were equally concerned to protect the voluntary nature of true church membership." And, "while in this way they paid tribute to the sovereignty of the State in church affairs, radical puritans and separatists both accepted the priority of the reformed provisio that obedience was due only so far as the Word of God allowed."[40] The seeds for a full-blown Calvinistic Baptist doctrine of religious liberty were already present and growing in Puritan-Separatism.

Not only can the roots of their teaching on toleration be found in their Puritan-Separatist heritage but, as was evident for their ecclesiology and doctrine of baptism, they can be found in their commitment to Scripture, and in particular to the New Testament precepts. Again Michael Novak has shown that these Baptists first of all based their notion of the separation of church and state on Scripture. He writes:

---

[38] George Selement, "The Covenant Theology of English Separatism and the Separation of Church and State," *Journal of American Academy of Religion*, 41 (1973), pp. 67-68.

[39] Manley, "Origins," p. 42.

[40] Brachlow, *Communion*, p. 270. See his chapter on this subject (*Ibid.*, pp. 230-267).

To substantiate their assertion that the realms of civil and spiritual authority must remain wholly distinct the Particular Baptist authors refer first of
all to the binding authority of the New Testament precedents. They reason
simply that because nowhere in the authoritative Gospel narratives does
Christ or the Apostles appeal to the secular office in the planting or maintenance of churches the magistrate can have no say in these matters. All ministers of the Gospel must follow the example set by the agents of Christ,
who first preached the Word and then gathered into fellowship those whom
conversion had made willing and able to profess Him in service. In the
blueprint established by Christ for His church there is no place whatsoever
for the sword.[41]

Moreover, not only are the roots of their doctrine of toleration
found in their commitment to Scripture and in their Puritan-Separatist heritage, but also in the simple logic of their ecclesiological
evolution. In his study of the first twenty years of Calvinistic Baptist
history Murray Tolmie maintains that their adherence to religious
liberty was the logical outcome of their ecclesiology and their teaching on baptism; he states that the Particular Baptist "theory of separation of church and state was closely bound to their notion of the
gathered church formed by believer's baptism, and it was largely
defined by its specific opposition to the idea of an established or
national church."[42]

In summary, Michael Novak makes clear from his study of the
writings of the Calvinistic Baptists of the first twenty years that their
espousal of religious liberty was a natural outcome of their assumptions, emphases, their understanding of a true church, their Puritan
heritage, and their New Testament hermeneutic. He writes,

The defense of religious toleration which these authors propose is in fact
grounded in precisely the same broader assumptions and special emphases
which have been shown to underlie their limitation first of church membership and then of baptism itself to believers. It also follows directly upon the
conception of the nature and purposes of New Covenant religious fellowship which they elaborate in their discussion of these two ordinances. In the
context defined by their own theological imperatives the Particular Baptist
authors' demand for the complete separation of church and state is as nec-

---

[41]   Novak, "Thy Will," p. 279. Novak again states, "As with their other ecclesiological innovations the Particular Baptist authors here ground their demand for religious
toleration on the absolute authority of the literal model established by Christ and the
Apostles" (*Ibid.*, p. 282).
[42]   Tolmie, "General," p. 213.

essary a corollary to their system as are their other major ecclesiological innovations. Although attacked by their contemporaries on a variety of grounds, this position is based largely on ideas which these authors share with their fellow Calvinists. On the question of toleration as on those of church membership and baptism, however, the special emphases which distinguish the Particular Baptist system itself also confirm these authors in their distinctive interpretation of the common New Testament source materials.[43]

As for Knollys, there is no evidence that his belief in the separation of Church and State was influenced by the Anabaptists. Like his fellow Calvinistic Baptists the prime influences on his thought in this area were his Puritan-Separatist heritage and his Bible.

Having examined the roots of the Calvinistic Baptists' ecclesiology, believer's baptism by immersion, and separation of church and state we conclude that though their understanding of these subjects is similar to that of the Anabaptists there is little evidence that these Baptists were influenced by them. In fact, as we have seen, there is much evidence to posit a Puritan-Separatist influence coupled with their own study of the Scriptures and strict adherence to them. We concur with B.R. White who argues that "when a plausible source of Separatist views is available in Elizabethan Puritanism and its natural developments, the onus of proof lies upon those who would

---

[43]   Novak, "Thy Will," pp. 278-279. Novak also states, "Their judgment that the examples of the New Testament bar the magistrate from interference in religious affairs is confirmed in their minds by the larger consideration that civil coercion simply cannot produce the true spiritual obedience which alone is acceptable to God under the New Covenant. Although such compulsion was valid under the Old Covenant it has no place whatsoever in [the] spiritual order of Christ. Because the nature of Gospel service is such that it can be rendered only by the regenerate, those who attempt by civil law to force people even to the true forms of worship violate the most basic terms of the New Covenant and dishonor rather than magnify the truths of God. Not only the precedents of Christ and the Apostles but also His larger purposes dictate that the magistrate protect the freedom of all to answer His call to conscience....

Conscience must ... remain free not because this is a natural right or because man has retained the capacity to choose the good, but rather because God has reserved to Himself the capacity to make it over in harmony with His will.... [These Baptists] insist that the consciences of all be left free from men because they believe that those whom He has chosen out of the world God Himself will bind perfectly to His truths" (*Ibid.*, pp. 288-290).

As a secondary factor we must also recognize the human element. Because of the sting of persecution in the 1640s these Baptists were emotionally positioned to argue for liberty of conscience in religious matters. For example, their political involvement in the 1650s was prompted by their desire for their own freedom of worship. Any policies that would take that freedom away they addressed in print.

affirm that the Anabaptists had any measurable influence upon the shaping of English Separatism."[44]

---

[44] White, *English Separatist*, p. 164. There are some dissenting voices about Anabaptist influence on the Calvinistic Baptists. For example, William Estep believes that there probably was an Anabaptist influence upon the Calvinistic Baptists either through the General Baptists or Mennonites evidenced in their *Confession* (1644, 1646), e.g., modification of their Calvinism and ecclesiology, change from a fourfold ministry to a twofold; but he recognizes there is no clear evidence of either groups' influence ("On the Origins of English Baptists," *Baptist History and Heritage*, 22, no. 2 [1987], pp. 21-22). Calvin Pater sees Anabaptist influence at several points, e.g., Blunt's baptism, Stassen's Mennonite hypothesis for the baptismal phrase "death, burial, and resurrection", toleration, and confessional subscription (*Karlstadt as the Father of the Baptist Movements: The Emergence of Lay Protestation* [Toronto, 1984], pp. 273-278). There is, however, general agreement that the main influence on the Calvinistic Baptists was Puritan-Separatism. Even Stassen agrees that the main influence and basic orientation of the Particular Baptists is non-separatist, Congregationalist Calvinism (Stassen, "Anabaptist Influence," p. 324). Michael Novak strongly maintains their connection to Puritan-Separatism (Novak, "Thy Will," pp. 4-6, 237-238). And Joseph Ban and Winthrop Hudson strongly reject any Anabaptist influence on the Calvinistic Baptists (Hudson, "Baptists were not Anabaptists," *The Chronicle* 16, no. 4 [1953], pp. 171-179, cited in Ban "Were the Earliest English Baptists Anabaptists?" in *In the Great Tradition* [Valley Forge, 1982], pp. 91, 104). Ban critiques Irvin B. Horst's thesis found in *The Radical Brethren: Anabaptism and the English Reformation to 1558* (Nieuwkoop, 1972) which according to Ban claims to have "discovered a historical link between the Anabaptists of the Lowlands and English Lollardy." If there is evidence of a link then Michael Watts concluded there is evidence of early Anabaptist influence upon the General Baptists (*The Dissenters*, vol. 1 [Oxford, 1978], p. 8). This link is quite speculative with very little evidence to back up the thesis (Ban, "English Baptists," pp. 96, 99-104). B.R. White believes the source of the commonalities between the Anabaptists and Baptists is the Bible (*English Separatist*, p. 163). Even if it could be proved that there was Anabaptist influence on the General Baptists, those scholars who posit Anabaptist influence on the Calvinistic Baptists see little evidence of connection between the General and Calvinistic Baptists (Estep, "Origins," p. 22; Stassen, "Mennonite Influence," pp. 322, 325).

Furthermore, Hugh Wamble also sees the Calvinistic Baptist roots in the Puritan-Separatist tradition, and believes they "were not immediately and institutionally related to continental Anabaptism or Mennonitism" ("Inter-Relations of Seventeenth Century English Baptists," *Review and Expositor*, 54 [1957], pp. 408, 407). See also Novak, "Thy Will," pp. 10, 277, 343, 344, 348.

APPENDIX C

SURVEY OF KNOLLYS' COMMENTARY ON REVELATION

According to Knollys the Book of Revelation could be divided into three parts or three principle visions; the seven candlesticks (Rev. 1-3), the seven seals, seven trumpets and seven vials (Rev. 6-19), and the new heavens and earth (Rev. 20-22).[1] Knollys believed that most of the Book was to be interpreted historically. Therefore, the Book dealt with the state of the church from the time of the reign of the Roman Emperor Domitan through to the end of the world.[2] This meant that the visions of the seals, the trumpets, and the vials were to be interpreted historically. According to Knollys the seven seals (Rev. 6:4-17) contained the judgements of God upon the Roman Pagan Idolators (the years prior to Constantine), the trumpets (Rev. 8:7-13; 9:1-21) contained the woes of God executed on the Arian apostate persecutors (the years prior to the fall of Rome), and the seven vials (Rev. 16; 18:8-21; 19:19) contained the last plagues of God in judgement against the Roman Antichristian Papal beast, whore and false prophet (the time of the destruction of Mystical Babylon).[3]

Knollys believed that the first three chapters of Revelation were addressed to the historical situation of the seven Asian churches.[4] These are "the things which are" according to Revelation 1:19. Chapters four to six deal with "the things which thou hast seen," that is, the condition of the church under the Roman Pagan state. And "the things which shall be hereafter" given in chapters seven to twenty-two refer to the condition of the church under the Antichristian Roman, Arian and Papal state.[5]

The first principle vision of the seven seals primarily signified the

---

[1] *Eleventh*, Preface.
[2] *Revelation*, Preface.
[3] Ibid.
[4] *Ibid.*, p. 15. Commenting on Rev. 1:19.
[5] *Ibid.*, p. 15.

sufferings of God's people under the Roman Pagan Emperors and the judgement of God on the European empire.[6] This judgement took place through Constantine the Great with the destruction of Paganism and the setting up of the worship of Christ throughout the empire.[7] This great day of God's wrath took place in the days of the tenth persecution of the Christians during Diocletian's reign.[8] From the eighth chapter through to the thirteenth is the seventh seal which begins the sounding of the seven trumpets.[9] But before the trumpets begin in verse eight there is peace in the church for half the reign of Constantine, fifteen years.[10] After this peace the great Arian heresy began in which the orthodox bishops, ministers and Christians were persecuted by the Arians.[11] The first angel who sounded the first trumpet represented the faithful ministers of Christ such as Athanasius and Hilarius; and it also included the kings of the Goths and Vandals. This angel sounded against the Roman Empire and Arianism.[12]

The second angel represented the faithful ministers of the fourth century in the Western church; he sounded the second trumpet concerning the preeminence of the Pope of Rome and the corruption of the worship and ordinances by the clergy.[13] The third angel represented the ministers of the fifth century such as Augustine and Hieronymus who sounded the third trumpet concerning Nestorius' corruption of worship and teachings; this is also when popery's teachings began.[14] The fourth angel represented Gregorius who opposed John, Bishop of Constantinople who took the name of universal bishop. It also includes all the faithful ministers who opposed innovations in worship and doctrine. This angel sounded the fourth trumpet concerning the corruption of the ministers.[15] After this the three woes against the Roman Papal church which is Mystical Babylon begin. The first woe takes place at the time of the sounding of the fifth trumpet. This trumpet sounds the judgement

---

[6]   *Ibid.*, pp. 79ff.
[7]   *Ibid.*, p. 87.
[8]   *Ibid.*, p. 88.
[9]   *Ibid.*, p. 97.
[10]   Ibid.
[11]   *Ibid.*, p. 98.
[12]   *Ibid.*, p. 100.
[13]   *Ibid.*, p. 101.
[14]   *Ibid.*, pp. 102-103.
[15]   *Ibid.*, p. 103.

of God upon the apostates which include an emminent apostate churchman (the man of sin) and those who follow after him. This is the beginning of Popedom and of the Antichristian Papal power, and the opening of the bottomless pit of idolatry.[16] This Antichristian Papal power will continue for 1260 years.[17]

The sixth angel and the second woe now follow. The sixth angel represents the orthodox ministers who sounded against Popish idolatry, image worship, and other superstitions of the Roman clergy. This angel also loosed the four angels of the river Euphrates representing the commanders of the armies of the Turkish Emperor who will judge the Roman empire for their idolatrous worship and departure from true worship.[18] Knollys cautiously suggests this takes place for some 390 years. We are told in the tenth chapter that when the seventh angel sounds two things will happen: the reign of the beast, whore, false prophet and all those kings that follow the beast will come to an end; and the mystery of God will be finished, that is, the conversion of the Jews to Christ and the restoring of the church to its primitive purity of worship and ordinances.[19]

In chapter eleven John is told that the church will be tread under foot for 42 months (1260 prophetic years) by false Christians who are atheists, Papists, all profane and ungodly persons, and unbelieving Jews.[20] This period of time coincides with the prophecy of the two witnesses (11:3-13), the woman in the wilderness (12:1-17), and the beast's presence out of the bottomless pit (13:1-5).[21] Knollys now comments on the two witnesses. According to him they are the ministers and true constituted gospel churches who are given prophetical power from God to preach the Word of God and to pray.[22] These witnesses are to prophecy 1260 prophetic years which began

---

[16]   *Ibid.*, pp. 105-106.
[17]   *Ibid.*, p. 108.
[18]   *Ibid.*, pp. 112-113. In this section Knollys lists numerous examples of idolatrous worship, e.g. their adoration of images, crosses, crucifixes; and their worship of the image of the virgin Mary and image of Christ upon a cross. In addition, they murder the souls of people who follow their false doctrines and worship; they worship their breaden God in the Mass; and they steal by getting money for the Roman church under pretence and pretext of giving pardons, indulgences and dispensations (*Ibid.*, pp. 115-116).
[19]   *Ibid.*, p. 118.
[20]   *Ibid.*, p. 125.
[21]   *Ibid.*, p. 126.
[22]   *Ibid.*, pp. 126-128. They are not given magisterial power and, therefore, they are not to use the sword (*Ibid.*, pp. 128, 129, 134).

about 407, 409, 410 or before 428 AD. Therefore, these 1260 years will end somewhere around 1688, although these are uncertain conjectures.[23]

Knollys believed that in 1688 when he wrote this commentary the witnesses were still suffering under the Roman Papal Beast, and that the end of their prophesying would come when the gospel is preached to the whole world.[24] Here he explains that the testimony of the witnesses is: proclamation of true doctrine, true worship, the kingship of Jesus; and condemnation of Papal false teaching and worship.[25] These witnesses will be killed near the end of the 1260 years by the beast out of the bottomless pit. This beast is Mystical Babylon who is also the beast of the eighth head (Rev. 17:8-11) who is also the Pope of Rome. This war with the two witnesess has recently been taking place; for example, the Popes and Emperors against the German Protestants, the edicts of the Papists in the days of Mary in England, Pope Alexander III against the Waldensians, and in 1464 the Roman persecution of the Lollards.[26] The witnesses eventually suffer a civil and ecclesiatical death which includes deprivation of livelihood, life, civil and ecclesiatical rights and liberties, estates, and imprisonment. They will also lose their spiritual vigour against the Antichrist, be deprived of the Spirit of Life, become lukewarm, and some will fall into the great apostasy; all of this is a kind of spiritual death that the church will experience during the days the witnesses are dead.[27] Their death takes place in "the street of the great city." This city is the whole Anitchristian kingdom of the beast; and according to Knollys the street is England and, in particular, London.[28] These witnesses will lie dead for 3 1/2 years. At the end of these years the two witnesses will be raised which means the testimony and witness of the church is restored. At this time the 1260 year period is completed and the end has come.

Knollys believed, contrary to most seventeenth-century expositors, that the witnesses had not yet been killed. He gave his reasons which included his conviction that the two witnesses likely began their prophesying in 428 so ending their prophetic ministry about

---

23 *Ibid.*, p. 130.
24 *Ibid.*, pp. 131, 135.
25 *Ibid.*, p. 136.
26 *Ibid.*, pp. 135-139.
27 *Ibid.*, pp. 138-139.
28 *Ibid.*, pp. 139-141.

1688.[29] According to Knollys when the witnesses ascend, a tenth part of the city will fall. He believed this meant that England, Scotland and Ireland would break away from following Papal Rome.[30] The sixth trumpet and the second woe have now ended.

The seventh angel sounds forth the seventh trumpet which signals the third woe when the Roman Antichristian beast will be destroyed. This will be accomplished by the seven vials of the wrath of God, which are the seven last plagues. Knollys believed contrary to many expositors that none of the seven vials had been poured out yet (1688).[31] When the vials are poured out the kingdoms of the world become the kingdom of our Lord and of His Christ. The kingdoms of this world are the kingdom of David (Judah and Israel), the kingdoms of the Roman Caesars (the fourth monarchy), and all the kingdoms of the earth. These kingdoms will become the kingdom of Christ by the preaching of the gospel, by the pouring out of the Spirit, and by the breaking to pieces of these kingdoms.[32]

Now chapter twelve goes back in time to the beginning of the church in the apostles' day. The "woman clothed with the sun" is the true visible constituted church, and the child is the many converts in the days of the apostles. The "great red dragon" is the Roman Pagan government that persecuted the saints from the time of Tiberius to Diocletian.[33] The "man-child" of verse five is Christ and His saints as well as, possibly, Constantine who ruled in those days of the early fourth century. The "war in heaven" of verse seven took place when the Christian emperors, kings and governors (especially Constantine) defeated the Roman Pagan empire with its idolatry.[34] Then, according to verse 13, the dragon began to persecute the true church through Arianism after the death of Constantine. The church at this time was preserved by the "two wings of a great eagle," that is, by Arcadius and Honorius, the two sons of Theodosius between whom the Roman empire was divided. Yet still the dragon tried to corrupt and destroy the church by means of the heresies of Arianism and Pelagianism.[35]

---

[29]   *Ibid.*, pp. 143-146.
[30]   *Ibid.*, p. 148.
[31]   *Ibid.*, pp. 149-151.
[32]   *Ibid.*, pp. 151-154.
[33]   *Ibid.*, pp. 159-161.
[34]   *Ibid.*, pp. 161-162, 164.
[35]   *Ibid.*, pp. 167-168.

According to chapter thirteen, verse one, the sea represents the barbarian nations under Alcaricus which invaded the Roman Empire. And the beast who rose up out of the sea is the Popedom of Papal Rome with its ten crowned horns, that is the ten Roman provinces. The rising of this beast is between 410 and 428 AD.[36] The power of the beast comes from the devil, and this power is his Poli-Ecclesiastical jurisdiction in all causes and over all persons, civil, military, maritime and ecclesiastical. The Roman Pope was wounded when Rome was sacked by the Barbarian armies. He was then healed by the Dragon and the world submitted to the Pope.[37] Then in verse eleven we are told of another beast who rose out of the earth. According to Knollys this was the same beast as the one who rose up out of the sea. The healing of his wound took place when Pope Boniface III returned to Rome about the year 606/7 AD, and Emperor Phocas declared him the universal bishop and head of the Catholic church. This latter year coincides with the number of the beast which is 666, that is, the beast begins his reign 666 years after the Roman empire began.[38] The woman, the true church, at that time fled into the wilderness for 1260 years. This wilderness signifies the persecution of the church by the Roman Papal powers.[39]

Now Knollys sees the visions in the chapters following the thirteenth as those events that will take place after the 1260 year period, even after the two witnesses have been raised.[40] At this time the judgement of God is announced against Papal Rome, the beast of the eighth head, the pope, the false prophet, the great whore, mystery Babylon and all the national, synodal and parochial false churches. This judgement is described as the wine of the wrath of God which is the seven vials of the seven last plagues. The wine-press is Armageddon where the saints trod on Babylon.[41] Chapter fifteen and following gives us the third principle vision of this prophecy which is the seven vials of the seven last plagues and the

---

[36]   *Ibid.*, p. 169. This is the same interpretation as that of Joseph Mede. The ten crowned horns are the Britans, Saxons, Franks, Burgundians, Wisigothes, Swedes, Vandals, Alemans, Ostrogoths, and Grecians.

[37]   *Ibid.*, pp. 170-171.

[38]   *Ibid.*, pp. 174-175, 179.

[39]   *Ibid.*, pp. 161-163.

[40]   *Ibid.*, p. 181.

[41]   *Ibid.*, pp. 184-188.

third woe. These judgements will be the means of the conversion of Jews and Gentiles.[42] The seven angels are to pour out the vials on all the earth, that is, upon the whole Roman Papal state, both political and ecclesiastical. The vials are poured out: first, against the earthly state of the Roman Papal kingdom; second, against all ecclesiastical, metropolitan and diocesian Sees; third, against all the political rulers under the Papal kingdom; fourth, against the Emperor of Germany, the French King, and the Pope of Rome; fifth, against the city of Rome; sixth, against the Turkish kingdom and power; and seventh, against all Satan's kingdom, and all kingdoms of Antichrist, both of Turk and Pope. At this time Mystical Babylon, the Roman Papal empire and power, and her daughters, the National churches of the Papists, of the Lord Bishops and of the Presbyterians are destroyed.[43] Between the sixth and seventh vial there was an interval in which the pope, the cardinals, etc. and the devil gather forces to make war against Christ. This is the great battle of Armageddon where the Turks will be utterly destroyed.[44] The Jews will be involved in this battle.[45]

Now the fifth angel, according to Knollys, declares God's judgement upon Mystery Babylon in chapters seventeen to nineteen. In chapter seventeen she is described as a great whore riding on a scarlet coloured beast. The beast is the Roman Papal Emperor with the kings of the earth who give their strength and power to the beast.[46] The seven kings of the fourth kingdom mentioned in verse eleven are the successive governments of the Roman empire. The first five that were before John's time were kings, consuls, decemvers, tribunes, and dictators. The "one that is" is the Roman Caesars of John's time, and the "one that is to come" is the Pope of Rome. This is the "beast that was, and is not," who is also the eighth head, the man of sin who reigns for fourty-two months or 1260 years.[47] He has ten kingdoms and kings under him. These ten kings shall in the end turn against the church of Rome.[48] Once Babylon has fallen, that is, the church of Rome is ruined, then

---

[42] *Ibid.*, p. 191.
[43] *Ibid.*, pp. 193-201.
[44] *Ibid.*, pp. 197-199.
[45] *Ibid.*, pp. 197, 198-199.
[46] *Ibid.*, pp. 201-202.
[47] *Ibid.*, p. 206.
[48] *Ibid.*, pp. 207, 208.

praise and rejoicing in heaven takes place as recorded in chapter nineteen; and the church is made ready for the marriage of the Lamb.

Verses eleven to the end of this chapter describe the battle of Armaggedon, which is the same battle as Ezekiel's Gog and Magog. Christ and the armies of heaven which include the angels and saints, war against the beast, the kings of the earth. Christ is victorious fighting this battle with two weapons, the Word of God (his word of threatened vengence) and his rod of iron.[49] At that time the beast and the false prophet are cast into the lake of fire.

After the destruction of Papal Rome Satan is bound for a literal thousand years where he is kept from tempting and deceiving the nations by himself or his instruments, i.e. pagan, Papal or Mohammedan false teaching.[50] Then Christ reigns with His suffering, overcoming saints. Those who had worshipped the beast were not raised until the thousand years were over. The first resurrection of verse five is the raising of the two witnesses, that is, those Christians who are alive at Christ's coming; they shall reign with Christ for a thousand years.[51] Satan is then released at the end of the thousand years at which time he deceives the nations, Gog and Magog, gathering them together to war against the New Jerusalem and the Church. Then God destroys Satan, and he is cast into the lake of fire forever.[52]

At this time Christ's Second Coming occurs and all stand before His judgement-seat. Here the wicked and righteous, both dead and alive, are judged.[53] They are judged out of the things written in those books which were opened, the Old and New Testaments, and the Book of life. The wicked are then cast into the lake of fire.[54]

The last two chapters are concerned with the millennial period. Chapter twenty-one gives us a vision of the world to come, that is, the world as it is during the thousand years on earth. This world to come is the newly created heavens and earth, and where the New

---

[49]   *Ibid.*, pp. 216-221.
[50]   *Ibid.*, pp. 222-223. Knollys states that this literal thousand years was held by Pareus and other expositors.
[51]   *Ibid.*, pp. 223-224.
[52]   *Ibid.*, pp. 224-225.
[53]   Ibid.
[54]   *Ibid.*, pp. 225-226.

Jerusalem, which is the church in her latter-day glory, is located.[55] The description of the New Jerusalem during these thousand years is given in the rest of the chapter and in the first five verses of chapter twenty-two. The rest of the last chapter looks to Christ's Second Coming which will be personal, visible and with all His saints.[56] This will occur at the end of the thousand years. During these years the Spirit and the bride call sinners to take Christ freely.[57] Knollys closes his commentary with an invitation to the readers to come out of Papal Rome.[58]

---

[55] *Ibid.*, pp. 227-228.
[56] *Ibid.*, p. 239.
[57] *Ibid.*, pp. 241-242.
[58] *Ibid.*, pp. 243-244.

SELECT BIBLIOGRAPHY

Knollys' Writings in Chronological Order

Knollys, Hanserd. *A Moderate Answer vnto Dr. BASTVVICKS BOOK Called,* Independency Gods Ordinance. *Wherein, is declared the manner how some CHVRCHES in this City were gathered, and upon what tearmes their Members were admitted; That so both the Dr. and the Reader may judge, how near some Beleevers who walk together in the Fellowship of the Gospell, do come in their practice to these Apostolicall rules which are propounded by the Dr. as Gods method in gathering Churches and admitting MEMBERS.* London, Printed by Iane Coe. 1645.

Knollys, Hanserd, Benjamin Coxe, and William Kiffin, &c. *A Declaration concerning the Publicke Dispute Which Should have been in the Publike Meeting House of Alderman-Bury, the 3d. of this instant Moneth of December; Concerning Infants-Baptisme.* London, Printed in the Year, 1645.

—. Letter to Mr. John Dutton. 1645. In Thomas Crosby, *The History of the English Baptists, from the Reformation to the Beginning of the Reign of George I.* London: 1738, I, 231-232.

—. *Christ exalted: in a sermon begun to be preached at Debenham in Suffolk, upon the 14. day of Febr. last, upon Coloss. 3. 11. By Hanserd Knollys. Who was stoned out of the pulpit (as he was preaching) by a company of rude fellowes, and poor women of that town; who were sent for, called together, and set on by a malignant high-constable, who lives in the same town. Also, another sermon, preached at Stradbrooke in Suffolk, the 13. day of Febr. last, concerning sanctification; upon Ephes. 1. 4.* London: 1645.

—. *Christ Exalted: A lost sinner Sought, and saved by Christ: Gods people are an Holy people. Being the summe of divers Sermons Preached in* Suffolk; *By Hanserd Knollys. Who for this Doctrine had the Meeting-house doores shut against him, and was stoned out of the Pulpit (as he was preaching) by a rude multitude; who were gathered together, and set on by a Malignant High-*Constable. *Which hath been proved by divers Witnesses of good reputation, before the Honourable Committee of Examination at* London. London, Printed by Jane Coe, according to Order. 1646.

—. *The Shining of a Flaming fire in Zion. Or, A clear Answer unto 13. Exceptions, against the Grounds of New Baptism; (so called) in Mr. Saltmarsh his Book; Intituled,* The Smoke in the Temple, *p. 15, &c. Which Exceptions, Were tendered by him to all Believers, to shew them, how little they have attained; and that there is a more glorious fulnesse to be revealed. Also, A Postscript; Wherein (to the like end) some Queries are propounded unto Believers.* London, Printed by Jane Coe, according to Order, 1646.

Knollys Hanserd, *et al. A Confession of Faith of seven Congregations or Churches of Christ in London, which are commonly (but uniustly) called Anabaptists Published For the vindication of the truth, and information of the ignorant; likewise for the taking off of those aspersions which are frequently both in Pulpit and Print unjustly cast upon them.* The Second Impression corrected and enlarged. Published according to Order. London printed by Matth. Simmons, and are to be sold by John Hancock in Popeshead Alley. 1646.

–. "To the Churches of God in London and elsewhere in all places with the Bishops and Deacons." In Robert Garner, *Mysteries Unvailed. Wherein the Doctrine of Redemption by Christ, flowing from the glorious Grace, and everlasting Love of God, the very fountain of Life and Salvation unto lost Sinners, is handled. The most usuall Scriptures explained, and Reasons answered, which are urged for the universality of the death of Christ for all Persons. Wherein the unsoundness of this opinion, together with divers other conclusions, as depending upon it, are discovered and the Truth unvailed.* Printed ... at the black sprad [*sic*] Eagle, at the west end of *Pauls.* 1646.

–. "Epistle to the Reader by Hanserd Knollys." In Thomas Collier, *The Exaltation of Christ in The dayes of the Gospel: As the alone High Priest, Prophet, and King, of Saints.... The Second Edition, corrected by the Author.* London, Printed, by R.L. for Giles Calvert, at the black Spred-Eagle, at the West end of Pauls. 1647.

Knollys, Hanserd, *et al. A Declaration by Congregational Societies in, and about the City of LONDON; as well as those commonly called* Anabaptists, *as others. In a way of* Vindication *of themselves. Touching, 1.* Liberty. *2.* Magistracy. *3.* Propriety. *4.* Polygamie. *Wherein their Judgments, concerning the particulars mentioned are tendred to consideration, to prevent misunderstanding.* 1647. In E.B. Underhill, ed., *Confessions of Faith and other Public Documents, Illustrative of the History of the Baptist Churches of England in the 17th Century.* London: 1854, pp. 273-287.

–. *The Rudiments of* Hebrew Grammar *in* English. *Published for the benefit of some friends, who being ignorant of the Latine, are desirous to understand the Bible in the Originall TONGUE.* London, Printed by Moses Bell, for William Larner at the Blackmore neere Bishopgate, and George Whittington at the blew Anchor In Cornhill neer the Exchange. 1648.

–. "To the Churches of God in London and elsewhere in all places with the Bishops and Deacons." In [Robert Garner], *Redemption By Jesus Christ Unto lost Sinners, Handled. Also, The Scriptures (alleadged by Mr. Den, Tho. Moor, Thomas Lamb, and others, to prove the Universality of the extent of the death of Christ) are freed from the corrupt sense which is put upon them. With an Epistle to the Churches of God in London, and elsewhere, by Hanserd Knollys.* London, Printed for Giles Calvert, at the black Spread-Eagle at the West-end of Pauls: 1653.

–. *An exposition of the first chapter of the Song of Solomon.* London: 1656.

Knollys, Hanserd, *et al. Address of the Anabaptist Ministers in London to the Lord Protector.* 1657. In E.B. Underhill, ed. *Confessions of Faith and other Public Documents, Illustrative of the History of the Baptist Churches of England in the 17th Century* London: 1854, pp. 335-338.

—. *Rhetoricae adumbratio opera & studio.* Londini : [s.n], 1663.

—. "Courteous Reader." In Katherine Sutton, *A Christian Womans Experiences of the glorious working of Gods free grace.* At Rotterdam, Printed by Henry Goddæus, Printer in the Newstreet, Anno 1663.

—. "Recommended to the use of all Parents and Schoolmasters, by H. Knowls." In Benjamin Keach, *Instructions for Children.* 1664.

—. *Radices simplicium vocum, flexilium maxime, Novi testamenti opera & studio.* Londini: [s.n], 1664.

—. *Grammaticae graecae compendium operâ & studio.* Londini : [s.n], 1664.

—. *Grammaticae Latinae compendium, or, An introduction to the Latine tongue.* London : [s.n], 1664.

—. *Linguae Hebricae delineatio opera & studio.* Londini : [s.n], 1664.

—. *Radices Hebraicae omnes, quae in S. Scriptura, Veteris testamenti occurrunt opera & studio.* Londini : [s.n], 1664.

—. *Grammaticae Latinae, Graecae, & Hebraicae. Compendium. Rhetoricæ adumbratio. Item Radices Græcæ & Hebraicæ omnes quæ in Sacra Scriptura Veteris & Novi Testamenti occurrunt. Opera & studio.* Londini : typis Tho. Roycroft, anno Dom. 1665.

—. *Apocalyptical Mysteries, Touching the Two WITNESSES, the Seven VIALS, and the Two KINGDOMS, to wit, of Christ, and of ANTICHRIST, EXPOUNDED. Wherein is contained some things necessary for the Saints in this present GENERATION to know. And therein is also shewed, what the ISRAEL of God ought to do in this DAY.* London, Printed in Year, 1667.

—. *The parable of the kingdom of heaven expounded, or an exposition of the first thirteen verses of the 25th chapter of Matthew.* London: printed for Benjamin Harris, and are to be sold at the Stationers Armes in Sweetings Rents, in Cornhill, near the Royal Exchange, 1674.

Knollys, Hanserd, Daniel Dike, Thomas Paul, William Kiffin, and Henry Forty. *The Quakers appeal answer'd, or a full Relation of the Occasion, Progress, and Issue of a Meeting held in Barbican, the 28th of August last past. Wherein the Allegations of William Pen in Two BOOKS lately Published by Him, against Thomas Hicks: were Answered and Disproved. And Tho. Hicks, his Quotations out of the Quakers own Books, Attested, by several, as being appeal'd unto.* Published for Common Information. London, Printed for Peter Parker, at the Leg and Star in Cornhil, over against the Royal Exchange, 1674. Where are Sold the three Diologues between a Christian and a Quaker.

Knollys, Hanserd, *et al.* Letter to Andrew Gifford. 1675. In Joseph Ivimey, *History of the English Baptists.* London: Printed for B.J. Holdsworth, 1811-1830, I, 417-420.

Knollys, Hanserd, William Kiffin, Dan Dyke, Jo Gosnold, Henry Forty, Thomas Delanne. *The Baptists Answer to Mr. Obed Wills, His appeal against Mr. H. Danvers.*

London : printed for Francis Smith, at the Elephant and Castle in Cornhill, near the Royal-Exchange, 1675.

Knollys, Hanserd, *et al. Confession of the Faith Put forth by the ELDERS and BRETH-REN Of many CONGREGATIONS OF Christians (bapized upon Profession of their Faith) in* London *and the Country.* Printed in the year, 1677. In William Lumpkin, *Baptist Confessions of Faith.* Philadelphia: The Judson Press, 1959, pp. 241-295.

—. *An Exposition of the Eleventh Chapter of the Revelation. Wherein All those Things therein Revealed, which must shortly come to pass, are Explained.* N.p. Printed, Anno Domini, 1679.

—. *Mystical Babylon Unveiled, Wherein is Proved, I. That* Rome*-Papal is mystical-Babylon. II. That the Pope of* Rome *is the Beast. III. That the Church of* Rome *is the great Whore. IV. That the Roman-Priests are the false Prophet. Also a Call To all the People of God to come out of Babylon.* N.p. Printed Anno Domini, 1679.

Knollys, Hanserd, *et al.* "Christian Reader." In John Russel, *A Brief Narrative of some Considerable Passages Concerning the First Gathering and further Progress of a Church of Christ in Gospel Order, in BOSTON.....IN NEW......ENGLAND. Commonly (though falsely) called by the Name of ANABAPTISTS: For the clearing their innocency from the Scandalous things laid to their charge.* 1680. In Nathan E. Wood, *The History of the First Baptist Church of Boston (1665-1899).* Philadelphia: American Baptist Publication Society, 1899, pp. 149-172.

—. *The world that now is; and the world that is to come: or the first and second coming of Jesus Christ. Wherein several prophecies not yet fulfilled are expounded.* 1681.

—. *An Exposition of the whole Book of the Revelation. Wherein The Visions and Prophecies of CHRIST Are opened and Expounded: Shewing The great Conquests of our LORD Jesus Christ for his Church over all His and Her Adversaries, PAGAN, ARIAN, and PAPAL; and the glorious State of the Church of God in the New Heavens and New Earth, in these Latter Days.* By Hanserd Knowles, Preacher of the Morning Lecture at Pinners-Hall. Licensed, September 12. 1688. London, Printed for the Author; and are to be Sold by William Barthall, at the Bible in Newgate-street, MDCLXXXIX.

Knollys, Hanserd, *et al.* "To the Congregation of Baptized Believers in *England* and *Wales,* Grace, Mercy and Peace be multiplied through the saving Knowledge of our Lord Jesus Christ." In [Benjamin Keach], *The Gospel Minister's Maintenance Vindicated. Wherein, A Regular Ministry in the Churches, is first Asserted, and the Objections against a Gospel Maintenance for Ministers, Answered. Also, The Dignity, Necessity, Difficulty, Use and Excellency of the Ministry of Christ is opened. Likewise, The Nature and VVeightiness of that Sacred VVork and Office clearly evinc'd.* London Printed, and are to be sold by John H ... at the Harrow, in the Poultrey, 1689.

—. *An Answer to a Brief Discourse concerning singing in the public worship of God in the Gospel-Church by I [Isaac]. M [Marlow]. 1690.*" 1691.

Knollys, Hanserd, *et al.* "A General Epistle." In *A Narrative of the proceedings of the General Assembly of the elders and messengers of the baptized Churches ... of England and Wales.* 1691.

—. *The Life and Death of that old Disciple of Jesus Christ, and eminent Minister of the Gospel, Mr. Hanserd Knollys, who died in the Ninety-third year of his age written with his own hand to the year 1672; and continued in general in an epistle by Mr. W. K. To which is added his last Legacy to the Church*. 1692; rpt. London: E. Huntington, High Street, Bloomsbury, 1812.

Primary Sources

Anon. *The Anabaptists Catechisme: with All their Practices, Meetings and Exercises: The names of their Pastors, their trades, and places of meeting, their Doctrine and Discipline; a Catalogue of such dishes as they usually make choice of at their Feasts: How, and by whom they are dipped: and all other things belonging to their Society and Brotherhood.... Published according to Order of their Conventicles*. Printed for R.A. 1645.

Anon. *A True Discovery of a Bloody Plot Contrived by ther Phanaticks against the Proceedings of the City of London*. 1661.

Anon. *A Door of Hope: or, A Call ... unto the Standard of our Lord, King Jesus*. 1661.

Adams, Thomas. *A Commentary or Exposition upon the Divine Second Epistle Generall, written by the Blessed Apostle St. Peter*. 1633.

A Declaration of Several Churches ... concerning the Kingly Interest of Christ. 1654.

Ames, William. *The Marrow of Theology*. Trans. By John Dykstra Eusden. 1968; rpt. Durham, NC: The Labyrinth Press, 1983.

Archer, Henry. *The Personall Reign of Christ upon Earth*. 1642.

Aspinwall, William. *A Brief Description of the Fifth Monarchy, or Kingdome*. 1653.

Baillie, Robert. *Anabaptisme, the true Fountaine of Independency, Brownisme, Antinomy, Familisme and Most of the Other Errours which for the time Doe Trouble the Church of England, Unsealed*. London: 1646.

—. *The Letters and Journals of Robert Baillie*. 3 vols. Ed. David Laing. Edinburgh: Printed for Robert Ogle, 1841.

Bastwick, John. *Independency not God's Ordinance*. 1645.

—. *The utter routing of the whole army of all the Independents and Sectaries ... and all the forces of the three generals and commanders of thesectaries, Hanserdo Knollys, J.S. & Henry Burton are all dissipated, with all their whibbling reserves*. 1646.

Baxter, Richard. *Reliquiae Baxterianae: or Mr. Baxters Narrative of The Most Memorable Passages of His Life and Times*, ed. Matthew Sylvester. London: 1696.

—. *The Saints Everlasting Rest: or a Treatise of the Blessed State of the Saints in their enjoyment of God in Glory*. 1650.

Bridge, William. *Christ's coming Opened in a Sermon Before the Honourable House of Commons in Margarets Westminster: May 17, 1648*. 1648.

Brightman, Thomas. *Revelation of the Revelation, that is the Revelation of St. John opened clearely, with a logicall Resolution and Exposition*. 1615.

Brine, John. *A Treatise on Various Subjects*. 4th ed. London: 1851.

—. *A Defence of the Doctrine of Eternal Justification from some Exceptions made to it by Mr. Bragge, and others*. 1732; rpt. Paris, Arkansas: The Baptist Standard Bearer, Inc., 1987.

—. *A Refutation of Arminian Principles, Delivered in a Pamphlet, intitled, the Modern Question concerning Repentance and Faith, examined with Candour, &c*. London: 1743.

–. *The Covenant of Grace open'd in a sermon Occasioned by the Death of Mrs. Margaret Busfield*. London: 1734.

–. Grace, proved to be at the Sovereign Disposal of GOD: *in a Discourse Preached* July *19, 1760*. London: 1760.

–. *Remarks upon a Pamphlet intitled*, Some Doctrines in the *Superlapsarian* Scheme impartially examin'd by the Word of God: *Containing a Defence of Several Evangelical Doctrines therein Objected to*. London: 1736.

–. *The Imputation of Christ's active Obedience to his People, and the Merit of it demonstrated*, in a Sermon. London: 1759.

–. *The Proper Eternity of the Divine Decrees, and of the Mediatorial Office, of Jesus Christ: Asserted and Proved*. London: 1754.

–. *The Doctrines of the Imputation of Sin to Christ, and the Imputation of his Righteousness to his People: Clearly stated, explained, and improved, in a Sermon*. London: 1757.

Bernard, Richard. *A Key of Knowledge for the Openning of the Secret Mysteries of St. Johns Mysticall Revelation*. 1617.

Calendar of State Papers, Domestic series,of the reigns of Edward VI, Mary,Elizabeth and James I. 12 vols. Ed. Mary Anne Everett Green. London : Longman, Brown, Green, Longmans, & Roberts, 1856-1872.

Calendar of State Papers, Domestic Series, Charles I, 1625-1649. 23 vols. Eds. John Bruce, W.D. Hamilton, and S.C. Lomas. London: Longmans, Green, Reader, and Dyer. 1858-1897.

Calendar of State Papers, Domestic Series, Interregnum, 1649-1660. 13 vols. Ed. Mary A.E. Green. London: Longmans and Co. 1879-1886.

Calendar of State Papers, Domestic Series, of the Reign of Charles II. 28 vols. Ed. Mary Anne Everett Green. London: Longman, Green, Longman, & Roberts, 1860-1939.

Calvin, John. *Institutes of the Christian Religion 1536 Edition*. Trans. F.L Battles. Grand Rapids: Wm. B. Eerdmans Publ. Co.,1989.

–. *Institutes of the Christian Religion*. 2 vols. Ed. John T. McNeill & trans. by Ford Lewis Battles. Philadelphia: The Westminster Press, 1977.

–. *Calvin's New Testament Commentaries*. 12 vols. Eds. David W. Torrance & Thomas F. Torrance. Grand Rapids: W. B. Eerdmans Publ. Co., 1974.

Canne, John. *Truth with Time: or, Certain reasons Proving That none of the seven last Plagues, or Vials, are yet poured out: neither will the time of their pouring out begin, till after the rising of the Two Witnesses, and the fourty two months of the Beast's reign be expired*. 1656.

–. *The Time of the End*. 1657.

–. *The Time of Finding*. 1658.

Cary, Mary. *Little Horns Doom & Downfall: or a Scripture Prophesie of King James, and King Charles*. 1651.

Chambers, Humphrey. *Animadversions on Mr. William Dells Book Intitled the Crucified and Quickned Christian*. 1652.

Cotton, John. *Bloudy Tenent, washed, and made white in the bloud of the Lambe*. 1647.

Cox, Benjamin. *An Appendix to a Confession of Faith; or a More Full Declaration of the Faith and Judgement of Baptized Beleevers*. London: 1646.

Crisp, Tobias. *Christ Alone Exalted*. 3 vols. Ed. By Robert Lancaster. London: 1643-1646.

Danvers, Henry. *Theopolis, or the City of God, New Jerusalem*. 1672.

Denne, Henry. *A Conference Between a Sick Man, and a Minister*. 1643.

—. *The Doctrine and Conversation of John Baptist*. 1641.

Dent, Arthur. *The Ruine of Rome:or An Exposition upon the whole Revelation*. 1603.

Durant, John. *The Salvation of the Saints By the Appearances of Christ 1. Now in Heaven, 2. Hereafter from Heaven*. 1653.

Eaton, John. *The Honey-Combe of Free Justification by Christ Alone*. 1642.

Edwards, Thomas. *The First and Second Part of Gangraena: or a Catalogue and Discovery of Many of the Errours, Heresies, Blasphemies, and Pernicious Practices of the Secretaries of This Time*. London: 1646.

Feake, Christopher. *Beam of Light, shining in the midst of much Darkness*. 1659.

Featley, Daniel. *Dippers dipt. Or, The Anabaptists Duck'd and Plung'd Over Head and Eares, at a Disputation in* Southwark. London: 1644/45.

Garner, Robert. *A Treatise on Baptism: Wherein is Clearly Proved the Lawfulness and Usefulness of Believer's Baptism*. 1645.

—. *Mysteries Unvailed, Wherein the Doctrine of Redemption by Christ, flowing from the glorious Grace, and everlasting Love of God, the very fountain of Life and Salvation unto lost Sinners, is handled. The most usuall Scriptures explained, and Reasons answered, which are urged for the universality of the death of Christ for all Persons. Wherein the unsoundness of this opinion, together with divers other conclusions, as depending upon it, are discovered and the Truth unvailed*. Printed ... at the black sprad [*sic*] Eagle, at the west end of *Pauls*. 1646.

[Garner, Robert]. *Redemption By Jesus Christ Unto lost Sinners, Handled. Also, The Scriptures (alleadged by Mr. Den, Tho. Moor, Thomas Lamb, and others, to prove the Universality of the extent of the death of Christ) are freed from the corrupt sense which is put upon them. With an Epistle to the Churches of God in London, and elsewhere, by Hanserd Knollys*. London: 1653

Geree, Stephen. *The Doctrine of the Antinomians by Evidence of Gods Truth, Plainly Confuted*. London: 1644.

Gill, John. *The Cause of God & Truth*. 1855; rpt. Edmonton: Still Waters Revival Books, n.d..

—. *Body of Divinity*. 1839; rpt. Atlanta: Turner Lassetter, 1957.

—. *Sermons and Tracts, by the late Reverend and Learned John Gill, D.D.*. 3 vols. 1814; rpt. Streamwood, IL: Primitive Baptist Press, 1981.

—. *An Exposition of the New Testament*. 3 vols. Philadelphia: Printed by and for William W. Woodward, 1811.

—. *A Collection of Sermons and Tracts: In Two Volumes*. London: 1773.

Goodwin, Thomas. *The Works of Thomas Goodwin*. Vol. III. Edinburgh: James Nichol, 1861.

Guild, William. *The Sealed Book Opened, or A cleer Explication of the Prophecies of the Revelation*. 1656.

Hall, Thomas. *A Practical and Polemical Commentary or Exposition Upon the the Third and Fourth Chapters of the latter Epistle of Saint Paul to Timothy*. 1658.

Harrison, Thomas. *A Sermon on the decease of Mr. Hanserd Knollis minister of the gospel. Preached at Pinners Hall, Octob. 4, 1691*. 1694.

Hicks, William. 'ΑΠΟΚΑΛΥΨΙΣ'ΑΠΟΚΑΛΥΨΕΩΣ *or, the Revelation Revealed: being a Practical Exposition on the Revelation of St. John*. 1659

Hussey, Joseph. *God's Operations of Grace: But no Offers of his Grace*. London: 1707.

Lawrence, Henry. *Of Baptism. The Heads and Order of Such things as are especially insisted on, you will find in the Table of Chapters.* London: 1646.

The Life and Death of Mr. Henry Jessey. 1671.

Lightfoot, John. *The Whole Works of the Rev. John Lightfoot, D.D..* Vol. XIII. Ed. John Rogers Pitman. London: Printed for J.F. Dove, 1824.

Llanvaedonon, William. *A Brief Exposition upon the Second Psalme.* 1655.

Love, Christopher. *Heavens Glory, Hells terror. Or Two treatisees; the one Concerning the glory of the Saints with Jesus Christ as a spur to Duty; the other, Of the Torments of the Damned, as a Preservative against Security.* 1653.

–. *The Penitent Pardoned ... Together with a Discourse Of Christ's Ascension into Heaven, and of his coming again from Heaven. Wherein the opinion of the Chiliasts is considered, and solidly confuted.* 1657.

Ludlow, E. *Memoirs.* 2 vols. Ed. C.H. Firth. Oxford: Oxford University Press, 1894.

Luther, Martin. *Luther's Works.* Eds. Robert C. Schultz. Philadelphia: Fortress Press, 1967.

Mede, Joseph. *The Works of ... Joseph Mede, B.D.* Ed. J. Worthington. 1672.

–. *The Apostacy of the Later Times; ... or, the Gentiles Theology of Deamons Revived in the Latter Times amongst Christians, in Worshipping of Angels, Deifying and Invocating of Saints, Adoring of Reliques, Bowing down to Images and Crosses, &C..* 1641.

–. *The Key of the Revelation searched and demonstrated out of the Naturall and proper Characters of the Visions.* 1643.

Minutes of the Sessions of the Westminster Assembly of Divines. Eds. Alex F. Mitchell & John Struthers. Edinburgh and London: William Blackwood and Sons, 1874.

Napier, John. *A Plaine Discovery of the whole Revelation of Saint John.* 1593.

Owen, John. *The Works of John Owen.* 16 vols. Edited by William H. Goold. Edinburgh: Banner of Truth Trust, 1968.

–. *An Exposition of the Epistle to the Hebrews.* 7 vols. W.H. Goold. Rpt.; Grand Rapids: Baker Book House, 1980.

Pagitt, Ephraim. *Heresiography: or, A Description of the Hereticks and Sectaries sprung up in this latter Age, &c.* 1647.

Perkins, William. *The Workes of That famous and Worthy Minister of Christ in the Universitie of Cambridge, M.W. Perkins.* 3 vols. 1626-31.

Pinnell, Robert. *A word of Prophecy concerning the Parliament, Generall and the Army.* 1648.

Richardson, Samuel. *Saints Desire; or a Cordiall for a Fainting Soule.* 1647.

–. *News from Heaven of a Treaty of Peace, or a Cordiall for a Fainting Heart.* 1643.

–. *Justification by Christ Alone, a Fountain of Life and Comfort.* 1647.

–. *Plain Dealing: or The unvailing of the opposers of the Present Government.* 1656.

–. *Some Brief Considerations on Dr. Featley His Book, entitled, the Dipper Dipt.* 1645.

Rogers, John. *Jegar-Sahadutha: An Oyled Pillar: Set up for Posterity.* 1657.

–. אהל *Ohel or Beth-shemesh. A Tabernacle for the Sun.* 1653.

–. *Sagrir. Or Doomes-day drawing nigh, with Thunder and Lightening to lawyers.* 1653.

Rutherford, Samuel. *A Survey of the Spiritual Antichrist.* !647.

Saltmarsh, John. *An end of one controversie ... an answer to Light for smoke.* 1646.

–. *The Smoke in the temple.* 1646.

–. *Sparkles of Glory, or, Some Beams of the Morning Star.* 1647.

–. *Free Grace: or, the Flowing of Christs Blood freely to Sinners.* 1645.

Seagar, John. *A Discoverie of the World to Come.* 1650.

Sedgwick, John. *Antinomianisme Anatomized. Or, A Glasse for the Lawless: Who deny the Ruling use of the Morall Law unto Christians under the Gospel.* 1643.

Sibbes, Richard. *The Brides Longing for her Bridegroomes second comming.* 1638.

Skepp, John. *Divine Energy or the Efficacious Operations of the Spirit of God upon the Soul of Man, in his Effectual Calling and Conversion, stated, Prov'd and Vindicated Wherein the real Weakness and Insufficiency of Moral Suasion ... for Faith and Conversion to God are fully evinced, Being an Antidote against the Pelagian Plague.* 1722.

Spittlehouse, John. *Certain Queries Propounded To the most serious Consideration of those Persons Now in Power.* 1654.

–. *Rome RUIN'D BY WHITEHALL.* 1649.

–. *An Answer to One Part of the Lord Protector's Speech.* 1654.

Strong, William. *The Vengeance of the Temple.* 1648.

–. *XXXI Select Sermons, Preached on Special Occasions.* 1656.

Sutton, Katherine. *A Christian Womans Experiences of the glorious working of Gods free grace. Published for the edification of others, by Katherine Sutton.* Rotterdam: 1663.

Thurloe, John. *A Collection of the State Papers of John Thurloe, Esq. &c.* 5 vols. Ed. T. Birch. 1742.

Tillam, Thomas. *The Two Witnesses.* 1651.

Tillinghast, John. *Generation-Worke. Or a Brief and Seasonable Word offered to the view and consideration of the Saints and people of God in this Generation, relating to the work of the present age, or generation wee live in.* 1653-54.

–. *Mr. Tillinghasts Eight Last Sermons.* 1655.

–. *Knowledge of the Times; or the resolution of the Question how long it shall be unto the end of Wonders.* 1654.

Towne, Robert. *The Assertion of Grace.* 1644.

–. *A Re-Assertion of Grace.* 1654.

Trapnell, Anna. *The Cry of a Stone.* 1654.

Ussher, James. *A Body of Divinitie, or the Summe and Substance of Christian Religion.* 1645.

Wills, Obed. *Vindiciae Vindiciarium, or a vindication of Infant baptism asserted ... in answer to a Treatise of Baptism lately published by Mr. Henry Danvers. The Bishop of Lincolns apologeticall letter: also, an appeal to the Baptists against Mr. Danvers; for his strange forgeries and misrepresentation of councils and divers authors.* 1675.

Secondary Sources

Ball, Bryan W. *A Great Expectation: Eschatological Thought in English Protestantism to 1660.* Leiden: E.J. Brill, 1975.

Ban, Joseph D. "Were the Earliest English Baptists Anabaptists." In *In the Great Tradition.* Valley Forge: Judson Press, 1982, pp. 91-106.

Battis, Emery. *Saints and Sectaries: Anne Hutchinson and the Antinomian Controversy in the Massachusetts Bay Colony.* Chapel Hill: University of North Carolina Press, 1962.

Beeke, Joel R. *Assurance of Faith: Calvin, English Puritanism, and the Dutch Second Reformation.* New York: Peter Lang Publishing, Inc., 1991.

Belcher, Richard P. and Anthony Mattia. *A Discussion of the Seventeenth Century Particular Baptist Confessions of Faith*. Southbridge,MA: Crowne Publications, Inc., 1990.

Bell, Charles H. *John Wheelwright: His Writings, Including His Fast Day Sermon, 1637 and His Mercurius Americanus, 1645 ... and a Memoir.* New York: Burt Franklin, 1876.

Bolam, C.G., Jeremy Goring, H.L. Short & Roger Thomas. *The English Presbyterians from Elizabethan Puritanism to Modern Unitarianism*. London: George Allen & Unwin Ltd., 1968.

Brachlow, Stephen. *The Communion of Saints: Radical Puritan and Separatist Ecclesiology 1570-1625*. Oxford: Oxford University Press, 1988.

Brackney, William H., ed. *Baptist Life and Thought 1600-1980*. Valley Forge: Judson Press, 1983.

—. *The Baptists*. Westport: Praegar Publishers, 1994.

—. "Knollys, Hanserd." In *The Baptists*. Westport, CT: Greenwood Press, Inc. 1988, pp. 214-215.

Brady, David. "The Number of the Beast in Seventeenth- and Eighteenth-Century England." *The Evangelical Quarterly*, 45 (1973): 219-240.

Brook, Benjamin. *The Lives of the Puritans*. 3 vols. 1813; rpt. Pittsburgh: Soli Deo Gloria, 1994.

Brown, J. Newton. "Hanserd Knollys 1638-1641." In *Annals of the American Baptist Pulpit*. Ed. William B. Sprague. New York: 1860, pp. 1-7.

Brown, Louise Fargo. *Political Activities of the Baptists and Fifth Monarchy Men in England During the Interregnum*. Washington: American Historical Association, 1913.

Brown, Raymond, *The English Baptists of the 18th Century*. London: The Baptist Historical Society, 1984.

Burrage, Champlain. *The Early English Dissenters*. 2 vols. Cambridge: Cambridge University Press, 1912.

—. "The Restoration of Immersion by the English Anabaptists and Baptists (1640-1700)." *The American Journal of Theology*, 16 (1912): 70-89.

—. "The Fifth Monarchy Insurrections," *English Historical Review*, 25 (1910): 722-747.

—, ed. "Early Welsh Baptist Doctrines, set forth in a Manuscript, ascribed to Vavasor Powell." *Transactions of the Baptist Historical Society*, 1 (1908): 3-20.

Capp, Bernard Stuart. *Fifth Monarchy Men: A Study in Seventeenth Century English Millenarianism*. Totowa, New Jersey: Rowman and Littlefield, 1972.

—. "Extreme Millenarianism." In *Puritans, The Millennium & the Future of Israel*. Ed. Peter Toon. Cambridge & London: James Clarke & Co. Ltd., 1970, pp. 66-90.

Carruthers, S.W. *The Everyday Work of the Westminster Assembly.* Philadelphia: The Presbyterian Society of England and America, 1943.

Christianson, Paul. *Reformers and Babylon. English apocalytic visions from the reformation to the eve of the civil war.* Toronto: University of Toronto Press, 1978.

Clements, K.W. "The Significance of 1679." *The Baptist Quarterly*, 28 (1979,80): 2-6.

Clouse, Robert. "The Millennium that Survived the Fifth Monarchy Men." In *Sixteenth Century Essays and Studies 8*, ed. Jerome Friedman. Kirksville, MI: Sixteenth Centuiry Journal Publishers, 1987, pp. 19-29.

Collinson, Patrick. "England and International Calvinism 1558-1640." In *International Calvinism 1541-1715*. Ed. Menna Prestwick. New York: Oxford University Press, 1985, pp. 197-223.

Crosby, Thomas. *The History of the English Baptists, from the Reformation to the Beginning of the Reign of George I*. 4 vols. London: 1738.

Culross, James. *Hanserd Knollys "A Minister and Witness of Jesus Christ 1598-1691*. London: Alexander and Shepheard, 1895.

Daniel, Curt. "Hyper-Calvinism and John Gill." Unpublished Ph.D. Dissertation, University of Edinburgh, 1983.

Davies, Horton. *Worship and Theology in England from Cranmer to Baxter and Fox, 1534-1690*. 1970 & 1975; rpt. Grand Rapids: Eerdmans, 1996.

Dexter, H.M. *Congregationalism of the Last Three Hundred Years*. New York: n.d.

Dowley, T.E. "A London Congregation during the Great Persecution." *The Baptist Quarterly*, 27 (1977,78): 233-239.

Duncan, Pope A. *Hanserd Knollys: Seventeenth-Century Baptist*. Nashville: Broadman Press, 1965.

Estep, William. *The Anabaptist Story*. Nashville: Broadman Press, 1963.

–. "On the Origins of English Baptists." *Baptist History and Heritage*, 22, No. 2 (1987): 19-26.

–. "The Nature and Use of Biblical Authority in Baptist Confessions of Faith, 1610-1963." *Baptist History and Heritage*, 22, No. 4 (1987): 3-16.

Ferguson, Sinclair B. *John Owen on the Christian Life*. 1987; Edinburgh: Banner of Truth Trust, 1995.

Fincham, Kenneth, ed. *The Early Stuart Church*. Stanford: Stanford University Press. 1993.

Fowler, Stanley. "Baptism As a Sacrament in 20th-Century British Baptist Theology." Unpublished Th.D. thesis, Wycliffe College, University of Toronto, 1998.

Froom, L.E. *The Prophetic Faith of our Fathers: The Historical Development of Prophetic Interpretation*. 4 vols. Washington: 1946-64.

Garrett, James Leo, Jr. "Restitution and Dissent Among Early English Baptists: Part II – Representative Late Sixteenth and Early Seventeenth Century Sources." *Baptist Heritage and History*, 13 (1978): 11-27.

George, Timothy. *John Robinson and the English Separatist Tradition*. Macon: Mercer University Press, 1982.

–. "Between Pacifism and Coercion: The English Baptist Doctrine of Religious Toleration." *The Mennonite Quarterly Review*, 58 (1984): 30-49.

–. "Predestination in a Separatist Context: The Case of John Robinson." *The Sixteenth Century Journal*, 15 (1984): 73-85.

–. "The Reformation Roots of the Baptist Tradition." *Review and Expositor*, 86 (1989): 9-22.

George, Timothy and David S. Dockery. *Baptist Theologians*. Nashville: Broadman Press, 1990.

Greaves, Richard & Robert Zaller. *Biographical Dictionary of British Radicals in the Seventeenth Century*. 3 vols. Brighton, England: Harvester Press, 1982-1984.

Greaves, Richard. *Saints and Rebels: Seven Nonconformists in Stuart England*. Macon: Mercer University Press. 1985.

Grislis, Egil. "Calvin's Doctrine of Baptism." *Church History*, 31 (1962): 46-65

Gritz, Paul Linton. "Samuel Richardson and the Religious and Political Controversies Confronting the London Particular Baptists, 1643 to 1658." Unpublished Ph.D. dissertation, Southwestern Baptist Theological Seminary, 1987.

Gura, Philip. *A Glimpse of Sion's Glory: Puritan Radicalism in New England, 1620-1660.* Middletown: Wesleyan University Press, 1984.

Hall, David D., ed. *The Antinomian Controversy, 1636-1638: A Documentary History.* Middletown: Wesleyan University Press, 1968.

Hannen, Robert B. "A Suggested Source of Some Expressions in the Baptist Confession of Faith, London 1644." *The Baptist Quarterly*, 12 (1948): 389-399.

–. "Historical Notes on the Name 'Baptist'." *Foundations*, 8 (1965): 62-71.

Hayden, Roger. "The Particular Baptist Confession 1689 and Baptists Today." *The Baptist Quarterly*, 32 (1987,88): 403-417.

–. *English Baptist History & Heritage.* N.p.: The Baptist Union of Great Britain. 1990.

–, ed. *The Records of a Church of Christ in Bristol 1640-1687.* N.p.: Bristol Record Society, 1974.

Haykin, Michael A.G., ed. *The Life and Thought of John Gill (1697-1771).* Leiden: E.J. Brill, 1997.

–. ed. *The British Particular Baptists 1638-1910.* Springfield, Missouri: Particular Baptist Press, 1998.

–. "The Nature and Purpose of the Lord's Supper According to Early Calvinistic Baptist Thought." Unpublished paper, 1995.

–. "Hanserd Knollys (ca. 1599-1691) on the Gifts of the Spirit." *Westminster Theological Journal*, 54 (1992): 99-113.

–. "The 1689 Confession: A Tercentennial Appreciation." *Reformation Canada*, 13, No. 4 (1990): 13-28.

–. "The 1689 Confession: A Tercentennial Appreciation." *Reformation Canada*, 14, No. 1 (1991): 11-25.

–. "The 1689 Confession: A Tercentennial Appreciation." *Reformation Canada*, 14, No.2 (1991): 10-18.

Hill, Christopher. *The World Turned Upside Down.* 1975; rpt. Harmondsworth: Penguin Books, 1991.

–. *Puritanism and Revolution: Studies in Interpretation of the English Revolution of the 17th Century.* Harmondsworth: Peregrine Books. 1986.

–. "Till the Conversion of the Jews." In *Millenarianism and Messianism in English Literature and Thought 1650-1800.* Ed. Richard H. Popkin. London: E.J. Brill, 1988, pp. 12-36.

–. *The Century of Revolution 1603-1714.* London: Cardinal Books, 1975.

–. *Antichrist in Seventeenth-Century England.* Revised ed. London: Verso, 1990

Holifield, E. Brooks. *The Covenant Sealed: The Development of Puritan Sacramental theology in Old and New England 1570-1720.* New Haven: Yale University Press, 1974.

Horle, Craig W. "Quakers and Baptists 1647-1660." *The Baptist Quarterly*, 26 (1975,76): 344-362.

Hudson, W.S., ed. *Baptist Conceptions of the Church.* Chicago: 1959.

–. "Who were the Baptists?" *The Baptist Quarterly*, 16 (1956): 303-312.

Huehns, Gertrude. *Antinomianism in English History with Special Reference to the Period 1640-1660.* London: Cresset Press, 1951.

Ivimey, Joseph. *A History of the English Baptists.* 4 Vols. London: Printed for B.J. Holdsworth, 1811-1830.

James, Muriel. *Religious Liberty on Trial: Hanserd Knollys—Early Baptist Hero.* Franklin, Tn: Providence House Publishers, 1997.

Jordan, W.K. *The Development of Religious Toleration in England.* 4 vols. London: George Allen & Unwin Ltd., 1932-1940.

Kendall, R.T. *Calvin and English Calvinism to 1649.* New York: Oxford University Press, 1979.

Kevan, Ernest F. *The Grace of Law: A Study in Puritan Theology.* 1963; rpt. Ligonier: Soli Deo Gloria, 1993.

Kingsley, Gordon. "Opposition to Early Baptists (1638-1645)." *Baptist History and Heritage,* 4 (1969): 18-30, 66.

Klaiber, Ashley J. *The Story of the Suffolk Baptists.* London: The Kingsgate Press, 1931.

Land, Richard D. "Doctrinal Controversies of English Particular Baptists (1644-1691) as Illustrated by the career and Writings of Thomas Collier." Unpublished D.Phil. dissertation, Oxford University, 1979.

Langley, Arthur S. "Seventeenth Century Baptist Disputations." *Transactions of the Baptist Historical Society,* 6 (1919): 216-243.

Letham, Robert. "Baptism in the Writings of the Reformers." *The Scottish Bulletin of Evangelical Theology,* 7 (1989): 21-44.

Lindberg, Richard. "The Westminster and Second London Baptist Confessions of Faith: A Historical-Theological Comparison." Unpublished M.Th. Thesis, Westminster Theological Seminary, 1980.

Liu, Tai. *Discord in Zion: The Puritan Divines and the Puritan Revolution 1640-1660.* The Hague: Martinus Nijoff, 1973.

Lumpkin, William L. *Baptist Confessions of Faith.* Philadelphia: The Judson Press, 1959.

–. "The Nature and Authority of Baptist Confessions of Faith." *Review and Expositor,* 76 (1979): 17-28.

MacDonald, M. D. "London Calvinistic Baptists 1689-1727: Tensions within a Dissenting Community under Toleration." Unpublished D. Phil. Dissertation, University of Oxford, 1982.

Manley, Kenneth Ross. "Origins of the Baptists: The Case for Development from Puritanism-Separatism." *Baptist History and Heritage,* 22, No. 4 (1987): 34-46.

Mathews, A. G. *Calamy Revised.* Oxford: 1934.

Mayor, S.H. "James II and the Dissenters." *The Baptist Quarterly,* 34 (1991): 180-190.

McBeth, H. Leon. *The Baptist Heritage.* Nashville: Broadman Press, 1987.

–. *A Sourcebook for Baptist Heritage.* Nashville: Roadman Press, 1990

–. *English Baptist Literature on Religious Liberty to 1689.* Th.D. Dissertation, Southwestern Baptist Theological Seminary, 1961; rpt. New York: Arno Press, 1980.

McGlothlin, W.J. "Dr. Daniel Featley and the First Calvinistic Baptist Confession." *The Review and Expositor,* 6 (1909): 579-589.

–. *Baptist Confessions of Faith.* London: Baptist Historical Society, 1911.

–. "Sources of the First Calvinistic Baptist Confession of Faith." *The Review and Expositor,* 13 (1916): 500-507.

McGregor, J.F. & B. Reay, eds. *Radical Religion in the English Revolution*. 1984; rpt. Oxford: Oxford University Press, 1988.

McLachlan, H. John. *Socinianism in Seventeenth-Century England*. London: Oxford University Press, 1951.

Murray, Iain H., ed. *The Reformation of the Church: A Collection of Reformed and Puritan Documents of Church Issues*. Edinburgh: Banner of Truth Trust, 1965.

–. *Spurgeon vs. Hyper-Calvinism: The Battle for Gospel Preaching*. Edinburgh: The Banner of Truth Trust, 1995.

–. *Antinomianism: New England's First Controversy*. Edinburgh: The Banner of Truth Trust Magazine, 1978.

Naylor, Peter. *Picking up a Pin for the Lord: English Particular Baptists from 1688 to the Early Nineteenth Century*. London: Grace Publications Trust, 1992.

Neal, Daniel. *The History of the Puritans; or, Protestant Nonconformists; from the Reformation in 1517 to The Revolution in 1688*. 5 vols. London: 1822.

Nelson, Stanley A. "Reflecting on Baptist Origins: The London Confession of Faith of 1644." *Baptist History and Heritage*, 29, No. 2 (1994): 33-46.

Nettles, Thomas J. *By His Grace and for His Glory: A Historical, Theological and Practical Study of the Doctrines of Grace in Baptist Life*. Grand Rapids: Baker Book House, 1986.

Novak, Michael J. '"Thy Will Be Done' The Theology of the English Particular Baptists, 1638-1660." Unpublished Ph.D. dissertation, Harvard University, 1979.

Nuttall, Geoffrey F. "Calvinism in Free Church History." *The Baptist Quarterly*, 22 (1967-68): 418-428.

–. *Visible Saints: The Congregational Way 1640-1660*. Oxford: Basil Blackwell, 1957.

–. "The Baptist Western Association 1653-1658." *Journal of Ecclesiatical History*, 11 (1960): 213-218.

–. "Northamptonshire and the Modern Question: A Turning-Point in Eighteenth-Century Dissent," *Journal of Theological Studies*, N.S., 16 (1965): 101-123.

Oliver, Robert. "Baptist Confession Making 1644 and 1689." Paper from the Strict Baptist Historical Society, March, 1989.

Parratt, J.K. "An Early Baptist on the Laying on of Hands." *The Baptist Quarterly*, 21 (1965,66): 325-327, 320.

Pater, Calvin. *Karlstadt as the Father of the Baptist Movements: The Emergence of Lay Protestantism*. Toronto: University of Toronto Press, 1984.

Patterson, W. Morgan. "The Lord's Supper in Baptist History." *Review and Expositor*, 66 (1969): 25-34.

Paul, Robert S. *The Assembly of the Lord*. Edinburgh: T.& T. Clark, 1985.

Payne, Ernest A. "Who Were the Baptists?" *The Baptist Quarterly*, 26 (1956): 339-342.

–. "Contacts Between Mennonites and Baptists." *Foundations*, 4 (1961): 39-55.

–. "More about the Sabbatarian Baptists." *The Baptist Quarterly*, 14 (1951,52): 161-166.

–. *The Fellowship of Believers*. 2nd ed. London: 1952.

Pennington, D.H. *Seventeenth Century Europe*. Singapore: Longman. 1970.

Pettit, Norman. *The Heart Prepared: Grace and Conversion in Puritan Spiritual Life*. 2nd ed. Middletown: Wesleyan University Press, 1989.

Poe, Harry L. "John Bunyan's Controversy with the Baptists." *Baptist History and Heritage*, 23, No. 2 (1988): 25-35.

Poole, Matthew. *A Commentary on the Holy Bible*, 3 vols. N.d.; rpt. McLean, VA: MacDonald Publ. Co., n.d.

Powicke, Fred T. "Richard Baxter's Relation to the Baptists and his Proposed Terms of Communion." *Transactions of the Baptist Historical Society*, 6 (1919): 193-215.

Roberts, R. Philip. *Continuity and Change: London Calvinistic Baptists and the Evangelical Revival 1760-1820.* Wheaton, IL: Richard Owen Roberts, Publishers, 1989.

Rogers, P.G. *The Fifth Monarchy Men.* London: Oxford University Press, 1966.

Schaff, Philip. *The Creeds of Christendom.* 3 vols. 1931; rpt. Grand Rapids: Baker Book House, 1990.

Schuldiner, Michael. *Gifts and Works: The Post-Conversion Paradigm and Spiritual Controversy in Seventeenth-Century Massachusetts.* Macon: Mercer University Press, 1991.

Selement, George. "The Covenant Theology of English Separatism and the Separation of Church and State." *Journal of American Academy of Religion*, 46 (1973): 66-74.

Solt, Leo F. "John Saltmarsh: New Model Army Chaplain." *Journal of Ecclesiastical History*, 2 (1951): 69-80.

–. *Saints in Arms: Puritanism and Democracy in Cromwell's Army.* London: Oxford University Press. 1959.

Sparkes, Douglas C. "The Test Act of 1673 and its aftermath." *The Baptist Quarterly*, 25 (1973,74): 74-85.

Sprunger, Keith L. "English Puritans and Anabaptists in Early Seventeenth-Century Amsterdam." *The Mennonite Quarterly Review*, 46 (1972): 113-128.

Starr, C.E. *A Baptist Bibliography.* 25 vols. Philadelphia and Rochester: 1947-1976.

Stassen, Glen H. "Anabaptist Influence in the Origin of The Particular Baptists." *The Mennonite Quarterly Review*, 36 (1962): 322-348.

–. "Opening Menno Simons's *Foundation Book* and Finding the Father of Baptist Origins Alongside the Mother—Calvinist Congregationalism." *Baptist History and Heritage*, 33, No. 1 (1998): 34-44.

–. "Revisioning Baptist Identity by Naming Our Origin and Character Rightly." *Baptist History and Heritage*, 33, No. 1 (1998): 45-54.

Stearns, Raymond P. *The Strenuous Puritan: Hugh Peter 1598-1660.* Urbana: University of Illinois Press. 1954.

Stephen, Leslie & Sidney Lee, eds. *The Dictionary of National Biography*, 22 vols. London: Oxford University Press. 1882-1938.

Stoever, William, K.B. *'A Faire and Easie Way to Heaven' Covenant Theology and Antinomianism in Early Massachusetts.* Middletown, CT: Weselyan University Press, 1978.

Tolmie, Murray. "General and Particular Baptists in the Puritan Revolution." Unpublished Ph.D. dissertation, Harvard University, 1960.

–. *The Triumph of the Saints.* Cambridge: Cambridge University Press, 1977.

Toon, Peter, ed. *Puritans, The Millennium & the Future of Israel.* Cambridge & London: James Clarke & Co. Ltd., 1970.

–. *Puritans and Calvinism.* Swengal, PA: Reiner Publications, 1973.

–. *The Emergence of Hyper-Calvinism in English Non-Conformity 1689-1765.* London: The Olive Tree, 1967.

Torbet, Robert G. *A History of the Baptists.* Philadelphia: The Judson Press, 1955.

Turretin, Francis. *Institutes of Elenctic Theology.* 3 vols. Ed. James T. Dennison, Jr. Phillipsburg: P & R Publishing, 1992.

Tyacke, Nicholas. *Anti-Calvinists: The Rise of English Arminianism, c. 1590-1640.* Oxford: Oxford University Press, 1987.

Underhill, E.B., ed. *Confessions of Faith, and other Public Documents ... of the Baptist Churches of England in the 17th Century.* London: Printed for the Hanserd Knollys Society by Haddon, Brothers, and Co., 1854.

Underwood, A.C. *A History of the English Baptists.* London: Carey Kingsgate Press, 1947.

Vaughn, J. Barry. "Public Worship and Practical Theology in the Work of Benjamin Keach (1640-1704)." Unpublished Ph.D. thesis, University of St. Andrews, 1989.

Venn, John & J.A. Venn. *Alumni Cantabrigienses. Part 1 from the earliest times to 1751.* 4 vols. Cambridge: 1922.

Von Rohr, John. "*Extra Ecclesiam nulla Salus*: An Early Congregational Version." *Church History*, 36 (1967): 107-121.

–. *Covenant of Grace in Puritan Thought.* Atlanta: Scholars Press, 1986.

Walker, David. "Thomas Goodwin and the Debate on Church Government." *Journal of Ecclesiastical History*, 34 (1983): 85- 99.

Walker, Michael J. "Baptist Theology of Infancy." *The Baptist Quarterly*, 21 (1965,66): 251-262.

Walker, Williston. *The Creeds and Platforms of Congregationalism.* New York: 1893.

Wallace, Dewey. *Puritans and Predestination.* Chapel Hill: University of North Carolina Press, 1982.

Wamble, Hugh. "Inter-relations of Seventeenth Century English Baptists." *Review and Expositor*, 54 (1957): 407-425.

–. "Early English Baptist Sectarianism." *Review and Expositor*, 55 (1958): 59-69.

–. "The Beginning of Associationalism Among English Baptists." *Review and Expositor*, 54 (1957): 545-559.

Watts. Michael R. *The Dissenters.* Vol. I. Oxford: Clarendon Press, 1978.

Westminster Confession of Faith. Inverness: The Publications Committee of the Free Presbyterian Church of Scotland, 1976.

White, B.R., ed. *Association Records of the Particular Baptists of England, Wales and Ireland to 1660.* London: The Baptist Historical Society, n.d.

–. *Hanserd Knollys and Radical Dissent in the Seventeenth Century.* London: Dr. Williams's Trust, 1977.

–. "The English Particular Baptists and the Great Rebellion." *Baptist History and Heritage*, 9, No. 1 (1974): 16-29.

–. "The Origins and Convictions of the First Calvinistic Baptists." *Baptist History and Heritage*, 25, No. 4 (1990): 39-47.

–. "Organization of the Particular Baptists, 1644-1660." *Journal of Ecclesiastical History*, 17 (1966): 209-226.

–. *The English Baptists of the Seventeenth Century.* London: Baptist Historical Society, 1983.

–. "John Pendavres, the Calvinistic Baptists and the Fifth Monarchy." *The Baptist Quarterly*, 25 (1974): 251-71.

–. "The Doctrine of the Church in the Particular Baptist Confession of 1644." *Journal of Theological Studies*, N.S. 19 (1968): 570-90.

–. "The London Calvinistic Baptist Leadership 1644-1660." *The Baptist Quarterly*, 32 (1987,88): s34-45.

–. "Thomas Collier and Gangraena Edwards." *The Baptist Quarterly*, 24 (1971,72): 99-110.

–. *The English Separatist Tradition*. Oxford: Oxford University Press, 1971.

–. "Who Really Wrote the 'Kiffin Manuscript'?" *Baptist History and Heritage*, 1, No. 3 (1966): 3-10,14.

–. "The Frontiers of Fellowship between English Baptists, 1609-1660." *Foundations*, 11 (1968): 244-256.

–. "How did William Kiffin join the Baptists." *The Baptist Quarterly*, 23 (1970): 201-207.

–. "Henry Jessey in the Great Rebellion." In *Reformation Conformity and Dissent*. Ed. R. Buick Knox. London:Epworth Press, 1977, pp. 132-153.

–. "Baptist Beginnings and the Kiffin Manuscript." *Baptist History and Heritage*, 2 , No. 1 (1967): 27-39.

–. "Early Baptist Arguments for Religious Freedom: Their Overlooked Agenda." *Baptist History and Heritage*, 24, No. 4 (1989): 3-10.

–. "Samuel Eaton (d.1639) Particular Baptist Pioneer." *The Baptist Quarterly*, 24 (1971,72): 10-21.

Whiting, C. *Studies in English Puritanism 1660-1688*. New York & Toronto: The MacMillan Co., 1931.

Whitley, W.T., ed. *A Baptist Bibliography*. London: The Kingsgate Press, 1916.

–. *A History of British Baptists*. London: Charles Griffin and Company, 1923

–. "The Seven Churches of London." *The Review and Expositor*, 7 (1910): 384-413.

–. *The Baptists of London: 1612-1928*. London: The Kingsgate Press, 1928.

–. "Baptist Meetings in the City of London." *Transactions of the Baptist Historical Society*, 5 (1916): 74-82.

–. "Debate on Infant Baptism, 1643." *Transactions of the Baptist Historical Society*, 1 (1910): 237-245.

–. "Records of the Jacob-Lathrop-Jessey Church 1616-1641." *Transactions of the Baptist Historical Society*, 1 (1910): 203-225.

–. "The Jacob-Jessey Church, 1616-1678." *Transactions of the Baptist Historical Society*, 1 (1910): 246-256.

–. "Militant Baptists 1660-1672." *Transactions of the Baptist Historical Society*, 1 (1909): 148-155.

–. "Baptist Churches till 1660." *Transactions of the Baptist Historical Society*, 2 (1911): 236-254.

–. "An Index to Notable Baptists, whose careers began within the British Empire before 1850." *Transactions of the Baptist Historical Society*, 7 (1921): 182-239.

–. "The Relation of Baptists to the Ejectment." In *The Enactment of 1662 and the Free churches*. London: National Council of Evangelical Free Churches, n.d., pp. 75-96.

–. "Rise of the Particular Baptists in London, 1633-1644." *Transactions of the Baptist Historical Society*, 1 (1910): 226-236.

–. "John Tombes as a Correspondent." *Transactions of the Baptist Historical Society*, 7 (1920): 13-18.

–. "Dissent in Worcestershire during the Seventeenth Century." Transactions *of the Baptist Historical Society*, 7 (1920): 1-12.

Williams, George H. *The Radical Reformation*. Philadelphia: The Westminster Press, 1962.

Wilson, John F. "Another look at John Canne." *Church History*, 33 (1964): 34-48.

–. *Pulpit in Parliament: Puritanism during the English Civil Wars 1640-1648*. Princeton: Princeton University Press. 1969.

Winthrop, John. *Winthrop's Journal: "History of New England."* 2 vols. Ed. James Kendall Hosmer. New York: Charles Scribner's Sons, 1908.

Winter, E.P. "The Lord's Supper." *The Baptist Quarterly*, 17 (1957,58): 272-281.

–. "Calvinist and Zwinglian Views of the Lord's Supper among the Baptists of the Seventeenth Century." *The Baptist Quarterly*, 15 (1953,54): 323-329.

Woodhouse, A.S.P., ed. *Puritanism and Liberty: Being the Army Debates (1647-49) from the Clarke Manuscripts*. 1974; rpt. London and Rutland: J.M. Dent & Sons Ltd., 1992.

Woolrych, Austin. *England Without a King 1649-1660*. London: Metheun & Co. 1983.

Yarbrough, Sladen A. "The Origins of Baptist Associations Among English Particular Baptists." *Baptist History and Heritage*, 23, No. 2 (1988): 14-25.

INDICES

INDEX OF PERSONS

Abbot, John   18, 97, 98n
Adams, Richard   77n
Adams, Thomas   253, 263, 274
Ainsworth, Henry   31
Alaric   266
Alcaricus   340
Alexander, Sir William   253
Allen, William   288n, 290
Alsted, Johann   243, 267, 277, 285
Ames, William   24n, 89, 138, 141, 148, 320n
Amyraut, M.   47n, 160
Aquinas   160
Arcadius, Emperor   267, 339
Archer, Henry   285
Archer, John   272n, 277, 282
Armacanus   215
Arminius, James   138, 160
Arrowsmith, John   55n, 56
Ash, John   171n
Aspinwall, Thomas   288, 297, 300
Athanasius   160, 336
Augustine   160, 336
Axtell, Lady   52n

Baillie, Robert   14, 39n, 80, 99, 194-196, 199-200, 202-211, 213, 214n
Bale, John   262
Ball, Bryan   292n, 294n, 304
Ball, John   100
Ban, Joseph   334n
Barber, Mr.   201
Barebone, Praise-God   35
Barrow, Henry   31, 319, 321
Bastwick, John   61n, 65, 224n, 225, 230n
Batten(Batte), John   325
Baxter, Richard   47n, 83, 99n, 101-

102, 150, 158, 253, 255
Beasts, Paul   210
Beddome, Benjamin   171n
Bedford, Thomas   101
Beeke, Joel   151-152
Belcher, John   291
Belcher, Mr.   48n
Belknap, Dr.   64n
Bennet, Robert   68n
Bentley, William   163
Berlinas, Christian Ravy   66n
Bernard, Richard   257, 258n
Beza, Theodore   138-140, 148, 152, 160
Blacklock, Mr.   36, 325
Blackwood, Christopher   40n, 41n, 318n
Blake, Thomas   200
Blunt, Richard   35-36, 324-325, 327
Bond, John   55n
Brachlow, Stephen   319-321, 331
Bradbury, Thomas   170
Bradford, John   55n, 252
Braggs, Mr.   70n
Brearley, Roger   97
Bridge, William   279-280
Bridges, Francis   98
Brightman, Thomas   243, 257-261, 262n, 266, 269-270, 271n, 273-274, 277, 282, 284, 303
Brine, John   14, 133-134, 158, 163, 167-172, 174-177, 179-180, 182-184, 187-192
Broughton, Hugh   276
Brown, J. Newton   64n
Brown, Louise Fargo   43n, 244n
Browne, Robert   30, 54n, 207, 319, 321-322, 330

Bryan, John   66n
Bucer, Martin   138
Bulkeley, Peter   86n, 92n
Bullinger, Heinrich   24n, 138, 262
Bunyan, John   17
Burdet, Captain   62n
Burgess, Anthony   63n, 82, 100
Burrage, Champlin   325n
Burroughs, Jeremiah   71n
Burton, Henry   19, 61n

Callamy, Edmund   63n, 65, 82-83, 199, 215, 253n
Calvin, John   14, 24, 89, 118, 134, 138-142, 145, 150-153, 160, 172, 176-177, 182, 186, 189, 252n, 326, 329-330
Calvert, Giles   69n
Calvert, Sir George   18
Canne, John   246, 293, 296-297, 303
Capp, Bernard   286n, 287, 289n, 290n, 291
Carew, John   289, 291
Carleton, Guy   50n
Cartwright, Thomas   320, 322, 331
Cary, Mary   297, 299
Chamberlen, Peter   287-288
Charles I   18-21, 286, 296-297
Charles II   2, 21-23, 43-44, 50n, 54n, 69, 290
Charles V   248, 298
Chauncey, Isaac   159
Cheare, Abraham   50n, 68n
Cheney, John   58, 72n
Christianson, Paul   268n
Clarendon, Lord   50n
Clayton, Thomas   65n
Clouse, Robert   285
Cole, Thomas   158
Collier, Thomas   12, 41n, 43, 47n, 65n, 80n, 157, 274, 318n
Collins, Hercules   48n, 77n
Collins, William   74, 77n, 182n
Constantine   261, 266, 335-336, 339
Cotton, John   81, 85-96, 99n, 116, 258, 262, 269, 271n, 274-275, 277, 282

Courtney, Hugh   289
Cox, Benjamin   41n, 43, 65, 66, 200, 215, 217, 318n
Coxe, Nehemiah   47n, 182n
Crandon, John   47n
Crisp, Samuel   76, 83-84, 102-103, 158-159
Crisp, Tobias   38n, 76, 83, 99-100, 102-103, 105-106, 109-112, 114n, 158, 168-169
Cromwell, Henry   38n
Cromwell, Oliver   21-22, 40, 44n, 67n, 68-69, 247, 286-290, 297, 300n
Cromwell, Richard   21, 69, 290
Crosby, Thomas   4-5, 60n, 201n
Crossley, David   171n
Culross, James   3, 7-8, 133, 137, 192

Daniel   266, 268, 274, 288, 292, 297, 298n, 304
Daniel, Curt   133, 163n,171n
Danvers, Henry   45, 47n, 49, 73, 300
Davies, Horton   321-322
Davis, John   167
Davis, Richard   159, 163n, 167-169, 173n
Defoe, Daniel   17
Delaune, Thomas   73
Dell, William   83, 100-101, 104, 110n, 113
Denne, Henry   38n, 99-100, 103n, 104-105, 107
Dent, Arthur   256-260, 269-270, 271n, 272-273, 276, 282, 284
Dewit, Prince   71n
Dickens, A.G.   30n
Diocletian   336, 339
Domitan   258, 335
Donne, John   253
Dove, Dr.   57
Drapes, Edward   318n
Duppa, Bishop Brian   253n
Dupper, Mr.   33, 34
Duncan, Pope   8-9
Durant, John   253n, 277, 280n
Dyke, Daniel   71, 73-74, 182n

Dyke, Jeremiah   19

Eaton, John   38n, 83, 96-100, 103-105, 108-111, 113
Eaton, Samuel   33-35
Edwards, Thomas   1, 14, 47n, 63n, 83, 101, 105, 132, 194-195, 198, 201-205, 207n, 213n
Eliot, John   86n
Elizabeth I   17, 259
Elton, Edward   100
Estep, William   28, 334n
Etsall, John   97-98
Eudoxias, Empress   267
Evans, Caleb   171n
Evans, Hugh   171n
Everard, John   97n
Ewins, Thomas   50n
Eyre, William   47n

Feake, Christopher   286, 288, 301
Featley, Daniel   14, 66, 80n, 195-197, 199, 202-206, 208-210, 213-215, 317
Ferman, Henry   98
Finch, Sir Henry   70n, 253, 272n, 274-275
Flavell, John   84, 103
Forty, Henry   45n, 73, 182n
Fowler, Stanley   329
Fownes, Pastor   51n
Foxe, John   243, 262n, 298, 320
Francis, B.   171n
Fuller, Andrew   158n, 170

Garner, Robert   66n, 121n, 157, 318n, 329
Gataker, Thomas   100
Gell, Robert   253n
Gerhard, Johannes   262
Gifford, Jr., Andrew   171n
Gifford, Sr., Andrew   48n, 73, 135
Gill, John   14, 133-134, 158, 163, 167-174, 176-179, 182-183, 186-187, 189-190, 192
Goodwin, John   55n, 56, 68, 71n, 139, 260, 261n, 262n, 266-267,

268n, 269, 271n, 273, 275-277, 282, 284, 303
Gosnold, John   73
Goths   266-267, 336
Greenwood, John   31, 319
Gregorius   336
Grew, Obadiah   66n
Griffin, Mr.   201
Gritz, Paul   11-12, 106, 117, 132, 288n
Groton, Samuel   99n
Guild, William   269-270, 277
Gunter, Peter   96-97
Gura, Philip   84, 132, 247

Haigh, Christopher   30n
Hall, Edmund   267, 277
Hall, Thomas   243n, 252, 256, 263-264, 277
Hammon, George   277
Hanserd, Jr., Richard   55n
Hardcastle, Thomas   50n, 52n
Harley, Sir Robert   19
Harris, John   74
Harrison, Edward   41n, 44, 71, 246n
Harrison, Robert   330
Harrison, Thomas   74, 77-78, 288-292
Hartlib, Samuel   253
Harvey, Mrs. Jane   75n
Haughton, Edward   272, 277
Hawkes, R.M.   152n
Hayden, Roger   52n
Haykin, Michael   3, 133, 135, 193
Hellier, John   50n
Helwys, Thomas   29, 31-32, 32n, 34, 318n
Henry IV   248, 299
Hewling, Benjamin   45
Hewling, William   45
Hicks, Thomas   74n, 182n
Hicks, William   277-280
Hieronymus   336
Hilarius   336
Hill, Christopher   17, 45n, 268n, 274n, 276, 283n
Hobson, Paul   1, 38n, 39n, 41n, 44,

80n, 83, 100-101, 103n, 104, 198, 200-201, 205n, 207n, 213, 318n
Hoe, Matthias   259, 261n
Holmes, Abraham   45
Homes, Nathaniel   258n, 267, 272n, 277-278, 285n, 303
Honorius   339
Hooker   17
Hopgood, Thomas   182n
Horst, Irvin B.   334n
How, Samuel   59, 81, 116, 324, 330
Howard, Henry   18
Howard, Luke   39n
Howe, John   84, 102
Hudson, Winthrop   28, 334n
Huehns, Gertrude   99, 101
Huit, Ephraim   267, 272n, 274-275
Hussey, Joseph   13, 133, 160-163, 167-170
Hutchinson, Anne   58n, 61, 81-82, 85-96, 99n, 116, 131
Hutchinson, Edward   86n
Hutchinson, Mary   86n
Hutchinson, William   86n
Hycrigg, James   182n
Hyde, Edward   74n

Ivimey, Joseph   3, 5-7, 74n, 133, 136, 192, 246

Jacob, Henry   32, 63n, 319-321, 324, 331
James I   17-19, 297
James II   22-23, 45, 51
James, Muriel   10n, 54n, 57n, 60n, 65n, 116n
James, William   293
Jeffreys, Chief Justice   45
Jessey, Henry   33, 33n, 35, 35n, 39n, 40n, 50n, 63-64, 68, 70, 243, 246-247, 288-289, 318n, 324-325, 330
Jews   250-251, 252n, 264-265, 274-276, 297-298, 312, 337, 341
John, Bishop of Constantinople   336
John of Leyden   131, 214
Johnson, Francis   31, 32n, 319, 321, 330

Jones, James   182n
Joye, George   252
Julian the Apostate   266

Kaye, William   44
Keach, Benjamin   12, 45n, 47n, 48n, 49n, 60n, 72, 75n, 240n
Kiffin, William   6, 13n, 29, 35, 38n, 39n, 40n, 43n, 45, 47n, 48n, 52n, 64-65, 57, 68n, 71-75, 77n, 182n, 197-198, 200, 207n-209, 213, 215, 217, 247, 318n, 326-327, 330
Kilcop, Thomas   41n, 318n
King, Daniel   42n, 43, 318n
Kingsley, Gordon   203n
Kliever, Lonnie   28
Knollys, Anne (Cheney)   58, 64, 72
Knollys, Cheney   65n
Knollys, Richard   54-55
Knutton, Immanuel   195

Lambe, Thomas   157
Lancaster, Robert   99-100
Land, Richard   11-12
Lane, Richard   98
Larke, Sampson   45
Larkham, Thomas   62n, 64n
Lathrop, John   33, 324
Latimer, Hugh   252
Laud, William   19-20, 61, 194
Laurence, Henry   318n, 329
Legge, Colonel   70n
Ley, Mr.   63n, 82
Lightfoot, John   99, 202n, 262n
Lilburne, John   67n
Lipscomb, G.   55n
Love, Christopher   253-254, 264, 276
Ludlow, E.   292
Lukar, Marke   34, 35n
Luther   160, 208, 252n, 262, 272

MacDonald, Murdina   163, 167n
MacGregor, J.F.   38
Magyars   272
Manley, K.R.   326n, 331
Marlowe, Isaac   48n, 76
Marshall, Stephen   101, 200

Martyr, Peter (Vermigli) 117, 138
Mather, Cotton 6
Mather, Nathaniel 158
Maton, Robert 253n, 274, 285
Matthew, Toby 18
Maurice, Matthias 169-170, 174, 179
McBeth, Leon 11, 28n, 34, 40, 247, 330
McLachlan, H. John 39n
McLoughlin, William 84n
Mede, Joseph 243, 253n, 257, 258n, 259-262, 266-267, 270, 272-274, 278, 282, 284-285, 303, 340n
Melanchthon, Philip 252n
Michael 260-261
Miles, John 41n, 43-44
Miller, Perry 94n
Milton, John 253
Mohammed 272
Monck, General 21, 290
Monmouth, Duke of 23, 45, 291
Montagu, Richard 19
Moore, John 168
Moore, Thomas 157
More, Henry 285n
More, John 297
Morrice, Roger 74n
Morton, Joseph 182n
Mudford, Henry 98
Munter, Jan 31
Muntzer 208
Murray, Iain 96n
Murton, John 34n

Napier, John 243, 253, 257, 258n, 259, 266-267, 269, 271n, 284, 303
Neal, Daniel 4
Nelson, Robert 103
Nelson, Stanley 320n, 326n
Nestorius 336
Novak, Michael 11-12, 221, 318n, 322-323, 327-329, 331-333, 334n

Oates, Titus 23
Oecolampadius 138
Olevanius 141

Olive, Ralph 50n
Overton, Robert 288n, 290-291
Owen, John 14, 47n, 133, 139, 141-143, 146, 149-150, 152, 192, 255, 322

Packer, J.I. 47n
Pagitt, Ephraim 1, 14, 101, 105, 110, 113, 195-196, 199, 202-205, 208, 214n
Pareus, David 259, 261n, 269, 272n, 276, 282
Parker, Thomas 267, 272n
Partridge, Susannah 72
Pater, Calvin 28-29, 334n
Patience, Thomas 41n, 71, 199n, 201, 318n
Payne, Ernest 28, 321, 325n
Pendaveres(Pendarves), John 41n, 243, 289, 318n
Penn, William 74n
Perkins, William 24n, 138-141, 152-153, 252, 264
Peter, Hugh 247
Petitt, Norman 153
Petrie, Alexander 285n
Phocas, Emperor 262, 269, 271, 340
Pinnell, Henry 106
Pompey 262
Poole, Matthew 142
Pope Alexander III 248n, 338
Pope Boniface III 340
Pope Innocent 267
Pope Sixtus III 267
Portman, John 289n, 291
Powell, Vavasor 44, 72, 243, 288, 289n, 290-291
Preston, John 18
Pretty, Samuel 97-98
Proud, Thomas 41n
Prynne, William 61n
Purnell, Robert 253n, 318n

Randall, Giles 100
Rich, Nathaniel 288n, 289-291
Richardson, Samuel 12, 41n, 80n, 106, 108, 110, 200, 204-205, 288,

289n, 317, 318n

Ritor, Andrew   318n

Robinson, John   31, 317, 319, 321, 330

Rogers, John   288, 290, 293, 297, 299, 300n

Rogers, Thomas   96n, 252

Rohr, John von   154, 319

Rous, Francis   19

Rumbold, Richard   45

Russell, John   74

Rutherford, Samuel   100-101, 109-110, 140

Saltmarsh, John   9, 38n, 66, 83, 100, 101, 104, 107-108, 110n, 111, 113n

Sandys, Edwin   55n, 252

Seagar, John   253n, 254-255

Seaman, Mr.   63n, 82

Sedgwick, John   100, 103n, 112

Selement, George   331

Servetus   210

Seymour, Edward   133

Shepard, Thomas   86n, 195

Sherwin, William   261n, 285n

Sibbes, Richard   55n, 57, 151n, 253, 256, 279-280, 324

Simons, Menno   326-327

Simpson, John   70, 80n, 83, 100, 243, 246, 288-289, 300

Skepp, John   2-3, 6-7, 133, 135-137, 157, 163-168, 182n, 192

Skinner, John   44

Smyth, John   29, 31-32, 317

Snelling, Robert   182n

Socinus   160

Solt, Leo   100n

Spilsbury, John   29, 34, 34n, 39n, 41n, 68, 200-201, 318n, 325

Spittlehouse, John   287-288, 294

Spurgeon, C.H.   137

Spurstow, William   55n, 63n, 82

Stassen, Glen   28, 326, 334n

Steed, Robert   76n

Stennet, Joseph   77n

Stephens, Nathaniel   243n, 262, 272n, 277

Stinton, Benjamin   167

Stockell, Samuel   163

Stoever, William   93-94

Storre, Marie   86n

Strange, Nathaniel   43, 291

Strong, William   55, 264, 270, 274

Stuart, Mary   23, 46n, 73

Sutcliffe, Christobel   55n

Sutton, Katherine   76

Symmes, Zachariah   86n

Taylor, Abraham   170

Taylor, Thomas   70n, 100, 111

Theodosis, Emperor   267, 339

Thomas, J   171n

Tiberius   339

Tillam, Thomas   39n, 41n, 299, 318n

Tillinghast, John   260, 261n, 277, 292, 294, 296, 303n, 304

Tipson, Baird   153

Tolmie, Murray   11, 34, 285n, 318-319, 327, 332

Tombes, John   40n, 44, 47, 200

Toon, Peter   133-134, 148, 159, 164-165, 274n

Torbet, Robert   28

Towne, Robert   100, 104, 109, 111, 113n

Townes, Thomas   98

Traill, Robert   47n

Trapnel, Anna   246, 288

Traske, John   97

Travers, Walter   320

Tuckney, Mr.   63n, 82

Tudor, Mary   30, 298, 338

Turks   250, 259, 263, 268, 272-273, 312, 341

Twisse, William   139n, 140

Underhill, John   62n, 82

Underwood, A.C.   14, 247

Ussher, James   270, 274

Valentinian   266

Vandals   259n, 336

Vane, Jr., Henry   87

Vaughn, Barry   11-12, 48n

Venner, Thomas   43, 69, 244, 246,
   290-291, 293, 301, 304
Vines, Mr.   63n, 82

Walker, Mr.   63n, 82
Wallace, Dewey   104, 148
Wallin, Edward   164
Wallis, Thomas   168
Walter, David   70n
Wamble, Hugh   28, 334n
Ward, Samuel   63n, 82, 86n
Warner, James   75n
Watts, Michael   334n
Wayman, Lewis   169
Weld, Thomas   86n
Whally, E.   67n
Wheelwright, John   58-61, 81-82, 85-
   96, 116, 131, 324, 330
White, B.R.   10-11, 42, 246, 318-320,
   322, 326n, 327, 333-334

Whitehead, G.   74n
Whitley, W.T.   11, 14, 34n, 170n,
   247
William of Orange   23, 45, 46n, 73
Williams, Daniel   158-159
Williams, John   58n
Williams, Roger   330
Willoughby, Lord   69
Wills, Obediah   73
Wilson, John   87
Winthrop, John   8, 62n, 81, 86-89,
   91, 131-132
Wise, Laurence   182n
Wither, John   253

Yarborough, Slayden   319

Zanchius, Jerome   105n, 140
Zwingli, Ulrich   24n, 138, 329

INDEX OF PLACES

Abergavenny 41n
Abingdon 41, 42n
Acton 47n
Alcaster 42n
Alderman-bury 217
Alford 86n
All Hallows the Great 246, 286
Amsterdam 31, 318
Anchor Lane 70n
Anderby 61n
Armageddon 250, 260, 263, 273, 275, 312, 340-341
Ashford 49n

Babylon 250, 260, 268-271, 283n, 293, 298, 335, 338, 340-341
Barnoldswick 170n
Belgrade 272
Bennington 58, 86n
Bilsby 58n
Bishopgate 71
Boston 52n, 58n, 61, 64n, 82, 85-88
Bourton-on-the-Water 42n
Breconshire 67n
Bristol 48n, 50n, 51n, 135
Britain 17, 43, 50, 287
Broadmead 50n
Broken Wharf 76n
Bunhill Fields 72n, 77

Cambridge 31, 55-57, 58n, 85, 86n, 163, 167, 171
Cambridgeshire 163
Canterbury 18, 61, 283n
Carmarthen 41n
Carolina 52n
Cawkwell 54-55
Charlestown 52n, 86n

Cheapside 5, 201
Constantinople 272-273
Cornhill 201, 330
Cornwall 68
Coventry 168
Cripplegate 76n, 163, 168

Dallinghoo 63n
Dalwood 45
Danube River 272
Dartmouth 52n
Derby 42n
Devonshire Square 168-169
Dover 61

East Anglia 290
England 21, 31, 32, 34, 26, 40-41, 42n, 45, 46, 47n, 52n, 53n, 54, 61n, 62-64, 68n, 79, 81, 82, 84-85, 96, 101, 104, 114-115, 131-132, 137-139, 151, 153, 170n, 194, 199, 223, 240n, 243, 248-250, 252, 263, 268, 276, 281, 283n, 284n, 286, 290, 298-299, 304n, 317, 318n, 320n, 324, 330, 338-339
Euphrates River 273, 337
Eversholt 42n
Exeter, NH 62n

Finsbury Fields 64
Finsbury Hills 63n
France 249, 271, 298, 341
Fulleby on the Hill 61n

Gainsborough 31, 54n, 56, 57, 69, 317
Geneva 30
George Yard 71

Germany   70, 200, 249, 261n, 271, 298, 341
Glamorgan   41n
Goulceby   58n
Great Eastcheap   167-168
Great St. Helens   63n, 64
Great Tower Hill   63
Grimsby   55
Grindleton   97

Hampton, NH   59n
Hampton Court   18
Hemel Hempstead   42n
Henly   42n
Hertfordshire   39n
Hexham   39n
Higham Ferrers   167
Hoddenham   42n
Holland   2, 32, 35, 36, 69-70, 77, 245n, 318n, 324-325, 327
Honiton   45
Hook Norton   42n
Horsleydown   48n, 167
Humberstone   57

Ilston   41n
Ipswich   66n, 67
Ireland   38n, 40-41, 42n, 46, 68n, 250, 284n, 298, 339
Italy   271

Jordan Well   168

Kensworth   39n, 42n
Kent   39n, 49n
Kettering   167-168, 170
Kimbolton   169
Kings Norton   252
Kingston   42n

Lancashire   99n
Leyden   31, 32
Lincoln   31, 57, 58n, 65n
Lincolnshire   54, 58n, 61, 85, 86n, 99n
Llanharan   41n
Llanigan   41n

London   21, 31-32, 34, 38n, 40-43, 48n, 51n, 52, 60n, 61-65, 67-71, 75, 99, 103, 135, 137, 163-164, 169, 170-171, 180, 195-204, 207n, 208-209, 213, 227, 238, 240, 244, 249, 281, 284n, 286, 289n, 290-291, 298-299, 318, 338
Long Island   61
Louth   54
Lyme   45

Maine   52n
Massachusetts   58n, 61, 62n, 81, 85, 86n, 88
Mentmore   55n
Middlesex   47n
Midlands   40, 42, 135n, 289
Moorfields   47n
Morton-in-the-Marsh   42n
Mulbus   208
Munster   7, 214

Netherlands   35, 325
Newbury   39n
Newcastle   39n
New England   6, 8, 13, 52n, 61, 77, 81, 82, 84-86, 89-90, 96, 104, 114-115, 131-132, 138, 151, 153, 247, 324
Newgate   2, 50n, 69-70, 75, 244, 245n, 304
New Hampshire   61, 62n, 82, 324
New Jerusalem   251, 277-278, 301-302, 342-343
Newtown (Cambridge)   86n, 87
Norfolk   286, 289
Northhampton   18
Northhamptonshire   167, 169, 171
North Warborough   42n
Norwich   30, 207n, 286

Oxford   10, 39n, 42n

Palestine   274
Parham   69
Peterborough   57, 86n
Pinner's Hall   78, 84, 102, 158

Piscattuah   61, 62n, 64n, 82
Pithay   48n, 135, 180
Plymouth   50n, 68n
Portsmouth   62n
Pyrton   42n

Radnor   67n
Reading   42n
Rhode Island   88
Rhodes   272
Rome   20, 73, 248-249, 256, 261-
    262, 266-268, 270-272, 283n, 298-
    299, 312, 335-336, 338-343
Rothwell   169-170
Rotterdam   71n, 76n
Roxbury   86n

Salter's Hall   158
Scartho   55, 57, 65, 67n
Scotland   20, 249-250, 284n, 290,
    298, 339
Scrooby Manor   31
Seekonk   35n, 52n
Somersetshire   52n
Somerton   52n
Southwark   32, 163n, 167, 197, 199,
    208n, 209n, 210, 319
Spain   271
Spitalfields   70n
St. Giles   65n

Storeditch   290
Suffolk   4-6, 63n, 82, 97, 201n
Sussex   49n
Swan Alley   41n
Swansea   52n
Switzerland   139

Taunton   45
Tewkesbury   42n
Tiverton   39n
Torbay   45
Turkey   272, 275

Virginia   33

Wainfleet   61n
Wales   7, 40-41, 42n, 44, 46, 52n,
    53n, 67, 68n, 77, 240n, 288-289
Wallington   42n
Wantage   42n
Warwich   42n
Waterford   42n
Watford   39n
Westminster   63n, 322
Whitechapel   50n
Wickham Market   97
Windsor   293

York   18, 58n, 283n

INDEX OF PLACES

Abergavenny 41n
Abingdon 41, 42n
Acton 47n
Alcaster 42n
Alderman-bury 217
Alford 86n
All Hallows the Great 246, 286
Amsterdam 31, 318
Anchor Lane 70n
Anderby 61n
Armageddon 250, 260, 263, 273, 275, 312, 340-341
Ashford 49n

Babylon 250, 260, 268-271, 283n, 293, 298, 335, 338, 340-341
Barnoldswick 170n
Belgrade 272
Bennington 58, 86n
Bilsby 58n
Bishopgate 71
Boston 52n, 58n, 61, 64n, 82, 85-88
Bourton-on-the-Water 42n
Breconshire 67n
Bristol 48n, 50n, 51n, 135
Britain 17, 43, 50, 287
Broadmead 50n
Broken Wharf 76n
Bunhill Fields 72n, 77

Cambridge 31, 55-57, 58n, 85, 86n, 163, 167, 171
Cambridgeshire 163
Canterbury 18, 61, 283n
Carmarthen 41n
Carolina 52n
Cawkwell 54-55
Charlestown 52n, 86n

Cheapside 5, 201
Constantinople 272-273
Cornhill 201, 330
Cornwall 68
Coventry 168
Cripplegate 76n, 163, 168

Dallinghoo 63n
Dalwood 45
Danube River 272
Dartmouth 52n
Derby 42n
Devonshire Square 168-169
Dover 61

East Anglia 290
England 21, 31, 32, 34, 26, 40-41, 42n, 45, 46, 47n, 52n, 53n, 54, 61n, 62-64, 68n, 79, 81, 82, 84-85, 96, 101, 104, 114-115, 131-132, 137-139, 151, 153, 170n, 194, 199, 223, 240n, 243, 248-250, 252, 263, 268, 276, 281, 283n, 284n, 286, 290, 298-299, 304n, 317, 318n, 320n, 324, 330, 338-339
Euphrates River 273, 337
Eversholt 42n
Exeter, NH 62n

Finsbury Fields 64
Finsbury Hills 63n
France 249, 271, 298, 341
Fulleby on the Hill 61n

Gainsborough 31, 54n, 56, 57, 69, 317
Geneva 30
George Yard 71

Hypercalvinism   2-3, 7-8, 11, 14,
    47-48, 133-193
    and John Brine   14, 163, 168-
        169, 171-172, 174-176, 179-
        180, 182-184, 187-192
    and John Gill   14, 163, 167-171,
        174, 176-179, 182-183, 186-
        187, 189-192
    and John Skepp   2-3, 6-7, 133,
        163-168, 177n, 192
    and Joseph Hussey   13-14, 160-
        164, 167-169
    modern question   169-170, 179,
        182
    origins   158-163

Increated grace   93-95, 122-123

Knollys, Hanserd
    and Antinomianism   211-213,
        241
    and Arminianism   210-211
    and assurance   115-118, 131,
        155, 157
    and charges of Anabaptism   1-4,
        200-202, 307
    and charges of Antinomianism
        2-4, 80-84, 241, 307
    and charges of Fifth Monarchism
        2-4, 244-247, 291-305, 307
    and church and state   236-241
    and Deity of Christ   235-236
    and doctrine of baptism   217-
        221, 241, 310
    and doctrine of ministry   229-
        235, 310-311
    and faith   118-119, 175-176, 180,
        184-185
    and hyper-Calvinism   2-3, 134-
        137, 171-193, 307
    and increated grace   122-123
    and law   128-132
    and perfectionism   125
    and preparationism   119-122,
        131-132, 156-157
    and sanctification   116-118, 124,
        131, 155, 309

and sin   123, 125-128
and singing   76
and Trinitarianism   235
and union with Christ   118-119
Anabaptist connections   317,
    324, 329-330, 333
baptism   54n, 63-64, 73
birth   54
calling to preach   60-61
character   8-9, 74, 77-78, 131
churches   57, 64-65, 76n
conversion   58-60
death   77
early spiritual experiences   56
ecclesiology   221-229, 241, 309-
    311
education   55-57
eschatology   2, 6, 8-11, 73, 75,
    311-312, 248-252
eschatology – date setting   267-
    268
eschatology – Jews   275-276
eschatology – millennium   277-
    279, 342-343
eschatology – nature of return
    255
eschatology – nearness of return
    253-254
eschatology – number 666   262-
    263
eschatology – Papacy   270-272
eschatology – signs of the
    end   265
eschatology – Turkey   273-274
family   54, 62, 70-72
High Calvinism   140-157
historiography   3-10
imprisonment   69, 71, 75
interpretation of Revelation
    260-263, 256, 258-259, 335-343
life in New England   61-62
ordination   57
reasons for eschatological writ-
    ings   282-284
soteriology   308-309
wife   58, 72
writings   65-76, 315-316

Orthodoxy   24-28

Particular Baptists
  Anabaptist connections   317-334
  associations   41-43
  charges of Anabaptism   3-4, 195-
    200, 203-204
  charges of Antinomianism   3-4,
    79-80, 211-213
  charges of Fifth Monarchism   3-
    4, 243
  hermeneutic   322-323, 327-329,
    331-333
  history 1640s-1660s   21, 37-43
  history 1660s-1689   43-53,
  origins   32-36
  persecutions   44-45, 50-52
  political involvement   37-38

  roots   28-31
  separation of church and state
    330-333
Pelagianism   139, 339
Puritanism   28, 30, 32, 55, 61, 89,
  108, 150, 154, 318-319, 322-324,
  326, 330, 332-334

Quakers   39, 43, 47, 74n

Radical Puritans   320-321, 331
Rynsburgers   35, 325

Separatism   28, 30-31, 318-319,
  321-324, 330-334
Seventh-day Baptists   39, 48
Socinianism   39, 139, 194

Studies in the History
of Christian Thought

EDITED BY HEIKO A. OBERMAN

1. McNEILL, J. J. *The Blondelian Synthesis*. 1966. Out of print
2. GOERTZ, H.-J. *Innere und äussere Ordnung in der Theologie Thomas Müntzers*. 1967
3. BAUMAN, Cl. *Gewaltlosigkeit im Täufertum*. 1968
4. ROLDANUS, J. *Le Christ et l'Homme dans la Théologie d'Athanase d'Alexandrie*. 2nd ed. 1977
5. MILNER, Jr., B. Ch. *Calvin's Doctrine of the Church*. 1970. Out of print
6. TIERNEY, B. *Origins of Papal Infallibility, 1150-1350*. 2nd ed. 1988
7. OLDFIELD, J. J. *Tolerance in the Writings of Félicité Lamennais 1809-1831*. 1973
8. OBERMAN, H. A. (ed.). *Luther and the Dawn of the Modern Era*. 1974. Out of print
9. HOLECZEK, H. *Humanistische Bibelphilologie bei Erasmus, Thomas More und William Tyndale*. 1975
10. FARR, W. *John Wyclif as Legal Reformer*. 1974
11. PURCELL, M. *Papal Crusading Policy 1244-1291*. 1975
12. BALL, B. W. *A Great Expectation*. Eschatological Thought in English Protestantism. 1975
13. STIEBER, J. W. *Pope Eugenius IV, the Council of Basel, and the Empire*. 1978. Out of print
14. PARTEE, Ch. *Calvin and Classical Philosophy*. 1977
15. MISNER, P. *Papacy and Development*. Newman and the Primacy of the Pope. 1976
16. TAVARD, G. H. *The Seventeenth-Century Tradition*. A Study in Recusant Thought. 1978
17. QUINN, A. *The Confidence of British Philosophers*. An Essay in Historical Narrative. 1977
18. BECK, J. *Le Concil de Basle (1434)*. 1979
19. CHURCH, F. F. and GEORGE, T. (ed.). *Continuity and Discontinuity in Church History*. 1979
20. GRAY, P. T. R. *The Defense of Chalcedon in the East (451-553)*. 1979
21. NIJENHUIS, W. *Adrianus Saravia (c. 1532-1613)*. Dutch Calvinist. 1980
22. PARKER, T. H. L. (ed.). *Iohannis Calvini Commentarius in Epistolam Pauli ad Romanos*. 1981
23. ELLIS, I. *Seven Against Christ*. A Study of 'Essays and Reviews'. 1980
24. BRANN, N. L. *The Abbot Trithemius (1462-1516)*. 1981
25. LOCHER, G. W. *Zwingli's Thought*. New Perspectives. 1981
26. GOGAN, B. *The Common Corps of Christendom*. Ecclesiological Themes in Thomas More. 1982
27. STOCK, U. *Die Bedeutung der Sakramente in Luthers Sermonen von 1519*. 1982
28. YARDENI, M. (ed.). *Modernité et nonconformisme en France à travers les âges*. 1983
29. PLATT, J. *Reformed Thought and Scholasticism*. 1982
30. WATTS, P. M. *Nicolaus Cusanus*. A Fifteenth-Century Vision of Man. 1982
31. SPRUNGER, K. L. *Dutch Puritanism*. 1982
32. MEIJERING, E. P. *Melanchthon and Patristic Thought*. 1983
33. STROUP, J. *The Struggle for Identity in the Clerical Estate*. 1984
34. 35. COLISH, M. L. *The Stoic Tradition from Antiquity to the Early Middle Ages*. 1.2. 2nd ed. 1990
36. GUY, B. *Domestic Correspondence of Dominique-Marie Varlet, Bishop of Babylon, 1678-1742*. 1986
37. 38. CLARK, F. *The Pseudo-Gregorian Dialogues*. I. II. 1987
39. PARENTE, Jr. J. A. *Religious Drama and the Humanist Tradition*. 1987
40. POSTHUMUS MEYJES, G. H. M. *Hugo Grotius, Meletius*. 1988
41. FELD, H. *Der Ikonoklasmus des Westens*. 1990
42. REEVE, A. and SCREECH, M. A. (eds.). *Erasmus' Annotations on the New Testament*. Acts — Romans — I and II Corinthians. 1990
43. KIRBY, W. J. T. *Richard Hooker's Doctrine of the Royal Supremacy*. 1990
44. GERSTNER, J. N. *The Thousand Generation Covenant*. Reformed Covenant Theology. 1990
45. CHRISTIANSON, G. and IZBICKI, T. M. (eds.). *Nicholas of Cusa*. 1991
46. GARSTEIN, O. *Rome and the Counter-Reformation in Scandinavia*. 1553-1622. 1992
47. GARSTEIN, O. *Rome and the Counter-Reformation in Scandinavia*. 1622-1656. 1992
48. PERRONE COMPAGNI, V. (ed.). *Cornelius Agrippa, De occulta philosophia Libri tres*. 1992
49. MARTIN, D. D. *Fifteenth-Century Carthusian Reform*. The World of Nicholas Kempf. 1992
50. HOENEN, M. J. F. M. *Marsilius of Inghen*. Divine Knowledge in Late Medieval Thought. 1993

51. O'MALLEY, J. W., IZBICKI, T. M. and CHRISTIANSON, G. (eds.). *Humanity and Divinity in Renaissance and Reformation.* Essays in Honor of Charles Trinkaus. 1993
52. REEVE, A. (ed.) and SCREECH, M. A. (introd.). *Erasmus' Annotations on the New Testament.* Galatians to the Apocalypse. 1993
53. STUMP, Ph. H. *The Reforms of the Council of Constance (1414-1418).* 1994
54. GIAKALIS, A. *Images of the Divine.* The Theology of Icons at the Seventh Ecumenical Council. With a Foreword by Henry Chadwick. 1994
55. NELLEN, H. J. M. and RABBIE, E. (eds.). *Hugo Grotius – Theologian.* Essays in Honour of G. H. M. Posthumus Meyjes. 1994
56. TRIGG, J. D. *Baptism in the Theology of Martin Luther.* 1994
57. JANSE, W. *Albert Hardenberg als Theologe.* Profil eines Bucer-Schülers. 1994
59. SCHOOR, R.J.M. VAN DE. *The Irenical Theology of Théophile Brachet de La Milletière (1588-1665).* 1995
60. STREHLE, S. *The Catholic Roots of the Protestant Gospel.* Encounter between the Middle Ages and the Reformation. 1995
61. BROWN, M.L. *Donne and the Politics of Conscience in Early Modern England.* 1995
62. SCREECH, M.A. (ed.). *Richard Mocket, Warden of All Souls College, Oxford, Doctrina et Politia Ecclesiae Anglicanae.* An Anglican Summa. Facsimile with Variants of the Text of 1617. Edited with an Introduction. 1995
63. SNOEK, G.J.C. *Medieval Piety from Relics to the Eucharist.* A Process of Mutual Inter-action. 1995
64. PIXTON, P.B. *The German Episcopacy and the Implementation of the Decrees of the Fourth Lateran Council, 1216-1245.* Watchmen on the Tower. 1995
65. DOLNIKOWSKI, E.W. *Thomas Bradwardine: A View of Time and a Vision of Eternity in Fourteenth-Century Thought.* 1995
66. RABBIE, E. (ed.). *Hugo Grotius, Ordinum Hollandiae ac Westfrisiae Pietas (1613).* Critical Edition with Translation and Commentary. 1995
67. HIRSH, J.C. *The Boundaries of Faith.* The Development and Transmission of Medieval Spirituality. 1996
68. BURNETT, S.G. *From Christian Hebraism to Jewish Studies.* Johannes Buxtorf (1564-1629) and Hebrew Learning in the Seventeenth Century. 1996
69. BOLAND O.P., V. *Ideas in God according to Saint Thomas Aquinas.* Sources and Synthesis. 1996
70. LANGE, M.E. *Telling Tears in the English Renaissance.* 1996
71. CHRISTIANSON, G. and T.M. IZBICKI (eds.). *Nicholas of Cusa on Christ and the Church.* Essays in Memory of Chandler McCuskey Brooks for the American Cusanus Society. 1996
72. MALI, A. *Mystic in the New World.* Marie de l'Incarnation (1599-1672). 1996
73. VISSER, D. *Apocalypse as Utopian Expectation (800-1500).* The Apocalypse Commentary of Berengaudus of Ferrières and the Relationship between Exegesis, Liturgy and Iconography. 1996
74. O'ROURKE BOYLE, M. *Divine Domesticity.* Augustine of Thagaste to Teresa of Avila. 1997
75. PFIZENMAIER, T.C. *The Trinitarian Theology of Dr. Samuel Clarke (1675-1729).* Context, Sources, and Controversy. 1997
76. BERKVENS-STEVELINCK, C., J. ISRAEL and G.H.M. POSTHUMUS MEYJES (eds.). *The Emergence of Tolerance in the Dutch Republic.* 1997
77. HAYKIN, M.A.G. (ed.). *The Life and Thought of John Gill (1697-1771).* A Tercentennial Appreciation. 1997
78. KAISER, C.B. *Creational Theology and the History of Physical Science.* The Creationist Tradition from Basil to Bohr. 1997
79. LEES, J.T. *Anselm of Havelberg.* Deeds into Words in the Twelfth Century. 1997
80. WINTER, J.M. VAN. *Sources Concerning the Hospitallers of St John in the Netherlands, 14th-18th Centuries.* 1998
81. TIERNEY, B. *Foundations of the Conciliar Theory.* The Contribution of the Medieval Canonists from Gratian to the Great Schism. Enlarged New Edition. 1998
82. MIERNOWSKI, J. *Le Dieu Néant.* Théologies négatives à l'aube des temps modernes. 1998
83. HALVERSON, J.L. *Peter Aureol on Predestination.* A Challenge to Late Medieval Thought. 1998.
84. HOULISTON, V. (ed.). *Robert Persons, S.J.: The Christian Directory (1582).* The First Booke of the Christian Exercise, appertayning to Resolution. 1998
85. GRELL, O.P. (ed.). *Paracelsus.* The Man and His Reputation, His Ideas and Their Transformation. 1998
86. MAZZOLA, E. *The Pathology of the English Renaissance.* Sacred Remains and Holy Ghosts. 1998.
87. 88. MARSILIUS VON INGHEN. *Quaestiones super quattuor libros sententiarum.* Super Primum. Bearbeitet von M. Santos Noya. 2 Bände. I. Quaestiones 1-7. II. Quaestiones 8-21. 2000
89. FAUPEL-DREVS, K. *Vom rechten Gebrauch der Bilder im liturgischen Raum.* Mittelalterliche Funktionsbestimmungen bildender Kunst im *Rationale divinorum officiorum* des Durandus von Mende (1230/1-1296). 1999

90. KREY, P.D.W. and SMITH, L. (eds.). *Nicholas of Lyra. the Senses of Scripture.* 2000
92. OAKLEY, F. *Politics and Eternity.* Studies in the History of Medieval and Early-Modern Political Thought. 1999
93. PRYDS, D. *The Politics of Preaching.* Robert of Naples (1309-1343) and his Sermons. 2000
94. POSTHUMUS MEYJES, G.H.M. *Jean Gerson – Apostle of Unity.* His Church Politics and Ecclesiology. Translated by J.C. Grayson. 1999
95. BERG, J. VAN DEN. *Religious Currents and Cross-Currents.* Essays on Early Modern Protestantism and the Protestant Enlightenment. Edited by J. de Bruijn, P. Holtrop, and E. van der Wall. 1999
96. IZBICKI, T.M. and BELLITTO, C.M. (eds.). *Reform and Renewal in the Middle Ages and the Renaissance.* Studies in Honor of Louis Pascoe, S.J. 2000
97. KELLY, D. *The Conspiracy of Allusion.* Description, Rewriting, and Authorship from Macrobius to Medieval Romance. 1999
98. MARRONE, S.P. *The Light of Thy Countenance.* Science and Knowledge of God in the Thirteenth Century. 2 volumes. 1. A Doctrine of Divine Illumination. 2. God at the Core of Cognition. 2001
99. HOWSON B.H. *Erroneous and Schismatical Opinions.* The Question of Orthodoxy regarding the Theology of Hanserd Knollys (c. 1599-1691). 2001
100 ASSELT, W.J. VAN. *The Federal Theology of Johannes Cocceius (1603-1669).* 2001

Prospectus available on request

BRILL — P.O.B. 9000 — 2300 PA LEIDEN — THE NETHERLANDS